EDITED BY

RICHARD K. BETTS

University

D0462614

Conflict After the Cold War

Arguments on Causes of War and Peace

Allyn and Bacon

Boston · London · Toronto · Sydney · Tokyo · Singapore

Editor: Robert Miller
Production Supervisor: Jane O'Neill
Production Manager: Su Levine
Text Designer: Robert Freese
Cover Designer: Russ Maselli
Cover Illustration: Tom Post

Printed in the United States of America

10 9 8 7 6 5 4   99 98 97 96

PREFACE

It has become a cliché among observers of international relations that we are living in amazing times. Until the stunning events of the past few years, we lived with the Cold War for more than four decades. That epochal worldwide conflict was tense, difficult, and occasionally frightening. The issues that dominated the agenda of those concerned with the danger of war and prospects for peace were a constant challenge, but they developed a familiar quality: How large should the defense budget be? What sorts of arms control agreements might improve the stability of the East–West relationship? Should the superpowers compete in political interventions in the Third World?

As issues in the Cold War became almost routinized, the basic framework and assumptions of international security came to be taken for granted. Then almost overnight the war ended, and international developments seemed to move in two directions—toward greater stability and peace in many areas, and toward fragmentation and chaotic violence in others. Which of these apparent trends is likely to prevail?

Much of the recent literature on international security, grounded as it was in the Cold War, does not provide a great deal of guidance to the answers. To get a sense of whether and how international conflict will develop after the Cold War, we need to look beneath the surface of current events and popular arguments and investigate competing ideas about the fundamental causes of war and peace. Many of these ideas go so far back and have been so thoroughly absorbed that people assume them to be self-evident—indeed, many people are often unaware that there are intellectually serious positions that contradict their assumptions.

This volume aims to help students sort out the main debates about whether war is likely to remain a major problem in international life. The collection of writings outlines contrasting arguments about the future of the post–Cold War world and puts them in philosophical and historical context.

It frames them in a topically organized and ideologically balanced survey of the most relevant schools of thought and arguments about what political, economic, social, and military factors tend to cause war and whether or not such causes can be made obsolete.

Bruce Nichols of Macmillan helped me decide that it was important to remedy the lack of a collection of this sort. He and Robert Miller shepherded the project. Columbia University's Institute of War and Peace Studies, and especially Susan Burgerman and Stuart Gottlieb, provided helpful logistical support in assembling the material. My thanks also go to the following colleagues who reviewed the manuscript: Timothy J. Lomperis, Duke University; Bruce D. Porter, Harvard University and Brigham Young University; Eric S. Einhorn, University of Massachusetts; Dale L. Smith, Florida State University; Bruce R. Drury, Lamar University; and Herbert K. Tillema, University of Missouri-Columbia. Most of all I am grateful to my wife, Adela Maria Bolet, and our children, Elena Christine, Michael Francis, and Diego Fitzpatrick Betts, for letting me give the project some of the time that they had a right to expect me to give them.

Richard K. Betts
Teaneck, New Jersey

CONTENTS

PART 4

Economics: Interests and Interdependence   173

PART 5

Politics: Ideology and Identity   247

PART 6

Strategy: Military Technology, Doctrine, and Stability   309

PART 1

Introduction: Does War Have a Future?

The titanic Cold War struggle is over. No power or idea of global significance exists to challenge the interests or ideals of the Western democracies.
Does this mean that war will no longer be the biggest danger in international re
lations? To many, that notion seemed obvious as we celebrated the collapse of
Communism and the rush to embrace Western political and economic values on
almost every continent. In step with the revolutions of 1989 and 1991 which liberated Eastern Europe and demolished the Soviet Union, conflicts all around the
world that had seemed intractable began to wind down: South Africa, Central
America, Cambodia, Afghanistan, the Middle East. Could euphoria about the
permanence of peace ever be better justified?

Other events gave cause for second thoughts: Iraq's invasion of Kuwait, ferocious communal violence in what used to be Yugoslavia and the Soviet Union,
internal chaos in Third World countries as diverse as Haiti, Peru, Burma, and So
malia. Will international civility be limited to the developed "core" of Western
Europe, Japan, and North America, while the poor countries of the "periphery"
continue to wallow in force and fury?[1] Or will even the core go bad? Some worry
that the durability of the new peace is doubtful in Europe too, despite the demise
of the Soviet threat. The Cold War standoff between the superpowers had im-

---

[1]See James M. Goldgeier and Michael McFaul, "A Tale of Two Worlds: Core and Periphery in
the Post-Cold War Era," *International Organization* 46, no. 2 (Spring 1992).

posed a cautionary discipline[2] on the traditional self-assertion of nations, and had forced them to cooperate in the interests of alliance security. Removal of the standoff reduces the incentives for caution and cooperation, making it easier for different states of the continent to rediscover old frictions and ambitions. Will the end of the East-West conflict bring the "end of history" and a world of unprecedented peace, or the return of history and old patterns of violence?[3]

To decide whether international relations in the next millennium will be fundamentally different from those of the past, we need to understand what forces made for war or peace in the past,[4] which of these are more important in the new world and which less, and what new forces may push events in uncharted directions. Without confronting the questions in this context, to assume that the end of the Cold War epoch points clearly toward either more peace or more conflict is an arrogant gamble for intellectuals and a potential source of tragic miscalculation for politicians.

Optimists sometimes overlook the fact that some current arguments for why international relations have become permanently peaceful are not very different from earlier explanations. These earlier theories have been jolted, if not discredited, by the catastrophes of the first half of this century (the two World Wars) and by the reinvigoration of the Cold War after the detente of the early 1970s. More than once, analysts have thought they discovered decisive shifts in the world, only to find that less had changed than met the eye.

Pessimists, on the other hand, overlook how much *has* changed. The recent demise of Marxism-Leninism everywhere but in a few puny enclaves is even more significant an elimination of ideological conflict than was the destruction of fascism in 1945. Even traditional dictatorships have been declining as an alternative to Western liberalism. Can political and economic change on this scale be irrelevant to the prospects for peace or war?

The readings in this volume explore competing ideas about present trends in the light of historic debates over the causes of war and peace. The Introduction presents the main current arguments about the prospects for conflict or cooperation offered by optimists and skeptics of various stripes. The next two sections sample the main arguments that have animated debate about whether the threat of war is inevitable or can be made obsolete. The two overarching theoretical traditions that subsume most of the arguments are *realism* (represented in Part 2) and *liberalism* (Part 3), both of which cover a wide variety of ideas. Not long ago, Marxism might have been considered a paradigm competing on the same level as

---

[2]See John L. Gaddis, *The Long Peace* (New York: Oxford University Press, 1987).

[3]See Robert Jervis, "The Future of World Politics: Will It Resemble the Past?" *International Security* 16, no. 3 (Winter 1991/92).

[4]For a comprehensive survey see Jack S. Levy, "The Causes of War: A Review of Theories and Evidence," in Philip E. Tetlock *et al.*, eds., *Behavior, Society, and Nuclear War* (New York: Oxford University Press, 1989), vol. I.

the other two, but, except to the degree that it shares some assumptions with realism,[5] it has fallen by the wayside intellectually as well as politically.

Parts 4 to 6 present contending views of how political, economic, and military factors may encourage decisions to resort to force or suppress them. Most of these entries reflect variations of the realist and liberal perspectives. (As editor I have tried to keep a balance between the two strands of argument, and I personally do not have complete faith in either one. Frankness, however, requires that I admit a tilt in favor of realism.) Part 7, which briefly considers potential sources of conflict that transcend borders, shows the extent to which newly salient issues may also cut across traditional lines of theoretical explanation. The Conclusion offers perspectives, lying between extreme realist and liberal views, on what should be done to cope with the post-Cold War world.

This collection does not represent all relevant points of view. One problem is, that like all too much of international relations theory, ideas in this volume are drawn primarily from the experience and interests of Europe and the developed industrial world. A selection of theories must draw from the best available. While there is ample literature on the history of war and peace on other continents, most attempts at rigorous theory (at least those written in English) have drawn their inspiration from European history and the Cold War, the heart of which was the NATO/Warsaw Pact confrontation. Another reason is that most people in the West who are interested in war are not worried about war in general, but about either big, potentially cataclysmic wars, or small ones that could escalate into a large conflict, like one of the World Wars. This concern still tends to focus attention on the great powers and areas where the concentrations of high-tech military capability, gross national product, and per capita wealth are highest. Finally, there is relatively little debate about whether violent disorder will persist in the so-called Third World. Even the most optimistic arguments about a new era of peace restrict themselves to the developed countries.

Another omission is the perspective of game theory or "rational choice" analysis. In deciding what to include among the limited number of selections that space allows here, I have chosen to expose several sets of ideas in depth, and to strive for some cohesion among the selections, rather than to include a selection from every body of literature. Moreover, while the emphasis in these selections is on theory, it is important to maintain as close a link as possible to evidence from history and current topics, so I have minimized selections that are purely deductive and abstract.

---

[5]If we substitute classes for states as the essential units in competition for power, Marxism has much of the materialist and determinist logic of realism. Both philosophies assert, in contrast to liberalism, that conflict rather than harmony is the natural condition of human relations. In opposition to realism, classical Marxism sees the state as only the superstructure of class interests; thus, transnational social alliances should have proved to be more significant than conflict between states. This idea was thoroughly knocked out by World War I. When Leninism came to dominate Marxism, and married it to Russian and Chinese nationalism, Communist statesmanship became eminently realist.

Some of the readings in this volume are reprinted in their entirety. Others have been edited to avoid repetition or discussion of matters not germane to the theme of the collection. Standard ellipses indicate where passages have been deleted. Some footnotes have also been deleted from passages that remain.

The four selections in the Introduction below present the pithiest views about whether traditional international conflict is obsolete. Francis Fukuyama[6] and John Mueller argue that societies in the Western world have evolved beyond the divisions and values traditionally associated with war. These writers emphasize changes in culture, sociology, and ideology as the central forces in this process. In response, Samuel Huntington questions the finality of the changes they cite, and how much it is fair to generalize from them, and argues that developments pointing in a different direction should be considered equally significant.

John Mearsheimer[7] presents the starkest challenge to optimistic conventional wisdom, with a pure distillation of the realist tradition represented in the readings that follow in Part 2. To him, the intellectual and cultural developments that Fukuyama and Mueller see as decisive forces actually matter very little. When push comes to shove, ideas give way to interests. Mearsheimer asserts not only that the new era of peace on the horizon is a mirage, but that the future will be worse than the recent past. The Cold War, not the new world, represents the most stable and peaceful order we are likely to see.

All four of these arguments are arresting, but in many important respects they reflect philosophical assumptions rooted in earlier and well-developed schools of thought. Those roots of the current argument are traced in more detail in the subsequent selections.

[6]For the full-length version of these arguments see Francis Fukuyama, *The End of History and the Last Man* (New York: Free Press, 1992). Responses to early attacks on the argument can be found in Fukuyama's "A Reply to My Critics," *The National Interest* No. 18 (Winter 1989/90).

[7]A more academic and detailed version of this argument can be found in John J. Mearsheimer, "Back to the Future: Instability in Europe After the Cold War," *International Security* 15, no. 4 (Spring 1990).

The End of History?

FRANCIS FUKUYAMA

In watching the flow of events over the past decade or so, it is hard to avoid the feeling that something very fundamental has happened in world history. The past year has seen a flood of articles commemorating the end of the Cold War, and the fact that "peace" seems to be breaking out in many regions of the world. Most of these analyses lack any larger conceptual framework for distinguishing between what is essential and what is contingent or accidental in world history, and are predictably superficial. If Mr. Gorbachev were ousted from the Kremlin or a new Ayatollah proclaimed the millennium from a desolate Middle Eastern capital, these same commentators would scramble to announce the rebirth of a new era of conflict.

And yet, all of these people sense dimly that there is some larger process at work, a process that gives coherence and order to the daily headlines. The twentieth century saw the developed world descend into a paroxysm of ideological violence, as liberalism contended first with the remnants of absolutism, then bolshevism and fascism, and finally an updated Marxism that threatened to lead to the ultimate apocalypse of nuclear war. But the century that began full of self-confidence in the ultimate triumph of Western liberal democracy seems at its close to be returning full circle to where it started: not to an "end of ideology" or a convergence between capitalism and socialism, as earlier predicted, but to an unabashed victory of economic and political liberalism.

The triumph of the West, of the Western *idea*, is evident first of all in the total exhaustion of viable systematic alternatives to Western liberalism. In the past decade, there have been unmistakable changes in the intellectual climate of the world's two largest communist countries, and the beginnings of significant reform movements in both. But this phenomenon extends beyond high politics and it can be seen also in the ineluctable spread of con-

Francis Fukuyama, "The End of History?" *The National Interest* No. 16 (Summer 1989). Copyright © 1989 by Francis Fukuyama.

sumerist Western culture in such diverse contexts as the peasants' markets
and color television sets now omnipresent throughout China, the cooperative restaurants and clothing stores opened in the past year in Moscow, the
Beethoven piped into Japanese department stores, and the rock music enjoyed alike in Prague, Rangoon, and Tehran.

What we may be witnessing is not just the end of the Cold War, or the passing of a particular period of postwar history, but the end of history as such:
that is, the end point of mankind's ideological evolution and the universalization of Western liberal democracy as the final form of human government. This is not to say that there will no longer be events to fill the pages of
Foreign Affairs's yearly summaries of international relations, for the victory of
liberalism has occurred primarily in the realm of ideas or consciousness and
is as yet incomplete in the real or material world. But there are powerful reasons for believing that it is the ideal that will govern the material world *in the
long run.* To understand how this is so, we must first consider some theoretical issues concerning the nature of historical change.

I

The notion of the end of history is not an original one. Its best known prop-
agator was Karl Marx, who believed that the direction of historical development was a purposeful one determined by the interplay of material forces,
and would come to an end only with the achievement of a communist utopia
that would finally resolve all prior contradictions. But the concept of history
as a dialectical process with a beginning, a middle, and an end was borrowed
by Marx from his great German predecessor, Georg Wilhelm Friedrich
Hegel.

For better or worse, much of Hegel's historicism has become part of our
contemporary intellectual baggage. The notion that mankind has progressed through a series of primitive stages of consciousness on his path to
the present, and that these stages corresponded to concrete forms of social
organization, such as tribal, slave-owning, theocratic, and finally democratic-
egalitarian societies, has become inseparable from the modern understanding of man. Hegel was the first philosopher to speak the language of modern
social science, insofar as man for him was the product of his concrete historical and social environment and not, as earlier natural right theorists would
have it, a collection of more or less fixed "natural" attributes. The mastery
and transformation of man's natural environment through the application
of science and technology was originally not a Marxist concept, but a
Hegelian one. Unlike later historicists whose historical relativism degener-
ated into relativism *tout court,* however, Hegel believed that history culmi-
nated in an absolute moment—a moment in which a final, rational form of
society and state became victorious.

It is Hegel's misfortune to be known now primarily as Marx's precursor, and it is our misfortune that few of us are familiar with Hegel's work from direct study, but only as it has been filtered through the distorting lens of Marxism. In France, however, there has been an effort to save Hegel from his Marxist interpreters and to resurrect him as the philosopher who most correctly speaks to our time. Among those modern French interpreters of Hegel, the greatest was certainly Alexandre Kojève, a brilliant Russian emigre who taught a highly influential series of seminars in Paris in the 1930s at the *Ecole Practique des Hautes Etudes*.[1] While largely unknown in the United States, Kojève had a major impact on the intellectual life of the continent. Among his students ranged such future luminaries as Jean-Paul Sartre on the Left and Raymond Aron on the Right; postwar existentialism borrowed many of its basic categories from Hegel via Kojève.

Kojève sought to resurrect the Hegel of the *Phenomenology of Mind,* the Hegel who proclaimed history to be at an end in 1806. For as early as this Hegel saw in Napoleon's defeat of the Prussian monarchy at the Battle of Jena the victory of the ideals of the French Revolution, and the imminent universalization of the state incorporating the principles of liberty and equality. Kojève, far from rejecting Hegel in light of the turbulent events of the next century and a half, insisted that the latter had been essentially correct. The Battle of Jena marked the end of history because it was at that point that the *vanguard* of humanity (a term quite familiar to Marxists) actualized the principles of the French Revolution. While there was considerable work to be done after 1806—abolishing slavery and the slave trade, extending the franchise to workers, women, blacks, and other racial minorities, etc.—the basic *principles* of the liberal democratic state could not be improved upon. The two world wars in this century and their attendant revolutions and upheavals simply had the effect of extending those principles spatially, such that the various provinces of human civilization were brought up to the level of its most advanced outposts, and of forcing those societies in Europe and North America at the vanguard of civilization to implement their liberalism more fully. . . .

II

For Hegel, the contradictions that drive history exist first of all in the realm of human consciousness, i.e. on the level of ideas—not the trivial election year proposals of American politicians, but ideas in the sense of large unifying world views that might best be understood under the rubric of ideology.

[1]Kojève's best-known work is his *Introduction à la lecture de Hegel* (Paris: Editions Gallimard, 1947), which is a transcript of the *Ecole Practique* lectures from the 1930s. This book is available in English entitled *Introduction to the Reading of Hegel* arranged by Raymond Queneau, edited by Allan Bloom, and translated by James Nichols (New York: Basic Books, 1969).

Ideology in this sense is not restricted to the secular and explicit political doctrines we usually associate with the term, but can include religion, culture, and the complex of moral values underlying any society as well.

Hegel's view of the relationship between the ideal and the real or material worlds was an extremely complicated one, beginning with the fact that for him the distinction between the two was only apparent. He did not believe that the real world conformed or could be made to conform to ideological preconceptions of philosophy professors in any simple-minded way, or that the "material" world could not impinge on the ideal. Indeed, Hegel the professor was temporarily thrown out of work as a result of a very material event, the Battle of Jena. But while Hegel's writing and thinking could be stopped by a bullet from the material world, the hand on the trigger of the gun was motivated in turn by the ideas of liberty and equality that had driven the French Revolution.

For Hegel, all human behavior in the material world, and hence all human history, is rooted in a prior state of consciousness—an idea similar to the one expressed by John Maynard Keynes when he said that the views of men of affairs were usually derived from defunct economists and academic scribblers of earlier generations. This consciousness may not be explicit and self-aware, as are modern political doctrines, but may rather take the form of religion or simple cultural or moral habits. And yet this realm of consciousness *in the long run* necessarily becomes manifest in the material world, indeed creates the material world in its own image. Consciousness is cause and not effect, and can develop autonomously from the material world; hence the real subtext underlying the apparent jumble of current events is the history of ideology.

Hegel's idealism has fared poorly at the hands of later thinkers. Marx reversed the priority of the real and the ideal completely, relegating the entire realm of consciousness—religion, art, culture, philosophy itself—to a "superstructure" that was determined entirely by the prevailing material mode of production. Yet another unfortunate legacy of Marxism is our tendency to retreat into materialist or utilitarian explanations of political or historical phenomena, and our disinclination to believe in the autonomous power of ideas. A recent example of this is Paul Kennedy's hugely successful *The Rise and Fall of the Great Powers,* which ascribes the decline of great powers to simple economic overextension. Obviously, this is true on some level: an empire whose economy is barely above the level of subsistence cannot bankrupt its treasury indefinitely. But whether a highly productive modern industrial society chooses to spend 3 or 7 percent of its GNP on defense rather than consumption is entirely a matter of that society's political priorities, which are in turn determined in the realm of consciousness.

The materialist bias of modern thought is characteristic not only of people on the Left who may be sympathetic to Marxism, but of many passionate anti-Marxists as well. Indeed, there is on the Right what one might label the *Wall Street Journal* school of deterministic materialism that discounts the importance of ideology and culture and sees man as essentially a rational, profit-maximizing individual. It is precisely this kind of individual and his pursuit of material incentives that is posited as the basis for economic life as such in economic textbooks. One small example will illustrate the problematic character of such materialist views.

Max Weber begins his famous book, *The Protestant Ethic and the Spirit of Capitalism,* by noting the different economic performance of Protestant and Catholic communities throughout Europe and America, summed up in the proverb that Protestants eat well while Catholics sleep well. Weber notes that according to any economic theory that posited man as a rational profit-maximizer, raising the piece-work rate should increase labor productivity. But in fact, in many traditional peasant communities, raising the piece-work rate actually had the opposite effect of *lowering* labor productivity: at the higher rate, a peasant accustomed to earning two and one-half marks per day found he could earn the same amount by working less, and did so because he valued leisure more than income. The choices of leisure over income, or of the militaristic life of the Spartan hoplite over the wealth of the Athenian trader, or even the ascetic life of the early capitalist entrepreneur over that of a traditional leisured aristocrat, cannot possibly be explained by the impersonal working of material forces, but come preeminently out of the sphere of consciousness—what we have labeled here broadly as ideology. And indeed, a central theme of Weber's work was to prove that contrary to Marx, the material mode of production, far from being the "base," was itself a "superstructure" with roots in religion and culture, and that to understand the emergence of modern capitalism and the profit motive one had to study their antecedents in the realm of the spirit.

As we look around the contemporary world, the poverty of materialist theories of economic development is all too apparent. The *Wall Street Journal* school of deterministic materialism habitually points to the stunning economic success of Asia in the past few decades as evidence of the viability of free market economics, with the implication that all societies would see similar development were they simply to allow their populations to pursue their material self-interest freely. Surely free markets and stable political systems are a necessary precondition to capitalist economic growth. But just as surely the cultural heritage of those Far Eastern societies, the ethic of work and saving and family, a religious heritage that does not, like Islam, place restrictions on certain forms of economic behavior, and other deeply ingrained moral qualities, are equally important in explaining their economic performance.[2] And yet the intellectual weight of materialism is such that not a single respectable contemporary theory of economic development ad-

[2]One need look no further than the recent performance of Vietnamese immigrants in the U.S. school system when compared to their black or Hispanic classmates to realize that culture and consciousness are absolutely crucial to explain not only economic behavior but virtually every other important aspect of life as well.

dresses consciousness and culture seriously as the matrix within which economic behavior is formed.

Failure to understand that the roots of economic behavior lie in the realm of consciousness and culture leads to the common mistake of attributing material causes to phenomena that are essentially ideal in nature. For example, it is commonplace in the West to interpret the reform movements first in China and most recently in the Soviet Union as the victory of the material over the ideal—that is, a recognition that ideological incentives could not replace material ones in stimulating a highly productive modern economy, and that if one wanted to prosper one had to appeal to baser forms of self-interest. But the deep defects of socialist economies were evident thirty or forty years ago to anyone who chose to look. Why was it that these countries moved away from central planning only in the 1980s? The answer must be found in the consciousness of the elites and leaders ruling them, who decided to opt for the "protestant" life of wealth and risk over the "Catholic" path of poverty and security. That change was in no way made inevitable by the material conditions in which either country found itself on the eve of the reform, but instead came about as the result of the victory of one idea over another. . . .

III

. . . In the past century, there have been two major challenges to liberalism, those of fascism and of communism. The former[3] saw the political weakness, materialism, anomie, and lack of community of the West as fundamental contradictions in liberal societies that could only be resolved by a strong state that forged a new "people" on the basis of national exclusiveness. Fascism was destroyed as a living ideology by World War II. This was a defeat, of course, on a very material level, but it amounted to a defeat of the idea as well. What destroyed fascism as an idea was not universal moral revulsion against it, since plenty of people were willing to endorse the idea as long as it seemed the wave of the future, but its lack of success. After the war, it seemed to most people that German fascism as well as its other European and Asian variants were bound to self-destruct. There was no material reason why new fascist movements could not have sprung up again after the war in other locales, but for the fact that expansionist ultranationalism, with its

---

[3]I am not using the term "fascism" here in its most precise sense, fully aware of the frequent misuse of this term to denounce anyone to the right of the user. "Fascism" here denotes any organized ultra-nationalist movement with universalistic pretensions—not universalistic with regard to its nationalism, of course, since the latter is exclusive by definition, but with regard to the movement's belief in its right to rule other people. Hence Imperial Japan would qualify as fascist while former strongman Stoessner's Paraguay or Pinochet's Chile would not. Obviously fascist ideologies cannot be universalistic in the sense of Marxism or liberalism, but the structure of the doctrine can be transferred from country to country.

promise of unending conflict leading to disastrous military defeat, had completely lost its appeal. The ruins of the Reich chancellory as well as the atomic bombs dropped on Hiroshima and Nagasaki killed this ideology on the level of consciousness as well as materially, and all of the proto-fascist movements spawned by the German and Japanese examples like the Peronist movement in Argentina or Subhas Chandra Bose's Indian National Army withered after the war.

The ideological challenge mounted by the other great alternative to liberalism, communism, was far more serious. Marx, speaking Hegel's language, asserted that liberal society contained a fundamental contradiction that could not be resolved within its context, that between capital and labor, and this contradiction has constituted the chief accusation against liberalism ever since. But surely, the class issue has actually been successfully resolved in the West. . . .

But the power of the liberal idea would seem much less impressive if it had not infected the largest and oldest culture in Asia, China. The simple existence of communist China created an alternative pole of ideological attraction, and as such constituted a threat to liberalism. But the past fifteen years have seen an almost total discrediting of Marxism Leninism as an economic system. Beginning with the famous third plenum of the Tenth Central Committee in 1978, the Chinese Communist party set about decollectivizing agriculture for the 800 million Chinese who still lived in the countryside. The role of the state in agriculture was reduced to that of a tax collector, while production of consumer goods was sharply increased in order to give peasants a taste of the universal homogenous state and thereby an incentive to work. The reform doubled Chinese grain output in only five years, and in the process created for Deng Xiao-ping a solid political base from which he was able to extend the reform to other parts of the economy. Economic statistics do not begin to describe the dynamism, initiative, and openness evident in China since the reform began.

China could not now be described in any way as a liberal democracy. At present, no more than 20 percent of its economy has been marketized, and most importantly it continues to be ruled by a self-appointed Communist party which has given no hint of wanting to devolve power. Deng has made none of Gorbachev's promises regarding democratization of the political system and there is no Chinese equivalent of *glasnost*. The Chinese leadership has in fact been much more circumspect in criticizing Mao and Maoism than Gorbachev with respect to Brezhnev and Stalin, and the regime continues to pay lip service to Marxism-Leninism as its ideological underpinning. But anyone familiar with the outlook and behavior of the new technocratic elite now governing China knows that Marxism and ideological principle have become virtually irrelevant as guides to policy, and that bourgeois consumerism has a real meaning in that country for the first time since the revolution. The various slowdowns in the pace of reform, the campaigns against "spiritual pollution" and crackdowns on political dissent are more properly seen as tactical adjustments made in the process of managing what is an extraordinarily difficult political transition. By ducking the question of political reform while putting the economy on a new footing, Deng has managed to avoid the breakdown of authority that has accompanied Gorbachev's *perestroika*. Yet the pull of the liberal idea continues to be very strong as economic power devolves and the economy becomes more open to the outside world. There are currently over 20,000 Chinese students studying in the U.S. and other Western countries, almost all of them the children of the Chinese elite. It is hard to believe that when they return home to run the country they will be content for China to be the only country in Asia unaffected by the larger democratizing trend. The student demonstrations in Beijing that broke out first in December 1986 and recurred recently on the occasion of Hu Yao-bang's death were only the beginning of what will inevitably be mounting pressure for change in the political system as well.

What is important about China from the standpoint of world history is not the present state of the reform or even its future prospects. The central issue is the fact that the People's Republic of China can no longer act as a beacon for illiberal forces around the world, whether they be guerrillas in some Asian jungle or middle class students in Paris. Maoism, rather than being the pattern for Asia's future, became an anachronism. . . .

If we admit for the moment that the fascist and communist challenges to liberalism are dead, are there any other ideological competitors left? Or put another way, are there contradictions in liberal society beyond that of class that are not resolvable? Two possibilities suggest themselves, those of religion and nationalism.

The rise of religious fundamentalism in recent years within the Christian, Jewish, and Muslim traditions has been widely noted. One is inclined to say that the revival of religion in some way attests to a broad unhappiness with the impersonality and spiritual vacuity of liberal consumerist societies. Yet while the emptiness at the core of liberalism is most certainly a defect in the ideology—indeed, a flaw that one does not need the perspective of religion to recognize—it is not at all clear that it is remediable through politics. Modern liberalism itself was historically a consequence of the weakness of religiously-based societies which, failing to agree on the nature of the good life, could not provide even the minimal preconditions of peace and stability. In the contemporary world only Islam has offered a theocratic state as a political alternative to both liberalism and communism. But the doctrine has little appeal for non-Muslims, and it is hard to believe that the movement will take on any universal significance. Other less organized religious impulses have been successfully satisfied within the sphere of personal life that is permitted in liberal societies.

The other major "contradiction" potentially unresolvable by liberalism is the one posed by nationalism and other forms of racial and ethnic consciousness. It is certainly true that a very large degree of conflict since the Battle of Jena has had its roots in nationalism. Two cataclysmic world wars in this century have been spawned by the nationalism of the developed world in various guises, and if those passions have been muted to a certain extent in post-war Europe, they are still extremely powerful in the Third World. Nationalism has been a threat to liberalism historically in Germany, and continues to be one in isolated parts of "post-historical" Europe like Northern Ireland.

But it is not clear that nationalism represents an irreconcilable contradiction in the heart of liberalism. In the first place, nationalism is not one single phenomenon but several, ranging from mild cultural nostalgia to the highly organized and elaborately articulated doctrine of National Socialism. Only systematic nationalisms of the latter sort can qualify as a formal ideology on the level of liberalism or communism. The vast majority of the world's nationalist movements do not have a political program beyond the negative desire of independence *from* some other group or people, and do not offer anything like a comprehensive agenda for socio-economic organization. As such, they are compatible with doctrines and ideologies that do offer such agendas. While they may constitute a source of conflict for liberal societies, this conflict does not arise from liberalism itself so much as from the fact that the liberalism in question is incomplete. Certainly a great deal of the world's ethnic and nationalist tension can be explained in terms of peoples who are forced to live in unrepresentative political systems that they have not chosen.

While it is impossible to rule out the sudden appearance of new ideologies or previously unrecognized contradictions in liberal societies, then, the present world seems to confirm that the fundamental principles of socio-political organization have not advanced terribly far since 1806. Many of the wars and revolutions fought since that time have been undertaken in the name of ideologies which claimed to be more advanced than liberalism, but whose pretensions were ultimately unmasked by history. In the meantime, they have helped to spread the universal homogenous state to the point where it could have a significant effect on the overall character of international relations.

IV

What are the implications of the end of history for international relations? Clearly, the vast bulk of the Third World remains very much mired in history, and will be a terrain of conflict for many years to come. But let us focus for the time being on the larger and more developed states of the world who after all account for the greater part of world politics. Russia and China are not likely to join the developed nations of the West as liberal societies any time in the foreseeable future, but suppose for a moment that Marxism-Leninism ceases to be a factor driving the foreign policies of these states—a prospect which, if not yet here, the last few years have made a real possibility.

How will the overall characteristics of a de-ideologized world differ from those of the one with which we are familiar at such a hypothetical juncture?

The most common answer is—not very much. For there is a very wide-spread belief among many observers of international relations that underneath the skin of ideology is a hard core of great power national interest that guarantees a fairly high level of competition and conflict between nations. Indeed, according to one academically popular school of international relations theory, conflict inheres in the international system as such, and to understand the prospects for conflict one must look at the shape of the system—for example, whether it is bipolar or multipolar—rather than at the specific character of the nations and regimes that constitute it. This school in effect applies a Hobbesian view of politics to international relations, and assumes that aggression and insecurity are universal characteristics of human societies rather than the product of specific historical circumstances.

Believers in this line of thought take the relations that existed between the participants in the classical nineteenth century European balance of power as a model for what a deideologized contemporary world would look like. Charles Krauthammer, for example, recently explained that if as a result of Gorbachev's reforms the USSR is shorn of Marxist-Leninist ideology, its behavior will revert to that of nineteenth century imperial Russia.[4] While he finds this more reassuring than the threat posed by a communist Russia, he implies that there will still be a substantial degree of competition and conflict in the international system, just as there was say between Russia and Britain or Wilhelmine Germany in the last century. This is, of course, a convenient point of view for people who want to admit that something major is changing in the Soviet Union, but do not want to accept responsibility for recommending the radical policy redirection implicit in such a view. But is it true?

In fact, the notion that ideology is a superstructure imposed on a substratum of permanent great power interest is a highly questionable proposition. For the way in which any state defines its national interest is not universal but rests on some kind of prior ideological basis, just as we saw that economic behavior is determined by a prior state of consciousness. In this century, states have adopted highly articulated doctrines with explicit foreign policy agendas legitimizing expansionism, like Marxism-Leninism or National Socialism.

The expansionist and competitive behavior of nineteenth-century European states rested on no less ideal a basis; it just so happened that the ideology driving it was less explicit than the doctrines of the twentieth century. For one thing, most "liberal" European societies were illiberal insofar as they believed in the legitimacy of imperialism, that is, the right of one nation to rule over other nations without regard for the wishes of the ruled. The justifications for imperialism varied from nation to nation, from a crude belief in

---

[4]See his article, "Beyond the Cold War," *New Republic,* December 19, 1988.

the legitimacy of force, particularly when applied to non-Europeans, to the White Man's Burden and Europe's Christianizing mission, to the desire to give people of color access to the culture of Rabelais and Molière. But whatever the particular ideological basis, every "developed" country believed in the acceptability of higher civilizations ruling lower ones—including, incidentally, the United States with regard to the Philippines. This led to a drive for pure territorial aggrandizement in the latter half of the century and played no small role in causing the Great War.

The radical and deformed outgrowth of nineteenth-century imperialism was German fascism, an ideology which justified Germany's right not only to rule over non-European peoples, but over *all* non-German ones. But in retrospect it seems that Hitler represented a diseased bypath in the general course of European development, and since his fiery defeat, the legitimacy of any kind of territorial aggrandizement has been thoroughly discredited.[5] Since the Second World War, European nationalism has been defanged and shorn of any real relevance to foreign policy, with the consequence that the nineteenth-century model of great power behavior has become a serious anachronism. The most extreme form of nationalism that any Western European state has mustered since 1945 has been Gaullism, whose self-assertion has been confined largely to the realm of nuisance politics and culture. International life for the part of the world that has reached the end of history is far more preoccupied with economics than with politics or strategy.

The developed states of the West do maintain defense establishments and in the post war period have competed vigorously for influence to meet a worldwide communist threat. This behavior has been driven, however, by an external threat from states that possess overtly expansionist ideologies, and would not exist in their absence. To take the "neo-realist" theory seriously, one would have to believe that "natural" competitive behavior would reassert itself among the OECD states were Russia and China to disappear from the face of the earth. That is, West Germany and France would arm themselves against each other as they did in the 1930s, Australia and New Zealand would send military advisers to block each others' advances in Africa, and the U.S.-Canadian border would become fortified. Such a prospect is, of course, ludicrous: minus Marxist-Leninist ideology, we are far more likely to see the "Common Marketization" of world politics than the disintegration of the EEC into nineteenth-century competitiveness. Indeed, as our experience in dealing with Europe on matters such as terrorism or Libya prove, they are much further gone than we down the road that denies the legitimacy of the use of force in international politics, even in self-defense.

---

[5]It took European colonial powers like France several years after the war to admit the illegitimacy of their empires, but decolonialization was an inevitable consequence of the Allied victory which had been based on the promise of a restoration of democratic freedoms.

The automatic assumption that Russia shorn of its expansionist communist ideology should pick up where the czars left off just prior to the Bolshe-
vik Revolution is therefore a curious one. It assumes that the evolution of
human consciousness has stood still in the meantime, and that the Soviets,
while picking up currently fashionable ideas in the realm of economics, will
return to foreign policy views a century out of date in the rest of Europe.
This is certainly not what happened to China after it began its reform
process. Chinese competitiveness and expansionism on the world scene
have virtually disappeared: Beijing no longer sponsors Maoist insurgencies
or tries to cultivate influence in distant African countries as it did in the
1960s. This is not to say that there are not troublesome aspects to contemporary Chinese foreign policy, such as the reckless sale of ballistic missile technology in the Middle East; and the PRC continues to manifest traditional
great power behavior in its sponsorship of the Khmer Rouge against Vietnam. But the former is explained by commercial motives and the latter is a
vestige of earlier ideologically-based rivalries. The new China far more resembles Gaullist France than pre-World War I Germany.

The real question for the future, however, is the degree to which Soviet
elites have assimilated the consciousness of the universal homogenous state
that is post-Hitler Europe. From their writings and from my own personal
contacts with them, there is no question in my mind that the liberal Soviet
intelligentsia rallying around Gorbachev has arrived at the end-of-history
view in a remarkably short time, due in no small measure to the contacts
they have had since the Brezhnev era with the larger European civilization
around them. "New political thinking," the general rubric for their views,
describes a world dominated by economic concerns, in which there are no
ideological grounds for major conflict between nations, and in which, consequently, the use of military force becomes less legitimate. As Foreign Minister Shevardnadze put it in mid-1988:

> The struggle between two opposing systems is no longer a determining ten-
> dency of the present-day era. At the modern stage, the ability to build up mate-
> rial wealth at an accelerated rate on the basis of front-ranking science and
> high-level techniques and technology, and to distribute it fairly, and through
> joint efforts to restore and protect the resources necessary for mankind's sur-
> vival acquires decisive importance.

The post-historical consciousness represented by "new thinking" is only
one possible future for the Soviet Union, however. There has always been a
very strong current of great Russian chauvinism in the Soviet Union, which
has found freer expression since the advent of *glasnost*. It may be possible to
return to traditional Marxism-Leninism for a while as a simple rallying point
for those who want to restore the authority that Gorbachev has dissipated.
But as in Poland, Marxism-Leninism is dead as a mobilizing ideology: under
its banner people cannot be made to work harder, and its adherents have
lost confidence in themselves. Unlike the propagators of traditional Marx-

ism-Leninism, however, ultra-nationalists in the USSR believe in their Slavophile cause passionately, and one gets the sense that the fascist alternative is not one that has played itself out entirely there.

The Soviet Union, then, is at a fork in the road: it can start down the path that was staked out by Western Europe forty-five years ago, a path that most of Asia has followed, or it can realize its own uniqueness and remain stuck in history. The choice it makes will be highly important for us, given the Soviet Union's size and military strength, for that power will continue to preoccupy us and slow our realization that we have already emerged on the other side of history.

V

The passing of Marxism-Leninism first from China and then from the Soviet Union will mean its death as a living ideology of world historical significance. For while there may be some isolated true believers left in places like Managua, Pyongyang, or Cambridge, Massachusetts, the fact that there is not a single large state in which it is a going concern undermines completely its pretensions to being in the vanguard of human history. And the death of this ideology means the growing "Common Marketization" of international relations, and the diminution of the likelihood of large-scale conflict between states.

This does not by any means imply the end of international conflict *per se*. For the world at that point would be divided between a part that was historical and a part that was post-historical. Conflict between states still in history, and between those states and those at the end of history, would still be possible. There would still be a high and perhaps rising level of ethnic and nationalist violence, since those are impulses incompletely played out, even in parts of the post-historical world. Palestinians and Kurds, Sikhs and Tamils, Irish Catholics and Walloons, Armenians and Azeris, will continue to have their unresolved grievances. This implies that terrorism and wars of national liberation will continue to be an important item on the international agenda. But large-scale conflict must involve large states still caught in the grip of history, and they are what appear to be passing from the scene.

The end of history will be a very sad time. The struggle for recognition, the willingness to risk one's life for a purely abstract goal, the worldwide ideological struggle that called forth daring, courage, imagination, and idealism, will be replaced by economic calculation, the endless solving of technical problems, environmental concerns, and the satisfaction of sophisticated consumer demands. In the post-historical period there will be neither art nor philosophy, just the perpetual caretaking of the museum of human history. I can feel in myself, and see in others around me, a powerful nostalgia for the time when history existed. Such nostalgia, in fact, will continue to fuel competition and conflict even in the post-historical world for some time to come. Even though I recognize its inevitability, I have the most ambivalent feelings for the civilization that has been created in Europe since 1945, with its north Atlantic and Asian offshoots. Perhaps this very prospect of centuries of boredom at the end of history will serve to get history started once again.

The Obsolescence of Major War

JOHN MUELLER

On May 15, 1984, the major countries of the developed world had managed to remain at peace with each other for the longest continuous stretch of time since the days of the Roman Empire. If a significant battle in a war had been fought on that day, the press would have bristled with it. As usual, however, a landmark crossing in the history of peace caused no stir: the most prominent story in the *New York Times* that day concerned the saga of a manicurist, a machinist, and a cleaning woman who had just won a big Lotto contest. . . .

For decades now, two massively armed countries, the United States and the Soviet Union, have dominated international politics, and during that time they have engaged in an intense, sometimes even desperate, rivalry over political, military, and ideological issues. Yet despite this enormous mutual hostility, they have never gone to war with each other. Furthermore, although they have occasionally engaged in confrontational crises, there have been only a few of these—and virtually none at all in the last two-thirds of the period. Rather than gradually drawing closer to armed conflict, as often happened after earlier wars, the two major countries seem to be drifting farther away from it.

Insofar as it is discussed at all, there appear to be two schools of thought to explain what John Lewis Gaddis has called the "long peace."[1]

John Mueller, *Retreat from Doomsday: The Obsolescence of Major War* (New York: Basic Books, 1989), Introduction. Copyright © 1989, 1990 by John Mueller. Excerpts reprinted by permission of Basic Books, a division of HarperCollins publishers.

[1]Gaddis 1987b. The calculations about eras of peace are by Paul Schroeder (1985, p. 88). The previous record, he notes, was chalked up during the period from the end of the Napoleonic Wars in 1815 to the effective beginning of the Crimean War in 1854. The period between the conclusion of the Franco-Prussian War in 1871 and the outbreak of World War I in 1914— marred by a major war in Asia between Russia and Japan in 1904—was an even longer era of peace among major European countries. That record was broken on November 8, 1988. On some of these issues, see also Nye 1987; Hinsley 1963, ch. 17; Luard 1986, pp. 395–99; Russett and Starr 1981, ch. 15.

One school concludes that we have simply been lucky. Since 1947, the *Bulletin of Atomic Scientists* has decorated its cover with a "doomsday" clock set ominously at a few minutes before midnight. From time to time the editors push the clock's big hand forward or backward a bit to demonstrate their pleasure with an arms control measure or their disapproval of what they perceive to be rising tension; but they never nudge it very far away from the fatal hour, and the message they wish to convey is clear. They believe we live perpetually on the brink, teetering on a fragile balance; if our luck turns a bit sour, we are likely at any moment to topple helplessly in cataclysmic war.[2] As time goes by, however, this point of view begins to lose some of its persuasiveness. When a clock remains poised at a few minutes to midnight for decades, one may gradually come to suspect that it isn't telling us very much.

The other school stresses paradox: It is the very existence of unprecedentedly destructive weapons that has worked, so far, to our benefit—in Winston Churchill's memorable phrase, safety has been the "sturdy child of [nuclear] terror."[3] This widely held (if minimally examined) view is, to say the least, less than fully comforting, because the very weapons that have been so necessary for peace according to this argument, also possess the capability of cataclysmic destruction, should they somehow be released. For many, this perpetual threat is simply too much to bear, and to them the weapons' continued existence seals our ultimate doom even as it perpetuates our current peace. In his influential best-seller, *The Fate of the Earth*, Jonathan Schell dramatically prophesies that if we do not "rise up and cleanse the earth of nuclear weapons," we will soon "sink into the final coma and end it all."[4]

This book develops a third explanation: The long peace since World War II is less a product of recent weaponry than the culmination of a substantial historical process. For the last two or three centuries major war—war among developed countries—has gradually moved toward terminal disrepute because of its perceived repulsiveness and futility.

---

[2]Said Herman Kahn in 1960: "I have a firm belief that unless we have more serious and sober thought on various aspects of the strategic problem . . . we are not going to reach the year 2000—and maybe not even the year 1965—without a cataclysm" (1960, p. x). Hans J. Morgenthau stated in 1979, "In my opinion the world is moving ineluctably towards a third world war—a strategic nuclear war. I do not believe that anything can be done to prevent it. The international system is too unstable to survive for long" (quoted, Boyle 1985, p. 73). And astronomer Carl Sagan commented in 1983: "I do not think our luck can hold out forever" (quoted, Schroeder 1985, p. 87). On the history of the doomsday clock, see Feld 1978.

[3]Churchill: Bartlett 1977, p. 104. Edward Luttwak says, "We have lived since 1945 without another world war precisely because rational minds . . . extracted a durable peace from the very terror of nuclear weapons" (1983b, p. 82). Kenneth Waltz: "Nuclear weapons have banished war from the center of international politics" (1988, p. 627). See also Knorr 1985, p. 79; Mearsheimer 1984/85, pp. 25–26; Art and Waltz 1983, p. 28; Gilpin 1981, pp. 213–19; Betts 1987, pp. 1–2; Joffe 1987, p. 37; F. Lewis 1987.

[4]Schell 1982, p. 231. For a discussion of expert opinion concluding that the chances of nuclear war by the year 2000 were at least fifty-fifty, see Russett 1983, pp. 3–4.

The book also concludes that nuclear weapons have not had an important impact on this remarkable trend—they have not crucially defined postwar stability, and they do not threaten to disturb it severely. They have affected rhetoric (we live, we are continually assured, in the atomic age, the nuclear epoch), and they certainly have influenced defense budgets and planning. However, they do not seem to have been necessary to deter major war, to cause the leaders of major countries to behave cautiously, or to determine the alliances that have been formed. Rather, it seems that things would have turned out much the same had nuclear weapons never been invented.

That something other than nuclear terror explains the long peace is suggested in part by the fact that there have been numerous nonwars since 1945 besides the nonwar that is currently being waged by the United States and the Soviet Union. With only one minor and fleeting exception (the Soviet invasion of Hungary in 1956), there have been no wars among the forty-four wealthiest (per capita) countries during that time.[5] Although there have been many wars since World War II, some of them enormously costly by any standard, these have taken place almost entirely within the third—or really the fourth—world. The developed countries have sometimes participated in these wars on distant turf, but not directly against each other.

Several specific nonwars are in their own way even more extraordinary than the one that has taken place between the United States and the Soviet Union. France and Germany are important countries which had previously spent decades—centuries even—either fighting each other or planning to do so. For this ages-old antagonism World War II indeed served as the war to end war: like Greece and Turkey, they have retained the creative ability to discover a motivation for war even under an overarching nuclear umbrella if they really wanted to, yet they have now lived side by side for decades, perhaps with some bitterness and recrimination, but without even a glimmer of war fever. The case of Japan is also striking: this formerly aggressive major country seems now to have fully embraced the virtues (and profits) of peace.

In fact, within the first and second worlds warfare of *all* sorts seems generally to have lost its appeal. Not only have there been virtually no international wars among the major and not-so-major countries, but the developed world has experienced virtually no civil war either. The only exception is the

---

[5]Wealth is calculated using 1978 data when Iran and Iraq were at their financial peak (World Bank 1980). If later data are used, the figure of forty-four would be greater. Countries like Monaco that have no independent foreign policy are not included in the count. The Soviet invasion of Hungary was in some sense requested by ruling politicians in Hungary and for that reason is sometimes not classified as an international war. On classification issues, see Small and Singer 1982, pp. 55, 305; Luard 1986, pp. 5–7. Small and Singer consider Saudi Arabia to have been a participant in the Yom Kippur War of 1973 because it committed 1,000 troops to the anti-Israeli conflict (p. 306); if one accepts their procedure here, that war would form another example of war among the top forty-four. Some might also include the bloodless "war" between the USSR and Czechoslovakia in 1968.

1944–49 Greek civil war—more an unsettled residue of World War II tha an autonomous event. The sporadic violence in Northern Ireland or th Basque region of Spain has not really been sustained enough to be consic ered civil war, nor have the spurts of terrorism carried out by tiny bands c self-styled revolutionaries elsewhere in Western Europe that have never coa lesced into anything bigger. Except for the fleeting case of Hungary in 1956 Europeans under Soviet rule have so far accepted their fate, no matter hov desperate their disaffection, rather than take arms to oppose it—thougl some sort of civil uprising there is certainly not out of the question.[6]

Because it is so quiet, peace often is allowed to carry on unremarked. W tend to delimit epochs by wars and denote periods of peace not for thei own character, but for the wars they separate. As Geoffrey Blainey has ob served, "For every thousand pages published on the causes of wars there i less than one page directly on the causes of peace."[7] But now, surely, with sc much peace at hand in so much of the world, some effort ought to be made to explain the unprecedented cornucopia. Never before in history have so many well-armed, important countries spent so much time not using their arms against each other. . . .

The Rising Costs of War

War is merely an idea. It is not a trick of fate, a thunderbolt from hell, a nat- ural calamity, or a desperate plot contrivance dreamed up by some sadistic puppeteer on high. And if war begins in the minds of men, as the UNESCO charter insists, it can end there as well. Over the centuries war opponents have been trying to bring this about by discrediting war as an idea. In part, their message . . . stresses that war is unacceptably costly, and they have pointed to two kinds of costs: (1) psychic ones—war, they argue, is repulsive, immoral, and uncivilized; and (2) physical ones—war is bloody, destructive, and expensive.

It is often observed that war's physical costs have risen. World War II was the most destructive in history, and World War I was also terrible. World War III, even if nuclear weapons were not used, could easily be worse; and a ther- monuclear war might, as Schell would have it, "end it all."

Rising physical costs do seem to have helped to discredit war. But there are good reasons to believe that this cannot be the whole story.

In 1889, Baroness Bertha von Suttner of Austria published a sentimental antiwar novel, *Die Waffen Nieder!*, that swiftly became an international best- seller—the *Uncle Tom's Cabin* of the nineteenth-century peace movement. In

---

[6]Even as dedicated a foe of the Soviet regime as Aleksandr Solzhenitsyn has said, "I have never advocated physical general revolution. That would entail such destruction of our people's life as would not merit the victory obtained" (quoted, S. Cohen 1985, p. 214).

[7]Blainey, 1973, p. 3.

it she describes the travails of a young Austrian woman who turns against war when her husband is killed in the Franco-Austrian War of 1859. Now, in historical perspective, that brief war was one of the least memorable in modern history, and its physical costs were minor in comparison with many other wars of that, or any other, era. But Suttner's fictional young widow was repelled not by the war's size, but by its existence and by the devastating personal consequences to her. Opposition to war has been growing in the developed world because more and more people have come to find war repulsive for what it *is*, not simply for the extent of the devastation it causes.

Furthermore, it is simply not true that cataclysmic war is an invention of the 20th century.[8] To annihilate ancient Carthage in 146 B.C., the Romans used weaponry that was primitive by today's standard, but even nuclear weapons could not have been more thorough. And, as Thucydides recounts with shattering calm, when the Athenians invaded Melos in 416 B.C., they "put to death all the grown men whom they took and sold the women and children for slaves, and subsequently sent out five hundred colonists and inhabited the place for themselves."[9]

During the Thirty Years War of 1618–48 the wealthy city of Magdeburg, together with its 20,000 inhabitants, was annihilated. According to standard estimates accepted as late as the 1930s, Germany's population in that war declined from 21 million to under 13.5 million—absolute losses far larger than it suffered in either world war of the twentieth century. Moreover, and more importantly, most people apparently *thought* things were even worse: for centuries a legend prevailed that Germany had suffered a 75 percent decline in population, from 16 million to 4 million.[10] Yet the belief that war could cause devastation of such enormous proportions did not lead to its abandonment. After the Thirty Years War, conflict remained endemic in Europe, and in 1756 Prussia fought the Seven Years War, which, in the estimate of its king and generalissimo, Frederick the Great, cost it 500,000 lives—one-

[9]To put things in somewhat broader perspective, it may be useful to note that war is not the century's greatest killer. Although there have been a large number of extremely destructive wars, totalitarian and extreme authoritarian governments have put more of their own people to death—three times more according to one calculation—than have died in all the century's international and civil wars combined (Rummel 1986). For example, the man-made famine in China between 1958 and 1962 apparently caused the deaths of 30 million people (see p. 165), far more than died during World War I. Governments at peace can also surpass war in their economic destruction as well; largely because of government mismanagement and corruption, the average Zairian's wages in 1988, after adjusting for inflation, were 10 percent of what they had been in 1960 (Greenhouse 1988).

[9]Thucydides 1934, p. 337.

[10]Wedgwood 1938, p. 516. German civilian and military deaths have been estimated at 3,160,000 in World War I and 6,221,000 in World War II (Sivard 1987, p. 29). For the latter-day argument that the losses in the Thirty Years War have been grossly overestimated, see Steinberg 1966, ch. 3. A recent estimate suggests a population decline from 20 million to 16 or 17 million (Parker 1984, p. 211).

ninth of its population, a proportion higher than almost any suffered by any combatant in the wars of the nineteenth or twentieth centuries.[11]

Wars in the past have often caused revolts and economic devastation as well. Historians have been debating for a century whether the Thirty Years War destroyed a vibrant economy in Germany or whether it merely administered the final blow to an economy that was already in decline—but destruction was the consequence in either case. The Seven Years War brought Austria to virtual bankruptcy, and it so weakened France that the conditions for revolution were established. When the economic costs of war are measured as a percentage of the gross national product of the combatants, observes Alan Milward, war "has not shown any discernible long-term trend towards greater costliness."[12]

And in sheer pain and suffering wars used to be far worse than ones fought by developed countries today. In 1840 or 1640 or 1240 a wounded or diseased soldier often died slowly and in intense agony. Medical aid was inadequate, and since physicians had few remedies and were unaware of the germ theory, they often only made things worse. War, indeed, was hell. By contrast, an American soldier wounded in the Vietnam jungle could be in a sophisticated, sanitized hospital within a half hour.

Consequently, if the revulsion toward war has grown in the developed world, this development cannot be due entirely to a supposed rise in its physical costs. Also needed is an appreciation for war's increased psychic costs. Over the last century or two, war in the developed world has come widely to be regarded as repulsive, immoral, and uncivilized. There may also be something of an interactive effect between psychic and physical costs here: If for moral reasons we come to place a higher value on human life— even to have a sort of reverence for it—the physical costs of war or any other life-taking enterprise will effectively rise as cost tolerance declines.

It may not be obvious that an accepted, time-honored institution that serves an urgent social purpose can become obsolescent and then die out because a lot of people come to find it obnoxious. But this book will argue that something like that has been happening to war in the developed world. To illustrate the dynamic and to set up a framework for future discussion, it will be helpful briefly to assess two analogies: the processes through which the once-perennial institutions of dueling and slavery have been virtually expunged from the earth.

[11]Luard 1986, p. 51. Small and Singer 1982, pp. 82–99. About 180,000 of the half-million were soldiers (Kennedy 1987, p. 115), giving a battle death rate of about 4 percent.
[12]Thirty Years War: Robb 1962. Seven Years War: Kennedy 1987, p. 114; Brodie 1973, pp. 248–49; Milward 1977, p. 3.

Dueling Ceases to Be a "Peculiar Necessity"

In some important respects war in the developed world may be following the example of another violent method for settling disputes, dueling, which up until a century ago was common practice in Europe and America among a certain class of young and youngish men who liked to classify themselves as gentlemen. When one man concluded that he had been insulted by another and therefore that his honor had been besmirched, he might well engage the insulter in a short, private, and potentially deadly battle. The duel was taken somehow to settle the matter, even if someone was killed in the process—or even if someone wasn't.[13]

At base, dueling was a matter of attitude more than of cosmology or technology; it was something someone might want to do, and in some respects was even expected to do, from time to time. The night before his famous fatal duel with Aaron Burr in 1804, the methodical Alexander Hamilton wrote out his evaluation of the situation. He could find many reasons to reject Burr's challenge—he really felt no ill will toward his challenger, he wrote, and dueling was against his religious and moral principles, as well as against the laws of New York (where he lived) and New Jersey (where the duel was to be held); furthermore, his death would endanger the livelihood of his wife, children, and creditors. In sum, "I shall hazard much, and can possibly gain nothing." Nevertheless, he still concluded he must fight. All these concerns were overwhelmed because he felt that "what men of the world denominate honor" imposed upon him a "peculiar necessity": his refusal to duel would reduce his political effectiveness by subjecting him to contempt and derision in the circles he considered important. Therefore, he felt that he had to conform with "public prejudice in this particular."[14] Although there were solid economic, legal, moral, and religious reasons to turn down the challenge of Vice President Burr, the prick of honor and the attendant fear of immobilizing ridicule—Hamilton's peculiar necessities—impelled him to venture out that summer morning to meet his fate, and his maker, at Weehawken, N.J.

Dueling died out as a general practice eighty years later in the United States after enjoying quite a vogue, especially in the South and in California. It finally faded, not so much because it was outlawed (like liquor—and war—in the 1920s), but because the "public prejudice" Hamilton was so fatally concerned about changed in this particular. Since dueling was an activity carried out by consenting adults in private, laws prohibiting it were difficult to enforce when the climate of opinion accepted the institution. But gradu-

---

[13]For other observations of the analogy between war and dueling, see Brodie 1973, p. 275; Angell 1914, pp. 202–3; Gooch 1911, p. 249; Cairnes 1865, p. 650n.
[14]Seitz 1929, pp. 98–101; Freeman 1884, pp. 345–48.

ally a consensus emerged that dueling was contemptible and stupid, and it came to be duelers, not nonduelers, who suffered ridicule. As one student of the subject has concluded, "It began to be clear that pistols at ten paces did not settle anything except who was the better shot. . . . Dueling had long been condemned by both statute book and church decree. But these could make no headway against public opinion." However, when it came to pass that "solemn gentlemen went to the field of honor only to be laughed at by the younger generation, that was more than any custom, no matter how sanctified by tradition, could endure. And so the code of honor in America finally died." One of the last duels was in 1877. After the battle (at which no blood was spilled), the combatants found themselves the butt of public hilarity, causing one of them to flee to Paris, where he remained in self-exile for several years.[15]

The American experience was reflected elsewhere. Although dueling's decline in country after country was due in part to enforced legislation against it, the "most effective weapon" against it, one study concludes, "has undoubtedly been ridicule."[16] The ultimate physical cost of dueling—death—did not, and could not rise. But the psychic costs did.

Men of Hamilton's social set still exist, they still get insulted, and they still are concerned about their self respect and their standing among their peers. But they don't duel. However, they do not avoid dueling today because they evaluate the option and reject it on cost–benefit grounds—to use the jargon of a later chapter, they do not avoid it because it has become rationally unthinkable. Rather, the option never percolates into their consciousness as something that is available—that is, it has become subrationally unthinkable. Dueling under the right conditions—with boxing gloves, for example—would not violate current norms or laws. And, of course, in other social classes duel-like combat, such as the street fight or gang war, persists. But the romantic, ludicrous institution of formal dueling has faded from the scene. Insults of the sort that led to the Hamilton-Burr duel often are simply ignored or, if applicable, they are settled with peaceful methods like litigation.[17]

A dueling manual from 1847 states that "dueling, like war, is the necessary consequence of offense."[18] By now, however, dueling, a form of violence famed and fabled for centuries, is avoided not merely because it has ceased to seem "necessary," but because it has sunk from thought as a viable, con-

---

[15]Stevens 1940, pp. 280–83. See also Cochran 1963, p. 287.

[16]Baldick 1965, p. 199.

[17]It is sometimes held that dueling died out because improved access to the legal system provided a nonviolent alternative. But most duels were fought over matters of "honor," not legality. Furthermore, lawyers, hardly a group alienated or disenfranchised from the legal system, were frequent duelists—in Tennessee 90 percent of all duels were fought between attorneys (Seitz 1929, p. 30).

[18]Stowe 1987, p. 15.

scious possibility. You can't fight a duel if the idea of doing so never occurs to you or your opponent.

The Prussian strategist Carl von Clausewitz opens his famous 1832 book, *On War,* by observing that "war is nothing but a duel on a larger scale."[19] If war, like dueling, comes to be viewed as a thoroughly undesirable, even ridiculous, policy, and if it can no longer promise gains or if potential combatants no longer value the things it can gain for them, then war could fade away first as a "peculiar necessity" and then as a coherent possibility, even if a truly viable substitute or "moral equivalent" for it were never formulated. Like dueling, it could become unfashionable and then obsolete.

Slavery Abruptly Becomes a "Peculiar Institution"

From the dawn of prehistory until about 1788 it had occurred to almost no one that there was anything the least bit peculiar about the institution of slavery. Like war, it could be found just about everywhere in one form or another, and it flourished in every age.[20] Here and there, some people expressed concern about excessive cruelty, and a few found slavery an unfortunate necessity. But the abolitionist movement that broke out at the end of the eighteenth century in Britain and the United States was something new, not the culmination of a substantial historical process.

Like war opponents, the antislavery forces had come to believe that the institution that concerned them was unacceptable because of both its psychic and its physical costs. For some time a small but socially active religious sect in England and the United States, the Quakers, had been arguing that slavery, like war, was repulsive, immoral, and uncivilized, and this sentiment gradually picked up adherents.

Slavery's physical costs, opponents argued, stemmed from its inefficiency. In 1776, Adam Smith concluded that the "work done by slaves . . . is in the end the dearest of any" because "a person who can acquire no property, can have no other interest but to eat as much and to labor as little as possible." Smith's view garnered adherents, but not, as it happens, among slaveowners. That is, either Smith was wrong, or slaveholders were bad businessmen. Clearly, if the economic argument had been correct, slavery would have eventually died of its own inefficiency. Although some have argued that this process was indeed under way, Stanley Engerman observes that in "the history of slave emancipation in the Americas, it is difficult to find any cases of slavery declining economically prior to the imposition of emancipation." Rather, he says, "it took political and military action to bring it to a halt," and

---

[19]Clausewitz 1976, p. 75.
[20]See Patterson 1982; Engerman 1986, pp. 318–19.

"political, cultural, and ideological factors" played crucial roles. In fact, at exactly the time that the antislavery movement was taking flight, the Atlantic slave economy, as Seymour Drescher notes, "was entering what was probably the most dynamic and profitable period in its existence."[21]

Thus, the abolitionists were up against an institution that was viable, profitable, and expanding, and one that had been uncritically accepted for thousands—perhaps millions—of years as a natural and inevitable part of human existence. To counter this time-honored institution, the abolitionists' principal weapon was a novel argument: it had recently occurred to them, they said, that slavery was no longer the way people ought to do things.

As it happened, it was an idea whose time had come. The abolition of slavery required legislative battles, international pressures, economic travail, and, in the United States, a cataclysmic war (but, notably, it did *not* require the fabrication of a functional equivalent or the formation of an effective supranational authority). Within a century slavery, and most similar institutions like serfdom, had been all but eradicated from the face of the globe. Slavery became controversial, then peculiar, and then obsolete.

War

Dueling and slavery no longer exist as effective institutions and have faded from human experience except as something one reads about in books. Although their reestablishment is not impossible, they show after a century of neglect no signs of revival. Other once-popular, even once admirable, institutions in the developed world have been, or are being, eliminated because at some point they began to seem repulsive, immoral, and uncivilized: bearbaiting, bareknuckle fighting, freak shows, casual torture, wanton cruelty to animals, the burning of heretics, Jim Crow laws, human sacrifice, family feuding, public and intentionally painful methods of execution, deforming corseting, infanticide, laughing at the insane, executions for minor crimes, eunuchism, flogging, public cigarette smoking. . . . War is not, of course, the same as dueling or slavery. Like war, dueling is an institution for settling disputes; but it usually involved only matters of "honor," not ones of physical gain. Like war, slavery was nearly universal and an apparently inevitable part of human existence, but it could be eliminated area by area: a country that abolished slavery did not have to worry about what other countries were doing. A country that would like to abolish war, however, must continue to be concerned about those that have kept it in their repertoire.

On the other hand, war has against it not only substantial psychic costs but also very obvious and widespread physical ones. Dueling brought death and

---

[21]Smith 1976, p. 387 (book 3, ch. 2). Engerman 1986, pp. 322—33, 339. Drescher 1987, p. 4; see also Eltis 1987.

injury, but only to a few people who, like Hamilton, had specifically volunteered to participate. And although slavery may have brought moral destruction, it generally was a considerable economic success in the view of those who ran the system, if not to every ivory-tower economist.

In some respects, then, the fact that war has outlived dueling and slavery is curious. But there are signs that, at least in the developed world, it has begun, like them, to succumb to obsolescence. Like dueling and slavery, war does not appear to be one of life's necessities—it is not an unpleasant fact of existence that is somehow required by human nature or by the grand scheme of things. One can live without it, quite well in fact. War may be a social affliction, but in important respects it is also a social affectation that can be shrugged off.

References

Angell, Norman. 1914. The Great Illusion: A Study of the Relation of Military Power to National Advantage. London: Heinemann.

———. 1933. *The Great Illusion 1933.* New York: Putnam's.

———. 1951. *After All: An Autobiography.* New York: Farrar, Straus and Young.

Art, Robert J., and Kenneth N. Waltz. 1983. Technology, Strategy, and the Uses of Force. In Robert J. Art and Kenneth N. Waltz (eds.), *The Use of Force.* Lanham, MD: University Press of America.

Baldick, Robert. 1965. *The Duel: A History of Dueling.* New York: Potter.

Bartlett, C. J. 1977. *A History of Postwar Britain, 1945–1974.* London: Longman.

Betts, Richard K. 1987. *Nuclear Blackmail and Nuclear Balance.* Washington: Brookings.

Boyle, Francis Anthony. 1985. *World Politics and International Law.* Durham, NC: Duke University Press.

Brodie, Bernard. 1946. The Weapon. In Bernard Brodie (ed.), *The Absolute Weapon.* New York: Harcourt, Brace, pp. 21–107.

———. 1959. *Strategy in the Missile Age.* Princeton, NJ: Princeton University Press.

———. 1966. *Escalation and the Nuclear Option.* Princeton, NJ: Princeton University Press.

———. 1973. *War and Politics.* New York: Macmillan.

———. 1976a. The Continuing Relevance of On War, and A Guide to the Reading of On War. In Carl von Clausewitz, *On War.* Princeton, NJ: Princeton University Press, pp. 45–58, 641–711.

———. 1976b. On the Objectives of Arms Control. *International Security,* vol. 1, no. 1 (Summer), pp. 17–36.

Cairnes, J. E. 1865. International Law. *Fortnightly Review,* vol. 2 (November 1), pp. 641–50.

Clausewitz, Carl von. 1976. *On War* (Edited and translated by Michael Howard and Peter Paret).

Cochran, Hamilton. 1963. *Noted American Duels and Hostile Encounters.* Philadelphia: Chilton.

Drescher, Seymour. 1987. *Capitalism and Antislavery: British Mobilization in Comparative Respective.* New York: Oxford University Press.

————. 1988. Brazilian Abolition in Comparative Perspective. *Hispanic American Historical Review,* vol. 68, no. 3 (August), pp. 429–60.

Eltis, David. 1987. *Economic Growth and the Ending of the Transatlantic Slave Trade.* New York: Oxford University Press.

Engerman, Stanley L. 1986. Slavery and Emancipation in Comparative Perspective: A Look at Some Recent Debates. *Journal of Economic History,* vol. 46, no. 2 (June), pp. 317–39.

Feld, Bernard T. 1978. To Move or Not to Move the Clock. *Bulletin of Atomic Scientists,* January, pp. 8–9.

Freeman, Major Ben C. 1884. *The Field of Honor: Being a Complete and Comprehensive History of Dueling in All Countries.* New York: Fords, Howard, and Hulbert.

Gaddis, John Lewis. 1972. *The United States and the Origins of the Cold War, 1941–1947.* New York: Columbia University Press.

————. 1974. Was the Truman Doctrine a Real Turning Point? *Foreign Affairs,* vol. 52, no. 2 (January), pp. 386–401.

————. 1982. *Strategies of Containment: A Critical Appraisal of Postwar American National Security Policy.* New York: Oxford University Press.

————. 1987a. Expanding the Data Base: Historians, Political Scientists, and the Enrichment of Security Studies. *International Security,* vol. 12, no. 1 (Summer), pp. 3–21.

————. 1987b. *The Long Peace: Inquiries into the History of the Cold War.* New York: Oxford University Press.

Gilpin, Robert. 1981. *War and Change in World Politics.* Cambridge: Cambridge University Press.

Gooch, B. P. 1911. *History of Our Time, 1885–1911.* London: Williams and Norgate.

Greenhouse, Steven. 1988. Zaire, The Manager's Nightmare, So Much Potential, So Poorly Harnessed. *New York Times,* May 23, p. 48. See also correction, May 26, p. A3.

Hinsley, F. H. 1963. *Power and the Pursuit of Peace: Theory and Practice in the History of Relations between States.* London: Cambridge University Press.

Joffe, Josef. 1987. Peace and Populism: Why the European Anti-Nuclear Movement Failed. *International Security,* vol. 11, no. 4 (Spring), pp. 3–40.

Kahn, Herman. 1960. *On Thermonuclear War.* Princeton, NJ: Princeton University Press.

————. 1970. Issues of Thermonuclear War Termination. *Annals of the American Academy of Political and Social Science,* vol. 390 (November), pp. 133–72.

Kennedy, Paul. 1987. *The Rise and Fall of the Great Powers.* New York: Random House.

Knorr, Klaus. 1966. *On the Uses of Military Power in the Nuclear Age.* Princeton, NJ: Princeton University Press.

————. 1985. Controlling Nuclear War. *International Security,* vol. 9, no. 4 (Spring), pp. 79–98.

Lewis, Flora. 1986. Step Back from Folly. *New York Times,* November 7, p. A35.

————. 1987. Don't Be Afraid of 'Da'. *New York Times,* April 17, p. A31.

Luard, Evan. 1986. *War in International Society: A Study in International Sociology.* New Haven, CT: Yale University Press.

Luttwak, Edward N. 1983a. *The Grand Strategy of the Soviet Union.* New York: St. Martin's.

————. 1983b. Of Bombs and Men. *Commentary,* August. pp. 77–82.

———. 1988. An Emerging Postnuclear Era? *Washington Quarterly,* vol. 11, no. 1 (Winter), pp. 5–15.

Mearsheimer, John J. 1983. *Conventional Deterrence.* Ithaca, NY: Cornell University Press.

———. 1984/85. Nuclear Weapons and Deterrence in Europe. *International Security,* vol. 9, no. 3 (Winter), pp. 19–47.

Milward, Alan S. 1977. *War, Economy and Society, 1939–1945.* Berkeley, CA. University of California Press.

Morgenthau, Hans J. 1948. *Politics among Nations: The Struggle for Power and Peace.* New York: Knopf.

Nye, Joseph S., Jr. 1987. Nuclear Learning and U.S.–Soviet Security Regimes. *International Organization,* vol. 41, no. 3 (Summer), pp. 371–402.

Parker, Geoffrey. 1984. *The Thirty Years War.* London: Routledge and Kegan Paul.

Patterson, Orlando. 1982. *Slavery and Social Death: A Comparative Study.* Cambridge, MA: Harvard University Press.

Robb, Theodore K. 1962. The Effects of the Thirty Years' War. *Journal of Modern History,* vol. 34 (March), pp. 40–51.

Rummel, Rudolph J. 1983. Libertarianism and International Violence. *Journal of Conflict Resolution,* vol. 27, no. 1 (March), pp. 27–71.

———. 1986. War Isn't This Century's Biggest Killer. *Wall Street Journal,* July 7, p. 12.

Russett, Bruce. 1963. The Calculus of Deterrence. *Journal of Conflict Resolution,* vol. 7 (June), pp. 97–109.

———. 1972. *No Clear and Present Danger: A Skeptical View of the United States' Entry into World War II.* New York: Harper and Row.

———. 1983. *The Prisoners of Insecurity: Nuclear Deterrence, the Arms Race, and Arms Control.* San Francisco: Freeman.

Russett, Bruce, and Harvey Starr. 1981. *World Politics: The Menu for Choice.* San Francisco: Freeman.

Sagan, Carl. 1983/84. Nuclear War and Climatic Catastrophe: Some Policy Implications. *Foreign Affairs,* vol. 62, no. 2 (Winter), pp. 257–92.

Schell, Jonathan. 1982. *The Fate of the Earth.* New York: Knopf.

Schroeder, Paul. 1985. Does Murphy's Law Apply to History? *Wilson Quarterly,* vol. 9, no. 1 (New Year's), pp. 84–93.

Seitz, Don C. 1929. *Famous American Duels.* New York: Crowell.

Sivard, Ruth Leger. 1985. *World Military and Social Expenditures 1985.* Washington: World Priorities.

———. 1987. *World Military and Social Expenditures 1987/88.* Washington: World Priorities.

Small, Melvin, and J. David Singer. 1982. *Resort to Arms: International Civil Wars, 1816–1980.* Beverly Hills, CA: Sage.

Smith, Adam. 1976. *An Inquiry into the Nature and Causes of the Wealth of Nations.* New York: Oxford University Press.

Steinberg, S. H. 1966. *The Thirty Years War and the Conflict for European Hegemony 1600–1660.* New York: Norton.

Stevens, William Oliver. 1940. *Pistols at Ten Paces: The Story of the Code of Honor in America.* Boston: Houghton Mifflin.

Stowe, Steven M. 1987. *Intimacy and Power in the Old South: Ritual in the Lives of the Planters.* Baltimore, MD: Johns Hopkins University Press.

Thucydides. 1934. *The Peloponnesian War.* New York: Modern Library.
Waltz, Kenneth. 1959. *Man, the State, and War.* New York: Columbia University Press.
———. 1979. *Theory of International Politics.* Reading, MA: Addison-Wesley.
———. 1988. The Origins of War in Neorealist Theory. *Journal of Interdisciplinary History,* vol. 18, no. 4 (Spring), pp. 615–28.
Wedgwood, C. V. 1938. *The Thirty Years War.* London: Jonathan Cape.
———. 1961. *The Thirty Years War.* Garden City, NY: Anchor.

The Errors of Endism

SAMUEL P. HUNTINGTON

For a second year serious discussion of international affairs has been dominated by a major theoretical and academic issue. In 1988 the issue was American decline. The theory of declinism, articulated by many thinkers, but
most notably by Paul Kennedy, became the focus of extended and intense
debate. Was the United States following in the path of Great Britain and declining as a great power? To what extent was its economic base being undermined by spending too much on defense and/or too much on consumption?

The major issue in 1989 is very different. The theory of declinism has been
displaced by the theory of endism. Its central element is that bad things are
coming to an end.[1] Endism manifests itself in at least three ways. At its most
specific level, endism hails the end of the Cold War. In the spring of 1989
the *New York Times* and the International Institute for Strategic Studies,
George Kennan and George Bush, all set forth this proposition in one form
or another. The end of the Cold War became the Foreign Policy Establishment's Established Truth.

At a second level, endism manifested itself in the more academic and
more general proposition that wars among nation states, or at least among
some types of nation states, were coming to an end. Many scholars pointed
to the historical absence of wars between democratic countries and saw the
multiplication of democratic regimes since 1974 as evidence that the probability of war was declining. In a related but somewhat different version of

Samuel P. Huntington, "No Exit—The Errors of Endism," *The National Interest* No. 17 (Fall
1989). Reprinted with permission. © *The National Interest*, Washington, D. C.

[1]Some have raised the question as to what extent endist writers are really serious in their arguments. The time and intellectual effort they have devoted to elaborating those arguments
suggest that they are, and I will assume this to be the case. The arguments also deserve to be
taken seriously because of their widespread popularity.

this proposition, Michael Doyle argued that wars were impossible between liberal states. In a still more sweeping formulation, John Mueller contended that the advance of civilization was making war obsolescent and that it would disappear the same way that slavery and duelling had disappeared in advanced societies.[2] Wars still might occur among backward Third World countries, but among developed countries, communist or capitalist, war was unthinkable.

The third and most extreme formulation of endism was advanced by Francis Fukuyama in a brilliant essay called "The End of History?" ... Fukuyama celebrates not just the end of the Cold War or the end of wars among developed nation states, but instead "the end of history as such." This results from the "unabashed victory of economic and political liberalism" and the "exhaustion of viable systematic alternatives." Like Mueller, Fukuyama concedes that wars may occur among Third World states still caught up in the historical process. But for the developed countries, the Soviet Union, and China, history is at an end.

Endism—the intellectual fad of 1989—contrasts rather dramatically with declinism—the intellectual fad of 1988. Declinism is conditionally pessimistic. It is rooted in the study of history and draws on the parallels between the United States in the late twentieth century, Britain in the late nineteenth century, and France, Spain, and other powers in earlier centuries. Its proponents and its critics debate the relevance of these parallels and argue over detailed, historical data concerning economic growth, productivity, defense spending, savings, and investment.[3] Endism, on the other hand, is oriented to the future rather than the past and is unabashedly optimistic. In its most developed form, as with Fukuyama, it is rooted in philosophical speculation rather than historical analysis. It is based not so much on evidence from history as on assumptions about history. In its extreme form, declinism is historically deterministic: nations naturally, and perhaps inevitably, evolve through phases of rise, expansion, and decline. They are caught in the inexorable grip of history. In the extreme form of endism, in contrast, nations escape from history.

---

[2]Michael W. Doyle, "Kant, Liberal Legacies, and Foreign Affairs," *Philosophy and Public Affairs,* vol. 12 (Summer, Fall 1983), pp. 205–235, 323–353, and "Liberalism and World Politics," *American Political Science Review,* vol. 80 (December 1986), pp. 1151–1169; John Mueller, *Retreat from Doomsday: The Obsolescence of Major War* (New York: Basic Books, 1989). Also see Dean V. Babst, "A Force for Peace," *Industrial Research,* vol. 14 (April 1972), pp. 55–58; R. J. Rummel, "Libertarianism and International Violence," *Journal of Conflict Resolution,* vol. 27 (March 1983), pp. 27–71; Ze'ev Maoz and Nasrin Abdolali, "Regime Types and International Conflict, 1816–1976," *Journal of Conflict Resolution,* vol. 33 (March 1989), pp. 3–35; Bruce Russett, "The Politics of an Alternative Security System: Toward a More Democratic and Therefore More Peaceful World," in Burns Weston, ed., *Alternatives to Nuclear Deterrence* (Boulder: Westview Press, forthcoming 1989).

[3]For a careful analysis of the evidence and arguments on this issue, see Joseph S. Nye, *Bound to Lead* (New York: Basic Books, 1990).

The message of declinism for Americans is "We're losing"; the message of endism is "We've won!" Despite or perhaps even because of its deterministic strand, declinism performs a useful historical function. It provides a warning and a goad to action in order to head off and reverse the decline that it says is taking place. It serves that purpose now as it did in its earlier manifestations in the 1950s, 1960s, and 1970s. Endism, in contrast, provides not a warning of danger but an illusion of well-being. It invites not corrective action but relaxed complacency. The consequences of its thesis being in error, hence, are far more dangerous and subversive than those that would result if the declinist thesis should be wrong.

The End of the Cold War

"The Cold War is over" was the prevailing cry in the spring of 1989. What does this mean? It typically referred to two related developments: the changes usually referred to as glasnost and perestroika in the Soviet Union and the improvements that were occurring in Soviet-American relations. "The cold war," as the *New York Times* put it, "of poisonous Soviet-American feelings, of domestic political hysteria, of events enlarged and distorted by East-West confrontation, of almost perpetual diplomatic deadlock is over."[4] Several questions can be raised about this proposition.

First, is it really true? The easing in Soviet-American relations in the late 1950s was followed by the Berlin and Cuban crises; detente in the early 1970s was followed by Angola and Afghanistan. How do we know that the current relaxation is not simply another swing of the cycle? One answer is that the changes occurring within the Soviet Union are far more fundamental than those that have occurred in the past, and this is certainly the case. The opening up of political debate, limited but real competition in elections, the formation of political groups outside the Party, the virtual abandonment, indeed, of the idea of a monolithic party, the assertion of power by the Supreme Soviet—all these will, if continued, lead to a drastically different Soviet political system. The price of attempting to reverse them increases daily, but it would be rash to conclude that they are as yet irreversible, and the costs of reversing them could decline in the future.

On the international level, the Soviets have cooperated in resolving regional conflicts in the Persian Gulf, southern Africa, and Indochina. They have promised to reduce their overall military forces and their deployments in Eastern Europe. As yet, however, no perceptible changes have taken place in Soviet force structure, Soviet deployments, or Soviet output of military equipment. Even if these do occur, the competition between the United States and the Soviet Union for influence and power in world affairs will still

[4]"The Cold War is Over," *New York Times*, April 2, 1989, p. E30.

go on. It has been continuing as President Bush and President Gorbachev attempt to woo Eastern and Western European publics. Europe, it is well to remember, is where the Cold War started. It is the overwhelmingly preeminent stake in the Cold War, and Gorbachev's public relations can be as much a threat to American interests in Europe as were Brezhnev's tanks (which, for the moment at any rate, Gorbachev also has).

Let us, however, concede that in some meaningful and not transitory sense the Cold War is over and that a real change has occurred in Soviet-American relations. How do the proponents of this thesis see the post-Cold War world? The "we-they world" that has existed, the editors of the *New York Times* assure us, is giving way "to the more traditional struggles of great powers." In a similar vein, George Kennan alleges that the Soviet Union "should now be regarded essentially as another great power, like other great powers." Its interests may differ from ours but these differences can be "adjusted by the normal means of compromise and accommodation."[5]

Russia was, however, just "another great power" for several centuries before it became a communist state. As a great power, Russia frequently deployed its armies into Europe and repeatedly crushed popular uprisings in central Europe. Soviet troops bloodily suppressed the Hungarian revolution in 1956 and trampled the embryonic Czech democracy in 1968. Russian troops bloodily suppressed the Hungarian revolution of 1848–49 and violently put down uprisings in Poland in 1831 and again in 1863–64. Soviet forces occupied Berlin in 1945; Russian troops occupied and burnt Berlin in 1760. In pursuit of Russia's interests as a great power, Russian troops appeared many places where as yet Soviet troops have not. In 1799 Russian troops occupied Milan and Turin and fought a battle on the outskirts of Zurich. The same year, they occupied the Ionian islands off Greece and stayed there until 1807. These excursions preceded Napoleon's invasion of Russia. As a great power, Russia regularly participated in the partitions of Poland. In 1914 Nicholas II directly ruled more of Europe (including most of Poland) than Gorbachev does today.

The past record of Russia as a "normal" great power, therefore, is not reassuring for either the liberty of Eastern Europe or the security of Western Europe. Some suggest that the liberalizing and democratizing trends in the Soviet Union will prevent that country from bludgeoning other countries in the manner of the tsars. One cannot assume, Fukuyama argues, that "the evolution of human consciousness has stood still" and that "the Soviets will return to foreign policy views a century out of date in the rest of Europe." Fukuyama is right: one cannot assume that the Soviets will revert to the bad old ways of the past. One also cannot assume that they will not. Gorbachev may be able to discard communism but he cannot discard geography and the geopolitical imperatives that have shaped Russian and Soviet behavior

---

[5]"Just Another Great Power," *New York Times,* April 9, 1989, p. E25.

for centuries. And, as any Latin American will quickly point out, even a truly democratic superpower is capable of intervening militarily in the affairs of its smaller neighbors.

The era of the Cold War, John Lewis Gaddis reminds us, has also been the era of the Long Peace, the longest period in history without hot war between major powers. Does the end of the Cold War mean the end of the Long Peace? Two central elements of both have been bipolarity and nuclear weapons: they have in considerable measure defined both the Soviet-American rivalry and its limits. The end of the Cold War will mean a loosening of bipolarity even if it does not mean, as some declinists predict, a world of five or more roughly equal major powers. The delegitimation of nuclear weapons and the increasing constraints on their deployment and potential use could increase the probability of conventional war.

Active American involvement in world affairs has been substantially limited to two world wars and one prolonged and ideologically-driven cold war. In the absence of the Kaiser, Hitler, Stalin, and Brezhnev, the American inclination may well be to relax and to assume that peace, goodwill, and international cooperation will prevail: that if the Cold War is over, American relations with the Soviet Union will be similar to its relations with Canada, France, or Japan. Americans tend to see competition and conflict as normal and even desirable features of their domestic economy and politics and yet perversely assume them to be abnormal and undesirable in relations among states. In fact, however, the history of the relations among great powers, when it has not been the history of hot wars, has usually been the history of cold wars.

The end of the Cold War does not mean the end of political, ideological, diplomatic, economic, technological, or even military rivalry among nations. It does not mean the end of the struggle for power and influence. It very probably does mean increased instability, unpredictability, and violence in international affairs. It could mean the end of the Long Peace.

The End of War

A second manifestation of endism postulates the end of war between certain types of nation states. A number of authors, including Dean V. Babst, R. J. Rummel, and Bruce Russett, have pointed to the fact that no significant interstate wars have occurred between democratic regimes since the emergence of such regimes in the early nineteenth century. Michael Doyle has similarly argued that a "pacific union" exists among liberal regimes (which includes and is slightly broader than the class of democratic regimes, as defined by most scholars). "*[C]onstitutionally secure liberal states,*" he says, "*have yet to engage in war with each other. Even threats of war have been regarded as illegitimate.*"

Given the large number of wars between non-democratic regimes and between democratic regimes and non-democratic regimes, the almost total absence of armed conflict between democratic regimes is indeed striking. It is, as Bruce Russett says, "perhaps the strongest non-trivial or non-tautological statement that can be made about international relations." It is also plausible to believe that this absence of war may stem from the nature of the regime. Democracy is a means for the peaceful resolution of disputes, involving negotiation and compromise as well as elections and voting. The leaders of democracies may well expect that they ought to be able to resolve through peaceful means their differences with the leaders of other democracies. In the years since World War II, for instance, several conflicts which could or did lead to war between countries tended to moderate when the countries became democratic. The controversies between Britain and Argentina, Guatemala, and Spain over the remnants of empire (one of which did lead to war and one of which produced significant military deployment) moderated considerably when those three countries became democratic. The conflict between Greece and Turkey similarly seemed to ease in the 1980s after both countries had democratically-elected regimes.

The democratic "zone of peace" is a dramatic historical phenomenon. If that relationship continues to hold and if democracy continues to spread, wars should become less frequent in the future than they have been in the past. This is one endist argument that has a strong empirical base. Three qualifications have to be noted, however, to its implications for the end of war.

First, democracies are still a minority among the world's regimes. The 1989 Freedom House survey classified 60 out of 167 sovereign states as "free" according to its rather generous definition of freedom. Multiple possibilities for war thus continue to exist among the 107 states that are not free, and between those states and the democratic states.

Second, the number of democratic states has been growing, but it tends to grow irregularly in a two-step forward, one-step backward pattern. A major wave of democratization occurred in the nineteenth century, but then significant reversals to authoritarianism took place in the 1920s and 1930s. A second wave of democratization after World War II was followed by several reversals in the 1960s and 1970s. A third wave of democratization began in 1974, with fifteen to twenty countries shifting in a democratic direction since then. If the previous pattern prevails, some of these new democracies are likely to revert to authoritarianism. Hence the possibility of war could increase rather than decrease in the immediate future, although still remaining less than it was prior to 1974.

Finally, peace among democratic states could be related to extraneous accidental factors and not to the nature of democracy. In the nineteenth century, for instance, wars tended to occur between geographical neighbors. Democratic states were few in number and seldom bordered on each other.

Hence the absence of war could be caused by the absence of propinquity.[6] Since World War II most democratic countries have been members of the alliance system led by the United States, which has been directed against an alliance of non-democratic regimes and within which the hegemonic position of the U.S. has precluded war between other alliance members (e.g., between Greece and Turkey). If American leadership weakens and the alliance system loosens, the probability of war between its erstwhile members, democratic or otherwise, could well increase.

The "democratic zone of peace" argument is thus valid as far as it goes, but it may not go all that far.

In his book, *Retreat from Doomsday,* John Mueller argues for the growing obsolescence of war on more general grounds. He sees the Long Peace since 1945 not as the result of bipolarity or nuclear weapons but rather as the result of a learning experience that wars do not pay and that there are few conflicts of interest among countries where it would be reasonable for either side to resort to war to achieve its goals. World War II was an aberration from the twentieth-century trend away from war due largely to the idiosyncratic and irrational personality of Hitler. As countries become more developed and civilized, they will become more peaceful. Denmark is the future model for individual countries, U.S.-Canadian relations the future model for relations between countries.

Mueller makes much of the argument that war will become "obsolete, subrationally unthinkable," and unacceptable in civilized society in the way slavery and duelling have become. Why, however, are those social practices the appropriate parallels to war? Why not murder? Murder has been unacceptable in civilized societies for millennia, and yet it seems unlikely that the murder rate in twentieth-century New York is less than it was in fifth-century Athens. While major wars between developed countries have not occurred since World War II, interstate and intrastate violence has been widespread with the casualties numbering in the tens of millions.

Mueller himself substantially qualifies his case. He agrees that wars will continue among less developed countries. He also concedes that irrational leaders on the Hitler model could involve their countries in future wars. Economic considerations motivate strongly against war, he says, but economic prosperity "is not always an overriding goal even now." Territorial issues exist even in the developed world that "could lead to wars of expansion or territorial readjustment." The Cold War is being resolved peacefully, "but there is no firm guarantee that this trend will continue."

A more general problem may also exist with the end-of-war or even a decline-in-war thesis. As Michimi Muranushi of Yale has pointed out, peace can be self-limiting rather than cumulative. If relations between two countries be-

[6]See J. David Singer and Melvin Small, "The War-Proneness of Democratic Regimes, 1815–1965," *Jerusalem Journal of International Relations,* vol. 1 (Summer 1976), p. 67.

come more peaceful, this may, in some circumstances, increase the probability that either or both of those countries will go to war with a third country. The Hitler-Stalin pact paves the way for the attacks on Poland; normalization of U.S.-China relations precipitates China's war with Vietnam. If the Soviet threat disappears, so also does an inhibitor of Greek-Turkish war.

In addition, if more countries become like Denmark, forswearing war and committing themselves to material comfort, that in itself may produce a situation which other countries will wish to exploit. History is full of examples of leaner, meaner societies over-running richer, less martial ones.

The End of History

"The end of history" is a sweeping, dramatic, and provocative phrase. What does Fukuyama mean by it? The heart of Fukuyama's argument is an alleged change in political consciousness throughout the principal societies in the world and the emergence of a pervasive consensus on liberal-democratic principles. It posits the triumph of one ideology and the consequent end of ideology and ideological conflict as significant factors in human existence. His choice of language suggests, however, that he may have something more sweeping in mind than simply the obsolescence of war highlighted by Mueller or the end of ideology predicted by Daniel Bell twenty-five years ago.

Insofar as it is focused on war, Fukuyama's argument suffers all the weaknesses that Mueller's does. He admits that "conflict between states still in history, and between those states and those at the end of history, would still be possible." At the same time he includes China and the Soviet Union among those states that are out of history. Current Soviet leaders, he says, have arrived at the "end-of-history view" and "assimilated the consciousness of the universal homogenous state that is post-Hitler Europe"; yet he also admits that the Soviet Union could turn to Slavophile Russian chauvinism and thus remain stuck in history.

Fukuyama ridicules the idea that Germany and France might fight each other again. That is a valid but irrelevant point. A hundred years ago one could have validly made the point that Pennsylvania and Virginia would not fight each other again. That did not prevent the United States, of which each was a part, from engaging in world wars in the subsequent century. One trend in history is the amalgamation of smaller units into larger ones. The probability of war between the smaller units declines but the probability of war between the larger amalgamated units does not necessarily change. A united European community may end the possibility of Franco-German war; it does not end the possibility of war between that community and other political units.

With respect to China, Fukuyama argues that "Chinese competitiveness and expansionism on the world scene have virtually disappeared" and, he implies strongly, will not reappear. A more persuasive argument, however, could be made for exactly the opposite proposition that Chinese expansionism has yet to appear on the world scene. Britain and France, Germany and Japan, the United States and the Soviet Union, all became expansionist and imperialist powers in the course of industrialization. China is just beginning seriously to develop its industrial strength. Maybe China will be different from all the other major powers and not attempt to expand its influence and control as it industrializes. But how can one be confident that it will pursue this deviant course? And if it follows the more familiar pattern, a billion Chinese engaged in imperial expansion are likely to impose a lot of history on the rest of the world.

Fukuyama quite appropriately emphasizes the role of consciousness, ideas, and ideology in motivating and shaping the actions of men and nations. He is also right in pointing to the virtual end of the appeal of communism as an ideology. Ideologically, communism has been "the grand failure" that Brzezinski labels it. It is erroneous, however, to jump from the decline of communism to the global triumph of liberalism and the disappearance of ideology as a force in world affairs.

First, revivals are possible. A set of ideas or an ideology may fade from the scene in one generation only to reappear with renewed strength a generation or two later. From the 1940s to the 1960s, dominant currents in economic thinking were Keynesianism, welfare statism, social democracy, and planning. It was hard to find much support for classical economic liberalism. By the late 1970s, however, the latter had staged an amazing comeback; economists and economic institutions were devoted to The Plan in the 1950s, they have been devoted to The Market in the 1980s. Somewhat similarly, social scientists in the decades immediately after World War II argued that religion, ethnic consciousness, and nationalism would all be done in by economic development and modernization. But in the 1980s these have been the dominant bases of political action in most societies. The revival of religion is now a global phenomenon. Communism may be down for the moment, but it is rash to assume that it is out for all time.

Second, the universal acceptance of liberal democracy does not preclude conflicts within liberalism. The history of ideology is the history of schism. Struggles between those who profess different versions of a common ideology are often more intense and vicious than struggles between those espousing entirely different ideologies. To a believer the heretic is worse than the nonbeliever. An ideological consensus on Christianity existed in Europe in 1500 but that did not prevent Protestants and Catholics from slaughtering each other for the next century and a half. Socialists and communists, Trotskyites and Leninists, Shi'ites and Sunnis have treated each other in similar fashion.

Third, the triumph of one ideology does not preclude the emergence of new ideologies. Nations and societies presumably will continue to evolve. New challenges to human well-being will emerge, and people will develop new concepts, theories, and ideologies as to how those challenges should be met. Unless all social, economic, and political distinctions disappear, people will also develop belief systems that legitimate what they have and justify their getting more. Among its other functions, for instance, communism historically legitimized the power of intellectuals and bureaucrats. If it is gone for good, it seems highly likely that intellectuals and bureaucrats will develop new sets of ideas to rationalize their claims to power and wealth.

Fourth, has liberal democracy really triumphed? Fukuyama admits that it has not won out in the Third world. To what extent, however, has it really been accepted in the Soviet Union and China? Between them these societies encompass well over one-quarter of the world's population. If any one trend is operative in the world today it is for societies to turn back toward their traditional cultures, values, and patterns of behavior. This trend is manifest in the revival of traditional identities and characters of Eastern European countries, escaping from the deadly uniformity of Soviet-imposed communism, and also in the increasing differentiation among the republics within the Soviet Union itself. Russia and China do not lack elements of liberalism and democracy in their histories. These are, however, minor chords, and their subordinate importance is underlined by the contemporary problems facing economic liberalism in the Soviet Union and political democracy in communist China.

More generally, Fukuyama's thesis itself reflects not the disappearance of Marxism but its pervasiveness. His image of the end of history is straight from Marx. Fukuyama speaks of the "universal homogeneous state," in which "all prior contradictions are resolved and all human needs are satisfied." What is this but the Marxist image of a society without class conflict or other contradictions organized on the basis of from each according to his abilities and to each according to his needs? The struggles of history, Fukuyama says, "will be replaced by economic calculation, the endless solving of technical problems, environmental concerns, and the satisfaction of sophisticated consumer demands." Engels said it even more succinctly: "The government of persons is replaced by the administration of things and the direction of the process of production." Fukuyama says liberalism is the end of history. Marx says communism "is the solution to the riddle of history." They are basically saying the same thing and, most importantly, they are thinking the same way. Marxist ideology is alive and well in Fukuyama's arguments to refute it.

Two Fallacies

The Soviet Union is increasingly preoccupied with its own problems and a significant political loosening has occurred in that country. The ideological intensity of the early Cold War has virtually disappeared, and the probability of hot war between the two superpowers is as low as it has ever been. War is even more unlikely between any of the advanced industrialized democracies. On these points, endist propositions are accurate. The more extensive formulations of the endist argument, however, suffer from two basic fallacies.

First, endism overemphasizes the predictability of history and the permanence of the moment. Current trends may or may not continue into the future. Past experience certainly suggests that they are unlikely to do so. The record of past predictions by social scientists is not a happy one. Fifteen years ago, just as the democratic wave was beginning, political analysts were elaborating fundamental reasons why authoritarianism had to prevail in the Third World. Ten years ago foreign policy journals were filled with warnings of the rise of Soviet military power and political influence throughout the world. Five years ago what analyst of the Soviet Union predicted the extent of the political changes that have occurred in that country? Given the limitations of human foresight, endist predictions of the end of war and ideological conflict deserve a heavy dose of skepticism. Indeed, in the benign atmosphere of the moment, it is sobering to speculate on the possible future horrors that social analysts are now failing to predict.

Second, endism tends to ignore the weakness and irrationality of human nature. Endist arguments often assume that because it would be rational for human beings to focus on their economic well-being, they will act in that way, and therefore they will not engage in wars that do not meet the tests of cost–benefit analysis or in ideological conflicts that are much ado about nothing. Human beings are at times rational, generous, creative, and wise, but they are also often stupid, selfish, cruel, and sinful. The struggle that is history began with the eating of the forbidden fruit and is rooted in human nature. In history there may be total defeats, but there are no final solutions. So long as human beings exist, there is no exit from the traumas of history.

To hope for the benign end of history is human. To expect it to happen is unrealistic. To plan on it happening is disastrous.

Why We Will Soon Miss the Cold War

JOHN J. MEARSHEIMER

Peace: It's wonderful. I like it as much as the next man, and have no wish to be willfully gloomy at a moment when optimism about the future shape of the world abounds. Nevertheless, my thesis in this essay is that we are likely soon to regret the passing of the Cold War.

To be sure, no one will miss such by-products of the Cold War as the Korean and Vietnam conflicts. No one will want to replay the U–2 affair, the Cuban missile crisis, or the building of the Berlin Wall. And no one will want to revisit the domestic Cold War, with its purges and loyalty oaths, its xenophobia and stifling of dissent. We will not wake up one day to discover fresh wisdom in the collected fulminations of John Foster Dulles.

We may, however, wake up one day lamenting the loss of the order that the Cold War gave to the anarchy of international relations. For untamed anarchy is what Europe knew in the forty-five years of this century before the Cold War, and untamed anarchy—Hobbes's war of all against all—is a prime cause of armed conflict. Those who think that armed conflicts among the European states are now out of the question, that the two world wars burned all the war out of Europe, are projecting unwarranted optimism onto the future. The theories of peace that implicitly undergird this optimism are notably shallow constructs. They stand up to neither logical nor historical analysis. You would not want to bet the farm on their prophetic accuracy.

The world is about to conduct a vast test of the theories of war and peace put forward by social scientists, who never dreamed that their ideas would be tested by the world-historic events announced almost daily in newspaper headlines. This social scientist is willing to put his theoretical cards on the table as he ventures predictions about the future of Europe. In the process, I hope to put alternative theories of war and peace under as much intellectual pressure as I can muster. My argument is that the prospect of major crises, even wars, in Europe is likely to increase dramatically now that the Cold War is receding into history. The next forty-five years in Europe are not likely to be so violent as the forty-five years before the Cold War, but they are likely to be substantially more violent than the past forty-five years, the era that we may someday look back upon not as the Cold War but as the Long Peace, in John Lewis Gaddis's phrase.

This pessimistic conclusion rests on the general argument that the distribution and character of military power among states are the root causes of war and peace. Specifically, the peace in Europe since 1945—precarious at first, but increasingly robust over time—has flowed from three factors: the bipolar distribution of military power on the Continent; the rough military equality between the polar powers, the United States and the Soviet Union; and the ritualistically deplored fact that each of these superpowers is armed with a large nuclear arsenal.

We don't yet know the entire shape of the new Europe. But we do know some things. We know, for example, that the new Europe will involve a return to the multipolar distribution of power that characterized the European state system from its founding, with the Peace of Westphalia, in 1648, until 1945. We know that this multipolar European state system was plagued by war from first to last. We know that from 1900 to 1945 some 50 million Europeans were killed in wars that were caused in great part by the instability of this state system. We also know that since 1945 only some 15,000 Europeans have been killed in wars; roughly 10,000 Hungarians and Russians, in what we might call the Russo-Hungarian War of October and November, 1956, and somewhere between 1,500 and 5,000 Greeks and Turks, in the July and August, 1974, war on Cyprus.

The point is clear: Europe is reverting to a state system that created powerful incentives for aggression in the past. If you believe (as the Realist school of international-relations theory, to which I belong, believes) that the prospects of international peace are not markedly influenced by the domestic political character of states—that it is the character of the state system, not the character of the individual units composing it, that drives states toward war—then it is difficult to share in the widespread elation of the moment about the future of Europe. Last year was repeatedly compared to 1789, the year the French Revolution began, as the Year of Freedom, and so it was. Forgotten in the general exaltation was that the hope-filled events of 1789 signaled the start of an era of war and conquest.

A "Hard" Theory of Peace

What caused the era of violence in Europe before 1945, and why has the postwar era, the period of the Cold War, been so much more peaceful? The two world wars before 1945 had myriad particular and unrepeatable causes, but to the student of international relations seeking to establish generalizations about the behavior of states in the past which might illuminate their behavior in the future, two fundamental causes stand out. These are the multi-polar distribution of power in Europe, and the imbalances of strength that often developed among the great powers as they jostled for supremacy or advantage.

There is something elementary about the geometry of power in international relations, and so its importance is easy to overlook. "Bipolarity" and "multipolarity" are ungainly but necessary coinages. The Cold War, with two superpowers serving to anchor rival alliances of clearly inferior powers, is our model of bipolarity. Europe in 1914, with France, Germany, Great Britain, Austria-Hungary, and Russia positioned as great powers, is our model of multipolarity.

If the example of 1914 is convincing enough evidence that multipolar systems are the more dangerous geometry of power, then perhaps I should rest my case. Alas for theoretical elegance, there are no empirical studies providing conclusive support for this proposition. From its beginnings until 1945 the European state system was multipolar, so this history is barren of comparisons that would reveal the differing effects of the two systems. Earlier history, to be sure, does furnish scattered examples of bipolar systems, including some—Athens and Sparta, Rome and Carthage—that were warlike. But this history is inconclusive, because it is incomplete. Lacking a comprehensive survey of history, we can't do much more than offer examples—now on this, now on that side of the debate. As a result, the case made here rests chiefly on deduction.

Deductively, a bipolar system is more peaceful for the simple reason that under it only two major powers are in contention. Moreover, those great powers generally demand allegiance from minor powers in the system, which is likely to produce rigid alliance structures. The smaller states are then secure from each other as well as from attack by the rival great power. Consequently (to make a Dick-and-Jane point with a wellworn social-science term), a bipolar system has only one dyad across which war might break out. A multipolar system is much more fluid and has many such dyads. Therefore, other things being equal, war is statistically more likely in a multipolar system than it is in a bipolar one. Admittedly, wars in a multipolar world that involve only minor powers or only one major power are not likely to be as devastating as a conflict between two major powers. But small wars always have the potential to widen into big wars.

Also, deterrence is difficult to maintain in a multipolar state system, because power imbalances are common-place, and when power asymmetries develop, the strong become hard to deter. Two great powers can join together to attack a third state, as Germany and the Soviet Union did in 1939, when they ganged up on Poland. Furthermore, a major power might simply bully a weaker power in a one-on-one encounter, using its superior strength to coerce or defeat the minor state. Germany's actions against Czechoslovakia in the late 1930s provide a good example of this sort of behavior. Ganging up and bullying are largely unknown in a bipolar system, since with only two great powers dominating center stage, it is impossible to produce the power asymmetries that result in ganging up and bullying.

There is a second reason that deterrence is more problematic under multipolarity. The resolve of opposing states and also the size and strength of opposing coalitions are hard to calculate in this geometry of power, because the shape of the international order tends to remain in flux, owing to the tendency of coalitions to gain and lose partners. This can lead aggressors to conclude falsely that they can coerce others by bluffing war, or even achieve outright victory on the battlefield. For example, Germany was not certain before 1914 that Britain would oppose it if it reached for Continental hegemony, and Germany completely failed to foresee that the United States would eventually move to contain it. In 1939 Germany hoped that France and Britain would stand aside as it conquered Poland, and again failed to foresee the eventual American entry into the war. As a result, Germany exaggerated its prospects for success, which undermined deterrence by encouraging German adventurism.

The prospects for peace, however, are not simply a function of the number of great powers in the system. They are also affected by the relative military strength of those major states. Bipolar and multipolar systems both are likely to be more peaceful when power is distributed equally in them. Power inequalities invite war, because they increase an aggressor's prospects for victory on the battlefield. Most of the general wars that have tormented Europe over the past five centuries have involved one particularly powerful state against the other major powers in the system. This pattern characterized the wars that grew from the attempts at hegemony by Charles V, Philip II, Louis XIV, Revolutionary and Napoleonic France, Wilhelmine Germany, and Nazi Germany. Hence the size of the gap in military power between the two leading states in the system is a key determinant of stability. Small gaps foster peace; larger gaps promote war.

Nuclear weapons seem to be in almost everybody's bad book, but the fact is that they are a powerful force for peace. Deterrence is most likely to hold when the costs and risks of going to war are unambiguously stark. The more horrible the prospect of war, the less likely war is. Deterrence is also more robust when conquest is more difficult. Potential aggressor states are given pause by the patent futility of attempts at expansion.

Nuclear weapons favor peace on both counts. They are weapons of mass destruction, and would produce horrendous devastation if used in any numbers. Moreover, they are more useful for self-defense than for aggression. If both sides' nuclear arsenals are secure from attack, creating an arrangement of mutual assured destruction, neither side can employ these weapons to gain a meaningful military advantage. International conflicts then become tests of pure will. Who would dare to use these weapons of unimaginable destructive power? Defenders have the advantage here, because defenders usually value their freedom more than aggressors value new conquests.

Nuclear weapons further bolster peace by moving power relations among states toward equality. States that possess nuclear deterrents can stand up to one another, even if their nuclear arsenals vary greatly in size, as long as both sides have an assured destruction capability. In addition, mutual assured destruction helps alleviate the vexed problem of miscalculation by leaving little doubt about the relative power of states.

No discussion of the causes of peace in the twentieth century would be complete without a word on nationalism. With "nationalism" as a synonym for "love of country" I have no quarrel. But hypernationalism, the belief that other nations or nation-states are both inferior and threatening, is perhaps the single greatest domestic threat to peace, although it is still not a leading force in world politics. Hypernationalism arose in the past among European states because most of them were nation-states—states composed mainly of people from a single ethnic group—that existed in an anarchic world, under constant threat from other states. In such a system people who love their own nation can easily come to be contemptuous of the nationalities inhabiting opposing states. The problem is worsened when domestic elites demonize a rival nation to drum up support for national-security policy.

Hypernationalism finds its most fertile soil under military systems relying on mass armies. These require sacrifices to sustain, and the state is tempted to appeal to nationalist sentiments to mobilize its citizens to make them. The quickening of hypernationalism is least likely when states can rely on small professional armies, or on complex high-technology military organizations that operate without vast manpower. For this reason, nuclear weapons work to dampen nationalism, because they shift the basis of military power away from mass armies and toward smaller, high-technology organizations.

Hypernationalism declined sharply in Europe after 1945, not only because of the nuclear revolution but also because the postwar occupation forces kept it down. Moreover, the European states, no longer providing their own security, lacked an incentive to whip up nationalism to bolster public support for national defense. But the decisive change came in the shift of the prime locus of European politics to the United States and the Soviet Union—two states made up of peoples of many different ethnic origins which had not exhibited nationalism of the virulent type found in Europe. This welcome absence of hypernationalism has been further helped by the greater stability of the postwar order. With less expectation of war, neither superpower felt compelled to mobilize its citizens for war.

Bipolarity, an equal balance of military power, and nuclear weapons—these, then, are the key elements of my explanation for the Long Peace.

Many thoughtful people have found the bipolar system in Europe odious and have sought to end it by dismantling the Soviet empire in Eastern Europe and diminishing Soviet military power. Many have also lamented the military equality obtaining between the superpowers; some have decried the indecisive stalemate it produced, recommending instead a search for military superiority; others have lamented the investment of hundreds of billions of dollars to deter a war that never happened, proving not that the investment, though expensive, paid off, but rather that it was wasted. As for nuclear weapons, well, they are a certifiable Bad Thing. The odium attached to these props of the postwar order has kept many in the West from recognizing a hard truth: they have kept the peace.

But so much for the past. What will keep the peace in the future? Specifically, what new order is likely to emerge if NATO and the Warsaw Pact dissolve, which they will do if the Cold War is really over, and the Soviets withdraw from Eastern Europe and the Americans quit Western Europe, taking their nuclear weapons with them—and should we welcome or fear it?

One dimension of the new European order is certain: it will be multipolar. Germany, France, Britain, and perhaps Italy will assume major-power status. The Soviet Union will decline from superpower status, not only because its military is sure to shrink in size but also because moving forces out of Eastern Europe will make it more difficult for the Soviets to project power onto the Continent. They will, of course, remain a major European power. The resulting four- or five-power system will suffer the problems endemic to multipolar systems—and will therefore be prone to instability. The other two dimensions—the distribution of power among the major states and the distribution of nuclear weapons—are less certain. Indeed, who gets nuclear weapons is likely to be the most problematic question facing the new Europe. Three scenarios of the nuclear future in Europe are possible.

The "Europe Without Nuclear Weapons" Scenario

Many Europeans (and some Americans) seek to eliminate nuclear weapons from Europe altogether. Fashioning this nuclear-free Europe would require that Britain, France, and the Soviet Union rid themselves of these talismans of their sovereignty—an improbable eventuality, to say the least. Those who wish for it nevertheless believe that it would be the most peaceful arrangement possible. In fact a nuclear-free Europe has the distinction of being the most dangerous among the envisionable post-Cold War orders. The pacifying effects of nuclear weapons—the caution they generate, the security they provide, the rough equality they impose, and the clarity of the relative power they create—would be lost. Peace would then depend on the other dimensions of the new order—the number of poles and the distribution of power among them. The geometry of power in Europe would look much as it did between the world wars—a design for tension, crisis, and possibly even war.

The Soviet Union and a unified Germany would likely be the most powerful states in a nuclear-free Europe. A band of small independent states in Eastern Europe would lie between them. These minor Eastern European powers would be likely to fear the Soviets as much as the Germans, and thus would probably not be disposed to cooperate with the Soviets to deter possible German aggression. In fact, this very problem arose in the 1930s, and the past forty-five years of Soviet occupation have surely done little to mitigate Eastern European fears of a Soviet military presence. Thus scenarios in which Germany uses force against Poland, Czechoslovakia, or even Austria enter the realm of the possible in a nuclear-free Europe.

Then, too, the Soviet withdrawal from Eastern Europe hardly guarantees a permanent exit. Indeed, the Russian presence in Eastern Europe has surged and ebbed repeatedly over the past few centuries. In a grave warning, a member of President Mikhail Gorbachev's negotiating team at the recent Washington summit said, "You have the same explosive mixture you had in Germany in the 1930s. The humiliation of a great power. Economic troubles. The rise of nationalism. You should not underestimate the danger."

Conflicts between Eastern European states might also threaten the stability of the new European order. Serious tensions already exist between Hungary and Romania over Romania's treatment of the Hungarian minority in Transylvania, a formerly Hungarian region that still contains roughly two million ethnic Hungarians. Absent the Soviet occupation of Eastern Europe, Romania and Hungary might have gone to war over this issue by now, and it might bring them to war in the future. This is not the only potential danger spot in Eastern Europe as the Soviet empire crumbles. The Polish-German border could be a source of trouble. Poland and Czechoslovakia have a border dispute. If the Soviets allow some of their republics to achieve independence, the Poles and the Romanians may lay claim to territory now in Soviet hands which once belonged to them. Looking farther south, civil war in Yugoslavia is a distinct possibility. Yugoslavia and Albania might come to blows over Kosovo, a region of Yugoslavia harboring a nationalistic Albanian majority. Bulgaria has its own quarrel with Yugoslavia over Macedonia, while Turkey resents Bulgaria's treatment of its Turkish minority. The danger that these bitter ethnic and border disputes will erupt into war in a supposedly Edenic nuclear-free Europe is enough to make one nostalgic for the Cold War.

Warfare in Eastern Europe would cause great suffering to Eastern Europeans. It also might widen to include the major powers, especially if disorder created fluid politics that offered opportunities for expanded influence, or threatened defeat for states friendly to one or another of the major powers. During the Cold War both superpowers were drawn into Third World conflicts across the globe, often in distant areas of little strategic importance. Eastern Europe is directly adjacent to both the Soviet Union and Germany, and it has considerable economic and strategic importance. Thus trouble in Eastern Europe would offer even greater temptations to these powers than past conflicts in the Third World offered to the superpowers. Furthermore, Eastern European states would have a strong incentive to drag the major powers into their local conflicts, because the results of such conflicts would be largely determined by the relative success of each party in finding external allies.

It is difficult to predict the precise balance of conventional military power that will emerge in post-Cold War Europe. The Soviet Union might recover its strength soon after withdrawing from Eastern Europe. In that case Soviet power would outmatch German power. But centrifugal national forces might pull the Soviet Union apart, leaving no remnant state that is the equal of a unified Germany. Finally, and probably most likely, Germany and the Soviet Union might emerge as powers of roughly equal strength. The first two geometrics of power, with their marked military inequality between the two leading countries, would be especially worrisome, although there would be cause for concern even if Soviet and German power were balanced.

A non-nuclear Europe, to round out this catalogue of dangers, would likely be especially disturbed by hypernationalism, since security in such an order would rest on mass armies, which, as we have seen, often cannot be maintained without a mobilized public. The problem would probably be most acute in Eastern Europe, with its uncertain borders and irredentist minority groups. But there is also potential for trouble in Germany. The Germans have generally done an admirable job of combating hypernationalism over the past forty-five years, and of confronting the dark side of their past. Nevertheless, a portent like the recent call of some prominent Germans for a return to greater nationalism in historical education is disquieting.

For all these reasons, it is perhaps just as well that a nuclear-free Europe, much as it may be longed for by so many Europeans, does not appear to be in the cards.

The "Current Ownership" Scenario

Under this scenario Britain, France, and the Soviet Union retain their nuclear weapons, but no new nuclear powers emerge in Europe. This vision of a nuclear-free zone in Central Europe, with nuclear weapons remaining on the flanks of the Continent, is also popular in Europe, but it, too, has doubtful prospects.

Germany will prevent it over the long run. The Germans are not likely to be willing to rely on the Poles or the Czechs to provide their forward defense against a possible direct Soviet conventional attack on their homeland. Nor are the Germans likely to trust the Soviet Union to refrain for all time from nuclear blackmail against a non-nuclear Germany. Hence they will eventually look to nuclear weapons as the surest means of security, just as NATO has done.

The small states of Eastern Europe will also have strong incentives to acquire nuclear weapons. Without them they would be open to nuclear blackmail by the Soviet Union, or by Germany if proliferation stopped there. Even if those major powers did not have nuclear arsenals, no Eastern European state could match German or Soviet conventional strength.

Clearly, then, a scenario in which current ownership continues, without proliferation, seems very unlikely.

The "Nuclear Proliferation" Scenario

The most probable scenario in the wake of the Cold War is further nuclear proliferation in Europe. This outcome is laden with dangers, but it also might just provide the best hope for maintaining stability on the Continent. Everything depends on how proliferation is managed. Mismanaged proliferation could produce disaster; well-managed proliferation could produce an order nearly as stable as that of the Long Peace.

The dangers that could arise from mismanaged proliferation are both profound and numerous. There is the danger that the proliferation process itself could give one of the existing nuclear powers a strong incentive to stop a nonnuclear neighbor from joining the club, much as Israel used force to stop Iraq from acquiring a nuclear capability. There is the danger that an unstable nuclear competition would emerge among the new nuclear states. They might lack the resources to make their nuclear forces invulnerable, which could create first-strike fears and incentives—a recipe for disaster in a crisis. Finally, there is the danger that by increasing the number of fingers on the nuclear trigger, proliferation would increase the risk that nuclear weapons would be fired by accident or captured by terrorists or used by madmen.

These and other dangers of proliferation can be lessened if the current nuclear powers take the right steps. To forestall preventive attacks, they can extend security guarantees. To help the new nuclear powers secure their deterrents, they can provide technical assistance. And they can help to socialize nascent nuclear societies to understand the lethal character of the forces they are acquiring. This kind of well-managed proliferation could help bolster peace.

Proliferation should ideally stop with Germany. It has a large economic base, and so could afford to sustain a secure nuclear force. Moreover, Germany would no doubt feel insecure without nuclear weapons, and if it felt insecure its impressive conventional strength would give it a significant capacity to disturb the tranquillity of Europe. But if the broader spread of nuclear weapons proves impossible to prevent without taking extreme steps, the current nuclear powers should let proliferation occur in Eastern Europe while doing all they can to channel it in safe directions.

However, I am pessimistic that proliferation can be well managed. The members of the nuclear club are likely to resist proliferation, but they cannot easily manage this tricky process while at the same time resisting it—and they will have several motives to resist. The established nuclear powers will be exceedingly chary of helping the new nuclear powers build secure deterrents, simply because it goes against the grain of state behavior to share military secrets with other states. After all, knowledge of sensitive military technology could be turned against the donor state if that technology were passed on to adversaries. Furthermore, proliferation in Europe will undermine the legitimacy of the 1968 Nuclear Non-Proliferation Treaty, and this could open the floodgates of proliferation worldwide. The current nuclear powers will not want that to happen, and so they will probably spend their energy trying to thwart proliferation, rather than seeking to manage it.

The best time for proliferation to occur would be during a period of relative international clam. Proliferation in the midst of a crisis would obviously be dangerous, since states in conflict with an emerging nuclear power would then have a powerful incentive to interrupt the process by force. However, the opposition to proliferation by citizens of the potential nuclear powers would be so vociferous, and the external resistance from the nuclear club would be so great, that it might take a crisis to make those powers willing to pay the domestic and international costs of building a nuclear force. All of which means that proliferation is likely to occur under international conditions that virtually ensure it will be mismanaged.

Is War Obsolete?

Many students of European politics will reject my pessimistic analysis of post-Cold War Europe. They will say that a multipolar Europe, with or without nuclear weapons, will be no less peaceful than the present order. Three specific scenarios for a peaceful future have been advanced, each of which rests on a well-known theory of international relations. However, each of these "soft" theories of peace is flawed.

Under the first optimistic scenario, a non-nuclear Europe would remain peaceful because Europeans recognize that even a conventional war would be horrific. Sobered by history, national leaders will take care to avoid war. This scenario rests on the "obsolescence of war" theory, which posits that modern conventional war had become so deadly by 1945 as to be unthinkable as an instrument of statecraft. War is yesterday's nightmare.

The fact that the Second World War occurred casts doubt on this theory: if any war could have persuaded Europeans to forswear conventional war, it should have been the First World War, with its vast casualties. The key flaw in this theory is the assumption that all conventional wars will be long and bloody wars of attrition. Proponents ignore the evidence of several wars since 1945, as well as several campaign-ending battles of the Second World War, that it is still possible to gain a quick and decisive victory on the conventional battlefield and avoid the devastation of a protracted conflict. Conventional wars can be won rather cheaply; nuclear war cannot be, because neither side can escape devastation by the other, regardless of what happens on the battlefield. Thus the incentives to avoid war are of another order of intensity in a nuclear world than they are in a conventional world.

There are several other flaws in this scenario. There is no systematic evidence demonstrating that Europeans believe war is obsolete. The Romanians and the Hungarians don't seem to have gotten the message. However, even if it were widely believed in Europe that war is no longer thinkable, attitudes could change. Public opinion on national-security issues is notoriously fickle and responsive to manipulation by elites as well as to changes in the international environment. An end to the Cold War, as we have seen, will be accompanied by a sea change in the geometry of power in Europe, which will surely alter European thinking about questions of war and peace. Is it not possible, for example, that German thinking about the benefits of controlling Eastern Europe will change markedly once American forces are withdrawn from Central Europe and the Germans are left to provide for their own security? Is it not possible that they would countenance a conventional war against a substantially weaker Eastern European state to enhance their position vis-á-vis the Soviet Union? Finally, only one country need decide that war is thinkable to make war possible.

Is Prosperity the Path to Peace?

Proponents of the second optimistic scenario base their optimism about the future of Europe on the unified European market coming in 1992—the realization of the dream of the European Community. A strong EC, they argue, ensures that the European economy will remain open and prosperous, which will keep the European states cooperating with one another. Prosperity will make for peace. The threat of an aggressive Germany will be removed by enclosing the newly unified German state in the benign embrace of the EC. Even Eastern Europe and the Soviet Union can eventually be brought into the EC. Peace and prosperity will then extend their sway from the Atlantic to the Urals.

This scenario is based on the theory of economic liberalism, which assumes that states are primarily motivated by the desire to achieve prosperity and that leaders place the material welfare of their publics above all other considerations, including security. Stability flows not from military power but from the creation of a liberal economic order.

A liberal economic order works in several ways to enhance peace and dampen conflict. In the first place, it requires significant political cooperation to make the trading system work—make states richer. The more prosperous states grow, the greater their incentive for further political cooperation. A benevolent spiral relationship sets in between political cooperation and prosperity. Second, a liberal economic order fosters economic interdependence, a situation in which states are mutually vulnerable in the economic realm. When interdependence is high, the theory holds, there is less temptation to cheat or behave aggressively toward other states, because all states can retaliate economically. Finally, some theorists argue, an international institution like the EC will, with every-increasing political cooperation, become so powerful that it will take on a life of its own, eventually evolving into a superstate. In short, Mrs. Thatcher's presentiments about the EC are absolutely right.

This theory has one grave flaw: the main assumption underpinning it is wrong. States are not primarily motivated by the desire to achieve prosperity. Although economic calculations are hardly trivial to them, states operate in both an international political and an international economic environment, and the former dominates the latter when the two systems come into conflict. Survival in an anarchic international political system is the highest goal a state can have.

Proponents of economic liberalism largely ignore the effects of anarchy on state behavior and concentrate instead on economic motives. When this omission is corrected, however, their arguments collapse for two reasons.

Competition for security makes it difficult for states to cooperate, which, according to the theory of economic liberalism, they must do. When security is scarce, states become more concerned about relative than about absolute gains. They ask of an exchange not "Will both of us gain?" but "Who will gain more?" They reject even cooperation that will yield an absolute economic gain if the other state will gain more, from fear that the other might convert its gain to military strength, and then use this strength to win by coercion in later rounds. Cooperation is much easier to achieve if states worry only about absolute gains. The goal, then, is simply to ensure that the overall economic pie is expanding and that each state is getting at least some part of the increase. However, anarchy guarantees that security will often be scarce; this heightens states' concerns about relative gains, which makes cooperation difficult unless the pie can be finely sliced to reflect, and thus not disturb, the current balance of power.

Interdependence, moreover, is as likely to lead to conflict as to cooperation, because states will struggle to escape the vulnerability that interdependence creates, in order to bolster their national security. In time of crisis or war, states that depend on others for critical economic supplies will fear cut-off or blackmail; they may well respond by trying to seize the source of supply by force of arms. There are numerous historical examples of states' pursuing aggressive military policies for the purpose of achieving economic autarky. One thinks of both Japan and Germany during the interwar period. And one recalls that during the Arab oil embargo of the early 1970s there was much talk in America about using military force to seize Arab oil fields.

In twentieth-century Europe two periods saw a liberal economic order with high levels of interdependence. According to the theory of economic liberalism, stability should have obtained during those periods. It did not.

The first case clearly contradicts the economic liberals. The years from 1890 to 1914 were probably the time of greatest economic interdependence in Europe's history. Yet those years of prosperity were all the time making hideously for the First World War.

The second case covers the Cold War years, during which there has been much interdependence among the EC states, and relations among them have been very peaceful. This case, not surprisingly, is the centerpiece of the economic liberals' argument.

We certainly see a correlation in this period between interdependence and stability, but that does not mean that interdependence has caused cooperation among the Western democracies. More likely the Cold War was the prime cause of cooperation among the Western democracies, and the main reason that intra-EC relations have flourished.

A powerful and potentially dangerous Soviet Union forced the Western democracies to band together to meet a common threat. This threat muted concerns about relative gains arising from economic cooperation among the EC states by giving each Western democracy a vested interest in seeing its alliance partners grow powerful. Each increment of power helped deter the Soviets. Moreover, they all had a powerful incentive to avoid conflict with one another while the Soviet Union loomed to the East, ready to harvest the grain of Western quarrels.

In addition, America's hegemonic position in NATO, the military counterpart to the EC, mitigated the effects of anarchy on the Western democracies and induced cooperation among them. America not only provided protection against the Soviet threat; it also guaranteed that no EC state would aggress against another. For example, France did not have to fear Germany as it re-armed, because the American presence in Germany meant that the Germans were contained. With the United States serving as a night watchman, fears about relative gains among the Western European states were mitigated, and furthermore, those states were willing to allow their economies to become tightly interdependent.

Take away the present Soviet threat to Western Europe, send the American forces home, and relations among the EC states will be fundamentally altered. Without a common Soviet threat or an American night watchman, Western European states will do what they did for centuries before the onset of the Cold War—look upon one another with abiding suspicion. Consequently, they will worry about imbalances in gains and about the loss of autonomy that results from cooperation. Cooperation in this new order will be more difficult than it was during the Cold War. Conflict will be more likely.

In sum, there are good reasons for being skeptical about the claim that a more powerful EC can provide the basis for peace in a multipolar Europe.

Do Democracies Really Love Peace?

Under the third scenario war is avoided because many European states have become democratic since the early twentieth century, and liberal democracies simply do not fight one another. At a minimum, the presence of liberal democracies in Western Europe renders that half of Europe free from armed conflict. At a maximum, democracy spreads to Eastern Europe and the Soviet Union, bolstering peace. The idea that peace is cognate with democracy is a vision of international relations shared by both liberals and neoconservatives.

This scenario rests on the "peace-loving democracies" theory. Two arguments are made for it.

First, some claim that authoritarian leaders are more likely to go to war than leaders of democracies, because authoritarian leaders are not accountable to their publics, which carry the main burdens of war. In a democracy the citizenry, which pays the price of war, has a greater say in what the government does. The people, so the argument goes, are more hesitant to start trouble, because it is they who must pay the bloody price; hence the greater their power, the fewer wars.

The second argument rests on the claim that the citizens of liberal democracies respect popular democratic rights—those of their countrymen, and those of people in other states. They view democratic governments as more legitimate than others, and so are loath to impose a foreign regime on a democratic state by force. Thus an inhibition on war missing from other international relationships is introduced when two democracies face each other.

The first of these arguments is flawed because it is not possible to sustain the claim that the people in a democracy are especially sensitive to the costs of war and therefore less willing than authoritarian leaders to fight wars. In fact the historical record shows that democracies are every bit as likely to fight wars as are authoritarian states, though admittedly, thus far, not with other democracies.

Furthermore, mass publics, whether in a democracy or not, can become deeply imbued with nationalistic or religious fervor, making them prone to support aggression and quite indifferent to costs. The widespread public support in post-Revolutionary France for Napoleon's wars is just one example of this phenomenon. At the same time, authoritarian leaders are often fearful of going to war, because war tends to unleash democratic forces that can undermine the regime. In short, war can impose high costs on authoritarian leaders as well as on their citizenry.

The second argument, which emphasizes the transnational respect for democratic rights among democracies, rests on a secondary factor that is generally overridden by other factors such as nationalism and religious fundamentalism. Moreover, there is another problem with the argument. The possibility always exists that a democracy, especially the kind of fledgling democracy emerging in Eastern Europe, will revert to an authoritarian state. This threat of backsliding means that one democratic state can never be sure that another democratic state will not turn on it sometime in the future. Liberal democracies must therefore worry about relative power among themselves, which is tantamount to saying that each has an incentive to consider aggression against another to forestall trouble. Lamentably, it is not possible for even liberal democracies to transcend anarchy.

Problems with the deductive logic aside, at first glance the historical record seems to offer strong support for the theory of peace-loving democracies. It appears that no liberal democracies have ever fought against each other. Evidentiary problems, however, leave the issue in doubt.

First, democracies have been few in number over the past two centuries, and thus there have not been many cases in which two democracies were in a position to fight with each other. Three prominent cases are usually cited: Britain and the United States (1832 to the present); Britain and France (1832–1849; 1871–1940); and the Western democracies since 1945.

Second, there are other persuasive explanations for why war did not occur in those three cases, and these competing explanations must be ruled out before the theory of peace-loving democracies can be accepted. Whereas relations between the British and the Americans during the nineteenth century were hardly blissful, in the twentieth century they have been quite harmonious, and thus fit closely with the theory's expectations. That harmony, however, can easily be explained by common threats that forced Britain and the United States to work together—a serious German threat in the first part of the century, and later a Soviet threat. The same basic argument applies to relations between France and Britain. Although they were not on the best of terms during most of the nineteenth century, their relations improved significantly around the turn of the century, with the rise of Germany. Finally, as noted above, the Soviet threat goes far in explaining the absence of war among the Western democracies since 1945.

Third, several democracies have come close to fighting each other, suggesting that the absence of war may be due simply to chance. France and Britain approached war during the Fashoda crisis of 1898. France and Weimar Germany might have come to blows over the Rhineland during the 1920s. The United States has clashed with a number of elected governments in the Third World during the Cold War, including the Allende regime in Chile and the Arbenz regime in Guatemala.

Last, some would classify Wilhelmine Germany as a democracy, or at least a quasi-democracy; if so, the First World War becomes a war among democracies.

While the spread of democracy across Europe has great potential benefits for human rights, it will not guarantee peaceful relations among the states of post-Cold War Europe. Most Americans will find this argument counterintuitive. They see the United States as fundamentally peace-loving, and they ascribe this peacefulness to its democratic character. From this they generalize that democracies are more peaceful than authoritarian states, which leads them to conclude that the complete democratization of Europe would largely eliminate the threat of war. This view of international politics is likely to be repudiated by the events of coming years.

Missing the Cold War

The implications of my analysis are straightforward, if paradoxical. Developments that threaten to end the Cold War are dangerous. The West has an interest in maintaining peace in Europe. It therefore has an interest in maintaining the Cold War order, and hence has an interest in continuing the Cold War confrontation. The Cold War antagonism could be continued at lower levels of East-West tension than have prevailed in the past, but a complete end to the Cold War would create more problems than it would solve.

The fate of the Cold War is mainly in the hands of the Soviet Union. The Soviet Union is the only superpower that can seriously threaten to overrun Europe, and the Soviet threat provides the glue that holds NATO together. Take away that offensive threat and the United States is likely to abandon the Continent; the defensive alliance it has headed for forty years may well then disintegrate, bringing an end to the bipolar order that has kept the peace of Europe for the past forty-five years.

There is little the Americans or the West Europeans can do to perpetuate the Cold War.

For one thing, domestic politics preclude it. Western leaders obviously cannot base national-security policy on the need to maintain forces in Central Europe simply to keep the Soviets there. The idea of deploying large numbers of troops in order to bait the Soviets into an order-keeping competition would be dismissed as bizarre, and contrary to the general belief that ending the Cold War and removing the Soviet yoke from Eastern Europe would make the world safer and better.

For another, the idea of propping up a declining rival runs counter to the basic behavior of states. States are principally concerned about their relative power in the system—hence they look for opportunities to take advantage of one another. If anything, they prefer to see adversaries decline, and invariably do whatever they can to speed up the process and maximize the distance of the fall. States, in other words, do not ask which distribution of power best facilitates stability and then do everything possible to build or maintain such an order. Instead, each pursues the narrower aim of maximizing its power advantage over potential adversaries. The particular international order that results is simply a by-product of that competition.

Consider, for example, the origins of the Cold War order in Europe. No state intended to create it. In fact the United States and the Soviet Union each worked hard in the early years of the Cold War to undermine the other's position in Europe, which would have needed the bipolar order on the Continent. The remarkably stable system that emerged in Europe in the late 1940s was the unintended consequence of an intense competition between the superpowers.

Moreover, even if the Americans and the West Europeans wanted to help the Soviets maintain their status as a superpower, it is not apparent that they could do so. The Soviet Union is leaving Eastern Europe and cutting its military forces largely because its economy is floundering badly. The Soviets don't know how to fix their economy themselves, and there is little that Western governments can do to help them. The West can and should avoid doing malicious mischief to the Soviet economy, but at this juncture it is difficult to see how the West can have a significant positive influence.

The fact that the West cannot sustain the Cold War does not mean that the United States should make no attempt to preserve the current order. It should do what it can to avert a complete mutual withdrawal from Europe. For instance, the American negotiating position at the conventional-arms-control talks should aim toward large mutual force reductions but should not contemplate complete mutual withdrawal. The Soviets may opt to withdraw all their forces unilaterally anyway; if so, there is little the United States can do to stop them.

Should complete Soviet withdrawal from Eastern Europe prove unavoidable, the West would confront the question of how to maintain peace in a multipolar Europe. Three policy prescriptions are in order.

First, the United States should encourage the limited and carefully managed proliferation of nuclear weapons in Europe. The best hope for avoiding war in post-Cold War Europe is nuclear deterrence; hence some nuclear proliferation is necessary, to compensate for the withdrawal of the Soviet and American nuclear arsenals from Central Europe. Ideally, as I have argued, nuclear weapons would spread to Germany but to no other state.

Second, Britain and the United States, as well as the Continental states, will have to counter any emerging aggressor actively and efficiently, in order to offset the ganging up and bullying that are sure to arise in post-Cold War Europe. Balancing in a multipolar system, however, is usually a problem-ridden enterprise, because of either geography or the problems of coordination. Britain and the United States, physically separated from the Continent, may conclude that they have little interest in what happens there. That would be abandoning their responsibilities and, more important, their interests. Both states failed to counter Germany before the two world wars, making war more likely. It is essential for peace in Europe that they not repeat their past mistakes.

Both states must maintain military forces that can be deployed against Continental states that threaten to start a war. To do this they must persuade their citizens to support a policy of continued Continental commitment. This will be more difficult than it once was, because its principal purpose will be to preserve peace, rather than to prevent an imminent hegemony, and the prevention of hegemony is a simpler goal to explain publicly. Furthermore, this prescription asks both countries to take on an unaccustomed task, given that it is the basic nature of states to focus on maximizing relative power, not on bolstering stability. Nevertheless, the British and the Americans have a real stake in peace, especially since there is the risk that a European war might involve the large-scale use of nuclear weapons. Therefore, it should be possible for their governments to lead their publics to recognize this interest and support policies that protect it.

The Soviet Union may eventually return to its past expansionism and threaten to upset the status quo. If so, we are back to the Cold War. However, if the Soviets adhere to status-quo policies, Soviet power could play a key role in countering Germany and in maintaining order in Eastern Europe. It is important in those cases where the Soviets are acting in a balancing capacity that the United States cooperate with its former adversary and not let residual distrust from the Cold War obtrude.

Third, a concerted effort should be made to keep hypernationalism at bay, especially in Eastern Europe. Nationalism has been contained during the Cold War, but it is likely to re-emerge once Soviet and American forces leave the heart of Europe. It will be a force for trouble unless curbed. The teaching of honest national history is especially important, since the teaching of false, chauvinist history is the main vehicle for spreading hypernationalism. States that teach a dishonestly self-exculpating or self-glorifying history should be publicly criticized and sanctioned.

None of these tasks will be easy. In fact, I expect that the bulk of my prescriptions will not be followed; most run contrary to important strains of domestic American and European opinion, and to the basic nature of state behavior. And even if they are followed, peace in Europe will not be guaranteed. If the Cold War is truly behind us, therefore, the stability of the past forty-five years is not likely to be seen again in the coming decades.

PART 2

International Realism: Anarchy and Power

The dominant tradition in thinking about international relations is known colloquially as "power politics," and in academic circles as "realism." The main themes in this school of thought are that in order to survive, states are driven to seek power, that moral and legal principles may govern relations among citizens within societies but cannot control the relations among states, and that wars occur because there is no sovereign in the international system to settle disputes peacefully and enforce judgments. States have no one but themselves to rely on for protection, or to obtain what they believe they are entitled to by right.

Thucydides' *Peloponnesian War*, the history of the conflict between Athens and Sparta, is the classic statement of these ideas. The selection included here the Melian Dialogue—is perhaps the most extreme and frank discussion of power politics, unclouded by diplomatic niceties, ever recorded. Taken alone, the dialogue can appear a caricature, so readers are encouraged to delve more deeply into the original work, which is rich in commentary on various aspects of balance of power politics, strategy, and the role of ideology and domestic conflict in international relations.[1]

The tradition of realism, in various forms, can be traced through Machiavelli, Hobbes, the German schools of *Realpolitik* and *Machtpolitik*, to E. H. Carr, Reinhold Niebuhr, Hans Morgenthau, and others in the mid-twentieth century. Morgenthau's *Politics Among Nations*[2] has been the most prominent textbook of

---

[1]Thucydides also presents examples that differ markedly from the Melian Dialogue, such as the Mytilene Debate. See Michael Walzer's comparison in *Just and Unjust Wars* (New York: Basic Books, 1977), pp. 5-11.

[2]Hans Morgenthau, *Politics Among Nations,* 5th edition (New York: Knopf, 1973).

realism in the United States. Carr's *Twenty Years Crisis,* on the other hand, is distinguished by its pungency, which helps to convey the essence of realism in brief selections. Before pigeon-holing Carr as a strident realist, however, note his eloquent discussion of the serious deficiencies of the theory in the concluding section of this volume.

The most prominent recent writings in this school have been dubbed "neorealism" to distinguish their more rigorously scientific formulation of the theory from classical realism. Neorealists focus less on the questions of human motivation or morality than on the security incentives posed by the structure of the international system. The selection below by Kenneth Waltz, the dean of neorealism, is close to a summary of his masterwork, *Theory of International Politics.*[3] Mearsheimer's hyper-realist argument in favor of the Cold War, in Part 1 above, derives directly from Waltz's reasoning about the stability of a bipolar world (discussed in this selection) and the pacifying effect of nuclear weapons (discussed in Waltz's selection in Part 6).

The favorable view of bipolarity among neorealists, however, contradicts traditional balance-of-power theory. In considering whether a world of only two great powers, as opposed to a world of many, should be less likely to lead to war, compare Waltz and Mearsheimer with Thucydides, Blainey, and Gilpin. The competition between Athens and Sparta, for example, unlike that between the United States and the Soviet Union, ended in disaster. Where Waltz sees bipolarity as imposing clarity and stability on the competition, others see it as inherently unstable, a delicate balance between contenders ever striving for primacy. Robert Gilpin sees history as a succession of struggles for hegemony between declining and rising powers, with the struggles normally resolved by a major war. Geoffrey Blainey considers a hierarchical system, in which differences in power are clear, as the most stable. When there is no doubt about who would prevail if disagreements were to lead to combat, there is little chance that the strong will need to resort to combat or that the weak will dare to. Blainey sees a world of rough parity, in contrast, as unstable, because it is easier for states to miscalculate the balance of power and their chances of being able to impose their will by either initiating or resisting the use of force.

How much do the structure of the international balance of power and competition for primacy determine the actions of states? We might ask how one could have predicted the end of the Cold War from realist theories. Is the Soviet Union's voluntary surrender of control over Eastern Europe in 1989, indeed its entire withdrawal from the power struggle with the West, consistent with such explanations of state behavior? Realists understand that politicians do not always act in accord with realist norms. But the enormity of the Gorbachev revolution is an uncomfortable exception for the theory to have to bear.

The greatest irony of the end of the Cold War, perhaps, is that it occurred be-

---

[3]Kenneth N. Waltz, *Theory of International Politics* (Reading, Mass.: Addison-Wesley, 1979). See also Waltz, *Man, the State, and War* (New York: Columbia University Press, 1959).

cause the leadership of the Soviet Union, the superpower that had so tenaciously opposed Western liberalism as a model for the world, itself adopted liberal ideas about international cooperation. The readings in Part 3 will present some tenets of the liberal tradition whose view of the possibilities of peace differs markedly from the one presented in this section.

The Melian Dialogue

THUCYDIDES

The Melians are a colony of Lacedaemon [Sparta] that would not submit to
the Athenians like the other islanders, and at first remained neutral and
took no part in the struggle, but afterwards upon the Athenians using violence and plundering their territory, assumed an attitude of open hostility.
Cleomedes, son of Lycomedes, and Tisias, son of Tisimachus, the generals,
encamping in their territory with the above armament, before doing any
harm to their land, sent envoys to negotiate. These the Melians did not
bring before the people, but bade them state the object of their mission to
the magistrates and the few; upon which the Athenian envoys spoke as follows:—

Athenians: 'Since the negotiations are not to go on before the people, in
order that we may not be able to speak straight on without interruption, and
deceive the ears of the multitude by seductive arguments which would pass
without refutation (for we know that this is the meaning of our being
brought before the few), what if you who sit there were to pursue a method
more cautious still! Make no set speech yourselves, but take us up at whatever you do not like, and settle that before going any farther. And first tell us
if this proposition of ours suits you.'

The Melian commissioners answered:—

Melians: 'To the fairness of quietly instructing each other as you propose
there is nothing to object; but your military preparations are too far advanced to agree with what you say, as we see you are come to be judges in
your own cause, and that all we can reasonably expect from this negotiation

Thucydides, *The Peloponnesian War*, Richard Crawley, trans. (New York: The Modern Library,
1934), Book V.

is war, if we prove to have right on our side and refuse to submit, and in the contrary case, slavery.'

Athenians: 'If you have met to reason about presentiments of the future, or for anything else than to consult for the safety of your state upon the facts that you see before you, we will give over; otherwise we will go on.'

Melians: 'It is natural and excusable for men in our position to turn more ways than one both in thought and utterance. However, the question in this conference is, as you say, the safety of our country; and the discussion, if you please, can proceed in the way which you propose.'

Athenians: 'For ourselves, we shall not trouble you with specious pretences—either of how we have a right to our empire because we overthrew the Mede, or are now attacking you because of wrong that you have done us—and make a long speech which would not be believed; and in return we hope that you, instead of thinking to influence us by saying that you did not join the Lacedaemonians, although their colonists, or that you have done us no wrong, will aim at what is feasible, holding in view the real sentiments of us both; since you know as well as we do that right, as the world goes, is only in question between equals in power, while the strong do what they can and the weak suffer what they must.'

Melians: 'As we think, at any rate, it is expedient—we speak as we are obliged, since you enjoin us to let right alone and talk only of interest—that you should not destroy what is our common protection, the privilege of being allowed in danger to invoke what is fair and right, and even to profit by arguments not strictly valid if they can be got to pass current. And you are as much interested in this as any, as your fall would be a signal for the heaviest vengeance and an example for the world to meditate upon.'

Athenians: 'The end of our empire, if end it should, does not frighten us: a rival empire like Lacedaemon, even if Lacedaemon was our real antagonist, is not so terrible to the vanquished as subjects who by themselves attack and overpower their rulers. This, however, is a risk that we are content to take. We will now proceed to show you that we are come here in the interest of our empire, and that we shall say what we are now going to say, for the preservation of your country; as we would fain exercise that empire over you without trouble, and see you preserved for the good of us both.'

Melians: 'And how, pray, could it turn out as good for us to serve as for you to rule?'

Athenians: 'Because you would have the advantage of submitting before suffering the worst, and we should gain by not destroying you.'

Melians: 'So that you would not consent to our being neutral, friends instead of enemies, but allies of neither side.'

Athenians: 'No; for your hostility cannot so much hurt us as your friendship will be an argument to our subjects of our weakness, and your enmity of our power.'

Melians: 'Is that your subjects' idea of equity, to put those who have nothing to do with you in the same category with peoples that are most of them your own colonists, and some conquered rebels?'

Athenians: 'As far as right goes they think one has as much of it as the other, and that if any maintain their independence it is because they are strong, and that if we do not molest them it is because we are afraid; so that besides extending our empire we should gain in security by your subjection; the fact that you are islanders and weaker than others rendering it all the more important that you should not succeed in baffling the masters of the sea.'

Melians: 'But do you consider that there is no security in the policy which we indicate? For here again if you debar us from talking about justice and invite us to obey your interest, we also must explain ours, and try to persuade you, if the two happen to coincide. How can you avoid making enemies of all existing neutrals who shall look at our case and conclude from it that one day or another you will attack them? And what is this but to make greater the enemies that you have already, and to force others to become so who would otherwise have never thought of it?'

Athenians: 'Why, the fact is that continentals generally give us but little alarm; the liberty which they enjoy will long prevent their taking precautions against us; it is rather islanders like yourselves, outside our empire, and subjects smarting under the yoke, who would be the most likely to take a rash step and lead themselves and us into obvious danger.'

Melians: 'Well then, if you risk so much to retain your empire, and your subjects to get rid of it, it were surely great baseness and cowardice in us who are still free not to try everything that can be tried, before submitting to your yoke.'

Athenians: 'Not if you are well advised, the contest not being an equal one, with honour as the prize and shame as the penalty, but a question of self-preservation and of not resisting those who are far stronger than you are.'

Melians: 'But we know that the fortune of war is sometimes more impartial than the disproportion of numbers might lead one to suppose; to submit is to give ourselves over to despair, while action still preserves for us a hope that we may stand erect.'

Athenians: 'Hope, danger's comforter, may be indulged in by those who have abundant resources, if not without loss at all events without ruin; but its nature is to be extravagant, and those who go so far as to put their all upon the venture see it in its true colours only when they are ruined; but so long as the discovery would enable them to guard against it, it is never found wanting. Let not this be the case with you, who are weak and hang on a single turn of the scale; nor be like the vulgar, who, abandoning such security as human means may still afford, when visible hopes fail them in extremity, turn to invisible, to prophecies and oracles, and other such inventions that delude men with hopes to their destruction.'

Melians: 'You may be sure that we are as well aware as you of the difficulty of contending against your power and fortune, unless the terms be equal.

But we trust that the gods may grant us fortune as good as yours, since we are just men fighting against unjust, and that what we want in power will be made up by the alliance of the Lacedaemonians, who are bound if only for very shame, to come to the aid of their kindred. Our confidence, therefore, after all is not so utterly irrational.'

Athenians: 'When you speak of the favour of the gods, we may as fairly hope for that as yourselves; neither our pretensions nor our conduct being in any way contrary to what men believe of the gods, or practise among themselves. Of the gods we believe, and of men we know, that by a necessary law of their nature they rule wherever they can. And it is not as if we were the first to make this law, or to act upon it when made: we found it existing before us, and shall leave it to exist for ever after us; all we do is to make use of it, knowing that you and everybody else, having the same power as we have, would do the same as we do. Thus, as far as the gods are concerned, we have no fear and no reason to fear that we shall be at a disadvantage. But when we come to your notion about the Lacedaemonians, which leads you to believe that shame will make them help you, here we bless your simplicity but do not envy your folly. The Lacedaemonians, when their own interests of their country's laws are in question, are the worthiest men alive; of their conduct towards others much might be said, but no clearer idea of it could be given than by shortly saying that of all the men we know they are most conspicuous in considering what is agreeable honourable, and what is expedient just. Such a way of thinking does not promise much for the safety which you now unreasonably count upon.'

Melians: 'But it is for this very reason that we now trust to their respect for expediency to prevent them from betraying the Melians, their colonists, and thereby losing the confidence of their friends in Hellas and helping their enemies.'

Athenians: 'Then you do not adopt the view that expediency goes with security, while justice and honour cannot be followed without danger; and danger the Lacedaemonians generally court as little as possible.'

Melians: 'But we believe that they would be more likely to face even danger for our sake, and with more confidence than for others, as our nearness to Peloponnese makes it easier for them to act, and our common blood insures our fidelity.'

Athenians: 'Yes, but what an intending ally trusts to, is not the goodwill of those who ask his aid, but a decided superiority of power for action; and the Lacedaemonians look to this even more than others. At least, such is their distrust of their home resources that it is only with numerous allies that they attack a neighbour; now is it likely that while we are masters of the sea they will cross over to an island?'

Melians: 'But they would have others to send. The Cretan sea is a wide one, and it is more difficult for those who command it to intercept others, than for those who wish to elude them to do so safely. And should the Lacedaemonians miscarry in this, they would fall upon your land, and upon those left of your allies whom Brasidas did not reach; and instead of places which are not yours, you will have to fight for your own country and your own confederacy.'

Athenians: 'Some diversion of the kind you speak of you may one day experience, only to learn, as others have done, that the Athenians never once yet withdrew from a siege for fear of any. But we are struck by the fact, that after saying you would consult for the safety of your country, in all this discussion you have mentioned nothing which men might trust in and think to be saved by. Your strongest arguments depend upon hope and the future, and your actual resources are too scanty, as compared with those arrayed against you, for you to come out victorious. You will therefore show great blindness of judgment, unless, after allowing us to retire, you can find some counsel more prudent than this. You will surely not be caught by that idea of disgrace, which in dangers that are disgraceful, and at the same time too plain to be mistaken, proves so fatal to mankind; since in too many cases the very men that have their eyes perfectly open to what they are rushing into, let the thing called disgrace, by the mere influence of a seductive name, lead them on to a point at which they become so enslaved by the phrase as in fact to fall wilfully into hopeless disaster, and incur disgrace more disgraceful as the companion of error, than when it comes as the result of misfortune. This, if you are well advised, you will guard against; and you will not think it dishonourable to submit to the greatest city in Hellas, when it makes you the moderate offer of becoming its tributary ally, without ceasing to enjoy the country that belongs to you; nor when you have the choice given you between war and security, will you be so blinded as to choose the worse. And it is certain that those who do not yield to their equals, who keep terms with their superiors, and are moderate towards their inferiors, on the whole succeed best. Think over the matter, therefore, after our withdrawal, and reflect once and again that it is for your country that you are consulting, that you have not more than one, and that upon this one deliberation depends its prosperity or ruin.'

The Athenians now withdrew from the conference; and the Melians, left to themselves, came to a decision corresponding with what they had maintained in the discussion, and answered, 'Our resolution, Athenians, is the same as it was at first. We will not in a moment deprive of freedom a city that has been inhabited these seven hundred years; but we put our trust in the fortune by which the gods have preserved it until now, and in the help of men, that is, of the Lacedaemonians; and so we will try and save ourselves. Meanwhile we invite you to allow us to be friends to you and foes to neither party, and to retire from our country after making such a treaty as shall seem fit to us both.'

Such was the answer of the Melians. The Athenians now departing from the conference said, 'Well, you alone, as it seems to us, judging from these resolutions, regard what is future as more certain than what is before your eyes, and what is out of sight, in your eagerness, as already coming to pass; and as you have staked most on, and trusted most in, the Lacedaemonians, your fortune, and your hopes, so will you be most completely deceived.'

The Athenian envoys now returned to the army; and the Melians showing no signs of yielding, the generals at once betook themselves to hostilities, and drew a line of circumvallation round the Melians, dividing the work among the different states. Subsequently the Athenians returned with most of their army, leaving behind them a certain number of their own citizens and of the allies to keep guard by land and sea. The force thus left stayed on and besieged the place. . . .

Summer was now over. The next winter the Lacedaemonians intended to invade the Argive territory, but arriving at the frontier found the sacrifices for crossing unfavourable, and went back again. This intention of theirs gave the Argives suspicions of certain of their fellow-citizens, some of whom they arrested; others, however, escaped them. About the same time the Melians again took another part of the Athenian lines which were but feebly garrisoned. Reinforcements afterwards arriving from Athens in consequence, under the command of Philocrates, son of Demeas, the siege was now pressed vigorously; and some treachery taking place inside, the Melians surrendered at discretion to the Athenians, who put to death all the grown men whom they took, and sold the women and children for slaves, and subsequently sent out five hundred colonists and inhabited the place themselves.

Realism and Idealism

EDWARD HALLETT CARR

In Europe after 1919, planned economy, which rests on the assumption that no natural harmony of interests exists and that interests must be artificially harmonised by state action, became the practice, if not the theory, of almost every state. In the United States, the persistence of an expanding domestic market stayed off this development till after 1929. The natural harmony of interests remained an integral part of the American view of life; and in this as in other respects, current theories of international politics were deeply imbued with the American tradition. Moreover, there was a special reason for the ready acceptance of the doctrine in the international sphere. In domestic affairs it is clearly the business of the state to create harmony if no natural harmony exists. In international politics, there is no organized power charged with the task of creating harmony; and the temptation to assume a natural harmony is therefore particularly strong. But this is no excuse for burking the issue. To make the harmonisation of interests the goal of political action is not the same thing as to postulate that a natural harmony of interests exist; and it is this latter postulate which has caused so much confusion in international thinking.

Politically, the doctrine of the identity of interests has commonly taken the form of an assumption that every nation has an identical interest in peace, and that any nation which desires to disturb the peace is therefore both irrational and immoral. This view bears clear marks of its Anglo-Saxon origin. It was easy after 1918 to convince that part of mankind which lives in English-speaking countries that war profits nobody. The argument did not seem particularly convincing to Germans, who had profited largely from the wars of 1866 and 1870, and attributed their more recent sufferings, not to the war of 1914, but to the fact that they had lost it; or to Italians, who

Edward Hallett Carr, *The Twenty Years Crisis, 1919–1939*, 2d edition (London: Macmillan, 1946), selections from chapters 4, 5, 8, 10, 11, and 13. Copyright © 1969. Reprinted with permission of St. Martin's Press Incorporated.

blamed not the war, but the treachery of allies who defrauded them in the peace settlement; or to Poles or Czecho-Slovaks who, far from deploring the war, owed their national existence to it; or to Frenchmen, who could not unreservedly regret a war which had restored Alsace-Lorraine to France; or to people of other nationalities who remembered profitable wars waged by Great Britain and the United States in the past. But these people had fortunately little influence over the formation of current theories of international relations, which emanated almost exclusively from the English-speaking countries. British and American writers continued to assume that the uselessness of war had been irrefutably demonstrated by the experience of 1914-18, and that an intellectual grasp of this fact was all that was necessary to induce the nations to keep the peace in the future; and they were sincerely puzzled as well as disappointed at the failure of other countries to share this view.

The confusion was increased by the ostentatious readiness of other countries to flatter the Anglo-Saxon world by repeating its slogans. In the fifteen years after the first world war, every Great Power (except, perhaps, Italy) repeatedly did lip-service to the doctrine by declaring peace to be one of the main objects of its policy.[1] But as Lenin observed long ago, peace in itself is a meaningless aim. "Absolutely everybody is in favour of peace in general", he wrote in 1915, "including Kitchener, Joffre, Hindenburg and Nicholas the Bloody, for everyone of them wishes to end the war."[2] The common interest in peace masks the fact that some nations desire to maintain the *status quo* without having to fight for it, and others to change the *status quo* without having to fight in order to do so. . . .

International Economic Harmony

. . . We find in the modern period an extraordinary divergence between the theories of economic experts and the practice of those responsible for the

---

[1] "Peace must prevail, must come before all" (Briand, *League of Nations: Ninth Assembly*, p. 83). "The maintenance of peace is the first objective of British foreign policy" (Eden, *League of Nations: Sixteenth Assembly*, p. 106). "Peace is our dearest treasure" (Hitler, in a speech in the German Reichstag on January 30, 1937, reported in *The Times*, February 1, 1937). "The principal aim of the international policy of the Soviet Union is the preservation of peace" (Chicherin in *The Soviet Union and Peace* (1929), p. 249). "The object of Japan, despite propaganda to the contrary, is peace" (Matsuoka, *League of Nations: Special Assembly 1932-33*, iii. p. 73). The paucity of Italian pronouncements in favour of peace was probably explained by the poor reputation of Italian troops as fighters: Mussolini feared that any emphatic expression of preference for peace would be construed as an admission that Italy had no stomach for war.

[2] Lenin, *Collected Works* (Engl. transl.), xviii. p. 264. Compare Spenser Wilkinson's dictum: "It is not peace but preponderance that is in each case the real object. The truth cannot be too often repeated that peace is never the object of policy: you cannot define peace except by reference to war, which is a means and never an end" (*Government and the War*, p. 121).

economic policies of their respective countries. Analysis will show that this divergence springs from a simple fact. The economic expert, dominated in the main by *laissez-faire* doctrine, considers the hypothetical economic interest of the world as a whole, and is content to assume that this is identical with the interest of each individual country. The politician pursues the concrete interest of his country, and assumes (if he makes any assumption at all) that the interest of the world as a whole is identical with it. Nearly every pronouncement of every international economic conference held between the two world wars was vitiated by this assumption that there was some "solution" or "plan" which, by a judicious balancing of interests, would be equally favourable to all and prejudicial to none. . . .

In the nineteenth century, Germany and the United States, by pursuing a "strictly nationalistic policy", had placed themselves in a position to challenge Great Britain's virtual monopoly of world trade. No conference of economic experts, meeting in 1880, could have evolved a "general plan" for "parallel or concerted action" which would have allayed the economic rivalries of the time in a manner equally advantageous to Great Britain, Germany and the United States. It was not less presumptuous to suppose that a conference meeting in 1927 could allay the economic rivalries of the later period by a "plan" beneficial to the interests of everyone. Even the economic crisis of 1930-33 failed to bring home to the economists the true nature of the problem which they had to face. The experts who prepared the "Draft Annotated Agenda" for the World Economic Conference of 1933 condemned the "world-wide adoption of ideals of national self-sufficiency which cut unmistakably athwart the lines of economic development".[3] They did not apparently pause to reflect that those so-called "lines of economic development", which might be beneficial to some countries and even to the world as a whole, would inevitably be detrimental to other countries, which were using weapons of economic nationalism in self-defence. . . . *Laissez-faire,* in international relations as in those between capital and labour, is the paradise of the economically strong. State control, whether in the form of protective legislation or of protective tariffs, is the weapon of self-defence invoked by the economically weak. The clash of interests is real and inevitable; and the whole nature of the problem is distorted by an attempt to disguise it.

The Foundations of Realism

. . . The three essential tenets implicit in Machiavelli's doctrine are the foundation-stones of the realist philosophy. In the first place, history is a sequence of cause and effect, whose course can be analysed and understood

---

[3]*League of Nations:* C.48, M.18, 1933, ii. p. 6.

by intellectual effort, but not (as the utopians believe) directed by "imagination". Secondly, theory does not (as the utopians assume) create practice, but practice theory. In Machiavelli's words, "good counsels, whencesoever they come, are born of the wisdom of the prince, and not the wisdom of the prince from good counsels". Thirdly, politics are not (as the utopians pretend) a function of ethics, but ethics of politics. Men "are kept honest by constraint". Machiavelli recognised the importance of morality, but thought that there could be no effective morality where there was no effective authority. Morality is the product of power.[4]

The extraordinary vigour and vitality of Machiavelli's challenge to orthodoxy may be attested by the fact that, more than four centuries after he wrote, the most conclusive way of discrediting a political opponent is still to describe him as a disciple of Machiavelli. . . .

. . . Theories of social morality are always the product of a dominant group which identifies itself with the community as a whole, and which possesses facilities denied to subordinate groups or individuals for imposing its view of life on the community. Theories of international morality are, for the same reason and in virtue of the same process, the product of dominant nations or groups of nations. For the past hundred years, and more especially since 1918, the English-speaking peoples have formed the dominant group in the world; and current theories of international morality have been designed to perpetuate their supremacy and expressed in the idiom peculiar to them. France, retaining something of her eighteenth-century tradition and restored to a position of dominance for a short period after 1918, has played a minor part in the creation of current international morality, mainly through her insistence on the role of law in the moral order. Germany, never a dominant Power and reduced to helplessness after 1918, has remained for these reasons outside the charmed circle of creators of international morality. Both the view that the English-speaking peoples are monopolists of international morality and the view that they are consummate international hypocrites may be reduced to the plain fact that the current canons of international virtue have, by a natural and inevitable process, been mainly created by them.

The Realist Critique of the Harmony of Interests

The doctrine of the harmony of interests yields readily to analysis in terms of this principle. It is the natural assumption of a prosperous and privileged class, whose members have a dominant voice in the community and are there-

---

[4]Machiavelli, *The Prince*, chs. 15 and 23 (Engl. transl., Everyman's Library, pp. 121, 193).

fore naturally prone to identify its interest with their own. In virtue of this identification, any assailant of the interests of the dominant group is made to incur the odium of assailing the alleged common interest of the whole community, and is told that in making this assault he is attacking his own higher interests. The doctrine of the harmony of interests thus serves as an ingenious moral device invoked, in perfect sincerity, by privileged groups in order to justify and maintain their dominant position. But a further point requires notice. The supremacy within the community of the privileged group may be, and often is, so overwhelming that there is, in fact, a sense in which its interests are those of the community, since its well-being necessarily carries with it some measure of well-being for other members of the community, and its collapse would entail the collapse of the community as a whole. In so far, therefore, as the alleged natural harmony of interests has any reality, it is created by the overwhelming power of the privileged group, and is an excellent illustration of the Machiavellian maxim that morality is the product of power.

   . . . British nineteenth-century statesmen, having discovered that free trade promoted British prosperity, were sincerely convinced that, in doing so, it also promoted the prosperity of the world as a whole. British predominance in world trade was at that time so overwhelming that there was a certain undeniable harmony between British interests and the interests of the world. British prosperity flowed over into other countries, and a British economic collapse would have meant world-wide ruin. British free traders could and did argue that protectionist countries were not only egotistically damaging the prosperity of the world as a whole, but were stupidly damaging their own, so that their behaviour was both immoral and muddle headed. In British eyes, it was irrefutably proved that international trade was a single whole, and flourished or slumped together. Nevertheless, this alleged international harmony of interests seemed a mockery to those under-privileged nations whose inferior status and insignificant stake in international trade were consecrated by it. The revolt against it destroyed that overwhelming British preponderance which had provided a plausible basis for the theory. Economically, Great Britain in the nineteenth century was dominant enough to make a bold bid to impose on the world her own conception of international economic morality. When competition of all against all replaced the domination of the world market by a single Power, conceptions of international economic morality necessarily became chaotic.

   Politically, the alleged community of interest in the maintenance of peace, whose ambiguous character has already been discussed, is capitalised in the same way by a dominant nation or group of nations. Just as the ruling class in a community prays for domestic peace, which guarantees its own security and predominance, and denounces class-war, which might threaten them, so international peace becomes a special vested interest of predominant Powers. In the past, Roman and British imperialism were commended to the world in the guise of the *pax Romana* and the *pax Britannica*. To-day, when no single Power is strong enough to dominate the world, and supremacy is vested in a group of nations, slogans like "collective security" and "resistance to aggression" serve the same purpose of proclaiming an identity of interest between the dominant group and the world as a whole in the maintenance of peace.

... It is a familiar tactic of the privileged to throw moral discredit on the under-privileged by depicting them as disturbers of the peace; and this tactic is as readily applied internationally as within the national community. "International law and order", writes Professor Toynbee of a recent crisis, "were in the true interests of the whole of mankind ... whereas the desire to perpetuate the region of violence in international affairs was an anti-social desire which was not even in the ultimate interests of the citizens of the handful of states that officially professed this benighted and anachronistic creed."[5] This is precisely the argument, compounded of platitude and falsehood in about equal parts, which did duty in every strike in the early days of the British and American Labour movements. It was common form for employers, supported by the whole capitalist press, to denounce the "anti-social" attitude of trade union leaders, to accuse them of attacking law and order and of introducing "the reign of violence", and to declare that "true" and "ultimate" interests of the workers lay in peaceful cooperation with the employers.[6] In the field of social relations, the disingenuous character of this argument has long been recognised. But just as the threat of class-war by the proletarian is "a natural cynical reaction to the sentimental and dishonest efforts of the privileged classes to obscure the conflict of interest between classes by a constant emphasis on the minimum interests which they have in common",[7] so the war-mongering of the dissatisfied Powers was the "natural, cynical reaction" to the sentimental and dishonest platitudinising of the satisfied Powers on the common interest in peace. When Hitler refused to believe "that God has permitted some nations first to acquire a world by force and then to defend this robbery with moralising theories"[8] he was merely echoing in another context the Marxist denial of a community of interest between "haves" and "have-nots", the Marxist exposure of the interested character of "*bourgeois* morality", and the Marxist demand for the expropriation of the expropriators. ...

Military Power

The supreme importance of the military instrument lies in the fact that the *ultima ratio* of power in international relations is war. Every act of the state,

---

[5]Toynbee, *Survey of International Affairs, 1935,* ii. p. 46.

[6]"Pray earnestly that right may triumph", said the representative of the Philadelphia coal-owners in an early strike organised by the United Mine Workers, "remembering that the Lord God Omnipotent still reigns, and that His reign is one of law and order, and not of violence and crime" (H. F. Pringle, *Theodore Roosevelt,* p. 267).

[7]R. Niebuhr, *Moral Man and Immoral Society,* p. 153.

[8]Speech in the Reichstag, January 30, 1939.

in its power aspect, is directed to war, not as a desirable weapon, but as a weapon which it may require in the last resort to use. Clausewitz's famous aphorism that "war is nothing but the continuation of political relations by other means" has been repeated with approval both by Lenin and by the Communist International[9] and Hitler meant much the same thing when he said that "an alliance whose object does not include the intention to fight is meaningless and useless".[10] In the same sense, Mr. Hawtrey defines diplomacy as "potential war".[11] These are half-truths. But the important thing is to recognise that they are true. War lurks in the background of international politics just as revolution lurks in the background of domestic politics. There are few European countries where, at some time during the past thirty years, potential revolution has not been an important factor in politics;[12] and the international community has in this respect the closest analogy to those states where the possibility of revolution is most frequently and most conspicuously present to the mind.

Potential war being thus a dominant factor in international politics, military strength becomes a recognised standard of political values. Every great civilisation of the past has enjoyed in its day a superiority of military power. . . .

Military power, being an essential element in the life of the state, becomes not only an instrument, but an end in itself. Few of the important wars of the last hundred years seem to have been waged for the deliberate and conscious purpose of increasing either trade or territory. The most serious wars are fought in order to make one's own country militarily stronger or, more often, to prevent another country from becoming militarily stronger, so that there is much justification for the epigram that "the principal cause of war is war itself".[13] Every stage in the Napoleonic Wars was devised to prepare the way for the next stage: the invasion of Russia was undertaken in order to make Napoleon strong enough to defeat Great Britain. The Crimean War was waged by Great Britain and France in order to prevent Russia from becoming strong enough to attack their Near Eastern possessions and interests at some future time. The origin of the Russo-Japanese War of 1904-5 is described as follows in a note addressed to the League of Nations by the Soviet Government in 1924: "When the Japanese torpedo-boats attacked the Russian fleet at Port Arthur in 1904, it was clearly an act of aggression from a technical point of view, but, politically speaking, it was an act caused by the aggressive policy of the Tsarist Government towards Japan, who, in order to

---

[9]Lenin, *Collected Works* (Engl. transl.), xviii. p. 97; Theses of the Sixth Congress of Comintern quoted in Taracouzio, *The Soviet Union and International Law*, p. 436.

[10]Hitler, *Mein Kampf,* p. 749.

[11]R. G. Hawtrey, *Economic Aspects of Sovereignty*, p. 107.

[12]It is perhaps necessary to recall the part played in British politics in 1914 by the threat of the Conservative Party to support revolutionary action in Ulster.

[13]R. G. Hawtrey, *Economic Aspects of Sovereignty*, p. 105.

forestall the danger, struck the first blow at her adversary".[14] In 1914, Austria sent an ultimatum to Servia because she believed that Servians were planning the downfall of the Dual Monarchy; Russia feared that Austria-Hungary, if she defeated Servia, would be strong enough to menace her; Germany feared that Russia, if she defeated Austria-Hungary, would be strong enough to menace her; France had long believed that Germany, if she defeated Russia, would be strong enough to menace her, and had therefore concluded the Franco-Russian alliance; and Great Britain feared that Germany, if she defeated France and occupied Belgium, would be strong enough to menace her. Finally, the United States came to fear that Germany, if she won the war would be strong enough to menace them. Thus the war, in the minds of all the principal combatants, had a defensive or preventive character. They fought in order that they might not find themselves in a more unfavourable position in some future war. Even colonial acquisitions have often been prompted by the same motive. The consolidation and formal annexation of the original British settlements in Australia were inspired by fear of Napoleon's alleged design to establish French colonies there. Military, rather than economic, reasons dictated the capture of German colonies during the war of 1914 and afterwards precluded their return to Germany.

It is perhaps for this reason that the exercise of power always appears to beget the appetite for more power. There is, as Dr. Niebuhr says, "no possibility of drawing a sharp line between the will-to-live and the will-to-power".[15] Nationalism, having attained its first objective in the form of national unity and independence, develops almost automatically into imperialism. International politics amply confirm the aphorisms of Machiavelli that "men never appear to themselves to possess securely what they have unless they acquire something further from another",[16] and of Hobbes that man "cannot assure the power and means to live well which he hath present, without the acquisition of more".[17] Wars, begun for motives of security, quickly become wars of aggression and self-seeking. President McKinley invited the United States to intervene in Cuba against Spain in order "to secure a full and final termination of hostilities between the Government of Spain and the people of Cuba and to secure on the island the establishment of a stable government."[18] But by the time the war was over the temptation to self-aggrandisement by the annexation of the Philippines had become irresistible. Nearly every country participating in the first world war regarded it initially as a war of self-defence; and this belief was particularly strong on the Allied side. Yet during

---

[14] *League of Nations: Official Journal*, May 1924, p. 578.
[15] R. Niebuhr, *Moral Man and Immoral Society*, p. 42.
[16] Machiavelli, *Discorsi*, I. i. ch. v.
[17] Hobbes, *Leviathan*, ch. xi.
[18] *British and Foreign State Papers*, ed. Hertslet, xc. p. 811.

the course of the war, every Allied Government in Europe announced war aims which included the acquisition of territory from the enemy Powers. In modern conditions, wars of limited objective have become almost as impossible as wars of limited liability. It is one of the fallacies of the theory of collective security that war can be waged for the specific and disinterested purpose of "resisting aggression". Had the League of Nations in the autumn of 1935, under the leadership of Great Britain, embarked on "military sanctions" against Italy, it would have been impossible to restrict the campaign to the expulsion of Italian troops from Abyssinia. Operations would in all probability have led to the occupation of Italy's East African colonies by Great Britain and France, of Trieste, Fiume and Albania by Yugoslavia, and of the islands of the Dodecanese by Greece or Turkey or both; and war aims would have been announced, precluding on various specious grounds the restoration of these territories to Italy. Territorial ambitions are just as likely to be the product as the cause of war.

Economic Power

Economic strength has always been an instrument of political power, if only through its association with the military instrument. Only the most primitive kinds of warfare are altogether independent of the economic factor. The wealthiest prince or the wealthiest city-state could hire the largest and most efficient army of mercenaries; and every government was therefore compelled to pursue a policy designed to further the acquisition of wealth. The whole progress of civilisation has been so closely bound up with economic development that we are not surprised to trace, throughout modern history, an increasingly intimate association between military and economic power. In the prolonged conflicts which marked the close of the Middle Ages in Western Europe, the merchants of the towns, relying on organised economic power, defeated the feudal barons, who put their trust in individual military prowess. The rise of modern nations has everywhere been marked by the emergence of a new middle class economically based on industry and trade. Trade and finance were the foundation of the short-lived political supremacy of the Italian cities of the Renaissance and later of the Dutch. The principal international wars of the period from the Renaissance to the middle of the eighteenth century were trade wars (some of them were actually so named). Throughout this period, it was universally held that, since wealth is a source of political power, the state should seek actively to promote the acquisition of wealth; and it was believed that the right way to make a country powerful was to stimulate production at home, to buy as little as possible from abroad, and to accumulate wealth in the convenient form of precious metals. Those who argued in this way afterwards came to be known as mercantilists. Mercantilism was a system of economic policy based on the hitherto unquestioned assumption that to promote the acquisition of wealth was part of the normal function of the state.

The Separation of Economics from Politics

The *laissez-faire* doctrine of the classical economists made a frontal attack on this assumption. The principal implications of *laissez-faire* have already been discussed. Its significance in the present context is that it brought about a complete theoretical divorce between economics and politics. The classical economists conceived a natural economic order with laws of its own, independent of politics and functioning to the greatest profit of all concerned when political authority interfered least in is automatic operation. This doctrine dominated the economic thought, and to some extent the economic practice (though far more in Great Britain than elsewhere), of the nineteenth century. . . .

Marx was overwhelmingly right when he insisted on the increasing importance of the role played by economic forces in politics; and since Marx, history can never be written again exactly as it was written before him. But Marx believed, just as firmly as did the *laissez-faire* liberal, in an economic system with laws of its own working independently of the state, which was its adjunct and its instrument. In writing as if economics and politics were separate domains, one subordinate to the other, Marx was dominated by nineteenth-century presuppositions in much the same way as his more recent opponents who are equally sure that "the primary laws of history are political laws, economic laws are secondary".[19] Economic forces are in fact political forces. Economics can be treated neither as a minor accessory of history, nor as an independent science in the light of which history can be interpreted. Much confusion would be saved by a general return to the term "political economy", which was given the new science by Adam Smith himself and not abandoned in favour of the abstract "economics", even in Great Britain itself, till the closing years of the nineteenth century.[20] The science of economics presupposes a given political order, and cannot be profitably studied in isolation from politics.

Some Fallacies of the Separation of Economics from Politics

. . . The most conspicuous practical failure caused by the persistence of this nineteenth-century illusion was the breakdown of League sanctions in 1936. Careful reading of the text of Article 16 of the Covenant acquits its framers

---

[19]Moeller van den Bruck, *Germany's Third Empire*, p. 50. The idea is a commonplace of National Socialist and Fascist writers.

[20]In Germany, "political economy" was at first translated *Nationalökonomie*, which was tentatively replaced in the present century by *Sozialökonomie*.

of responsibility for the mistake. Paragraph 1 prescribes the economic weapons, paragraph 2 the military weapons, to be employed against the violator of the Covenant. Paragraph 2 is clearly complementary to paragraph 1, and assumes as a matter of course that, in the event of an application of sanctions, "armed forces" would be required "to protect the Covenants of the League". The only difference between the two paragraphs is that, whereas all members of the League would have to apply the economic weapons, it would be natural to draw the necessary armed forces from those members which possessed them in sufficient strength and in reasonable geographical proximity to the offender.[21] Subsequent commentators, obsessed with the assumption that economics and politics were separate and separable things, evolved the doctrine that paragraphs 1 and 2 of Article 16 were not complementary, but alternative, the difference being that "economic sanctions" were obligatory and "military sanctions" optional. This doctrine was eagerly seized on by the many who felt that the League might conceivably be worth a few million pounds worth of trade, but not a few million human lives; and in the famous 1934 Peace Ballot in Great Britain, some two million deluded voters expressed simultaneously their approval of economic, and their disapproval of military, sanctions. "One of the many conclusions to which I have been drawn", said Lord Baldwin at this time, "is that there is no such thing as a sanction which will work, which does not mean war."[22] But the bitter lesson of 1935-36 was needed to drive home the truth that in sanctions, as in war, the only motto is "all or nothing", and that economic power is impotent if the military weapon is not held in readiness to support it.[23] Power is indivisible; and the military and economic weapons are merely different instruments of power.[24]

---

[21]This interpretation is confirmed by the report of the Phillimore Committee, on whose proposals the text of Article 16 was based. The Committee "considered financial and economic sanctions as being simply the contribution to the work of preventing aggression which might properly be made by countries which were not in a position to furnish actual military aid" (*International Sanctions: Report by a Group of Members of the Royal Institute of International Affairs*, p. 115 where the relevant texts are examined).

[22]House of Commons, May 18, 1934; *Official Report*, col. 2139.

[23]It is not, of course, suggested that the military weapon must always be used. The British Grand Fleet was little used in the first world war. But it would be rash to assume that the result would have been much the same if the British Government had not been prepared to use it. What paralyzed sanctions in 1935-36 was the common knowledge that the League Powers were not prepared to use the military weapon.

[24]It is worth noting that Stresemann was fully alive to this point when Germany entered the League of Nations. When the Secretary-General argued that Germany, if she contracted out of military sanctions, could still participate in economic sanctions, Stresemann replied: "We cannot do that either; if we take part in an economic boycott of a powerful neighbour, a declaration of war against Germany might be the consequence, since the exclusion of another country from intercourse with a nation of sixty million citizens would be a hostile act" (*Stresemann's Diaries and Papers* (Engl. Transl.), ii. p. 69).

A different, and equally serious, form in which this illusory separation of politics and economics can be traced is the popular phraseology which distinguishes between "power" and "welfare", between "guns" and "butter". "Welfare arguments are 'economic'", remarks an American writer, "power arguments are 'political'."[25] This fallacy is particularly difficult to expose because it appears to be deducible from a familiar fact. Every modern government and every parliament is continually faced with the dilemma of spending money on armaments or social services; and this encourages the illusion that the choice really lies between "power" and "welfare", between political guns and economic butter. Reflexion shows, however, that this is not the case. The question asked never takes the form, Do you prefer guns or butter? For everyone (except a handful of pacifists in those Anglo-Saxon countries which have inherited a long tradition of uncontested security) agrees that, in case of need, guns must come before butter. The question asked is always either, Have we already sufficient guns to enable us to afford some butter? or, Granted that we need x guns, can we increase revenue sufficiently to afford more butter as well? But the neatest exposure of this fallacy comes from the pen of Professor Zimmern; and the exposure is none the less effective for being unconscious. Having divided existing states on popular lines into those which pursue "welfare" and those which pursue "power", Professor Zimmern revealingly adds that "the welfare states, taken together, enjoy a preponderance of power and resources over the power states"[26] thereby leading us infallibly to the correct conclusion that "welfare states" are states which, already enjoying a preponderance of power, are not primarily concerned to increase it, and can therefore afford butter, and "power states" those which, being inferior in power, are primarily concerned to increase it, and devote the major part of their resources to this end. In this popular terminology, "welfare states" are those which possess preponderant power, and "power states" those which do not. Nor is this classification as illogical as it may seem. Every Great Power takes the view that the minimum number of guns necessary to assert the degree of power which it considers requisite takes precedence over butter, and that it can only pursue "welfare" when this minimum has been achieved. For many years prior to 1933, Great Britain, being satisfied with her power, was a "welfare state". After 1935, feeling her power contested and inadequate, she became a "power state"; and even the Opposition ceased to press with any insistence the prior claim of the social services. The contrast is not one between "power" and "welfare", and still less between "politics" and "economics", but between different degrees of power. In the pursuit of power, military and economic instruments will both be used....

[25]F. L. Schuman, *International Politics*, p. 356.
[26]Zimmern, *Quo Vadimus?* p. 41.

The Nature of International Law

International law differs from the municipal law of modern states in being the law of an undeveloped and not fully integrated community. It lacks three institutions which are essential parts of any developed system of municipal law: a judicature, an executive and a legislature.

(1) International law recognises no court competent to give on any issue of law or fact decisions recognised as binding by the community as a whole. It has long been the habit of some states to make special agreements to submit particular disputes to an international court for judicial settlement. The Permanent Court of International Justice, set up under the Covenant of the League, represents an attempt to extend and generalise this habit. But the institution of the court has not changed international law: it has merely created certain special obligations for states willing to accept them.

(2) International law has no agents competent to enforce observance of the law. In certain cases, it does indeed recognise the right of an aggrieved party, where a breach of the law has occurred, to take reprisals against the offender. But this is the recognition of a right of self-help, not the enforcement of a penalty by an agent of the law. The measures contemplated in Article 16 of the Covenant of the League, in so far as they can be regarded as punitive and not merely preventive, fall within this category.

(3) Of the two main sources of law—custom and legislation—international law knows only the former, resembling in this respect the law of all primitive communities. To trace the stages by which a certain kind of action or behaviour, from being customary, comes to be recognised as obligatory on all members of the community is the task of the social psychologist rather than of the jurist. But it is by some such process that international law has come into being. In advanced communities, the other source of law—direct legislation—is more prolific, and could not possibly be dispensed with in any modern state. So serious does this lack of international legislation appear that, in the view of some authorities, states do on certain occasions constitute themselves a legislative body, and many multilateral agreements between states are in fact "law-making treaties" (*traités-lois*).[27] This view is open to grave objections. A treaty, whatever its scope and content, lacks the essential quality of law: it is not automatically and unconditionally applicable to all members of the community whether they assent to it or not. Attempts have been made from time to time to embody customary international law in multilateral treaties between states. But the value of such attempts has been

---

[27]The Carnegie Endowment has, for example, given the title *International Legislation* to a collection published under its auspices of "multipartite instruments of general interest".

largely nullified by the fact that no treaty can bind a state which has not accepted it. The Hague Conventions of 1907 on the rules of war are sometimes treated as an example of international legislation. But these conventions were not only not binding on states which were not parties to them, but were not binding on the parties *vis-à-vis* states which were not parties. The Briand-Kellogg Pact is not, as is sometimes loosely said, a legislative act prohibiting war. It is an agreement between a large number of states "to renounce war as an instrument of national policy in their relations with one another". International agreements are contracts concluded by states with one another in their capacity as subjects of international law, and not laws created by states in the capacity of international legislators. International legislation does not yet exist. . . .

In June 1933, the British Government ceased to pay the regular installments due under its war debt agreement, substituting minor "token payments"; and a year later these token payments came to an end. Yet in 1935 Great Britain and France once more joined in a solemn condemnation of Germany for unilaterally repudiating her obligations under the disarmament clauses of the Versailles Treaty. Such inconsistencies are so common that the realist finds little difficulty in reducing them to a simple rule. The element of power is inherent in every political treaty. The contents of such a treaty reflect in some degree the relative strength of the contracting parties. Stronger states will insist on the sanctity of the treaties concluded by them with weaker states. Weaker states will renounce treaties concluded by them with stronger states so soon as the power position alters and the weaker state feels itself strong enough to reject or modify the obligation. Since 1918, the United States have concluded no treaty with a stronger state, and have therefore unreservedly upheld the sanctity of treaties. Great Britain concluded the war debt agreement with a country financially stronger than herself, and defaulted. She concluded no other important treaty with a stronger Power and, with this single exception, upheld the sanctity of treaties. The countries which had concluded the largest number of treaties with states stronger than themselves, and subsequently strengthened their position, were Germany, Italy and Japan; and these are the countries which renounced or violated the largest number of treaties. But it would be rash to assume any *moral* distinction between these different attitudes. There is no reason to assume that these countries would insist any less strongly than Great Britain or the United States on the sanctity of treaties favourable to themselves concluded by them with weaker states.

The case is convincing as far as it goes. The rule *pacta sunt servanda* is not a moral principle, and its application cannot always be justified on ethical grounds. It is a rule of international law; and as such it not only is, but is universally recognised to be, necessary to the existence of an international society. But law does not purport to solve every political problem; and where it fails, the fault often lies with those who seek to put it to uses for which it was never intended. It is no reproach to law to describe it as a bulwark of the existing order. The essence of law is to promote stability and maintain the existing framework of society; and it is perfectly natural everywhere for conservatives to describe themselves as the party of law and order, and to denounce radicals as disturbers of the peace and enemies of the law. The history of every society reveals a strong tendency on the part of those who want important changes in the existing order to commit acts which are illegal and which can plausibly be denounced as such by conservatives. It is true that in highly organised societies, where legally constituted machinery exists for bringing about changes in the law, this tendency to illegal action is mitigated. But it is never removed altogether. Radicals are always more likely than conservatives to come into conflict with the law.

Before 1914, international law did not condemn as illegal resort to war for the purpose of changing the existing international order; and no legally constituted machinery existed for bringing about changes in any other way. After 1918 opinion condemning "aggressive" war became almost universal, and nearly all the nations of the world signed a pact renouncing resort to war as an instrument of policy. While therefore resort to war for the purpose of altering the *status quo* now usually involves the breach of a treaty obligation and is accordingly illegal in international law, no effective international machinery has been constituted for bringing about changes by pacific means. The rude nineteenth-century system, or lack of system, was logical in recognising as legal the one effective method of changing the *status quo*. The rejection of the traditional method as illegal and the failure to provide any effective alternative have made contemporary international law a bulwark of the existing order to an extent unknown in previous international law or in the municipal law of any civilised country. This is the most fundamental cause of the recent decline of respect for international law; and those who, in deploring the phenomenon, fail to recognise its origin, not unnaturally expose themselves to the charge of hypocrisy or of obtuseness.

Of all the considerations which render unlikely the general observance of the legal rule of the sanctity of treaties, and which provide a plausible moral justification for the repudiation of treaties, this last is by far the most important. Respect for international law and for the sanctity of treaties will not be increased by the sermons of those who, having most to gain from the maintenance of the existing order, insist most firmly on the morally binding character of the law. Respect for law and treaties will be maintained only in so far as the law recognises effective political machinery through which it can itself be modified and superseded. There must be a clear recognition of that play of political forces which is antecedent to all law. Only when these forces are in stable equilibrium can the law perform its social function without becoming a tool in the hands of the defenders of the *status quo*. The achievement of this equilibrium is not a legal, but a political task. . . .

Peaceful Change

... The attempt to make a moral distinction between wars of "aggression" and wars of "defence" is misguided. If a change is necessary and desirable, the use or threatened use of force to maintain the *status quo* may be morally more culpable than the use or threatened use of force to alter it. Few people now believe that the action of the American colonists who attacked the *status quo* by force in 1776, or of the Irish who attacked the *status quo* by force between 1916 and 1920, was necessarily less moral than that of the British who defended it by force. The moral criterion must be not the "aggressive" or "defensive" character of the war, but the nature of the change which is being sought and resisted. ...

... When the change is effected by legislation, the compulsion is that of the state. But where the change is effected by the bargaining procedure, the *force majeure* can only be that of the stronger party. The employer who concedes the strikers' demands pleads inability to resist. The trade union leader who calls off an unsuccessful strike pleads that the union was too weak to continue. "Yielding to threats of force", which is sometimes used as a term of reproach, is therefore a normal part of the process. ...

The defence of the *status quo* is not a policy which can be lastingly successful. It will end in war as surely as rigid conservatism will end in revolution. "Resistance to aggression", however necessary as a momentary device of national policy, is no solution; for readiness to fight to prevent change is just as unmoral as readiness to fight to enforce it. To establish methods of peaceful change is therefore the fundamental problem of international morality and of international politics. We can discard as purely utopian and muddle-headed plans for a procedure of peaceful change dictated by a world legislature or a world court. We can describe as utopian in the right sense (i.e. performing the proper function of a utopia in proclaiming an ideal to be aimed at, though not wholly attainable) the desire to eliminate the element of power and to base the bargaining process of peaceful change on a common feeling of what is just and reasonable. But we shall also keep in mind the realist view of peaceful change as an adjustment to the changed relations of power; and since the party which is able to bring most power to bear normally emerges successful from operations of peaceful change, we shall do our best to make ourselves as powerful as we can. In practice, we know that peaceful change can only be achieved through a compromise between the utopian conception of a common feeling of right and the realist conception of a mechanical adjustment to a changed equilibrium of forces. That is why a successful foreign policy must oscillate between the apparently opposite poles of force and appeasement.

The Origins of War in Neorealist Theory

KENNETH N. WALTZ

Like most historians, many students of international politics have been skeptical about the possibility of creating a theory that might help one to understand and explain the international events that interest us. Thus Morgenthau, foremost among traditional realists, was fond of repeating Blaise Pascal's remark that "the history of the world would have been different had Cleopatra's nose been a bit shorter" and then asking "How do you systemize that?"[1] His appreciation of the role of the accidental and the occurrence of the unexpected in politics dampened his theoretical ambition.

The response of neorealists is that, although difficulties abound, some of the obstacles that seem most daunting lie in misapprehensions about theory. Theory obviously cannot explain the accidental or account for unexpected events; it deals in regularities and repetitions and is possible only if these can be identified. A further difficulty is found in the failure of realists to conceive of international politics as a distinct domain about which theories can be fashioned. Morgenthau, for example, insisted on "the autonomy of politics," but he failed to apply the concept to international politics. A theory is a depiction of the organization of a domain and of the connections among its parts. A theory indicates that some factors are more important than others and specifies relations among them. In reality, everything is related to every-

Kenneth N. Waltz, "The Origins of War in Neorealist Theory," *Journal of Interdisciplinary History*, vol. 18 (1988), 615–628. Reprinted with permission of the editors of *The Journal of Interdisciplinary History* and the MIT Press, Cambridge, Massachusetts. © 1988 by the Massachusetts Institute of Technology and the editors of *The Journal of Interdisciplinary History*.

[1]Hans J. Morgenthau, "International Relations: Quantitative and Qualitative Approaches," in Norman D. Palmer (ed.), *A Design for International Relations Research: Scope, Theory, Methods, and Relevance* (Philadelphia, 1970), 78.

thing else, and one domain cannot be separated from others. But theory isolates one realm from all others in order to deal with it intellectually. By defining the structure of international political systems, neorealism establishes the autonomy of international politics and thus makes a theory about it possible.[2]

In developing a theory of international politics, neorealism retains the main tenets of *realpolitik,* but means and ends are viewed differently, as are causes and effects. Morgenthau, for example, thought of the "rational" statesman as ever striving to accumulate more and more power. He viewed power as an end in itself. Although he acknowledged that nations at times act out of considerations other than power, Morgenthau insisted that, when they do so, their actions are not "of a political nature."[3] In contrast, neorealism sees power as a possibly useful means, with states running risks if they have either too little or too much of it. Excessive weakness may invite an attack that greater strength would have dissuaded an adversary from launching. Excessive strength may prompt other states to increase their arms and pool their efforts against the dominant state. Because power is a possibly useful means, sensible statesmen try to have an appropriate amount of it. In crucial situations, however, the ultimate concern of states is not for power but for security. This revision is an important one.

An even more important revision is found in a shift of causal relations. The infinite materials of any realm can be organized in endlessly different ways. Realism thinks of causes as moving in only one direction, from the interactions of individuals and states to the outcomes that their acts and interactions produce. Morgenthau recognized that, when there is competition for scarce goods and no one to serve as arbiter, a struggle for power will ensue among the competitors and that consequently the struggle for power can be explained without reference to the evil born in men. The struggle for power arises simply because men want things, not because of the evil in their desires. He labeled man's desire for scarce goods as one of the two roots of conflict, but, even while discussing it, he seemed to pull toward the "other root of conflict and concomitant evil"—"the *animus dominandi,* the desire for power." He often considered that man's drive for power is more basic than the chance conditions under which struggles for power occur. This attitude is seen in his statement that "in a world where power counts, no nation pursuing a rational policy has a choice between renouncing and wanting

[2]Morgenthau, *Politics among Nations* (New York, 1973; 5th ed.), 11. Ludwig Boltzman (trans. Rudolf Weingartner), "Theories as Representations," excerpted in Arthur Danto and Sidney Morgenbesser (eds.), *Philosophy of Science* (Cleveland, 1960), 245-252. Neorealism is sometimes dubbed structural realism. I use the terms interchangeably and, throughout this article, refer to my own formulation of neorealist theory. See Waltz, *Theory of International Politics* (Reading, Mass., 1979); Robert Keohane (ed.), *Neorealism and its Critics* (New York, 1986).
[3]Morgenthau, *Politics among Nations,* 27.

power; *and, if it could,* the lust for power for the individual's sake would still confront us with its less spectacular yet no less pressing moral defects."[4]

Students of international politics have typically inferred outcomes from salient attributes of the actors producing them. Thus Marxists, like liberals, have linked the outbreak of war or the prevalence of peace to the internal qualities of states. Governmental forms, economic systems, social institutions, political ideologies—these are but a few examples of where the causes of war have been found. Yet, although causes are specifically assigned, we know that states with widely divergent economic institutions, social customs, and political ideologies have all fought wars. More striking still, many different sorts of organizations fight wars, whether those organizations be tribes, petty principalities, empires, nations, or street gangs. If an identified condition seems to have caused a given war, one must wonder why wars occur repeatedly even though their causes vary. Variations in the characteristics of the states are not linked directly to the outcomes that their behaviors produce, nor are variations in their patterns of interaction. Many historians, for example, have claimed that World War I was caused by the interaction of two opposed and closely balanced coalitions. But then many have claimed that World War II was caused by the failure of some states to combine forces in an effort to right an imbalance of power created by an existing alliance.

Neorealism contends that international politics can be understood only if the effects of structure are added to the unit-level explanations of traditional realism. By emphasizing how structures affect actions and outcomes, neorealism rejects the assumption that man's innate lust for power constitutes a sufficient cause of war in the absence of any other. It reconceives the causal link between interacting units and international outcomes. According to the logic of international politics, one must believe that some causes of international outcomes are the result of interactions at the unit level, and, since variations in presumed causes do not correspond very closely to variations in observed outcomes, one must also assume that others are located at the structural level. Causes at the level of units interact with those at the level of structure, and, because they do so, explanation at the unit level alone is bound to be misleading. If an approach allows the consideration of both unit-level and structural-level causes, then it can cope with both the changes and the continuities that occur in a system.

Structural realism presents a systemic portrait of international politics depicting component units according to the manner of their arrangement. For the purpose of developing a theory, states are cast as unitary actors wanting at least to survive, and are taken to be the system's constituent units. The essential structural quality of the system is anarchy—the absence of a central monopoly of legitimate force. Changes of structure and hence of system occur with variations in the number of great powers. The range of expected

---

[4]*Idem, Scientific Man vs. Power Politics* (Chicago, 1946), 192, 200. Italics added.

outcomes is inferred from the assumed motivation of the units and the structure of the system in which they act.

A systems theory of international politics deals with forces at the international, and not at the national, level. With both systems-level and unit-level forces in play, how can one construct a theory of international politics without simultaneously constructing a theory of foreign policy? An international-political theory does not imply or require a theory of foreign policy any more than a market theory implies or requires a theory of the firm. Systems theories, whether political or economic, are theories that explain how the organization of a realm acts as a constraining and disposing force on the interacting units within it. Such theories tell us about the forces to which the units are subjected. From them, we can draw some inferences about the expected behavior and fate of the units: namely, how they will have to compete with and adjust to one another if they are to survive and flourish. To the extent that the dynamics of a system limit the freedom of its units, their behavior and the outcomes of their behavior become predictable. How do we expect firms to respond to differently structured markets, and states to differently structured international-political systems? These theoretical questions require us to take firms as firms, and states as states, without paying attention to differences among them. The questions are then answered by reference to the placement of the units in their system and not by reference to the internal qualities of the units. Systems theories explain why different units behave similarly and, despite their variations, produce outcomes that fall within expected ranges. Conversely, theories at the unit level tell us why different units behave differently despite their similar placement in a system. A theory about foreign policy is a theory at the national level. It leads to expectations about the responses that dissimilar polities will make to external pressures. A theory of international politics bears on the foreign policies of nations although it claims to explain only certain aspects of them. It can tell us what international conditions national policies have to cope with.

From the vantage point of neorealist theory, competition and conflict among states stem directly from the twin facts of life under conditions of anarchy: States in an anarchic order must provide for their own security, and threats or seeming threats to their security abound. Preoccupation with identifying dangers and counteracting them become a way of life. Relations remain tense; the actors are usually suspicious and often hostile even though by nature they may not be given to suspicion and hostility. Individually, states may only be doing what they can to bolster their security. Their individual intentions aside, collectively their actions yield arms races and alliances. The uneasy state of affairs is exacerbated by the familiar "security dilemma," wherein measures that enhance one state's security typically diminish that of others.[5] In an anarchic domain, the source of one's own com-

---

[5] See John H. Herz, "Idealist Internationalism and the Security Dilemma," *World Politics,* II (1950), 157-180.

fort is the source of another's worry. Hence a state that is amassing instruments of war, even for its own defensive, is cast by others as a threat requiring response. The response itself then serves to confirm the first state's belief that it had reason to worry. Similarly, an alliance that in the interest of defense moves to increase cohesion among its members and add to its ranks inadvertently imperils an opposing alliance and provokes countermeasures.

Some states may hunger for power for power's sake. Neorealist theory, however, shows that it is not necessary to assume an innate lust for power in order to account for the sometimes fierce competition that marks the international arena. In an anarchic domain, a state of war exists if all parties lust for power. But so too will a state of war exist if all states seek only to ensure their own safety.

Although neorealist theory does not explain why particular wars are fought, it does explain war's dismal recurrence through the millennia. Neorealists point not to the ambitions or the intrigues that punctuate the outbreak of individual conflicts but instead to the existing structure within which events, whether by design or accident, can precipitate open clashes of arms. The origins of hot wars lie in cold wars, and the origins of cold wars are found in the anarchic ordering of the international arena.

The recurrence of war is explained by the structure of the international system. Theorists explain what historians know: War is normal. Any given war is explained not by looking at the structure of the international-political system but by looking at the particularities within it: the situations, the characters, and the interactions of states. Although particular explanations are found at the unit level, general explanations are also needed. Wars vary in frequency, and in other ways as well. A central question for a structural theory is this: How do changes of the system affect the expected frequency of war?

Keeping Wars Cold: The Structural Level

In an anarchic realm, peace is fragile. The prolongation of peace requires that potentially destabilizing developments elicit the interest and the calculated response of some or all of the system's principal actors. In the anarchy of states, the price of inattention or miscalculation is often paid in blood. An important issue for a structural theory to address is whether destabilizing conditions and events are managed better in multipolar or bipolar systems.

In a system of, say, five great powers, the politics of power turns on the diplomacy by which alliances are made, maintained, and disrupted. Flexibility of alignment means both that the country one is wooing may prefer another suitor and that one's present alliance partner may defect. Flexibility of alignment limits a state's options because, ideally, its strategy must please potential allies and satisfy present partners. Alliances are made by states that have some but not all of their interests in common. The common interest is ordinarily a negative one: fear of other states. Divergence comes when positive interests are at issue. In alliances among near equals, strategies are always the product of compromise since the interests of allies and their notions of how to secure them are never identical.

If competing blocs are seen to be closely balanced, and if competition turns on important matters, then to let one's side down risks one's own destruction. In a moment of crisis the weaker or the more adventurous party is likely to determine its side's policy. Its partners can afford neither to let the weaker member be defeated nor to advertise their disunity by failing to back a venture even while deploring its risks.

The prelude to World War I provides striking examples of such a situation. The approximate equality of partners in both the Triple Alliance and Triple Entente made them closely interdependent. This interdependence, combined with the keen competition between the two camps, meant that, although any country could commit its associates, no one country on either side could exercise control. If Austria-Hungary marched, Germany had to follow; the dissolution of the Austro-Hungarian Empire would have left Germany alone in the middle of Europe. If France marched, Russia had to follow; a German victory over France would be a defeat for Russia. And so the vicious circle continued. Because the defeat or the defection of a major ally would have shaken the balance, each state was constrained to adjust its strategy and the use of its forces to the aims and fears of its partners.

In alliances among equals, the defection of one member threatens the security of the others. In alliances among unequals, the contributions of the lesser members are at once wanted and of relatively small importance. In alliances among unequals, alliance leaders need worry little about the faithfulness of their followers, who usually have little choice anyway. Contrast the situation in 1914 with that of the United States and Britain and France in 1956. The United States could dissociate itself from the Suez adventure of its two principal allies and subject one of them to heavy financial pressure. Like Austria-Hungary in 1914, Britain and France tried to commit or at least immobilize their ally by presenting a fait accompli. Enjoying a position of predominance, the United States could continue to focus its attention on the major adversary while disciplining its two allies. Opposing Britain and France endangered neither the United States nor the alliance because the security of Britain and France depended much more heavily on us than our security depended on them. The ability of the United States, and the inability of Germany, to pay a price measured in intra-alliance terms is striking.

In balance-of-power politics old style, flexibility of alignment led to rigidity of strategy or the limitation of freedom of decision. In balance-of-power politics new style, the obverse is true: Rigidity of alignment in a two-power world results in more flexibility of strategy and greater freedom of decision. In a multipolar world, roughly equal parties engaged in cooperative endeavors must look for the common denominator of their policies. They risk finding the lowest one and easily end up in the worst of all possible worlds. In a bipolar world, alliance leaders can design strategies primarily to advance their own interests and to cope with their main adversary and less to satisfy their own allies.

Neither the United States nor the Soviet Union has to seek the approval of other states, but each has to cope with the other. In the great-power politics of a multipolar world, who is a danger to whom and who can be expected to deal with threats and problems are matters of uncertainty. In the great-power politics of a bipolar world, who is a danger to whom is never in doubt. Any event in the world that involves the fortunes of either of the great powers automatically elicits the interest of the other. President Harry S. Truman, at the time of the Korean invasion, could not very well echo Neville Chamberlain's words in the Czechoslovakian crisis by claiming that the Americans knew nothing about the Koreans, a people living far away in the east of Asia. We had to know about them or quickly find out.

In a two-power competition, a loss for one is easily taken to be a gain for the other. As a result, the powers in a bipolar world promptly respond to unsettling events. In a multipolar world, dangers are diffused, responsibilities unclear, and definitions of vital interests easily obscured. Where a number of states are in balance, the skillful foreign policy of a forward power is designed to gain an advantage without antagonizing other states and frightening them into united action. At times in modern Europe, the benefits of possible gains have seemed to outweigh the risks of likely losses. Statesmen have hoped to push an issue to the limit without causing all of the potential opponents to unite. When there are several possible enemies,unity of action among them is difficult to achieve. National leaders could therefore think— or desperately hope, as did Theobald Von Bethmann Hollweg and Adolf Hitler before two world wars—that a united opposition would not form.

If interests and ambitions conflict, the absence of crises is more worrisome than their presence. Crises are produced by the determination of a state to resist a change that another state tries to make. As the leaders in a bipolar system, the United States and the Soviet Union are disposed to do the resisting, for in important matters they cannot hope that their allies will do it for them. Political action in the postwar world has reflected this condition. Communist guerrillas operating in Greece prompted the Truman Doctrine. The tightening of Soviet control over the states of Eastern Europe led to the Marshall Plan and the Atlantic Defense Treaty, and these in turn gave rise to the Cominform and the Warsaw Pact. The plan to create a West German government produced the Berlin blockade. During the past four decades, our responses have been geared to the Soviet Union's actions, and theirs to ours.

Miscalculation by some or all of the great powers is a source of danger in a multipolar world; overreaction by either or both of the great powers is a source of danger in a bipolar world. Which is worse: miscalculation or overreaction? Miscalculation is the greater evil because it is more likely to permit an unfolding of events that finally threatens the status quo and brings the powers to war. Overreaction is the lesser evil because at worst it costs only money for unnecessary arms and possibly the fighting of limited wars. The dynamics of a bipolar system, moreover, provide a measure of correction. In a world in which two states united in their mutual antagonism overshadow any others, the benefits of a calculated response stand out most clearly, and the sanctions against irresponsible behavior achieve their greatest force. Thus two states, isolationist by tradition, untutored in the ways of international politics, and famed for impulsive behavior, have shown themselves— not always and everywhere, but always in crucial cases—to be wary, alert, cautious, flexible, and forbearing. . . .

Wars, Hot and Cold

Wars, hot and cold, originate in the structure of the international political system. Most Americans blame the Soviet Union for creating the Cold War, by the actions that follow necessarily from the nature of its society and government. Revisionist historians, attacking the dominant view, assign blame to the United States. Some American error, or sinister interest, or faulty assumption about Soviet aims, they argue, is what started the Cold War. Either way, the main point is lost. In a bipolar world, each of the two great powers is bound to focus its fears on the other, to distrust its motives, and to impute offensive intentions to defensive measures. The proper question is what, not who, started the Cold War. Although its content and virulence vary as unit-level forces change and interact, the Cold War continues. It is firmly rooted in the structure of postwar international politics, and will last as long as that structure endures.

Hegemonic War and International Change

ROBERT GILPIN

Because of the redistribution of power, the costs to the traditional dominant state of maintaining the international system increase relative to its capacity to pay; this, in turn, produces the severe fiscal crisis. . . . By the same token, the costs to the rising state of changing the system decrease; it begins to appreciate that it can increase its own gains by forcing changes in the nature of the system. Its enhanced power position means that the relative costs of changing the system and securing its interests have decreased. Thus, in accordance with the law of demand, the rising state, as its power increases, will seek to change the status quo as the perceived potential benefits begin to exceed the perceived costs of undertaking a change in the system.

As its relative power increases, a rising state attempts to change the rules governing the international system, the division of the spheres of influence, and, most important of all, the international distribution of territory. In response, the dominant power counters this challenge through changes in its policies that attempt to restore equilibrium in the system. The historical record reveals that if it fails in this attempt, the disequilibrium will be resolved by war. Shepard Clough, in his book *The Rise and Fall of Civilization,* drew on a distinguished career in historical scholarship to make the point: "At least in all the cases which we have passed . . . in review in these pages, cultures with inferior civilization but with growing economic power have always attacked the most civilized cultures during the latters' economic decline" (1970, p. 263). The fundamental task of the challenged dominant

Robert Gilpin, *War and Change in World Politics* (New York: Cambridge University Press, 1981), Chapter 5. Copyright © 1981, Cambridge University Press. Reprinted with the permission of Cambridge University Press.

state is to solve what Walter Lippmann once characterized as the fundamental problem of foreign policy—the balancing of commitments and resources (Lippmann, 1943, p. 7). An imperial, hegemonic, or great power has essentially two courses of action open to it as it attempts to restore equilibrium in the system. The first and preferred solution is that the challenged power can seek to increase the resources devoted to maintaining its commitments and position in the international system. The second is that it can attempt to reduce its existing commitments (and associated costs) in a way that does not ultimately jeopardize its international position. Although neither response will be followed to the exclusion of the other, they may be considered analytically as separate policies. The logic and the pitfalls of each policy will be considered in turn.

Historically, the most frequently employed devices to generate new resources to meet the increasing costs of dominance and to forestall decline have been to increase domestic taxation and to exact tribute from other states. Both of these courses of action have inherent dangers in that they can provoke resistance and rebellion. The French Revolution was triggered in part by the effort of the monarchy to levy the higher taxes required to meet the British challenge (von Ranke, 1950, p. 211). Athens's "allies" revolted against Athenian demands for increased tribute. Because higher taxes (or tribute) mean decreased productive investment and a lowered standard of living, in most instances such expedients can be employed for only relatively short periods of time, such as during a war.

The powerful resistance within a society to higher taxes or tribute encourages the government to employ more indirect methods of generating additional resources to meet a fiscal crisis. Most frequently, a government will resort to inflationary policies or seek to manipulate the terms of trade with other countries. As Carlo Cipolla observed (1970, p. 13), the invariable symptoms of a society's decline are excessive taxation, inflation, and balance-of-payments difficulties as government and society spend beyond their means. But these indirect devices also bring hardship and encounter strong resistance over the long run.

The most satisfactory solution to the problem of increasing costs is increased efficiency in the use of existing resources. Through organizational, technological, and other types of innovations, a state can either economize with respect to the resources at its disposal or increase the total amount of disposable resources. Thus, as Mark Elvin explained, the fundamental reason that imperial China survived intact for so long was its unusually high rate of economic and technological innovation; over long periods China was able to generate sufficient resources to finance the costs of protection against successive invaders (Elvin, 1973). Conversely, the Roman economy stagnated and failed to innovate. Among the reasons for the decline and destruction of Rome was its inability to generate resources sufficient to stave off barbarian invaders. More recently, the calls for greater industrial productivity in contemporary America derive from the realization that technological innovation and more efficient use of existing resources are needed to meet the increasing demands of consumption, investment, and protection.

This innovative solution involves rejuvenation of the society's military, economic, and political institutions. In the case of declining Rome, for example, a recasting of its increasingly inefficient system of agricultural production and a revised system of taxation were required. Unfortunately, social reform and institutional rejuvenation become increasingly difficult as a society ages, because this implies more general changes in customs, attitudes, motivation, and sets of values that constitute a cultural heritage (Cipolla, 1970, p. 11). Vested interests resist the loss of their privileges. Institutional rigidities frustrate abandonment of "tried and true" methods (Downs, 1967, pp. 158-66). One could hardly expect it to be otherwise: "Innovations are important not for their immediate, actual results but for their potential for future development, and potential is very difficult to assess" (Cipolla, 1970, pp. 9-10).

A declining society experiences a vicious cycle of decay and immobility, much as a rising society enjoys a virtuous cycle of growth and expansion. On the one hand, decline is accompanied by lack of social cooperation, by emphasis on rights rather than emphasis on duty, and by decreasing productivity. On the other hand, the frustration and pessimism generated by this gloomy atmosphere inhibit renewal and innovation. The failure to innovate accentuates the decline and its psychologically debilitating consequences. Once caught up in this cycle, it is difficult for the society to break out (Cipolla, 1970, p. 11). For this reason, a more rational and more efficient use of existing resources to meet increasing military and productive needs is seldom achieved.

There have been societies that have managed their resources with great skill for hundreds of years and have rejuvenated themselves in response to external challenges, and this resilience has enabled them to survive for centuries in a hostile environment. In fact, those states that have been notable for their longevity have been the ones most successful in allocating their scarce resources in an optimal fashion in order to balance, over a period of centuries, the conflicting demands of consumption, protection, and investment. An outstanding example was the Venetian city-state. Within this aristocratic republic the governing elite moderated consumption and shifted resources back and forth between protection and investment as need required over the centuries (Lane, 1973). The Chinese Empire was even more significant. Its longevity and unity were due to the fact that the Chinese were able to increase their production more rapidly than the rise in the costs of protection (Elvin, 1973, pp. 92-3, 317). The progressive nature of the imperial Chinese economy meant that sufficient resources were in most cases available to meet external threats and preserve the integrity of the empire for centuries. In contrast to the Romans, who were eventually inundated and destroyed by the barbarians, the Chinese "on the whole . . . managed to keep one step ahead of their neighbours in the relevant technical skills, military, economic and organizational" (Elvin, 1973, p. 20).

An example of social rejuvenation intended to meet an external challenge was that of revolutionary France. The point has already been made that European aristocracies were reluctant to place firearms in the hands of the lower social orders, preferring to rely on small professional armies. The French Revolution and the innovation of nationalism made it possible for the French state to tap the energies of the masses of French citizens. The so-called *levée en masse* greatly increased the human resources available to the republic and, later, to Napoleon. Although this imperial venture was ultimately unsuccessful, it does illustrate the potentiality for domestic rejuvenation of a society in response to decline.

The second type of response to declining fortunes is to bring costs and resources into balance by reducing costs. This can be attempted in three general ways. The first is to eliminate the reason for the increasing costs (i.e., to weaken or destroy the rising challenger). The second is to expand to a more secure and less costly defensive perimeter. The third is to reduce international commitments. Each of these alternative strategies has its attractions and its dangers.

The first and most attractive response to a society's decline is to eliminate the source of the problem. By launching a preventive war the declining power destroys or weakens the rising challenger while the military advantage is still with the declining power. Thus, as Thucydides explained, the Spartans initiated the Peloponnesian War in an attempt to crush the rising Athenian challenger while Sparta still had the power to do so. When the choice ahead has appeared to be to decline or to fight, statesmen have most generally fought. However, besides causing unnecessary loss of life, the greatest danger inherent in preventive war is that it sets in motion a course of events over which statesmen soon lose control (see the subsequent discussion of hegemonic war).

Second, a state may seek to reduce the costs of maintaining its position by means of further expansion.[1] In effect, the state hopes to reduce its long-term costs by acquiring less costly defensive positions. As Edward Luttwak (1976) demonstrated in his brilliant study of Roman grand strategy, Roman expansion in its later phases was an attempt to find more secure and less costly defensive positions and to eliminate potential challengers. Although this response to declining fortunes can be effective, it can also lead to further overextension of commitments, to increasing costs, and thereby to ac-

---

[1]This cause of expansion is frequently explained by the "turbulent-frontier" thesis. A classic example was Britain's steady and incremental conquest of India in order to eliminate threatening political disturbances on the frontier of the empire. Two recent examples are the American invasion of Cambodia during the Vietnam War and the Soviet invasion of Afghanistan.

celeration of the decline. It is difficult for a successful and expanding state to break the habit of expansion, and it is all too easy to believe that "expand or die" is the imperative of international survival. Perhaps the greatest danger for every imperial or hegemonic power, as it proved eventually to be for Rome, is overextension of commitments that gradually begin to sap its strength (Grant, 1968, p. 246).[2]

The third means of bringing costs and resources into balance is, of course, to reduce foreign-policy commitments. Through political, territorial, or economic retrenchment, a society can reduce the costs of maintaining its international position. However, this strategy is politically difficult, and carrying it out is a delicate matter. Its success is highly uncertain and strongly dependent on timing and circumstances. The problem of retrenchment will be considered first in general terms; then a case of relatively successful retrenchment by a great power will be discussed.

The most direct method of retrenchment is unilateral abandonment of certain of a state's economic, political, or military commitments. For example, a state may withdraw from exposed and costly strategic positions. Venice, as was pointed out, pursued for centuries a conscious policy of alternating advance and retreat. The longevity of the later roman Empire or Byzantine Empire may be partially explained by its withdrawal from its exposed and difficult-to-defend western provinces and consolidation of its position on a less costly basis in its eastern provinces; its survival for a thousand years was due to the fact that it brought the scale of empire and resources into balance (Cipolla, 1970, p. 82; Rader, 1971, p. 54). In our own time, the so-called Nixon doctrine may be interpreted as an effort on the part of the United States to disengage from vulnerable commitments and to shift part of the burden of defending the international status quo to other powers (Hoffmann, 1978, pp. 46-7).

A second standard technique of retrenchment is to enter into alliances with or seek rapprochement with less threatening powers. In effect, the dominant but declining power makes concessions to another state and agrees to share the benefits of the status quo with that other state in exchange for sharing the costs of preserving the status quo. Thus the Romans brought the Goths into the empire (much to their later regret) in exchange for their assistance in defending the frontiers of the empire. As will be pointed out in a moment, the policy of entente or rapprochement was pursued by the British prior to World War I as they sought to meet the rising German challenge. The American rapprochement with Communist China is a late-twentieth-century example. In exchange for weakening the American commitment to Taiwan, the Americans seek Chinese assistance in containing the expanding power of the Soviet Union.

---

[2]As Raymond Aron argued (1974), defeat in Vietnam may, in the long run, save the United States from the corrupting and ultimately weakening vice of overexpansion of commitments.

Unfortunately, there are several dangers associated with this response to decline. First, in an alliance between a great power and a lesser power there is a tendency for the former to overpay in the long run, as has occurred with the United States and the North Atlantic Treaty Organization (NATO); the great power increases its commitments without a commensurate increase in the resources devoted by its allies to finance those commitments. Further, the ally is benefited materially by the alliance, and as its capabilities increase, it may turn against the declining power. Thus the Romans educated the Goths in their military techniques only to have the latter turn these techniques against them. Second, the utility of alliances is limited by Riker's theory of coalitions: An increase in the number of allies decreases the benefits to each. Therefore, as an alliance increases in number, the probability of defection increases (Riker, 1962). Third, the minor ally may involve the major ally in disputes of its own from which the latter cannot disengage itself without heavy costs to its prestige. For these reasons, the utility of an alliance as a response to decline and a means to decrease costs is severely restricted.

The third and most difficult method of retrenchment is to make concessions to the rising power and thereby seek to appease its ambitions. Since the Munich conference in 1938, "appeasement" as a policy has been in disrepute and has been regarded as inappropriate under every conceivable set of circumstances. This is unfortunate, because there are historical examples in which appeasement has succeeded. Contending states have not only avoided conflict but also achieved a relationship satisfactory to both. A notable example was British appeasement of the rising United States in the decades prior to World War I (Perkins, 1968). The two countries ended a century-long hostility and laid the basis for what has come to be known as the "special relationship" of the two Anglo-Saxon powers.

The fundamental problem with a policy of appeasement and accommodation is to find a way to pursue it that does not lead to continuing deterioration in a state's prestige and international position. Retrenchment by its very nature is an indication of relative weakness and declining power, and thus retrenchment can have a deteriorating effect on relations with allies and rivals. Sensing the decline of their protector, allies try to obtain the best deal they can from the rising master of the system. Rivals are stimulated to "close in," and frequently they precipitate a conflict in the process. Thus World War I began as a conflict between Russia and Austria over the disposition of the remnants of the retreating Ottoman Empire (Hawtrey, 1952, pp. 75-81).

Because retrenchment signals waning power, a state seldom retrenches or makes concessions on its own initiative. Yet, not to retrench voluntarily and then to retrench in response to threats or military defeat means an even more severe loss of prestige and weakening of one's diplomatic standing. As a consequence of such defeats, allies defect to the victorious party, opponents press their advantage, and the retrenching society itself becomes demoralized. Moreover, if the forced retrenchment involves the loss of a "vital interest," then the security and integrity of the state are placed in jeopardy.

For these reasons, retrenchment is a hazardous course for a state; it is a course seldom pursued by a declining power. However, there have been cases of a retrenchment policy being carried out rather successfully.

An excellent example of a declining hegemon that successfully brought its resources and commitments into balance is provided by Great Britain in the decades just prior to World War I. Following its victory over France in the Napoleonic wars, Great Britain had become the world's most powerful and most prestigious state. It gave its name to a century of relative peace, the Pax Britannica. British naval power was supreme on the high seas, and British industry and commerce were unchallengeable in world markets. An equilibrium had been established on the European continent by the Congress of Vienna (1814), and no military or industrial rivals then existed outside of Europe. By the last decades of the century, however, a profound transformation had taken place. Naval and industrial rivals had risen to challenge British supremacy both on the Continent and overseas. France, Germany, the United States, Japan, and Russia, to various degrees, had become expanding imperial powers. The unification of Germany by Prussia had destroyed the protective Continental equilibrium, and Germany's growing naval might threatened Britain's command of the seas.

As a consequence of these commercial, naval, and imperial challenges, Great Britain began to encounter the problems that face every mature or declining power. On the one hand, external demands were placing steadily increasing strains on the economy; on the other hand, the capacity of the economy to meet these demands had deteriorated. Thus, at the same time that the costs of protection were escalating, both private consumption and public consumption were also increasing because of greater affluence. Superficially the economy appeared strong, but the rates of industrial expansion, technological innovation, and domestic investment had slowed. Thus the rise of foreign challenges and the climacteric of the economy had brought on disequilibrium between British global commitments and British resources.

As the disequilibrium between its global hegemony and its limited resources intensified, Britain faced the dilemma of increasing its resources or reducing its commitments or both. In the national debate on this critical issue the proponents of increasing the available resources proposed two general courses of action. First, they proposed a drawing together of the empire and drawing on these combined resources, as well as the creation of what John Seeley (1905) called Greater Britain, especially the white dominions. This idea, however, did not have sufficient appeal at home or abroad. Second, reformers advocated measures to rejuvenate the declining British economy and to achieve greater efficiency. Unfortunately, as W. Arthur Lewis argued, all the roads that would have led to industrial innovation and a higher rate of economic growth were closed to the British for social, political, or ideological reasons (Lewis, 1978, p. 133). The primary solution to the problem of decline and disequilibrium,therefore, necessarily lay in the reduction of overseas diplomatic and strategic commitments.

The specific diplomatic and strategic issue that faced British leadership was whether to maintain the global position identified with the Pax Britannica or to bring about a retrenchment of its global commitments. By the last decade of the century, Great Britain was confronted by rival land and sea powers on every continent and every sea. European rivals were everywhere: Russia in the Far East, south Asia, and the Middle East; France in Asia, the Middle East, and north Africa; Germany in the Far East, the Middle East, and Africa. Furthermore, in the Far East, Japan had suddenly emerged as a great power; the United States also was becoming a naval power of consequence and was challenging Great Britain in the Western Hemisphere and the Pacific Ocean.

At the turn of the century, however, the predominant problem was perceived to be the challenge of German naval expansionism. Whereas all the other challenges posed limited and long-term threats, the danger embodied in Germany's decision to build a battle fleet was immediate and portentous. Despite intense negotiations, no compromise of this naval armaments race could be reached. The only course open to the British was retrenchment of their power and commitments around the globe in order to concentrate their total efforts on the German challenge.

Great Britain settled its differences with its other foreign rivals one after another. In the 1890s came the settlement of the Venezuela-British Guiana border dispute in accordance with American desires; in effect, Britain acquiesced in America's primacy in the Caribbean Sea. A century of American-British uneasiness came to an end, and the foundation was laid for the Anglo-American alliance that would prevail in two world wars. Next, in the Anglo-Japanese alliance of 1902, Great Britain gave up its policy of going it alone and took Japan as its partner in the Far East. Accepting Japanese supremacy in the northwestern Pacific as a counterweight to Russia, Great Britain withdrew to the south. This was immediately followed in 1904 by the *entente cordiale,* which settled the Mediterranean and colonial confrontation between France and Great Britain and ended centuries of conflict. In 1907 the Anglo-Russian agreement resolved the British-Russian confrontation in the Far East, turned Russia's interest toward the Balkans, and eventually aligned Russia, Great Britain, and France against Germany and Austria. Thus, by the eve of World War I, British commitments had been retrenched to a point that Britain could employ whatever power it possessed to arrest further decline in the face of expanding German power.

Thus far we have described two alternative sets of strategies that a great power may pursue in order to arrest its decline: to increase resources or to decrease costs. Each of these policies has succeeded to some degree at one time or another. Most frequently, however, the dominant state is unable to generate sufficient additional resources to defend its vital commitments; alternatively, it may be unable to reduce its cost and commitments to some manageable size. In these situations, the disequilibrium in the system becomes increasingly acute as the declining power tries to maintain its position and the rising power attempts to transform the system in ways that will advance its interests. As a consequence of this persisting disequilibrium, the international system is beset by tensions, uncertainties, and crises. However, such a stalemate in the system seldom persists for a long period of time.

Throughout history the primary means of resolving the disequilibrium between the structure of the international system and the redistribution of power has been war, more particularly, what we shall call a hegemonic war. In the words of Raymond Aron, describing World War I, a hegemonic war "is characterized less by its immediate causes or its explicit purposes than by its extent and the stakes involved. It affected all the political units inside one system of relations between sovereign states. Let us call it, for want of a better term, a war of hegemony, hegemony being, if not conscious motive, at any rate the inevitable consequence of the victory of at least one of the states or groups" (Aron, 1964, p. 359). Thus, a hegemonic war is the ultimate test of change in the relative standings of the powers in the existing system.

Every international system that the world has known has been a consequence of the territorial, economic, and diplomatic realignments that have followed such hegemonic struggles. The most important consequence of a hegemonic war is that it changes the system in accordance with the new international distribution of power; it brings about a reordering of the basic components of the system. Victory and defeat reestablish an unambiguous hierarchy of prestige congruent with the new distribution of power in the system. The war determines who will govern the international system and whose interests will be primarily served by the new international order. The war leads to a redistribution of territory among the states in the system, a new set of rules of the system, a revised international division of labor, etc. As a consequence of these changes, a relatively more stable international order and effective governance of the international system are created based on the new realities of the international distribution of power. In short, hegemonic wars have (unfortunately) been functional and integral parts of the evolution and dynamics of international systems.

It is not inevitable, of course, that a hegemonic struggle will give rise immediately to a new hegemonic power and a renovated international order. As has frequently occurred, the combatants may exhaust themselves, and the "victorious" power may be unable to reorder the international system. The destruction of Rome by barbarian hordes led to the chaos of the Dark Ages. The Pax Britannica was not immediately replaced by the Pax Americana; there was a twenty year interregnum, what E. H. Carr called the "twenty years' crisis." Eventually, however, a new power or set of powers emerges to give governance to the international system.

What, then, are the defining characteristics of a hegemonic war? How does it differ from more limited conflicts among states? In the first place, such a war involves a direct contest between the dominant power or powers in an international system and the rising challenger or challengers. The conflict becomes total and in time is characterized by participation of all the major states and most of the minor states in the system. The tendency, in fact, is for every state in the system to be drawn into one or another of the opposing camps. Inflexible bipolar configurations of power (the Delian League versus the Peloponnesian League, the Triple Alliance versus the Triple Entente) frequently presage the outbreak of hegemonic conflict.

Second, the fundamental issue at stake is the nature and governance of the system. The legitimacy of the system may be said to be challenged. For this reason, hegemonic wars are unlimited conflicts; they are at once political, economic, and ideological in terms of significance and consequences. They become directed at the destruction of the offending social, political, or economic system and are usually followed by religious, political, or social transformation of the defeated society. The leveling of Carthage by Rome, the conversion of the Middle East to Islam by the Arabs, and the democratization of contemporary Japan and West Germany by the United States are salient examples. . . .

Third, a hegemonic war is characterized by the unlimited means employed and by the general scope of the warfare. Because all parties are drawn into the war and the stakes involved are high, few limitations, if any, are observed with respect to the means employed; the limitations on violence and treachery tend to be only those necessarily imposed by the state of technology, the available resources, and the fear of retaliation. Similarly, the geographic scope of the war tends to expand to encompass the entire international system; these are "world" wars. Thus, hegemonic wars are characterized by their intensity, scope, and duration.

From the premodern world, the Peloponnesian War between Athens and Sparta and the Second Punic War between Carthage and Rome meet these criteria of hegemonic war. In the modern era, several wars have been hegemonic struggles: the Thirty Years' War (1618-48); the wars of Louis XIV (1667-1713); the wars of the French Revolution and Napoleon (1792-1814); World Wars I and II (1914-18, 1939-45) (Mowat, 1928, pp. 1-2). At issue in each of these great conflicts was the governance of the international system.

In addition to the preceding criteria that define hegemonic war, three preconditions generally appear to be associated with the outbreak of hegemonic war. In the first place, the intensification of conflicts among states is a consequence of the "closing in" of space and opportunities. With the aging of an international system and the expansion of states, the distance between states decreases, thereby causing them increasingly to come into conflict with one another. The once-empty space around the centers of power in the system is appropriated. The exploitable resources begin to be used up, and opportunities for economic growth decline. The system begins to encounter limits to the growth and expansion of member states; states increasingly come into conflict with one another. Interstate relations become more and more a zero-sum game in which one state's gain is another's loss.

Marxists and realists share a sense of the importance of contracting frontiers and their significance for the stability and peace of the system. As long as expansion is possible, the law of uneven growth (or development) can operate with little disturbing effect on the overall stability of the system. In time, however, limits are reached, and the international system enters a period of crisis. The clashes among states for territory, resources, and markets increase in frequency and magnitude and eventually culminate in hegemonic war. Thus, as E. H. Carr told us, the relative peace of nineteenth-century Europe and the belief that a harmony of interest was providing a basis for increasing economic interdependence were due to the existence of "continuously expanding territories and markets" (1951, p. 224). The closing in of political and economic space led to the intensification of conflict and the final collapse of the system in the two world wars.

The second condition preceding hegemonic war is temporal and psychological rather than spatial; it is the perception that a fundamental historical change is taking place and the gnawing fear of one or more of the great powers that time is somehow beginning to work against it and that one should settle matters through preemptive war while the advantage is still on one's side. It was anxiety of this nature that Thucydides had in mind when he wrote that the growth of Athenian power inspired fear on the part of the Lacedaemonians and was the unseen cause of the war. The alternatives open to a state whose relative power is being eclipsed are seldom those of waging war versus promoting peace, but rather waging war while the balance is still in that state's favor or waging war later when the tide may have turned against it. Thus the motive for hegemonic war, at least from the perspective of the dominant power, is to minimize one's losses rather than to maximize one's gains. In effect, a precondition for hegemonic war is the realization that the law of uneven growth has begun to operate to one's disadvantage.

The third precondition of hegemonic war is that the course of events begins to escape human control. Thus far, the argument of this study has proceeded as if mankind controlled its own destiny. The propositions presented and explored in an attempt to understand international political change have been phrased in terms of rational cost/benefit calculations. Up to a point, rationality does appear to apply; statesmen do explicitly or implicitly make rational calculations and then attempt to set the course of the ship of state accordingly. But it is equally true that events, especially those associated with the passions of war, can easily escape from human control.

"What is the force that moves nations?" Tolstoy inquires in the concluding part of *War and Peace,* and he answers that ultimately it is the masses in motion (1961, Vol. II, p. 1404). Leadership, calculation, control over events— these are merely the illusions of statesmen and scholars. The passions of men and the momentum of events take over and propel societies in novel and unanticipated directions. This is especially true during times of war. As the Athenians counseled the Peloponnesians in seeking to forestall war, "consider the vast influence of accident in war, before you engage in it. As it continues, it generally becomes an affair of chances, chances from which neither of us is exempt, and whose event we must risk in the dark. It is a common mistake in going to war to begin at the wrong end, to act first, and wait for disaster to discuss the matter" (Thucydides, 1951, p. 45).

Indeed, men seldom determine or even anticipate the consequences of hegemonic war. Although in going to war they desire to increase their gains or minimize their losses, they do not get the war they want or expect; they fail to recognize the pent-up forces they are unleashing or the larger historical significance of the decisions they are taking. They underestimate the eventual scope and intensity of the conflict on which they are embarking and its implications for their civilization. Hegemonic war arises from the structural conditions and disequilibrium of an international system, but its consequences are seldom predicted by statesmen. As Toynbee suggested, the law governing such conflicts would appear to favor rising states on the periphery of an international system rather than the contending states in the system itself. States directly engaged in hegemonic conflict, by weakening themselves, frequently actually eliminate obstacles to conquest by a peripheral power.

The great turning points in world history have been provided by these hegemonic struggles among political rivals; these periodic conflicts have reordered the international system and propelled history in new and uncharted directions. They resolve the question of which state will govern the system, as well as what ideas and values will predominate, thereby determining the ethos of succeeding ages. The outcomes of these wars affect the economic, social, and ideological structures of individual societies as well as the structure of the larger international system.

In contrast to the emphasis placed here on the role of hegemonic war in changing the international system, it might be argued that domestic revolution can change the international system. This is partially correct. It would be foolish to suggest, for example, that the great revolutions of the twentieth century (the Russian, Chinese, and perhaps Iranian) have not had a profound impact on world politics. However, the primary consequence of these social and political upheavals (at least of the first two) has been to facilitate the mobilization of the society's resources for purposes of national power. In other words, the significance of these revolutions for world politics is that they have served to strengthen (or weaken) their respective states and thereby cause a redistribution of power in the system.

As the distinguished French historian Elie Halévy put it, "all great convulsions in the history of the world, and more particularly in modern Europe, have been at the same time wars and revolutions" (1965, p. 212). Thus the Thirty Years' War was both an international war among Sweden, France, and the Hapsburg Empire and a series of domestic conflicts among Protestant and Catholic parties. The wars of the French Revolution and the Napoleonic period that pitted France against the rest of Europe triggered political upheavals of class and national revolutions throughout Europe. World Wars I and II represented not only the decay of the European international political order but also an onslaught against political liberalism and economic laissez-faire. The triumph of American power in these wars meant not only American governance of the system but also reestablishment of a liberal world order.

References

Aron, Raymond. *Peace and War—A Theory of International Relations.* Garden City, N. Y.: Doubleday, 1966.

———. "War and Industrial Society." In *War—Studies from Psychology, Sociology, Anthropology,* edited by Leon Bramson and George W. Goethals, pp. 351-394. New York: Basic Books, 1964.

———. *The Imperial Republic.* Englewood Cliffs, N. J.: Prentice-Hall, 1974.

Beer, Francis A. *Peace Against War—The Ecology of International Violence.* San Francisco: W. H. Freeman, 1981.

Carr, Edward Hallett, *The Twenty Years' Crisis, 1919-1939. An Introduction to the Study of International Relations.* London: Macmillan, 1951.

Cipolla, Carlo M. *Guns, Sails and Empires—Technological Innovation and the Early Phases of European Expansion 1400-1700.* New York: Minerva Press, 1965.

———. ed. *The Economic Decline of Empires.* London: Methuen, 1970.

Clark, George. *War and Society in the Seventeenth Century.* Cambridge University Press, 1958.

Clough, Shepard B. *The Rise and Fall of Civilization.* New York: Columbia University Press, 1970.

Downs, Anthony. *An Economic Theory of Democracy.* New York: Harper & Row, 1957. *Inside Bureaucracy.* Boston: Little, Brown, 1967.

Elvin, Mark. *The Pattern of the Chinese Past.* Stanford: Stanford University Press, 1973.

Grant, Michael. *The Climax of Rome, the Final Achievements of the Ancient World.* London: Weidenfeld and Nicolson, 1968.

Halévy, Elie. *The Era of Tyrannies.* New York: Doubleday, 1965.

Hawtrey, Ralph G. *Economic Aspects of Sovereignty.* London: Longmans, Green, 1952.

Hoffmann, Stanley, ed. *Contemporary Theory in International Relations.* Englewood Cliffs, N. J.: Prentice-Hall, 1960.

———. International Systems and International Law." In *The State of War—Essays on the Theory and Practice of International Politics,* edited by Stanley Hoffmann, pp. 88-122. New York: Praeger, 1965.

———. "Choices." *Foreign Policy* 12 (1973):3-42.

———. "An American Social Science: International Relations." *Daedalus* 1 (1977):41-60.

————. *Primacy or World Order—American Foreign Policy since the Cold War*. New York: McGraw-Hill, 1978.

Lane, Frederic C. "The Economic Meaning of War and Protection." *Journal of Social Philosophy and Jurisprudence* 7 (1942):254-70.

————. "Economic Consequences of Organized Violence." *The Journal of Economic History* 18 (1958):401-17.

————. *Venice and History: The Collected Papers of Frederic C. Lane*. Baltimore: Johns Hopkins University Press, 1966.

————. *Venice—A Maritime Republic*. Baltimore: Johns Hopkins University Press, 1973.

Lewis, W. Arthur. *The Theory of Economic Growth*. New York: Harper & Row, 1970.

————. *Growth and Fluctuations 1870-1913*. London: George Allen and Unwin, 1978.

Lippmann, Walter. *U.S. Foreign Policy: Shield of the Republic*. Boston: Little, Brown, 1943.

Luttwak, Edward. *The Grand Strategy of the Roman Empire—From the First Century A.D. to the Third*. Baltimore: Johns Hopkins University Press, 1976.

Mensch, Gerhard. *Stalemate in Technology—Innovations Overcome the Depression*. Cambridge, Mass.: Ballinger Publishing, 1979.

Modelski, George. "Agraria and Industria: Two Models of the International System." *World Politics* 14(1961):118-43.

————. *Principles of World Politics*. New York: Free Press, 1972.

"The Long Cycle of Global Politics and the Nation-State." *Comparative Studies in Society and History* 20 (1978):214-35.

Mowat, R. B. *A History of European Diplomacy 1451-1789*. New York: Longmans, Green, 1928.

Perkins, Bradford. *The Great Rapprochement—England and the United States, 1895-1914*. New York: Atheneum, 1968.

Rader, Trout. *The Economics of Feudalism*. New York: Gordon & Breach, 1971.

Riker, William H. *The Theory of Political Coalitions*. New Haven: Yale University Press, 1962.

Rostow, W. W. *Politics and the Stages of Growth*. Cambridge University Press, 1971.

————. *Getting from Here to There*. New York: McGraw-Hill, 1978.

————. *Why the Poor Get Richer and the Rich Slow Down: Essays in the Marshallian Long Period*. Austin: University of Texas Press, 1980.

Seeley, John. *The Expansion of England—Two Courses of Lectures*. Boston: Little, Brown, 1905.

Thucydides. *The Peloponnesian War*. New York: Modern Library, 1951.

Tolstoy, L. N. *War and Peace*. 2 vols. Baltimore: Penguin Books, 1961.

Toynbee, Arnold J. *Survey of International Affairs 1930*. London: Oxford University Press, 1931.

————. *A Study of History*. Vols. 3 and 12. London: Oxford University Press, 1961.

von Ranke, Leopold. "The Great Powers." In *Leopold Ranke—The Formative Years*, edited by Theodore H. von Laue, pp. 181-218. Princeton: Princeton University Press, 1950.

Walbank, F. W. *The Awful Revolution: The Decline of the Roman Empire in the West*. Liverpool: Liverpool University Press, 1969.

Wright, Quincy. *A Study of War*. 2 vols. Chicago: University of Chicago Press, 1942.

Power, Culprits, and Arms

GEOFFREY BLAINEY

The Abacus of Power

I

The Prussian soldier, Carl von Clausewitz, died of cholera in 1831, while leading an army against Polish rebels. He left behind sealed packets containing manuscripts which his widow published in the following year. The massive dishevelled books, entitled *On War*, could have been called *On War and Peace,* for Clausewitz implied that war and peace had much in common. In his opinion the leisurely siege of the eighteenth century was not much more than a forceful diplomatic note; that kind of war was 'only diplomacy somewhat intensified'.[1] In essence diplomatic despatches breathed deference, but their courtesy was less effective than the silent threats which underwrote them. The threat might not be mentioned, but it was understood. The blunt words of Frederick the Great had similarly summed up the way in which military power influenced diplomacy: 'Diplomacy without armaments is like music without instruments'.[2]

Clausewitz had fought for Prussia in many campaigns against the French but he had more influence on wars in which he did not fight. He is said to have been the talisman of the German general who planned the invasions of

Geoffrey Blainey, *The Causes of War,* 3rd edition (New York: Free Press, 1988), selections from chapters 8 and 10. Reprinted with permission of The Free Press, a division of Macmillan, Inc. Copyright © 1973, 1977, 1988 by Geoffrey Blainey.

[1]A siege likened to diplomacy: Clausewitz, III 97.
[2]'Diplomacy without armaments': Gooch, *Studies in Diplomacy,* p. 226.

France in 1870 and 1914. His books were translated into French just before the Crimean War and into English just after the Franco-Prussian War, and in military academies in many lands the name of this man who had won no great battles became more famous than most of those names inseparably linked with victorious battles. His writings however had less influence outside military circles. He was seen as a ruthless analyst who believed that war should sometimes be 'waged with the whole might of national power'.[3] His views therefore seemed tainted to most civilians; he appeared to be the sinister propagandist of militarism. Those who studied a war's causes, as distinct from its course, ignored him. And yet one of the most dangerous fallacies in the study of war is the belief that the causes of a war and the events of a war belong to separate compartments and reflect completely different principles. This fallacy, translated into medicine, would require the causes and course of an illness to be diagnosed on quite different principles.

Clausewitz's tumble of words was overwhelmingly on warfare, and the index of the three English volumes of his work points to only one sentence on peace. Nevertheless some of his views on peace can be inferred from lonely sentences. He believed that a clear ladder of international power tended to promote peace. 'A conqueror is always a lover of peace', he wrote.[4] His statement at first sight seems preposterous, but at second sight it commands respect.[5]

II

Power is the crux of many explanations of war and peace, but its effects are not agreed upon. Most observers argue that a nation which is too powerful endangers the peace. A few hint, like Clausewitz, that a dominant nation can preserve the peace simply by its ability to keep inferior nations in order. There must be an answer to the disagreement. The last three centuries are studded with examples of how nations behaved in the face of every extremity of military and economic power.

That a lopsided balance of power will promote war is probably the most popular theory of international relations. It has the merit that it can be turned upside down to serve as an explanation of peace. It is also attractive because it can be applied to wars of many centuries, from the Carthaginian wars to the Second World War. The very phrase, 'balance of power', has the soothing sound of the panacea: it resembles the balance of nature and the balance of trade and other respectable concepts. It therefore suggests that

---

[3]'Waged with the whole might': Leonard, p. 25.
[4]'A conqueror': Clausewitz, II 155.
[5]Clausewitz on peace: On first reading Clausewitz I noticed no comment on peace. Later, realizing that he must have commented by implication, I skimmed through his work again. As his references to peace seem sparse, I cannot be sure that I have interpreted his views correctly.

an even balance of power is somehow desirable. The word 'balance', unfortunately, is confusing. Whereas at one time it usually signified a set of weighing scales—in short it formerly signified either equality or inequality—it now usually signifies equality and equilibrium. In modern language the assertion that 'Germany had a favourable balance of power' is not completely clear. It is rather like a teacher who, finding no equality of opportunity in a school, proceeded to denounce the 'unfavourable equality of opportunity'. The verbal confusion may be partly responsible for the million vague and unpersuasive words which have been written around the concept of the balance of power.

The advantages of an even balance of power in Europe have been stressed by scores of historians and specialists in strategy. The grand old theory of international relations, it is still respected though no longer so venerated. According to Hedley Bull, who was a director of a research unit on arms control in the British foreign office before becoming professor of international relations at the Australian National University, 'The alternative to a stable balance of military power is a preponderance of power, which is very much more dangerous'.[6] Likewise, Alastair Buchan, director of London's Institute for Strategic Studies, suggested in his excellent book *War in Modern Society:* 'certainly we know from our experience of the 1930s that the lack of such a balance creates a clear temptation to aggression'.[7] Many writers of history have culled a similar lesson from past wars.

Most believers in the balance of power think that a world of many powerful states tends to be more peaceful. There an aggressive state can be counterbalanced by a combination of other strong states. Quincy Wright, in his massive book, *A Study of War,* suggested with some reservations that 'the probability of war will decrease in proportion as the number of states in the system increases'.[8] Arnold Toynbee,[9] observing that the world contained eight major powers on the eve of the First World War and only two—the United States and the Soviet Union—at the close of the Second World War, thought the decline was ominous. A chair with only two legs, he argued, had less balance. As the years passed, and the two great powers avoided major war, some specialists on international affairs argued that a balance of terror had replaced the balance of power. In the nuclear age, they argued, two great powers were preferable to eight. The danger of a crisis that slipped from control was diminished if two powers dominated the world.[10] Neverthe-

---

[6]Bull: cited in Buchan, p. 34.
[7]Buchan, p. 177.
[8]Wright, abridged edn., p. 122.
[9]Toynbee, *A Study of History,* IX 244.
[10]The preference for a bi-polar system often seems to hinge on the idea that wars are often the result of situations which go further than either nation intended.
[11]Scholars' preference for a multi-polar system before 1945 and bi-polar system thereafter: G. H. Snyder in Pruitt and Snyder, p. 124.

less even those who preferred to see two powers dominant in the nuclear age still believed, for the most part, that in the pre-nuclear era a world of many strong powers was safer.[11]

To my knowledge no historian or political scientist produced evidence to confirm that a power system of seven strong states was more conducive to peace than a system of two strong states. The idea relies much on analogies. Sometimes it resembles the kind of argument which old men invoked in European cities when the two-wheeled bicycle began to supersede the tricycle. At other times it resembles a belief in the virtues of free competition within an economic system. It parallels the idea that in business many strong competitors will so function that none can win a preponderance of power; if one seems likely to become predominant, others will temporarily combine to subdue him. It is possibly significant that this doctrine of flexible competition in economic affairs was brilliantly systematised at the time when a similar doctrine was refined in international affairs. While Adam Smith praised the virtues of the free market in economic affairs, the Swiss jurist Emerich de Vattel praised it in international affairs. In one sense both theories were reactions against a Europe in which powerful monarchs hampered economic life with meddlesome regulations and disturbed political life with frequent wars.

It is axiomatic that a world possessing seven nations of comparable strength, each of which values its independence, will be a substantial safeguard against the rise of one world-dominating power. Even two nations of comparable strength will be a useful safeguard. When all this has been said we possess not an axiom for peace but an axiom for national independence. And that in fact was the main virtue of a balance of power in the eyes of those who originally practiced it. It was not primarily a formula for peace: it was a formula for national independence. Edward Gulick,[12] Massachusetts historian, was adamant that its clearest theorists and practitioners—the Metternichs and Castlereaghs—'all thought of war as an instrument to preserve or restore a balance of power'. In essence a balance of power was simply a formula designed to prevent the rise of a nation to world dominance. It merely masqueraded as a formula for peace.

III

The idea that an even distribution of power promotes peace has gained strength partly because it has never been accompanied by tangible evidence. Like a ghost it has not been captured and examined for pallor and pulsebeat. And yet there is a point of time when the ghost can be captured. The actual distribution of power can be measured at the end of the war.

[12]Gulick, p. 36.

The military power of rival European alliances was most imbalanced, was distributed most unevenly, at the end of a decisive war. And decisive wars tended to lead to longer periods of international peace. Indecisive wars, in contrast, tended to produce shorter periods of peace. Thus the eighteenth century was characterised by inconclusive wars and by short periods of peace. During the long wars one alliance had great difficulty in defeating the other. Many of the wars ended in virtual deadlock: military power obviously was evenly balanced. Such wars tended to lead to short periods of peace. The War of the Polish Succession—basically an ineffectual war between France and Austria—was followed within five years by the War of the Austrian Succession. That war after eight years was so inconclusive on most fronts that the peace treaty signed in 1748 mainly affirmed the status quo. That ineffectual war was followed only eight years later by another general war, the Seven Years War, which ended with Britain the clear victor in the war at sea and beyond the seas, though on European soil the war was a stalemate. But even the Anglo-French peace which followed the Treaty of Paris in 1763 was not long; it ended after fifteen years. It ended when the revolt of the American colonies against Britain removed Britain's preponderance of power over France.

The French Revolutionary Wars which, beginning in 1792, raged across Europe and over the sea for a decade were more decisive than any major war for more than a century. They ended with France dominant on the continent and with England dominant at sea and in America and the East. They thus failed to solve the crucial question: was England or France the stronger power? The Peace of Amiens, which England and France signed in 1802, lasted little more than a year. So began the Napoleonic Wars which at last produced undisputed victors.

This is not to suggest that a general war which ended in decisive victory was the sole cause of a long period of peace. A decisive general war did not always lead to a long period of peace. This survey of the major wars of the period 1700 to 1815 does suggest however that the traditional theory which equates an even balance of power with peace should be reversed. Instead a clear preponderance of power tended to promote peace.

Of the general wars fought in Europe in the last three centuries those with the most decisive outcome were the Napoleonic (1815), Franco-Prussian (1871), First World War (1918), and Second World War (1945). The last days of those wars and the early years of the following periods of peace marked the height of the imbalance of power in Europe. At the end of those wars the scales of power were so tilted against the losers that Napoleon Bonaparte was sent as a captive to an island in the South Atlantic, Napoleon III was captured and permitted to live in exile in England, Kaiser Wilhelm II went into exile in Holland and Adolf Hitler committed suicide. Years after the end of those wars, the scales of power were still strongly tilted against the losers. And yet those years of extreme imbalance marked the first stages of perhaps the most pronounced periods of peace known to Europe in the last three or more centuries.

Exponents of the virtues of an even distribution of military power have concentrated entirely on the outbreak of war. They have ignored however the conditions surrounding the outbreak of peace. By ignoring the outbreak of peace they seem to have ignored the very period when the distribution of military power between warring nations can be accurately measured. For warfare is the one convincing way of measuring the distribution of power. The end of a war produces a neat ledger of power which has been duly audited and signed. According to that ledger an agreed preponderance of power tends to foster peace. In contrast the exponents of the orthodox theory examine closely the prelude to a war, but that is a period when power is muffled and much more difficult to measure. It is a period characterised by conflicting estimates of which nation or alliance is the most powerful. Indeed one can almost suggest that war is usually the outcome of a diplomatic crisis which cannot be solved because both sides have conflicting estimates of their bargaining power.

The link between a diplomatic crisis and the outbreak of war seems central to the understanding of war. That link however seems to be misunderstood. Thus many historians, in explaining the outbreak of war, argue that 'the breakdown in diplomacy led to war'. This explanation is rather like the argument that the end of winter led to spring: it is a description masquerading as an explanation. In fact that main influence which led to the breakdown of diplomacy—a contradictory sense of bargaining power—also prompted the nations to fight. At the end of a war the situation was reversed. Although I have not come across the parallel statement—'so the breakdown of war led to diplomacy'—it can be explained in a similar way. In essence the very factor which made the enemies reluctant to continue fighting also persuaded them to negotiate. That factor was their agreement about their relative bargaining position.

It is not the actual distribution or balance of power which is vital: it is rather the way in which national leaders *think* that power is distributed. In contrast orthodox theory assumes that the power of nations can be measured with some objectivity. It assumes that, in the pre-nuclear era, a statesman's knowledge of the balance of international power rested mainly on an 'objective comparison of military capabilities'.[13] I find it difficult however to accept the idea that power could ever be measured with such objectivity. The clear exception was at the end of wars—the points of time which theorists ignore. Indeed, it is the problem of accurately measuring the relative power of nations which goes far to explain why wars occur. War is a dispute about the measurement of power. War marks the choice of a new set of weights and measures.

---

[13]'The objective comparison of military capabilities': G. H. Snyder in Pruitt and Snyder, p. 117. According to Wright, p. 116, the term 'balance of power' implies that fluctuations in power 'can be observed and measured'.

IV

In peace time the relations between two diplomats are like relations between two merchants. While the merchants trade in copper or transistors, the diplomats' transactions involve boundaries, spheres of influence, commercial concessions and a variety of other issues which they have in common. A foreign minister or diplomat is a merchant who bargains on behalf of his country. He is both buyer and seller, though he buys and sells privileges and obligations rather than commodities. The treaties he signs are simply more courteous versions of commercial contracts.

The difficulty in diplomacy, as in commerce, is to find an acceptable price for the transaction. Just as the price of merchandise such as copper roughly represents the point where the supply of copper balances the demand for it, the price of a transaction in diplomacy roughly marks the point at which one nation's willingness to pay matches the price demanded by the other. The diplomatic market however is not as sophisticated as the mercantile market. Political currency is not so easily measured as economic currency. Buying and selling in the diplomatic market is much closer to barter, and so resembles an ancient bazaar in which the traders have no accepted medium of exchange. In diplomacy each nation has the rough equivalent of a selling price—a price which it accepts when it sells a concession—and the equivalent of a buying price. Sometimes these prices are so far apart that a transaction vital to both nations cannot be completed peacefully; they cannot agree on the price of the transaction. The history of diplomacy is full of such crises. The ministers and diplomats of Russia and Japan could not agree in 1904, on the eve of the Russo-Japanese War; the Germans could not find acceptable terms with British and French ministers on the eve of the Second World War.

A diplomatic crisis is like a crisis in international payments; like a crisis in the English pound or the French franc. In a diplomatic crisis the currency of one nation or alliance is out of alignment with that of the others. These currencies are simply the estimates which each nation nourishes about its relative bargaining power. These estimates are not easy for an outsider to assess or to measure; and yet these estimates exist clearly in the minds of the ministers and diplomats who bargain.

For a crisis in international payments there are ultimate solutions which all nations recognise. If the English pound is the object of the crisis, and if its value is endangered because England is importing too much, the English government usually has to admit that it is living beyond its present means. As a remedy it may try to discourage imports and encourage exports. It may even have to declare that the value of the English pound is too high in relation to the French franc, the German mark and all other currencies, and accordingly it may fix the pound at a lower rate. Whichever solution it follows is not pleasant for the national pride and the people's purse. Fortunately there is less shame and humiliation for a nation which has to confess that its monetary currency is overvalued than for a country which has to confess that its diplomatic currency is overvalued. It is almost as if the detailed statistics which record the currency crisis make it seem anonymous and unemotional. In contrast a diplomatic crisis is personal and emotional. The opponent is not a sheet of statistics representing the sum of payments to and from all nations: the opponent is an armed nation to which aggressive intentions can be attributed and towards whom hatred can be felt.

A nation facing a payments crisis can *measure* the extent to which it is living beyond its means. As the months pass by, moreover, it can measure whether its remedies have been effective, for the statistics of its balance of payments are an accurate guide to the approach of a crisis and the passing of crisis. On the other hand a deficit in international power is not so easy to detect. A nation with an increasing deficit in international power may not even recognise its weaknesses. A nation may so mistake its bargaining power that it may make the ultimate appeal to war, and then learn through defeat in warfare to accept a humbler assessment of its bargaining position.

The death-watch wars of the eighteenth century exemplified such crises. A kingdom which was temporarily weakened by the accession of a new ruler or by the outbreak of civil unrest refused to believe that it was weaker. It usually behaved as if its bargaining position were unaltered. But its position, in the eyes of rival nations, was often drastically weaker. Negotiations were therefore frustrated because each nation demanded far more than the other was prepared to yield. Likewise the appeal to war was favoured because each side believed that it would win.

In diplomacy some nations for a longer period can live far beyond their means: to live beyond their means is to concede much less than they would have to concede if the issue was resolved by force. A government may be unyielding in negotiations because it predicts that its adversary does not want war. It may be unyielding because it has an inflated idea of its own military power. Or it may be unyielding because to yield to an enemy may weaken its standing and grip within its own land. Whereas an endangered nation facing a currency crisis cannot escape some punishment, in a diplomatic crisis it can completely escape punishment so long as the rival nation or alliance does not insist on war. Thus diplomacy may become more unrealistic, crises may become more frequent, and ultimately the tension and confusion may end in war. . . .

War itself provides the most reliable and most objective test of which nation or alliance is the most powerful. After a war which ended decisively, the warring nations agreed on their respective strength. The losers and the winners might have disagreed about the exact margin of superiority; they did agree however that decisive superiority existed. A decisive war was therefore usually followed by an orderly market in political power, or in other words peace. Indeed one vital difference between the eighteenth and nineteenth centuries was that wars tended to become more decisive. This is part of the explanation for the war-studded history of one century and the relative peacefulness of the following century. Whereas the eighteenth century more often had long and inconclusive wars followed by short periods of peace, the century after 1815 more often had short and decisive wars and long periods of peace.

Nevertheless, during both centuries, the agreement about nations' bargaining power rarely lasted as long as one generation. Even when a war had ended decisively the hierarchy of power could not last indefinitely. It was blurred by the fading of memories of the previous war, by the accession of new leaders who blamed the old leaders for the defeat, and by the legends and folklore which glossed over past defeats. It was blurred by the weakening effects of internal unrest or the strengthening effects of military reorganisation, by economic and technical change, by shifts in alliances, and by a variety of other influences. So the defeated nation regained confidence. When important issues arose, war became a possibility. The rival nations believed that each could gain more by fighting than by negotiating. Those contradictory hopes are characteristic of the outbreak of war. . . .

VII

Wars usually end when the fighting nations *agree* on their relative strength, and wars usually begin when fighting nations *disagree* on their relative strength. Agreement or disagreement is shaped by the same set of factors. Thus each factor that is a prominent cause of war can at times be a prominent cause of peace. Each factor can oscillate between war and peace, and the oscillation is most vivid in the history of nations which decided to fight because virtually everything was in their favour and decided to cease fighting because everything was pitted against them. . . .

Aims and Arms

I

A culprit stands in the centre of most generalised explanations of war. While there may be dispute in naming the culprit, it is widely believed that the culprit exists.

In the eighteenth century many philosophers thought that the ambitions of absolute monarchs were the main cause of war: pull down the mighty, and wars would become rare. Another theory contended that many wars came from the Anglo-French rivalry for colonies and commerce: restrain that quest, and peace would be more easily preserved. The wars following the French Revolution fostered an idea that popular revolutions were becoming the main cause of international war. In the nineteenth century, monarchs who sought to unite their troubled country by a glorious foreign war were widely seen as culprits. At the end of that century the capitalists' chase for markets or investment outlets became a popular villain. The First World War convinced many writers that armaments races and arms salesmen had become the villains, and both world wars fostered the idea that militarist regimes were the main disturbers of the peace.

Most of these theories of war have flourished, then fallen away, only to appear again in new dress. The eighteenth-century belief that mercantilism was the main cause of war was re-clothed by the Englishman, J. A. Hobson, and the Russian exile, V. I. Lenin, in the Boer War and in the First World War; and the theme that manufacturers of armaments were the chief plotters of war was revived to explain the widening of the war in Vietnam. The resilience of this type of explanation is probably aided by the fact that it carries its own solution to war. Since it points to a particular culprit, we only have to eliminate the culprit in order to abolish war. By abolishing dictators, capitalists, militarists, manufacturers of armaments or one of the other villains, peace would be preserved. Indeed it is often the passion for the antidote—whether democracy, socialism or free trade—rather than an analysis of the illness that popularises many of these theories of war.

These theories assume that ambitions and motives are the dominant cause of wars. As war is increasingly denounced as the scarlet sin of civilisation, it is understandable that the search for the causes of war should often become a search for villains. The search is aided by the surviving records of war. So many of the documents surrounding the outbreak of every war—whether the War of Spanish Succession or the recent War of the Saigon Succession—are attempts to blame the other side. The surviving records of wars are infected with insinuations and accusations of guilt, and some of that infection is transmitted to the writings of those who, generations or centuries later, study those wars. Since so much research into war is a search for villains, and since the evidence itself is dominated by attempts to apportion blame, it is not surprising that many theories of war and explanations of individual wars are centred on the aims of 'aggressors'.

Most controversies about the causes of particular wars also hinge on the aims of nations. What did France and England hope to gain by aiding the Turks against the Russians in the Crimean War? What were the ambitions of Bismarck and Napoleon III on the eve of the Franco-Prussian War of 1870? Who deserves most blame for the outbreak of the First World War? The evergreen examination-question at schools and universities—were the main causes of a certain war political or economic or religious—reflects the strong tradition that ambitions are the key to understanding war.

The running debate on the causes of the Vietnam War is therefore in a rich tradition. Measured by the mileage of words unrolled it must be the most voluminous which any war has aroused, but it is mainly the traditional debate about ambitions and motives. The war in Vietnam is variously said to have been caused by the desire of United States' capitalists for markets and investment outlets, by the pressures of American military suppliers, by the American hostility to communism, by the crusading ambitions of Moscow and Peking, the aggressive nationalism or communism of Hanoi, the corrup-

tion or aggression of Saigon, or the headlong clash of other aims. The ker-
nel of the debate is the assumption that pressures or ambitions are the main
causes of the war.

II

The idea that war is caused simply by a clash of aims is intrinsically satisfying.
It is easy to believe that historians will ultimately understand the causes of
war if only they can unravel the ambitions held on the eve of a war by the relevant monarchs, prime ministers, presidents, chiefs of staff, archbishops, editors, intellectuals and cheering or silent crowds. Explanations based on
ambitions however have a hidden weakness. They portray ambitions which
were so strong that war was inevitable. It is almost a hallmark of such interpretations to describe ambitions—whether for prestige, ideology, markets
or empire—as the fundamental causes, the basic causes, the deepseated, underlying or long-term causes. Such causes merely need the provocation of
minor events to produce war. The minor events are usually referred to as the
occasion for war as distinct from the causes of war. Sometimes the incidents
which immediately precede the war are called the short-term causes: the assumption is that long-term causes are more powerful.

This idea of causation has a distinctive shape. Its exponents see conflict as
a volcano which, seeming to slumber, is really approaching the day of terror.
They see conflict as water which slowly gathers heat and at last comes to the
boil. The events which happen on the eve of a war add the last few degrees of
heat to the volcano or kettle. It is a linear kind of argument: the causes of
war are like a graph of temperatures and the last upward movement on the
graph marks the transition from peace to war. If in fact such a graph were a
valid way of depicting the coming of war, one would also expect to see the
temperature curve move downwards in the last days of a war. One would also
expect that if, on the eve of a war, minor incidents could convert the long-
term causes of conflict into war, similar incidents could activate the transition from war to peace. No such explanations however are offered for the
end of a war. If one believes that the framework of an explanation of war
should also be valid for an explanation of peace, the volcano or kettle theories are suspect.

For any explanation the framework is crucial. In every field of knowledge
the accepted explanations depend less on the marshalling of evidence than
on preconceptions of what serves as a logical framework for the evidence.
The framework dominates the evidence, because it dictates what evidence
should be sought or ignored. Our idea of a logical framework is often unconscious, and this elusiveness enhances its grip. One may suggest that the
explanations of war which stress ambitions are resting on a persuasive but
rickety framework.

The policies of a Frederick the Great, a Napoleon and a President Lincoln
were clearly important in understanding wars. So too were the hopes of the
inner circles of power in which they moved and the hopes of the people

whom they led. Likewise the aims of all the surrounding nations—irrespective of their eagerness or reluctance to fight—were important. It is doubtful however whether a study of the aims of many wars will yield useful patterns. There is scant evidence to suggest that century after century the main aims of nations which went to war could be packaged into a simple economic, religious or political formula. There is no evidence that, over a long period, the desire for territory or markets or the desire to spread an ideology tended to dominate all other war aims. It is even difficult to argue that certain kinds of aims were dominant in one generation. Admittedly it is often said that the main 'causes'—meaning the main aims—of war were religious in the sixteenth century, dynastic or mercantile in various phases of the eighteenth century and nationalist or economic in the nineteenth century. It seems more likely, however, that those who share in a decision to wage war pursued a variety of aims which even fluctuated during the same week and certainly altered during the course of the war.

One generalisation about war aims can be offered with confidence. The aims are simply varieties of power. The vanity of nationalism, the will to spread an ideology, the protection of kinsmen in an adjacent land, the desire for more territory or commerce, the avenging of a defeat or insult, the craving for greater national strength or independence, the wish to impress or cement alliances—all these represent power in different wrappings. The conflicting aims of rival nations are always conflicts of power. Not only is power the issue at stake, but the decision to resolve that issue by peaceful or warlike methods is largely determined by assessments of relative power.

III

The explanations that stress aims are theories of rivalry and animosity and not theories of war. They help to explain increasing rivalry between nations but they do not explain why the rivalry led to war. For a serious rift between nations does not necessarily end in war. It may take other forms: the severing of diplomatic relations; the peaceful intervention of a powerful outside nation; an economic blockade; heavy spending on armaments; the imposing of tariffs; an invasion accomplished without bloodshed; the enlisting of allies; or even the relaxing of tension through a successful conference. Of course these varieties of conflict may merely postpone the coming of war but serious rivalry and animosity can exist for a century without involving warfare. France and Britain were serious rivals who experienced dangerous crises between 1815 and 1900, but the war so often feared did not eventuate.

One may suggest that this kind of interpretation is hazy about the causes of peace as well as war. Its exponents usually ignore the question of why a war came to an end. They thus ignore the event which would force them to revise their analysis of the causes of war. Consider for instance the popular but dubious belief that the main cause of the First World War was Berlin's desire to dominate Europe. Now if such an explanation is valid, what were the main causes of the peace which ensued in 1918? It would be consistent

with this interpretation to reply that the crumbling of German ambitions led
to peace. And why had those ambitions crumbled? Because by October 1918
Germany's military power—and morale is a vital ingredient of power—was
no longer adequate. As the emphasis on aims cannot explain Germany's desire for peace in 1918, it would be surprising if the emphasis on aims could
explain Germany's decision for war in 1914. Indeed Germany's aims would
not have been high in 1914 if her leaders then had believed that Germany
lacked adequate power. Bethmann Hollweg, chancellor of Germany at the
outbreak of war, confessed later that Germany in 1914 had overvalued her
strength. 'Our people', he said, 'had developed so amazingly in the last
twenty years that wide circles succumbed to the temptation of overestimat-
ing our enormous forces in relation to those of the rest of the world.'[14]

One conclusion seems clear. It is dangerous to accept any explanation of
war which concentrates on ambitions and ignores the means of carrying out
those ambitions. A government's aims are strongly influenced by this assessment of whether it has sufficient strength to achieve these aims. Indeed the
two factors interact quietly and swiftly. When Hitler won power in 1933 and
had long-term hopes of reviving German greatness, his ambitions could not
alone produce a forceful foreign policy. Hitler's foreign policy in 1933 was
no more forceful than his means, in his judgment, permitted. His military
and diplomatic weapons, in his opinion, did not at first permit a bold foreign policy. A. J. P. Taylor's *The Origins of the Second World War,* one of the
most masterly books on a particular war, reveals Hitler as an alert oppor-
tunist who tempered his objectives to the available means of achieving them.
When Hitler began to rearm Germany he was guided not only by ambitions
but by his sense of Germany's bargaining position in Europe. He would not
have rearmed if he had believed that France or Russia would forcefully prevent him from building aircraft, submarines and tanks. In the main decisions which Hitler made between 1933 and the beginning of war in 1939, his
short-term objectives and his sense of Germany's bargaining position
marched so neatly in step that it is impossible to tell whether his aims or his
oscillating sense of Germany's strength beat the drum. Opportunity and ambition—or aims and arms—so acted upon one another that they were virtually inseparable. The interaction was not confined to Berlin; it occurred in
the 1930s in London, Paris, Warsaw, Moscow, Rome, Prague and all the
cities of power. . . .

---

[14]'Our people': Fischer, p. 637.

References

Buchan, Alastair, *War in Modern Society: an introduction* (London, 1968).

Clausewitz, Carl von. *On War,* ed. by F. N. Maude, tr. from German, 3 vols. (London, 1940).

Fischer, Fritz, *Germany's Aims in the First World War,* tr. from German (London, 1967).

Gooch, G. P., *Studies in Diplomacy and Statecraft* (London, 1942).

_____. *Louis XV: the monarchy in decline* (London, 1956).

Gulick, E. V., *Europe's Classical Balance of Power* (New York, 1967).

Leonard, Roger A., ed., *A Short Guide to Clausewitz on War* (London, 1967).

Pruitt, Dean G. and Snyder, R. C., eds., *Theory and Research on the Causes of War* (Englewood Cliffs, New Jersey, 1969).

Toynbee, Arnold, *Experiences* (London, 1969).

_____. *A Study of History,* 12 vols. (London, 1934-61).

Wright, Quincy, *A Study of War,* 2 vols. (Chicago, 1942).

_____. *A Study of War,* abridged by Louis L. Wright (Chicago, 1965).

PART 3

International Liberalism: Institutions and Cooperation

In the previous section, E. H. Carr presented idealism as the alternative to realism. Many sorts of ideals can drive people toward war or away from it; for example, religious militance (the Crusades, the Thirty Years War); religious pacifism (Quakerism); racist ideology (German fascism); or militarist moral codes (Japanese Bushido). At the moment, however, liberalism—the idealism of the contemporary Western world—is the only major challenge to realism. Many theorists also believe that liberal ideas about international relations are no less grounded in reality than is realism—that liberalism is not wishful thinking about the "harmony of interests," as Carr presented it, but a description of how the world sometimes *does* work, as well as how it *should* work. The newest variants of these theories are now known in academic jargon as "neoliberal institutionalism."[1]

"Liberal" in the sense used here is not synonymous with "left of center," its colloquial meaning in U.S. politics. Rather, it means the broad philosophical tradition that enshrines the values of individual political and economic liberty, the free market of ideas and enterprise—the basic values that unite what passes for left and right in American politics, from George McGovern to Ronald Reagan. The United States has been so fundamentally liberal a country in this general

---

[1] See Robert Keohane, *International Institutions and State Power* (Boulder: Westview Press, 1989).

sense that most Americans take the basic principles utterly for granted, and are not even conscious of their liberalism as a distinct ideology.[2]

Three general points distinguish liberal views of international conflict from realism or, in some respects, from Marxism:

First, ideas matter. A society's political and economic values will make it more or less prone to peace, no matter what the structure of the international balance of power may be. "Good" states—liberal republics—are likely to use force only for what they believe to be self-defense, not to rule others. Societies devoted to free trade will seek profit through exchange and comparative advantage in production rather than through conquest and plunder. These themes are elaborated in Parts 4 and 5 of this volume.

Second, history is *progress*, a process of development in which the right ideas steadily drive out the wrong, not a cycle in which nations are fated to repeat the same follies. With allowances for exceptions and backsliding, the world has been developing from primitive, parochial, and destructive behavior toward modern, cosmopolitan, efficient interchange. This is the conviction that animates Fukuyama's "End of History" and Kant's "Perpetual Peace."

Third, the fact that the international system is anarchic does not bar civility among nations. Under certain conditions, norms of cooperation can help keep countries from each others' throats, because governments recognize their mutual interest in avoiding conflict.[3] To realists, insecurity and the possibility of war are inherent in a system of separate states without an overarching authority. To liberals, anarchy is a necessary, but not a sufficient, cause of war. The proximate cause of war is usually that people who are bad, backward, or deluded decide to start it. The causes can be exposed as unnecessary, and inimical to selfish material interests as well as to moral ones, and can thus be overcome by the spread of liberal values and institutions.

Kant's "Perpetual Peace" is as classic a statement of some aspects of the liberal paradigm as Thucydides' *Peloponnesian War* is of the realist.[4] Kant claims that the tendency to progress is inherent in nature, and that as people and republics improve themselves, they will create perpetual peace. Kant's logic is the primary ingredient in Michael Doyle's discussion of why democracy breeds peace (Part 5).

Among the contemporary authors in this section, Hedley Bull argues that the international system, even without a sovereign, has become more civil than the state of nature. Keohane and Nye present the case for why modern interdepen-

---

[2]See Louis Hartz, *The Liberal Tradition in America* (New York: Harcourt, Brace, 1955). The deep roots of liberal assumptions lie behind much of the American behavior that realists criticize as legalistic and moralistic. See George F. Kennan, *American Diplomacy, 1900-1950* (Chicago: University of Chicago Press, 1951).

[3]See Kenneth A. Oye ed., *Cooperation Under Anarchy* (Princeton: Princeton University Press, 1986) and Robert Axelrod, *The Evolution of Cooperation* (New York: Basic Books, 1984).

[4]For an argument that reconciles Kant with realism see Kenneth N. Waltz, "Kant, Liberalism, and War," *American Political Science Review* 56, no. 2 (June 1962).

dence among states reduced the utility of force in their interrelations, even before the end of the Cold War.[5] Richard Ullman offers a scheme for adapting the idea of collective security to codify the current outbreak of peace and triumph of liberalism in Europe, and insulating it from disturbances to come.

Liberal arguments of various sorts about the obsolescence of war, the declining significance of the nation state, and the growing import of cooperative supranational institutions, have periodically been popular in the past. Most recent was the resurgence of such ideas in the 1970s, just after the protracted and inconclusive Vietnam War soured many observers on the utility of force, and before the collapse of U.S.-Soviet detente made optimism about basic changes in international relations seem premature. With reinvigoration of the Cold War, realism once again became the dominant school of thought. As intellectual fashions seem to coincide with actual trends in world politics, and the end of the Cold War is celebrated and widely seen as a fundamentally new departure in world development, the liberal paradigm is again ascendant in the 1990s.

[5]For an earlier essay in this vein see Klaus Knorr, *On the Utility of Force in the Nuclear Age* (Princeton: Princeton University Press, 1966). Knorr later had second thoughts about how far his argument was being taken in literature of the early 1970s, and qualified his views. See Knorr, "Is International Coercion Waning or Rising?" *International Security* 1, no. 4 (Spring 1977) and "On the International Uses of Force in the Contemporary World," *Orbis* 21, no. 1 (Spring 1977).

Perpetual Peace

IMMANUEL KANT

Section II: Containing the Definitive Articles for Perpetual Peace among States

The state of peace among men living side by side is not the natural state (*status naturalis*); the natural state is one of war. This does not always mean open hostilities, but at least an unceasing threat of war. A state of peace, therefore, must be *established*, for in order to be secured against hostility it is not sufficient that hostilities simply be not committed; and, unless this security is pledged to each by his neighbor (a thing that can occur only in a civil state), each may treat his neighbor, from whom he demands this security, as an enemy.

First Definitive Article for Perpetual Peace

"THE CIVIL CONSTITUTION OF EVERY STATE SHOULD BE REPUBLICAN" The only constitution which derives from the idea of the original compact, and on which all juridical legislation of a people must be based, is the republican.

... The republican constitution, besides the purity of its origin (having sprung from the pure source of the concept of law), also gives a favorable prospect for the desired consequence, i.e., perpetual peace. The reason is this: if the consent of the citizens is required in order to decide that war should be declared (and in this constitution it cannot but be the case), nothing is more natural than that they would be very cautious in commencing such a poor game, decreeing for themselves all the calamities of war. Among the latter would be: having to fight, having to pay the costs of war from their

Immanuel Kant, "Perpetual Peace," in *Immanuel Kant: On History*, Lewis White Beck, ed. and trans. (Indianapolis: Bobbs-Merrill, 1963), originally published in 1795. Copyright © 1963 by Macmillan Publishing Company. © 1957 by Bobbs-Merrill Publishing Company.

own resources, having painfully to repair the devastation war leaves behind, and, to fill up the measure of evils, load themselves with a heavy national debt that would embitter peace itself and that can never be liquidated on account of constant wars in the future. But, on the other hand, in a constitution which is not republican, and under which the subjects are not citizens, a declaration of war is the easiest thing in the world to decide upon, because war does not require of the ruler, who is the proprietor and not a member of the state, the least sacrifice of the pleasures of his table, the chase, his country houses, his court functions, and the like. He may, therefore, resolve on war as on a pleasure party for the most trivial reasons, and with perfect indifference leave the justification which decency requires to the diplomatic corps who are ready to provide it. . . .

Second Definitive Article for a Perpetual Peace

"THE LAW OF NATIONS SHALL BE FOUNDED ON A FEDERATION OF FREE STATES"
Peoples, as states, like individuals, may be judged to injure one another merely by their coexistence in the state of nature (i.e., while independent of external laws). Each of them may and should for the sake of its own security demand that the others enter with it into a constitution similar to the civil constitution, for under such a constitution each can be secure in his right. This would be a league of nations, but it would not have to be a state consisting of nations. That would be contradictory, since a state implies the relation of a superior (legislating) to an inferior (obeying) i.e., the people, and many nations in one state would then constitute only one nation. This contradicts the presupposition, for here we have to weigh the rights of nations against each other so far as they are distinct states and not amalgamated into one.

When we see the attachment of savages to their lawless freedom, preferring ceaseless combat to subjection to a lawful constraint which they might establish, and thus preferring senseless freedom to rational freedom, we regard it with deep contempt as barbarity, rudeness, and a brutish degradation of humanity. Accordingly, one would think that civilized people (each united in a state) would hasten all the more to escape, the sooner the better, from such a depraved condition. But, instead, each state places its majesty (for it is absurd to speak of the majesty of the people) in being subject to no external juridical restraint, and the splendor of its sovereign consists in the fact that many thousands stand at his command to sacrifice themselves for something that does not concern them and without his needing to place himself in the least danger. The chief difference between European and American savages lies in the fact that many tribes of the latter have been eaten by their enemies, while the former know how to make better use of their conquered enemies than to dine off them; they know better how to use them to increase the number of their subjects and thus the quantity of instruments for even more extensive wars.

When we consider the perverseness of human nature which is nakedly revealed in the uncontrolled relations between nations (this perverseness being veiled in the state of civil law by the constraint exercised by government), we may well be astonished that the word "law" has not yet been banished from war politics as pedantic, and that no state has yet been bold enough to advocate this point of view. Up to the present, Hugo Grotius, Pufendorf, Vattel, and many other irritating comforters have been cited in justification of war, though their code, philosophically or diplomatically formulated, has not and cannot have the least legal force, because states as such do not stand under a common external power. There is no instance on record that a state has ever been moved to desist from its purpose because of arguments backed up by the testimony of such great men. But the homage which each state pays (at least in words) to the concept of law proves that there is slumbering in man an even greater moral disposition to become master of the evil principle in himself (which he cannot disclaim) and to hope for the same from others. Otherwise the word "law" would never be pronounced by states which wish to war upon one another; it would be used only ironically, as a Gallic prince interpreted it when he said, "It is the prerogative which nature has given the stronger that the weaker should obey him."

States do not plead their cause before a tribunal; war alone is their way of bringing suit. But by war and its favorable issue in victory, right is not decided, and though by treaty of peace this particular war is brought to an end, the state of war, of always finding a new pretext to hostilities, is not terminated. Nor can this be declared wrong, considering the fact that in this state each is the judge of his own case. Notwithstanding, the obligation which men in a lawless condition have under the natural law, and which requires them to abandon the state of nature, does not quite apply to states under the law of nations, for as states they already have an internal juridical constitution and have thus outgrown compulsion from others to submit to a more extended lawful constitution according to their ideas of right. This is true in spite of the fact that reason, from its throne of supreme moral legislating authority, absolutely condemns war as a legal recourse and makes a state of peace a direct duty, even though peace cannot be established or secured except by a compact among nations.

For these reasons there must be a league of a particular kind, which can be called a league of peace (*foedus pacificum*), and which would be distinguished from a treaty of peace (*pactum pacis*) by the fact that the latter terminates only one war, while the former seeks to make an end of all wars forever. This league does not tend to any dominion over the power of the state but only to the maintenance and security of the freedom of the state itself and of other states in league with it, without there being any need for them to submit to civil laws and their compulsion, as men in a state of nature must submit.

The practicability (objective reality) of this idea of federation, which should gradually spread to all states and thus lead to perpetual peace, can be proved. For if fortune directs that a powerful and enlightened people can make itself a republic, which by its nature must be inclined to perpetual peace, this gives a fulcrum to the federation with other states so that they may adhere to it and thus secure freedom under the idea of the law of nations. By more and more such associations, the federation may be gradually extended.

We may readily conceive that a people should say, "There ought to be no war among us, for we want to make ourselves into a state; that is, we want to establish a supreme legislative, executive, and judiciary power which will reconcile our differences peaceably." But when this state says, "There ought to be no war between myself and other states, even though I acknowledge no supreme legislative power by which our rights are mutually guaranteed," it is not at all clear on what I can base my confidence in my own rights unless it is the free federation, the surrogate of the civil social order, which reason necessarily associates with the concept of the law of nations—assuming that something is really meant by the latter.

The concept of a law of nations as a right to make war does not really mean anything, because it is then a law of deciding what is right by unilateral maxims through force and not by universally valid public laws which restrict the freedom of each one. The only conceivable meaning of such a law of nations might be that it serves men right who are so inclined that they should destroy each other and thus find perpetual peace in the vast grave that swallows both the atrocities and their perpetrators. For states in their relation to each other, there cannot be any reasonable way out of the lawless condition which entails only war except that they, like individual men, should give up their savage (lawless) freedom, adjust themselves to the constraints of public law, and thus establish a continuously growing state consisting of various nations (*civitas gentium*), which will ultimately include all the nations of the world. But under the idea of the law of nations they do not wish this, and reject in practice what is correct in theory. If all is not to be lost, there can be, then, in place of the positive idea of a world republic, only the negative surrogate of an alliance which averts war, endures, spreads, and holds back the stream of those hostile passions which tear the law though such an alliance is in constant peril of their breaking loose again. *Furor impius intus . . . fremit horridus ore cruento* (Virgil). . . .

First Supplement: Of the Guarantee for Perpetual Peace

The guarantee of perpetual peace is nothing less than that great artist, nature (*natura daedala rerum*). In her mechanical course we see that her aim is to produce a harmony among men, against their will and indeed through their discord. As a necessity working according to laws we do not know, we call it destiny. But considering its design in world history, we call it "providence," inasmuch as we discern in it the profound wisdom of a higher cause which predetermines the course of nature and directs it to the objective final end of the human race.

. . . Before we more narrowly define the guarantee which nature gives, it is necessary to examine the situation in which she has placed her actors on her vast stage, a situation which finally assures peace among them. Then we shall see how she accomplishes the latter. Her preparatory arrangements are:

1. In every region of the world she has made it possible for men to live.
2. By war she has driven them even into the most inhospitable regions in order to populate them.
3. By the same means, she has forced them into more or less lawful relations with each other. . . .

The first instrument of war among the animals which man learned to tame and to domesticate was the horse (for the elephant belongs to later times, to the luxury of already established states). The art of cultivating certain types of plants (grain) whose original characteristics we do not know, and the increase and improvement of fruits by transplantation and grafting (in Europe perhaps only the crab apple and the wild pear), could arise only under conditions prevailing in already established states where property was secure. Before this could take place, it was necessary that men who had first subsisted in anarchic freedom by hunting, fishing, and sheepherding should have been forced into an agricultural life. Then salt and iron were discovered. These were perhaps the first articles of commerce for the various peoples and were sought far and wide; in this way a peaceful traffic among nations was established, and thus understanding, conventions, and peaceable relations were established among the most distant peoples.

As nature saw to it that men *could* live everywhere in the world, she also despotically willed that they *should* do so, even against their inclination and without this *ought* being based on a concept of duty to which they were bound by a moral law. She chose war as the means to this end. So we see peoples whose common language shows that they have a common origin. For instance, the Samoyeds on the Arctic Ocean and a people with a similar language a thousand miles away in the Altaian Mountains are separated by a Mongolian people adept at horsemanship and hence at war; the latter drove the former into the most inhospitable arctic regions where they certainly would not have spread of their own accord. Again, it is the same with the Finns who in the most northerly part of Europe are called Lapps; Goths and Sarmatians have separated them from the Hungarians to whom they are related in language. What can have driven the Eskimos, a race entirely distinct form all others in America and perhaps descended from primeval European adventurers, so far into the North, or the Pescherais as far south as Tierra del Fuego, if it were not war which nature uses to populate the whole earth?

War itself requires no special motive but appears to be engrafted on human nature; it passes even for something noble, to which the love of glory impels men quite apart from any selfish urges. Thus among the American savages, just as much as among those of Europe during the age of chivalry, military valor is held to be of great worth in itself, not only during war (which is natural) but in order that there should be war. Often war is waged only in order to show valor; thus an inner dignity is ascribed to war itself, and even some philosophers have praised it as an ennoblement of humanity, forgetting the pronouncement of the Greek who said, "War is an evil inasmuch as it produces more wicked men than it takes away." So much for the measures nature takes to lead the human race, considered as a class of animals, to her own end.

Now we come to the question concerning that which is most essential in the design of perpetual peace: What has nature done with regard to this end which man's own reason makes his duty? That is, what has nature done to favor man's moral purpose, and how has she guaranteed (by compulsion but without prejudice to his freedom) that he shall do that which he ought to but does not do under the laws of freedom? This question refers to all three phases of public law, namely, civil law, the law of nations, and the law of citizenship. If I say of nature that she wills that this or that occur, I do not mean that she imposes a duty on us to do it, for this can be done only by free practical reason; rather I mean that she herself does it, whether we will or not (*fata volentem ducunt, nolentem trahunt*).

1. Even if a people were not forced by internal discord to submit to public laws, war would compel them to do so, for we have already seen that nature has placed each people near another which presses upon it, and against this it must form itself into a state in order to defend itself. Now the republican constitution is the only one entirely fitting to the rights of man. But it is the most difficult to establish and even harder to preserve, so that many say a republic would have to be a nation of angels, because men with their selfish inclinations are not capable of a constitution of such sublime form. But precisely with these inclinations nature comes to the aid of the general will established on reason, which is revered even though impotent in practice. Thus it is only a question of a good organization of the state (which does lie in man's power), whereby the powers of each selfish inclination are so arranged in opposition that one moderates or destroys the ruinous effect of the other. The consequence for reason is the same as if none of them existed, and man is forced to be a good citizen even if not a morally good person.

The problem of organizing a state, however hard it may seem, can be solved even for a race of devils, if only they are intelligent. The problem is: "Given a multitude of rational beings requiring universal laws for their preservation, but each of whom is secretly inclined to exempt himself from them, to establish a constitution in such a way that, although their private intentions conflict, they check each other, with the result that their public conduct is the same as if they had no such intentions."

A problem like this must be capable of solution; it does not require that we know how to attain the moral improvement of men but only that we should know the mechanism of nature in order to use it on men, organizing the conflict of the hostile intentions present in a people in such a way that they must compel themselves to submit to coercive laws. Thus a state of peace is established in which laws have force. We can see, even in actual states, which are far from perfectly organized, that in their foreign relations they approach that which the idea of right prescribes. This is so in spite of the fact that the intrinsic element of morality is certainly not the cause of it. (A good constitution is not to be expected from morality, but, conversely, a good moral condition of a people is to be expected only under a good constitution.) Instead of genuine morality, the mechanism of nature brings it to pass through selfish inclinations, which naturally conflict outwardly but which can be used by reason as a means for its own end, the sovereignty of law, and, as concerns the state, for promoting and securing internal and external peace.

This, then, is the truth of the matter: Nature inexorably wills that the right should finally triumph. What we neglect to do comes about by itself, though with great inconveniences to us. "If you bend the reed too much, you break it; and he who attempts too much attempts nothing" (Bouterwek).

2. The idea of international law presupposes the separate existence of many independent but neighboring states. Although this condition is itself a state of war (unless a federative union prevents the outbreak of hostilities), this is rationally preferable to the amalgamation of states under one superior power, as this would end in one universal monarchy, and laws always lose in vigor what government gains in extent; hence a soulless despotism falls into anarchy after stifling the seeds of the good. Nevertheless, every state, or its ruler, desires to establish lasting peace in this way, aspiring if possible to rule the whole world. But nature wills otherwise. She employs two means to separate peoples and to prevent them from mixing: differences of language and of religion. These differences involve a tendency to mutual hatred and pretexts for war, but the progress of civilization and men's gradual approach to greater harmony in their principles finally leads to peaceful agreement. This is not like that peace which despotism (in the burial ground of freedom) produces through a weakening of all powers; it is, on the contrary, produced and maintained by their equilibrium in liveliest competition.

3. Just as nature wisely separates nations, which the will of every state, sanctioned by the principles of international law, would gladly unite by artifice or force, nations which could not have secured themselves against violence and war by means of the law of world citizenship unite because of mutual interest. The spirit of commerce, which is incompatible with war, sooner or later gains the upper hand in every state. As the power of money is perhaps the most dependable of all the powers (means) included under the state power, states see themselves forced, without any moral urge, to promote

honorable peace and by mediation to prevent war wherever it threatens to break out. They do so exactly as if they stood in perpetual alliances, for great offensive alliances are in the nature of the case rare and even less often successful.

In this manner nature guarantees perpetual peace by the mechanism of human passions. Certainly she does not do so with sufficient certainty for us to predict the future in any theoretical sense, but adequately from a practical point of view, making it our duty to work toward this end, which is not just a chimerical one.

Society and Anarchy in International Relations[1]

HEDLEY BULL

I

Whereas men within each state are subject to a common government, sovereign states in their mutual relations are not. This anarchy it is possible to regard as the central fact of international life and the starting-point of theorizing about it.[2] A great deal of the most fruitful reflection about international life has been concerned with tracing the consequences in it of this absence of government. We can, indeed, give some account in these terms of what it is that distinguishes the international from the domestic field of politics, morals and law.

One persistent theme in the modern discussion of international relations has been that as a consequence of this anarchy states do not form together any kind of society; and that if they were to do so it could only be by subordinating themselves to a common authority. One of the chief intellectual supports of this doctrine is what may be called the domestic analogy, the argument from the experience of individual men in domestic society to the ex-

Hedley Bull, "Society and Anarchy in International Relations," in Herbert Butterfield and Martin Wight, eds., *Diplomatic Investigations: Essays in the Theory of International Politics* (Cambridge: Harvard University Press, 1968). Reprinted by permission of Allen & Unwin and International Thomson Publishing Services.

[1]A number of the leading ideas in this essay derive, in a process in which they may have lost their original shape, from Martin Wight; and a number of others from C. A. W. Manning.

[2]Anarchy: 'Absence of rule; disorder; confusion' (*O.E.D.*). The term here is used exclusively in the first of these senses. The question with which the essay is concerned is whether in the international context it is to be identified also with the second and the third.

perience of states, according to which the need of individual men to stand in awe of a common power in order to live in peace is a ground for holding that states must do the same. The conditions of an orderly social life, on this view, are the same among states as they are within them: they require that the institutions of domestic society be reproduced on a universal scale. . . .

The view that anarchy is incompatible with society among nations has been especially prominent in the years since the First World War. It was the First World War that gave currency to the doctrine of a 'fresh start' in international relations and set the habit of disparaging the past. Nineteenth century thought had regarded both the existence of international society and its further consolidation as entirely consistent with the continuation of international anarchy. The ideas of 1919 were in part a mere extension of the liberal, progressive strand of this nineteenth century anarchist view: the strengthening of international law, the creation of new procedures for arbitration, the establishment of permanent institutions for cooperation among sovereign states, a reduction and limitation of armaments, the pressure of public opinion, the aspiration that states should be popularly based and that their boundaries should coincide with the boundaries of nations. But there was now voiced also a view that is not to be found in Cobden or Gladstone or Mazzini: a rejection of international anarchy itself, expressed on the one hand in the view that the true value of the League and the United Nations lay not in themselves, but in their presumed final cause, a world government; and on the other hand in the endorsement of world government as an immediately valid objective, and a depreciation of the League and its successor as destined to 'failure' on account of their preservation of state sovereignty.

The twentieth century view of international anarchy is not, however, something new. Such a doctrine was stated at the outset of modern international history and has since found a succession of embodiments. The European system of sovereign states did not, of course, arise as a result of the outward growth and collision of hitherto isolated communities. Its origin lay in the disintegration of a single community: the waning on the one hand of central authorities, and on the other hand of local authorities, within Western Christendom, and the exclusion of both from particular territories by the princely power. Throughout its history modern European international society has been conscious of the memory of the theoretical imperium of Pope and Emperor and the actual imperium of Rome. When in the sixteenth and early seventeenth centuries the question was raised of the nature of relationships between sovereign princes and states, order and justice on a universal scale were readily associated with the idea of a universal state: not merely because the supremacy of the prince was observed to be a condition of order within the confines of the state, but also because order throughout Western Christendom as a whole was associated with the vanished authority of the Papacy and the Holy Roman Empire. The idea that international anarchy has as its consequence the absence of society among states, and the associated but opposite idea of the domestic analogy, became and have remained persistent doctrines about the international predicament.

The first of these doctrines describes international relations in terms of a Hobbesian state of nature, which is a state of war. Sovereign states, on this view, find themselves in a situation in which their behavior in relation to one another, although it may be circumscribed by considerations of prudence, is not limited by rules or law or morality. Either, as in the Machiavellian version of this doctrine, moral and legal rules are taken not to impinge on the sphere of action of the state: the political life and the moral life being presented as alternatives, as in the theory of quietism. Or, as in the Hegelian version, moral imperatives are thought to exist in international relations, but are believed to endorse the self-assertion of states in relation to one another, and to be incapable of imposing limits upon it. In this first doctrine the conditions of social life are asserted to be the same for states as they are for individuals. In the case of Hobbes, whose views we shall examine more closely, government is stated to be a necessary condition of social life among men, and the same is said to hold of sovereign princes. But the domestic analogy stops short at this point; it is not the view of Hobbes, or of other thinkers of this school, that a social contract of states that would bring the international anarchy to an end either should or can take place.

The second doctrine accepts the description of international relations embodied in the first, but combines with it the demand that the international anarchy be brought to an end. Where the domestic analogy is employed to buttress this doctrine, it is taken further, to embrace the concept of the social contract as well as that of the state of nature. This search for an alternative to international anarchy may be sustained by the memory of an alternative actually experienced, as in the backward-looking tradition of a return to Roman or to Western Christian unity. The other variety, the forward-looking tradition of which we may take Kant to be representative, finds its sustenance in the belief in human progress, in the possibility of achieving in the future what has not been achieved in the past.

Even as these two doctrines were taking shape there was asserted against them both the third possibility of a society of sovereign states; and along with it the beginnings of the idea that the conditions of order among states were different from what they were among individual men. Like the two doctrines against which it has been directed, this third doctrine consists in part of a description of what is taken to be the actual character of relations between states, and in part of a set of prescriptions. The description is one which sees sovereign states in intercourse with one another as consciously united together for certain purposes, which modify their conduct in relation to one another. The salient fact of international relations is taken to be not that of conflict among states within the international anarchy, as on the Hobbesian view; nor that of the transience of the international anarchy and the availability of materials with which to replace it, as on the Kantian view;

but co-operation among sovereign states in a society without government. The prescriptions which accompany this account of the nature of international relations enjoin respect for the legal and moral rules upon which the working of the international society depends. In place of the Hobbesian view that states are not limited by legal or moral rules in their relations with one another, and the Kantian view that the rules to which appeal may be had derive from the higher morality of a cosmopolitan society and enjoin the overthrow of international society, there are asserted the duties and right attaching to states as members of international society.

Two traditions, in particular, have advanced this third conception on an international society. One is the body of theory to which modern international law is the heir, which depicts states as constituting a society in the course of showing them to be bound of a system of legal rules: whether these rules are thought to derive from natural law or positive law, whether the subjects of the rules are taken to be states or the men who rule them, and whether the rules are regarded as universally valid or as binding only upon the states of Christendom or Europe. In the system of sixteenth century writers like Vitoria and Suarez, and of seventeenth century thinkers like Grotius and Pufendorf, the idea of the domestic analogy was still strong; the alternative notion of the uniqueness of international society was fully worked out only by the positivist international lawyers of the nineteenth century. The other tradition is that of the analysis of the political relations of states in terms of the system of balance of power. According to such analyses states throughout modern history have been engaged in the operation of a 'political system' or 'states-system', which makes its own demands upon their freedom of action and requires them in particular to act so as to maintain a balance of power as a product of policies consciously directed towards it, and in so far as they have asserted that states are obliged to act so as to maintain it, they must be taken also to embody the idea of international society and of rules binding upon its members. In the sixteenth and seventeenth centuries the predominant theories of the law of nations and of the balance of power were held by different groups of persons and in their respective content were largely antithetical. But in the eighteenth century the two streams converged, as in the writings of Vattel international law came to take account of the balance of power, and in the writings of Burke and later Gentz the political maxim enjoining the preservation of a balance of power came to be defined in a more legalistic way. In the nineteenth century the predominant doctrines moved close together: although it may still be doubted whether either theory can be reconciled to the other without sacrifice of an essential part of its content.

It is the validity of this third conception of an international society, either as a description of the past or as a guide for the present and the future, that is called in question by the doctrine that the international anarchy is, or has become, intolerable.

II

... The theorists of international society have been able to question the applicability to relations between states of each of the three elements in Hobbes' account of the state of nature. In the first place they have often remarked that sovereign states do not so exhaust their strength and invention in providing security against one another that industry and other refinements of living do not flourish. States do not as a rule invest resources in war and military preparations to such an extent that their economic fabric is ruined; even if it may be argued that the allocation of resources to war and armaments is not the best allocation from the point of view of economic development. On the contrary the armed forces of the state by providing security against external attack and internal disorder, establish the conditions under which economic improvement may take place within its borders. The absence of universal government and the fragmentation among sovereign states of responsibility for military security is not incompatible, moreover, with economic interdependence. The relative economic self-sufficiency of states as compared with individuals, has often been taken to explain why states are able to tolerate a looser form of social organization than that enjoyed by individuals within the modern state. At the same time, these theorists may point to the mutual advantages which states derive from economic relationships; and argue that trade, symbolic as it is of the existence of overlapping through different interests, is the activity most characteristic of international relationships as a whole.

As regards the second feature of the Hobbesian state of nature, the absence in it of notions of right and wrong, it is a matter of observation that this is not true of modern international relations. The theorist of international society has often begun his inquiries, as Grotius did, by remarking the extent to which states depart from rules of law and morality, and by uttering a protest against this situation in asserting the binding character of the rules. However, he has also been able to draw attention to the recognition of legal and moral rules by statesmen themselves, and to traditions of positive law and morality which have been a continuous feature of international life. International action which, although it is contrary to recognized principles of international law and morality, is accompanied by pretexts stated in terms of those principles, attests the force in international relations of notions of right and wrong, just as does action which conforms to them. By contrast, action which in addition to involving a violation of the legal and moral rules of international society is accompanied by no legal and moral pretext, action which, to use Grotius' terms, is 'not persuasive' as well as 'not justifiable', is widely taken by legal theorists to be quite uncharacteristic of the behavior of member states of modern international society (as well as to be hostile to its working in a way in which illegal behavior accompanied by a pretext is not).

The element in the Hobbesian state of nature which appears most clearly to apply to international relations is the third. It is the fact of war which appears to provide the chief evidence for the view that states do not form a society. On the one hand, if we take the modern state to illustrate the idea of a society, one of its salient features is that in it, apart from certain residual rights of self-defense, the private use of force is proscribed. But on the other hand, it cannot be denied that sovereign states in relation to one another are in a state of war, in Hobbes' sense that they are disposed to it over a period of time. It must be conceded also that this war is one of all against all. At any single moment in the history of the modern states-system, it is true, certain states will not be disposed to war against certain other states. That is to say, certain pairs of states will be pursuing common purposes and will be allied to one another; certain other pairs of states will be pursuing purposes which are different but do not cross, and will therefore treat one another with indifference; and certain pairs of states, although they have purposes which are conflicting, nevertheless share such a sense of community that (as now among the English-speaking states) war is not contemplated as a possible outcome of the conflict. But if we consider the states-system not at a single moment but in motion throughout the whole of its life (say, from 1648) then we shall find that every state that has survived the period has at some point or other been disposed to war with every other one.

The theorist of international society has sought to deal with this difficulty not by denying the ubiquity of war, but by questioning the relevance of the model of the modern state. If sovereign states are understood to form a society of a different sort from that constituted by the modern state—one, in particular, whose operation not merely tolerates certain private uses of force but actually requires them—then the fact of a disposition to war can no longer be regarded as evidence that international society does not exist. Theorists of the law of nations and of the system of balance of power have thus sought to show that war does not indicate the absence of international society, or its break-down, but can occur as a part of its functioning. Thus some international legal writers have seen in war a means by which the law of international society is enforced by individual members; others have seen in it a means of settling political conflicts. Theorists of the balance of power have seen war as the ultimate means by which threats to the international equilibrium are redressed. It may even be argued, in line with these theories, that the element in international relations of a 'war of all against all' so far from being detrimental to the working of international society, is in a certain sense positively favorable to it. For if the enforcement of law depends upon the willingness of particular law-abiding states to undertake war against particular law-breaking ones, then the prospects of law enforcement will be best if every state is willing to take up arms against any state that breaks the law. The fact that at any one time certain states are unwilling to contemplate war with certain other states, either because they are allied to them, or because they are indifferent to one another's policies, or because they are bound by a particular sense of community, is an obstacle to the enforcement of international law. In the same way the balance of power is best preserved if states are willing to take up arms against any state that threatens the balance, to focus their attention upon its recalcitrance in this respect and to disregard all special claims it may have on them.

If, then, we were tempted to compare international relations with a precontractual state of nature among individual men, it might be argued that we should choose not Hobbes' description of that condition, but Locke's. In the conception of a society without government, whose members must themselves judge and enforce the law, which is therefore crude and uncertain, we can recognize the international society of many thinkers in the tradition of international law. And although Locke's speculations about life of men in anarchy will leave us dissatisfied, we may turn to modern anthropological studies of actual societies of this kind, which have been forced to consider what, in the absence of explicit forms of government, could be held to constitute the political structure of a people.[3] Such studies widen our view of the devices for cohesion in a society, and suggest a number of parallels in the international field.

There are a number of these which are worth exploring. One which has received some attention from international lawyers is the principle of the 'hue and cry'. Another is the place of ritual. Another is the principle of loyalty—among kinsmen in primitive society, among allies in international society. International society and certain sorts of primitive society would seem also to be alike in respect of the function performed within them by the principle that might is right. This we are inclined to dismiss as the contrary of a moral principle, a mere way of saying that the question of right does not arise. This, indeed, is what, according to Thucydides, the Athenians said to the Melians: they did not appeal to the principle that might is right, but said that the question of right arose only when the parties were equal, which in this case they were not. Yet in international relations the parties are frequently not equal, and the society of states has had to evolve principles which will take account of this fact and lead to settlements. The rule that the will of the stronger party should be accepted provides a means of going directly to what the outcome of a violent struggle would be, without actually going through that struggle. To say that the principle that might is right fulfills a function in international society is not to provide a justification of it or to regard it as a necessary element in international life; but it is to argue that the working of a social order may be recognized even in a feature of rela-

---

[3]M. Fortes and E. E. Evans-Pritchard, *African Political Systems* (Oxford University Press, 1940), p. 6.

[4]On the functioning of the principle that might is right in primitive and in international society, see Ernest Gellner, 'How to Live in Anarchy', *The Listener*, April 3, 1958, pp. 579-83.

tions between states sometimes taken to demonstrate the absence of any kind of order.[4]

We must, however, at some point abandon the domestic analogy altogether. Not only is this because the attempt to understand something by means of analogies with something else is a sign of infancy in a subject, an indication of lack of familiarity with our own subject matter. But also because international society is unique, and owes its character to qualities that are peculiar to the situation of sovereign states, as well as to those it has in common with the lives of individuals in domestic society. One of the themes that has accompanied the statement of the idea of international society has been that anarchy among states is tolerable to a degree to which among individuals it is not. This has been recognized in some measure even by those who originated the description of international relations in terms of the Hobbesian state of nature.

In the first place, as we have noted, it is not consequent upon the international anarchy that in it there can be no industry or other refinements of living; unlike the individual in Hobbes' state of nature, the state does not find its energies so absorbed in the pursuit of security that the life of its activities is that of mere brutes. Hobbes himself recognizes this when having observed that persons of sovereign authority are in 'a posture of war', he goes on to say: 'But because they uphold thereby the industry of their subjects, there does not follow from it that misery which accompanies the liberty of particular men.'[5] The same sovereigns that find themselves in the state of nature in relation to one another have provided with particular territories, the conditions in which the refinements of life can flourish.

In the second place states have not been vulnerable to violent attack to the same degree that individuals are. Spinoza, echoing Hobbes in his assertion that 'two states are in the same relation to one another as two men in the condition of nature,' goes on to add 'with this exception, that a commonwealth can guard itself against being subjugated by another, as a man in the state of nature cannot do. For, of course, a man is overcome by sleep every day, is often afflicted by disease of body or mind, and is finally prostrated by old age; in addition, he is subject to other troubles against which a commonwealth can make itself secure.'[6] One human being in the state of nature cannot make himself secure against violent attack; and this attack carries with it the prospect of sudden death. Groups of human beings organized as states, however, may provide themselves with a means of defense that exists independently of the frailties of any one of them. And armed attack by one state upon another has not brought with it a prospect comparable to the killing of one individual by another. For one man's death may be brought about

[5]Hobbes, *Leviathan* (Everyman ed.), p. 65.
[6]Spinoza, *Tractatus Politicus*, ch. iii, para. 11, *The Political Works*, ed. A. G. Wernham (Clarendon Press, 1958), p. 295).

suddenly, in a single act; and once it has occurred, it cannot be undone. But war has only occasionally resulted in the physical extinction of the vanquished people. In modern history it has been possible to take Clausewitz's view that 'war is never absolute in its results' and that defeat in it may be merely 'a passing evil which can be remedied'. Moreover, war in the past, even if it could in principle lead to the physical extermination of one or both of the belligerent peoples, could not be thought capable of doing so at once in the course of a single act. Clausewitz, in holding that war does not consist of a single instantaneous blow, but always of a succession of separate actions, was drawing attention to something that in the past has always held true and has rendered public violence distinct from private. It is only in the context of recent military technology that it has become pertinent to ask whether war could not now both be 'absolute in its results' and 'take the form of a single, instantaneous blow,' in Clausewitz's understanding of these terms; and whether therefore violence does not now confront the state with the same sort of prospect it has always held for the individual.[7]

This second difference, that states have been less vulnerable to violent attack by one another than individual men, is reinforced by a third contingency of great importance; that in so far as states have been vulnerable in this sense they have not been equally so. Hobbes builds his account of the state of nature upon the proposition that 'Nature hath made men so equal, in the faculties of body and mind ... (that) the weakest has strength enough to kill the strongest.'[8] It is this equal vulnerability of every man to every other that, in Hobbes' view, renders the condition of anarchy intolerable. In modern international society, however, there has been a persistent distinction between Great Powers and small. Great Powers have been secure against the attacks of small Powers; and have had to fear only other Great Powers, and hostile combinations of Powers. We have only to think of the security enjoyed by Great Britain in the nineteenth century to appreciate that the insecurity which is a feature of the Hobbesian state of nature, in so far as it exists in international society, is not distributed equally among all its members. It is interesting to find Gentz writing of 'the European Commonwealth' that 'The original inequality of the parties in such a union as is here described is not an accidental circumstance, much less a casual evil; but is in a certain degree to be considered as the previous condition and foundation of the whole system.[9] A footnote follows: 'Had the surface of the globe been divided into equal parts, no such union would ever have taken place; and an eternal war of each against the whole is probably the only event we should

---

[7] I have deliberately excluded from this essay any consideration of how far recent military technology should lead us to alter the answers that have been given to these questions in the past.

[8] Hobbes, *op. cit.*, p. 63.

[9] Friedrich von Gentz, *Fragments upon the Balance of Power in Europe* (London, Peltier, 1806), p. 63.

have heard of.' If Great Powers are relatively safe from attack and do not stand in need of the protection of a central authority, then by the same token they are themselves in a position to attack others and to withstand the pressures which other states may seek to bring to bear upon them. If an even distribution of strength among states would seem unfavorable to the development of international society, it is also true that great discrepancies in strength may obstruct its working or even prove irreconcilable with it. One of the central contentions of theorists of the balance of power has been that if international society is to be maintained, no one state may be in a position to dominate the rest. Other writers have gone beyond this, to assert with Gentz himself, in a doctrine in which the principle of the balance of power becomes difficult to disentangle from that of collective security, 'That if that system is not merely to exist, but to be maintained without constant perils and violent concussions, each member which infringes it must be in a condition to be coerced, not only by the collective strength of the other members, but by any majority of them, if not by one individual.'[10] Ancillon, writing sixteen years later, saw the same principle at work in the early development in Italy of the principle of equilibrium: 'Le voisinage d'un grand nombre d'états, trop inégaux pour résister l'un à l'autre, y avait fait saisir, suivre et appliquer de bonne heure ces maximes de prudence qui servent de sauvegarde au droit, et qui allaient passer de ce petit théâtre sur un théâtre plus vaste.'[11]

A fourth point of contrast that has often been remarked is that states in their economic lives enjoy a degree of self-sufficiency beyond comparison with that of individual men. Thus while it has been one of the themes of theorists of international society to stress the mutual dependence of states in trade, at the same time their relative economic independence of one another, by contrast with individuals, has provided support for the argument that states are able to tolerate a form of society looser than that which is crowned by a government.

As against the Hobbesian view that states find themselves in a state of nature which is a state of war, it may be argued, therefore, that they constitute a society without a government. This society may be compared with the anarchical society among individual men of Locke's imagining, and also with primitive anarchical societies that have been studied by anthropologists. But although we may employ such analogies, we must in the end abandon them, for the fact that states form a society without a government reflects also the features of their situation that are unique. The working of international society must be understood in terms of its own, distinctive institutions. These include international law, diplomacy and the system of balance of power.

---

[10] *Ibid.*, p. 62.
[11] J. P. F. Ancillon, *Tableau des Révolutions du Système Politique de l'Europe, depuis la Fin du Quinzième Siècle* (Paris, Anselin et Pochard, 1823), vol. i, pp. 262-3.

There may be others which should be ranked alongside these; it is arguable, for example, that collaboration among the Great Powers to manage the affairs of international society as a whole and impart to them a degree of central direction—seen in operation in the series of conferences from Westphalia to Potsdam, and finding its most perfect embodiment in the Concert of Europe—also represents such an institution, even though it has functioned only intermittently.

III

The idea that sovereign states find themselves in a Hobbesian state of nature, as well as standing on its own as a description of what international politics is like, is also to be found linked to demands for the establishment of a universal state. In doctrines like that of Kant in *Perpetual Peace,* the Hobbesian domestic analogy is applied to international relations, but in this case taken further to embrace not only the idea of the state of nature but also that of the social contract.

The Kantian view of international relations involves a dilemma. If states are indeed in a Hobbesian state of nature, the contract by means of which they are to emerge from it cannot take place. For if covenants without the sword are but words, this will be true of covenants directed towards the establishment of universal government, just as it will hold true of agreements on other subjects. The difficulty with the Kantian position is that the description it contains of the actual condition of international relations, and the prescription it provides for its improvement, are inconsistent with one another. Action within the context of continuing international anarchy is held to be of no avail; but at the same time it is in the international anarchy that the grand solution of the international social contract is held to take place.

The advocate of a universal state can show his scheme to be feasible as well as desirable only by admitting that international relations do not resemble a Hobbesian state of nature; that in it covenants without the sword are more than words and the materials may be found with which to bring about collaboration between sovereign governments. But to make this admission is to weaken the case for bringing the international anarchy to an end. For the establishment of a universal government cannot then be regarded as a *sine qua non* of the world order. If a Hobbesian description of the international state of nature is abandoned for a Lockean one, then the case for a fundamental change is simply that which Locke presents for a contract of government: that to crown the anarchical society with a government would be to render it more efficient.

However, such a case might still be a quite formidable one. It may rest essentially on something which the Lockean description of international society itself admits: that in it the private use of force is tolerated or even in certain circumstances required. The international society described by the international lawyers and the theorists of balance of power is one in which war has a permanent and perhaps even a necessary place. The argument for proceeding from anarchy to government may therefore be stated, as Kant states it, in terms of the possibility and desirability of perpetual peace.

It is a facile view according to which a universal state would abolish war because war is a relationship between sovereign states and sovereign states would have been abolished. Either we may take war to mean any kind of organized violence between large groups of human beings, in which case the statement is false. Or we may understand the term in the narrow sense of a contention between sovereign states, in which case although the statement is true it is misleading. War in this latter sense comprises only one area of the spectrum of possible violence; if the elimination of war in this special sense of public war were to occasion the re-establishment of the various forms of private war, this could not necessarily be counted a gain.

If, however, a universal state should be understood as providing, just as does the system of sovereign states, a particular solution to the problem of the management of violence, rather than a means of transcending it, this is not to say that it is an inferior solution. It may be argued that the propensities for violence that are inherent in any form of political organization on a world-scale, will be better managed through the medium of a single authority entrusted with the legitimate exercise of force, than through many such authorities; just as this is the case in the smaller geographical context of the nation-state. Such an argument might well be sustained; yet the traditional arguments upholding international society against universal government would first have to be met.

These arguments have often rested on a preference for liberty in international relations over order or security: the liberty of states and nations from domination by a central power, and of individuals from the reach of a tyrannical government whose ubiquitous authority must deny them the right of foreign asylum. It may well be replied to this that order or security is the prime need of international society, and that liberty should if necessary be sacrificed to it. International anarchy, however, may be preferred on grounds of order also.

Government, involving as it does a legal monopoly of the use of force, provides a means for maintaining order; but it is also a source of dissension among conflicting groups in society, which compete for its control. If government authority, once it is captured, may be wielded so as to deny the resort to force by private individuals or groups, it is also the case that the existence of the governmental mechanism constitutes a prize in political conflict, which raises the stakes in such conflict to a level above that it would otherwise be. In the typical modern nation-state order is best preserved when conflict takes the form of a competition between the contending forces for control of a single government, rather than that of competition among governments. Yet the political community is also familiar in which the reverse is the case; in which the dangers to order arising from the coexistence of sovereign governments are less than those involved in the attempt to hold hostile communities in the framework of a single polity. The partition of India in 1947 had this *rationale*. It is possible also to view the problem of order in the world community in this way. Formidable though the classic dangers are of a plurality of sovereign states, these have to be reckoned against those inherent in the attempt to contain disparate communities within the framework of a single government. It is an entirely reasonable view of world order at the present time that it is best served by living with the former dangers rather than by attempting to face the latter.

Power and Interdependence

ROBERT O. KEOHANE AND JOSEPH S. NYE

For political realists, international politics, like all other politics, is a struggle for power but, unlike domestic politics, a struggle dominated by organized violence. In the words of the most influential postwar textbook, "All history shows that nations active in international politics are continuously preparing for, actively involved in, or recovering from organized violence in the form of war."[1] Three assumptions are integral to the realist vision. First, states as coherent units are the dominant actors in world politics. This is a double assumption: states are predominant; and they act as coherent units. Second, realists assume that force is a usable and effective instrument of policy. Other instruments may also be employed, but using or threatening force is the most effective means of wielding power. Third, partly because of their second assumption, realists assume a hierarchy of issues in world politics, headed by questions of military security: the "high politics" of military security dominates the "low politics" of economic and social affairs.

These realist assumptions define an ideal type of world politics. They allow us to imagine a world in which politics is continually characterized by active or potential conflict among states, with the use of force possible at any time. Each state attempts to defend its territory and interests from real or perceived threats. Political integration among states is slight and lasts only as long as it serves the national interests of the most powerful states. Transnational actors either do not exist or are politically unimportant. Only the

[1]Hans J. Morgenthau, *Politics Among Nations: The Struggle for Power and Peace*, 4th ed. (New York: Knopf, 1967), p. 36.

adept exercise of force or the threat of force permits states to survive, and only while statesmen succeed in adjusting their interests, as in a well-functioning balance of power, is the system stable.

Each of the realist assumptions can be challenged. If we challenge them all simultaneously, we can imagine a world in which actors other than states participate directly in world politics, in which a clear hierarchy of issues does not exist, and in which force is an ineffective instrument of policy. Under these conditions—which we call the characteristics of complex interdependence—one would expect world politics to be very different than under realist conditions. . . .

We do not argue, however, that complex interdependence faithfully reflects world political reality. Quite the contrary: both it and the realist portrait are ideal types. Most situations will fall somewhere between these two extremes. Sometimes, realist assumptions will be accurate, or largely accurate, but frequently complex interdependence will provide a better portrayal of reality. Before one decides what explanatory model to apply to a situation or problem, one will need to understand the degree to which realist or complex interdependence assumptions correspond to the situation.

The Characteristics of Complex Interdependence

Complex interdependence has three main characteristics:

1. *Multiple channels* connect societies, including: informal ties between governmental elites as well as formal foreign office arrangements; informal ties among non-governmental elites (face-to-face and through telecommunications); and transnational organizations (such as multinational banks or corporations). These channels can be summarized as interstate, trans-governmental, and transnational relations. *Interstate* relations are the normal channels assumed by realists. *Transgovernmental* applies when we relax the realist assumption that states act coherently as units; *transnational* applies when we relax the assumption that states are the only units.

2. The agenda of interstate relationships consists of multiple issues that are not arranged in a clear or consistent hierarchy. This *absence of hierarchy among issues* means, among other things, that military security does not consistently dominate the agenda. Many issues arise from what used to be considered domestic policy, and the distinction between domestic and foreign issues becomes blurred. These issues are considered in several government departments (not just foreign offices), and at several levels. Inadequate policy coordination on these issues involves significant costs. Different issues generate different coalitions, both within governments and across them, and involve different degrees of conflict. Politics does not stop at the waters' edge.

3. Military force is not used by governments toward other governments within the region, or on the issues, when complex interdependence prevails. It may, however, be important in these governments' relations with governments outside that region, or on other issues. Military force could, for instance, be irrelevant to resolving disagreements on economic issues among members of an alliance, yet at the same time be very important for that alliance's political and military relations with a rival bloc. For the former relationships this condition of complex interdependence would be met; for the latter, it would not. . . .

Minor Role of Military Force

Political scientists have traditionally emphasized the role of military force in international politics. . . . Force dominates other means of power: *if* there are no constraints on one's choice of instruments (a hypothetical situation that has only been approximated in the two world wars), the state with superior military force will prevail. If the security dilemma for all states were extremely acute, military force, supported by economic and other resources, would clearly be the dominant source of power. Survival is the primary goal of all states, and in the worst situations, force is ultimately necessary to guarantee survival. Thus military force is always a central component of national power.

Yet particularly among industrialized, pluralist countries, the perceived margin of safety has widened: fears of attack in general have declined, and fears of attack *by one another* are virtually nonexistent. France has abandoned the *tous azimuts* (defense in all directions) strategy that President de Gaulle advocated (it was not taken entirely seriously even at the time). Canada's last war plans for fighting the United States were abandoned half a century ago. Britain and Germany no longer feel threatened by each other. Intense relationships of mutual influence exist between these countries, but in most of them force is irrelevant or unimportant as an instrument of policy.

Moreover, force is often not an appropriate way of achieving other goals (such as economic and ecological welfare) that are becoming more important. It is not impossible to imagine dramatic conflict or revolutionary change in which the use or threat of military force over an economic issue or among advanced industrial countries might become plausible. Then realist assumptions would again be a reliable guide to events. But in most situations, the effects of military force are both costly and uncertain.[2]

Even when the direct use of force is barred among a group of countries, however, military power can still be used politically. Each superpower continues to use the threat of force to deter attacks by other superpowers on itself or its allies; its deterrence ability thus serves an indirect, protective role,

---

[2]For a valuable discussion, see Klaus Knorr, *The Power of Nations: The Political Economy of International Relations* (New York: Basic Books, 1975).

which it can use in bargaining on other issues with its allies. This bargaining tool is particularly important for the United States, whose allies are concerned about potential Soviet threats and which has fewer other means of influence over its allies than does the Soviet Union over its Eastern European partners. The United States has, accordingly, taken advantage of the Europeans' (particularly the Germans') desire for its protection and linked the issue of troop levels in Europe to trade and monetary negotiations. Thus, although the first-order effect of deterrent force is essentially negative—to deny effective offensive power to a superpower opponent—a state can use that force positively—to gain political influence.

Thus, even for countries whose relations approximate complex interdependence, two serious qualifications remain: (1) drastic social and political change could cause force again to become an important direct instrument of policy; and (2) even when elites' interests are complementary, a country that uses military force to protect another may have significant political influence over the other country.

In North-South relations, or relations among Third World countries, as well as in East-West relations, force is often important. Military power helps the Soviet Union to dominate Eastern Europe economically as well as politically. The threat of open or covert American military intervention has helped to limit revolutionary changes in the Caribbean, especially in Guatemala in 1954 and in the Dominican Republic in 1965. Secretary of State Kissinger, in January 1975, issued a veiled warning to members of the Organization of Petroleum Exporting Countries (OPEC) that the United States might use force against them "where there is some actual strangulation of the industrialized world."[3]

Even in these rather conflictual situations, however, the recourse to force seems less likely now than at most times during the century before 1945. The destructiveness of nuclear weapons makes any attack against a nuclear power dangerous. Nuclear weapons are mostly used as a deterrent. Threats of nuclear action against much weaker countries may occasionally be efficacious, but they are equally or more likely to solidify relations between one's adversaries. The limited usefulness of conventional force to control socially mobilized populations has been shown by the United States failure in Vietnam as well as by the rapid decline of colonialism in Africa. Furthermore, employing force on one issue against an independent state with which one has a variety of relationships is likely to rupture mutually profitable relations on other issues. In other words, the use of force often has costly effects on non-security goals. And finally, in Western democracies, popular opposition to prolonged military conflicts is very high.[4]

---

[3]*Business Week,* January 13, 1975.

[4]Stanley Hoffmann, "The Acceptability of Military Force," and Laurence Martin, "The Utility of Military Force," in *Force in Modern Societies: Its Place in International Politics* (Adelphi Paper, International Institute for Strategic Studies, 1973). See also Knorr, *The Power of Nations.*

It is clear that these constraints bear unequally on various countries, or on the same countries in different situations. Risks of nuclear escalation affect everyone, but domestic opinion is far less constraining for communist states, or for authoritarian regional powers, than for the United States, Europe, or Japan. Even authoritarian countries may be reluctant to use force to obtain economic objectives when such use might be ineffective and disrupt other relationships. Both the difficulty of controlling socially mobilized populations with foreign troops and the changing technology of weaponry may actually enhance the ability of certain countries, or nonstate groups, to use terrorism as a political weapon without effective fear of reprisal.

The fact that the changing role of force has uneven effects does not make the change less important, but it does make matters more complex. This complexity is compounded by differences in the usability of force among issue areas. When an issue arouses little interest or passion, force may be unthinkable. In such instances, complex interdependence may be a valuable concept for analyzing the political process. But if that issue becomes a matter of life and death—as some people thought oil might become—the use or threat of force could become decisive again. Realist assumptions would then be more relevant.

It is thus important to determine the applicability of realism or of complex interdependence to each situation. Without this determination further analysis is likely to be confused. Our purpose in developing an alternative to the realist description of world politics is to encourage a differentiated approach that distinguishes among dimensions and areas of world politics—not (as some modernist observers do) to replace one oversimplification with another.

The Political Processes of Complex Interdependence

Three main characteristics of complex interdependence give rise to distinctive political processes, which translate power resources into power as control of outcomes. As we argued earlier, something is usually lost or added in the translation. Under conditions of complex interdependence the translation will be different than under realist conditions, and our predictions about outcomes will need to be adjusted accordingly.

In the realist world, military security will be the dominant goal of states. It will even affect issues that are not directly involved with military power or territorial defense. Nonmilitary problems will not only be subordinated to military ones; they will be studied for their politico-military implications. Balance of payments issues, for instance, will be considered at least as much in the light of their implications for world power generally as for their purely financial ramifications. McGeorge Bundy conformed to realist expectations when he argued in 1964 that devaluation of the dollar should be seriously considered if necessary to fight the war in Vietnam.[5] To some extent, so did former Treasury Secretary Henry Fowler when he contended in 1971 that the United States needed a trade surplus of $4 billion to $6 billion in order to lead in Western defense.[6]

In a world of complex interdependence, however, one expects some officials, particularly at lower levels, to emphasize the *variety* of state goals that must be pursued. In the absence of a clear hierarchy of issues, goals will vary by issue, and may not be closely related. Each bureaucracy will pursue its own concerns; and although several agencies may reach compromises on issues that affect them all, they will find that a consistent pattern of policy is difficult to maintain. Moreover, transnational actors will introduce different goals into various groups of issues.

Linkage Strategies

Goals will therefore vary by issue area under complex interdependence, but so will the distribution of power and the typical political processes. Traditional analysis focuses on *the* international system, and leads us to anticipate similar political processes on a variety of issues. Militarily and economically strong states will dominate a variety of organizations and a variety of issues, by linking their own policies on some issues to other states' policies on other issues. By using their overall dominance to prevail on their weak issues, the strongest states will, in the traditional model, ensure a congruence between the overall structure of military and economic power and the pattern of outcomes on any one issue area. Thus world politics can be treated as a seamless web.

Under complex interdependence, such congruence is less likely to occur. As military force is devalued, militarily strong states will find it more difficult to use their overall dominance to control outcomes on issues in which they are weak. And since the distribution of power resources in trade, shipping, or oil, for example, may be quite different, patterns of outcomes and distinctive political processes are likely to vary from one set of issues to another. If force were readily applicable, and military security were the highest foreign policy goals, these variations in the issue structures of power would not matter very much. The linkages drawn from them to military issues would ensure consistent dominance by the overall strongest states. But when military force is largely immobilized, strong states will find that linkage is less effec-

[5]Henry Brandon, *The Retreat of American Power* (New York: Doubleday, 1974), p. 218.
[6]*International Implications of the New Economic Policy*, U.S. Congress, House of Representatives, Committee on Foreign Affairs, Subcommittee on Foreign Economic Policy, Hearings, September 16, 1971.

tive. They may still attempt such links, but in the absence of a hierarchy of issues, their success will be problematic.

Dominant states may try to secure much the same result by using overall economic power to affect results on other issues. If only economic objectives are at stake, they may succeed: money, after all, is fungible. But economic objectives have political implications, and economic linkage by the strong is limited by domestic, transnational, and transgovernmental actors who resist having their interests traded off. Furthermore, the international actors may be different on different issues, and the international organizations in which negotiations take place are often quite separate. Thus it is difficult, for example, to imagine a militarily or economically strong state linking concessions on monetary policy to reciprocal concessions in oceans policy. On the other hand, poor weak states are not similarly inhibited from linking unrelated issues, partly because their domestic interests are less complex. Linkage of unrelated issues is often a means of extracting concessions or side payments from rich and powerful states. And unlike powerful states whose instrument for linkage (military force) is often too costly to use, the linkage instrument used by poor, weak states—international organization—is available and inexpensive.

Thus as the utility of force declines, and as issues become more equal in importance, the distribution of power within each issue will become more important. If linkages become less effective on the whole, outcomes of political bargaining will increasingly vary by issue area.

The differentiation among issue areas in complex interdependence means that linkages among issues will become more problematic and will tend to reduce rather than reinforce international hierarchy. Linkage strategies, and defense against them, will pose critical strategic choices for states. Should issues be considered separately or as a package? If linkages are to be drawn, which issues should be linked, and on which of the linked issues should concessions be made? How far can one push a linkage before it becomes counterproductive? For instance, should one seek formal agreements or informal, but less politically sensitive, understandings? The fact that world politics under complex interdependence is not a seamless web leads us to expect that efforts to stitch seams together advantageously, as reflected in linkage strategies, will, very often, determine the shape of the fabric.

The negligible role of force leads us to expect states to rely more on other instruments in order to wield power. For the reasons we have already discussed, less vulnerable states will try to use asymmetrical interdependence in particular groups of issues as a source of power; they will also try to use international organizations and transnational actors and flows. States will approach economic interdependence in terms of power as well as its effects on citizens' welfare, although welfare considerations will limit their attempts to maximize power. Most economic and ecological interdependence involves the possibility of joint gains, or joint losses. Mutual awareness of potential gains and losses and the danger of worsening each actor's position through overly rigorous struggles over the distribution of the gains can limit the use of asymmetrical interdependence.

Agenda Setting

Our second assumption of complex interdependence, the lack of clear hierarchy among multiple issues, leads us to expect that the politics of agenda formation and control will become more important. Traditional analyses lead statesmen to focus on politico-military issues and to pay little attention to the broader politics of agenda formation. Statesmen assume that the agenda will be set by shifts in the balance of power, actual or anticipated, and by perceived threats to the security of states. Other issues will only be very important when they seem to affect security and military power. In these cases, agendas will be influenced strongly by considerations of the overall balance of power.

Yet, today, some nonmilitary issues are emphasized in interstate relations at one time, whereas others of seemingly equal importance are neglected or quietly handled at a technical level. International monetary politics, problems of commodity terms of trade, oil, food, and multinational corporations have all been important during the last decade; but not all have been high on interstate agendas throughout that period.

Traditional analysts of international politics have paid little attention to agenda formation: to how issues come to receive sustained attention by high officials. The traditional orientation toward military and security affairs implies that the crucial problems of foreign policy are imposed on states by the actions or threats of other states. These are high politics as opposed to the low politics of economic affairs. Yet, as the complexity of actors and issues in world politics increases, the utility of force declines and the line between domestic policy and foreign policy becomes blurred: as the conditions of complex interdependence are more closely approximated, the politics of agenda formation becomes more subtle and differentiated.

The Changed Premises of European Security

RICHARD H. ULLMAN

The Declining Value of Territory

The traditional functions of military power have been three: to seize territory, to hold it, and to defend territories and regimes against the depredations of others. Perhaps the most important change that has affected international politics in the course of the twentieth century is the steady diminution in the utility of military power for all but the third of these functions . . .

Because military power has traditionally been so closely linked with territory, the diminution in the utility of military power in the late twentieth century is due in large measure to the fact that, in much of the world, territory—land as such—has lost the paramount importance it once had.

That importance stemmed from a number of factors. One, of course, is the relationship between territory and living space. As the citizens of Hong Kong or Singapore can attest, there are, ultimately, upper limits to the number of persons who can dwell in a given geographic space. Neither city-state has yet reached those limits, but there surely must be days in which the sheer press of persons leads residents to worry that the limits are near. Hong Kong and Singapore are scarcely typical, however. Even in densely populated countries like Japan or Germany, no serious argument can be made, now or in the foreseeable future, about the shortage of living space. That is because nearly all their population now lives in cities or suburbs and works in offices

Richard H. Ullman, *Securing Europe* (Princeton: Princeton University Press, 1991), a Twentieth Century Fund Book; selections from chapters 2 and 4, pp. 23–25, 40–42, 63–79. Copyright 1991 by the Twentieth Century Fund.

or factories rather than on the land. In all the advanced industrialized countries there are, in fact, large expanses of open land on which new conurbations could be built.

A second reason why territory has been valued is for the defensive utility of natural barriers—mountains, rivers, marshes, forests, and the like—or simply of vast amounts of space as such. The armies of Napoleon and Hitler discovered the value for the defense of Russia of sheer territorial extent. Such physical characteristics—particularly natural barriers, which slow or channel attacking forces—are still of some importance. But the range, accuracy, load-carrying capability, and destructive power of modern weapons have made them much less so.

A third reason for valuing land as such is for the resources that lie beneath the surface. The twentieth century has seen two trends that have substantially diminished that importance, however. One is the large value added by industrial processing as compared with the actual market prices of nearly all mineral resources. Japan is the quintessential example of a resource-poor nation that has grown rich on the value a highly educated, industrious population has added to the materials it imports. The second trend is the relative ease with which substitutes for most natural resources can now be found. The low relative value and the easy substitutability of those resources is a source of enormous distress to Third World states whose economies depend upon their production. It is also the reason why nearly all scenarios depicting resource wars are so inherently implausible.

The principal exception, of course, is petroleum, where satisfactory substitutes are not available at competitive prices, the value added by processing is not so large, and the geographic location of the largest reserves is relatively concentrated. Yet it is only a partial exception. During the oil shocks of the 1970s, analysts put forward scenarios involving competitive big power intervention to seize the oil fields of the Middle East. All the scenarios, however, posited seizure of the oil fields by external powers, either the Soviet Union or the West, not by states within the region. None of them ever seemed fully plausible: the predicted costs of interventions by outside powers always exceeded the putative benefits.

That would-be aggressors from within the region might apply a different calculus was demonstrated by Iraq's forcible seizure of Kuwait in August 1990. President Saddam Hussein was evidently counting on a combination of fear of Iraq's formidably large army and resentment of oil-rich, family-run mini-states like Kuwait to secure the Arab world's acquiescence in his instant fait accompli. It was not his first effort to seize neighboring territory. In 1980 he attacked Iran in order to acquire the border waterway known as the Shatt al-Arab, and with it more secure access to the sea for Iraq. In doing so he unleashed an eight-year war. But the Shatt al-Arab was a sparsely populated tract whose ownership was disputed between the two states. Kuwait, a fully functioning (if territorially small) state, was an altogether different matter. This instance may be the exception that makes the rule, however: the very strong international reaction to Saddam's action will surely be a deterrent against similar invasions in the future.

A fourth reason for valuing land is for the living that can be made from farming its surface. Until the present century, the vast majority of mankind lived on and worked the land for the subsistence it could provide. The right to extract produce from a tiny tract of land, passed on from generation to generation, was the crucial factor in the histories of countless millions of families in every region of the globe. Today, in many parts of the world, that pattern continues almost unchanged. In other regions, however, it has changed beyond recognition. In the industrialized countries there is still a living to be earned from the land, but the number of persons engaged in doing so is a small fraction—in the technologically most advanced countries, a very small fraction—of the total population. . . .

Softening the Impact of the Security Dilemma

. . . A primary function of a new security regime in Europe will be to continue the process of removing from the continent the weight of the security dilemma. So long as the international system contains separate states capable of projecting force beyond their borders, other states will have at least a theoretical reason to worry about that capability. Among Western European states, despite the formidable military power that some currently wield, any such worries have since the late 1940s been at most only theoretical. Despite heavy historical legacies such as the longstanding Franco-German antagonism, the use of force between France and the Federal Republic became inconceivable. Similarly, it strains the imagination to put forward plausible scenarios involving the use of force between France and a reunified German state. Liberal democratic states, as Michael Doyle has so convincingly argued, may pick fights with authoritarian states, but they do not make war on one another.

Therefore, central to any scenario positing violent conflict between Germany and its democratic neighbors would surely be the atrophy of democratic politics in Germany and their replacement by the institutional structures of an authoritarian state. Anything is possible in political life, but such a transformation is scarcely likely. The forces for democracy in the Federal Republic are very strong. If anything, they will be augmented by the wholehearted East German embrace of democratic institutions. In the present and foreseeable European political context, characterized by the wholesale rejection of totalitarianism, a German flight from democracy would be, to say the least, ahistorical.

The Premises of a New European Security Regime

Three premises supply the foundation for a new security regime in Europe. First is that there is now less perceived conflict of interest among the major European states than has been the case since the beginning of the modern state system nearly half a millennium ago. This does not mean that European states will not come into conflict with one another. Conflicts will certainly occur, especially when, as is likely to be the case for some time in much of Eastern Europe, economic distress is widespread. Rather, it means that the major powers—if not all of the minor ones—will not see their relations in zero-sum terms. Their conflicts, when they occur, will not escalate across the threshold into violence. Instead, they will be channeled toward peaceful solutions.

The second premise is the obverse of the first. There exists among European states today a stronger impetus than ever before to seek security through cooperation. That is because of an acute and widespread awareness of both the devastation and the unprofitability of war. The enormous power of modern weapons, even non-nuclear ones, would make any European war one of unparalleled destruction. And there seems to be a steadily growing realization among all the major European governments that, now and for the foreseeable future, they face no problems that they might be able to solve by using military force to expand the extent of their political control. This new willingness to seek cooperative solutions means that states can now be freed from much of the burden of military preparedness that until now they have taken for granted as a necessary concomitant of independence. Instead, they will be able to arrive at agreed limitations on military forces that will provide greater security at much lower costs.

The third premise is an extension of the second. European states will rest their security upon cooperative relationships with others, yet they will be more able than ever before to detect efforts by others to subvert or evade those regimes of cooperation. That is because modern technology is increasingly making transparent what has traditionally been opaque. Ronald Reagan made a slogan of the admonition, "Trust but verify." His point was valid, however. Contemporary sensing technologies make it possible for relatively affluent European states, such as Britain, France, or Germany, to follow the former president's advice by placing in space reconnaissance satellites, like those already deployed by the United States and the Soviet Union, to monitor military forces worldwide. In that respect they could, if they wished to expend the resources, be substantially self-reliant.

It may well be, however, that they will choose instead to join with other European states, and with the two superpowers as well, in forming a multinational monitoring and verification agency whose function it would be to assure all that no one of them is preparing to launch a surprise attack. Such an agency might be a central part of a new institutional structure for the organization of European security. It is to this new structure—the so-called architecture of European security—that this analysis will now turn.

Building on CSCE and the WEU

... The end of the conflict between the Soviet Union and the West makes the division of Europe into military blocs not only purposeless but potentially harmful: it perpetuates adversarial images and behavior, and it impedes the processes by which what was once a deeply divided continent can be knit together to form a political whole. The case for the creation of a new European Security Organization, linking together the members and former members of both alliances, is therefore both clear and compelling.

The conceptual bases for such an organization are already present in the form and functions of two existing institutions, the Conference on Security and Cooperation in Europe (CSCE) and the Western European Union. Those who would seek to set up a new pan-European security organization should draw selectively upon the architecture and the experience of both. CSCE continues to be more a conference than an organization. It has convened in both general and specialized sessions at frequent intervals since 1973, meetings that have given rise to agreements of considerable importance on issues of principle or of practice, such as the inviolability of state frontiers, confidence- and security-building measures, human rights, economic cooperations, and environmental safeguards. As important as the concrete agreements themselves has been the so-called CSCE process, which has repeatedly brought together representatives of thirty-five states (now reduced to thirty-four by German unification) to discuss past compliance and to agree on new standards by which to measure future action. The two North American members of NATO, the United States and Canada, are full participants in CSCE, as is the Soviet Union.[1] Membership in a new European Security Organization of the two superpowers, if not of Canada, would be essential. It seems certain, however, that all current NATO and WTO members would wish to take part. So would many, if not all, CSCE members from the neutral and nonaligned bloc.

From the outset, decision making in CSCE has been by consensus. That, also, is what is meant by the "CSCE process." On more than one occasion, to the distress of the majority, individual states have withheld their assent to a given measure until they have received a concession on another. Until its November 1990 summit meeting in Paris, CSCE had no executive capability nor any continuity between conference sessions. As the chairman of the U.S.

---

[1]For an informative analysis of CSCE's accomplishments and of its place in U.S.-Soviet and interbloc diplomacy, see Karl E. Birnbaum and Ingo Peters, "The CSCE: A Reassessment of its Role in the 1980s," *Review of International Studies*, Vol. 16, No. 4, October 1990, pp. 305-19.

House Foreign Affairs Committee approvingly put it, CSCE "has never had a headquarters or a staff, or even a mailing address.[2] But the Paris meeting established a small CSCE secretariat located in Prague, a Center for the Prevention of Conflict in Vienna, and an election-monitoring office in Warsaw. And there were suggestions that the task of monitoring compliance with the treaty on conventional force reductions in Europe (CFE), also signed at the Paris summit, be turned over to CSCE, to which a powerful verification agency would report.[3]

Whenever CSCE is suggested as the possible foundation stone of a new European security order, critics immediately point to its requirement of unanimity for all its decisions as a reason for declaring the model impossible. In that respect it would indeed be. The WEU, by contrast, offers a model of a very different sort. The Brussels Treaty and its supplementary protocols would require remarkably few changes to become the charter of a European Security Organization (ESO). As the previous chapter explained, because the WEU was originally intended to be a nondiscriminatory watchdog over West German rearmament, it was endowed by its creators with quite sweeping powers—which it has never used—over the composition and deployment of the military forces of all of its member-states. For example, WEU's charter conferred upon its Agency for the Control of Armaments an absolute right to make its inspections. Any veto by a member government would have been impermissible under the WEU's rules, and it should be equally impermissible in a new pan-European security organization. Because the WEU proved from its outset to be so intimate and clubby in its workings, it is often forgotten that its constitution provides for limited supranationality. That is another reason why the WEU is an apposite model for the ESO. On most issues, WEU decisions require simple or weighted majorities of the organization's members, not unanimity. Indeed, the only WEU decisions requiring unanimity are those connected with the relaxation of its stringencies: the release of any member-state from the agreed-upon force ceilings and of the FRG from its additional commitments not to acquire nuclear, biological, or chemical weapons.

One function of the WEU—the function for which it was in fact established—is arms control. Another is collective security. On this issue the Brussels Treaty mandates very far-reaching commitments. Indeed, the collective-security obligation it imposes on members is total. It permits no wobbling. If any signatory state "should be the object of an armed attack in Europe," the treaty states, the others "will . . . afford the Party so attacked all the military and other aid and assistance in their power." There is no room

---

[2]Dante B. Fascell, "The CSCE: Properly Homeless," *International Herald Tribune,* September 28, 1990. "The secret of the organization's success," Fascell continued, "has been precisely that there has been no bureaucracy to which the real decision-makers in the capitals of the CSCE countries . . . could delegate their responsibility or authority."

[3]*New York Times,* November 22, 1990, p. 1.

left for national discretion, such as the NATO treaty's provision that, in responding to an attack, each ally should take "such action as it deems necessary."

This commitment by WEU members may be impressively obligatory, but it is—inevitably—also only declaratory. A spiraling crisis might reveal that even the most fervent declarations of solidarity are merely expressions of wishful thinking. By contrast, the NATO treaty's weaker formulation is made more solid and might in practice have been more difficult for governments to disavow because of the existence of the alliance's integrated military organization. Hypothetically, at least, by the time a government had made the decision to opt out, its NATO forces might already have been committed to combat by SACEUR. Such an eventuality is indeed hypothetical: the reality now—and this is an issue to which I will return—is that the political conditions that have transformed the problem of security in Europe may also make it impossible, and perhaps even undesirable, to maintain for long an integrated military organization such as NATO's.

If one were to rely on the historical record of generalized commitments to collective security, one could not be hopeful regarding the prospects of a European Security Organization based upon the model of the WEU. The security organizations that have been most successful have been alliances directed (in rare instances explicitly, usually tacitly) against a specified state not itself a member of the alliance. But it is arguable that the conditions now emerging in Europe make the past a poor predictor.

As has been seen in earlier chapters, a central characteristic of the emerging configuration of international politics in Europe is that no major state has revisionist ambitions that its leaders think they could satisfy by sending troops across borders. In particular, neither the Soviet nor the German government will face problems whose solution it will perceive as likely to come from the external use of military force. A genuine congruence of interests and goals sharply distinguishes the present from previous eras and makes it possible to contemplate a security organization that incorporates within its membership all the European states.

This transformation of European politics means that it is unlikely that the great powers will soon find their commitment to collective security put to the test of a large, searing, and escalating crisis.[4] They should have reason to be thankful for that window of opportunity. For the less dangerous circumstances that are likely to prevail will make it much easier for them to put into place the other aspects of a WEU-like pan European security regime. These would include substantial reductions in the military forces wielded by the major members of a European Security Organization and the arming, training, and deploying of those forces in ways that minimize their abilities to

---

[4]Iraq's invasion of Kuwait was not such a crisis. It was geographically "out of area" and did not directly involve any of the members of a potential ESO.

conduct offensive operations in Europe. And they will provide valuable time for governments and publics to develop confidence in the institution that would be crucially necessary for the security regime's success, the monitoring and verifying organization that would be the ESO's equivalent of the WEU's Agency for the Control of Armaments. . . .

Collective Security and Collective Confidence

Like members of the WEU, members of an ESO would commit themselves to come to each other's defense. Logically, such a commitment should be unbounded, but reasonably it could not extend beyond Europe with anything resembling automaticity. The United States (or Sweden) could plausibly be depended upon to support a Germany attacked by the Soviet Union. It is more difficult to imagine Europeans (or Americans) defending a Soviet Union attacked by China. The United Nations or perhaps an (eventual) Asian security organization would be a more appropriate forum than the ESO for handling such a conflict. Similarly, Japan would look to its alliance with the United States for whatever assurance it needs against the threat of a Soviet attack. The U.S.-Japan mutual security treaty is, and should continue to be, a central feature of Asia's security architecture. . . .

In Europe, an important role for an ESO would be in walling off and damping conflicts among or within smaller states—for example, an outbreak of warfare between Hungary and Romania or Greece and Turkey, or between two Yugoslav republics. Here a paradox arises: The principal members of a post-NATO ESO might well unite forcibly to oppose expansionist aggression by a recidivist Soviet Union. But their response to war between two small powers would probably be limited to the extension of good offices for damping the conflict—for example, through an agency like the CSCE conflict-prevention center, although at the outset, at least, it will have more limited duties.[5] In the instance of flagrant aggression, they might apply economic pressure such as trade sanctions or even a freeze of the aggressor's assets. But more would be unlikely.

In other words, if a conflict or crisis involved large powers, other states would feel much more impelled to respond assertively than if the antagonists were relatively weak and if their dispute appeared to endanger no one but themselves. In the latter instance, for other states to risk the lives of their own citizens in attempting to impose a settlement would put too severe a strain on their own domestic politics. NATO or the Warsaw Treaty Organization would have been most unlikely to do more if two lesser members of either alliance had come to blows, as Greece and Turkey almost did on more

---

[5]The functions that will initially be assigned to the conflict-prevention center will be confined to the monitoring and verification of agreed-upon confidence- and security-building measures. (*The Economist*, November 24, 1990, p. 53.)

than one occasion. Why should anyone expect more from a new organization that combines the former members of both?

Among academic analysts and practitioners as well—at least those in both groups who regard themselves as "realists"—the notion of collective security is currently in bad repute, evoking the image of an impotent League of Nations whose members were unable to agree on collective action to resist aggression in the 1930s. But critics should blame the governments of the era, not the design of the League as an institution. At the core of any effective collective security organization, it should be remembered, is not its formal charter or its voting mechanism but agreement upon what constitutes danger and a shared willingness to use military power to resist a major attempt to challenge the status quo. That consensus, so obviously lacking in the 1930s, was present in 1950 when North Korea invaded South Korea and in 1990 when Iraq invaded Kuwait. In both instances the United Nations Security Council happened to be unanimous, and the governments seeking to organize resistance to the invasions had their hands strengthened. But the majorities in favor of action were so strong in any case that had a veto intervened, they would have proceeded to act regardless. . . .

The new order would depend upon continued confidence. Once confidence began to erode—once inspectors observed behavior for which they did not receive satisfactory explanations—the process of coalescing against the potentially offending state would begin to take the place of confidence. Indeed, the likelihood of the coalescence of effective opposition by the other members of an ESO could never be absent from the calculations of planners in Moscow (or any other capital) contemplating aggression. Along with the nuclear weapons that would continue to remain under American, British, and French control, that prospect would provide considerable deterrence.

Because deterrence would no longer stem from a tightly integrated military organization, this may seem a prescription for anxiety. It is not, and for reasons that have already been seen: politics are likely to reinforce, rather than undermine, a regime of confidence-building measures. The example of the WEU is the limiting case. So rapidly and completely was the Federal Republic integrated into Western Europe that the formidable array of WEU controls over its military forces soon ceased to have a raison d'etre. The inspection mechanisms of an ESO would need to be even more intrusive than the WEU's as originally agreed. Unlike those of the WEU, however, they would be unlikely to atrophy for lack of work. But it is not naive optimism to suggest that, at least so far as the great powers are concerned, they would have a fairly tranquil existence.

European states already have more than a decade and a half of experience of confidence-building measures (now formally referred to as "confidence- and security-building measures," or CSBMs) across the East-West fault line. As applied in Europe thus far they are restraints on peacetime military operations designed to reduce the possibility of a potential aggressor being able successfully to launch a surprise attack. They have been one of the principal results of the CSCE process. As stipulated in the first CSCE agreement, the Helsinki accords of 1975, these CSBMs began with the requirement that state give advance notice of the large-scale movement of military forces and that they permit observers at maneuvers. A series of follow-on agreements have made the requirements both more extensive and more rigorous, with compliance subject to on-site challenge verification, so that all but quite minor movements of military forces now require advance notification, and there has developed an expectation not only of a high degree of transparency but of substantial cooperation among military forces to assure it. Thus, as one summary account puts it, no CSCE state can mobilize for war and stay within the terms of the agreements; "unpredicted movements automatically [constitute] evidence of bad faith" and thus warn of the possibility of imminent danger.[6]

Alongside the CSCE regime of CSBMs has grown a parallel process that began with the 1987 treaty between the United States and the Soviet Union, providing for the elimination of their intermediate- and shorter-range nuclear forces and mandating deeply intrusive measures to monitor compliance with the treaty and to give each side confidence that the other is not making clandestine efforts to violate it. The 1990 conventional forces treaty (CFE) carried these measures a stage further, and the U.S.-Soviet agreement reducing their long-range nuclear forces (the product of the so-called START talks) will strengthen the verification regime even more. Thus the CSCE member-states, especially the two superpowers, are now thoroughly at home with the previously revolutionary notion that one of the normal roles of a military organization is providing verifiable assurances to others that it is not marshalling forces for a surprise attack, nor even acquiring the capabilities that would make such an attack possible.

The purpose of an Agency for the Control of Armaments within a European Security Organization would be much the same as that of the prototype agency within the WEU. Its inspectors—drawn, as in the WEU, from all the member-states—would monitor the members' military forces along a number of dimensions: locations of units, frequency and scope of exercises, numbers of personnel, numbers and types of major weapons systems, and the like.[7]

The ACA, of course, would not establish national figures for maximum force levels. That would be an issue for negotiation by governments. A pre-

---

[6]Ian M. Cuthbertson and David Robertson, *Enhancing European Security* (New York: St. Martin's, for the Institute for East-West Security Studies, 1990), pp. 193-94. For a wide-ranging discussion of CSBMs, see the collection of essays in R. B. Byers, F. Stephen Larrabee, and Allen Lynch, eds., *Confidence-Building Measures and International Security* (New York: Institute for East-West Security Studies, 1987).

[7]The duties of the ESO's ACA would necessarily be more extensive than those of the WEU prototype. That is because "with respect to forces and depots under NATO authority"—and that meant all FRG forces—the protocol creating the WEU agency formally devolved its monitoring tasks upon NATO inspectors, whose reports would in turn be supplied to the WEU Council. (*American Foreign Policy 1950-1955*, Vol. 2, p. 986).

requisite for agreement on force levels would be agreement regarding the purposes for which they retained military forces. At a rhetorical level that would never have been difficult. No matter when the question was asked, all the governments with a stake in European security would have claimed—not disingenuously—that the purpose of their own military forces was deterrence and defense. Until now, however, their actual force structures would have belied that claim. Both alliances had substantial offensive capabilities. Both subscribed to military doctrines asserting, in essence, that only the ability to carry a war deep into the territory of a potential aggressor would deter aggression.

That was also a prescription for an endless arms race, as states attempted (in the case of the West) to use technology as a means to overcome personnel deficits or (in the East) to keep from falling even further behind, if not to catch up. The way out of this competitive spiral is not simply through quantitative arms control of the kind represented by the Washington Naval agreement or the START and CFE agreements. Quantitative limits are indeed necessary: large imbalances may be destabilizing in a crisis and, in any case, are politically unacceptable. But quantitative limits are in themselves not sufficient. To be most effective, they should be accompanied by changes in military doctrine to emphasize defensive rather than offensive strategies.

Much has been written during the last few years about "nonoffensive defense." The concept has attracted strong advocates ranging from a number of former military officers to political leaders like Mikhail Gorbachev. Applied to the conditions prevailing in Europe it involves such measures as large reductions in numbers of ground-attack aircraft or of heavy armored vehicles (e.g., tanks and large self-propelled guns) and an emphasis on light antitank weapons; zones near borders where some types of weapons, such as armored attack vehicles, are altogether prohibited and other military forces are present in substantially reduced numbers; limits on stored supplies of munitions, fuel, and other military consumables, so as to curtail the ability of highly mechanized, high-firepower forces to fight prolonged campaigns; construction of physical barriers against attacks; strategies such as the one dubbed "spider in the web," in which attacking forces (themselves first reduced by quantitative arms control) are allowed to penetrate defenders' territory before becoming ensnared and then destroyed; restrictions on the content of training manuals, published operational concepts, and training routines so as to drill forces in defensive rather than offensive operations; and so forth.[8]

---

[8]For an excellent, brief treatment of these issues, see John Grin, "Eliminating Offensive Capabilities: Exploring Multilateral Mechanisms Beyond Arms Reductions," in John Grin and Henny J. van der Graaf, eds., *Unconventional Approaches to Conventional Arms Control Verification* (New York: St. Martin's, 1990), pp. 72-92. For a comprehensive treatment, see Studiengruppe Alternative Sicherheitspolitik (Hrsg.), *Vertrauensbildende Verteidigung: Reform deutscher Sicherheitspolitik* (Gerlingen, FRG: Bleicher, 1989). For a sympathetic but critical review of the latter by a former West German minister of defense, see Rupert Scholz, "Alternative Verteidigung? Die Strategie der 'Spinne im Netz,'" *Europäische Wehrkunde*, November 1989, pp. 643-46.

The idea of nonoffensive defense has also given rise to skeptical criticism from specialists who argue that nearly any weapon can be used offensively as well as defensively, that the Soviet Union would be able to evade the accompanying quantitative restrictions and launch a sudden, devastating attack, or that the Soviet political leadership does not exert sufficient control over the military leaders so as really to follow through on a meaningful (as distinct from rhetorical) change in doctrine. Moreover, as one Hungarian analyst writes, "It is very difficult to maintain a counteroffensive capability that is sufficient for destroying the forces of the possible aggressor without threatening an unprovoked attack.[9] But the skeptical comments for the most part antedated the profound political changes of 1989-90 that seem certain to lead to the drastic reduction, if not the elimination, of any Soviet military presence beyond the borders of the USSR itself. There will now be a vast buffer zone between the Soviet Union and Germany that, especially when accompanied by changes in force composition to deemphasize heavy armored vehicles, should considerably increase Western confidence in the practicability of agreed doctrinal shifts toward nonoffensive defense.

Properly employed, however, such a buffer zone—perhaps even augmented with physical barriers—should be the most effective confidence-building measure of all. That would obviously be the case for Western nations, who for four decades stood nose-to-nose with powerful Soviet forces at the inter-German border. But a buffer zone in Eastern Europe should be equally reassuring for the Soviet Union. Moscow will no longer have open-ended commitments to maintain in power unpopular client governments. And, because of the transparency of the security regime, it will know that nowhere within the region are there forces gathering that might suddenly jeopardize Soviet security.

From NATO to ESO

"We need to arrive at an all-European security system in a few years, through some transitional steps," the chief of the international department of the Soviet Communist Party Central Committee, Valentin M. Falin, told an interviewer in April 1990 before Moscow had agreed that a unified Germany might be a member of NATO. At that point the Soviets were contemplating that "for a certain time" the western part of Germany might remain in NATO and its eastern part in the Warsaw Pact. But Germany's most important role would be to act as "a motor to help to extract the best out of these two organizations and then meld them into an all-European security structure."[10]

---

[9]Pal Dunay, *Military Doctrine: Change in the East?* (New York: Institute for East-West Security Studies, 1990), p. 45.
[10]*New York Times,* April 11, 1990, p. A1.

Yet, as Edward Mortimer observed, the Soviet leaders would surely have agreed with Foreign Minister Jiri Dienstbier of the Czech and Slovak Federal Republic, who on a visit to London at about the same time noted: "There's nothing wrong with NATO except that we don't belong to it.[11] Indeed, it is difficult to escape the conclusion that it is only the name and the connotations it carries that prevent the Soviet Union and its Warsaw Pact partners from formally applying to join NATO. That is what Gorbachev and Shevardnadze seem to have had in mind when they urged the formation of "a qualitatively new security system in Europe to be achieved through a consistent transformation of the existing military-political alliances."[12]

That "new security system" would be NATO transformed. The final declaration of the July 1990 NATO summit conference promised that the alliance would "reach out to the countries of the East which were our adversaries in the cold war, and extend to them the hand of friendship."[13] But the division of Europe will have been fully overcome only when NATO evolves into something like the European Security Organization whose nature and purposes have been explored here, an organization that includes within its membership the Soviet Union and the other members of the Warsaw Pact. That evolution will scarcely occur overnight. It should occur only when it seems to entail no increase in risk for those states that have long looked to NATO to guarantee their security. Therefore, although it is much too early even to speculate about a date for the completion of the process, the transformation of NATO into the ESO should nevertheless be made an explicit goal of NATO policy, and member governments should take it seriously as such....[14]

NATO has not always been assiduous in its insistence that member-states adhere to the democratic values the alliance proclaims. Portugal under Salazar, Greece under the colonels, and Turkey under a number of governments could not have passed the democratic test. But NATO's principal members have always been able to do so, and in recent years, especially as the threat from the East has visibly diminished, it has been taken for granted that the practices of NATO members must without exception conform to those of liberal democracy. Only democratic polities would have the openness that is the precondition of confidence. Only democracies share a commitment both

---

[11]Edward Mortimer in "Creating a New Alliance," *Financial Times,* April 17, 1990, p. 19.

[12]From Shevardnadze's news conference statement on April 6, 1990, following the conclusion of his talks in Washington, *New York Times,* April 7, 1990, p. 6. See his "Towards a Greater Europe—the Warsaw Treaty Organization and NATO in a Renewing Europe," *NATO's Sixteen Nations,* Vol. 35, No. 3, June 1990, pp. 16–19.

[13]The text of the declaration, issued in London on July 6, 1990, is in *New York Times,* July 7, 1990, p. 5.

[14]For a Soviet proposal along similar lines, see Major General A. I. Vladimorov and Colonel S. A. Posokhov, "Obscheevropeiskii Soyuz Bezopasnosti" (All-European Union for Security), *Mezhdunarodnaya Zhizn,* No. 6, 1990, pp. 78-80.

domestically and internationally to the rule of law and to the peaceful settlement of disputes. It would be neither hypocritical nor ideologically imperialistic to make genuine adherence to democratic values and forms a condition for membership in a new European Security Organization.

That, of course, is scarcely an insignificant criterion. Not all of the current participants in CSCE could clearly meet it; Bulgaria, Romania, and the Soviet Union itself are still far from fully functioning democracies, and Turkish governments sometimes still deal arbitrarily and roughly with their opponents. A striking change, however, is that the governments in all these states seem genuinely committed to democratization. Nevertheless, severe economic hardships in the years that lie ahead could lead these and other states to revert to more authoritarian rule. Such an occurrence, once they had become members of an ESO, would be grounds for their suspension, just as the Council of Europe forced Greece to withdraw in 1969 because of human rights violations by its military government and came close to doing the same with Turkey in 1981. (The council readmitted Greece when civilian rule was restored in 1974.) By far the most important of these states is the Soviet Union. That is why the formation of an ESO must wait until the USSR, or at least Russia and some of its other core republics, seem unquestionably democratic. The ESO could afford the exclusion of one or more of the other states in Central or Eastern Europe, but without the full participation of the Soviet Union, Europe's greatest military power, it would lack the bedrock of confidence necessary to make an all-European security organization viable.

If a democratic USSR were to revert to anything like the repressive government it has had in the past, it would present other members of an ESO with a real dilemma. Exclusion from "Europe" might merely further isolate the regime and therefore make it more repressive. On the other hand, it might affect the internal debate and move the regime in desirable directions. Regardless, if a government in Moscow began to turn its back on openness, other states would inevitably place it on probation. If their suspicions were confirmed, they would begin to take measures to insure themselves against any renewed military threat. Such measures would include consultation, coordination of military planning, and perhaps augmentation of armaments. In such a manner, with warning bells sounding, would a collective security system begin to function.

Any organizational structure runs a risk of unraveling. The question is whether Europe would be more secure with the Soviet Union in or out of an organization for common security. The argument in these pages is that European security would be more firmly assured by bringing the USSR in, and counting on inclusion to help the process of entrenching democracy there, than by keeping the Soviets out.

These are momentous questions. For NATO members, transition to the ESO would almost certainly mean the end of the alliance's integrated military organization that has been built up and honed for so many years. In one sense that would be a profound change, but in another much less so. I have already noted that in the environment of much lower force levels that would follow from successful arms control (not merely one but two or more rounds of conventional force negotiations) and from general movement away from a strategy based upon forward defense, an integrated alliance command would no long be so necessary militarily. In its place might be put a set of carefully meshed bilateral (or, conceivably, multilateral) agreements that would provide, for example, for the continued presence of the forces of some member-states on the territory of others. That continuity would, in particular, ease security concerns that the Germans might feel.

The European Security Organization that would emerge could be an umbrella covering a variety of institutional arrangements. At one level—that of the entire membership—there would be a generalized commitment to collective security. Each member-state would commit itself not to use force against any other, and to come to the aid of any other if it is the victim of an armed attack. Similarly, all members of the ESO would participate in the arms control arrangements that would be one of its principal functions. Force-level ceilings would be generally negotiated and agreed. Monitoring and verification would be the responsibility of a corps of inspectors drawn from all the member-states, acting under the instructions of the ESO's governing body.

At the same time, however, there might be special relationships among particular states. These might arise from regional groupings. Thus, the United Kingdom, France, Italy, the Benelux countries, and Germany—the original WEU partners—might enter into agreements to coordinate closely their defense programs, including stationing some forces in each other's territory. So might the Scandinavian states. It is difficult, however, to imagine the Soviet union taking part in any such cluster, or others wishing to do so with it. History and the USSR's sheer size would make that unlikely. Moscow's former Central European partners, perhaps with the addition of Austria, might instead form a regional grouping of their own. Among its purposes might be coordinating the construction of physical defensive obstacles, or making arrangements for destroying bridges or blocking tunnels that could be implemented at the approach of invading forces from any direction. There might also be a regional grouping of Balkan states.

Yet another architectural configuration might revive the idea, now four decades old, of a European Defense Community with a single command structure and a single multinational force, this time perhaps integrated down to a level that would make brigades, rather than divisions, the basic building blocks. Such a new defense community, composed perhaps of the West European core of the EC (the original seven members of the WEU), might result from the further intensification of the processes of political integration within the existing European Community following the implementation of the Single European Act in 1992. Its participation in the ESO might be more like that of a single entity than that of a collection of separate sovereign states. Thus, while NATO in its present form could not readily be absorbed into the ESO because it would seem too much like an anti-Soviet alliance, something like this reborn EDC might be. Such an evolution would be a natural concomitant of the increasing integration of the EC that is likely to take place over the course of the 1990s.

PART 4

Economics: Interests and Interdependence

Liberal economic theory opposes mercantilism, imperialism, fascism, and Marxism in arguing that war should be obsolete, not just because it is evil, but because it profits no one. Mercantilists and imperialists throughout history have believed that nations' wealth and prosperity increase with their control of territory, and that war is the main way to gain or keep territory. Marxists saw violent conflict as the natural and inevitable result of conflicting economic interests. In the Soviet Union, Marxism joined with nationalism and fostered the most serious attempt, apart from fascism, to become a viable autarky—a state that is economically self-sufficient.

Unabashed mercantilism no longer exists as a serious philosophical challenge to liberal economics or as an overt political movement. To varying degrees, though, it comes alive in other forms of economic nationalism, and may even be gaining in effective influence.[1] Marxism, until recently a quite potent challenge to international liberalism and a serious contender for wave of the future, is nearly defunct. Excerpts from Lenin's theory of imperialism are included here,

---

[1]See Robert Gilpin with the assistance of Jean M. Gilpin, *The Political Economy of International Relations* (Princeton: Princeton University Press, 1987), and James Kurth, "The Pacific Basin versus the Atlantic Alliance: Two Paradigms of International Relations," *Annals of the American Academy of Political and Social Sciences* 505 (September 1989).

nevertheless, because it represents a major school of thought in the evolution of ideas on the subject, and makes a specific argument about why the dynamics of capitalism actually push governments toward war and conquest in an effort to control foreign markets, instead of toward peaceful trade. Nonliberal interpretations could become more interesting again if current problems in the world economy and conversion of formerly Communist states become overwhelming. It is far from inconceivable that bitter disillusionment with attempts to move to liberal capitalism could promote a Marxist revival (it is certainly no more unlikely than the end of the Cold War seemed a few years before it happened).

Still, the liberal theory of political economy is dominant among Western elites. It holds that free trade in open markets yields the most efficient production and exchange of goods, and ultimately makes everyone wealthier than if governments interfere with commerce. Trade based on specialization and comparative advantage promotes efficient growth and interdependence among nations, which in turn gives them all a stake in each other's security and prosperity. Control of territory does not matter, because it does not create wealth, which is generated only by production and exchange. Interdependence makes war counterproductive and wasteful for all, not only because it destroys property, but because it deranges the international market and distorts global economic efficiency.

If peace is the path to profit, greed should discourage war rather than promote it. In this respect, liberal theory does not see itself as idealistic, relying on noble motives to suppress war. Just like realism, mercantilism, or Marxism, this theory focuses on material interest as the driving force, but sees the interest in a different way. Norman Angell summarizes this view in the selection included here, from one of the most popular tracts of the pre-World War I period.[2] If this logic is valid, the persistence of war after the arrival of industrial capitalism can only be irrational. What would account for such irrationality?

Joseph Schumpeter provides a sociological explanation, attributing militarist policies to cultural atavism, the continuing sway of feudal elites and their values in societies where capitalism had displaced them. Another source of irrationality, in terms of liberal theory, would be the nationalist ideologies of interwar fascism which promoted autarky and conquest for the direct economic exploitation of subjugated populations. The rationales behind this alternative are discussed in Alan Milward's piece below. The renewed appeal of liberal theories that tout the pacifying effect of international economic interdependence is not surprising, since the challenge of fascism and feudal militarism are even further gone than Marxism.

Realism, however, is not as far gone, and it offers different explanations for the failure of capitalism to prevent war. Some of these criticisms are noted in the

---

[2]Angell has often been pilloried by realists for having foolishly said that commercial interdependence made war impossible. He maintained that he never said that, and had argued only that war would be irrational. See Angell's post-World War I revision, *The Great Illusion, 1933* (New York: G. P. Putnam's Sons, 1933), pp. 267-270, and *After All: The Autobiography of Norman Angell* (New York: Farrar, Straus and Young, 1951), pp. 143-161.

pieces by Blainey and Waltz. Blainey argues that enthusiasts for the view that free trade, cultural exchange, and better communication foster peace confused cause and effect when these phenomena coincided in the nineteenth century. Most notably, Waltz argues that interdependence actually fosters conflict rather than amity, because nations fear dependence and seek to overcome it. He cites data indicating that the level of interdependence among the great powers is actually lower in the contemporary world than it was in the earlier part of the century, and considers it a good thing. Richard Rosecrance then argues that the specific type of interdependence is what matters, and the type that naturally fosters cooperation and peace has risen substantially in recent times.

The Great Illusion

NORMAN ANGELL

What are the fundamental motives that explain the present rivalry of armaments in Europe, notably the Anglo-German? Each nation pleads the need for defense; but this implies that someone is likely to attack, and has therefore a presumed interest in so doing. What are the motives which each State thus fears its neighbors may obey?

They are based on the universal assumption that a nation, in order to find outlets for expanding population and increasing industry, or simply to ensure the best conditions possible for its people, is necessarily pushed to territorial expansion and the exercise of political force against others (German naval competition is assumed to be the expression of the growing need of an expanding population for a larger place in the world, a need which will find a realization in the conquest of English Colonies or trade, unless these are defended); it is assumed, therefore, that a nation's relative prosperity is broadly determined by its political power; that nations being competing units, advantage, in the last resort, goes to the possessor of preponderant military force, the weaker going to the wall, as in the other forms of the struggle for life.

The author challenges this whole doctrine. He attempts to show that it belongs to a stage of development out of which we have passed; that the commerce and industry of a people no longer depend upon the expansion of its political frontiers; that a nation's political and economic frontiers do not now necessarily coincide; that military power is socially and economically futile, and can have no relation to the prosperity of the people exercising it; that it is impossible for one nation to seize by force the wealth or trade of another—to enrich itself by subjugating, or imposing its will by force on an-

Norman Angell, *The Great Illusion: A Study of the Relation of Military Power to National Advantage*, 4th edition (New York: Putnam's, 1913), Synopsis.

other; that, in short, war, even when victorious, can no longer achieve those aims for which peoples strive.

He establishes this apparent paradox, in so far as the economic problem is concerned, by showing that wealth in the economically civilized world is founded upon credit and commercial contract (these being the outgrowth of an economic interdependence due to the increasing division of labor and greatly developed communication). If credit and commercial contract are tampered with in an attempt at confiscation, the credit-dependent wealth is undermined, and its collapse involves that of the conqueror; so that if conquest is not to be self-injurious it must respect the enemy's property, in which case it becomes economically futile. Thus the wealth of conquered territory remains in the hands of the population of such territory. When Germany annexed Alsatia, no individual German secured a single mark's worth of Alsatian property as the spoils of war. Conquest in the modern world is a process of multiplying by x, and then obtaining the original figure by dividing by x. For a modern nation to add to its territory no more adds to the wealth of the people of such nation than it would add to the wealth of Londoners if the City of London were to annex the county of Hertford.

The author also shows that international finance has become so interdependent and so interwoven with trade and industry that the intangibility of an enemy's property extends to his trade. It results that political and military power can in reality do nothing for trade; the individual merchants and manufacturers of small nations, exercising no such power, compete successfully with those of the great. Swiss and Belgian merchants drive English from the British Colonial market; Norway has, relatively to population, a greater mercantile marine than Great Britain; the public credit (as a rough-and-ready indication, among others, of security and wealth) of small States possessing no political power often stands higher than that of the Great Powers of Europe, Belgian Three per Cents. standing at 96, and German at 82; Norwegian Three and a Half per Cents. at 102, and Russian Three and a Half per Cents. at 81.

The forces which have brought about the economic futility of military power have also rendered it futile as a means of enforcing a nation's moral ideals or imposing social institutions upon a conquered people. Germany could not turn Canada or Australia into German colonies—i. e., stamp out their language, law, literature, traditions, etc.—by "capturing" them. The necessary security in their material possessions enjoyed by the inhabitants of such conquered provinces, quick intercommunication by a cheap press, widely-read literature, enable even small communities to become articulate and effectively to defend their special social or moral possessions, even when military conquest has been complete. The fight for ideals can no longer take the form of fight between nations, because the lines of division on moral questions are within the nations themselves and intersect the political frontiers. There is no modern State which is completely Catholic or Protestant, or liberal or autocratic, or aristocratic or democratic, or socialist or individualist; the moral and spiritual struggles of the modern world go on between citizens of the same State in unconscious intellectual co-operation with corresponding groups in other States, not between the public powers of rival States.

This classification by strata involves necessarily a redirection of human pugnacity, based rather on the rivalry of classes and interests than on State divisions. War has no longer the justification that it makes for the survival of the fittest; it involves the survival of the less fit. The idea that the struggle between nations is a part of the evolutionary law of man's advance involves a profound misreading of the biological analogy.

The warlike nations do not inherit the earth; they represent the decaying human element. The diminishing role of physical force in all spheres of human activity carries with it profound psychological modifications.

These tendencies, mainly the outcome of purely modern conditions (e. g. rapidity of communication), have rendered the problems of modern international politics profoundly and essentially different from the ancient; yet our ideas are still dominated by the principles and axioms, images and terminology of the bygone days.

The author urges that these little-recognized facts may be utilized for the solution of the armament difficulty on at present untried lines—by such modification of opinion in Europe that much of the present motive to aggression will cease to be operative, and by thus diminishing the risk of attack, diminishing to the same extent the need for defense. He shows how such a political reformation is within the scope of practical politics, and the methods which should be employed to bring it about.

Paradise Is a Bazaar

GEOFFREY BLAINEY

The mystery of why the nineteenth century enjoyed unusually long eras of peace did not puzzle some powerful minds. They believed that intellectual and commercial progress were soothing those human misunderstandings and grievances which had caused many earlier wars. The followers of this theory were usually democrats with an optimistic view of human nature. Though they had emerged earlier in France than in England they became most influential in the English-speaking world and their spiritual home was perhaps the industrial city of Manchester, which exported cotton goods and the philosophy of free trade to every corner of the globe.

Manchester's disciples believed that paradise was an international bazaar.[1] They favored the international flow of goods and ideas and the creation of institutions that channeled that flow and the abolition of institutions that blocked it. Nations, they argued, now grew richer through commerce than through conquest. Their welfare was now enhanced by rational discussion rather than by threats. The fortresses of peace were those institutions and inventions which promoted the exchange of ideas and commodities: parliaments, international conferences, the popular press, compulsory education, the public reading room, the penny postage stamp, railways, submarine telegraphs, three funnelled ocean liners, and the Manchester cotton exchange.

The long peace that followed the Battle of Waterloo was increasingly explained as the result of the international flow of commodities and ideas. 'It is something more than an accident which has turned the attention of mankind to international questions of every description in the same age that

Geoffrey Blainey, *The Causes of War,* 3rd edition (New York: Free Press, 1988), Chapter 2. Reprinted with the permission of the Free Press, a Division of Macmillan, Inc. Copyright © 1973, 1977, 1988 by Geoffrey Blainey.

[1]The Manchester creed: in selecting this name my main reasons were Manchester's reputation as a symbol of free trade and the popularity of the creed among free-trade economists.

established freedom of commerce in the most enlightened nations.'[2] So wrote one of the early biographers of Richard Cobden, merchant of Manchester and citizen of the world. Variations of the same idea were shared by Sir Robert Peel, William Gladstone, John Stuart Mill, scores of economists and poets and men of letters, and by England's Prince Consort, Albert the Good. His sponsorship of the Great Exhibition in the new Crystal Palace in London in 1851 popularised the idea that a festival of peace and trade fair were synonymous. The Crystal Palace was perhaps the world's first peace festival.

In that palace of glass and iron the locomotives and telegraphic equipment were admired not only as mechanical wonders; they were also messengers of peace and instruments of unity. The telegraph cable laid across the English Channel in 1850 had been welcomed as an underwater cord of friendship. The splicing of the cable that snaked beneath the Atlantic in 1858 was another celebration of brotherhood, and the first message tapped across the seabed was a proclamation of peace: 'Europe and America are united by telegraphic communication. Glory to God in the Highest, On Earth Peace, Goodwill towards Men.'[3] That cable of peace was soon snapped, and so was unable to convey the news in the following year that France and Austria were at war, or the news in 1861 that the United States was split by war.

Henry Thomas Buckle was one of many influential prophets of the idea that telegraphs and railways and steamships were powerfully promoting peace. Buckle was a wealthy young London bachelor who in the 1850s studied beneath the skylight of his great London library, writing in powerful prose a vast survey of the influences which, to his mind, were civilising Europe. A brilliant chess player who had competed with Europe's champions at the palace of peace, Buckle thought human affairs obeyed rules that were almost as clear cut as the rules of chess; and those rules permeated his writings. The first volume of the *History of Civilisation in England* appeared in 1857, the second volume in 1861, and they were devoured by thousands of English readers, published in French, Spanish, German, Hungarian and Hebrew editions, and translated four times into Russian.[4]

One of Buckle's themes was the decline of the warlike spirit in western Europe. As a freethinker he attributed that decline not to moral influences but to the progress of knowledge and intellectual activity. The invention of gunpowder had made soldiering the specialist activity of the few rather than the occasional activity of the many, thereby releasing talent for peaceful pursuits. Similarly Adam Smith's *The Wealth of Nations,* 'probably the most important book that has ever been written',[5] had perceived and popularised

[2]'It is something': Apjohn, p. 234.
[3]The Atlantic telegraph: Cruikshank, p. 72.
[4]Buckle's career: *D.N.B.*, III 208-11.
[5]Praise of Adam Smith: Buckle, I, 214.

the idea that a nation gained most when its commercial policy enriched rather than impoverished its neighbours: free trade had replaced war and aggressive mercantilism as the road to commercial prosperity. Buckle argued that the new commercial spirit was making nations depend on one another whereas the old spirit had made them fight one another.

Just as commerce now linked nations, so the steamship and railway linked peoples: 'the greater the contact', argued Buckle, 'the greater the respect'. Frenchmen and Englishmen had curbed their national prejudices because they had done more than railways and steamships to increase their friendship. As he affirmed in his clear rolling prose: 'every new railroad which is laid down, and every fresh steamer which crosses the Channel, are additional guarantees for the preservation of that long and unbroken peace which, during forty years, has knit together the fortunes and the interests of the two most civilised nations of the earth'.[6] Buckle thought foreign travel was the greatest of all educations as well as a spur to peace; and it was while he was travelling near Damascus in 1862 that he caught the typhoid fever which ended his life.

Many readers must have thought that the outbreak of the Crimean War rather dinted Buckle's argument that the warlike spirit was declining in Europe. Buckle was composing that chapter of his book when war was raging in the Crimea, and he foresaw the criticism and met it head on:

> For the peculiarity of the great contest in which we are engaged is, that it was produced, not by the conflicting interests of civilised countries, but by a rupture between Russia and Turkey, the two most barbarous monarchies now remaining in Europe. This is a very significant fact. It is highly characteristic of the actual condition of society, that a peace of unexampled length should have been broken, not, as former peaces were broken, by a quarrel between two civilised nations, but by the encroachments of the uncivilised Russians on the still more uncivilised Turks.[7]

Buckle still had to explain why France and England, his heroes of civilisation, had exultantly joined in the barbarians' war. He explained that simply; the departure of their armies to the distant Crimea was a sign of their civilisation. France and England, he wrote, 'have drawn the sword, not for selfish purposes, but to protect the civilised world against the incursions of a barbarous foe'.

The shattering civil war which began in the United States in the last year of Buckle's life should have been a blow to his theory. On the contrary it seems to have heartened his supporters. They interpreted that war as another crusade against barbarism and the barbaric practice of slavery. At the end of that four-years' war Professor J. E. Cairnes, an Irish economist, wrote

[6]'Every new railroad': ibid., p. 223.
[7]'For the peculiarity of the great contest'; ibid., p. 195.
[8]'All the leading currents': Cairnes, p. 123.

a powerful article reaffirming the idea that 'all the leading currents of modern civilisation' were running steadily in the direction of peace.[8] He thought that the way in which the North craved the sympathy of foreign nations during the war was a sign of the increasing force of public opinion in international affairs. He believed that the enlightened public opinion was coming mainly from the expansion of free commerce, the railways and steamships, and the study of modern languages. Henry Thomas Buckle would have sympathized with the emphasis on modern languages; he spoke nineteen.

The idea that ignorance and misunderstanding were the seeds of war inspired the hope that an international language would nourish peace—so long as the chosen language was purged of nationalism. In 1880 a south German priest, J. M. Schleyer, published a neutral language of his own manufacture and called it Volapük. It spread with the speed of rumour to almost every civilised land, claiming one million students within a decade. To Paris in 1889 came the delegates of 283 Volapük societies, and even the waiters at the dining tables of the congress could translate the following manifesto into Volapük:

> I love all my fellow-creatures of the whole world, especially those cultivated ones who believe in Volapük as one of the greatest means of nation-binding.[9]

The rival nation-binding language of Esperanto was then two years old. Its inventor, a Russian physician named Zamenhof, had come from a feuding region where Polish, German, Yiddish, and Russian were all spoken; and he trusted that his Esperanto would ameliorate dissensions between races. Before long, however, many supporters of Esperanto and Volapük were feuding. Even the disciples of Volapük tongue discovered that their universal language did not necessarily lead to harmony. They split after a quarrel about grammar.

In the generation before the First World War there were abundant warnings that the Manchester gospel was not infallible. The very instruments of peace—railways and international canals and steamships and bills of lading—were conspicuous in the background to some wars. The Suez Canal was a marvelous artery of international exchange, but for that reason England and France were intensely interested in controlling it; without the canal it is doubtful if there would have been an Egyptian War in 1882. The Trans-Siberian railway was a great feat of construction and a powerful link between Europe and Asia, but without that railway it is doubtful whether there could have been a Russo-Japanese war in 1904-5. This is not to argue that these new arteries of commerce *caused* those two wars; but certainly they illustrated the hazards of assuming that whatever drew nations together was an

[9]Volapük: Henry Sweet, *Encyclopedia Britannica, 1910-11*, XXVIII 178.

instrument of peace. The Manchester creed, to many of its adherents, was a dogma; and so contrary evidence was dismissed. . . .

A war lasting four years and involving nearly all the 'civilised' nations of the world contradicted all the assumptions of the crusaders. Admittedly most had envisaged that the movement towards international peace could meet occasional setbacks. Wars against barbarians and autocrats might have to be fought before the millennium arrived. Indeed, if the First World War had been fought by Britain, France and Germany on the one hand and Russia and Serbia on the other, the belief in the millennium might have been less shaken. Such a war could have seemed a replay of the Crimean or American Civil War and thus been interpreted as a war against the barbarians. It was, however, more difficult for learned Frenchmen, Englishmen and Russians to interpret the war against Germany as simply a war against the ignorant and uncivilised: for Germany in 1914 was the homeland of Albert Einstein, Max Planck, Max Weber and a galaxy of great contemporary intellects. On the other hand German liberals at least had the intellectual satisfaction that the Tsar of Russia was one enemy they were fighting; but another of their enemies was France which in some eyes, was the lamp of civilisation.

There was a peculiar irony in the war which divided Europe. If the length and bitterness of the war had been foreseen, the efforts to preserve the peace in 1914 would have been far more vigorous and might have even succeeded. But one of the reasons why so many national leaders and followers in 1914 could not imagine a long war was their faith in the steady flow of that civilising stream that had seemed to widen during the peaceful nineteenth century. The Great War of 1914 would be short, it was widely believed, partly because civilised opinion would rebel against the war if it began to create chaos. The willingness of hundreds of millions of Europeans to tolerate chaos, slaughter and an atmosphere of hatred was an additional surprise to those who had faith in civilisation.

Despite the shock of a world war, versions of the Manchester creed survived. Indeed that creed may have been partly responsible for the outbreak of another world war only two decades later. The military revival of Germany had complicated causes, but in many of those causes one can detect the mark of Manchester.

Germany could not have revived, militarily, without the willing or reluctant sanction of some of the victors of the First World War. In particular the United States and Britain allowed Germany to revive. As they were themselves protected by ocean they tended to be careless of threats within Europe; as they were democracies they tended to have trouble spending adequately on defense in years of peace, for other calls on revenue were more persuasive. A secure island democracy is of course the haven of the Manchester creed; its optimism about human nature and distrust of excessive force reflect the security of its home environment.

One sign of optimism in England and the United States was the wide-spread belief that another world war was virtually impossible. The idea of a war to end war had been one of the popular slogans in those democracies from 1914 to 1918, and the idea lived long after the slogan dissolved in the mouths of orators and faded on recruiting billboards. The prediction that the world would not again experience a war of such magnitude aided the neglect of armaments among some of the main victors of the previous war. It was probably in England too that there was the deepest faith that the League of Nations would become an efficient substitute for the use of force in inter-national affairs; this was not surprising, for the League in a sense was a de-scendant of the House of Commons, the Manchester Cotton Exchange, and the old crusade for free trade. In England public opinion, more than official opinion, tended to expect more of the League of Nations than it was capable of giving. That misplaced faith indirectly helped the Germans to recover their bargaining position in Europe, for in crises the League of Nations proved to be powerless. Likewise in England the widespread mistrust of ar-maments in the 1920s was more than the normal reaction after a major war; it mirrored the belief that the armaments race had been a major cause of the previous war. The Great War, it was argued, had come through misunder-standing; it had been an unwanted war. This interpretation of 1914, to my mind quite invalid, matched the optimistic tenets of the Manchester creed. And since it was widely believed in England it affected future events. It also was a restraint on the English government's ability to match German re-arm-ing for part of the 1930s: to enter again into an armaments race was to en-danger peace, it was believed, even more than to neglect armaments. The ways in which the Manchester creed affected Europe between the two world wars represents only one strand in the rope which raised Germany from her enforced meekness of 1919 to her might of 1939, but it was still an important strand.

In the nineteenth century the Manchester creed in all its hues was favored more by public opinion than by the reigning ministry in England. On the eve of the Second World War however it was powerful in Whitehall. Man-chester had taken office, even if it was disguised as a former mayor of Birm-ingham. Neville Chamberlain, England's prime Minister from 1937 to 1940, is now often seen as a naïve individualist, an eccentric out of step with British traditions, but he represented one of the most influential traditions of British thought. Though he was rearming Britain he did not trust primarily in arms. He saw, not an evil world which reacted only to force or threats, but a world of rational men who reacted to goodwill and responded to discus-sion.[10] He believed that most modern wars were the result of misunderstand-ings or of grievances. Accordingly there were rational remedies for the

---

[10]Chamberlain's faith in rational discussion: Taylor, *The Origins of the Second World War,* pp. 172, 217.

causes of war. As he believed that Germany suffered unfairly from the Versailles Peace of 1919, he was prepared to make concessions in the belief that they would preserve the peace. He was eager to hurry to Germany—not summon Germany to England—in the belief that the conference table was the only sane field of battle. He believed Hitler would respond to rational discussion and to appeasement; so did many Englishmen in 1938.

. . . The optimistic theory of peace is still widespread. Within the United States it pervades much of the criticism of the war in Vietnam. Within the western world it is visible in the school of thought which expects quick results from the fostering of friendly contacts with Russia and China. It pervades many of the plans by which richer countries aid poorer countries. It permeates a host of movements and ventures ranging from the Olympic Games, Rotary and Telstar to international tourism and peace organizations. Irrespective of whether the creed rests on sound or false premises of human behaviour, it still influences international relations. In the short term it is a civilising influence. Whether it actually promotes peace or war, however, is open to debate. If it is based on false generalizations about the causes of war and the causes of peace its influence in promoting peace is likely to be limited and indeed haphazard. Moreover, if it is inspired by a strong desire for peace, but gnaws at the skin rather than the core of international relations, the results will be meagre.

Something is missing in that theory of peace which was shaped and popularised by so many gifted men in the nineteenth century. One may suggest that, like many other explanations of war and peace, it relied much on coincidence. Those living in the three generations after Waterloo had wondered at the long peace and sought explanations in events that were happening simultaneously.[11] They noticed that international peace coincided with industrialism, steam engines, foreign travel, freer and stronger commerce and advancing knowledge. As they saw specific ways in which these changes could further peace, they concluded that the coincidence was causal. Their explanation, however, was based on one example or one period of peace. They ignored the earlier if shorter periods of peace experience by a Europe which had no steam trains, few factories, widespread ignorance and restricted commerce. Their explanation of the cluster of European wars in the period 1848-71 was also shaky. These wars were relatively short, and to their mind the shortness of most wars in the century after Waterloo was evidence that Europe's warlike spirit was ebbing. On the contrary one can argue that most of these wars were shortened not by civilising restraints but by unusual political conditions and by new technological factors which the philosophers of peace did not closely investigate. If neglect of war led them into

[11]Likewise one explanation of the relative peace in Europe since 1945—the influence of nuclear weapons—seems to rely often on coincidence.

error their attitude was nonetheless a vital reaction to those studies of war which neglected peace.

Most of the changes which were hailed as causes of peace in the nineteenth century were probably more the effects of peace. The ease with which ideas, people and commodities flowed across international borders was very much an effect of peace though in turn the flow may have aided peace. Similarly the optimistic assessment of man's nature and the belief that civilisation was triumphing was aided by the relative peacefulness of the nineteenth century. That optimism would not have been so flourishing if wars had been longer and more devastating. In one sense the Manchester theory of peace was like the mountebank's diagnosis that shepherds were healthy simply because they had ruddy cheeks: therefore the cure for a sick shepherd was to inflame his cheeks.

It is difficult to find evidence that closer contacts between nations promoted peace. Swift communications which drew nations together did not necessarily promote peace: it is indisputable that during the last three centuries most wars have been fought by neighbouring countries—not countries which are far apart. The frequency of civil wars shatters the simple idea that people who have much in common will remain at peace. Even the strain of idealism which characterized most versions of the Manchester creed cannot easily be identified as an influence favoring peace, perhaps because in practice the creed is not idealistic. Thus Neville Chamberlain's concessions to Germany in 1938 were no doubt influenced partly by Germany's increasing strength: moreover his concessions were not so idealistic because they were mainly at the expense of Czechoslovakia's independence.

The conclusion seems unmistakable: the Manchester creed cannot be a vital part of a theory of war and peace. One cannot even be sure whether those influences which it emphasizes actually have promoted peace more than war.

Kenneth Boulding, an Anglo-American economist who brilliantly builds bridges across the chasms that divide regions of knowledge, made one observation which indirectly illuminates the dilemma of the Manchester brotherhood. 'Threat systems', wrote Boulding, 'are the basis of politics as exchange systems are the basis of economics.'[12] The Manchester idealists emphasized exchange and minimized the importance of threats. Believing that mankind contained much more good than evil, they thought that threats were becoming unnecessary in a world which seemed increasingly civilised. Indeed they thought that threats were the tyrannical hallmark of an old order which was crumbling. They despised the open or veiled threat as the weapon of their enemies. Thus they opposed czars and dictators who relied visibly on force and threats. For the same reason they opposed slavery,

[12]'Threat systems': Boulding, *Beyond Economics*, p. 105.

serfdom, militarism and harsh penal codes. And they mostly opposed the idea of hell, for hell was a threat.

They did not realize, nor perhaps do we, that a democratic country depends on threats and force, even if they are more veiled and more intermittent than in an autocracy. They did not realize that intellectual and commercial liberty were most assured in those two nations—Britain and the United States—which were economically strong and protected by ocean from the threat of foreign invasion. The preference of Anglo-Saxon nations for democratic forms of government had owed much to the military security which the ocean provided. On the rare occasions in the last two centuries when Britain was threatened by a powerful enemy it abandoned temporarily many of its democratic procedures; thus in the Second World War Churchill and the war cabinet probably held as much power as an autocracy of the eighteenth century. Mistakenly the Manchester creed believed that international affairs would soon repeat effortlessly the achievements visible in the internal affairs of a few favored lands. . . .

References

Apjohn, Lewis, *Richard Cobden and the Fee Traders* (London, c. 1880).

Boulding, Kenneth, *Conflict and Defense* (New York, 1962).

———. *Beyond Economics: essays on society, religion and ethics* (Ann Arbor, 1968).

Buckle, Henry Thomas, *History of Civilization in England,* 3 vols. (London, 1885).

Cairnes, J. E., 'International Law'. *Fortnightly Review* (November 1865)

Cruikshank, R. J., *Roaring Century* (London, 1946).

Dictionary of National Biography, The, 27 vols. (Oxford, 1968).

Taylor, A. J. P., 'Otto Bismarck', *Encyclopaedia Britannica,* 1962,. III 659-68.

———. *The Struggle for Mastery in Europe 1848-1918* (Oxford, 1954).

———. *The Origins of the Second World War* (London, 1961).

Imperialism, the Highest Stage of Capitalism

V. I. LENIN

The Export of Capital

Under the old capitalism, when free competition prevailed, the export of goods was the most typical feature. Under modern capitalism, when monopolies prevail, the export of capital has become the typical feature.

Capitalism is commodity production at the highest stage of development, when labour power itself becomes a commodity. The growth of internal exchange, and particularly of international exchange, is the characteristic distinguishing feature of capitalism. The uneven and spasmodic character of the development of individual enterprises, of individual branches of industry and individual countries, is inevitable under the capitalist system. England became a capitalist country before any other, and in the middle of the nineteenth century, having adopted free trade, claimed to be the "workshop of the world," the great purveyor of manufactured goods to all countries, which in exchange were to keep her supplied with raw materials. But in the last quarter of the nineteenth century, *this* monopoly was already undermined. Other countries, protecting themselves by tariff walls, had developed into independent capitalist states. On the threshold of the twentieth century, we see a new type of monopoly coming into existence. Firstly, there are monopolist capitalist combines in all advanced capitalist countries; secondly, a few rich countries, in which the accumulation of capital reaches gigantic proportions, occupy a monopolist position. An enormous "super-abundance of capital" has accumulated in the advanced countries.

V. I. Lenin, *Imperialism, the Highest Stage of Capitalism* (New York: International Publishers, 1939), originally published in 1917; selections from chapters 4-7. Reprinted with permission of International Publishers.

It goes without saying that if capitalism could develop agriculture, which today lags far behind industry everywhere, if it could raise the standard of living of the masses, who are everywhere still poverty-stricken and underfed, in spite of the amazing advance in technical knowledge, there could be no talk of a superabundance of capital. This "argument" the petty-bourgeois critics of capitalism advance on every occasion. But if capitalism did these things it would not be capitalism; for uneven development and wretched conditions of the masses are fundamental and inevitable conditions and premises of this mode of production. As long as capitalism remains what it is, surplus capital will never be utilized for the purpose of raising the standard of living of the masses in a given country, for this would mean a decline in profits for the capitalists; it will be used for the purpose of increasing those profits by exporting capital abroad to the backward countries. In these backward countries profits are usually high, for capital is scarce, the price of land is relatively low, wages are low, raw materials are cheap. The possibility of exporting capital is created by the fact that numerous backward countries have been drawn into international capitalist intercourse; main railways have either been built or are being built there; the elementary conditions for industrial development have been created, etc. The necessity for exporting capital arises from the fact that in a few countries capitalism has become "over-ripe" and (owing to the backward state of agriculture and the impoverished state of the masses) capital cannot find "profitable" investment. . . .

The Division of the World Among Capitalist Combines

Monopolist capitalist combines—cartels, syndicates, trusts—divide among themselves, first of all, the whole internal market of a country, and impose their control, more or less completely, upon the industry of that country. But under capitalism the home market is inevitably bound up with the foreign market. Capitalism long ago created a world market. As the export of capital increased, and as the foreign and colonial relations and the "spheres of influence" of the big monopolist combines expanded, things "naturally" gravitated towards an international agreement among these combines, and towards the formation of international cartels. . . .

International cartels show to what point capitalist monopolies have developed, and they *reveal the object* of the struggle between the various capitalist groups. This last circumstance is the most important; it alone shows us the historic-economic significance of events; for the *forms* of the struggle may and do constantly change in accordance with varying, relatively particular, and temporary causes, but the *essence* of the struggle, its class *content, cannot* change while classes exist. It is easy to understand, for example, that it is in the interests of the German bourgeoisie, whose theoretical arguments have now been adopted by Kautsky (we will deal with this later), to obscure the *content* of the present economic struggle (the division of the world) and to emphasise this or that *form* of the struggle. Kautsky makes the same mistake. Of course, we have in mind not only the German bourgeoisie, but the bourgeoisie all over the world. The capitalists divide the world, not out of any particular malice, but because the degree of concentration which has been reached forces them to adopt this method in order to get profits. And they divide it in proportion to "capital," in proportion to "strength," because there cannot be any other system of division under commodity production and capitalism. But strength varies with the degree of economic and political development. In order to understand what takes place, it is necessary to know what questions are settled by this change of forces. The question as to whether these changes are "purely" economic or *non*-economic (*e.g.*, military) is a secondary one, which does not in the least affect the fundamental view on the latest epoch of capitalism. To substitute for the question of the *content* of the struggle and agreements between capitalist combines the question of the *form* of these struggles and agreements (today peaceful, tomorrow war-like, the next day war-like again) is to sink to the role of a sophist.

The epoch of modern capitalism shows us that certain relations are established between capitalist alliances, *based* on the economic division of the world; while parallel with this fact and in connection with it, certain relations are established between political alliances, between states, on the basis of the territorial division of the world, of the struggle for colonies, of the "struggle for economic territory."

The Division of the World Among the Great Powers

In his book, *The Territorial Development of the European Colonies*, A. Supan, the geographer, gives the following brief summary of this development at the end of the nineteenth century:

Percentage of Territories Belonging to the European
Colonial Powers (Including United States)

	1876	1900	Increase or Decrease
Africa	10.8	90.4	+79.6
Polynesia	56.8	98.9	+42.1
Asia	51.5	56.6	+ 5.1
Australia	100.0	100.0	—
America	27.5	27.2	−0.3

"The characteristic feature of this period," he concludes, "is therefore, the division of Africa and Polynesia."

As there are no unoccupied territories—that is, territories that do not belong to any state—in Asia and America, Mr. Supan's conclusion must be carried further, and we must say that the characteristic feature of this period is the final partition of the globe—not in the sense that a *new* partition is impossible—on the contrary, new partitions are possible and inevitable—but in the sense that the colonial policy of the capitalist countries has *completed* the seizure of the unoccupied territories on our planet. For the first time the world is completely divided up, so that in the future *only* redivision is possible; territories can only pass from one "owner" to another, instead of passing as unowned territory to an "owner."

Hence, we are passing through a peculiar period of world colonial policy, which is closely associated with the "latest stage in the development of capitalism," with finance capital. For this reason, it is essential first of all to deal in detail with the facts, in order to ascertain exactly what distinguishes this period from those preceding it, and what the present situation is. In the first place, two questions of fact arise here. Is an intensification of colonial policy, an intensification of the struggle for colonies, observed precisely in this period of finance capital? And how, in this respect, is the world divided at the present time?

The American writer, Morris, in his book on the history of colonization[1] has made an attempt to compile data on the colonial possessions of Great Britain, France and Germany during different periods of the nineteenth century. The following is a brief summary of the results he has obtained:

Colonial Possessions

	(Million square miles and million inhabitants)					
	Great Britain		France		Germany	
	Area	Pop.	Area	Pop.	Area	Pop
1815-30	?	126.4	0.02	0.5	-	-
1860	2.5	145.1	0.2	3.4	-	-
1880	7.7	267.9	0.7	7.5		-
1899	9.3	309.0	3.7	56.4	1.0	14.7

For Great Britain, the period of the enormous expansion of colonial conquests is that between 1860 and 1880, and it was also very considerable in the last twenty years of the nineteenth century. For France and Germany this period falls precisely in these last twenty years. We saw above that the apex of premonopoly capitalist development, of capitalism in which free competition was predominant, was reached in the 'sixties and 'seventies of the last

[1] Henry C. Morris, *The History of Colonization*, New York, 1900, II, p. 88; I, pp. 304, 419.

century. We now see that it is *precisely after that period* that the "boom" in colonial annexations begins, and that the struggle for the territorial division of the world becomes extraordinarily keen. It is beyond doubt, therefore, that capitalism's transition to the stage of monopoly capitalism, to finance capital, is *bound up* with the intensification of the struggle for the partition of the world.

Hobson, in his work on imperialism, marks the years 1884-1900 as the period of the intensification of the colonial "expansion" of the chief European states. According to his estimate, Great Britain during these years acquired 3,700,000 square miles of territory with a population of 57,000,000; France acquired 3,600,000 square miles with a population of 16,700,000; Belgium 900,000 square miles with 30,000,000 inhabitants; Portugal 800,000 square miles with 9,000,000 inhabitants. The quest for colonies by all the capitalist states at the end of the nineteenth century and particularly since the 1880's is a commonly known fact in the history of diplomacy and of foreign affairs.

When free competition in Great Britain was at its zenith, *i.e.*, between 1840 and 1860, the leading British bourgeois politicians were opposed to colonial policy and were of the opinion that the liberation of the colonies and their complete separation from Britain was inevitable and desirable. M. Beer, in an article, "Modern British Imperialism,"[2] published in 1898, shows that in 1852, Disraeli, a statesman generally inclined towards imperialism, declared: "The colonies are millstones round our necks." But at the end of the nineteenth century the heroes of the hour in England were Cecil Rhodes and Joseph Chamberlain, open advocates of imperialism, who applied the imperialist policy in the most cynical manner.

It is not without interest to observe that even at the time these leading British bourgeois politicians fully appreciated the connection between what might be called the purely economic and the politico-social roots of modern imperialism. Chamberlain advocated imperialism by calling it a "true, wise and economical policy," and he pointed particularly to the German, American and Belgian competition which Great Britain was encountering in the world market. Salvation lies in monopolies, said the capitalists as they formed cartels, syndicates and trusts. Salvation lies in monopolies, echoed the political leaders of the bourgeoisie, hastening to appropriate the parts of the world not yet shared out. The journalist, Stead, relates the following remarks uttered by his close friend Cecil Rhodes, in 1895, regarding his imperialist ideas:

> I was in the East End of London yesterday and attended a meeting of the unemployed. I listened to the wild speeches, which were just a cry for 'bread,' 'bread,' 'bread,' and on my way home I pondered over the scene and I became more than ever convinced of the importance of imperialism.... My cherished idea is a solution for the social problem, *i.e.*, in order to save the 40,000,000 in-

[2]*Die Neue Zeit*, XVI, I, 1898, p. 302.

habitants of the United Kingdom from a bloody civil war, we colonial statesmen must acquire new lands to settle the surplus population, to provide new
markets for the goods produced by them in the factories and mines. The Empire, as I have always said, is a bread and butter question. If you want to avoid
civil war, you must become imperialists. . . .[3]

Imperialism as a Special Stage of Capitalism

We must now try to sum up and put together what has been said above on
the subject of imperialism. Imperialism emerged as the development and direct continuation of the fundamental attributes of capitalism in general. But
capitalism only became capitalist imperialism at a definite and very high
stage of its development, when certain of its fundamental attributes began to
be transformed into their opposites, when the features of a period of transition from capitalism to a higher social and economic system began to take
shape and reveal themselves all along the line. Economically, the main thing
in this process is the substitution of capitalist monopolies for capitalist free
competition. Free competition is the fundamental attribute of capitalism,
and of commodity production generally. Monopoly is exactly the opposite of
free competition; but we have seen the latter being transformed into monopoly before our very eyes, creating large-scale industry and eliminating
small industry, replacing large-scale industry by still larger-scale industry, finally leading to such a concentration of production and capital that monopoly has been and is the result: cartels, syndicates and trusts, and merging
with them, the capital of a dozen or so banks manipulating thousands of millions. At the same time monopoly, which has grown out of free competition,
does not abolish the latter, but exists over it and alongside of it, and thereby
gives rise to a number of very acute, intense antagonisms, friction and conflicts. Monopoly is the transition from capitalism to a higher system.

If it were necessary to give the briefest possible definition of imperialism
we should have to say that imperialism is the monopoly stage of capitalism.
Such a definition would include what is most important, for, on the one
hand, finance capital is the bank capital of a few big monopolist banks,
merged with the capital of the monopolist combines of manufacturers; and,
on the other hand, the division of the world is the transition from a colonial
policy which has extended without hindrance to territories unoccupied by
any capitalist power, to a colonial policy of monopolistic possession of the
territory of the world which has been completely divided up.

But very brief definitions, although convenient, for they sum up the main
points, are nevertheless inadequate, because very important features of the
phenomenon that has to be defined have to be especially deduced. And so,

---

[3] *Ibid.*, p. 304.

without forgetting the conditional and relative value of all definitions, which can never include all the concatenations of a phenomenon in its complete development, we must give a definition of imperialism that will embrace the following five essential features:

1) The concentration of production and capital developed to such a high stage that it created monopolies which play a decisive role in economic life.

2) The merging of bank capital with industrial capital, and the creation, on the basis of this "finance capital," of a "financial oligarchy."

3) The export of capital, which has become extremely important, as distinguished from the export of commodities.

4) The formation of international capitalist monopolies which share the world among themselves.

5) The territorial division of the whole world among the greatest capitalist powers is completed. . . .

Finance capital and the trusts are increasing instead of diminishing the differences in the rate of development of the various parts of world economy. When the relation of forces is changed, how else, *under capitalism,* can the solution of contradictions be found, except by resorting to *violence?* Railway statistics provide remarkably exact data on the different rates of development of capitalism and finance capital in world economy. In the last decades of imperialist development, the total length of railways has changed as follows:

Railways (*thousand kilometres*)

	1890		1913		Increase	
Europe	224		346		122	
U.S.A.	268		411		143	
Colonies (total)	82		210		128	
Independent and semi-dependent states of Asia and America	43	} 125	137	} 347	94	} 222
Total	617		1,104			

Thus, the development of railways has been more rapid in the colonies and in the independent (and semi-dependent) states of Asia and America. Here, as we know, the finance capital of the four or five biggest capitalist states reigns undisputed. Two hundred thousand kilometres of new railways in the colonies and in the other countries of Asia and America represent more than 40,000,000,000 marks in capital, newly invested on particularly advantageous terms, with special guarantees of a good return and with profitable orders for steel works, etc., etc.

Capitalism is growing with the greatest rapidity in the colonies and in overseas countries. Among the latter, *new* imperialist powers are emerging (*e.g.*, Japan). The struggle of world imperialism is becoming more acute. The tribute levied by finance capital on the most profitable colonial and overseas enterprises is increasing. In sharing out this "booty," an exceptionally large part goes to countries which, as far as the development of productive forces is concerned, do not always stand at the top of the list. In the case of the biggest countries, considered with their colonies, the total length of railways was as follows (in thousands of kilometres):

	1890	*1913*	*Increase*
U.S.A.	268	413	145
British Empire	107	208	101
Russia	32	78	46
Germany	43	68	25
France	41	63	22
Total	491	830	339

Thus, about 80 per cent of the total existing railways are concentrated in the hands of the five Great Powers. But the concentration of the *ownership* of these railways of finance capital, is much greater still: French and English millionaires, for example, own an enormous amount of stocks and bonds in American, Russian and other railways.

Thanks to her colonies, Great Britain has increased the length of "her" railways by 100,000 kilometres, four times as much as Germany. And yet, it is well known that the development of productive forces in Germany, and especially the development of the coal and iron industries, has been much more rapid during this period than in England—not to mention France and Russia. In 1892, Germany produced 4,900,000 tons of pig iron and Great Britain produced 6,800,000 tons; in 1912 Germany produced 17,600,000 tons and Great Britain 9,000,000 tons. Germany, therefore, had an overwhelming superiority over England in this respect. We ask, is there *under capitalism* any means of removing the disparity between the development of productive forces and the accumulation of capital on the one side, and the division of colonies and "spheres of influence" for finance capital on the other side—other than by resorting to war?

Imperialism and Capitalism

JOSEPH SCHUMPETER

Our analysis of the historical evidence has shown, first, the unquestionable fact that "objectless" tendencies toward forcible expansion, without definite, utilitarian limits—that is, non-rational and irrational, purely instinctual inclinations toward war and conquest—play a very large role in the history of mankind. It may sound paradoxical, but numberless wars—perhaps the majority of all wars—have been waged without adequate "reason"—not so much from the moral viewpoint as from that of reasoned and reasonable interest. The most herculean efforts of the nations, in other words, have faded into the empty air. Our analysis, in the second place, provides an explanation for this drive to action, this will to war—a theory by no means exhausted by mere references to the "urge" or an "instinct." The explanation lies, instead, in the vital needs of situations that molded peoples and classes into warriors—if they wanted to avoid extinction—and in the fact that psychological dispositions and social structures acquired in the dim past in such situations, once firmly established, tend to maintain themselves and to continue in effect long after they have lost their meaning and their life-preserving function. Our analysis, in the third place, has shown the existence of subsidiary factors that facilitate the survival of such dispositions and structures—factors that may be divided into two groups. The orientation toward war is mainly fostered by the domestic interests of ruling classes, but also by the influence of all those who stand to gain individually from war policy, whether economically or socially. Both groups of factors are generally overgrown by elements of an altogether different character, not only in terms of political phraseology, but also of psychological motivation. Imperialisms dif-

Joseph Schumpeter, "Imperialism and Capitalism," in *Imperialism/Social Classes: Two Essays by Joseph Schumpeter,* Heinz Norden, trans. (Cleveland: World, 1968), originally published in 1919.

fer greatly in detail, but they all have at least these traits in common, turning them into a single phenomenon in the field of sociology, as we noted in the introduction.

Imperialism thus is atavistic in character. It falls into that large group of surviving features from earlier ages that play such an important part in every concrete social situation. In other words, it is an element that stems from the living conditions, not of the present, but of the past—or, put in terms of the economic interpretation of history, from past rather than present relations of production. It is an atavism in the social structure, in individual, psychological habits of emotional reaction. Since the vital needs that created it have passed away for good, it too must gradually disappear, even though every warlike involvement, no matter how non-imperialist in character, tends to revive it. It tends to disappear as a structural element because the structure that brought it to the fore goes into a decline, giving way, in the course of social development, to other structures that have no room for it and eliminate the power factors that supported it. It tends to disappear as an element of habitual emotional reaction, because of the progressive rationalization of life and mind, a process in which old functional needs are absorbed by new tasks, in which heretofore military energies are functionally modified. If our theory is correct, cases of imperialism should decline in intensity the later they occur in the history of a people and of a culture. Our most recent examples of unmistakable, clear-cut imperialism are the absolute monarchies of the eighteenth century. They are unmistakably "more civilized" than their predecessors.

It is from absolute autocracy that the present age has taken over what imperialist tendencies it displays. And the imperialism of absolute autocracy flourished before the Industrial Revolution that created the modern world, or rather, before the consequences of that revolution began to be felt in all their aspects. These two statements are primarily meant in a historical sense, and as such they are no more than self-evident. We shall nevertheless try, within the framework of our theory, to define the significance of capitalism for our phenomenon and to examine the relationship between present-day imperialist tendencies and the autocratic imperialism of the eighteenth century.

The flood tide that burst the dams in the Industrial Revolution had its sources, of course, back in the Middle Ages. But capitalism began to shape society and impress its stamp on every page of social history only with the second half of the eighteenth century. Before that time there had been only islands of capitalist economy imbedded in an ocean of village and urban economy. True, certain political influences emanated from these islands, but they were able to assert themselves only indirectly. Not until the process we term the Industrial Revolution did the working masses, led by the entrepreneur, overcome the bonds of older life-forms—the environment of peasantry, guild, and aristocracy. The causal connection was this: a transformation in the basic economic factors (which need not detain us here) created the objective opportunity for the production of commodities, for large-scale industry, working for a market of customers whose individual identities were unknown, operating solely with a view to maximum financial profit. It was this opportunity that created an economically oriented leadership—personalities whose field of achievement was the organization of such commodity production in the form of capitalist enterprise. Successful enterprises in large numbers represented something new in the economic and social sense. They fought for and won freedom of action. They compelled state policy to adapt itself to their needs. More and more they attracted the most vigorous leaders from other spheres, as well as the manpower of those spheres, causing them and the social strata they represented to languish. Capitalist entrepreneurs fought the former ruling circles for a share in state control, for leadership in the state. The very fact of their success, their position, their resources, their power, raised them in the political and social scale. Their mode of life, their cast of mind became increasingly important elements on the social scene. . . .

A purely capitalist world therefore can offer no fertile soil to imperialist impulses. That does not mean that it cannot still maintain an interest in imperialist expansion. We shall discuss this immediately. The point is that its people are likely to be essentially of an unwarlike disposition. Hence we must expect that anti-imperialist tendencies will show themselves wherever capitalism penetrates the economy and, through the economy, the mind of modern nations—most strongly, of course, where capitalism itself is strongest, where it has advanced furthest, encountered the least resistance, and preeminently where its types and hence democracy—in the "bourgeois" sense—come closest to political dominion. We must further expect that the types formed by capitalism will actually be the carriers of these tendencies. Is such the case? The facts that follow are cited to show that this expectation, which flows from our theory, is in fact justified.

1. Throughout the world of capitalism, and specifically among the elements formed by capitalism in modern social life, there has arisen a fundamental opposition to war, expansion, cabinet diplomacy, armaments, and socially entrenched professional armies. This opposition had its origin in the country that first turned capitalist—England—and arose coincidentally with that country's capitalist development. "Philosophical radicalism" was the first politically influential intellectual movement to represent this trend successfully, linking it up, as was to be expected, with economic freedom in general and free trade in particular. Molesworth became a cabinet member, even though he had publicly declared—on the occasion of the Canadian revolution—that he prayed for the defeat of his country's arms. In step with the advance of capitalism, the movement also gained adherents elsewhere—though at first only adherents without influence. It found support in Paris—indeed, in a circle oriented toward capitalist enterprise (for example, Frédéric Passy). True, pacifism as a matter of principle had existed before, though only among a few small religious sects. But modern pacifism, in its

political foundations if not its derivation, is unquestionably a phenomenon of the capitalist world.

2. Wherever capitalism penetrated, peace parties of such strength arose that virtually every war meant a political struggle on the domestic scene. The exceptions arc rare—Germany in the Franco-Prussian war of 1870-1871, both belligerents in the Russo-Turkish war of 1877-1878. That is why every war is carefully justified as a defensive war by the governments involved, and by all the political parties, in their official utterances—indicating a realization that a war of a different nature would scarcely be tenable in a political sense. (Here too the Russo-Turkish war is an exception, but a significant one.) In former times this would not have been necessary. Reference to an interest or pretense at moral justification was customary as early as the eighteenth century, but only in the nineteenth century did the assertion of attack, or the threat of attack, become the only avowed occasion for war. In the distant past, imperialism had needed no disguise whatever, and in the absolute autocracies only a very transparent one; but today imperialism is carefully hidden from public view—even though there may still be unofficial appeal to warlike instincts. No people and no ruling class today can openly afford to regard war as a normal state of affairs or a normal element in the life of nations. No one doubts that today it must be characterized as an abnormality and a disaster. True, war is still glorified. But glorification in the style of King Tuglâti-palisharra is rare and unleashes such a storm of indignation that every practical politician carefully dissociates himself from such things. Everywhere there is official acknowledgment that peace is an end in itself—though not necessarily an end overshadowing all purposes that can be realized by means of war. Every expansionist urge must be carefully related to a concrete goal. All this is primarily a matter of political phraseology, to be sure. But the necessity for this phraseology is a symptom of the popular attitude. And that attitude makes a policy of imperialism more and more difficult—indeed, the very word imperialism is applied only to the enemy, in a reproachful sense, being carefully avoided with reference to the speaker's own policies. . . .

Capitalism is by nature anti-imperialist. Hence we cannot readily derive from it such imperialist tendencies as actually exist, but must evidently see them only as alien elements, carried into the world of capitalism from the outside, supported by non-capitalist factors in modern life. The survival of interest in a policy of forcible expansion does not, by itself, alter these facts—not even, it must be steadily emphasized, from the viewpoint of the economic interpretation of history. For objective interests become effective—and, what is important, become powerful political factors—only when they correspond to attitudes of the people or of sufficiently powerful strata.

. . . The national economy as a whole, of course, is impoverished by the tremendous excess in consumption brought on by war. It is, to be sure, conceivable that either the capitalists or the workers might make certain gains as a class, namely, if the volume either of capital or of labor should decline in such a way that the remainder receives a greater share in the social product and that, even from the absolute viewpoint, the total sum of interest or wages becomes greater than it was before. But these advantages cannot be considerable. They are probably, for the most part, more than outweighed by the burdens imposed by war and by losses sustained abroad. Thus the gain of the capitalists as a class cannot be a motive for war—and it is this gain that counts, for any advantage to the working class would be contingent on a large number of workers falling in action or otherwise perishing. There remain the entrepreneurs in the war industries, in the broader sense, possibly also the large landowner—a small but powerful minority. Their war profits are always sure to be an important supporting element. But few will go so far as to assert that this element alone is sufficient to orient the people of the capitalist world along imperialist lines. At most, an interest in expansion may make the capitalist allies of those who stand for imperialist trends.

It may be stated as being beyond controversy that where free trade prevails *no* class has an interest in forcible expansion as such. For in such a case the citizens and goods of every nation can move in foreign countries as freely as though those countries were politically their own—free trade implying far more than mere freedom from tariffs. In a genuine state of free trade, foreign raw materials and foodstuffs are as accessible to each nation as though they were within its own territory. Where the cultural backwardness of a region makes normal economic intercourse dependent on colonization, it does not matter, assuming free trade, which of the "civilized" nations undertakes the task of colonization. . . .

The gain lies in the enlargement of the commodity supply by means of the division of labor among nations, rather than in the profits and wages of the export industry and the carrying trade. For these profits and wages would be reaped even if there were no export, in which case import, the necessary complement, would also vanish. Not even monopoly interests—if they existed—would be disposed toward imperialism in such a case. For under free trade only *international* cartels would be possible. Under a system of free trade there would be conflicts in economic interest neither among different nations nor among the corresponding classes of different nations. And since protectionism is not an essential characteristic of the capitalist economy—otherwise the English national economy would scarcely be capitalist—it is apparent that any economic interest in forcible expansion on the part of a people or a class is not necessarily a product of capitalism. . . .

Consider which strata of the capitalist world are actually economically benefitted by protective tariffs. They do harm to both workers and capitalists—in contrast to entrepreneurs—not only in their role as consumers, but also as producers. The damage to consumers is universal, that to producers almost so. As for entrepreneurs, they have benefitted only by the tariff that happens to be levied on their own product. But this advantage is substantially reduced by the countermeasures adopted by other countries—universally, except in the case of England—and by the effect of the tariff on the prices of other articles, especially those which they require for their own productive process. Why, then, are entrepreneurs so strongly in favor of protective tariffs? The answer is simple. Each industry hopes to score *special* gains in the struggle of political intrigue, thus enabling it to realize a net gain. Moreover, every decline in freight rates, every advance in production abroad, is likely to affect the economic balance, making it necessary for domestic enterprises to adapt themselves, indeed often to turn to other lines of endeavor. This is a difficult task to which not everyone is equal. Within the industrial organism of every nation there survive antiquated methods of doing business that would cause enterprises to succumb to foreign competition—because of poor management rather than lack of capital, for before 1914 the banks were almost forcing capital on the entrepreneurs. If, still, in most countries virtually *all* entrepreneurs are protectionists, this is owing to a reason which we shall presently discuss. Without that reason, their attitude would be different. The fact that all industries today demand tariff protection must not blind us to the fact that even the entrepreneur interest is not unequivocally protectionist. For this demand is only the consequence of a protectionism already in existence, of a protectionist spirit springing from the economic interests of relatively small entrepreneur groups and from non-capitalist elements—a spirit that ultimately carried along all groups, occasionally even the representatives of working-class interests. Today the protective tariff confers its full and immediate benefits—or comes close to conferring them—only on the large landowners. . . .

Trade and industry of the early capitalist period . . . remained strongly pervaded with precapitalist methods, bore the stamp of autocracy, and served its interests, either willingly or by force. With its traditional habits of feeling, thinking, and acting molded along such lines, the bourgeoisie entered the Industrial Revolution. It was shaped, in other words, by the needs and interests of an environment that was essentially noncapitalist, or at least precapitalist—needs stemming not from the nature of the capitalist economy as such but from the fact of the coexistence of early capitalism with another and at first overwhelmingly powerful mode of life and business. Established habits of thought and action tend to persist, and hence the spirit of guild and monopoly at first maintained itself, and was only slowly undermined, even where capitalism did not fully prevail *anywhere* on the Continent. Existing economic interests, "artificially" shaped by the autocratic state, remained dependent on the "protection" of the state. The industrial organism, such as it was, would not have been able to withstand free competition. Even where the old barriers crumbled in the autocratic state, the people did not all at once flock to the clear track. They were creatures of mercantilism and even earlier periods, and many of them huddled together and protested against the affront of being forced to depend on their own ability. They cried for paternalism, for protection, for forcible restraint of strangers, and above all for tariffs. They met with partial success, particularly because capitalism failed to take radical action in the agrarian field.

Capitalism did bring about many changes on the land, springing in part from its automatic mechanisms, in part from the political trends it engendered—abolition of serfdom, freeing the soil from feudal entanglements, and so on—but initially it did not alter the basic outlines of the social structure of the countryside. Even less did it affect the spirit of the people, and least of all their political goals. This explains why the features and trends of autocracy—including imperialism—proved so resistant, why they exerted such a powerful influence on capitalist development, why the old export monopolism could live on and merge into the new.

These are facts of fundamental significance to an understanding of the soul of modern Europe. Had the ruling class of the Middle Ages—the war-oriented nobility—changed its profession and function and become the ruling class of the capitalist world; or had developing capitalism swept it away, put it out of business, instead of merely clashing head-on with it in the agrarian sphere—then much would have been different in the life of modern peoples. But as things actually were, neither eventuality occurred; or, more correctly, both are taking place, only at a very slow pace. The two groups of landowners remain social classes clearly distinguishable from the groupings of the capitalist world. The social pyramid of the present age has been formed, not by the substance and laws of capitalism alone, but by two different social substances, and by the laws of two different epochs. Whoever seeks to understand Europe must not forget this and concentrate all attention on the indubitably basic truth that one of these substances tends to be absorbed by the other and thus the sharpest of all class conflicts tends to be eliminated. Whoever seeks to understand Europe must not overlook that even today its life, its ideology, its politics are greatly under the influence of the feudal "substance," that while the bourgeoisie can assert its interests everywhere, it "rules" only in exceptional circumstances, and then only briefly. The bourgeois outside his office and the professional man of capitalism outside his profession cut a very sorry figure. Their spiritual leader is the rootless "intellectual," a slender reed open to every impulse and a prey to unrestrained emotionalism. The "feudal" elements, on the other hand, have both feet on the ground, even psychologically speaking. Their ideology is as stable as their mode of life. They believe certain things to be really true, others to be really false. This quality of possessing a definite character and cast of mind as a class, this simplicity and solidity of social and spiritual position extends their power far beyond their actual bases, gives them the ability to assimilate new elements, to make others serve their purposes—in a word, gives them *prestige,* something to which the bourgeois, as is well known, always looks up, something with which he tends to ally himself, despite all actual conflicts.

The nobility entered the modern world in the form into which it had been shaped by the autocratic state—the same state that had also molded the bourgeoisie. It was the sovereign who disciplined the nobility, instilled loyalty into it, "statized" it, and, as we have shown, imperialized it. He turned its nationalist sentiments—as in the case of the bourgeoisie—into an aggressive nationalism, and then made it a pillar of his organization, particularly his war machine. It had not been that in the immediately preceding period. Rising absolutism had at first availed itself of much more dependent organs. For that very reason in his position as leader of the feudal powers and as warlord, the sovereign survived the onset of the Industrial Revolution, and as a rule—except in France—won victory over political revolution. The bourgeoisie did not simply supplant the sovereign, nor did it make him its leader, as did the nobility. It merely wrested a portion of his power from him and for the rest submitted to him. It did not take over from the sovereign the state as an abstract form of organization. The state remained a special social power, confronting the bourgeoisie. In some countries it has continued to play that role to the present day. It is in the *state* that the bourgeoisie with its interests seeks refuge, protection against external and even domestic enemies.The bourgeoisie seeks to win over the state for itself, and in return serves the state and state interests that are different from its own. Imbued with the spirit of the old autocracy, trained by it, the bourgeoisie often takes over its ideology, even where, as in France, the sovereign is eliminated and the official power of the nobility has been broken. Because the sovereign needed soldiers, the modern bourgeois—at least in his slogans—is an even more vehement advocate of an increasing population. Because the sovereign was in a position to exploit conquests, needed them to be a victorious warlord, the bourgeoisie thirsts for national glory—even in France, worshiping a headless body, as it were. Because the sovereign found a large gold hoard useful, the bourgeoisie even today cannot be swerved from its bullionist prejudices. Because the autocratic state paid attention to the trader and manufacturer chiefly as the most important sources of taxes and credits, today even the intellectual who has not a shred of property looks on international commerce, not from the viewpoint of the consumer, but from that of the trader and exporter. Because pugnacious sovereigns stood in constant fear of attack by their equally pugnacious neighbors, the modern bourgeois attributes aggressive designs to neighboring peoples. All such modes of thought are essentially noncapitalist. Indeed, they vanish most quickly wherever capitalism fully prevails. They are survivals of the autocratic alignment of interests, and they endure wherever the autocratic state endures on the old basis and with the old orientation, even though more and more democratized and otherwise transformed. They bear witness to the extent to which essentially imperialist absolutism has patterned not only the economy of the bourgeoisie but also its mind—in the interests of autocracy and against those of the bourgeoisie itself.

This significant dichotomy in the bourgeois mind—which in part explains its wretched weakness in politics, culture and life generally; earns it the understandable contempt of the Left and the Right; and proves the accuracy of our diagnosis—is best exemplified by two phenomena that are very close to our subject: present-day nationalism and militarism. Nationalism is affirmative awareness of national character, together with an aggressive sense of superiority. It arose from the autocratic state. In conservatives, nationalism in general is understandable as an inherited orientation, as a mutation of the battle instincts of the medieval knights, and finally as a political stalking horse on the domestic scene; and conservatives are fond of reproaching the bourgeois with a lack of nationalism, which from their point of view, is evaluated in a positive sense. Socialists, on the other hand, equally understandably exclude nationalism from their general ideology, because of the essential interests of the proletariat, and by virtue of their domestic opposition to the conservative stalking horse; they, in turn, not only reproach the bourgeoisie with an excess of nationalism (which they, of course, evaluate in a negative sense) but actually identify nationalism and even the very idea of the nation with bourgeois ideology. The curious thing is that both of these groups are right in their criticism of the bourgeoisie. For, as we have seen, the mode of life that flows logically from the nature of capitalism necessarily implies an anti-nationalist orientation in politics and culture. This orientation actually prevails. We find a great many anti-nationalist members of the middle class, and even more who merely parrot the catchwords of nationalism. In the capitalist world it is actually not big business and industry at all that are the carriers of nationalist trends, but the intellectual, and the content of *his* ideology is explained not so much from definite class interests as from chance emotion and individual interest. But the submission of the bourgeoisie to the powers of autocracy, its alliance with them, its economic and psychological patterning by them—all these tend to push the bourgeois in a nationalist direction; and this too we find prevalent, especially among the chief exponents of export monopolism. The relationship between the bourgeoisie and militarism is quite similar. Militarism is not necessarily a foregone conclusion when a nation maintains a large army, but only when high military circles become a political power. The criterion is whether leading generals as such wield political influence and whether the responsible statesmen can act only with their consent. That is possible only when the officer corps is linked to a definite social class, as in Japan, and can assimilate to its position individuals who do not belong to it by birth. Militarism too is rooted in the autocratic state. And again the same reproaches are made against the bourgeois from both sides—quite properly too. According to the "pure" capitalist mode of life, the bourgeois is unwarlike. The alignment of capitalist interests should make him utterly reject military methods, put him in opposition to the professional soldier. Significantly, we see this in the example of England where, first, the struggle against a standing army generally and, next, opposition to its elaboration, furnished bourgeois politicians with their most popular slogan: "retrenchment." Even naval appropriations have encountered resistance. We find similar trends in other countries, though they are less strongly developed. The continental bourgeois, however, was used to the sight of troops. He regarded an army almost as a necessary component of the social order, ever since it had been his terrible taskmaster in the Thirty Years' War. He had no power at all to abolish the army. He might have done so if he had had the power; but not having it, he considered the fact that the army might be useful to him. In his "artificial" economic situation and because of his submission to the sovereign, he thus grew disposed toward militarism, especially where export monopolism flourished. The intellectuals, many of whom still maintained special relationships with feudal elements, were so disposed to an even greater degree.

Just as we once found a dichotomy in the social pyramid, so now we find everywhere, in every aspect of the bourgeois portion of the modern world, a dichotomy of attitudes and interests. Our examples also show in what way the two components work together. Nationalism and militarism, while not creatures of capitalism, become "capitalized" and in the end draw their best energies from capitalism. Capitalism involves them in its workings and thereby keeps them alive, politically as well as economically. And they, in turn, affect capitalism, cause it to deviate from the course it might have followed alone, support many of its interests.

Here we find that we have penetrated to the historical as well as the sociological sources of modern imperialism. It does not *coincide* with nationalism and militarism, though it *fuses* with them by supporting them as it is supported by them. It too is—not only historically, but also sociologically—a heritage of the autocratic state, of its structural elements, organizational forms, interest alignments, and human attitudes, the outcome of precapitalist forces which the autocratic state has reorganized, in part by the methods of early capitalism. It would never have been evolved by the "inner logic" of capitalism itself. This is true even of mere export monopolism. It too has its sources in absolutist policy and the action habits of an essentially precapitalist environment. That it was able to develop to its present dimensions is owing to the momentum of a situation once created, which continued to engender ever new "artificial" economic structures, that is, those which maintain themselves by political power alone. In most of the countries addicted to export monopolism it is also owing to the fact that the old autocratic state and the old attitude of the bourgeoisie toward it were so vigorously maintained. But export monopolism, to go a step further, is not yet imperialism. And even if it had been able to arise without protective tariffs, it would never have developed into imperialism in the hands of an unwarlike bourgeoisie. If this did happen, it was only because the heritage included the war machine, together with its sociopsychological aura and aggressive bent, and because a class oriented toward war maintained itself in a ruling position. This class clung to its domestic interest in war, and the promilitary interests among the bourgeoisie were able to ally themselves with it. This alliance kept alive war instincts and ideas of overlordship, male supremacy, and triumphant glory—ideas that would have otherwise long since died. It led to social conditions that, while they ultimately stem from the conditions of production, cannot be explained from capitalist production methods alone. And it often impresses its mark on present-day politics, threatening Europe with the constant danger of war. . . .

The only point at issue here was to demonstrate, by means of an important example, the ancient truth that the dead always rule the living.

War as Policy

ALAN S. MILWARD

> For Warre, consisteth not in Battell onely, or the act of fighting; but in a tract of time,
> wherein the will to contend by Battell is sufficiently known: and therefore the notion of
> Time, is to be considered in the nature of Warre; as it is in the nature of Weather. For as
> the nature of Foule weather, lyeth not in a shower or two of rain; but in an inclination
> thereto of many days together: So the nature of Warre, consisteth not in actual fighting;
> but in the known disposition thereto, during all the time there is no assurance to the
> contrary. All other time is Peace.
>
> —Thomas Hobbes, Leviathan, 1651

There are two commonly accepted ideas about war which have little foundation in history. One is that war is an abnormality. The other is that with the
passage of time warfare has become costlier and deadlier. The first of these
ideas established itself in the eighteenth century, when the theory of natural
law was used to demonstrate that peace was a logical deduction from the material laws governing the universe or, sometimes, from the psychological
laws governing mankind. The second of these ideas came to reinforce the
first, which might otherwise have been weakened by the weight of contrary
evidence, towards the end of the nineteenth century. The historical record
of that century had not been such as to substantiate the logical deductions
of eighteenth-century philosophy, for it was a century of unremitting warfare. But after 1850 a large body of economic literature began to reconcile
agreeable predictions with unpleasant facts by demonstrating that in spite of
the prevalence of warfare it would eventually cease to be a viable economic

Alan S. Milward, *War, Economy and Society: 1939–1945* (Berkeley: University of California Press,
1977), Chapter 1. Copyright © 1977 Alan S. Milward. Reprinted with permission of University of
California Press.

policy because it would price itself out of the market, a process which, it was agreed, had already begun.

Neither of these ideas has ever been completely accepted by economists but their influence on economic theory has been so powerful as to focus the operation of a substantial body of that theory on to the workings of a peace-time economy only. In spite of the fact that the world has practically never been at peace since the eighteenth century peace has usually been seen as the state of affairs most conducive to the achievement of economic aims and the one which economic theory seeks to analyze and illuminate. In the early nineteenth century, indeed, it was seen as the goal to which economic theory tended.

The frequency of war is in itself the best argument against accepting the idea of its abnormality. The second idea, that war has become more costly, is based less on a refusal to consider history than on a mistaken simplification of it. It was an idea which first gained wide credence with the development of more complicated technologies. War itself was an important stimulus to technological development in many industries in the late nineteenth century such as shipbuilding, the manufacture of steel plate and the development of machine tools. The construction of complex weapons which could only be manufactured by states at a high level of economic development seemed to change the economic possibilities of war. The first heavily armed steel battleships only narrowly preceded the adaptation of the internal combustion engine to military and then to aerial use, and these new armaments coincided with a period of enormous and growing standing armies. The productive capacities which economic development had placed in the hands of developed economies raised prospects of warfare on an absolute scale of cost and deadliness never before conceived. And these prospects in themselves seemed to indicate the economic mechanism by which war would disappear after its rather disappointing persistence in the nineteenth century. These ideas were succinctly expressed by de Molinari, one of the few economists who tried to integrate the existence of war into classical economic theory.

> Can the profits of war still cover its cost? The history of all wars which have occurred between civilized peoples for a number of centuries attests that these costs have progressively grown, and, finally that any war between members of the civilized community today costs the victorious nation more than it can possibly yield it.[1]

In the half century after de Molinari so firmly expressed his opinion there were two world wars, each of a far higher absolute cost and each responsible for greater destruction than any previous war. There is, to say the least, circumstantial evidence that de Molinari's judgement was a superficial one and

[1]M. G. de Molinari, *Comment se résoudra la question sociale?*, Guillaumin, Paris, 1896, p. 126.

that nations did not continue to go to war merely because they were ignorant of what had become its real economic consequences. War not only continued to meet the social, political and economic circumstances of states but, furthermore, as an instrument of policy, it remained, in some circumstances, economically viable. War remains a policy and investment decision by the state and there seem to be numerous modern examples of its having been a correct and successful decision. The most destructive of modern technologies have not changed this state of affairs. Their deployment by those states sufficiently highly developed economically to possess them is limited by the rarity of satisfactory strategic opportunity. The strategic synthesis by which the Vietnam war was conducted on the American side, for example, is very like the rational decisions frequently taken by all combatants in the First World War against the use of poison gas. The existence of the most costly and murderous armaments does not mean that they will be appropriate or even usable in any particular war, much less that all combinations of combatants will possess them.

The question of the economic cost of war is not one of absolutes. The cost and the effectiveness of a long-range bomber at the present time must be seen in relation to that of a long-range warship in the eighteenth century and both seen in relation to the growth of national product since the eighteenth century. In each case we are dealing with the summation of many different technological developments, and the armament itself is in each of these cases pre-eminently the expression of an extremely high relative level of economic development. The meaningful question is whether the cost of war has absorbed an increasing proportion of the increasing Gross National Products of the combatants. As an economic choice war, measured in this way, has not shown any discernible long-term trend towards greater costliness. As for its deadliness, the loss of human life is but one element in the estimation of cost. There are no humane wars, and where the economic cost of the war can be lowered by substituting labour for capital on the battlefield such a choice would be a rational one. It has been often made. The size of the Russian armies in the First World War reflected the low cost of obtaining and maintaining a Russian soldier and was intended to remedy the Russian deficiencies in more expensive capital equipment. It may be argued that modern technology changes the analysis because it offers the possibility of near-to-total destruction of the complete human and capital stock of the enemy. But numerous societies were so destroyed in the past by sword, fire and pillage and, more appositely, by primitive guns and gunpowder. The possibility of making a deliberate choice of war as economic policy has existed since the late eighteenth century and exists still.

The origins of the Second World War lay in the deliberate choice of warfare as an instrument of policy by two of the most economically developed states. Far from having economic reservations about warfare as policy, both the German and Japanese governments were influenced in their decisions for war by the conviction that war might be an instrument of economic gain.

Although economic considerations were in neither case prime reasons in the decision to fight, both governments held a firmly optimistic conviction that war could be used to solve some of their more long-term economic difficulties. Instead of shouldering the economic burden of war with the leaden and apprehensive reluctance of necessity, like their opponents, both governments kept their eyes firmly fixed on the short-term social and economic benefits which might accrue from a successful war while it was being fought, as well as on the long-term benefits of victory. In making such a choice the ruling elites in both countries were governed by the difference between their own political and economic ideas and those of their opponents. The government of Italy had already made a similar choice when it had attacked Ethiopia.

This difference in economic attitudes to warfare was partly attributable to the influence of fascist political ideas. Because these ideas were also of some importance in the formulation of Axis strategy and the economic and social policies pursued by the German occupying forces it is necessary briefly to consider some of their aspects here in so far as they relate to the themes considered in this book. Whether the National Socialist government in Germany and the Italian Fascist party are properly to be bracketed together as fascist governments and indeed whether the word fascist itself has any accurate meaning as a definition of a set of precise political and economic attitudes are complicated questions which cannot be discussed here.[2] Although the Japanese government had few hesitations in using war as an instrument of political and economic policy there is no meaningful definition of the word fascist which can include the ruling elites in Japan. There was a small political group in that country whose political ideas resembled those of the Fascists and the National Socialists but they had practically no influence in the Home Islands although they did influence the policy of the Japanese military government in Manchuria.[3] But for the German and Italian rulers war had a deeper and more positive social purpose and this was related to certain shared ideas. Whether the word fascism is a useful description of the affinities of political outlook between the Italian and German governments is less important than the fact that this affinity existed and extended into many areas of political and economic life. The differences between National Socialism in Germany and Fascism in Italy partly consisted, in fact, of the more unhesitating acceptance of the ideas of Italian Fascism by the National Socialist party and the linking of these ideas to concepts of racial purity.

The basis of Fascist and National Socialist political and economic thought was the rejection of the ideas of the eighteenth-century Enlightenment. In the submergence of the individual will in common instinctive action, which

---

[2]The reader is referred for a recent, short and relatively unbiased discussion of these issues to W. Wippermann, *Faschismustheorien. Zum Stand der gegenwärtigen Diskussion*, Wissenschaftliche Buchgesellschaft, Darmstadt, 1972.

[3]G. M. Wilson, 'A New Look at the Problem of "Japanese Fascism"', in *Comparative Studies in Society and History*, no. 10, 1968.

warfare represented, rational doubts and vacillations, which were regarded as a trauma on human society produced by the Enlightenment, could be suppressed. War was seen as an instrument for the healing of this trauma and for the restoration of human society to its pristine state. Both Hitler and Mussolini, whose writings in general not only subscribed to but advanced the political ideas of fascism, referred to war constantly in this vein, seeing it as a powerful instrument for forging a new and more wholesome political society. 'Fascism', wrote Mussolini,

> the more it considers and observes the future and the development of humanity, quite apart from the political considerations of the moment, believes neither in the possibility nor the utility of perpetual peace.... War alone brings up to its highest tension all human energy and puts the stamp of nobility upon the peoples who have the courage to meet it.[4]

Hitler similarly wrote and spoke of war and preparation for war as an instrument of the spiritual renewal of the German people, a device for eliminating the corrupting egotistical self-seeking which he saw as the concomitant of false ideas of human liberty, progress and democracy. The basis of existence in Hitler's view was a struggle of the strong for mastery and war was thus an inescapable, necessary aspect of the human condition.[5]

What made this not uncommon viewpoint especially dangerous and what gave to the Second World War its unique characteristic of a war for the political and economic destiny of the whole European continent was the way in which the ideas of fascism were developed by Hitler and the theorists of the National Socialist party. The wound that had been inflicted on European civilization could, they argued, only be healed by a process of spiritual regeneration. That process of regeneration must begin from the small surviving still uncorrupted elite. But politics was not a matter of debate and persuasion but of the instinctive recognition of social obligations, community ideas which were held to be carried not in the brain but in the blood. The elite was also a racial elite and the restoration of the lost European civilization was also a search for a lost racial purity. The nationalist conceptions of race had been derived from the rational mainstream of European politics. What now replaced them was an irrational concept of racial purity as the last hope for the salvation of European society.[6]

Within Germany, the National Socialist party from its earliest days had identified those of Jewish race as the source of corruption and racial pollu-

---

[4]Quoted in W. G. Welk, *Fascist Economic Policy. An Analysis of Italy's Economic Experiment* (Harvard Economic Studies, no. 62), Harvard University Press, Cambridge, Mass., 1938, p. 190.

[5]The connections between Hitler's political thought and his strategy are developed in an interesting way by E. Jäckel, *Hitlers Weltanschauung. Entwurf einer Herrschaft*, Rainer Wunderlich Verlag Hermann Leins, Tübingen, 1969.

[6]The most comprehensive discussion remains A. Kolnai's *The War against the West* (Gollancz, London, 1938), but E. Weber, in *Varieties of Fascism, Doctrines of Revolution in the Twentieth Century* (Van Nostrand, Princeton, 1964), draws out the further implications of these ideas.

tion. But it was scarcely possible that the 'problem' of the German Jews could be solved as an entirely domestic issue. The spiritual regeneration of Germany and, through Germany, the continent, also required a great extension of Germany's territorial area—*Lebensraum*. This area had to be sufficiently large to enable Germany militarily to play the role of a great power and to impose her will on the rest of the continent and perhaps on an even wider front. This expansion could also take the form of the destruction of what was seen as the last and most dangerous of all the European political heresies, communism and the Soviet state. The need to achieve these goals and the messianic urgency of the political programme of National Socialism meant that war was an unavoidable part of Hitler's plans.

But it was not the intellectual antagonism to communism which determined that the ultimate target of Germany's territorial expansion should be the Ukraine. That choice was more determined by economic considerations. The task of materially and spiritually rearming the German people had meant that Germany after 1933 pursued an economic policy radically different from that of other European states. A high level of state expenditure, of which military expenditure, before 1936, was a minor part, had sharply differentiated the behaviour of the German economy from that of the other major powers. The maintenance of high levels of production and full employment in a depressed international environment had necessitated an extensive battery of economic controls which had increasingly isolated the economy. After 1936 when expenditure for military purposes was increased to still higher levels there was no longer any possibility that the German economy might come back, by means of a devaluation, into a more liberal international payments and trading system. Rather, the political decisions of 1936 made it certain that trade, exchange, price and wage controls would become more drastic and more comprehensive, and the German economy more insulated from the influence of the other major economies. This was particularly so because of the large volume of investment allocated in the Four Year Plan to the production, at prices well above prevailing world prices, of materials of vital strategic importance, such as synthetic fuel, rubber and aluminum.[7]

The National Socialist party did not support the idea of restoring the liberal international order of the gold exchange standard. But neither did they have any clear positive alternative ideas. Economic policy was dictated by political expediency and each successive stage of controls was introduced to cope with crises as they arose. Nevertheless the political ideas of National Socialism favored an autarkic as opposed to a liberal economic order and it was not difficult to justify the apparatus of economic controls as a necessary and beneficial aspect of the National Socialist state. The international aspects of the controlled economy—exchange controls and bilateral trading treaties—

---

[7]The best account is D. Petzina's *Autarkiepolitik im Dritten Reich. Der nationalsozialistische Vierjahresplan* (Schriftenreihe der Vj.f.Z., no. 16, Deutsche Verlags-Anstalt, Stuttgart, 1968).

could readily be assimilated to an expansionist foreign policy. Indeed Hitler himself regarded a greater degree of self-sufficiency of the German economy as a necessity if he were to have the liberty of strategic action which he desired, and also as a justification of his policy of territorial expansion. The memory of the effectiveness of the Allied naval blockade during the First World War, when Germany had controlled a much larger resource base than was left to her after the Treaty of Versailles, strengthened this line of thought.

National Socialism elaborated its own theory to justify international economic policies which were in fact only the outcome of a set of domestic economic decisions which had been accorded priority over all international aspects. This was the theory of *Grossraumwirtschaft* (the economics of large areas). Although it was only a rhetorical justification after the event of economic necessities, it also played its part in the formulation of strategy and economic policy. On the basis of these economic ideas, it was hoped that the war would bring tangible economic gain, rather than the more spiritual benefits of a transformation of civilization. At an early stage in his political career, Hitler had come to the conclusion that the Ukraine was economically indispensable to Germany if she was to be, in any worthwhile sense, independent of the international economy and thus free to function as a great power. As the insulation of the German economy from the international economy became more complete in the 1930s the economic relationship of Germany to the whole of the continent came to be reconsidered, and National Socialist writers were advocating not merely a political and racial reconstruction of Europe but an economic reconstruction as well.

National Socialist economists argued that the international depression of 1929 to 1933 had brought the 'liberal' phase of economic development, associated with diminishing tariffs and an increasing volume of international trade, to an end. On the other hand, the extent to which the developed economies of Europe still depended on access to raw materials had not diminished. They argued that the epoch of the economic unit of the national state, itself the creation of liberalism, was past, and must be replaced by the concept of large areas (*Grossräume*) which had a classifiable economic and geographical unity. Such areas provided a larger market at a time of failing demand and could also satisfy that demand from their own production and resources. Improving employment levels and increasing *per capita* incomes depended therefore, not on a recovery in international trade, which could only in any case be temporary and inadequate, but on a reordering of the map of the world into larger 'natural' economic areas. The United States and the Soviet Union each represented such an area. Germany too had its own 'larger economic area' which it must claim.[8]

[8]Typical of this line of argument are, F. Fried, *Die Zukunft des Welthandels*, Knorr und Hirth, Munich, 1941; R. W. Krugmann, *Südosteuropa und Grossdeutschland. Entwicklung und Zukunftsmöligchkeiten der Wirtschaftsbeziehungen*, Breslauer Verlag, Breslau, 1939; H. Marschner, ed., *Deutschland in der Wirtschaft der Welt*, Deutscher Verlag für Politik und Wirtschaft, Berlin, 1937; J. Splettstoesser, *Der deutsche Wirtschaftsraum im Osten*, Limpert, Berlin, 1939; H. F. Zeck, *Die deutsche Wirtschaft und Südosteuropa*, Teubner, Leipzig, 1939.

The future economy of this area would be distinguished by its autarkic nature. The international division of labour would be modified into specialization of function within each *Grossraum.* Germany would be the manufacturing heartland of its own area, together with its bordering industrial areas of northeastern France, Belgium and Bohemia. The peripheral areas would supply raw materials and foodstuffs to the developed industrial core.

There were close links between these economic ideas and the political and racial ones. Such large areas were considered to have a racial unity in the sense that central Europe was developed because of the racial superiority of its inhabitants, the 'Aryans'; the periphery would always be the supplier of raw materials because its population was racially unsuitable for any more sophisticated economic activity.[9] For a time it seemed that Germany might create her *Grossraumwirtschaft* and dominate international economic exchanges in Europe through peaceful means; a series of trade agreements was signed between Germany and the underdeveloped countries of southeastern Europe after 1933. Germany was able to get better terms in bilateral trading from these lands than from more developed European economies who were able to threaten, and even, like Britain, to carry out the threat, to sequestrate German balances in order to force Germany to pay at once on her own (import) side of the clearing balance, and German trade with south-eastern Europe increased in relation to the rest of German and world trade in the thirties. But German-Russian trade after 1933 became insignificant and it was clear that a re-ordering of Europe's frontiers to correspond with Germany's economic ambitions would ultimately have to involve large areas of Russian territory. South-eastern Europe, without Russia, could make only a very limited contribution to emancipating Germany from her worldwide network of imports. A war against the Soviet Union seemed to be the necessary vehicle for political and economic gain.

Many scholars, particularly in the Soviet Union and eastern Europe, maintain that there was a further economic dimension to German policy and that the Second World War represented an even more fundamental clash over the economic and social destiny of the continent. Although the definition of fascism in Marxist analysis has varied greatly with time and place it has nevertheless been more consistent than definitions made from other standpoints. The tendency has been to represent it as the political expression of the control of 'state-monopoly capital' over the economy. It is seen as a stage of capitalism in decline, when it can survive only by a brutal and determined imperialism and through a monopolistic control over domestic and foreign markets by the bigger capitalist firms backed by the government. The changes in the German economy after 1933 are explained as following these lines: the readiness to go to war by the bigger profits it might bring and also by the ultimate necessity for an imperialist domination of other economies.

[9]W. Daitz, *Der Weg zur völkischen Wirtschaft und zur europäischen Grossraumwirtschaft,* Meinhold, Dresden, 1938.

Warfare, it is argued, had become an economic necessity for Germany and its ultimate purpose was the preservation of state capitalism, for which both territorial expansion and the destruction of the communist state were essential. The argument is succinctly put by Eichholtz:

> Towards the close of the twenties Germany stood once more in the ranks of the most developed and economically advanced of the imperialist powers. The strength and aggression necessary for expansion grew with the development of her economic strength. German imperialism was an imperialism which had been deprived of colonies, and imperialism whose development was limited by financial burdens stemming from the war and by the limitations and controls, onerous to the monopolies, which the victorious powers had imposed, especially on armaments, finances, etc. On that account extreme nationalism and chauvinism were characteristic of the development of the fascist movement in Germany from the start; once in power fascism maintained from its first days an overweening purposeful imperialistic aggression—which had been obvious for a long time—towards the outside world. With fascism a ruling form of state monopoly capital had been created which aimed at overcoming the crisis of capitalism by domestic terror and, externally, by dividing the world anew.[10]

Such a theory offers not merely a serious economic explanation of the war but also implies that the most fundamental causes of the war were economic. The major German firms, it is argued, had definite plans to gain from a war of aggression and supported the National Socialist government in many of its economic aims.

> Thus the results of research on the period immediately preceding the war, although still fragmentary, already show that German monopoly capital was pursuing a large and complex programme of war aims to extend its domination over Europe and over the world. The kernel of this programme was the destruction of the Soviet Union. Two main aims of war and expansion united the Hitler clique and all important monopolies and monopoly groups from the beginning: the 'dismantling of Versailles' and the 'seizure of a new living space (*Lebensraum*) in the east'. By the 'dismantling of Versailles' the monopolies understood, as they often expressed it later, the 'recapture' of all the economic and political positions which had been lost and the 'restitution' of all the damage to the sources of profit and monopoly situations which the Versailles system had inflicted on them. As an immediate step they planned to overrun the Soviet Union, to liquidate it and appropriate its immeasurable riches to themselves, and to erect a European 'economy of large areas' (*Grossraumwirtschaft*), if possible in conjunction with a huge African colonial empire.[11]

How the *Grossraumwirtschaft* eventually functioned in practice will be examined later. But as far as pre-war plans were concerned it was a concept

---

[10]D. Eichholtz, *Geschichte der deutschen Kriegswirtschaft, 1939-1945*, vol. 1, 1939-1941, Akademie-Verlag, Berlin, 1969, p. 1.

[11]D. Eichholtz, *Geschichte*, p. 63.

which attracted sympathy and support from certain business circles in Germany. Some German firms were able to benefit from the government's drive towards a greater level of autarky and hoped to expand their new interests to the limits of the future frontiers of the Reich. This was true, in spite of its extensive extra-European connections, of the large chemical cartel, I. G. Farben. Its profits increasingly came from the massive state investment in synthetic petrol and synthetic rubber production. Several of its important executives had high rank in the Four-Year Plan Organization which was entrusted with these developments, and the company had plans ready in the event of an expansion of German power over other European states.[12] These plans stemmed in part from the German trade drive into south-eastern Europe after 1933 and the consequent penetration of German capital into that region, but there were also unambiguous proposals, some part of which were later put into effect, to recapture the supremacy of the German dyestuffs industry in France, which had been lost as a result of the First World War.[13] Nor was this the only such firm with similar plans prepared.[14] Other firms regarded the expansionist foreign policy as a possible way of securing supplies of raw materials. Such was the case with the non-ferrous metal company, Mansfeld, and with the aluminum companies, who understandably were able to get a very high level of priority because of the great importance of aluminum for aircraft manufacture and the power which the Air Ministry exercised in the German government.[15]

However, the support for the National Socialist party came in large measure from a section of the population whose political sympathies were in many ways antipathetic to the world of big business. It drew its support from a protest against the apparently inexorably increasing power both of organized labour and of organized business. Its urban support came mainly from the lower income groups of the middle classes, such as clerical workers, artisans and shopkeepers, and was combined with massive rural support in Protestant areas after 1931. This support was maintained by a persistent anticapitalist rhetoric but also by a certain amount of legislation which cannot by any shift of argument be explained by a theory which assumes National Socialism to be a stage of state capitalism. Attempts to establish hereditary inalienable peasant tenures, to show favor to artisan enterprises, to restrict

---

[12]D. Eichholtz, *Geschichte*, p. 248 ff.; H. Radandt, 'Die I G Farben-industrie und Südosteuropa 1938 bis zum Ende des zweiten Weltkriegs', in *Jahrbuch für Wirtschaftgeschichte*, no. 1, 1967.

[13]A. S. Milward, *The New Order and the French Economy*, Oxford University Press, London, 1970, p. 100 ff.

[14]W. Schumann, "Das Kriegsprogramm des Zeiss-Konzerns', in *Zeitschrift für Geschichtswissenschaft*, no. 11, 1963.

[15]H. Radandt, *Kriegsverbrecherkonzern Mansfeld. Die Rolle des Mansfeld-Konzerns bei der Vorbereitung und während des zweiten Weltkriegs* (Geschichte der Fabriken und Werke, vol. 3), Akademie-Verlag, Berlin, 1957; A. S. Milward, *The Fascist Economy in Norway*, Clarendon Press, Oxford, 1972, p. 86.

the size of retail firms, to restrict the movement of labour out of the agricultural sector, all of which were futile in the face of a massive state investment in reflation which produced a rapid rate of growth of Gross National Product, show the curious ambivalence of National Socialist economic attitudes.[16] On the whole such legislation did little to affect the profits which accrued to the business world in Germany after 1933, some part of which came also from the severe controls on money wages and the destruction of the organized labour movements. But the National Socialist movement kept its inner momentum, which was driving towards a different horizon from that of the business world, a horizon both more distant and more frightening. It was in some ways a movement of protest against modern economic development and became a center of allegiance for all who were displaced and uprooted by the merciless and seemingly ungovernable swings of the German economy after 1918. National Socialism was as much a yearning for a stable utopia of the past as a close alliance between major capital interests and an authoritarian government.

These fundamental economic contradictions and tensions within the movement could only be exacerbated, not resolved, by a war of expansion. The idea—held in some conservative nationalist German business circles—that Germany must eventually dominate the exchanges of the continent if her economy was to find a lasting equilibrium, had a lineage dating from the 1890s and had found some expression in economic policy during the First World War.[17] The theory of *Grossraumwirtschaft* was only a reformulation of these ideas in terms of National Socialist foreign policy. The much more radical idea of a social and racial reconstruction of European society—accepted by some parts of the National Socialist movement—ran directly counter to it, and raised the possibility of a Europe where the 'business climate' would, to say the least, have been unpropitious.

Although, therefore, the German government in choosing war as an instrument of policy was anticipating an economic gain from that choice, it was by no means clear as to the nature of the anticipated gain. It has been argued that it was the irreconcilable contradictions in the National Socialist economy which finally made a war to acquire more resources (*ein Raubkrieg*) the only way out, and that the invasion of Poland was the last desperate attempt to sustain the Nazi economy.[18] But it is hard to make out a case that the Nazi economy was in a greater state of crisis in the autumn of 1939 than

[16]They are well described in D. Schoenbaum's *Hitler's Social Revolution: Class and Status in Nazi Germany 1933-1939* (Weidenfeld & Nicolson, London, 1966).

[17]The history is traced by J. Freymond, *Le IIIe Reich et la réorganisation économique de l'Europe 1940-1942: origines et projets* (Institut Universitaire de Hautes Etudes, Geneva, Collection de Relations Internationales, 3), Sithoff, Leiden, 1974.

[18]T. W. Mason, 'Innere Krise und Angriffskrieg 1938/1939', in F. Forstmeier and H. E. Volkmann (eds.), *Wirtschaft und Rustung am Vorabend des zweiten Weltkrieges*, Droste, Düsseldorf, 1975.

it had been on previous occasions particularly in 1936. Most of the problems which existed in 1939 had existed from the moment full employment had been reached, and some of them, on any calculation, could only be made worse by a war—as indeed they were.

In Italy there were episodes in the 1930s when foreign and economic policy seemed to be directed towards the creation of an Italian *Grossraumwirtschaft* in Europe as a solution to Italy's economic problems. But in the face of the powerful expansion of German trade in the south-east such aspirations were unattainable. In Italy, also, there were attempts at creating by protection and subsidy synthetic industries which might prove strategically necessary in war. But there was little resemblance between these tendencies and the full-scale politico-economic ambitions of Germany. If the Italian government viewed war as a desirable instrument of policy it did not contemplate a serious and prolonged European war and made no adequate preparations for one.

In Japan, however, the choice in favour of war was based on economic considerations which had a certain similarity to those of Germany. It lacked the radical social and racial implications but it was assumed that investment in a war which was strategically well-conceived would bring a substantial accretion to Japan's economic strength. The Japanese government hoped to establish a zone of economic domination which, under the influence of German policy, it dignified by the title 'Co-Prosperity Sphere'. As an economic bloc its trading arrangements would be like those of the *Grossraumwirtschaft*, a manufacturing core supplied by a periphery of raw material suppliers.[19] If the Co-Prosperity Sphere was to be created in the full extent that would guarantee a satisfactory level of economic self-sufficiency, war and conquest would be necessary. Germany's decision for war and early victories over the colonial powers gave Japan the opportunity to establish a zone of domination by military force while her potential opponents were preoccupied with other dangers. After the initial successes the boundaries of the Co-Prosperity Sphere were widened to include a more distant periphery, a decision which had serious strategic consequences, but the original Japanese war aims represented a positive and realistic attempt at the economic reconstruction of her own economic area in her own interests. All the peripheral areas produced raw materials and foodstuffs and semi-manufactures which were imported in large quantities into Japan; rice from Korea, iron ore, coal and foodstuffs from Manchuria, coal and cotton from Jehol, oil and bauxite from the Netherlands East Indies, tin and rubber from Malaya and sugar from Formosa. The variety of commodities and the scope for further developments in the future made the Co-Prosperity Sphere potentially more

[19]F. C. Jones, *Japan's New Order in East Asia: Its Rise and Fall, 1937-45,* Oxford University Press, London, 1954; M. Libal, *Japans Weg in den Krieg. Die Aussenpolitik der Kabinette Konoye 1940-41,* Droste-Verlag, Düsseldorf, 1971.

economically viable and more economically realistic than a European *Gross-raumwirtschaft* still heavily dependent on certain vital imports.[20] The Japanese decision for war, like the German, was taken under the persuasion that in Japan's situation, given the correct timing and strategy, war would be economically beneficial.

Of course such plans could only have been formulated where a harshly illiberal outlook on the problems of international economic and political relationships prevailed. But in the government circles of Japan proper the ready acceptance of war had no ideological connotations beyond this generally prevailing political attitude of mind. The major influence on the Japanese decision for war was the strategic conjuncture; with German military successes in Europe, the pressure on the European empires in the Pacific became unbearable and this in turn intensified the strategic dilemma of the United States. If Japan's ambitions were to be achieved it seemed that the opportune moment had arrived.

The probable and possible opponents of the Axis powers viewed this bellicosity with dismay. In these countries the First World War and its aftermath were seen as an economic disaster. Consequently the main problem of a future war, if it had to be fought, was thought to be that of avoiding a similar disaster. The components of that disaster were seen as a heavy loss of human beings and capital, acute and prolonged inflation, profound social unrest, and almost insuperable problems, both domestic and international, of economic readjustment once peace was restored. It was almost universally believed that the unavoidable aftermath of a major war would be a short restocking boom followed by worldwide depression and unemployment. When the *American Economic Review* devoted a special issue in 1940 to a consideration of the economic problems of war the problem of post-war readjustment was regarded by all contributors as the most serious and unavoidable. That the major economies after 1945 would experience a most remarkable period of stability and economic growth was an outcome which was quite unforeseen and unpredicted. The western European powers and the United States were as much the prisoners of their resigned pessimism about the unavoidable economic losses of war as Germany and Japan were the prisoners of their delusions about its possible economic advantages.

In fact the economic experience of the First World War had been for all combatants a chequered one. The First World War had not been a cause of unalloyed economic loss; it had on occasions brought economic and social advantages. What is more it had demonstrated to all the combatant powers that it lay in the hands of government to formulate strategic and economic policies which could to some extent determine whether or not a war would be economically a cause of gain or loss; they were not the hopeless prisoners

---

[20]J. R. Cohen, *Japan's Economy in War and Reconstruction,* University of Minnesota Press, Minneapolis, 1949, p. 7.

of circumstance. The extreme importance of what governments had learned of their own potential in this way during the 1914-18 war can be observed in almost every aspect of the Second World War. Nevertheless in most countries this learning process had been thought of as an ingenious economic improvisation to meet a state of emergency, having no connection with peacetime economic activity nor with the 'normal' functioning of government, which in 1939 had often only to be reached for and dusted, the influence of wartime events on economic attitudes in the inter-war period had been small.

Faced with a decision for war by two important powers the other major powers accepted the fact reluctantly and with much economic foreboding. The reluctance seems to have been greatest in the Soviet Union, which was in the throes of a violent economic and social transformation, and in the United States, which was less immediately threatened by German policy. The strategic initiative lay with the Axis powers; the strategies of the other powers were only responses to the initial decisions of their enemies. This fact, and the difference in economic attitudes toward warfare, operated decisively to shape each combatant power's strategic plans for fighting the war. By shaping strategy at every turn they also shaped economic policy and economic events. For the combatants the national economy had to be accommodated to a strategic plan and had to play its part in that plan. The economic dimension of the strategy was, however, only one part of the whole strategic synthesis, and the variety of the strategic and economic syntheses which were devised by the combatant powers show how complex and varied the economic experience of warfare can be.

Structural Causes and Economic Effects

KENNETH N. WALTZ

In a self-help system, interdependence tends to loosen as the number of parties declines, and as it does so the system becomes more orderly and peaceful. As with other international political concepts, interdependence looks different when viewed in the light of our theory. Many seem to believe that a growing closeness of interdependence improves the chances of peace. But close interdependence means closeness of contact and raises the prospect of occasional conflict. The fiercest civil wars and the bloodiest international ones are fought within arenas populated by highly similar people whose affairs are closely knit. It is impossible to get a war going unless the potential participants are somehow linked. Interdependent states whose relations remain unregulated must experience conflict and will occasionally fall into violence. If interdependence grows at a pace that exceeds the development of central control, then interdependence hastens the occasion for war. . . .

Interdependence as Sensitivity

. . . As now used, "interdependence" describes a condition in which anything that happens anywhere in the world may affect somebody, or everybody, elsewhere. To say that interdependence is close and rapidly growing closer is to suggest that the impact of developments anywhere on the globe are rapidly registered in a variety of far-flung places. This is essentially an economist's

Kenneth N. Waltz, *Theory of International Politics* (Reading, MA: Addison-Wesley, 1979), Chapter 7. Reprinted with permission of McGraw Hill, Inc.

definition. In some ways that is not surprising. Interdependence has been discussed largely in economic terms. The discussion has been led by Americans, whose ranks include nine-tenths of the world's living economists (Strange 1971, p. 223). Economists understandably give meaning to interdependence by defining it in market terms. Producers and consumers may or may not form a market. How does one know when they do? By noticing whether changes in the cost of production, in the price of goods, and in the quality of products in some places respond to similar changes elsewhere. Parties that respond sensitively are closely interdependent. Thus Richard Cooper defines interdependence as "quick responsiveness to differential earning opportunities resulting in a sharp reduction in differences in factor rewards"(1968, p. 152)....

In defining interdependence as sensitivity of adjustment rather than as mutuality of dependence, Richard Cooper unwittingly reflects the lesser dependence of today's great powers as compared to those of earlier times. Data excerpted from Appendix Table I graphically show this.

Exports plus Imports as a Percentage of GNP

| 1909-13 | U.K., France, Germany, Italy | 33-52% |
| 1975 | U.S., Soviet Union | 8-14% |

To say that great powers then depended on one another and on the rest of the world much more than today's great powers do is not to deny that the adjustment of costs across borders is faster and finer now. Interdependence as sensitivity, however, entails little vulnerability. The more automatically, the more quickly, and the more smoothly factor costs adjust, the slighter the political consequences become. Before World War I, as Cooper says, large differences of cost meant that "trade was socially very profitable" but "less sensitive to small changes in costs, prices, and quality" (1968, p. 152). Minor variations of cost mattered little. Dependence on large quantities of imported goods and materials that could be produced at home only with difficulty, if they could be produced at all, mattered much. States that import and export 15 percent or more of their gross national products yearly, as most of the great powers did then and as most of the middle and smaller powers do now, depend heavily on having reliable access to markets outside their borders. Two or more parties involved in such relations are interdependent in the sense of being mutually vulnerable to the disruption of their exchanges. Sensitivity is a different matter.

As Cooper rightly claims, the value of a country's trade is more likely to vary with its magnitude than with its sensitivity. Sensitivity is higher if countries are able to move back and forth from reliance on foreign and on domestic production and investment "in response to relatively small margins of advantage." Under such conditions, the value of trade diminishes. If domestic substitutions for foreign imports cannot be made, or can be made only at high cost, trade becomes of higher value to a country and of first importance to those who conduct its foreign policy. The high value of Japan's trade, to use Cooper's example, "led Japan in 1941 to attack the Philippines and the United States fleet at Pearl Harbor to remove threats to its oil trade with the East Indies." His point is that high sensitivity reduces national vulnerability while creating a different set of problems. The more sensitive countries become, the more internal economic policies have to be brought into accord with external economic conditions. Sensitivity erodes the autonomy of states, but not of all states equally. Cooper's conclusion, and mine, is that even though problems posed by sensitivity are bothersome, they are easier for states to deal with than the interdependence of mutually vulnerable parties, and that the favored position of the United States enhances both its autonomy and the extent of its influence over others (1972, pp. 164, 176-80).

Defining interdependence as sensitivity leads to an economic interpretation of the world. To understand the foreign-policy implications of high or of low interdependence requires concentration on the politics of international economics, not on the economics of international politics. The common conception of interdependence omits inequalities, whether economic or political. And yet inequality is what much of politics is about. The study of politics, theories about politics, and the practice of politics have always turned upon inequalities, whether among interest groups, among religious and ethnic communities, among classes, or among nations. Internally, inequality is more nearly the whole of the political story. Differences of national strength and power and of national capability and competence are what the study and practice of international politics are almost entirely about. This is so not only because international politics lacks the effective laws and the competent institutions found within nations but also because inequalities across nations are greater than inequalities within them (Kuznets 1951). A world of nations marked by great inequalities cannot usefully be taken as the unit of one's analysis.

Most of the confusion about interdependence follows from the failure to understand two points: first, how the difference of structure affects the meaning, the development, and the effects of the interactions of units nationally and internationally; and second, how the interdependence of nations varies with their capabilities. Nations are composed of differentiated parts that become integrated as they interact. The world is composed of like units that become dependent on one another in varying degrees. The parts of a polity are drawn together by their differences; each becomes dependent on goods and services that all specialize in providing. Nations pull apart as each of them tries to take care of itself and to avoid becoming dependent on others. How independent they remain, or how dependent they become, varies with their capabilities. . . . To define interdependence as a sensitivity, then, makes two errors. First, the definition treats the world as a whole, as reflected in the clichés cited earlier. Second, the definition compounds relations and interactions that represent varying degrees of independence for some, and of dependence for others, and lumps them all under the rubric of interdependence.

Interdependence as Mutual Vulnerability

A politically more pertinent definition is found in everyday usage. Interdependence suggests reciprocity among parties. Two or more parties are interdependent if they depend on one another about equally for the supply of goods and services. They are interdependent if the costs of breaking their relations or of reducing their exchanges are about equal for each of them. Interdependence means that the parties are mutually dependent. The definition enables one to identify what is politically important about relations of interdependence that are looser or tighter. Quantitatively, interdependence tightens as parties depend on one another for larger supplies of goods and services; qualitatively, interdependence tightens as countries depend on one another for more important goods and services that would be harder to get elsewhere. The definition has two components: the aggregate gains and losses states experience through their interactions and the equality with which those gains and losses are distributed. States that are interdependent at high levels of exchange experience, or are subject to, the common vulnerability that high interdependence entails.

Because states are like units, interdependence among them is low as compared to the close integration of the parts of a domestic order. States do not interact with one another as the parts of a polity do. Instead, some few people and organizations in one state interact in some part of their affairs with people and organizations abroad. Because of their similarity, states are more dangerous than useful to one another. Being functionally undifferentiated, they are distinguished primarily by their greater or lesser capabilities for performing similar tasks. This states formally what students of international politics have long noticed. The great powers of an era have always been marked off from others by both practitioners and theorists.

. . . Many believe that the mere mutualism of international exchange is becoming a true economic-social-political integration. One point can be made in support of this formulation. The common conception of interdependence is appropriate only if the inequalities of nations are fast lessening and losing their political significance. If the inequality of nations is still the dominant political fact of international life, then interdependence remains low. Economic examples in this section, and military examples in the next one, make clear that it is.

In placid times, statement and commentator employ the rich vocabulary of clichés that cluster around the notion of global interdependence. Like a flash of lightning, crises reveal the landscape's real features. What is revealed by the oil crisis following the Arab-Israeli War in October of 1973? Because that crisis is familiar to all of us and will long be remembered, we can concentrate on its lessons without rehearsing the details. Does it reveal states being squeezed by common constraints and limited to applying the remedies they can mutually contrive? Or does it show that the unequal capabilities of states continue to explain their fates and to shape international-political outcomes?

Recall how Kissinger traced the new profile of power. "Economic giants can be militarily weak," he said, "and military strength may not be able to obscure economic weakness. Countries can exert political influence even when they have neither military nor economic strength." . . . Economic, military, and political capabilities can be kept separate in gauging the ability of nations to act. Low politics, concerned with economic and such affairs, has replaced military concerns at the top of the international agenda. Within days the Arab-Israeli War proved that reasoning wrong. Such reasoning had supported references made in the early 1970s to the militarily weak and politically disunited countries of Western Europe as constituting "a great civilian power." Recall the political behavior of the great civilian power in the aftermath of the war. Not Western Europe as any kind of a power, but the separate states of Western Europe, responded to the crisis—in the metaphor of *The Economist*—by behaving at once like hens and ostriches. They ran around aimlessly, clucking loudly while keeping their heads buried deeply in the sand. How does one account for such behavior? Was it a failure of nerve? Is it that the giants of yesteryear—the Attlees and Bevins, the Adenauers and de Gaulles—have been replaced by men of lesser stature? Difference of persons explains some things; difference of situations explains more. In 1973 the countries of Western Europe depended on oil for 60 percent of their energy supply. Much of that oil came from the Middle East. . . . Countries that are highly dependent, countries that get much of what they badly need from a few possibly unreliable suppliers, must do all they can to increase the chances that they will keep getting it. The weak, lacking leverage, can plead their cause or panic. Most of the countries in question unsurprisingly did a little of each.

The behavior of nations in the energy crisis that followed the military one revealed the low political relevance of interdependence defined as sensitivity. Instead, the truth of the propositions I made earlier was clearly shown. Smooth and fine economic adjustments cause little difficulty. Political interventions that bring sharp and sudden changes in prices and supplies cause problems that are economically and politically hard to cope with. The crisis also revealed that, as usual, the political clout of nations correlates closely with their economic power and their military might. In the winter of 1973—74 the policies of West European countries had to accord with economic necessities. The more dependent a state is on others, and the less its leverage over them, the more it must focus on how its decisions affect its access to supplies and markets on which its welfare or survival may depend. This describes the condition of life for states that are no more than the equal of many others. In contrast, the United States was able to make its policy according to political and military calculations. Importing but two percent of its total energy supply from the Middle East, we did not have to appease Arab countries as we would have had to do if our economy had depended heavily on them and if we had lacked economic and other leverage. The United States could manipulate the crisis that others made in order to promote a balance of interests and forces holding some promise of peace. The unequal incidence of shortages led to the possibility of their manipulation. What does it mean then to say that the world is an increasingly interdependent one in which all nations are constrained, a world in which all nations lose control? Very little. To trace the effects that follow from inequalities, one has to unpack the word "interdependent" and identify the varying mixtures of relative dependence for some nations and of relative independence for others. As one should expect in a world of highly unequal nations, some are severely limited while others have wide ranges of choice; some have little ability to affect events outside of their borders while others have immense influence.

The energy crisis should have made this obvious, but it did not. Commentators on public affairs continue to emphasize the world's interdependence and to talk as though all nations are losing control and becoming more closely bound. Transmuting concepts into realities and endowing them with causal force is a habit easily slipped into. Public officials and students of international affairs once wrote of the balance of power causing war or preserving peace. They now attribute a comparable reality to the concept of interdependence and endow it with strong causal effect. Thus Secretary Kissinger, who can well represent both groups, wondered "whether interdependence would foster common progress or common disaster" (January 24, 1975, p.1). He described American Middle-East policy as being to reduce Europe's and Japan's vulnerability, to engage in dialogue with the producers, and "to give effect to the principle of interdependence on a global basis" (January 16, 1975, p. 3). Interdependence has become a thing in itself: a "challenge" with its own requirements, "a physical and moral imperative" (January 24, 1975, p. 2; April 20, 1974, p. 3).

When he turned to real problems, however, Kissinger emphasized America's special position. The pattern of his many statements on such problems as energy, food, and nuclear proliferation was first to emphasize that our common plight denies all possibility of effective national action and then to place the United States in a separate category. Thus, two paragraphs after declaring our belief in interdependence, we find this query: "In what other country could a leader say, 'We are going to solve energy; we're going to solve food; we're going to solve the problem of nuclear war,' and be taken seriously?" (October 13, 1974, p. 2)

In coupling his many statements about interdependence with words about what we can do to help ourselves and others, was Kissinger not saying that we are much less dependent than most countries are? We are all constrained but, it appears, not equally. Gaining control of international forces that affect nations is a problem for all of them, but some solve the problem better than others. The costs of shortages fall on all of us, but in different proportion. Interdependence, one might think, is a euphemism used to obscure the dependence of most countries (cf. Goodwin 1976, p. 63). Not so, Kissinger says. Like others, we are caught in the web because failure to solve major resource problems would lead to recession in other countries and ruin the international economy. That would hurt all of us. Indeed it would, but again the uneven incidence of injuries inflicted on nations is ignored. Recession in some countries hurts others, but some more and some less so. An unnamed Arab oil minister's grip on economics appeared stronger than Kissinger's. If an oil shortage should drive the American economy into recession, he observed, all of the world would suffer. "Our economies, our regimes, our very survival, depend on a healthy U.S. economy" (*Newsweek*, March 25, 1974, p. 43). How much a country will suffer depends roughly on how much of its business is done abroad. As Chancellor Schmidt said in October of 1975, West Germany's economy depends much more than ours does on a strong international economic recovery because it exports 25 percent of its GNP yearly (October 7, 1975). The comparable figure for the United States was seven percent.

No matter how one turns it, the same answer comes up: We depend somewhat on the external world, and most other countries depend on the external world much more so. Countries that are dependent on others in important respects work to limit or lessen their dependence if they can reasonably hope to do so.* From late 1973 onward, in the period of oil embargo and increased prices, Presidents Nixon and Ford, Secretary Kissinger, and an endless number of American leaders proclaimed both a new era of interdependence and the goal of making the United States energy-independent by 1985. This is so much the natural behavior of major states that not only the speakers but seemingly also their audiences failed to notice the humor. Because states are in a self-help system, they try to avoid becoming dependent on others for vital goods and services. To achieve energy independence would be costly. Economists rightly point out that by their definition of interdependence the cost of achieving the goal is a measure of how much international conditions affect us. But that is to think of interdependence merely as sensitivity. Politically the important point is that only the few industrial countries of greatest capability are able to think seriously of becoming independent in energy supply. As Kissinger put it: "We have greater latitude than the others because we can do much on our own. The others can't" (January 13, 1975, p. 76)....

---

*Notice the implication of the following statement made by Leonid Brezhnev: "Those who think that we need ties and exchanges in the economic and scientific-technical fields more than elsewhere are mistaken. The entire volume of USSR imports from capitalist countries comes to less than 1.5% of our gross social product. It is clear that this does not have decisive importance for the Soviet economy's development" (October 5, 1976, p.3).

When the great powers of the world were small in geographic compass, they did a high proportion of their business abroad. The narrow concentration of power in the present and the fact that the United States and the Soviet Union are little dependent on the rest of the world produce a very different international situation. The difference between the plight of great powers in the new bipolar world and the old multipolar can be seen by contrasting America's condition with that of earlier great powers. When Britain was the world's leading state economically, the portion of her wealth invested abroad far exceeded the portion that now represents America's stake in the world. In 1910 the value of total British investment abroad was one-and-one-half times larger than her national income. In 1973 the value of total American investments abroad was one-fifth as large as her national income. In 1910 Britain's return on investment abroad amounted to eight percent of national income; in 1973 the comparable figure for the United States was 1.6 percent (British figures computed from Imlah 1958, pp. 70-75, and Woytinsky and Woytinsky 1953, p. 791, Table 335; American figures computed from CIEP, March 1976, pp. 160-62, Tables 42, 47, and *US Bureau of the Census,* 1975, p. 384, and *Survey of Current Business,* October 1975, p. 48). Britain in its heyday had a huge stake in the world, and that stake loomed large in relation to her national product. From her immense and far-flung activities, she gained a considerable leverage. Because of the extent to which she depended on the rest of the world, wise and skillful use of that leverage was called for. Great powers in the old days depended on foodstuffs and raw materials imported from abroad much more heavily than the United States and the Soviet Union do now. Their dependence pressed them to make efforts to control the sources of their vital supplies.

Today the myth of interdependence both obscures the realities of international politics and asserts a false belief about the conditions that promote peace, as World War I conclusively showed. "The statistics of the economic interdependence of Germany and her neighbors," John Maynard Keynes remarked, "are overwhelming." Germany was the best customer of six European states, including Russia and Italy; the second best customer of three, including Britain; and the third best customer of France. She was the largest source of supply for ten European states, including Russia, Austria-Hungary, and Italy; and the second largest source of supply for three, including Britain and France (Keynes 1920, p. 17). And trade then was proportionately much higher than now. Then governments were more involved internationally than they were in their national economies. Now governments are more involved in their national economies than they are internationally. This is fortunate.

Economically, the low dependence of the United States means that the costs of, and the odds on, losing our trading partners are low. Other countries depend more on us than we do on them. If links are cut, they suffer more than we do. Given this condition, sustained economic sanctions against us would amount to little more than economic self-mutilation. The

United States can get along without the rest of the world better than most of its parts can get along without us. But, someone will hasten to say, if Russia, or anyone, should be able to foreclose American trade and investment in successively more parts of the world, we could be quietly strangled to death. To believe that, one has to think not in terms of politics but in terms of the apocalypse. If some countries want to deal less with us, others will move economically closer to us. More so than any other country, the United States can grant or withhold a variety of favors, in matters of trade, aid, loans, the supply of atomic energy for peaceful purposes, and military security. If peaceful means for persuading other countries to comply with preferred American policies are wanted, the American government does not have to look far to find them. The Soviet Union is even less dependent economically on the outside world than we are, but has less economic and political leverage on it. We are more dependent economically on the outside world than the Soviet Union is, but have more economic and political leverage on it.

The size of the two great powers gives them some capacity for control and at the same time insulates them with some comfort from the effect of other states' behavior. The inequality of nations produces a condition of equilibrium at a low level of interdependence. This is a picture of the world quite different from the one that today's transnationalists and interdependers paint. They cling to an economic version of the domino theory: Anything that happens anywhere in the world may damage us directly or through its repercussions, and therefore we have to react to it. This assertion holds only if the politically important nations are closely coupled. We have seen that they are not. Seldom has the discrepancy been wider between the homogeneity suggested by "interdependence" and the heterogeneity of the world we live in. A world composed of greatly unequal units is scarcely an interdependent one. A world in which a few states can take care of themselves quite well and most states cannot hope to do so is scarcely an interdependent one. A world in which the Soviet Union and China pursue exclusionary policies is scarcely an interdependent one. A world of bristling nationalism is scarcely an interdependent one. The confusion of concepts works against clarity of analysis and obscures both the possibilities and the necessities of action. Logically it is wrong, and politically it is obscurantist, to consider the world a unit and call it "interdependent."

References

Brezhnev, L. I. (October 5, 1976). "Brezhnev gives interview on French TV." In *The Current Digest of the Soviet Press*, vol. 28. Columbus: Ohio State University, November 3, 1976.

CIEP: Council on International Economic Policy (December 1974). (March 1976). *International Economic Report of the President*. Washington, D.C.: GPO

———. (January 1977). *International Economic Report of the President.* Washington, D.C.: GPO.

Cooper, Richard N. (1968). *The Economics of Interdependence.* New York: McGraw-Hill.

———. (January 1972). "Economic interdependence and foreign policy in the seventies." World Politics, vol. 24.

Finney, John W. (January 18, 1976). "Dreadnought or dinosaur." *New York Times Magazine.*

Goodwin, Geoffrey L. (1976). "International institutions and the limits of interdependence." In Avi Shlaim (ed.), *International Organizations in World Politics: Yearbook, 1975.* London: Croom Helm.

Imlah, A. H. (1958). *Economic Elements in the Pax Britannica.* Cambridge: Harvard University Press.

Keynes, John Maynard (1920). *The Economic Consequences of the Peace.* New York: Harcourt, Brace and Howe.

———. (September 1, 1926). "The end of laissez-faire—II." *New Republic,* vol 48.

———. (n.d.) *The General Theory of Employment, Interest, and Money.* New York: Harcourt, Brace.

Kissinger, Henry A. (1957). *Nuclear Weapons and Foreign Policy.* New York: Harper.

———. (1964). *A World Restored.* New York: Grosset and Dunlap.

———. (1965). *The Troubled Partnership.* New York: McGraw-Hill.

———. (Summer 1968). "The white revolutionary: reflections on Bismarck." *Daedalus,* vol. 97.

———. (April 24, 1973). "Text of Kissinger's talk at A.P. meeting here on U.S. relations with Europe." *New York Times.*

———. (October 10, 1973). "At Pacem in Terris conference." *News Release.* Bureau of Public Affairs: Department of State.

———. (April 20, 1974). "Good partner policy for Americas described by Secretary Kissinger." *New Release.* Bureau of Public Affairs: Department of State.

———. (October 13, 1974). "Interview by James Reston of the *New York Times.*" The Secretary of State. Bureau of Public Affairs: Department of State.

———. (January 13, 1975). "Kissinger on oil, food, and trade." *Business Week.*

———. (January 16, 1975). "Interview: for Bill Moyers' Journal." *The Secretary of State.* Bureau of Public Affairs: Department of State.

———. (January 24, 1975). "A new national partnership." *The Secretary of State.* Bureau of Public Affairs: Department of State.

———. (September 13, 1975). "Secretary Henry A. Kissinger interviewed by William F. Buckley, Jr." *The Secretary of State.* Bureau of Public Affairs: Department of State.

———. (December 23, 1975). "Major topics: Angola and detente." *The Secretary of State.* Bureau of Public Affairs: Department of State.

———. (September 30, 1976). "Toward a new understanding of community." *The Secretary of State.* Bureau of Public Affairs: Department of State.

———. (January 10, 1977). "Laying the foundations of a long-term policy." *The Secretary of State.* Bureau of Public Affairs:Department of State.

Kuznets, Simon (Winter 1951). "The state as a unit in study of economic growth." *Journal of Economic History,* vol. 11.

———. (1966). *Modern Economic Growth.* New Haven: Yale University Press.

———. (January 1967). "Quantitative aspects of the economic growth of nations: Paper X." *Economic Development and Cultural Change,* vol. 15.

Marx, Karl, and Frederick Engels (1848). *Communist Manifesto.* Translator unnamed. Chicago: Charles H. Kerr, 1946.

Newsweek (March 25, 1974). "Oil embargo: the Arab's compromise."

Schmidt, Helmut (October 7, 1975). "Schmidt, Ford 'cautiously optimistic' on world's economic recovery." *The Bulletin.* Bonn: Press and Information Office, Government of the Federal Republic of Germany, vol. 23.

Snyder, Glenn H. (1966). *Stockpiling Strategic Materials.* San Francisco: Chandler.

Strange, Susan (January 1971). "The politics of international currencies." *World Politics,* vol. 22.

Survey of Current Business (various issues). U.S. Department of Commerce, Bureau of Economic Analysis. Washington, D.C.: GPO.

UN Department of Economic Affairs (1949). *International Capital Movements During the Inter-War Period.* New York.

———. Department of Economic and Social Affairs (1961). *International Flow of Long Term Capital and Official Donations.* New York.

———. Statistical Office (1957, 1961, 1970, 1974). *Yearbook of National Accounts Statistics.* New York.

———. (1966). *Demographic Yearbook,* 1965, New York.

———. (1976). *Statistical Yearbook,* 1975, vol. 27. New York.

———. (1977). *Statistical Yearbook,* 1976, vol. 28. New York.

US Agency for International Development, Statistics and Reports Divisions (various years). *US Overseas Loans and Grants: July 1, 1945*. Washington, D.C.: GPO.

———. Bureau of the Census (1975). *Statistical Abstract, 1974.* Washington, D.C.: GPO.

———. Bureau of the Census (1976). *Historical Statistics of the United States: Colonial Times to 1970.* Washington, D.C.: GPO.

———. Department of Commerce, Bureau of Economic Analysis (1975). *Revised Data Series on US Direct Investment Abroad, 1966-1974.* Washington, D.C.: GPO.

———. Department of the Interior (June 1976). *Energy Perspectives 2.* Washington, D.C.: GPO.

———. Senate Committee on Finance (February 1973). *Implications of Multinational Firms for World Trade and Investment and for U.S. Trade and Labor.* Washington, D.C.: GPO.

———. Senate Committee on Government Operations, Permanent Subcommittee on Investigations (August 1974). *Selected Readings on Energy Self-Sufficiency and the Controlled Materials Plan.* Washington, D.C.: GPO.

Woytinsky, W. S., and E. S. Woytinsky (1953). *World Population and Production.* New York: Twentieth Century Fund.

Trade and Power

RICHARD ROSECRANCE

In the age of mercantilism—an era in which power and wealth combined—statesmen and stateswomen (for who dares to slight Elizabeth I or Catherine the Great) sought not only territory but also a monopoly of markets of particular goods highly valued in Europe, gold, silver, spices, sugar, indigo, tobacco. Who controlled local production and sales also determined the market in Europe and obtained a monopoly return. Initially, Venice and Genoa vied for dominance of the spice trade from the twelfth to the fourteenth centuries, a struggle that was interrupted by Portuguese navigators, sailors, and soldiers who temporarily established control of the Indies at their source. Later Holland ousted Portugal in the East Indies, and England and France took her place in India. By the seventeenth century, Spain could no longer hold her position in the Caribbean and the New World as Holland, England, and France disputed her monopoly, first by capturing her bullion fleets, then by seizing sugar islands as well as parts of the North American mainland. In the eighteenth century Britain won victory practically everywhere, though Holland was left with the Dutch East Indies, France with her sugar islands in the Caribbean, and Spain with a reduced position in North and South America. As William Pitt the Elder pointed out, "commerce had been made to flourish by war"[1]—English monopolies of colonial produce won her great dividends in trade with the continent. Her near monopoly of overseas empire and tropical products produced a great flow of continuing revenue that supported British military and naval exploits around the world. From either standpoint—territorial or economic—military force could be used to conquer territories or commodity-producing areas that would contribute greater revenue and power in Europe. With a

Richard Rosecrance, *The Rise of the Trading State: Commerce and Conquest in the Modern World* (New York: Basic Books, 1986), excerpts from chapters 1 and 7. Copyright © 1986 by Richard Rosecrance. Reprinted by permission of Basic Books, a division of HarperCollins Publishers.

[1]Quoted in Walter L. Dorn, *Competition for Empire* (New York: Harper & Row, 1940), p. 370.

monopoly on goods or territories, one nation or kingdom could forge ahead of others.

Thus we have one basic means by which nations have made their way in the world—by increasing their territories and maintaining them against other states. Sometimes, less cultured or civilized nations have by this means upset ruling empires or centers of civilization. In the past the barbarian invasions disrupted Rome; Attila the Hun and his followers intruded upon Mediterranean civilization; Genghis Khan and his military nomads ranged into Eastern Europe; Islam and the Turks dynamically transformed the culture of the Mediterranean and Southern Europe. In fact, it was not until the relatively recent period that highly developed economic centers could hold their own against military and agrarian peoples. The waging of war and the seizure of territory have been relatively easy tasks for most of Western history. It is not surprising that when territorial states began to take shape in the aftermath of the Reformation, they were organized for the purpose both of waging and of resisting war, and the seventeenth century became the most warlike of epochs. Kings and statesmen could most rapidly enhance their positions through territorial combat.

Associated with the drive for territory is an allied system of international relations which we will here call the "military political or territorial" system The more nations choose to conquer territory, the more dominant the allied system of international politics will be. Because territorial expansion has been the dominant mode of national policy since 1648 and the Peace of Westphalia, it is not surprising that the military-political and territorial system has been the prevailing system of international relations since then. In this system, war and the threat of war are the omnipresent features of interstate relationships, and states fear a decisive territorial setback or even extinction. This has not been an idle concern, if one considers that 95 percent of the state-units which existed in Europe in the year 1500 have now been obliterated, subdivided, or combined into other countries.

Whatever else a nation-state does, therefore, it must be concerned with the territorial balance in international politics and no small part of its energies will be absorbed by defense. But defense and territory are not the only concerns of states, nor is territorial expansion the only means by which nations hope to improve their fortunes. If war provides one means of national advancement, peace offers another.

The Oil Crisis, 1973–1980

Probably more important in the long-term than the battles of the fourth Arab-Israeli war was the oil crisis and embargo of 1973-74. While the war was being fought, the Organization of Petroleum Exporting Countries (OPEC) announced on October 16, 1973, its first unilateral increase of 70 percent, bringing the cost of a barrel of oil to $5.12. At the end of the year it had been raised to $11.65 (a further 128 percent increase), and by 1980 had risen to almost $40.00 a barrel, about twenty times the price in early 1970. In addition, the Arabs announced oil production cutbacks and on October 20, embargoed all oil exports to the United States and The Netherlands, the two countries closest to Israel.

These decisions stimulated different responses in America and abroad. Most European allies and Japan quickly made it clear that they sympathized with the Arab cause and distanced themselves from the United States. Nixon in response announced "Project Independence" on November 7, which committed the United States to free itself from the need to import oil by 1980. This difficult goal was to be accomplished by conservation and the development of alternative sources of energy. The objective was not achieved, of course, for the United States imported roughly the same 36 to 37 percent of its oil needs in 1980 as it had in 1973. No evolution would allow it to return to the nearly self-sufficient 8.1 percent level of 1947.

There were four ways in which the oil crisis might have been overcome. The first was through the traditional method used by the United States in the Middle East crises of 1956 and 1967. In response to an oil embargo, the United States could simply increase its domestic production of oil, allocating stockpiles to its allies. The United States had had the leverage to do this in previous years because excess domestic capacity more than provided for national requirements, leaving a surplus to be exported abroad, if need arose. In 1956, the United States imported 11 percent of its oil but had a reserve domestic production capacity that could provide for an additional 25 percent of its needs. In 1967, while oil imports had risen to 19 percent of its oil consumption, the United States possessed a similar ability to expand its production by 25 percent, more than replacing imported oil. By 1973, however, the low price of oil and past domestic production had eroded United State reserves. It now imported 35 percent of its needs and could increase production only by an additional 10 percent.[2] When the Arabs embargoed oil shipments to the United States, there was no way for the country to increase domestic production to cover the shortfall. If a solution was to be found, it depended upon reallocating production abroad. As it turned out, the embargo caused no difficulty or shortage in America, because the oil companies simply re-routed production, sending Arab production to compliant European states and Japan, and non-Arab production to the United States and Holland. This measure solved the supply problem, but it did nothing to alleviate the high price. Extra United States production would not be sufficient to create a glut in the world marketplace and thus force a drop in the OPEC price.

A second method of coping with the crisis was to form a cartel of buyers of oil, principally the United States, Europe, and Japan, together with a few developing countries. If all could agree to buy oil at a fixed low price, OPEC

[2]See R. Keohane, *After Hegemony* (Princeton: Princeton University Press, 1984), p. 199.

would not be able to sell abroad on its terms and would have to reduce the price. Since it was the formation of the producers' cartel (OPEC) which had forced up the price of oil, many thought that only a consumers' cartel could offset its bargaining leverage and bring the price down. Despite American attempts to organize such a consumers' group in 1973 and 1974, the other nations preferred to play an independent role. France, Germany, and Japan negotiated separate oil contracts with individual Arab countries, guaranteeing access to Middle Eastern oil over the long term. They would not cooperate with the United States. When the American-sponsored International Energy Agency was finally set up in 1974, it became an information gathering agency which could allocate supplies of oil only in a crisis and had no monopoly bargaining power.

A third means of overcoming the oil crisis and reducing the real price of oil was through military intervention. This was considered at the end of 1974 and the beginning of 1975 when Secretary of State Kissinger hinted intervention if "actual strangulation of the West" was threatened. Some concluded that the Persian Gulf fields should be seized by United States marines or units of a Rapid Deployment Force. Occupation of such thinly populated areas was possible. The question, however, was whether production could be started up and maintained in the face of determined sabotage by Arab resistance groups, including the Palestine Liberation Organization. Would pipelines be cut or harbors mined? Would oil tankers have free passage through the Gulf? These uncertainties could not be resolved over the long period that would be required to break the Arab embargo and reduce the price of petroleum.

The final and ultimately successful means of overcoming the crisis came through diplomacy and the mechanism of the world market. After the success of the Israeli-Egyptian shuttle negotiations producing a withdrawal of forces on the Sinai front, the very beginning of talks on the Golan with Syria and Israel led the Arabs to end the oil embargo on March 18, 1974.[3] This had no impact on oil prices or supply and therefore did not change the OPEC bargaining position. That awaited complex developments in the world market for oil and for industrial products. In 1973—74, it was generally believed that the market for oil was inelastic, that demand would not decline greatly with an increase in the oil price. If it did not, the Arabs would gain an incredible premium, and a huge surplus of funds. It was estimated that as much as $600 billion might flow to Arab producers over a ten-year period. They would never be able to spend that much importing goods from the industrial and oil-consuming countries; hence, huge Arab surpluses would build up—funds that could have no economic use in the Arab states themselves. The flow of funds from importing countries to OPEC was partly offset when about half the surplus was used to buy Western imports and

[3]Henry A. Kissinger, *Years of Upheaval* (Boston: Little Brown, 1982), pp. 891-95, 939-45, 975-78.

another large portion was invested in the world financial market, largely in the form of short-term deposits in Western banks. The banks and international financial agencies could then lend funds to the consuming countries, enabling them to finance their oil purchases. At the same time consumers became unwilling or unable to pay the high price. Even in the traditionally energy-extravagant United States, the amount of energy needed to produce one dollar of the gross national product declined 25 percent from 1973 to 1983. The average gas consumption of American-made automobiles almost doubled in the same period to reach 24.6 miles per gallon. Most of the leading industrial corporations instituted energy-conservation programs. The demand for oil dropped.

Between 1973 and 1979 industrial prices in the developed world increased more than oil prices. In the wake of the oil crisis and the ensuing inflation, many governments resorted to freely fluctuating exchange rates for their currencies. No longer under the discipline of gold flows, they could experiment with domestic economic expansion, convinced that their currencies values would not get out of line or their trade balance deteriorate. The result was further inflation of wages, prices, and industrial products. This had two effects on the Arab oil countries. First, it meant that they had to pay a great deal more to buy industrial goods, using up the oil surplus that they were beginning to accumulate. Second, as inflation advanced in the West and Japan, industrial entrepreneurs hesitated to invest, uncertain of their long-run return. Western economies ground to a halt and unemployment mounted. For a decade after 1973, the industrialized world grew at only 2 percent per year, and the number of jobless workers doubled. As a result, Arab investments in the developed countries were threatened by declines in Western profits and wages. Too high oil prices temporarily forced the industrial world into economic stagnation in which it would buy little Middle Eastern oil. The oil price increase, with the exception of the sudden rise of 1979-80, halted and reversed. Even the Iran-Iraq war did not lead to a new jump in prices. Oil consumption of the advanced industrial countries fell by seven million barrels a day between 1979 and 1982. In addition new oil production outside of OPEC increased, and OPEC production declined by twelve million barrels a day. Oil came into surplus, and the price fell back to $28 per barrel by 1983. The oil countries, which also suffered from the worldwide inflation, found they did not have sufficient export surplus to meet their needs in food and industrial imports. In 1982, eight Middle Eastern producers faced a deficit of $23 to $26 billion. Even Ayatollah Ruhollah Khomeini's Iran had to increase its oil production to finance imports and its war with Iraq.

The strange outcome was that the oil and energy crisis abated. The Arabs saw reason for increasing production while holding down the price, but the collapse in international demand for oil was so great, that the price could not be maintained. Consumers emerged in a much better position. The developing countries, which had borrowed to cover oil and industrial imports, found high interest rates imperilling their financial solvency in the first half of the 1980s. Paradoxically, there was then too little Arab money and too small an oil surplus to cover their borrowing needs.

The oil crisis underscored another means of dealing with conflict among nation-states. Instead of defending or fighting over territorial claims, nations found a way to reach a compromise through an international flow of funds, domestic economic adjustments, and world trade. The imbalance in payments threatened by the huge Arab oil surpluses in 1973-74 was reversed by the first years of the 1980s. Despite Kissinger's threats, force was not used to assure Western access to oil, and overarching cooperation was the ruling principle between industrial and oil-producing regions of the world. Each benefitted from the exchange, and consuming countries did not have to adopt policies of national self-sufficiency, reducing income and employment to the point where energy needs could be met on a national basis. Each side, instead, relied upon the other for the products it required.

Territorial gain is not the only means of advancing a nation's interest, and, in the nuclear age, wars of territorial expansion are not only dangerous, they are costly and threatening to both sides. Much more tenable is a policy of economic development and progress sustained by the medium of international trade. If national policies of economic growth depend upon an expanding world market, one country can hardly expect to rely primarily upon territorial aggression and aggrandizement. To attack one's best customers is to undermine the commercial faith and reciprocity in which exchange takes place. Thus, while the territorial and military-political means to national improvement causes inevitable conflict with other nations, the trading method is consistent with international cooperation. No other country's territory is attacked; the benefits that one nation gains from trade can also be realized by others.

If this is true, and two means of national advancement do indeed exist, why is it that Western and world history is mainly a narrative of territorial and military expansion, of unending war, to the detriment of the world's economic and trading system? Louis XIV and Napoleon would easily understand the present concern with territorial frontiers and the military balance, to the degree that one is hard put to explain what has changed in the past three hundred years.

The answer is that states have not until recently had to depend upon one another for the necessities of daily existence. In the past, trade was a tactical endeavor, a method used between wars, and one that could easily be sacrificed when military determinants so decreed. The great outpouring of trade between nations in the latter half of the nineteenth century did not prevent the First World War; it could be stanched as countries resorted to military means to acquire the territory or empire that would make them independent of others. No national leader would sacrifice territory to gain trade, unless the trade constituted a monopoly. Leaders aimed to have all needed resources in their own hands and did not wish to rely upon others.

As long as a state could get bigger and bigger, there was no incentive to re-gard trade with others as a strategic requirement, and for most of European history since the Renaissance, state units appeared to be growing larger. The five hundred or so units in Europe in 1500 were consolidated into about twenty-five by the year 1900.[4] If this process continued, statesmen and peo-ples could look forward to the creation of a few huge states like those in Or-well's *1984* which together controlled the globe. The process of imperialism in the late nineteenth century forwarded this conception: ultimately a few empires would become so enormous that they would not have to depend upon anyone else. Thus, the failure of the imperialist drive and the rapid de-colonization of recent years have meant a change of direction in world poli-tics. Since 1900, and especially after 1945, the number of nation-states has greatly increased, even more swiftly than the number belonging to the United Nations organizations. Between 170 and 180 states exist, and the number is growing. If contemporary nationalist and ethnic separatist move-ments succeed, some states in Europe, Africa, Asia, and Oceania may be fur-ther subdivided into new independent states or autonomous regions. These small and even weak states will scarcely be self-reliant; increasingly they will come to depend on others for economic and even military necessities, trad-ing or sharing responsibilities with other nations. The age of the indepen-dent, self-sufficient state will be at an end. Among such states, the method of international development sustained by trade and exchange will begin to take precedence over the traditional method of territorial expansion and war. . . .

The Trading World

. . .The role of Japan and Germany in the trading world is exceedingly inter-esting because it represents a reversal of past policies in both the nineteenth century and the 1930s. It is correct to say that the two countries experi-mented with foreign trade because they had been disabused of military ex-pansion by World War II. For a time they were incapable of fighting war on a major scale; their endorsement of the trading system was merely an adop-tion of the remaining policy alternative. But that endorsement did not change even when the economic strength of the two nations might have sus-tained a much more nationalistic and militaristic policy. Given the choice between military expansion to achieve self-sufficiency (a choice made more difficult by modern conventional and nuclear weapons in the hands of other powers) and the procurement of necessary markets and raw materials through international commerce, Japan and Germany chose the latter.

---

[4]Charles Tilly, ed., *The Formation of National States in Western Europe* (Princeton: Princeton Uni-versity Press, 1975), p. 24.

It was not until the nineteenth century that this choice became available. During the mercantilist period (1500-1775) commerce was hobbled by restrictions, and any power that relied on it was at the mercy of the tariffs and imperial expansion of other nations. Until the late eighteenth century internal economic development was slow, and there seemed few means of adding to national wealth and power except by conquering territories which contained more peasants and grain. With the Industrial Revolution the link between territory and power was broken; it then became possible to gain economic strength without conquering new lands.[5] New sources of power could be developed within a society, simply by mobilizing them industrially. When combined with peaceful international trade, the Industrial Revolution allowed manufactured goods to find markets in faraway countries. The extra demand would lengthen production runs and increase both industrial efficiency (through economies of scale) and financial return. Such a strategy, if adhered to by all nations, could put an end to war. There was no sense in using military force to acquire power and wealth when they could be obtained more efficiently through peaceful economic development and trade.

The increasing prevalence of the trading option since 1945 raises peaceful possibilities that were neglected during the late nineteenth century and the 1930s. It seems safe to say that an international system composed of more than 160 states cannot continue to exist unless trade remains the primary vocation of most of its members. Were military and territorial orientations to dominate the scene, the trend to greater numbers of smaller states would be reversed, and larger states would conquer small and weak nations.

The possibility of such amalgamations cannot be entirely ruled out. Industrialization had two possible impacts: it allowed a nation to develop its wealth peacefully through internal economic growth, but it also knit new sinews of strength that could coerce other states. Industrialization made territorial expansion easier but also less necessary. In the mid-nineteenth century the Continental states pursued the expansion of their territories while Britain expanded her industry. The industrialization of Prussia and the development of her rail network enabled her armies to defeat Denmark, Austria, and France. Russia also used her new industrial technology to strengthen her military. In the last quarter of the century, even Britain returned to a primarily military and imperialist policy. In his book on imperialism Lenin declared that the drive for colonies was an imminent tendency of the capitalist system. Raw materials would run short and investment capital would pile up at home. The remedy was imperialism with colonies providing new sources for the former and outlets for the latter. But Lenin did not fully understand that an open international economy and intensive

---

[5]It is true that the greatest imperial edifices were constructed after the start of the Industrial Revolution. It was precisely that revolution, however, which prepared the groundwork for their demise.

economic development at home obviated the need for colonies even under a capitalist, trading system.

The basic effect of World War II was to create much higher world interdependence as the average size of countries declined. The reversal of past trends toward a consolidation of states created instead a multitude of states that could not depend on themselves alone. They needed ties with other nations to prosper and remain viable as small entities. The trading system, as a result, was visible in defense relations as well as international commerce. Nations that could not stand on their own sought alliances or assistance from other powers, and they offered special defense contributions in fighting contingents, regional experience, or particular types of defense hardware. Dutch electronics, French aircraft, German guns and tanks, and British ships all made their independent contribution to an alliance in which no single power might be able to meet its defense needs on a self-sufficient basis. Israel developed a powerful and efficient small arms industry, as well as a great fund of experience combating terrorism. Israeli intelligence added considerably to the information available from Western sources, partly because of its understanding of Soviet weapons systems accumulated in several Arab-Israeli wars.

Defense interdependencies, however, are only one means of sharing the burdens placed upon the modern state. Perhaps more important is economic interdependence among countries. One should not place too much emphasis upon the existence of interdependence per se. European nations in 1913 relied upon the trade and investment between them; that did not prevent the political crisis which led to a breakdown of the international system and to World War I. Interdependence only constrains national policy if leaders accept and agree to work within its limits. In 1914 Lloyds of London had insured the German merchant marine but that did not stop Germany attacking Belgium, a neutral nation, or England from joining the war against Berlin.[6] The United States was Japan's best customer and source of raw materials in the 1930s, but that did not deter the Japanese attack on Pearl Harbor.

At least among the developed and liberal countries, interdependent ties since 1945 have come to be accepted as a fundamental and unchangeable feature of the situation. This recognition dawned gradually, and the United States may perhaps have been the last to acknowledge it, which was not surprising. The most powerful economy is ready to make fewer adjustments, and America tried initially to pursue its domestic economic policies without taking into account the effect on others, on itself, and on the international financial system as a whole. Presidents Kennedy and Lyndon B. Johnson tried to detach American domestic growth strategies from the deteriorating United States balance of payments, but they left a legacy of needed eco-

---

[6]Paul Kennedy, *Strategy and Diplomacy 1870-1945* (London: Fontana Paperbacks 1984), pp.95-96.

nomic change to their successors. Finally, in the 1980s two American administrations accepted lower United States growth in order to control inflation and begin to focus on the international impact of United States policies. The delay in fashioning a strategy of adjustment to international economic realities almost certainly made it more difficult. Smaller countries actively sought to find a niche in the structure of international comparative advantage and in the demand for their goods. Larger countries with large internal markets postponed that reckoning as long as they could. By the 1980s, however, such change could no longer be avoided, and the United States leaders embarked upon new industrial and tax policies designed to increase economic growth and enable America to compete more effectively abroad.

The acceptance of new approaches was a reflection of the decline in economic sovereignty. As long as governments could control all the forces impinging upon their economies, welfare states would have no difficulty in implementing domestic planning for social ends. But as trade, investment, corporations, and to some degree labor moved from one national jurisdiction to another, no government could insulate and direct its economy without instituting the extreme protectionist and "beggar thy neighbor" policies of the 1930s. Rather than do this, the flow of goods and capital was allowed to proceed, and in recent years it has become a torrent. In some cases the flow of capital has increased to compensate for barriers or rigidities to the movement of goods.

In both cases the outcome is the result of modern developments in transportation and communications. Railway and high-speed highway networks now allow previously landlocked areas to participate in the international trading network that once depended on rivers and access to the sea. Modern communications and computers allow funds to be instantaneously transferred from one market to another, so that they may earn interest twenty-four hours a day. Transportation costs for a variety of goods have reached a new low, owing to container shipping and handling. For the major industrial countries (member countries of the Organization for Economic Cooperation and Development, which include the European community, Austria, Finland, Iceland, Portugal, Norway, Spain, Sweden, Switzerland, Turkey, Australia, Canada, Japan, New Zealand, and the United States), exports have risen much faster than either industrial production or gross domestic product since 1965, with the growth of GDP (in constant prices) at 4 percent and that of exports at 7.7 percent.[7] Only Japan's domestic growth has been able to keep pace with the increase in exports (see Table 6).

Foreign trade (the sum of exports and imports) percentages were roughly twice as large as these figures in each case. The explosion of foreign trade since 1945 has, if anything, been exceeded by the enormous movement of capital.

[7]Michael Stewart, *The Age of Interdependence* (Cambridge, Mass: MIT Press, 1984), p. 20.

In 1950 the value of the stock of direct foreign investment held by U.S. companies was $11.8 billions, compared with $7.2 billions in 1935, $7.6 billions in 1929 and $3.9 billions in 1914. In the following decade, these investments increased by $22.4 billions, and at the end of 1967 their total value stood at $59 billions.[8]

In 1983, it had reached $226 billions.[9] And direct investment (that portion of investment which buys a significant stake in a foreign firm) was only

TABLE 6
Exports of Goods and Services
(as a Percentage of GDP)

Country	1965	1979
United States	5	9
Japan	11	12
Germany	18	26
United Kingdom	20	29
France	14	22

NOTE: Michael Stewart, The Age of Interdependence (Cambridge, Mass: MIT Press, 1981). p. 21 (derived from United Nations *Yearbook of National Accounts Statistics*, 1980, vol. 2, table 2A).

one part of total United States investment overseas. In 1983 United States private assets abroad totaled $774 billion, or about three times as much.

The amounts, although very large, were not significant in themselves. In 1913, England's foreign investments, equaled one and one-half times her GNP as compared to present American totals of one-quarter of United States GNP. England's foreign trade was more than 40 percent of her national income as compared with contemporary American totals of 15-17 percent. England's pre-World War I involvement in international economic activities was greater than America's today.

Part of what must be explained in the evolution of interdependence is not the high level reached post-1945, but how even higher levels in 1913 could have fallen in the interim. Here the role of industrialization is paramount. As Karl Deutsch, following the work of Werner Sombart, has shown, in the early stages of industrial growth nations must import much of their needed machinery: rail and transportation networks are constructed with equip-

[8]John H. Dunning, *Studies in International Investment* (London: George Allen and Unwin, 1970), p. 1.
[9]"International Investment Position of the United States at Year End" in *Survey of Current Business* (Washington, D.C.: Department of Commerce, June 1984).

ment and materials from abroad. Once new industries have been created, in a variety of fields, ranging from textiles to heavy industry, the national economy can begin to provide the goods that previously were imported.[10] The United States, the Scandinavian countries, and Japan reached this stage only after the turn of the century, and it was then that the gasoline-powered automobile industry and the manufacturing of electric motors and appliances began to develop rapidly and flourish. The further refinement of agricultural technology also rested on these innovations. Thus, even without restrictions and disruptions of trade, the 1920s would not have seen a rehabilitation of the old interdependent world economy of the 1890s. The further barriers erected in the 1930s confirmed and extended this outcome. If new industrial countries had less need for manufacturing imports, the growth and maintenance of general trade would then come to depend upon an increase in some other category of commerce than the traditional exchange of raw materials for finished goods. In the 1920s, as Albert Hirschman shows, the reciprocal exchange of industrial goods increased briefly, but fell again in the 1930s.[11] That decrease was only made up after 1945 when there was a striking and continuing growth in the trade of manufactured goods among industrial countries.[12] Some will say that this trade is distinctly expendable because countries could produce the goods they import on their own. None of the trade that the United States has today with Western Europe or Japan could really be dubbed "critical" in that the United States could not get along without it. American alternatives exist to almost all industrial products from other developed economies. Thus if interdependence means a trading link which "is costly to break,"[13] there is a sense that the sheer physical dependence of one country upon another, or upon international trade as a whole, has declined since the nineteenth century.

But to measure interdependence in this way misses the essence of the concept. Individuals in a state of nature can be quite independent if they are willing to live at a low standard of living and gather herbs, nuts, and fruits. They are not forced to depend on others but decide to do so to increase their total amount of food and security. Countries in an international state of nature (anarchy) can equally decide to depend only on themselves. They can limit what they consume to what they can produce at home, but they will

[10]Karl W. Deutsch and Alexander Eckstein, "National Industrialism and the Declining Share of the International Economic Sector, 1890-1959" in *World Politics,* 13 (January 1961), pp. 267-99.

[11]*National Power and the Structure of Foreign Trade* (Berkeley: University of California Press, 1980), pp. 129-43.

[12]Richard Rosecrance and Arthur Stein, "Interdependence: Myth or Reality" in *World Politics* (July 1973), pp. 7-9.

[13]Kenneth Waltz, "The Myth of National Interdependence" in Charles Kindleberger, ed., *The International Corporation* (Cambridge, Mass.: MIT Press, 1970), p. 206.

thereby live less well than they might with specialization and extensive trade and interchange with other nations.

There is no shortage of energy in the world, for example, and all energy needs that previously have been satisfied by imported petroleum might be met by a great increase in coal and natural gas production, fission, and hydropower. But coal-generated electric power produces acid rain, and coal liquification (to produce fuel for automobiles) is expensive. Nuclear power leaves radioactive wastes which have to be contained. Importing oil is a cheaper and cleaner alternative. Thus even though a particular country, like the United States, might become energy self-sufficient if it wanted to, there is reason for dependence on the energy supplies of other nations. Does this mean creating a "tie that is costly to break"? Yes, in the sense that we live less well if we break the tie; but that doesn't mean that the tie could not be broken. Any tie can be broken. In this respect, all ties create "vulnerability interdependence" if they are in the interest of those who form them. One could get along without Japanese cars or European fashions, but eliminating them from the market restricts consumer choice and in fact raises opportunity costs. In this manner, trade between industrial countries may be equally important as trade linking industrial and raw material producing countries.

There are other ways in which interdependence has increased since the nineteenth century. Precisely because industrial countries imported agricultural commodities and sold their manufactured goods to less developed states, their dependence upon each other was much less in the nineteenth century and the 1920s than it is today. Toward the end of the nineteenth century Britain increasingly came to depend upon her empire for markets, food, and raw materials or upon countries in the early stages of industrialization. As Continental tariffs increased, Britain turned to her colonies, the United States, and Latin America to find markets for her exports. These markets provided

> ready receptacles for British goods when other areas became too competitive or unattractive; for example, Australia, India, Brazil and Argentina took the cotton, railways, steel and machinery that could not be sold in European markets. In the same way, whilst British capital exports to the latter dropped from 52 percent in the 1860s to 25 percent in the few years before 1914, those to the empire rose from 36 percent to 46 percent, and those to Latin America from 10.5 percent to 22 percent.[14]

The British foreign trade which totalled 43.5 percent of GNP in 1913 went increasingly to the empire; thus, if one takes Britain and the colonies as a single economic unit, that unit was much less dependent upon the outside world than, say, Britain is today with a smaller (30.4 percent) ratio of trade to GNP. And Britain alone had much less stake in Germany, France, and the

[14]Paul Kennedy, *The Rise and Fall of British Naval Mastery* (London: Allen Lane, 1976), pp. 187-88.

Continental countries' economies than she does today as a member of the European Common Market.

In the nineteenth century trade was primarily vertical in character, taking place between countries at different stages of industrial development, and involving an exchange of manufactured goods on the one hand for food and raw materials on the other. But trade was not the only element in vertical interdependence.

British investment was also vertical in that it proceeded from the developed center, London, to less developed capitals in the Western Hemisphere, Oceania, and the Far East. Such ties might contribute to community feeling in the British Empire, later the Commonwealth of Nations, but it would not restrain conflicts among the countries of Western Europe. Three-quarters of foreign investment of all European countries in 1914 was lodged outside of Europe. In 1913, in the British case 66 percent of her foreign investment went to North and South America and Australia, 28 percent to the Middle and Far East, and only 6 percent to Europe.

In addition, about 90 percent of foreign investment in 1913 was portfolio investment, that is, it represented small holdings of foreign shares that could easily be disposed of on the stock exchange. Direct investment, or investment which represented more than a 10 percent share of the total ownership of a foreign firm, was only one-tenth of the total. Today the corresponding figure for the United States is nearly 30 percent. The growth of direct foreign investment since 1945 is a reflection of the greater stake that countries have in each other's well-being in the contemporary period.

In this respect international interdependence has been fostered by a growing interpenetration of economies, in the sense that one economy owns part of another, sends part of its population to live and work in it, and becomes increasingly dependent upon the progress of the latter.[15] The multinational corporation which originates in one national jurisdiction, but operates in others as well, is the primary vehicle for such investment ownership. Stimulated by the demands and incentives of the product life cycle, the multinational corporation invests and produces abroad to make sure of retaining its market share. That market may be in the host country, or it may be in the home country, once the foreign production is imported back into the home economy. Foreign trade has grown enormously since 1945. But its necessary growth has been reduced by the operation of multinational companies in foreign jurisdictions: production abroad reduces the need for exports. In this way an interpenetrative stake has increased between

[15]Nothing could be more misleading than to equate these interrelations with those of nineteenth-century imperialism. Then imperial dictates went in one direction—military, economic, and social. The metropole dominated the colony. Today, does North America become a colony when Chicanos and Hispanics move to it in increasing numbers or England a tributary of the West Indies? Does Chinese or Korean investment in the United States render it a peripheral member of the system? The point is that influence goes in both directions just as does investment and trade in manufactured goods.

developed economies even when tariffs and other restrictions might appear to have stunted the growth of exports. The application of a common external tariff to the European Economic Community in the 1960s greatly stimulated American foreign investment in Europe, which became such a massive tide that Europeans reacted against the "American challenge," worrying that their prized national economic assets might be preempted by the United States.

They need not have worried. The reverse flow of European and Japanese investment in the United States is reaching such enormous proportions that America has become a net debtor nation: a country that has fewer assets overseas than foreigners have in the United States. The threatened imposition of higher American tariffs and quotas on imports led foreign companies to invest in the United States in gigantic amounts, thereby obviating the need to send exports from their home nation. Such direct investment represents a much more permanent stake in the economic welfare of the host nation than exports to that market could ever be. Foreign production is a more permanent economic commitment than foreign sales, because large shares of a foreign company or subsidiary could not be sold on a stock exchange. The attempt to market such large holdings would only have the effect of depressing the value of the stock. Direct investment is thus illiquid, as opposed to the traditional portfolio investment of the nineteenth century.

After 1945 one country slowly developed a stake in another, but the process was not initially reciprocal. Until the beginning of the 1970s, the trend was largely for Americans to invest abroad, in Europe, Latin America, and East Asia. As the American dollar cheapened after 1973, however, a reverse flow began, with Europeans and Japanese placing large blocs of capital in American firms and acquiring international companies. Third World multinationals, from Hong Kong, the OPEC countries, and East Asia also began to invest in the United States. By the end of the 1970s world investment was much more balanced, with the European stake in the American economy nearly offsetting the American investment in Europe. Japan also moved to diversify her export offensive in the American market by starting to produce in the United States. But Japan did not benefit from a reciprocal stake in her own economy. Since foreign investors have either been kept out of the Japanese market or have been forced to accept cumbersome joint ventures with Japanese firms, few multinationals have a major commitment to the Japanese market. Japan imports the smallest percentage of manufactured goods of any leading industrial nation. Thus when economic policy makers in America and Europe formulate growth strategies, they are not forced to consider the Japanese economy on a par with their own because American and Europeans have little to lose if Japan does not prosper. In her own self-interest Japan will almost certainly have to open her capital market and economy to foreign penetration if she wishes to enjoy corresponding access to economies of other nations. Greater Japanese foreign direct investment will only partly mitigate the pressures on Tokyo in this respect.

PART 5

Politics: Ideology and Identity

When E. H. Carr's *Twenty Years Crisis* was first published in 1939, many saw its case for realism as an argument for accommodation with German power. Liberal idealism interfered with what Carr saw as sensible policy by placing principle over prudence, and by confusing the particular morality of international relations that coincided with the self-interest of World War I's victorious powers with a disinterested universal morality.

Western liberalism was not the only visionary philosophy interfering with realist behavior. The unfolding of World War II made clear to most that Hitler was not just another opportunistic realist statesman who could be contained or deterred by traditional balance-of-power politics.[1] As Stanley Kober points out below, Nazi Germany showed that idealism can exert awesome force in international politics, and that Hitler must be understood as an idealist, rather than a pragmatist, in order to appreciate the unlimited nature of Nazi aims. It is also quite doubtful that realism, rather than imprudent idealism and wishful thinking, could have justified either Churchill's defiant refusal to make peace or his stirring insistence on pursuit of victory against all odds, in the dark days between the fall of France and Hitler's reckless decisions to take on the Soviet

---

[1] For the notorious yet not altogether unconvincing argument to the contrary, see A. J. P. Taylor, *The Origins of the Second World War* (New York: Atheneum, 1962).

Union and United States. Whether or not ideology should matter in relations between states, it is clear that it often does.

The triumph of liberal political principles in the post-Communist era has so far been less decisive than that of liberal economic models. Command economies have given way to the market almost everywhere, yet authoritarian polities have been slower to follow; consider China. Nevertheless, the burgeoning of democracy has been one of the major world changes since the mid-1980s. If we believe Kant's philosophy, this trend must be a force for peace.

Michael W. Doyle supplements Kant's theory with impressive empirical evidence that although democratic states have fought many wars with alacrity, they do not go to war with each other. If the illiberal states that democracies tend to fight with are disappearing, there should soon be fewer occasions for war. Three questions stand in the way of this optimistic conclusion about the impact of the liberalization of political regimes on international conflict.

First, will the post-Communist trend to democratization survive? Or will the crushing economic problems of conversion and reconstruction in Eastern Europe and the former Soviet Union be too much for new democracies to bear, yielding disillusionment, authoritarian populism, dictatorship, a search for scapegoats, and temptations to project frustration outward? Political liberalism may subvert economic liberalism by empowering people to resist the distribution of pain that goes with tearing down the rickety old economy before a sleek new one is constructed to take its place.The consequent disappointment with economic results may in turn subvert political liberalism.

Second, will democratization unleash violent forms of nationalism, and will national divisions compound a decline of democracy? One accomplishment of Marxism-Leninism, in institutionalizing regimes based in principle (even if not in practice) on class solidarity, was the delegitimizing of divisive nationalism and its forced suppression. Now, the resurgence of nationalism marks the new world just as much as the proliferation of democratic political forms. Indeed, the norm of self-determination tends to promote nationalism. Events in the former Yugoslavia and southern parts of the former Soviet Union have dramatically highlighted the problem.

Third, if ethnic violence, civil war, and regional chaos result from unconstrained nationalist impulses, can such small wars be kept limited in scope? Or will they contaminate relations among great powers, thereby creating anxieties about instability, power vacuums, or intervention by others that could catalyze a crisis and escalation to large-scale conflict (in a manner reminiscent of the situation of 1914)?

Nationalism need not contradict liberalism. Indeed, in the nineteenth century the two tidal forces moved together. And if giving each nation its own state prevents civil war in multinational states, the result should favor peace. But the map does not make that solution easy. Should all nations get their own states when we are sometimes unsure what constitutes a "nation," or when doing so would truncate other states—for example, a Kurdistan carved from Turkey, Iran, Iraq, and Syria? Or when the intermingling of minorities would produce awkward gerrymandering for South Ossetians in Georgia, Armenians in Azerbaijan, Trans-Dniester Russians in Moldova, or Serbs in Croatia and Bosnia? Or when it could mean endless redivision into tribal mini-states, as in Africa? The selection from Ernest Gellner describes some of the conceptual problems in dealing with nationalism, and differences between its benign and malignant forms. Stephen Larrabee's piece traces just a sample of the actual problems left by the dissolution of the Soviet empire.

Neoliberal institutionalism focuses attention on movement in the other direction. Integration rather than independence, through the evolution of organizations such as the European Economic Community, has more often seemed the wave of the future to liberal theorists in recent times. Realists too have often assumed that balance of power imperatives naturally pushed the international system toward agglomeration rather than toward fractionation of states.[2] Which trends will prove to be the wave of the future—integration in Western Europe, or disintegration in Eastern Europe?

---

[2]E. H. Carr's *Nationalism and After* (New York: Macmillan, 1945) is a fascinating example of reasoning that partakes of both perspectives. It is particularly interesting considering that it was written during the closing days of World War II, and for its conviction that the war had made nationalism obsolete—hardly a view that most expect from an author so associated with realism.

Idealpolitik

STANLEY KOBER

A revolution is sweeping the world—a revolution of democracy. The success of this democratic revolution has shaken Europe to its foundatior ; and shattered the strategic guideposts used to chart American foreign policy for more than 40 years. Groping through this new landscape, foreign policy specialists are struggling to develop policies to encourage democratic change while safeguarding strategic stability.

The failure to anticipate these changes, however, has understandably introduced a note of caution into the American response. The events were unexpected but they should not have been if the policy framework had been correct. Throughout the postwar era, American foreign policy has been dominated by a philosophy of realism, which views international politics as a struggle for power in which the interests of the great powers must be in conflict. This was a natural vision of foreign policy during a time in which then Soviet Foreign Minister Andrei Gromyko declared that "the world outlook and the class goals of the two social systems are opposite and irreconcilable."

It is precisely this "realistic" approach to foreign policy that is now being challenged, however, as Soviet President Mikhail Gorbachev and his allies in the Soviet leadership explicitly repudiate Gromyko's position. "Coexistence," proclaimed Foreign Minister Eduard Shevardnadze in July 1988, "cannot be identified with the class struggle." Instead, it "should have universal interests as a common denominator." The realignment of the Soviet Union's foreign policy has been accompanied by an even more fundamental transformation of its domestic political structure. Indeed, Gorbachev himself has described *perestroika* (restructuring) not as economic reform but as "a legal revolution" designed to keep excessive power from being concentrated in the hands of a few people and to govern society according to the rule of law.

Stanley Kober, "Idealpolitik," *Foreign Policy* No. 79 (Summer 1990). Reprinted with permission. Copyright © 1990 by the Carnegie Endowment for International Peace.

Until November 1989, debate in the West centered on the sincerity of these intentions. However, with the collapse of the Berlin Wall, attention is turning to the survivability of Gorbachev and his reforms, with the attendant question of what the United States and its allies should do. This debate, in turn, is affected by another more fundamental issue: What makes nations adversaries? Are the United States and the Soviet Union doomed by geopolitics to remain enemies? Or does the prospective transformation of the Soviet Union into a parliamentary democracy herald an end to the danger of superpower conflict? The answers should be sought in the competing philosophies of American foreign policy: realism or idealism.

At the end of World War I, President Woodrow Wilson traveled to Europe to help develop a structure assuring that "the war to end wars" would be just that. Wilson's approach consisted of two main parts. First, the Central European empires were dismantled and new states based on the principle of national self-determination were established. Second, Wilson proposed the creation of the League of Nations to handle future threats to international security.

Wilson's ideas were immediately challenged by the great British geopolitician Sir Halford Mackinder. In *Democratic Ideals and Reality*, which was first published in 1919, Mackinder argued that Wilson's democratic idealism might be noble but failed to deal with world realities. "Idealists are the salt of the earth," he wrote condescendingly; but, he warned, "democracy is incompatible with the organization necessary for war against autocracies." Mackinder asserted that "political moralists" like Wilson "refused to reckon with the realities of geography and economics." Mackinder defined these realities in his famous formulation: "Who rules East Europe commands the Heartland: Who rules the Heartland commands the World-Island: Who rules the World-Island commands the World." Given the importance of Eastern Europe, the prevention of another world war would depend on the establishment of "a tier of independent states between Germany and Russia." The political structure of these states did not concern him; what interested him was the balance of power....

Postwar Realism

Mackinder's "realistic" critique of Wilson's idealism found an echo in U.S. policy in the late 1940s. Haunted by the failure of democracies to prevent World War II, American political leaders decided to assume the burden of world leadership they had abandoned in the interwar period. "Soviet pressure against the free institutions of the Western World," wrote George Kennan in his famous "X" article of 1947, "is something that can be contained by the adroit and vigilant application of counterforce at a series of constantly shifting geographical and political points, corresponding to the shifts and maneuvers of Soviet policy." This definition of containment was purely reactive, however. The United States not only had to respond to the "shifts and maneuvers of Soviet policy," it had to anticipate them. What mechanism could it use for understanding the Kremlin's designs?

According to the political realist, the answer was simple. "The main signpost that helps political realism to find its way through the landscape of international politics is the concept of interest defined in terms of power," wrote Hans Morgenthau, probably the foremost exponent of the realist school. Morgenthau's book, *Politics Among Nations: The Struggle for Power and Peace* (1948), helped provide the intellectual basis for America's engagement in power politics. "Politics, like society in general, is governed by objective laws that have their roots in human nature," observed Morgenthau. Since these laws are objective, they are necessarily universal, and consequently it is futile and deceptive to examine foreign policy exclusively by looking at the motives of government officials. Instead, it is assumed that "statesmen think and act in terms of interest defined as power." On this assumption, "we put ourselves in the position of a statesman who must meet a certain problem of foreign policy under certain circumstances, and we ask ourselves what the rational alternatives are from which a statesman may choose . . . and which of these rational alternatives this particular statesman, acting under these circumstances, is likely to choose."

Morgenthau placed little emphasis on appeals to ideals as a way of gaining influence in the world. It was only in the preface to his second edition, published in 1954, that he acknowledged, as a result of decolonization, "the struggle for the minds of men as a new dimension of international politics to be added to the traditional dimensions of diplomacy and war." Although Morgenthau acknowledged "the attractiveness . . . of its political philosophy, political institutions, and political policies" as one element of a state's power, in the final analysis "the state has no right to let its moral disapprobation of the infringement of liberty get in the way of successful political action." Rather than viewing the clash of ideologies as basic to politics, the realist sees it as an unfortunate intrusion into his relatively stable world. "This struggle for the minds of men," lamented Morgenthau,

> has dealt the final, fatal blow to that social system of international intercourse within which for almost three centuries nations lived together in constant rivalry, yet under the common roof of shared values and universal standards of action. . . . Beneath the ruins of that roof lies buried the mechanism that kept the walls of that house of nations standing: the balance of power.

By acknowledging that the effective functioning of international politics depends on the existence of "shared values," Morgenthau admitted that the "laws" of power politics are not so objective after all. Yet if Morgenthau grieved for a world order that was no more, former Secretary of State Henry Kissinger insists that it still exists and is irreplaceable. "To have stability," he wrote in a recent *Washington Post* article, "an international system must have two components: a balance of power and a generally accepted principle of legitimacy." Like Morgenthau, Kissinger believes that the study of policy statements is misguided and bound to lead to error. He wrote in an essay in 1968:

> If we focus our policy discussions on Soviet purposes, we confuse the debate in two ways: Soviet trends are too ambiguous to offer a reliable guide—it is possible that not even Soviet leaders fully understand the dynamics of their system; it deflects us from articulating the purposes we should pursue, whatever Soviet intentions.... Confusing foreign policy with psychotherapy deprives us of criteria by which to judge the political foundations of international order.

Similarly, Kissinger shares Morgenthau's conviction that the realities of power politics compel the subordination of a nation's ideology to more basic interests. "National security concerns should be in harmony with traditional American values," he explained in a 1986 article, but "this ideal cannot always prevail, imposing the necessity to strike a balance." Underlying this view is Kissinger's assessment, expressed at a 1977 lecture at New York University, that "the United States is now as vulnerable as any other nation." Not only is it subject to the danger of nuclear annihilation, but American "prosperity is to some extent hostage to the decisions on raw materials, prices, and investment in distant countries whose purposes are not necessarily compatible with ours." Thus, although "our morality and our power should not be antithetical," in the final analysis "all serious foreign policy must begin with the need for survival."

The New Idealism

In contrast to geopolitics and realism, idealism has never had a distinct line of philosophical development. The German philosopher Immanuel Kant wrote that the rule of law would result in "perpetual peace," but he provided little guidance on how governments should behave until that day arrives. By contrast, the Manchester school in the nineteenth century, putting its trust in economic self-interest, believed that free trade would make war irrational. Yet the outbreak of World War I demonstrated that governments do not always behave rationally. It is not surprising, therefore, that historian E. H. Carr, in his 1939 volume *The Twenty Years' Crisis, 1919–1939*, described the alternative to realism as utopianism, which he characterized as "the primitive ... stage of the political sciences."

Viewed in this manner, it is no wonder that the idealist alternative fell into disrepute. Unfortunately, idealism is still seen as a naive philosophy that fails to understand the realities of power politics. Because of the uncompromising moralism with which it is endowed by its opponents, idealism is viewed as leading either to withdrawal from an imperfect world or to unrestrained interventionism to right all the world's wrongs. It is time for a new, more rigorous idealist alternative to realism.

A proper understanding of idealism, therefore, begins with the recognition that ideologies matter, and that the foreign policy of a state is an outgrowth of the values embodied in its domestic institutions. In the idealist view, the structure of a government determines how aggressive it can be. Specifically, dictatorships will be more aggressive than parliamentary democracies, since dictators can undertake military actions on their own initiative without having to obtain prior consent from popularly elected legislatures.

In taking this position, idealists recognize that democracies have behaved aggressively in the past but add that they are also evolving institutions. Democracy embodies strict criteria for majority rule and minority rights. Majority rule means that all the people are entitled to vote, and that those elected are accountable to the voters at frequent and regular intervals. The idealist views a democracy in which women, minorities, or other groups are excluded as more likely to be aggressive, since those making the decisions for war or peace are not accountable to everyone affected. In order to be accountable, representatives must provide the voters with the information they need to exercise their authority properly, and the people must have some mechanism for obtaining this information if it is being improperly withheld.

Minority rights are widely regarded as contradictory to majority rule, but this view is misguided. As recent ethnic conflicts demonstrate, majorities can change over time, and majority rule in the absence of guaranteed minority rights is a prescription for catastrophe. More to the point, however, guarantees of minority rights, which can be enforced only by the voluntary consent of the majority, signify respect for the weak by the strong. This value system of respect for law rather than for power is the best assurance of order and stability, both domestically and internationally.

Thus, the idealist is an unabashed proponent of democracy, seeing democracy as the best guarantee of world peace. While admitting that there is little historical experience of democracies of the sort described, the idealist would point to the relationship between the United States and Canada as instructive. Although these two countries were at war with each other at the beginning of the nineteenth century, they now share the longest undefended border in the world. The idealist would attribute this outcome to their mutual development of democratic institutions and would challenge the realist to explain why, if the balance of power is so important, Canadians do not tremble in fear at the prospect of an American invasion. The realist might reply that although there is an imbalance of power between the United States and Canada, they share an accepted principle of legitimacy. This answer is incomplete, for what is the source of that accepted principle of legitimacy if it is not the democratic values and respect for law both countries share?

In short, if it is democratic values that bring peace, one should say so forthrightly and not pretend that one principle of legitimacy is as good as another so long as it is generally accepted. If the balance of power cannot explain the peaceful U.S.–Canadian relationship, neither can it explain the outbreak of World War II. No geopolitical arrangement achievable at the time could have deterred Adolf Hitler because he saw war as the glorious means for achieving his objective, the occupation and subjugation of lands to the east. "No one will ever again have the confidence of the whole German people as I have," Hitler observed in August 1939. "All these favorable circumstances will no longer prevail in two or three years' time. No one knows how much longer I shall live." Whereas normal people are afraid of war, Hitler was afraid he would die before he could start a war.

The cause of World War II, therefore, must be sought not in the geopolitics of Europe, but in the domestic politics of Germany. The question is not how Hitler could have been deterred, because it is impossible to deter an absolute ruler who is seeking war. Rather, the question is how Hitler could have led a reluctant German people into war. Although many factors contributed to the outbreak of World War II, one overlooked cause is the imperfection of the Weimar Constitution. Instead of the American concept of inalienable rights, the Weimar Assembly placed individual rights at the "service of the collectivity," as René Brunet wrote in his 1922 book *The New German Constitution*. "Individual liberties are no longer an end in themselves, nor do they constitute any longer an independent good," he explained. "They have no value and are not protected except in the measure that they serve for the accomplishment of this social duty."

Because of this fundamental constitutional defect, Hitler was able to destroy the Weimar democracy and create in its place an instrument of domestic terror and foreign aggression. A democracy that does not have ironclad guarantees of individual rights cannot endure. As Abraham Lincoln observed, "a majority, held in restraint by constitutional checks and limitations . . . is the only true sovereign of a free people. Whoever rejects it does, out of necessity, fly to anarchy or to despotism." Weimar, born of military defeat, had the additional misfortune of being subject to a worldwide economic depression beyond its control. Its political and legal institutions were too new, too fragile, too unprotected to resist Hitler's assault once he came to power.

The outbreak of World War II, therefore, cannot be explained by realism. Indeed, if anything, British Prime Minister Neville Chamberlain followed realist analysis too closely. A realist assumes that because of objective laws of human behavior, all rational people will solve a given problem of foreign policy alike. But this leaves two problems. First, what is the problem of foreign policy the statesman is trying to solve? By defining Hitler's objective as the national self-determination of the German people, Chamberlain and his supporters totally missed the enormity of Hitler's ambition.

Second, what is the definition of rationality? The realist might respond that Hitler was irrational and therefore outside the bounds of realist analysis, but that answer is too glib. Intent on starting a war of expansion, Hitler initiated a massive military buildup while using diplomacy to hide his true intention. On the eve of war, he reached an agreement with the Soviet

Union, his greatest enemy, thereby easing enormously the military challenge immediately confronting him. In other words, Hitler's purposes were certainly irrational, but the purposefulness with which he pursued his objectives cannot be so easily dismissed. And indeed, if Hitler falls outside realist analysis because of his irrationality, how useful is realism as an analytical tool?

Hitler demonstrates the folly of relying on objective laws of human behavior in determining foreign policy. Hitler's methods make perfect sense once one understands his objectives. But to understand those objectives, one would have to look not to his assurances to Chamberlain at Munich, but to statements he made elsewhere and especially to his destruction of Germany's democracy. To the realist such an investigation is meaningless; to the idealist it is of fundamental importance: Hitler's treatment of the Jews and others he disliked foreshadowed how he would behave in the international arena once he was strong enough. If the people of Europe and their leaders had been aware of idealist analysis, they would have readily understood the purpose behind Hitler's military buildup and therefore the danger confronting them.

Idealist analysis provides criteria for assessing whether a military buildup is the result of perceptions of insecurity or the product of a drive for military supremacy to achieve political objectives by the threat or use of arms. The difference is crucial in determining the proper response. If the former, policy should focus on alleviating the political causes of insecurity. In this case, arms control has its greatest effect by building confidence. In the latter case, however, political measures are of limited, if any, use since there is no insecurity to alleviate. On the contrary, policy here should focus on a countervailing arms buildup, both to safeguard one's own security and to convince the arming power that it cannot achieve its objective. Arms control in this case can play a modest role by directing the competition away from the most destabilizing weapons, but it cannot achieve its ultimate objective of building confidence.

Faced with the need to choose between these two causes of an arms race, realism is helpless, since either cause might be rational depending on the policy objectives of a country's leaders. Unwilling to trust policy statements and rejecting the connection between domestic and foreign policy, realists ultimately base their assessments on their own value biases with no independent test. The idealist, on the other hand, insists that policy statements, particularly those designed for domestic officials, are revealing. More to the point, the idealist believes that even if such statements are too ambiguous to be a guide for formulating a response, the values embodied in a country's domestic policy and institutions provide invaluable insight into its purposes in foreign policy.

It is incorrect, therefore, to say that idealism rejects the balance of power. In fact, idealism recognizes that in the face of a military threat, there is no alternative to maintaining a balance, or even a preponderance, of power.

What idealism rejects is the idea that international peace is solely the product of a balance of power. For the idealist, a country can have friends as well as interests. The ultimate objective of idealism is to broaden the circle of friendship by fostering the spread of democratic values and institutions. In the meantime, recognizing the dangers of the world as it exists, idealism provides a mechanism for assessing the degree of threat posed by hostile regimes, in particular the threat posed by a military buildup.

But if idealism is more effective than realism in providing timely and accurate warning of military threats, it is also careful not to exaggerate them. For example, the idealist would disagree with Kissinger's assessment that the United States is as vulnerable as any other country. The only credible threat to America's national survival at this time comes from Soviet nuclear weapons; assuming the Kremlin is not suicidal, the United States has more than enough retaliatory power to deter such an attack. Conventional military threats to American interests do not threaten U.S. survival. Perhaps most important, the United States does not have to depend on any other country to assure its security.

Similarly, the idealist would question the idea that the United States is economically vulnerable. While recognizing America's dependence on imports, the idealist believes that so long as the sources of commodities are diversified and market forces are in operation, a cutoff of supplies from one country or a group of countries should be manageable. If further protection is needed, stockpiles of critical goods can be accumulated.

This is not to say that economic sanctions cannot have an effect against relatively small countries, for they ultimately did in Rhodesia and may now be having an effect in South Africa. But these are special cases rather than universal examples. When then President Jimmy Carter embargoed American grain exports to the Soviet Union following the invasion of Afghanistan, Moscow was easily able to find alternative suppliers. Similarly, when tin producers formed a cartel to duplicate the success of the Organization of Petroleum Exporting Countries in the 1970s, the effort collapsed.

In contrast to the realist, the idealist does not believe that U.S. imports of vital commodities pose a security risk so long as proper economic policies are followed. Idealists see American economic security in a vibrant economy producing goods that other people want, rather than in a government-directed policy of import substitution, let alone in military intervention.

This difference in the assessment of American economic vulnerability also extends to policy toward the Soviet Union; underlying the doctrine of containment is the assumption that Soviet expansionism will necessarily increase Soviet power. This assumption reflects the geopolitician's mistaken evaluation of the sources of economic wealth. As the British economic historian Eric Hobsbawm observed in *Industry and Empire* (1969), the imperial expansion that occurred in the late nineteenth century was for Britain "a step back. She exchanged the informal empire over most of the underdeveloped world for the formal empire of a quarter of it, plus the older satellite economies."

For the idealist it is free trade rather than empire that sustains economic growth. One's trade must be protected against attack, but that is different from developing an exclusive economic zone that does not depend upon the goodwill of others. Idealists believe that the wealth of a nation depends not on the extent or characteristics of the territory directly under its control, but as Adam Smith states, "first, [on] the skill, dexterity, and judgment with which its labour is generally applied; and, secondly, [on] the proportion between the number of those who are employed in useful labour, and that of those who are not so employed." Since prosperity "seems to depend more upon the former of those two circumstances than upon the latter," it is important that the labor force of the most advanced country constantly improve its skills so that it can continue to produce innovative goods and services with high added value. Otherwise, it will inevitably fall behind.

Continuing economic prosperity requires a flexible economic system. The problem with empires, as Carlo Cipolla notes in *The Economic Decline of Empires* (1970), is that "all empires seem eventually to develop an intractable resistance to the change needed for the required growth of production. . . . An empire is inevitably characterized by a large number of sclerotic institutions. They hinder change for their very existence." Hobsbawm, assessing the British condition at the time Mahan and Mackinder wrote, agrees with this judgment. "Britain had escaped from the Great Depression (1873-96). . . not by modernizing her economy, but by exploiting the remaining possibilities of her traditional situation," he wrote. "When the last great receptacles of cotton goods developed their own textile industries—India, Japan and China—the hour of Lancashire tolled. For not even political control could permanently keep India non-industrial."

Hobsbawm's analysis points to the second fundamental reason why the geopolitical interpretation of the wealth of nations is flawed: Political control over people who resent that control is an unstable basis for continuing economic growth. It is not enough to assert that "who rules the Heartland commands the World-Island." The idealist, mindful of Machiavelli's warning that "princes. . . . must first try not to be hated by the mass of the people," will immediately inquire whether that rule is by popular consent or in spite of it. If the latter, it must be a source of economic weakness rather than strength over the long run. Not only will a sullen people be relatively unproductive, but the effort to keep them under control will over time amount to a huge drain on the government's resources.

Revolution in the '90s

Viewed in this manner, idealism provides a fundamental challenge to realism and geopolitics. It is no longer possible to dismiss idealists as utopian dreamers who do not understand the harsh reality of power. On the contrary, idealists can respond that it is realists and geopoliticians who have oversimplified the concept of power and misunderstood the lessons of history. The debate between them is of critical importance in formulating policy to respond to the revolutionary changes now confronting the world.

Of all the momentous changes now occurring, the most dramatic is the transformation of the Soviet bloc. It is worth noting that the Soviets have always accepted some principles of idealism. Unlike realists, the Soviets have always stressed the importance of ideology and insisted that it is impossible to understand the foreign policy of a country without appreciating its domestic values and institutions. Similarly, like idealists, the Soviets professed to see the ultimate guarantee of world peace in the domestic structure of states. However, they saw that domestic structure in the communist principles of Karl Marx and V. I. Lenin, rather than in the democratic institutions of Thomas Jefferson and James Madison.

What is so revolutionary about the current changes in the Soviet Union is that they are based on the acknowledgement that the guarantee of world peace lies not in the spread of socialism, but in parliamentary control over war-making power. According to a January 1988 article in *Kommunist*, the theoretical journal of the Soviet communist party, "there are no politically influential forces in either Western Europe or the U.S." that contemplate "military aggression against socialism." But even if there were, America's democratic institutions would make such large-scale aggression impossible. The article emphasizes that "bourgeois democracy serves as a definite barrier in the path of unleashing such a war. . . . The history of the American intervention in Indochina clearly demonstrated this. . . . The Pentagon now cannot fail to recognize the existence of limits placed on its actions by democratic institutions." By formulating the question of war and peace in this way, the authors posed, albeit implicitly, an extremely profound question: If it is democratic institutions like those in the West that prevent war, then where is the threat to peace? Logically, it must come from those countries without such democratic institutions—countries like the Soviet Union. Astonishing as it may seem, this realization is one of the foundations on which *perestroika* is being built.

"The use of armed forces outside the country without sanction from the Supreme Soviet or the congress is ruled out categorically, once and for all," Gorbachev affirmed in assuming his new powers as president in March 1990. This statement reflects the fundamental nature of the changes taking place in the Soviet Union, which have little, if anything, to do with Marxism-Leninism. Indeed, as the former head of the Soviet Institute of State and Law, Vladimir Kudryavtsev, has forthrightly acknowledged, "Marxists criticized the 'separation of powers' theory which drew a clear dividing line between legislative and executive power." Now Soviets are recognizing their mistake and embracing the separation of powers and the rule of law. The philosophical basis for these changes can be found in the writings of Kant. "The philosophical foundation of the rule-of-law state was formulated by Kant," Kudryavtsev and Yelena Lukasheva, a doctor of juridical science, flatly stated in a *Kommunist* article following the June–July 1988 19th party conference, which established the rule of law as a major objective of *perestroika*. Soviet officials from Gorbachev on down now routinely refer to Kant, and Shevard-nadze has specifically identified Kant's 1795 booklet *Perpetual Peace* as a work deserving special attention.

Perpetual Peace was a major contribution to idealist philosophy. An admirer of the principles behind the American Revolution, Kant saw perpetual peace as a product not of the balance of power, but of republican government. Similarly, he rejected economic mercantilism, which is the foundation of geopolitics, in favor of Adam Smith's promotion of free trade. These themes are now commonplace in the Soviet media.

Viewed from the realist perspective, Gorbachev's actions, particularly in Eastern Europe, are puzzling; viewed from an idealist position, however, they are easily explicable. Since it is commerce rather than control of re-sources that is the source of wealth, better to abandon the territory where people are resentful of occupation. Free trade will provide more economic benefits than occupation. Nor is there any security risk; Soviet security is, in the final analysis, assured not by the territorial glacis or even by the might of the Soviet armed forces, but by the institutions of Western democracy.

The point is so startling to realists, who emphasize the balance of power, that it deserves elaboration. The Soviets are not de-ideologizing policy, but rather *re*-ideologizing it on a new basis. The Soviets are not replacing the value-laden system of Marx and Lenin with the value-neutral system of the balance of power, but are instead turning to a new set of values, those of the Enlightenment and especially of Kant. As Gorbachev told the 19th party conference in words that anticipated the revolutionary changes in Eastern Europe: "A key factor in the new thinking is the concept of freedom of choice. . . . To oppose freedom of choice is to come out against the objective tide of history itself. That is why power politics in all their forms and mani-festations are historically obsolescent."

Underlying this shift in the Soviet world view is a reassessment of its do-mestic value system. "The image of a state," Shevardnadze has proclaimed, "is its attitude to its own citizens, respect for their rights and freedoms and recognition of the sovereignty of the individual." By emphasizing the sover-eignty of the individual, Shevardnadze is turning communist philosophy up-side down. In addition, he is paying an extraordinary compliment to the principles of the American Revolution. The European tradition has been one of national self-determination. "The basis of all sovereignty lies, essen-tially, in the Nation," states the French Declaration of the Rights of Man and the Citizen. But the pursuit of national self-determination has proved to be a chimera. What, after all, is a nation? How can it be defined? And the most painful question, which the Soviet Union is now confronting: How can na-tional self-determination be achieved in a multi-ethnic state?

The American principle, on the other hand, is *individual* self-determina-tion, not national self-determination. Americans believe in *e pluribus unum:* one out of many. So long as rights are guaranteed on an individual basis, the concept of a nation is irrelevant. In a multi-ethnic state—and, one is tempted to say, in a multinational world—there can be no other basis for preserving peace.

The changes in Eastern Europe go to the heart of the debate between realism and idealism. Since realists maintain that it is power rather than ideology that matters, they view Gorbachev's changes with suspicion. Realists are concerned that if Gorbachev is successful, the result could be a stronger Soviet Union and thus an even greater threat to the United States. Realists do not see a necessary link between the Soviet Union's domestic changes and its foreign policy. "*Glasnost* [openness] and *perestroika* represent attempts to modernize the Soviet state," Kissinger wrote in a January 1988 article in the *Washington Post*. "This is an internal Soviet matter, relevant to the democracies only if accompanied by a change in Soviet foreign policy." Indeed, Kissinger worries "whether Americans can be brought to see foreign policy in terms of equilibrium rather than as a struggle between good and evil." In his view, this was the problem with former President Ronald Reagan's policy toward the Soviet Union, which in a few years went from denunciations of an evil empire to an embrace of Gorbachev. "Such an approach," Kissinger stressed in another *Washington Post* article in February 1989, "neglects the realities of power, ambition and national interest."

For the idealist, on the other hand, there are no immutable "realities of power, ambition and national interest." All these must be viewed through the prism of policy, which changes as people change. Policy will be affected by a society's values, which in turn are embodied in its domestic institutions. Thus, the idealist rejects the notion that there is no connection between *perestroika* and Soviet foreign policy. Whereas the realist is in perpetual pursuit of a stabilizing equilibrium—believing, in former President Richard Nixon's words, that "the only time in the history of the world that we have had any extended periods of peace is when there has been balance of power"—the idealist seeks the spread of freedom, which ultimately would eliminate the need for a balance of power. . . .

The realist perspective has gone unchallenged long enough. Idealism is not naïve utopianism but a rigorous approach to the conduct of foreign policy. Moreover, it is idealism that is the great American tradition. As Washington declared in his Farewell Address:

> Observe good faith and justice toward all nations. Cultivate peace and harmony with all. Religion and morality enjoin this conduct. And can it be that good policy does not equally enjoin it? It will be worthy of a free, enlightened, and at no distant period a great nation to give mankind the magnanimous and too novel example of a people always guided by an exalted justice and benevolence. Who can doubt that in the course of time and things the fruits of such a plan would richly repay any temporary advantages which might be lost by a steady adherence to it?

Americans should not fear that the spread of the democratic system created by the founders of their republic could present a threat to their security. They should instead follow Washington's advice and reject the realist's compromises as leading only to those "temporary advantages" of which he spoke. The long-term interests of the United States are fulfilled when it is true to its ideals, thus setting an example for the rest of the world. "We shall be as a City upon a Hill, the Eyes of all people are upon us," John Winthrop proclaimed in 1630. More than 350 years later, our revolutionary world demonstrates that it is the power of America's ideals, and not the might of its armies, that is the real source of U.S. influence in the world.

Liberalism and
World Politics

MICHAEL W. DOYLE

Promoting freedom will produce peace, we have often been told. In a speech before the British Parliament in June of 1982, President Reagan proclaimed that governments founded on a respect for individual liberty exercise "restraint" and "peaceful intentions" in their foreign policy. He then announced a "crusade for freedom" and a "campaign for democratic development" (Reagan, June 9, 1982).

In making these claims the president joined a long list of liberal theorists (and propagandists) and echoed an old argument: the aggressive instincts of authoritarian leaders and totalitarian ruling parties make for war. Liberal states, founded on such individual rights as equality before the law, free speech and other civil liberties, private property, and elected representation, are fundamentally against war, this argument asserts. When the citizens who bear the burdens of war elect their governments, wars become impossible. Furthermore, citizens appreciate that the benefits of trade can be enjoyed only under conditions of peace. Thus the very existence of liberal states, such as the U.S., Japan, and our European allies, makes for peace.

Building on a growing literature in an international political science, I reexamine the liberal claim President Reagan reiterated for us. I look at three distinct theoretical traditions of liberalism, attributable to three theorists: Schumpeter, a brilliant explicator of the liberal pacifism the president invoked; Machiavelli, a classical republican whose glory is an imperialism we often practice; and Kant.

Michael W. Doyle, "Liberalism and World Politics," *The American Political Science Review* Vol. 80, no. 4 (December 1986). Reprinted with permission of Michael W. Doyle and the American Political Science Association.

Despite the contradictions of liberal pacifism and liberal imperialism, I find, with Kant and other liberal republicans, that liberalism does leave a coherent legacy on foreign affairs. Liberal states are different. They are indeed peaceful, yet they are also prone to make war, as the U.S. and our "freedom fighters" are now doing, not so covertly, against Nicaragua. Liberal states have created a separate peace, as Kant argued they would, and have also discovered liberal reasons for aggression, as he feared they might. I conclude by arguing that the differences among liberal pacifism, liberal imperialism, and Kant's liberal internationalism are not arbitrary but rooted in differing conceptions of the citizen and the state.

Liberal Pacifism

There is no canonical description of liberalism. What we tend to call liberal resembles a family portrait of principles and institutions, recognizable by certain characteristics—for example, individual freedom, political participation, private property, and equality of opportunity—that most liberal states share, although none has perfected them all. Joseph Schumpeter clearly fits within this family when he considers the international effects of capitalism and democracy. . . .

Democratic capitalism leads to peace. As evidence, Schumpeter claims that throughout the capitalist world an opposition has arisen to "war, expansion, cabinet diplomacy"; that contemporary capitalism is associated with peace parties; and that the industrial worker of capitalism is "vigorously anti-imperialist." In addition, he points out that the capitalist world has developed means of preventing war, such as the Hague Court and that the least feudal, most capitalist society—the United States—has demonstrated the least imperialistic tendencies (Schumpeter, 1955, pp. 95-96). An example of the lack of imperialistic tendencies in the U.S., Schumpeter thought, was our leaving over half of Mexico unconquered in the war of 1846—48.

Schumpeter's explanation for liberal pacifism is quite simple: Only war profiteers and military aristocrats gain from wars. No democracy would pursue a minority interest and tolerate the high costs of imperialism. When free trade prevails, "no class" gains from forcible expansion because

> foreign raw materials and food stuffs are as accessible to each nation as though they were in its own territory. Where the cultural backwardness of a region makes normal economic intercourse dependent on colonization it does not matter, assuming free trade, which of the "civilized" nations undertakes the task of colonization. (Schumpeter, 1955, pp. 75-76)

Schumpeter's arguments are difficult to evaluate. In partial tests of quasi-Schumpeterian propositions, Michael Haas (1974, pp. 464-65) discovered a cluster that associates democracy, development, and sustained modernization with peaceful conditions. However, M. Small and J. D. Singer (1976) have discovered that there is no clearly negative correlation between democracy and war in the period 1816-1965—the period that would be central to Schumpeter's argument (see also Wilkenfeld, 1968; Wright, 1942, p. 841).

Later in his career, in *Capitalism, Socialism, and Democracy,* Schumpeter (1950, pp. 127-28) acknowledged that "almost purely bourgeois commonwealths were often aggressive when it seemed to pay—like the Athenian or the Venetian commonwealths." Yet he stuck to his pacifistic guns, restating the view that capitalist democracy "steadily tells . . . against the use of military force and for peaceful arrangements, even when the balance of pecuniary advantage is clearly on the side of war which, under modern circumstances, is not in general very likely" (Schumpeter, 1950, p. 128). A recent study by R. J. Rummel (1983) of "libertarianism" and international violence is the closest test Schumpeterian pacifism has received. "Free" states (those enjoying political and economic freedom) were shown to have considerably less conflict at or above the level of economic sanctions than "nonfree" states. The free states, the partly free states (including the democratic socialist countries such as Sweden), and the nonfree states accounted for 24%, 26%, and 61%, respectively, of the international violence during the period examined.

These effects are impressive but not conclusive for the Schumpeterian thesis. The data are limited, in this test, to the period 1976 to 1980. It includes, for example, the Russo-Afghan War, the Vietnamese invasion of Cambodia, China's invasion of Vietnam, and Tanzania's invasion of Uganda but just misses the U.S., quasi-covert intervention in Angola (1975) and our not so covert war against Nicaragua (1981). More importantly, it excludes the cold war period, with its numerous interventions, and the long history of colonial wars (the Boer War, the Spanish-American War, the Mexican Intervention, etc.) that marked the history of liberal, including democratic capitalist, states (Doyle, 1983b; Chan, 1984; Weede, 1984).

The discrepancy between the warlike history of liberal states and Schumpeter's pacifistic expectations highlights three extreme assumptions. First, his "materialistic monism" leaves little room for noneconomic objectives, whether espoused by states or individuals. Neither glory, nor prestige, nor ideological justification, nor the pure power of ruling shapes policy. These nonmaterial goals leave little room for positive-sum gains, such as the comparative advantages of trade. Second, and relatedly, the same is true for his states. The political life of individuals seems to have been homogenized at the same time as the individuals were "rationalized, individualized, and democratized." Citizens—capitalists and workers, rural and urban—seek material welfare. Schumpeter seems to presume that ruling makes no difference. He also presumes that no one is prepared to take those measures (such as stirring up foreign quarrels to preserve a domestic ruling coalition) that enhance one's political power, despite detrimental effects on mass welfare. Third, like domestic politics, world politics are homogenized. Materially monistic and democratically capitalist, all states evolve toward free trade and liberty together. Countries differently constituted seem to disappear from Schumpeter's analysis. "Civilized" nations govern "culturally backward" *regions*. These assumptions are not shared by Machiavelli's theory of liberalism.

Liberal Imperialism

Machiavelli argues, not only that republics are not pacifistic, but that they are the best form of state for imperial expansion. Establishing a republic fit for imperial expansion is, moreover, the best way to guarantee the survival of a state.

Machiavelli's republic is a classical mixed republic. It is not a democracy—which he thought would quickly degenerate into a tyranny—but is characterized by social equality, popular liberty, and political participation (Machiavelli, 1950, bk. 1, chap. 2, p. 112; see also Huliung, 1983, chap. 2; Mansfield, 1970; Pocock, 1975, pp. 198-99; Skinner, 1981, chap. 3). The consuls serve as "kings," the senate as an aristocracy managing the state, and the people in the assembly as the source of strength.

Liberty results from "disunion"—the competition and necessity for compromise required by the division of powers among senate, consuls, and tribunes (the last representing the common people). Liberty also results from the popular veto. The powerful few threaten the rest with tyranny, Machiavelli says, because they seek to dominate. The mass demands not to be dominated, and their veto thus preserves the liberties of the state (Machiavelli, 1950, bk. 1, chap. 5, p. 122). However, since the people and the rulers have different social characters, the people need to be "managed" by the few to avoid having their recklessness overturn or their fecklessness undermine the ability of the state to expand (Machiavelli, 1950, bk. 1, chap. 53, pp. 249-50). Thus the senate and the consuls plan expansion, consult oracles, and employ religion to manage the resources that the energy of the people supplies.

Strength, and then imperial expansion, results from the way liberty encourages increased population and property, which grow when the citizens know their lives and goods are secure from arbitrary seizure. Free citizens equip large armies and provide soldiers who fight for public glory and the common good because these are, in fact, their own (Machiavelli, 1950, bk. 2, chap. 2, pp. 287-90). If you seek the honor of having your state expand, Machiavelli advises, you should organize it as a free and popular republic like Rome, rather than as an aristocratic republic like Sparta or Venice. Expansion thus calls for a free republic.

"Necessity"—political survival—calls for expansion. If a stable aristocratic republic is forced by foreign conflict "to extend her territory, in such a case we shall see her foundations give way and herself quickly brought to ruin"; if, on the other hand, domestic security prevails, "the continued tranquility would enervate her, or provoke internal dissensions, which together, or either of them separately, will apt to prove her ruin" (Machiavelli, 1950, bk. 1, chap. 6, p. 129). Machiavelli therefore believes it is necessary to take the constitution of Rome, rather than that of Sparta or Venice, as our model.

Hence, this belief leads to liberal imperialism. We are lovers of glory, Machiavelli announces. We seek to rule or, at least, to avoid being oppressed. In either case, we want more for ourselves and our states than just material welfare (materialistic monism). Because other states with similar aims thereby threaten us, we prepare ourselves for expansion. Because our fellow citizens threaten us if we do not allow them either to satisfy their ambition or to release their political energies through imperial expansion, we expand.

There is considerable historical evidence for liberal imperialism. Machiavelli's (Polybius's) Rome and Thucydides' Athens both were imperial republics in the Machiavellian sense (Thucydides, 1954, bk. 6). The historical record of numerous U.S. interventions in the postwar period supports Machiavelli's argument (Aron, 1973, chaps. 3-4; Barnet, 1968, chap. 11), but the current record of liberal pacifism, weak as it is, calls some of his insights into question. To the extent that the modern populace actually controls (and thus unbalances) the mixed republic, its diffidence may outweigh elite ("senatorial") aggressiveness.

We can conclude either that (1) liberal pacifism has at least taken over with the further development of capitalist democracy, as Schumpeter predicted it would or that (2) the mixed record of liberalism   pacifism and imperialism—indicates that some liberal states are Schumpeterian democracies while others are Machiavellian republics. Before we accept either conclusion, however, we must consider a third apparent regularity of modern world politics.

Liberal Internationalism

Modern liberalism carries with it two legacies. They do not affect liberal states separately, according to whether they are pacifistic or imperialistic, but simultaneously.

The first of these legacies is the pacification of foreign relations among liberal states. During the nineteenth century, the United States and Great Britain engaged in nearly continual strife; however, after the Reform Act of 1832 defined actual representation as the formal source of the sovereignty of the British parliament, Britain and the United States negotiated their disputes. They negotiated despite, for example, British grievances during the Civil War against the North's blockade of the South, with which Britain had close economic ties. Despite several Anglo-French colonial rivalries, liberal France and liberal Britain formed an entente against illiberal

Germany before World War I. And from 1914 to 1915, Italy, the liberal member of the Triple Alliance with Germany and Austria, chose not to fulfill its obligations under that treaty to support its allies. Instead, Italy joined in an alliance with Britain and France, which prevented it from having to fight other liberal states and then declared war on Germany and Austria. Despite generations of Anglo-American tension and Britain's wartime restrictions on American trade with Germany, the United States leaned toward Britain and France from 1914 to 1917 before entering World War I on their side.

Beginning in the eighteenth century and slowly growing since then, a zone of peace, which Kant called the "pacific federation" or "pacific union," has begun to be established among liberal societies. More than 40 liberal states currently make up the union. Most are in Europe and North America, but they can be found on every continent, as Appendix 1 indicates.

Here the predictions of liberal pacifists (and President Reagan) are borne out: liberal states do exercise peaceful restraint, and a separate peace exists among them. This separate peace provides a solid foundation for the United States' crucial alliances with the liberal powers, e.g., the North Atlantic Treaty Organization and our Japanese alliance. This foundation appears to be impervious to the quarrels with our allies that bedeviled the Carter and Reagan administrations. It also offers the promise of a continuing peace among liberal states, and as the number of liberal states increases, it announces the possibility of global peace this side of the grave or world conquest.

Of course, the probability of the outbreak of war in any given year between any two given states is low. The occurrence of a war between any two adjacent states, considered over a long period of time, would be more probable. The apparent absence of war between liberal states, whether adjacent or not, for almost 200 years thus may have significance. Similar claims cannot be made for feudal, fascist, communist, authoritarian, or totalitarian forms of rule (Doyle, 1983a, p. 222), nor for pluralistic or merely similar societies. More significant perhaps is that when states are forced to decide on which side of an impending world war they will fight, liberal states all wind up on the same side despite the complexity of the paths that take them there. These characteristics do not prove that the peace among liberals is statistically significant nor that liberalism is the sole valid explanation for the peace. They do suggest that we consider the possibility that liberals have indeed established a separate peace—but only among themselves.

Liberalism also carries with it a second legacy: international "imprudence" (Hume, 1963, pp. 346-47). Peaceful restraint only seems to work in liberals' relations with other liberals. Liberal states have fought numerous wars with nonliberal states. (For a list of international wars since 1816 see Appendix 2.)

Many of these wars have been defensive and thus prudent by necessity. Liberal states have been attacked and threatened by nonliberal states that do not exercise any special restraint in their dealings with the liberal states. Authoritarian rulers both stimulate and respond to an international political environment in which conflicts of prestige, interest, and pure fear of what other states might do all lead states toward war. War and conquest have thus characterized the careers of many authoritarian rulers and ruling parties, from Louis XIV and Napoleon to Mussolini's fascists, Hitler's Nazis, and Stalin's communists.

Yet we cannot simply blame warfare on the authoritarians or totalitarians, as many of our more enthusiastic politicians would have us do. Most wars arise out of calculations and miscalculations of interest, misunderstandings, and mutual suspicions, such as those that characterized the origins of World War I. However, aggression by the liberal state has also characterized a large number of wars. Both France and Britain fought expansionist colonial wars throughout the nineteenth century. The United States fought a similar war with Mexico from 1846 to 1848, waged a war of annihilation against the American Indians, and intervened militarily against sovereign states many times before and after World War II. Liberal states invade weak nonliberal states and display striking distrust in dealings with powerful nonliberal states (Doyle, 1983b).

Neither realist (statist) nor Marxist theory accounts well for these two legacies. While they can account for aspects of certain periods of international stability (Aron, 1968, pp. 151-54; Russett, 1985), neither the logic of the balance of power nor the logic of international hegemony explains the separate peace maintained for more than 150 years among states sharing one particular form of governance—liberal principles and institutions. Balance-of-power theory expects—indeed is premised upon—flexible arrangements of geostrategic rivalry that include preventive war. Hegemonics wax and wane, but the liberal peace holds. Marxist "ultra-imperialists" expect a form of peaceful rivalry among capitalists, but only liberal capitalists maintain peace. Leninists expect liberal capitalists to be aggressive toward nonliberal states, but they also (and especially) expect them to be imperialistic toward fellow liberal capitalists.

Kant's theory of liberal internationalism helps us understand these two legacies. . . .

[See the selection by Kant in Part 3. (Ed.)]

Liberal republics will progressively establish peace among themselves by means of the pacific federation, or union (foedus pacificum), described in Kant's Second Definitive Article. The pacific union will establish peace within a federation of free states and securely maintain the rights of each state. The world will not have achieved the "perpetual peace" that provides the ultimate guarantor of republican freedom until "a late stage and after many unsuccessful attempts" (Kant, *UH*, p. 47). At that time, all nations will have learned the lessons of peace through right conceptions of the appropriate constitution, great and sad experience, and good will. Only then will individuals enjoy perfect republican rights or the full guarantee of a global and just peace. In the meantime, the "pacific federation" of liberal republics—"an enduring and gradually expanding federation likely to prevent war"—brings within it more and more republics—despite republican collapses, backsliding, and disastrous wars—creating an ever-expanding separate peace (Kant, *PP*, p. 105). Kant emphasizes that

> it can be shown that this idea of federalism, extending gradually to encompass all states and thus leading to perpetual peace, is practicable and has objective reality. For if by good fortune one powerful and enlightened nation can form a republic (which is by nature inclined to seek peace), this will provide a focal point for federal association among other states. These will join up with the first one, thus securing the freedom of each state in accordance with the idea of international right, and the whole will gradually spread further and further by a series of alliances of this kind. (Kant, *PP*, p. 104)

The pacific union is not a single peace treaty ending one war, a world state, nor a state of nations. Kant finds the first insufficient. The second and third are impossible or potentially tyrannical. National sovereignty precludes reliable subservience to a state of nations; a world state destroys the civic freedom on which the development of human capacities rests (Kant, *UH*, p. 50). Although Kant obliquely refers to various classical interstate confederations and modern diplomatic congresses, he develops no systematic organizational embodiment of this treaty and presumably does not find institutionalization necessary (Riley, 1983, chap. 5; Schwarz, 1962, p. 77). He appears to have in mind a mutual nonaggression pact, perhaps a collective security agreement, and the cosmopolitan law set forth in the Third Definitive Article. . . .

Perpetual peace, for Kant, is an epistemology, a condition for ethical action, and, most importantly, an explanation of how the "mechanical process of nature visibly exhibits the purposive plan of producing concord among men, even against their will and indeed by means of their very discord" (Kant, *PP*, p. 108; *UH*, pp. 44-45). Understanding history requires an epistemological foundation, for without a teleology, such as the promise of perpetual peace, the complexity of history would overwhelm human understanding (Kant, *UH*, pp. 51-53). Perpetual peace, however, is not merely a heuristic device with which to interpret history. It is guaranteed, Kant explains in the "First Addition" to *Perpetual Peace* ("On the Guarantee of Perpetual Peace"), to result from men fulfilling their ethical duty or, failing that, from a hidden plan. Peace is an ethical duty because it is only under conditions of peace that all men can treat each other as ends, rather than means to an end (Kant, *UH*, p. 50; Murphy, 1970, chap. 3). In order for this duty to be practical, Kant needs, of course, to show that peace is in fact possible. The widespread sentiment of approbation that he saw aroused by the early success of the French revolutionaries showed him that we can indeed be moved by ethical sentiments with a cosmopolitan reach (Kant, *CF*, pp. 181-82; Yovel, 1980, pp. 153-54). This does not mean, however, that perpetual peace is certain ("prophesiable"). Even the scientifically regular course of the planets could be changed by a wayward comet striking them out of orbit. Human freedom requires that we allow for much greater reversals in the course of history. We must, in fact, anticipate the possibility of backsliding and destructive wars—though these will serve to educate nations to the importance of peace (Kant, *UH*, pp. 47-48).

In the end, however, our guarantee of perpetual peace does not rest on ethical conduct. As Kant emphasizes,

> we now come to the essential question regarding the prospect of perpetual peace. What does nature do in relation to the end which man's own reason prescribes to him as a duty, i.e. how does nature help to promote his *moral purpose*? And how does nature guarantee that what man *ought* to do by the laws of his freedom (but does not do) will in fact be done through nature's compulsion, without prejudice to the free agency of man? . . . This does not mean that nature imposes on us a *duty* to do it, for duties can only be imposed by practical reason. On the contrary, nature does it herself, whether we are willing or not: *facta volentem ducunt, nolentem tradunt. (PP, p. 112)*

The guarantee thus rests, Kant argues, not on the probable behavior of moral angels, but on that of "devils, so long as they possess understanding" (*PP*, p. 112). In explaining the sources of each of the three definitive articles of the perpetual peace, Kant then tells us how we (as free and intelligent devils) could be motivated by fear, force, and calculated advantage to undertake a course of action whose outcome we could reasonably anticipate to be perpetual peace. Yet while it is possible to conceive of the Kantian road to peace in these terms, Kant himself recognizes and argues that social evolution also makes the conditions of moral behavior less onerous and hence more likely (*CF*, pp. 187-89; Kelly, 1969, pp. 106-13). In tracing the effects of both political and moral development, he builds an account of why liberal states do maintain peace among themselves and of how it will (by implication, has) come about that the pacific union will expand. He also explains how these republics would engage in wars with nonrepublics and therefore suffer the "sad experience" of wars that an ethical policy might have avoided. . . .

Kant shows how republics, once established, lead to peaceful relations. He argues that once the aggressive interests of absolutist monarchies are tamed and the habit of respect for individual rights engrained by republic government, wars would appear as the disaster to the people's welfare that he and the other liberals thought them to be. . . . Yet these domestic republican restraints do not end war. If they did, liberal states would not be warlike, which is far from the case. They do introduce republican caution—Kant's "hesitation"—in place of monarchical caprice. Liberal wars are only fought for popular, liberal purposes. The historical liberal legacy is laden with popular wars fought to promote freedom, to protect private property, or to support liberal allies against nonliberal enemies. Kant's position is ambiguous. He regards these wars as unjust and warns liberals of their susceptibility to them (Kant, *PP*, p. 106). At the same time, Kant argues that each nation "can and ought to" demand that its neighboring nations enter into the pacific union of liberal states (*PP*, p. 102)....

A further cosmopolitan source of liberal peace is the international market's removal of difficult decisions of production and distribution from the direct sphere of state policy. A foreign state thus does not appear directly responsible for these outcomes, and states can stand aside from, and to some degree above, these contentious market rivalries and be ready to step in to resolve crises. The interdependence of commerce and the international contacts of state officials help create crosscutting transnational ties that serve as lobbies for mutual accommodation. According to modern liberal scholars, international financiers and transnational and transgovernmental organizations create interests in favor of accommodation. Moreover, their variety has ensured that no single conflict sours an entire relationship by setting off a spiral of reciprocated retaliation (Brzezinski and Huntington, 1963, chap. 9; Keohane and Nye, 1977, chap. 7; Neustadt, 1970; Polanyi, 1944, chaps. 1-2). Conversely, a sense of suspicion, such as that characterizing relations between liberal and nonliberal governments, can lead to restrictions on the range of contacts between societies, and this can increase the prospect that a single conflict will determine an entire relationship.

No single constitutional, international, or cosmopolitan source is alone sufficient, but together (and only together) they plausibly connect the characteristics of liberal polities and economies with sustained liberal peace. Alliances founded on mutual strategic interest among liberal and nonliberal states have been broken; economic ties between liberal and nonliberal states have proven fragile; but the political bonds of liberal rights and interests have proven a remarkably firm foundation for mutual nonaggression. A separate peace exists among liberal states.

In their relations with nonliberal states, however, liberal states have not escaped from the insecurity caused by anarchy in the world political system considered as a whole. Moreover, the very constitutional restraint, international respect for individual rights, and shared commercial interests that establish grounds for peace among liberal states establish grounds for additional conflict in relations between liberal and nonliberal societies.

Conclusion

... Unlike Machiavelli's republics, Kant's republics are capable of achieving peace among themselves because they exercise democratic caution and are capable of appreciating the international rights of foreign republics. These international rights of republics derive from the representation of foreign individuals, who are our moral equals. Unlike Schumpeter's capitalist democracies, Kant's republics—including our own—remain in a state of war with nonrepublics. Liberal republics see themselves as threatened by aggression from nonrepublics that are not constrained by representation. Even though wars often cost more than the economic return they generate, liberal republics also are prepared to protect and promote—sometimes forcibly—democracy, private property, and the rights of individuals overseas against nonrepublics, which, because they do not authentically represent the rights of individuals, have no rights to noninterference. These wars may liberate oppressed individuals overseas; they also can generate enormous suffering.

Preserving the legacy of the liberal peace without succumbing to the legacy of liberal imprudence is both a moral and a strategic challenge. The bipolar stability of the international system, and the near certainty of mutual devastation resulting from a nuclear war between the superpowers, have created a "crystal ball effect" that has helped to constrain the tendency toward miscalculation present at the outbreak of so many wars in the past (Carnesale, Doty, Hoffmann, Huntington, Nye, and Sagan, 1983, p. 44; Waltz, 1964). However, this "nuclear peace" appears to be limited to the superpowers. It has not curbed military interventions in the Third World. Moreover, it is subject to a desperate technological race designed to overcome its constraints and to crises that have pushed even the superpowers to the brink of war. We must still reckon with the war fevers and moods of appeasement that have almost alternately swept liberal democracies.

Yet restraining liberal imprudence, whether aggressive or passive, may not be possible without threatening liberal pacification. Improving the strategic acumen of our foreign policy calls for introducing steadier strategic calculations of the national interest in the long run and more flexible responses to changes in the international political environment. Constraining the indiscriminate meddling of our foreign interventions calls for a deeper appreciation of the "particularism of history, culture, and membership" (Walzer, 1983, p. 5), but both the improvement in strategy and the constraint on intervention seem, in turn, to require an executive freed from the restraints of a representative legislature in the management of foreign policy and a political culture indifferent to the universal rights of individuals. These conditions, in their turn, could break the chain of constitutional guarantees, the respect for representative government, and the web of transnational contact that have sustained the pacific union of liberal states.

Perpetual peace, Kant says, is the end point of the hard journey his republics will take. The promise of perpetual peace, the violent lessons of war, and the experience of a partial peace are proof of the need for and the possibility of world peace. They are also the grounds for moral citizens and statesmen to assume the duty of striving for peace.

Appendix 1. Liberal Regimes and the Pacific Union, 1700-1982

Period	Period	Period
18th Century	**1900-1945** (cont.)	**1945** (cont.)
Swiss Cantons[a]	Netherlands, -1940	Austria, 1945-
French Republic, 1790-	Argentina, -1943	Brazil, 1945-1954; 1955-
1795	France, -1940	1964
United States,[a] 1776-	Chile, -1924, 1932-	Belgium, 1946-
Total = 3	Australia, 1901	Luxemburg, 1946-
	Norway, 1905-1940	Netherlands, 1946-
1800-1850	New Zealand, 1907-	Italy, 1946-
Swiss Confederation	Colombia, 1910-1949	Philippines, 1946-1972
United States	Denmark, 1914-1940	India, 1947-1975, 1977-
France, 1830-1849	Poland, 1917-1935	Sri Lanka, 1948-1961;
Belgium, 1830-	Latvia, 1922-1934	1963-1971; 1978-
Great Britain, 1832-	Germany, 1918-1932	Ecuador, 1948-1963;
Netherlands, 1848-	Austria, 1918-1934	1979-
Piedmont, 1848-	Estonia, 1919-1934	Israel, 1949-
Denmark, 1849-	Finland, 1919-	West Germany, 1949-
Total = 8	Uruguay, 1919-	Greece, 1950-1967; 1975-
	Costa Rica, 1919-	Peru, 1950-1962; 1963-
1850-1900	Czechoslovakia, 1920-	1968; 1980–
Switzerland	1939	El Salvador, 1950-1961
United States	Ireland, 1920-	Turkey, 1950-1960; 1966-
Belgium	Mexico, 1928-	1971
Great Britain	Lebanon, 1944-	Japan, 1951-
Netherlands	Total = 29	Bolivia 1956-1969; 1982-
Piedmont, -1861		Colombia, 1958-
Italy, 1861-	**1945-[b]**	Venezuela, 1959-
Denmark, -1866	Switzerland	Nigeria, 1961-1964;
Sweden, 1864-	United States	1979-1984
Greece, 1864-	Great Britain	Jamaica, 1962-
Canada, 1867-	Sweden	Trinidad and Tobago,
France, 1871-	Canada	1962-
Argentina, 1880-	Australia	Senegal, 1963-
Chile, 1891-	New Zealand	Malaysia, 1963-
Total = 14	Finland	Botswana, 1966-
	Ireland	Singapore, 1965-
1900-1945	Mexico	Portugal, 1976-
Switzerland	Uruguay, -1973	Spain, 1978-
United States	Chile, -1973	Dominican Republic,
Great Britain	Lebanon, -1975	1978-
Sweden	Costa Rica, -1948; 1953-	Honduras, 1981-
Canada	Iceland, 1944-	Papua New Guinea,
Greece, -1911; 1928-1936	France, 1945-	1982-
Italy, -1922	Denmark, 1945	Total = 50
Belgium, -1940	Norway, 1945	

NOTE: I have drawn up this approximate list of "Liberal Regimes" according to the four institutions Kant described as essential: market and private property economies; polities that are externally sovereign; citizens who possess juridical rights; and "republican" (whether republican or parliamentary monarchy), representative government. This latter includes the requirement that the legislative branch have an effective role in public policy and be formally and competitively (either inter- or intra-party) elected. Furthermore, I have taken into account whether male suffrage is wide (i.e., 30%) or, as Kant (*MM*, p. 139) would have had it, open by "achievement" to inhabitants of the national or metropolitan territory (e.g., to poll-tax payers or householders). This list of liberal regimes is thus more inclusive than a list of democratic regimes, or polyarchies (Powell, 1982, p. 5). Other conditions taken into account here are that female suffrage is granted within a generation of its being demanded by an extensive female suffrage movement and that representative government is internally sovereign (e.g., including, and especially over military and foreign affairs) as well as stable (in existence for at least three years). Sources for these data are Banks and Overstreet (1983), Gastil (1985), *The Europa Yearbook, 1985* (1985), Langer (1968), U.K. Foreign and Commonwealth Office (1980), and U.S. Department of State (1981). Finally, these lists exclude ancient and medieval "republics," since none appears to fit Kant's commitment to liberal individualism (Holmes, 1979).

[a]There are domestic variations within these liberal regimes: Switzerland was liberal only in certain cantons; the United States was liberal only north of the Mason-Dixon line until 1865, when it became liberal throughout.

[b]Selected list, excludes liberal regimes with populations less than one million. These include all states categorized as "free" by Gastil and those "partly free" (four-fifths or more free) states with a more pronounced capitalist orientation.

Appendix 2. International Wars Listed Chronologically

British-Maharattan (1817-1818)
Greek (1821-1828)
Franco-Spanish (1823)
First Anglo-Burmese (1823-1826)
Javanese (1825-1830)
Russo-Persian (1826-1828)
Russo-Turkish (1828-1829)
First Polish (1831)
First Syrian (1831-1832)
Texas (1835-1836)
First British-Afghan (1838-1842)
Second Syrian (1839-1940)
Franco-Algerian (1839-1847)
Peruvian-Bolivian (1841)
First British-Sikh (1845-1846)
Mexican-American (1846-1848)
Austro-Sardinian (1848-1849)
First Schleswig-Holstein (1848-1849)
Hungarian (1848-1849)
Second British-Sikh (1848-1849)
Roman Republic (1849)
La Plata (1851-1852)
First Turco-Montenegran (1852-1853)
Crimean (1853-1856)
Anglo-Persian (1856-1857)
Sepoy (1857-1859)
Second Turco-Montenegran (1858-1859)
Italian Unification (1859)
Spanish-Moroccan (1859-1860)
Italo-Roman (1860)
Italo-Sicilian (1860-1861)
Franco-Mexican (1862-1867)
Ecuadorian-Colombian (1863)
Second Polish (1863-1864)
Spanish-Santo Dominican (1863-1865)
Second Schleswig Holstein (1864)
Lopez (1864-1870)
Spanish-Chilean (1865-1866)
Seven Weeks (1866)
Ten Years (1868-1878)
Franco-Prussian (1870-1871)
Dutch-Achinese (1873-1878)
Balkan (1875-1877)
Russo-Turkish (1877-1878)
Bosnian (1878)
Second British-Afghan (1878-1880)
Pacific (1879-1883)
British-Zulu (1879)
Franco-Indochinese (1882-1884)

Mahdist (1882-1885)
Sino-French (1884-1885)
Central American (1885)
Serbo-Bulgarian (1885)
Sino-Japanese (1894-1895)
Franco-Madagascan (1894-1895)
Cuban (1895-1898)
Italo-Ethiopian (1895-1896)
First Philippine (1896-1898)
Greco-Turkish (1897)
Spanish-American (1898)
Second Philippine (1899-1902)
Boer (1899-1902)
Boxer Rebellion (1900)
Ilinden (1903)
Russo-Japanese (1904-1905)
Central American (1906)
Central American (1907)
Spanish-Moroccan (1909-1910)
Italo-Turkish (1911-1912)
First Balkan (1912-1913)
Second Balkan (1913)
World War I (1914-1918)
Russian Nationalities (1917-1921)
Russo-Polish (1919-1920)
Hungarian-Allies (1919)
Greco-Turkish (1919-1922)
Riffian (1921-1926)
Druze (1925-1927)
Sino-Soviet (1929)
Manchurian (1931-1933)
Chaco (1932-1935)
Italo-Ethiopian (1935-1936)
Sino-Japanese (1937-1941)
Changkufeng (1938)
Nomohan (1939)
World War II (1939-1945)
Russo-Finnish (1939-1940)
Franco-Thai (1940-1941)
Indonesian (1945-1946)
Indochinese (1945-1954)
Madagascan (1947-1948)
First Kashmir (1947-1949)
Palestine (1948-1949)
Hyderabad (1948)
Korean (1950-1953)
Algerian (1954-1962)
Russo-Hungarian (1956)
Sinai (1956)
Tibetan (1956-1959)

(continued)

Appendix 2. International Wars Listed Chronologically

Sino-Indian (1962)	Ethiopian-Eritrean (1974-)
Vietnamese (1965-1975)	Vietnamese-Cambodian (1975-)
Second Kashmir (1965)	Timor (1975-)
Six Day (1967)	Saharan (1975-)
Israeli-Egyptian (1969-1970)	Ogaden (1976-)
Football (1969)	Ugandan-Tanzanian (1978-1979)
Bangladesh (1971)	Sino-Vietnamese (1979)
Philippine-MNLF (1972-)	Russo-Afghan (1979-)
Yom Kippur (1973)	Iran-Iraqi (1980-)
Turco-Cypriot (1974)	

NOTE: This table is taken from Melvin Small and J. David Singer (1982, pp. 79-80). This is a partial list of international wars fought between 1816 and 1980. In Appendices A and B, Small and Singer identify a total of 575 wars during this period, but approximately 159 of them appear to be largely domestic, or civil wars.

This list excludes covert interventions, some of which have been directed by liberal regimes against other liberal regimes—for example, the United States' effort to destabilize the Chilean election and Allende's government. Nonetheless, it is significant that such interventions are not pursued publicly as acknowledged policy. The covert destabilization campaign against Chile is recounted by the Senate Select Committee to Study Governmental Operations with Respect to Intelligence Activities (1975, *Covert Action in Chile, 1963-73*).

Following the argument of this article, this list also excludes civil wars. Civil wars differ from international wars, not in the ferocity of combat, but in the issues that engender them. Two nations that could abide one another as independent neighbors separated by a border might well be the fiercest of enemies if forced to live together in one state, jointly deciding how to raise and spend taxes, choose leaders, and legislate fundamental questions of value. Notwithstanding these differences, no civil wars that I recall upset the argument of liberal pacification.

References

Aron, Raymond. 1966. *Peace and War: A Theory of International Relations*. Richard Howard and Annette Baker Fox, trans. Garden City, NY: Doubleday.

———. 1974. Aron, Raymond. 1974. *The Imperial Republic*. Frank Jellinek, trans. Englewood Cliffs, NJ: Prentice Hall.

Banks, Arthur, and William Overstreet, eds. 1983. *A Political Handbook of the World; 1982-1983*. New York: McGraw Hill.

Barnet, Richard. 1968. *Intervention and Revolution*. Cleveland: World Publishing Co.

Brzezinski, Zbigniew, and Samuel Huntington. 1963. *Political Power: USA/USSR*. New York: Viking Press.

Carnesale, Albert, Paul Doty, Stanley Hoffmann, Samuel Huntington, Joseph Nye, and Scott Sagan. 1983. *Living With Nuclear Weapons.* New York: Bantam.

Chan, Steve. 1984. Mirror, Mirror on the Wall . . . : Are Freer Countries More Pacific? *Journal of Conflict Resolution,* 28:617-48.

Doyle, Michael W. 1983a. Kant, Liberal Legacies, and Foreign Affairs: Part 1. *Philosophy and Public Affairs,* 12:205-35.

———. 1983b. Kant, Liberal Legacies, and Foreign Affairs: Part 2. *Philosophy and Public Affairs,* 12:323-53.

———. 1986. *Empires.* Ithaca: Cornell University Press.

The Europa Yearbook for 1985. 1985. 2 vols. London: Europa Publications.

Friedrich, Karl. 1948. *Inevitable Peace.* Cambridge, MA: Harvard University Press.

Gastil, Raymond. 1985. The Comparative Survey of Freedom 1985. *Freedom at Issue,* 82:3-16.

Haas, Michael. 1974. *International Conflict.* New York: Bobbs-Merrill.

Hermens, Ferdinand A. 1944. *The Tyrants' War and the People's Peace.* Chicago: University of Chicago Press.

Holmes, Stephen. 1979. Aristippus in and out of Athens. *American Political Science Review,* 73:113-28.

Huliung, Mark. 1983. *Citizen Machiavelli.* Princeton: Princeton University Press.

Hume, David. 1963. Of the Balance of Power. *Essays: Moral, Political and Literary.* Oxford: Oxford University Press.

Kant, Immanuel. 1970. *Kant's Political Writings.* Hans Reiss, ed. H. B. Nisbet, trans. Cambridge: Cambridge University Press.

Kelly, George A. 1969. *Idealism, Politics, and History.* Cambridge: Cambridge University Press.

Keohane, Robert, and Joseph Nye. 1977. *Power and Interdependence.* Boston: Little Brown.

Langer, William L., ed. 1968. *The Encyclopedia of World History.* Boston: Houghton Mifflin.

Machiavelli, Niccolo. 1950. *The Prince and the Discourses.* Max Lerner, ed. Luigi Ricci and Christian Detmold, trans. New York: Modern Library.

Mansfield, Harvey C. 1970. Machiavelli's New Regime. *Italian Quarterly,* 13:63-95.

Murphy, Jeffrie. 1970. *Kant: The Philosophy of Right.* New York: St. Martins.

Neustadt, Richard. 1970. *Alliance Politics.* New York: Columbia University Press.

Pocock, J. G. A. 1975. *The Machiavellian Moment.* Princeton: Princeton University Press.

Polanyi, Karl. 1944. *The Great Transformation.* Boston: Beacon Press.

Posen, Barry, and Stephen Van Evera. 1980. Over-arming and Underwhelming. *Foreign Policy,* 40:99-118.

Powell, G. Bingham. 1982. *Contemporary Democracies.* Cambridge, MA: Harvard University Press.

Riley, Patrick. 1983. *Kant's Political Philosophy.* Totowa, NJ: Rowman and Littlefield.

Rummel, Rudolph J. 1979. *Understanding Conflict and War,* 5 vols. Beverly Hills: Sage Publications.

Russett, Bruce. 1985. The Mysterious Case of Vanishing Hegemony. *International Organization,* 39:207-31.

Schumpeter, Joseph. 1950. *Capitalism, Socialism, and Democracy.* New York: Harper Torchbooks.

————. Schumpeter, Joseph. 1955. The Sociology of Imperialism. In *Imperialism and Social Classes.* Cleveland: World Publishing Co. (Essay originally published in 1919.)

Schwarz, Wolfgang. 1962. Kant's Philosophy of Law and International Peace. *Philosophy and Phenomenonological Research,* 23:71-80.

Shell, Susan. 1980. *The Rights of Reason.* Toronto: University of Toronto Press.

Skinner, Quentin. 1981. *Machiavelli.* New York: Hill and Wang.

Small, Melvin, and J. David Singer. 1976. The War-Proneness of Democratic Regimes. *The Jerusalem Journal of International Relations,* 1(4):50-69.

————. Small, Melvin, and J. David Singer, 1982. *Resort to Arms.* Beverly Hills: Sage Publications.

Thucydides. 1954. *The Peloponnesian War.* Rex Warner, ed. and trans. Baltimore: Penguin.

U.K. Foreign and Commonwealth Office. 1980. *A Yearbook of the Commonwealth 1980.* London: HMSO.

U.S. Congress, Senate. Select Committee to Study Governmental Operations with Respect to Intelligence Activities. 1975. *Covert Action in Chile, 1963-74.* 94th Cong., 1st sess., Washington, D.C.: U.S. Government Printing Office.

U.S. Department of State. 1981. *Country Reports on Human Rights Practices.* Washington, D.C.: U.S. Government Printing Office.

Waltz, Kenneth. 1964. The Stability of a Bipolar World. *Daedalus,* 93:881-909.

Walzer, Michael. 1983. *Spheres of Justice.* New York: Basic Books.

Weede, Erich 1984. Democracy and War Involvement. *Journal of Conflict Resolution,* 28:649-64.

Wilkenfield, Jonathan. 1968. Domestic and Foreign Conflict Behavior of Nations. *Journal of Peace Research,* 5:56-69.

Wright, Quincy. 1942. *A Study of History.* Chicago: Chicago University Press.

Yovel, Yirmiahu. 1980. *Kant and the Philosophy of History.* Princeton: Princeton University Press.

Nations and Nationalism

ERNEST GELLNER

Definitions

Nationalism is primarily a political principle, which holds that the political and the national unit should be congruent.

Nationalism as a sentiment, or as a movement, can best be defined in terms of this principle. Nationalist *sentiment* is the feeling of anger aroused by the violation of the principle, or the feeling of satisfaction aroused by its fulfillment. A nationalist *movement* is one actuated by a sentiment of this kind.

There is a variety of ways in which the nationalist principle can be violated. The political boundary of a given state can fail to include all the members of the appropriate nation; or it can include them all but also include some foreigners; or it can fail in both these ways at once, not incorporating all the nationals and yet also including some non-nationals. Or again, a nation may live, unmixed with foreigners, in a multiplicity of states, so that no single state can claim to be *the* national one.

But there is one particular form of the violation of the nationalist principle to which nationalist sentiment is quite particularly sensitive; if the rulers of the political unit belong to a nation other than that of the majority of the ruled, this, for nationalists, constitutes a quite outstandingly intolerable breach of political propriety. This can occur either through the incorporation of the national territory in a larger empire, or by the local domination of an alien group.

In brief, nationalism is a theory of political legitimacy, which requires that ethnic boundaries should not cut across political ones, and, in particular,

Ernest Gellner, *Nations and Nationalism* (Ithaca: Cornell University Press, 1983), selections from chapters 1, 4, and 7. Copyright © 1983 by Ernest Gellner. Reprinted with permission of Cornell University Press.

that ethnic boundaries within a given state—a contingency already formally excluded by the principle in its general formulation—should not separate the power holders from the rest.

The nationalist principle can be asserted in an ethical, 'universalistic' spirit. There could be, and on occasion there have been, nationalists-in-the-abstract, unbiased in favour of any special nationality of their own, and generously preaching the doctrine for all nations alike: let all nations have their own political roofs, and let all of them also refrain from including non-nationals under it. There is no formal contradiction in asserting such non-egoistic nationalism. As a doctrine it can be supported by some good arguments, such as the desirability of preserving cultural diversity, of a pluralistic international political system, and of the diminution of internal strains within states.

In fact, however, nationalism has often not been so sweetly reasonable, nor so rationally symmetrical. It may be that, as Immanuel Kant believed, partiality, the tendency to make exceptions on one's own behalf or one's own case, is *the* central human weakness from which all others flow; and that it infects national sentiment as it does all else, engendering what the Italians under Mussolini called the *sacro egoismo* of nationalism. It may also be that the political effectiveness of national sentiment would be much impaired if nationalists had as fine a sensibility to the wrongs committed by their nation as they have to those committed against it.

But over and above these considerations there are others, tied to the specific nature of the world we happen to live in, which militate against any impartial, general, sweetly reasonable nationalism. To put it in the simplest possible terms: there is a very large number of potential nations on earth. Our planet also contains room for a certain number of independent or autonomous political units. On any reasonable calculation, the former number (of potential nations) is probably much, *much* larger than that of possible viable states. If this argument or calculation is correct, not all nationalisms can be satisfied, at any rate at the same time. The satisfaction of some spells the frustration of others. This argument is further and immeasurably strengthened by the fact that very many of the potential nations of this world live, or until recently have lived, not in compact territorial units but intermixed with each other in complex patterns. It follows that a territorial political unit can only become ethnically homogeneous, in such cases, if it either kills, or expels, or assimilates all non-nationals. Their unwillingness to suffer such fates may make the peaceful implementation of the nationalist principle difficult.

These definitions must, of course, like most definitions, be applied with common sense. The nationalist principle, as defined, is not violated by the presence of *small* numbers of resident foreigners, or even by the presence of the occasional foreigner in, say, a national ruling family. Just how many resident foreigners or foreign members of the ruling class there must be before the principle is effectively violated cannot be stated with precision. There is no sacred percentage figure, below which the foreigner can be benignly tolerated, and above which he becomes offensive and his safety and life are at peril. No doubt the figure will vary with circumstances. The impossibility of providing a generally applicable and precise figure, however, does not undermine the usefulness of the definition.

State and Nation

Our definition of nationalism was parasitic on two as yet undefined terms: state and nation.

Discussion of the state may begin with Max Weber's celebrated definition of it, as that agency within society which possesses the monopoly of legitimate violence. The idea behind this is simple and seductive: in well-ordered societies, such as most of us live in or aspire to live in, private or sectional violence is illegitimate. Conflict as such is not illegitimate, but it cannot rightfully be resolved by private or sectional violence. Violence may be applied only by the central political authority, and those to whom it delegates this right. Among the various sanctions of the maintenance of order, the ultimate one—force—may be applied only by one special, clearly identified, and well centralized, disciplined agency within society. That agency or group of agencies *is* the state.

The idea enshrined in this definition corresponds fairly well with the moral intuitions of many, probably most, members of modern societies. Nevertheless, it is not entirely satisfactory. There are 'states'—or, at any rate, institutions which we would normally be inclined to call by that name—which do not monopolize legitimate violence within the territory which they more or less effectively control. A feudal state does not necessarily object to private wars between its fief-holders, provided they also fulfill their obligations to their overlord; or again, a state counting tribal populations among its subjects does not necessarily object to the institution of the feud, as long as those who indulge in it refrain from endangering neutrals on the public highway or in the market. The Iraqi state, under British tutelage after the First World War, tolerated tribal raids, provided the raiders dutifully reported at the nearest police station before and after the expedition, leaving an orderly bureaucratic record of slain and booty. In brief, there are states which lack either the will or the means to enforce their monopoly of legitimate violence, and which nonetheless remain, in many respects, recognizable 'states'.

Weber's underlying principle does, however, seem valid *now*, however strangely ethnocentric it may be as a general definition, with its tacit assumption of the well-centralized Western state. The state constitutes one highly distinctive and important elaboration of the social division of labour. Where there is no division of labour, one cannot even begin to speak of the state. But not any or every specialism makes a state: the state is the specialization and concentration of order maintenance. The 'state' is that institution or set of institutions specifically concerned with the enforcement of order (whatever else they may also be concerned with). The state exists where specialized order-enforcing agencies, such as police forces and courts, have separated out from the rest of social life. They *are* the state.

Not all societies are state-endowed. It immediately follows that the problem of nationalism does not arise for stateless societies. If there is no state, one obviously cannot ask whether or not its boundaries are congruent with the limits of nations. If there are no rulers, there being no state, one cannot ask whether they are of the same nation as the ruled. When neither state nor rulers exist, one cannot resent their failure to conform to the requirements of the principle of nationalism. One may perhaps deplore statelessness, but that is another matter. Nationalists have generally fulminated against the distribution of political power and the nature of political boundaries, but they have seldom if ever had occasion to deplore the absence of power and of boundaries altogether. The circumstances in which nationalism has generally arisen have not normally been those in which the state itself, as such, was lacking, or when its reality was in any serious doubt. The state was only too conspicuously present. It was its boundaries and/or the distribution of power, and possibly of other advantages, within it which were resented.

This in itself is highly significant. Not only is our definition of nationalism parasitic on a prior and assumed definition of the state: it also seems to be the case that nationalism emerges only in milieux in which the existence of the state is already very much taken for granted. The existence of politically centralized units, and of a moral-political climate in which such centralized units are taken for granted and are treated as normative, is a necessary though by no means a sufficient condition of nationalism.

By way of anticipation, some general historical observations should be made about the state. Mankind has passed through three fundamental stages in its history: the pre-agrarian, the agrarian, and the industrial. Hunting and gathering bands were and are too small to allow the kind of political division of labour which constitutes the state; and so, for them, the question of the state, of a stable specialized order-enforcing institution, does not really arise. By contrast, most, but by no means all, agrarian societies have been state-endowed. Some of these states have been strong and some weak, some have been despotic and others law-abiding. They differ a very great deal in their form. The agrarian phase of human history is the period during which, so to speak, the very existence of the state is an option. Moreover, the form of the state is highly variable. During the hunting-gathering stage, the option was not available.

By contrast, in the post-agrarian, industrial age there is, once again, no option; but now the *presence*, not the absence of the state is inescapable. Paraphrasing Hegel, once none had the state, then some had it, and finally all have it. The form it takes, of course, still remains variable. There are some traditions of social thought—anarchism, Marxism—which hold that even, or

especially, in an industrial order the state is dispensable, at least under
favourable conditions or under conditions due to be realized in the fullness
of time. There are obvious and powerful reasons for doubting this: industrial societies are enormously large, and depend for the standard of living to
which they have become accustomed (or to which they ardently wish to become accustomed) on an unbelievably intricate general division of labour
and cooperation. Some of this co-operation might under favourable conditions be spontaneous and need no central sanctions. The idea that all of it
could perpetually work in this way, that it could exist without any enforcement and control, puts an intolerable strain on one's credulity.

So the problem of nationalism does not arise when there is no state. It
does not follow that the problem of nationalism arises for each and every
state. On the contrary, it arises only for *some* states. It remains to be seen
which ones do face this problem.

The Nation

The def'inition of the nation presents difficulties graver than those attendant on the definition of the state. Although modern man tends to take the
centralized state (and, more specifically, the centralized national state) for
granted, nevertheless he is capable, with relatively little effort, of seeing its
contingency, and of imagining a social situation in which the state is absent.
He is quite adept at visualizing the 'state of nature'. An anthropologist can
explain to him that the tribe is not necessarily a state writ small, and that
forms of tribal organization exist which can be described as stateless. By contrast, the idea of a man without a nation seems to impose a far greater strain
on the modern imagination. Chamisso, an *emigré* Frenchman in Germany
during the Napoleonic period, wrote a powerful proto-Kafkaesque novel
about a man who lost his shadow: though no doubt part of the effectiveness
of this novel hinges on the intended ambiguity of the parable, it is difficult
not to suspect that, for the author, the Man without a Shadow was the Man
without a Nation. When his followers and acquaintances detect his aberrant
shadowlessness they shun the otherwise well-endowed Peter Schlemiehl. A man
without a nation defies the recognized categories and provokes revulsion.

Chamisso's perception—if indeed this is what he intended to convey—was
valid enough, but valid only for one kind of human condition, and not for
the human condition as such anywhere at any time. A man must have a nationality as he must have a nose and two ears; a deficiency in any of these
particulars is not inconceivable and does from time to time occur, but only
as a result of some disaster, and it is itself a disaster of a kind. All this seems
obvious, though, alas, it is not true. But that it should have come to *seem* so
very obviously true is indeed an aspect, or perhaps the very core, of the problem of nationalism. Having a nation is not an inherent attribute of humanity, but it has now come to appear as such.

In fact, nations, like states, are a contingency, and not a universal necessity. Neither nations nor states exist at all times and in all circumstances. Moreover, nations and states are not the *same* contingency. Nationalism holds that they were destined for each other; that either without the other is incomplete, and constitutes a tragedy. But before they could become intended for each other, each of them had to emerge, and their emergence was independent and contingent. The state has certainly emerged without the help of the nation. Some nations have certainly emerged without the blessings of their own state. It is more debatable whether the normative idea of the nation, in its modern sense, did not presuppose the prior existence of the state.

What then is this contingent, but in our age seemingly universal and normative, idea of the nation? Discussion of two very makeshift, temporary definitions will help to pinpoint this elusive concept.

1. Two men are of the same nation if and only if they share the same culture, where culture in turn means a system of ideas and signs and associations and ways of behaving and communicating.
2. Two men are of the same nation if and only if they recognize each other as belonging to the same nation. In other words, *nations make the man*; nations are the artifacts of men's convictions and loyalties and solidarities. A mere category of persons (say, occupants of a given territory, or speakers of a given language, for example) becomes a nation if and when the members of the category firmly recognize certain mutual rights and duties to each other in virtue of their shared membership of it. It is their recognition of each other as fellows of this kind which turns them into a nation, and not the other shared attributes, whatever they might be, which separate that category from nonmembers.

Each of these provisional definitions, the cultural and the voluntaristic, has some merit. Each of them singles out an element which is of real importance in the understanding of nationalism. But neither is adequate. Definitions of culture, presupposed by the first definition, in the anthropological rather than the normative sense, are notoriously difficult and unsatisfactory. It is probably best to approach this problem by using this term without attempting too much in the way of formal definition, and looking at what culture does . . . .

A Note on the Weakness of Nationalism

It is customary to comment on the strength of nationalism. This is an important mistake, though readily understandable since, whenever nationalism has taken root, it has tended to prevail with ease over other modern ideologies.

Nevertheless, the clue to the understanding of nationalism is its weakness at least as much as its strength. It was the dog who failed to bark who provided the vital clue for Sherlock Holmes. The numbers of potential nationalisms which failed to bark is far, far larger than those which did, though *they* have captured all our attention.

We have already insisted on the dormant nature of this allegedly powerful monster during the pre-industrial age. But even within the age of nationalism, there is a further important sense in which nationalism remains astonishingly feeble. Nationalism has been defined, in effect, as the striving to make culture and polity congruent, to endow a culture with its own political roof, and not more than one roof at that. Culture, an elusive concept, was deliberately left undefined. But an at least provisionally acceptable criterion of culture might be language, as at least a sufficient, if not a necessary touchstone of it. Allow for a moment a difference of language to entail a difference of culture (though not necessarily the reverse).

If this is granted, at least temporarily, certain consequences follow. I have heard the number of languages on earth estimated at around 8000. The figure can no doubt be increased by counting dialects separately. If we allow the 'precedent' argument, this becomes legitimate: if a kind of differential which in some places defines a nationalism is allowed to engender a 'potential nationalism' wherever else a similar difference is found, then the number of potential nationalisms increases sharply. For instance, diverse Slavonic, Teutonic and Romance languages are in fact often no further apart than are the mere dialects within what are elsewhere conventionally seen as unitary languages. Slav languages, for instance, are probably closer to each other than are the various forms of colloquial Arabic, allegedly a single language.

The 'precedent' argument can also generate potential nationalisms by analogies invoking factors other than language. For instance, Scottish nationalism indisputably exists. (It may indeed be held to contradict my model.) It ignores language (which would condemn some Scots to Irish nationalism, and the rest to English nationalism), invoking instead a shared historical experience. Yet if such additional links be allowed to count (as long as they don't contradict the requirement of my model, that they can serve as a base for an *eventually* homogeneous, internally mobile culture/polity with one educational machine servicing that culture under the surveillance of that polity), then the number of potential nationalisms goes up even higher.

However, let us be content with the figure of 8000, once given to me by a linguist as a rough number of languages based on what was no doubt rather an arbitrary estimate of language alone. The number of states in the world at present is some figure of the order of 200. To this figure one may add all the irredentist nationalisms, which have not yet attained their state (and perhaps never will), but which are struggling in that direction and thus have a legitimate claim to be counted among actual, and not merely potential, nationalisms. On the other hand, one must also subtract all those states which have come into being without the benefit of the blessing of nationalist en-

dorsement, and which do not satisfy the nationalist criteria of political legitimacy, and indeed defy them; for instance, all the diverse mini-states dotted
about the globe as survivals of a pre-nationalist age, and sometimes brought
forth as concessions to geographical accident or political compromise. Once
all these had been subtracted, the resulting figure would again, presumably,
not be too far above 200. But let us, for the sake of charity, pretend that we
have four times that number of reasonably effective nationalisms on earth,
in other words, 800 of them. I believe this to be considerably larger than the
facts would justify, but let it pass.

This rough calculation still gives us only *one* effective nationalism for *ten*
potential ones! And this surprising ratio, depressing presumably for any enthusiastic pan-nationalist, if such a person exists, could be made much larger
if the 'precedent' argument were applied to the full to determine the number of potential nationalisms, and if the criteria of entry into the class of effective nationalisms were made at all stringent.

What is one to conclude from this? That for every single nationalism
which has so far raised its ugly head, nine others are still waiting in the
wings? That all the bomb-throwing, martyrdoms, exchange of populations,
and worse, which have so far beset humanity, are still to be repeated tenfold?

I think not. For every effective nationalism, there are *n* potential ones,
groups defined either by shared culture inherited from the agrarian world
or by some other link (on the 'precedent' principle) which *could* give hope
of establishing a homogeneous industrial community, but which nevertheless do not bother to struggle, which fail to activate their potential nationalism, which do not even try.

So it seems that the urge to make mutual cultural substitutability the basis
of the state is not so powerful after all. The members of *some* groups do indeed feel it, but members of most groups, with analogous claims, evidently
do not.

To explain this, we must return to the accusation made against nationalism; that it insists on imposing homogeneity on the populations unfortunate
enough to fall under the sway of authorities possessed by the nationalist ideology. The assumption underlying this accusation is that traditional, ideologically uninfected authorities, such as the Ottoman Turks, had kept the
peace and extracted taxes, but otherwise tolerated, and been indeed profoundly indifferent to, the diversity of faiths and cultures which they governed. By contrast, their gunman successors seem incapable of resting in
peace till they have imposed the nationalist principle of *cuius regio, eius lin-
gua*. They do not want merely a fiscal surplus and obedience. They thirst after the cultural and linguistic souls of their subjects.

This accusation must be stood on its head. It is not the case that nationalism imposes homogeneity out of a wilful cultural *Machtbedürfniss;* it is the
objective need for homogeneity which is reflected in nationalism. If it is
the case that a modern industrial state can only function with a mobile, liter-
ate, culturally standardized, interchangeable population, as we have argued,
then the illiterate, half-starved populations sucked from their erstwhile

rural cultural ghettoes into the melting pots of shanty-towns yearn for incorporation into some one of those cultural pools which already has, or looks as if it might acquire, a state of its own, with the subsequent promise of full cultural citizenship, access to primary schools, employment, and all. Often, these alienated, uprooted, wandering populations may vacillate between diverse options, and they may often come to a provisional rest at one or another temporary and transitional cultural resting place.

But there are some options which they will refrain from trying to take up. They will hesitate about trying to enter cultural pools within which they know themselves to be spurned; or rather, within which they expect to *continue* to be spurned. Poor newcomers are, of course, almost always spurned. The question is whether they will continue to be slighted, and whether the same fate will await their children. This will depend on whether the newly arrived and hence least privileged stratum possesses traits which its members and their offspring cannot shed, and which will continue to identify them: genetically transmitted or deeply engrained religious cultural habits are impossible or difficult to drop.

The alienated victims of early industrialism are unlikely to be tempted by cultural pools that are very small—a language spoken by a couple of villages offers few prospects—or very diffused or lacking in any literary traditions or personnel capable of carrying skills, and so on. They require cultural pools which are large, and/or have a good historic base, or intellectual personnel well equipped to propagate the culture in question. It is impossible to pick out any single qualification, or set of qualifications, which will either guarantee the success as a nationalist catalyst of the culture endowed with it (or them), or which on the contrary will ensure its failure. Size, historicity, reasonably compact territory, a capable and energetic intellectual class: all these will obviously help; but no single one is necessary, and it is doubtful whether any firm predictive generalization can be established in these terms. That the principle of nationalism will be operative can be predicted; just which groupings will emerge as its carriers can be only loosely indicated, for it depends on too many historic contingencies.

Nationalism as such is fated to prevail, but not any one particular nationalism. We know that reasonably homogeneous cultures, each of them with its own political roof, its own political servicing, are becoming the norm, widely implemented but for few exceptions; but we cannot predict just which cultures, with which political roofs, will be blessed by success. On the contrary, the simple calculations made above, concerning the number of cultures or potential nationalisms and concerning the room available for proper national states, clearly show that most potential nationalisms must either fail, or, more commonly, will refrain from even trying to find political expression.

This is precisely what we do find. Most cultures or potential national groups enter the age of nationalism without even the feeblest effort to benefit from it themselves. The number of groups which in terms of the 'precedent' argument could try to become nations, which could define themselves by the kind of criterion which in some other place does in fact define some real and effective nation, is legion. Yet most of them go meekly to their doom, to see their culture (though not themselves as individuals) slowly disappear, dissolving into the wider culture of some new national state. Most cultures are led to the dust heap of history by industrial civilization without offering any resistance. The linguistic distinctiveness of the Scottish Highlands within Scotland is, of course, incomparably greater than the cultural distinctiveness of Scotland within the UK; but there is no Highland nationalism. Much the same is true of Moroccan Berbers. Dialectal and cultural differences within Germany or Italy are as great as those between recognized Teutonic or Romance languages. Southern Russians differ culturally from Northern Russians, but, unlike Ukrainians, do not translate this into a sense of nationhood.

Does this show that nationalism is, after all, unimportant? Or even that it is an ideological artifact, an invention of febrile thinkers which has mysteriously captured some mysteriously susceptible nations? Not at all. To reach such a conclusion would, ironically, come close to a tacit, oblique acceptance of the nationalist ideologue's most misguided claim: namely, that the 'nations' are there, in the very nature of things, only waiting to be 'awakened' (a favourite nationalist expression and image) from their regrettable slumber, by the nationalist 'awakener'. One would be inferring from the failure of most potential nations ever to 'wake up', from the lack of deep stirrings waiting for reveille, that nationalism was not important after all. Such an inference concedes the social ontology of 'nations', only admitting, with some surprise perhaps, that some of them lack the vigour and vitality needed if they are to fulfill the destiny which history intended for them.

But nationalism is *not* the awakening of an old, latent, dormant force, though that is how it does indeed present itself. It is in reality the consequence of a new form of social organization, based on deeply internalized, education-dependent high cultures, each protected by its own state. It uses some of the pre-existent cultures, generally transforming them in the process, but it cannot possibly use them all. There are too many of them. A viable higher culture-sustaining modern state cannot fall below a certain minimal size (unless in effect parasitic on its neighbours); and there is only room for a limited number of such states on this earth.

The high ratio of determined slumberers, who will not rise and shine and who refuse to be woken, enables us to turn the tables on nationalism-as-seen-by-itself. Nationalism sees itself as a natural and universal ordering of the political life of mankind, only obscured by that long, persistent and mysterious somnolence. As Hegel expressed this vision: 'Nations may have had a long history before they finally reach their destination—that of forming themselves into states'.[1] Hegel immediately goes on to suggest that this pre-state period is really 'pre-historical' (*sic*): so it would seem that on this view the

---

[1] G.W.F. Hegel, *Lectures on the Philosophy of World History,* tr. H.B. Nisbet, Cambridge, 1975, p. 134.

real history of a nation only begins when it acquires its own state. If we invoke the sleeping-beauty nations, neither possessing a state nor feeling the lack of it, against the nationalist doctrine, we tacitly accept its social metaphysic, which sees nations as the bricks of which mankind is made up. Critics of nationalism who denounce the political movement but tacitly accept the existence of nations, do not go far enough. Nations as a natural, God-given way of classifying men, as an inherent though long-delayed political destiny, are a myth; nationalism, which sometimes takes pre-existing cultures and turns them into nations, sometimes invents them, and often obliterates pre-existing cultures: *that* is a reality, for better or worse, and in general an inescapable one. Those who are its historic agents know not what they do, but that is another matter.

But we must not accept the myth. Nations are not inscribed into the nature of things, they do not constitute a political version of the doctrine of natural kinds. Nor were national states the manifest ultimate destiny of ethnic or cultural groups. What do exist are cultures, often subtly grouped, shading into each other, overlapping, intertwined; and there exist, usually but not always, political units of all shapes and sizes. In the past the two did not generally converge. There were good reasons for their failing to do so in many cases. Their rulers established their identity by differentiating themselves downwards, and the ruled micro-communities differentiated themselves laterally from their neighbors grouped in similar units.

But nationalism is not the awakening and assertion of these mythical, supposedly natural and given units. It is, on the contrary, the crystallization of new units, suitable for the conditions now prevailing, though admittedly using as their raw material the cultural, historical and other inheritances from the pre-nationalist world. . . .

Two Types of Nationalism

. . . [In nineteenth-century Europe] most Italians were ruled by foreigners, and in that sense were politically underprivileged. The Germans, most of them, lived in fragmented states, many of them small and weak, at any rate by European great power standards, and thus unable to provide German culture, as a centralized modern medium, with its political roof. (By a further paradox, multi-national great power Austria was endeavoring to do something of that kind, but much to the displeasure of some of its citizens.)

So the political protection of Italian and German culture was visibly and, to the Italians and Germans offensively, inferior to that which was provided for, say, French or English culture. But when it came to access to education, the facilities provided by these two high cultures, to those who were born into dialectal variants of it, were not really in any way inferior. Both Italian and German were literary languages, with an effective centralized standardization of their correct forms and with flourishing literatures, technical vocabularies and manners, educational institutions and academies. There was little if any cultural inferiority. Rates of literacy and standards of education were not significantly lower (if lower at all) among Germans than they were among the French; and they were not significantly low among the Italians, when compared with the dominant Austrians. German in comparison with French, or Italian in comparison with the German used by the Austrians, were not disadvantaged cultures, and their speakers did not need to correct unequal access to the eventual benefits of a modern world. All that needed to be corrected was that inequality of power and the absence of a political roof over a culture (and over an economy), and institutions which would be identified with it and committed to its maintenance. The Risorgimento and the unification of Germany corrected these imbalances.

There is a difference, however, between this kind of unificatory nationalism, on behalf of a fully effective high culture which only needs an improved bit of political roofing, and the classical Habsburg-and-east-and-south type of nationalism. This difference is the subject of a fascinating and rather moving essay by the late Professor John Plamenatz, an essay which might well have been called 'The Sad Reflections of a Montenegrin in Oxford'.[2] Plamenatz called the two kinds of nationalism the Western and the Eastern, the Western type being of the Risorgimento or unificatory kind, typical of the nineteenth century and with deep links to liberal ideas, while the Eastern, though he did not stress it in so many words, was exemplified by the kind of nationalism he knew to exist in his native Balkans. There can be no doubt but that he saw the Western nationalism as relatively benign and nice, and the Eastern kind as nasty, and doomed to nastiness by the conditions which gave rise to it. (It would be an interesting question to ask him whether he would have considered the markedly un-benign forms taken by these once-benign or relatively liberal and moderate Western nationalisms in the twentieth century, as accidental and avoidable aberrations or not.)

The underlying logic of Plamenatz's argument is clear. The relatively benign Western nationalisms were acting on behalf of well-developed high cultures, normatively centralized and endowed with a fairly well-defined folk clientele: all that was required was a bit of adjustment in the political situation and in the international boundaries, so as to ensure for these cultures, and their speakers and practitioners, the same sustained protection as that which was already enjoyed by their rivals. This took a few battles and a good deal of sustained diplomatic activity but, as the making of historical omelettes goes, it did not involve the breaking of a disproportionate or unusual number of eggs, perhaps no more than would have been broken anyway in the course of the normal political game within the general political framework and assumptions of the time.

[2]John Plamenatz, 'Two types of Nationalism', in E. Kamenka (ed.), *Nationalism, The Nature and Evolution of an Idea*, London, 1973.

By way of contrast, consider the nationalism designated as Eastern by Plamenatz. Its implementation did, of course, require battles and diplomacy, to
at least the same extent as the realization of Western nationalisms. But the
matter did not end there. This kind of Eastern nationalism did not operate
on behalf of an already existing, well-defined and codified high culture,
which had as it were marked out and linguistically pre-converted its own territory by sustained literary activities ever since the early Renaissance or since
the Reformation, as the case might be. Not at all. This nationalism was active
on behalf of a high culture as yet not properly crystallized, a merely aspirant
or in-the-making high culture. It presided, or strove to preside, in ferocious
rivalry with similar competitors, over a chaotic ethnographic map of many
dialects, with ambiguous historical or linguo-genetic allegiances, and containing populations which had only just begun to identify with these emergent national high cultures. Objective conditions of the modern world were
bound, in due course, to oblige them to identify with one of them. But till
this occurred, they lacked the clearly defined cultural basis enjoyed by their
German and Italian counterparts.

These populations of eastern Europe were still locked into the complex
multiple loyalties of kinship, territory and religion. To make them conform
to the nationalist imperative was bound to take more than a few battles and
some diplomacy. It was bound to take a great deal of very forceful cultural
engineering. In many cases it was also bound to involve population exchanges or expulsions, more or less forcible assimilation, and sometimes liq-
uidation, in order to attain that close relation between state and culture
which is the essence of nationalism. And all these consequences flowed, not
from some unusual brutality of the nationalists who in the end employed
these measures (they were probably no worse and no better than anyone
else), but from the inescapable logic of the situation.

Long Memories and Short Fuses: Change and Instability in the Balkans

F. STEPHEN LARRABEE

The Balkans have traditionally been a region of instability and ferment, and with the end of the Cold War, longstanding conflicts are likely to re-emerge. During the nineteenth century the region was continually a site of great power rivalry, as Britain, Russia, and Austria sought to extend their influence in the area—or to block other powers from doing so. The volatile combination of great power ambition and assertive nationalism in the area contributed directly to the outbreak of World War I, and earned the region the reputation as "the powder keg of Europe."

The collapse of the Ottoman and Hapsburg empires at the end of World War I left a host of ethnic and territorial conflicts unresolved and created a number of new ones. The Cold War, with its emphasis on "tight" bipolarity, tended to dampen many of these tensions and conflicts, though it did not entirely eliminate them. Polemics between Bulgaria and Yugoslavia over Macedonia periodically flared up; the Romanian treatment of the Hungarian minority was a source of disagreement between Romania and Hungary; discontent among the Turkish minority in Bulgaria led to several waves of emigration and poisoned Bulgarian-Turkish relations; and Yugoslav-Albanian relations were marred by differences over the Albanian minority in the Yugoslav area of Kosovo.

Still, as long as the bloc system existed, it acted as a residual, if diminishing, constraint on these tensions. The end of the Cold War, however, threat-

F. Stephen Larrabee, "Long Memories and Short Fuses: Change and Instability in the Balkans," *International Security* Vol. 15, no. 3 (Winter 1990/91). Reprinted with permission of the MIT Press, Cambridge, Massachusetts. Copyright © 1990 by the President and Fellows of Harvard College and of the Massachusetts Institute of Technology.

ens to remove this constraint. As both superpowers are increasingly preoccupied with other pressing agendas and less inclined—or able—to act as hegemonic powers, there is a danger that many long-submerged regional conflicts could intensify. Moreover, by allowing more open expression of ethnic grievances, the process of democratization in the post-communist countries of the Balkans may exacerbate rather than ameliorate some of these conflicts.

Indeed, Europe may witness two diametrically opposed trends in the coming decade: while Western Europe moves toward greater integration and multilateral cooperation, Eastern Europe, particularly Southeastern Europe, may witness greater political fragmentation and a "renationalization" of politics. In the 1990s the main threat to European security is likely to come not from Soviet military power but from ethnic conflict and political fragmentation in the Balkans. In short, the end of the Cold War may not mean the end of conflict in Europe. The source of conflict and instability may simply shift southward. Indeed, the Balkans could emerge as a major stumbling block to the creation of a stable security order in Europe in the coming decade. . . .

Democratization and Change

. . . Unlike other countries in Europe that underwent transitions from authoritarian to democratic systems (such as Spain, Greece, and Portugal), the post-communist states in the Balkans and the rest of Eastern Europe will have to undergo a "dual transition": that is, they will have to change both their political systems and their economic systems at the same time. This dual transition will significantly complicate the transition process and will increase the possibility of political instability in many of these states.

Second, none of the countries in the post-communist Balkans has any lengthy experience with democracy. For most of the interwar period Romania, Bulgaria, Albania, and Yugoslavia were under authoritarian rule of one form or another.[1] The few democratic institutions that did exist were largely destroyed under communist rule. Thus these countries will have to begin practically from scratch to build new democratic institutions.

Third, nationalism has historically been a strong force in the Balkans.[2] The erosion of communist rule in Eastern Europe may, as Zbigniew Brzezin-

[1]For developments in the interwar periods see Barbara Jelavich, *History of the Balkans,* 2 vols. (Cambridge: Cambridge University Press, 1983); Paul Lendvai, *Eagles in the Cobwebs: Nationalism and Communism in the Balkans* (New York: Doubleday, 1969); Hugh Seton-Watson, *Eastern Europe Between the Wars 1918-1941* (New York: Harper Torchbooks, 1967); and Robert L. Wolff, *The Balkans in Our Time* (Cambridge: Harvard University Press, 1956).

[2]On the role of nationalism in the Balkans, see in particular the selections in Peter F. Sugar and Ivo J. Lederer, eds., *Nationalism in Eastern Europe* (Seattle: University of Washington Press, 1969).

ski and others have argued, lead to the resurgence of nationalism,[3] particularly in the Balkans. The anti-Turkish demonstrations in Bulgaria in January 1990 and the clashes in Transylvania between the Romanian population and the Hungarian minority in March 1990 indicate that nationalism is far from dead in both countries. Indeed, both could witness a re-nationalization of politics, in which weak semi-democratic regimes seek to bolster their popular support through appeals to nationalism. . . .[4]

Fourth, Bulgaria and Romania, unlike the post-communist countries of Central Europe, lack a strong "civil society."[5] Romanian leader Nicolae Ceausescu managed to stamp out all organized opposition in Romania through the brutal use of the secret police and a clever policy of "rotation of cadres."[6] Only in the last few years did Bulgaria witness any significant expressions of political dissent. This was limited, however, to a relatively small group of intellectuals and environmentalists.[7]

This lack of a strong civil society has important implications for the process of democratization and consolidation. In Poland, Czechoslovakia, and Hungary, there were organized political forces—Solidarity, Civil Forum, and Democratic Forum—to pick up the reins of power when the old order collapsed or was voted out of office. In Romania and Bulgaria, by contrast, the opposition was weak and fragmented and was unable to fill the power vacuum. Hence in these countries the former Communists have been able to cling to power by changing the name of their party and draping themselves in the mantle of reform. . . .

[3]See Zbigniew Brzezinski, "Post-Communist Nationalism," *Foreign Affairs*, Vol. 68, No. 5 (Winter 1989/90), pp. 1-25.

[4]This pattern has traditionally been so prevalent in the Balkans that Myron Weiner has termed it the "Macedonian Syndrome." See Weiner, "The Macedonian Syndrome: An Historical Model of International Relations and Political Development," *World Politics*, Vol. 23, No. 4 (July 1971), pp. 665-683.

[5]By "civil society" I mean the existence of autonomous political groups, institutions, and activities that are not entirely controlled by the established government. For a comprehensive treatment see John Keane, *Democracy and Civil Society* (London: Verso, 1988); and John Keane, ed., *Civil Society and the State* (London: Verso, 1988).

[6]"Rotation of cadres" involved switching party and government officials from one post to another at regular intervals. While its ostensible purpose was to give officials wide experience in a number of areas, in fact it was used to prevent any particular official from obtaining a powerbase from which he might challenge Ceausescu's rule. For a good discussion see James F. Brown, *Eastern Europe and Communist Rule* (Durham, N.C.: Duke University Press, 1988), pp. 279-289.

[7]See Richard Crampton, "The Intelligentsia, Ecology and the Opposition in Bulgaria," *The World Today*, February 1990, pp. 23-26.

Regional and Ethnic Conflicts

The problems of political development in the Balkans are compounded by the existence of a number of unresolved regional and ethnic conflicts with deep historical roots. While communist rule did not eliminate these conflicts, it did often act as a constraint on them. However, with the collapse of communist rule and the re-nationalization of politics in a number of states in the region, many of these disputes could re-emerge with increased intensity. To be sure, these conflicts are not likely to spark a world war, as the assassination of Austrian Archduke Franz Ferdinand did in 1914. At that time the Balkans were the seat of intense great-power rivalry. Today none of the major powers . . . has a strong interest in trying to exploit these conflicts for its own purposes.

This does not mean, however, that such conflicts can be ignored. In many instances their intensification could seriously complicate the process of democratic consolidation in the region, in the same way as Basque separatism hindered the consolidation of democracy in Spain in the late 1970s. Moreover, some of the disputes, like the Macedonian issue, involve more than one country. Thus there is a danger that an intensification of the disputes could have a "ripple effect" throughout the region, exacerbating other conflicts. Finally, the possibility of an actual shooting war, such as that which occurred between Greece and Turkey over Cyprus in 1974, while remote cannot entirely be excluded. Thus these conflicts could seriously hinder the construction of a stable security order in the "new Europe." With these considerations in mind it may be useful to take a more detailed look at some of these disputes and their potential impact on regional and European security.

The Kosovo Problem

Yugoslavia's disintegration could exacerbate Belgrade's dispute with Albania over the fate of the nearly two million Albanians living in Yugoslavia, most of whom live in Kosovo. The roots of the dispute can be traced back to the defeat of Turkey in the Balkan wars of 1912-13, which led to the creation of Albania as an independent state. At the London Conference (1913), the great powers decided to create a "rump Albania," which included only about half of the Albanian population in the area.[8] More than 50 percent of the Albanian population was left outside the boundaries of the newly created Albanian state. Serbia acquired most of what is now Kosovo, while Montenegro and Macedonia received small parts.

---

[8]For a detailed discussion of the London Conference and the creation of Albania, see R.J. Crampton, *The Hollow Detente: Anglo-German Relations in the Balkans 1911-1914* (London: George Prior, 1977).

The national conflict re-emerged during the course of World War II. The Albanian Communist Party, which spearheaded the resistance against the Germans, was controlled by the Yugoslav Communist Party (YCP) under Tito and was little more than an extension of the Yugoslav Party. During the war the Albanian Communist Party (ACP) had initially supported the Mukaj agreement, which called for the inclusion of Kosovo into a "Greater Albania." Under pressure from Yugoslavia, however, the Albanian Party was forced to repudiate its support for the Mukaj agreement and accept the incorporation of Kosovo into Yugoslavia, a move which undercut popular support for the Party in Albania and was resented by many members in the Albanian Party. After the Yugoslav-Soviet break in 1948, Albania quickly joined the cavalcade of criticism of Yugoslavia. The break led not only to a purge of alleged "Yugoslav agents" in the Albanian party,[9] but to a strong upsurge of anti-Yugolslav (or more accurately anti-Serb) feeling within Albania. Under Enver Hoxha, who emerged as the undisputed leader of the Albanian party after 1949, the struggle against "Titoism" became the cornerstone of Albania's policy and the litmus test of Albania's relations with other communist parties. In particular, Hoxha tirelessly attacked the repression and "exploitation" of the Albanian minority by Belgrade. Although Hoxha never *expressis verbis* demanded the return of Kosovo, the Albanian charges were regarded in Belgrade as little more than undisguised territorial claims against Yugoslavia.

Hoxha's successor, Ramiz Alia, . . . continued more or less unchanged the policy he inherited from Hoxha regarding Kosovo.[10] Like Hoxha he . . . persistently accused Yugoslavia of conducting an "anti-Albanian policy" and of repressing the Albanian minority in Yugoslavia, though like Hoxha, he . . . stopped short of actually demanding the return of Kosovo. Belgrade, in turn . . . , continued to accuse Albania of spreading "anti-Yugoslav propaganda" and stirring up unrest among the Albanian population of Kosovo.

Relations deteriorated after popular unrest in Kosovo in 1968, which led to a virtual cessation of all cultural and tourist exchanges. Since 1988, however, there have been signs that Tirana is interested in improving relations with Yugoslavia. In February 1988 a cultural agreement was signed between the two countries. And in a speech in May 1990 Foreign Minister Reis Malile, one of the chief architects of Albania's new foreign policy, suggested that Albania might relax its restrictions and allow families to visit relatives in neighboring countries.[11]

---

[9]The chief victim was Koci Xoxe, the Interior Minister, who had headed the "Yugoslav faction" in the party. Xoxe was arrested and executed in 1949 as part of the wave of purge trials that swept Eastern Europe in the aftermath of the Stalin-Tito break.

[10]See Jens Reuter, "Das Kosovo-Problem in Kontext der jugoslawisch-albanischen Beziehungen," *Südosteuropa,* Heft 11/12 (1987), pp. 718-727. Also by the same author, "Die jugoslawischalbanischen Beziehungen nach Enver Hoxha," *Südosteuropa,* Heft 1 (1987), pp. 10-18.

[11]*Zeri i Popullit* (Tirana), May 16, 1990. For a fuller discussion see Louis Zanga, "Albania's New Path," RFE, *Report on Eastern Europe,* June 15, 1990, pp. 1-5.

A liberalization of travel restrictions could have an important impact on the internal situation in both countries. On the one hand, greater contact with the process of democratization in Kosovo could whet the appetite of the Albanian population for more sweeping reforms at home, thus accelerating the process of change in Albania. On the other, it could create a growing feeling of "togetherness" between the two Albanian communities and lead to increased pressures for unification, especially if Serb repression of Albanian political rights continues and centrifugal forces within Yugoslavia as a whole intensify.

The Macedonian Question

The Macedonian problem has been a long-standing source of conflict in the Balkans.[12] The "Greater Bulgaria" established by the Treaty of San Stefano in March 1878 included most of Macedonia, but this was quickly lost at the Congress of Berlin three months later, greatly reducing Bulgaria's size. At the end of World War I Macedonia was divided among four states: Greece, which got the largest portion, Bulgaria, Yugoslavia, and Albania, which received a small part on its eastern border. During the interwar period the Internal Macedonia Revolutionary Organization (IMRO), operating from Bulgarian soil, conducted a campaign of terror against both Bulgarian officials and Yugoslavia in support of an independent Macedonia.[13]

In 1944 a completely new dimension was given to the problem with the establishment of the People's Republic of Macedonia as one of the federal units of Yugoslavia. In Yugoslavia the Macedonians were recognized as a separate Slavic nation, with their own separate language. Neither Greece nor Bulgaria, however, recognizes a separate Macedonian nation or nationality.

The focus of the postwar conflict between Yugoslavia and Bulgaria has been over the disputed ethnic identity of the Slavic majority in Macedonia. Yugoslavia asserts that this majority constitutes a Macedonian nation and insists that Bulgaria recognize the basis of Yugoslavia's ethnic claim to Macedonia and grant special minority rights to the Macedonian minority in southwestern Bulgaria, known as Pirin Macedonia. Bulgaria, on the other hand, claims that the Slavic population of Macedonia is ethnically and historically Bulgarian, while denying that Bulgaria has any territorial aspira-

---

[12]For a comprehensive treatment see Elisabeth Barker, *Macedonia: Its Place in Balkan Power Politics* (London: Royal Institute of International Affairs, 1950); Stephen Palmer and Robert King, *Yugoslav Communism and the Macedonian Question* (Hamden, Conn.: Shoestring Press, 1971); Patrick Moore, "Macedonia: Perennial Balkan Apple of Discord," *The World Today,* October 1979, pp. 427-428; and Wolf Oschlies, "Zur Mazedonian-Frage: Am Anfang war das Wort," *Europaische Rundschau,* No. 2 (Spring 1983), pp. 91-102.

[13]For a good discussion of IMRO's terrorist activities during the interwar period, see Seton-Watson, *Europe Between the Wars,* pp. 243-253.

tions against Yugoslavia—a position that the Yugoslavs find threateningly ambiguous.[14]

Moscow has often seen the dispute as a useful means of indirectly putting pressure on Yugoslavia. Indeed, the dispute was often a fairly accurate barometer of Soviet-Yugoslav relations. The problem, however, also developed an important Bulgarian domestic dimension. After 1967 it was increasingly linked to the Zhivkov regime's emphasis on nationalism and patriotism. In this capacity it served as a form of "surrogate nationalism" or "safety valve" for national aspirations that were otherwise largely subordinated to the dictates of Soviet foreign policy.

Since Zhivkov's removal in 1989 there has been a general re-nationalization of Bulgarian political life, and a number of independent political groups concerned with the Macedonian issue have emerged.[15] Some, such as the Ilinden Society, call for the recognition of the Macedonian minority. The majority, however, such as the Vardar Discussion Club and the Macedonian Cultural-Educational Society, promote the Bulgarian identity of the Macedonians. The Macedonian issue, moreover, has re-emerged as an issue in the internal Bulgarian debate. Some elements in the non-communist opposition have accused the Bulgarian Communist Party (BCP) of "selling out" Bulgarian national interests regarding Macedonia in the early postwar period.[16]

In early 1990 polemics between Bulgaria and Yugoslavia over Macedonia again flared up, prompted, it appears, by the passage of a resolution by the Yugoslav parliament on February 16 deploring the "forced assimilation" of the Macedonians in the Pirin region of Bulgaria.[17] To be sure, such polemics are hardly new. They take on added significance in the current context, however, because of the re-emergence of nationalist trends in both countries. There is thus a danger that one or the other government—or both—

---

[14]Initially Bulgaria recognized a Macedonian minority—a legacy of the early postwar cooperation between Dimitrov and Tito. However, since 1965 the Bulgarian census has not included a category for Macedonians.

[15]One of the most interesting examples of the re-emergence of the Macedonian theme was the broadcast in late June 1990 of an hour-long interview—the first ever—with Vance Mikhaylov, the leader of IMRO, the Macedonian nationalist terrorist organization. Mikhaylov, now 94, was forced to go underground in 1934 and had been living in Rome since 1959. In the interview Mikhaylov, apparently now less fervent a Macedonian nationalist than in his younger years, blamed the revival of Macedonian separatism on Yugoslavia. See Foreign Broadcast Information Service (FBIS), EEU-90-123, June 26, 1990, p. 7.

[16]For details see Wolf Oschlies, "Die 'unbulgarische Positionen' verlassen—endlich!" *Aktuellen Analysen,* Bundesinstitut für ostwissenschaftliche und internationale Studien, No. 24, April 4, 1990, pp. 1-8.

[17]See Patrick Moore, "The Macedonian Question Resurfaces," RFE, *Report on Eastern Europe,* April 6, 1990, pp. 46-49.

may seek to exploit the dispute to bolster popular support and compensate for its own domestic weakness.

The Macedonian issue has also more recently led to increased friction between Greece and Yugoslavia. Since late 1988 the Macedonians in Yugoslavia have begun to raise the issue of the rights of the Macedonian minority in Greece more aggressively. Greece has vigorously rejected these complaints. Greece contends that there is no separate Macedonian nationality and that those people living in the Macedonian part of Greece are "Slavophone Greeks," that is, Greeks who speak a Slavic language.[18]

The dispute took an important new turn in 1989–90. In the past it was mainly the authorities in Skopje, the capital of the Yugoslav Macedonian Republic, that raised the issue of the rights of the Macedonian minority most vigorously. The central government in Belgrade, by contrast, remained largely aloof from the dispute or gave it only lukewarm backing. Since the end of 1989, however, the government in Belgrade has begun to back the Macedonian claims more vigorously and has sought to internationalize the dispute, formally raising it at international fora such as the United Nations General Assembly and the UN Human Rights Commission in Geneva.

Border incidents between Greece and Yugoslavian Macedonia have also increased.[19] In May 1990, for instance, more than 50,000 Macedonians blocked several border crossings between Yugoslavia and Greece to demand that the Greek government recognize the Macedonian minority in Greece, and that it lift visa requirements for Greek citizens who wish to travel to Yugoslavia, and visa restrictions on those Yugoslav citizens who fought (or whose parents fought) in the Greek Civil War on the side of the Greek communists. Relations have also been strained by increased problems over truck permits and currency rules....[20]

The Turkish Minority in Bulgaria

Regional stability has also been disrupted in recent years by conflicts between Turkey and Bulgaria over the Bulgarian government's treatment of the Turkish minority in Bulgaria. There are about 800,000 ethnic Turks in Bulgaria; remnants of centuries of Turkish occupation, they comprise about

---

[18]For a good discussion of the Greek point of view and the role of the Macedonian question in postwar Greek-Yugoslav relations, see Evangelos Kofos, *The Macedonian Question: The Politics of Mutation* (Thessaloniki: Institute for Balkan Studies, 1987), pp. 1-16.

[19]See Milan Andrejevich, "Yugoslav Macedonians Demand Greece's Recognition of Aegean Macedonians," RFE, *Report on Eastern Europe*, June 1, 1990, pp. 45-49. Kerin Hope, "Greek-Yugoslav Row Blows Over Macedonian Issue," *Financial Times*, June 22, 1990; and Viktor Meier, "Wieder die mazedonische Frage," *Frankfurter Allgemeine Zeitung*, June 22, 1990.

[20]From the Greek point of view, the escalation of the Macedonian issue is particularly worrying because of its potential impact on Greek-Turkish relations: Greek officials fear that it will encourage Turkish complaints about Greek treatment of the Turkish minority in Western Thrace.

ten percent of the population. They are mostly located in the economically important tobacco-growing regions of Bulgaria.

The Turkish minority was treated relatively well during the interwar years, but they ... fared less well under the communist regime, which has sought to restrict their rights and curtail their religious and cultural opportunities.[21] These restrictions have led to discontent and periodic pressures for emigration.[22] In 1950-51 some 150,000 Bulgarian Turks left for Turkey in a series of mass expulsions. Another 120,000-130,000 were allowed to leave as a result of an agreement signed with Ankara in February 1968. The agreement expired in 1978 and thereafter emigration was reduced to a trickle until 1989 when a new round of expulsions occurred. . . .

Recent difficulties should be seen against the background of Bulgaria's general attempt to pursue a policy of national assimilation designed to break down the exclusiveness of the Turkish minority. This campaign gained intensity during the 1960s and especially the 1970s as a result of Zhivkov's efforts to create "a unified Bulgarian Socialist nation." The effort reached new heights in 1984-85, when the Bulgarian government began to compel all ethnic Turks to adopt Bulgarian names.[23] The speaking of Turkish was also forbidden in public places. The government justified the moves on the grounds that the Turks were actually ethnic Bulgarians who had been compelled to adopt Islam during the Ottoman occupation, now they were simply being "re-Bulgarianized."[24]

The campaign provoked widespread resistance among the Turkish population in Bulgaria, and led to bloody clashes with the authorities that resulted in hundreds of deaths.[25] Turkey's reaction was initially relatively restrained, probably because Ankara did not want to jeopardize a growing economic relationship with Sofia, but also out of fear that a sharp deterioration of bilateral relations would lead to a renewed emigration of the Turkish minority, which would exacerbate Turkey's internal social and economic problems. Pressure from public opinion, however, gradually forced the

---

[21]J.F. Brown, *Bulgaria Under Communist Rule* (New York: Praeger, 1970), pp. 293-295; Brown, *Eastern Europe and Communist Rule*, pp. 427-429.

[22]For detailed discussion of the causes of the emigration and its impact on Bulgarian-Turkish relations in the postwar period, see Wolfgang Höpken, "Im Schatten der nationalen Frage: die bulgarisch-türkischen Beziehungen," *Südosteuropa*, Heft 2/3 (1987), pp. 75-95; and by the same author, "Im Schatten der nationalen Frage: die bulgarisch-türkischen Beziehungen (II)," *Südosteuropa*, Heft 4 (1987), pp. 178-194.

[23]The drive seems to have been the final stage of a five-year campaign to issue Bulgarian citizens new identity cards before the next census, scheduled to be held at the end of 1985.

[24]The Turkish minority, who are ethnic Turks, are distinct from the Pomaks, Slavic-speaking ethnic Bulgarians who adopted Turkish names and converted to Islam during the Ottoman reign. There are about 150-200,000 Pomaks living in Bulgaria today.

[25]Reliable figures on the actual number of deaths are hard to come by. Turkish sources put them as high as 1,000. The real number, however, is probably closer to several hundred.

Turkish government to take stronger action, including an effort to internationalize the issue, which led to a sharp deterioration of relations.

Relations between the two countries improved for a short while after the signing of a "Protocol on the Promotion of Good Neighborliness, Friendship, and Cooperation" on the eve of the Belgrade meeting of Balkan foreign ministers in February 1988. Thereafter several working groups were set up to deal with outstanding bilateral problems, including the Turkish minority. However, the decision by the Bulgarian government at the end of May 1989 to force thousands of ethnic Turks to emigrate created new tensions in relations and caused severe domestic problems for Turkey, which was forced to absorb more than 300,000 refugees on short notice....[26]

Zhivkov's ouster in November 1989 led to a reversal of the policy of Bulgarianization. At the end of December, the Bulgarian State Council and Council of Ministers condemned Zhivkov's policy depriving the Turks of their rights and promised that these rights would be fully restored.[27] In March 1990 the Bulgarian Parliament passed a law restoring the names of the Turkish minority. Turks returning to Bulgaria have also been allowed to reclaim property and jobs.

The decision at the end of December 1989 to restore rights and property to the Turkish minority provoked widespread violent protests by Bulgarians in Sofia, Plovdiv, and several other cities in Bulgaria in early January 1990. The protests owed their strength as much to the way the decision was presented as to its contents.[28] The decision was taken in secret with little prior public discussion, and this caught many Bulgarians off-guard. Some of the protests also appear to have been organized by local party officials opposed to the changes instituted after Zhivkov's ouster, and intended to inhibit the reform process. Whatever the mix of causes, the strong backlash underscored the deep-seated sensitivities surrounding the Turkish minority issue and the degree to which nationalism remains a powerful force that could shape Bulgarian politics in the future.

At the same time, the deepening of the process of democratization is likely to provide greater opportunities for the Turkish minority to articulate its interests politically. In the elections in June, for instance, the newly formed Movement for Rights and Freedoms (MRF), which unofficially represents the interests of the Turkish minority, won 23 seats in the National As-

---

[26]The reasons for the Zhivkov government's decision remain unclear. Ethnic unrest among the Turkish community in Bulgaria had been growing and the government may well have thought that it could defuse the pressure by allowing some of the Turks to emigrate. It did not expect, however, the flood of emigration that actually occurred.

[27]Thomas Goltz, "Bulgaria Ends Campaign to Assimilate Turks," *Washington Post,* December 30, 1989; also "Turks Win Right to Use the Muslim Names They Were Forced to Change," *New York Times,* December 30, 1989.

[28]For a detailed discussion of the background and reasons for the unrest see Stephen Ashley, "Ethnic Unrest During January," RFE, *Report on Eastern Europe,* February 9, 1990, pp. 4-11.

sembly. Thus for the first time there will be a "Muslim bloc" in the parliament.

In the future the Turkish minority seems likely to press its demands for separate schools and language instruction more vigorously, primarily through the MRF. This could intensify ethnic tensions within Bulgaria as well as exacerbate relations with Turkey. A weak and fragmented Bulgarian government could be tempted to play the "national card" in order to bolster its domestic support. In addition, the growth of Muslim fundamentalism and Pan-Turkism could have a spill-over effect on Bulgaria, exacerbating the minority problem.

Over the long term these developments could have an impact on alignments within the Balkans, particularly on relations between Bulgaria and Greece. Both countries share a fear of Turkey, and in recent years ties between the two have warmed visibly. In 1986 they signed a "Declaration on Good Neighborliness, Friendship, and Cooperation," and more recently they have sought to develop common strategies toward Turkey, including limited military cooperation. . . .[29]

The Hungarian Minority in Romania

The Hungarian-Romanian dispute over the Hungarian minority in Romania is another source of tension in the Balkans.[30] The dispute had its origins in the aftermath of World War I. Following the defeat of the Austro-Hungarian Empire, governmental authority in Hungary collapsed and Yugoslavia, Czechoslovakia, and Romania occupied areas inhabited by their various nationalities. The Hungarian communist, Bela Kun, seized power in Budapest and launched attacks on the Romanians in Transylvania, but Hungary's armies were soundly defeated. As a result of the Treaty of Trianon (1920), Hungary was forced to cede nearly two-thirds of its territory: Transylvania, the age-old home of Hungarian culture, was given to Romania, parts of Slovakia inhabited by Hungarians were also ceded to Czechoslovakia, while Croatia and the Vojvodina were given to Yugoslavia. As a result nearly three million Hungarians found themselves living outside their former borders.

During the interwar period the Romanians did not deprive the Hungarians of their schools or language, though they did require all civil servants to pass a Romanian language examination, which was often used to discriminate against Hungarians. Ironically, in the Stalinist period the situation of the Hungarian minority considerably improved. In 1952 the Hungarian Autonomous Region was established, which gave its 600,000 Hungarians— about one-third of the Hungarian population in Romania at the time—

[29]Paul Anastasi, "Greece and Bulgaria Plan Anti-Turkey Strategies," *New York Times,* February 7, 1990.
[30]There are nearly 2 million ethnic Hungarians living in Romania. They comprise about 9-10 percent of the country's population.

considerable administrative freedom. In 1960, however, the Hungarian Autonomous Region was partially dismantled, and in 1968 it was abolished altogether, leading to a fragmentation of the Hungarian community. The number of Hungarian language schools declined, as did the number of institutions of advanced learning where subjects were taught in Hungarian.[31] Moreover, as a result of demographic changes and Ceausescu's policy of forced assimilation or "Romanization," many Transylvanian cities, the historical focal points of Hungarian culture, gradually lost their Hungarian character.

The Hungarian minority reacted to these developments, especially the closing of Hungarian language schools, with increasing alarm because it is upon them that not only Hungarian culture but a distinct Hungarian identity in Romania depends. Beginning in the 1970s the Hungarian minority began to speak out more vocally against repression and discrimination, and sought to call international attention to their plight. The number of Hungarian dissident journals and *samizdat* publications in Transylvania, many of them sharply critical of Ceausescu and his policy toward the minority, also increased visibly.[32]

Initially the government of János Kádár in Hungary sought to obtain an improvement of the minority's situation through quiet diplomacy. However, this policy failed to achieve any visible results and during the 1980s the situation of the minority continued to decline. As it did, intellectuals and dissident groups in Hungary began to take up the issue, pressing the Kádár government to speak out more forcefully about the plight of the minority in Romania.[33] Pressure from these groups forced the government to confront the issue more openly, including a reference to it for the first time in the Central Committee report approved at the Party Congress in March 1986.

The issue moved more directly into the open in 1988 as a result of two events. The first was Kádár's ouster as party leader in May 1988 and his replacement by Károly Grósz. Kádár had always been a reluctant nationalist, especially on the minority issue. His departure removed an important constraint on public debate and Hungarian diplomacy. The second event was Ceausescu's decision to raze some 6000-7000 villages, many of them located in Transylvania, as part of his industrialization campaign. This caused an

---

[31]In 1947 there were some 1800 Hungarian schools in Romania. By 1980 there were only 12, though 108 other schools still offered some courses in Hungarian. See Judith Pataki, "Free Hungarians in a Free Romania: Dream or Reality?" RFE, *Report on Eastern Europe*, February 23, 1990, p. 22.

[32]For background see F. Stephen Larrabee, *The Challenge to Soviet Interests in Eastern Europe*, R-3190-AF (Santa Monica, Calif.: RAND, December 1984), pp. 38-40.

[33]One of the most ardent champions of the cause of the Hungarian minority abroad was Gyula Illyes, one of Hungary's best known authors (*Children of the Puszta*). On a number of occasions he used his great prestige to put pressure on the Hungarian leadership, including Kádár himself, to take a stronger public stand on the minority issue.

outcry in Hungary and led to a serious deterioration of relations between the two countries.[34] Hungary also sought to internationalize the issue by raising it directly at the Conference on Security and Cooperation in Europe (CSCE) meeting in Vienna.

The overthrow of Ceausescu in December 1989 initially led to an improvement in Hungarian-Romanian relations. The National Salvation Front in Romania promised to guarantee the rights of minorities and in the first few months took a number of steps to improve their conditions, including a decision to reintroduce Hungarian language instruction in some high schools in Transylvania. This move, however, provoked strong criticism from parts of the Romanian population, and as a result, the implementation of the decision was postponed.[35]

Tensions reached a climax in mid-March when ethnic unrest broke out in the Transylvanian city of Tirgu Mures, which had been the capital of the Hungarian Autonomous Region. The unrest led to at least eight deaths and nearly 300 injuries. It appears to have been provoked by attacks on Hungarians by supporters of *Vatra Romaneasca* (Romanian Hearth), an ultra-nationalist group, which seeks the continuation of the Ceausescu regime's policies of forced assimilation of the ethnic minority and of creating a homogeneous Romanian society.[36]

The emergence of *Vatra* and its role in the Tirgu Mures disturbances underscores the fact that the forces of nationalism are by no means dead despite Ceausescu's departure. *Vatra* has strong support among the *nomenklatura* under Ceausescu as well as among former members of the *Securitate*. The problem is compounded by the fact that in the countryside, particularly in Transylvania, many of the key political and administrative posts are still occupied by holdovers from the Ceausescu period.

The process of democratization, however, has strengthened the hand of the Hungarian minority, giving it an official forum for articulating its interests. In the May 1990 elections the Hungarian Democratic Federation (UDF), which represents the interests of the Hungarian minority, won 7.5 percent of the vote—more than any other party except the National Salvation Front. The UDF's strong showing ensures that the question of

---

[34]Only a small number of these villages were ever actually razed. Nevertheless, the decision caused a major outcry not just in Hungary but also in Romania because many historic Romanian monuments and buildings were to be destroyed.

[35]On the role of the education issue in the outbreak of violence in Tirgu Mures, see Pataki, "Free Hungarians in a Free Romania: Dream or Reality?," pp. 18-26.

[36]For a detailed discussion of the causes of the unrest and the role of *Vatra* in it, see Vladimir Socor, "Forces of Old Resurface in Romania: The Ethnic Clashes in Tirgu Mures," RFE, *Report on Eastern Europe*, April 13, 1990, pp. 36-42. See also Celestine Bohlen, "The Romanian Revolution Over: It's Back to Old Hatreds in Transylvania," *New York Times*, March 21, 1990; Judith Dempsey, "Hungarian Protest Against Ethnic Violence in Romania," *Financial Times*, March 21, 1990; and Michael Shafer, "The Romanian Authorities' Reactions to the Violence in Tirgu Mures," RFE, *Report on Eastern Europe*, April 13, 1990, pp. 43-47.

minority rights will remain an important domestic issue in Romanian political life.

Changes within Hungary, moreover, seem likely to ensure that the issue of the Hungarian minority remains on the front burner. The Hungarian Democratic Forum, the major winner in the parliamentary elections in March and April 1990, has put a strong emphasis on Hungarian national pride and traditions. In a speech shortly after winning the election, Jozsef Antall, the leader of the Hungarian Democratic Forum, made clear that the party intended to be a spokesman for "all Hungarians," suggesting that it would concern itself more forcefully with the situation of Hungarians abroad, particularly those in Romania.[37] The party has a strong "populist" wing, for whom the issue of the Hungarian minority abroad is a strong emotional concern. Thus, while there is little likelihood that Hungary will raise irredentist territorial claims against Romania, the treatment of the Hungarian minority is likely to remain a major issue in Romanian-Hungarian relations.[38]

Bessarabia

The Bessarabian issue could also re-emerge more forcefully in the 1990s. Bessarabia, currently a part of the Moldavian Republic . . . has been a bone of contention between Russia and Romania for several hundred years.[39] For centuries the area was part of the Romanian principality of Moldavia. In 1812 it was annexed by the Russians. After World War I Bessarabia and Bukovina chose to join Romania. The Soviet Union, however, refused to recognize Romanian sovereignty over Bessarabia. The Molotov-Ribbentrop Pact, signed in August 1939, implicitly ceded Bessarabia to the Soviet Union, and in June 1940 Moscow formally annexed both Bessarabia and northern Bukovina. Romania recaptured the territories in 1941, only to lose them again in 1944 when both provinces were overrun by the Soviet Army.

After World War II Bessarabia was incorporated into the newly established Moldavian Soviet Socialist Republic. However, northern Bukovina, three historical counties of Bessarabia, and eight *raions* (small districts) of the Moldavian republic were ceded on Stalin's orders to the Ukraine—a decision regarded with considerable resentment by the Moldavians. In order to jus-

---

[37]See Blaine Harden, "National Pride Back in Style," *Washington Post,* April 11, 1990; Carol J. Williams, "Hungarian Patriotism Carried Conservatives to Victory," *Los Angeles Times,* April 11, 1990.

[38]In June 1990, on the seventieth anniversary of the signing of the Trianon Peace Treaty, the six parties represented in Hungary's parliament issued a statement specifically reaffirming Hungary's commitment to the 1975 Helsinki Final Act, which prohibits changing existing borders by force. At the same time they said that they expected the rights of ethnic Hungarians living outside Hungary's borders to be guaranteed. See Alfred Reisch, "Hungarian Parties Seek to Reassure Romania on Border Issue," RFE, *Report on Eastern Europe,* June 15, 1990, pp. 28-33.

[39]On the historical background of the dispute see Michael Sturdza, "Changes in the International Status of Bessarabia," RFE, *Report on Eastern Europe,* May 25, 1990.

tify the annexation, Stalin sought to emphasize the "separateness" of the Moldavians from the Romanians. Soviet authors were directed to stress the distinctiveness of the Moldavian language—which is in fact a dialect of Romanian—and Moldavia was forced to adopt the Cyrillic alphabet.

After 1945 Romania did not seek to reclaim the territories or challenge the Soviet borders. Although the issue continued to be a subject of historical controversy and academic debate, it never attained the political intensity or significance that characterized the dispute between Yugoslavia and Bulgaria over Macedonia. Indeed, Ceausescu was relatively cautious about Bessarabia, perhaps out of a desire not to give Moscow a ready-made excuse for increasing pressure on Romania at a time when relations were already strained.

The escalation of nationality tensions in the Soviet Union in the last several years, however, has cast the issue in a new light. The Moldavian National Front, which has spearheaded the nationalist revival in the Moldavian Republic and which is today the strongest political force there, has begun to raise the issue as part of its long list of grievances against the Soviet leadership. In June 1989 it organized a large rally in Kishinev to mourn the annexation of Bessarabia and the partition of the Moldavian lands. The rally approved several resolutions condemning the annexation of Bessarabia in 1940 and proclaiming June 28, the day the Soviet army entered Bessarabia in 1940, a "day of national mourning." One of the resolutions also demanded "the return to the Moldavian SSR of ancient territories of the Moldavian people that were unjustly incorporated into the Ukrainian SSR in 1940."[40]

While the Front has called for closer contacts with Romania, including an open border like the one between East Germany and West Germany after the collapse of the Berlin Wall, it has stopped short of demanding full independence or reunification. In the short term, any calls for territorial revision are more likely to be aimed at recovering northern Bukovina and the other territories given to the Ukraine after the 1940 annexation than at seeking reunification with Romania. As Moldavia emancipates itself from Soviet tutelage, however, the sense of cultural and spiritual unity with Romania could intensify and possibly lead to calls for some form of closer association, possibly even unification. . . .[41]

---

[40]See Vladimir Socor, "Rallies in Kishinev Mourn Soviet Annexation, Escalate National Demands," RFE, *Report on the USSR*, July 21, 1989, pp. 21-24.

[41]The strength of this feeling of "spiritual unity" was underscored in June 1990, when thousands of Moldavians and Romanians converged for a symbolic linking of hands at the Moldavian-Romanian border. Chanting "One nation!" and "United we cannot be conquered!" many demonstrators clearly saw the event as a manifestation of national unity. See Quentin Peel, "Border Spirit Fires Moldavia's Defiance," *Financial Times*, June 25, 1990.

PART 6

Strategy:
Military Technology,
Doctrine, and Stability

Military capabilities can exert an independent influence on decisions for or against war. Depending on which side has the edge in a conflict, the military factors make it easier or harder for a government to resort to force against the status quo. Military forces, and particular technical aspects of their composition, can also become causes of conflict in their own right, by altering the balance of power and perceptions of threats, aggravating anxieties, and creating incentives for preemptive attack. A state is not likely to start a war, however, unless one of the following two conditions exists:

The first concerns a government that wishes to overturn the status quo and is willing to take offensive action to do so. This government's leaders must also believe that they can win a war if they attack, and can do so at a cost more bearable than the cost borne by continuing to live with the existing situation. If they think that their would-be victim can defend its own territory successfully, or can retaliate and inflict costly damage on them if attacked, peace should remain preferable to war.

The other condition exists when leaders whose objectives are mainly defensive believe that if they do not strike first, their enemy will do so, forcing war upon them on less favorable terms and increasing the chances of defeat. On the other hand, if they know the enemy would like to attack, but believe that they can fight more effectively by waiting to parry the blow when it falls, they will not have reason to initiate the war themselves.

These notions are the foundation of deterrence theory, which became prominent in the Cold War. When the basic source and dimensions of international conflict are clear, as they were once the East–West confrontation became institutionalized in the decade after World War II, attention turns to the instrumental questions. At first, theorists wanted to design strategies that would put the revolutionary power of nuclear weapons to the purpose of deterring enemy attack. Then, when fear of overreliance on nuclear weapons came to the fore, strategists turned to applying the logic of deterrence to conventional military power. Since the Soviet collapse, deterrence seems beside the point among the great powers. If political tensions reemerge, however, so will the salience of military strategy. How good a guide can we get from the ideas spawned in the Cold War?

More specifically, how should conventional military power affect the odds of war or peace from now on? Some will want to be able to use force actively to change situations that they do not approve of (as the United States has often done, including twice since the end of the Cold War, in Panama and the Persian Gulf). Strategists who have that option in mind will focus on maintaining superior military capabilities, the capacity to defeat and dictate to opponents. For Americans, that should not be difficult even with major cuts in the defense budget, since no other country now has anywhere near the military capacity of the United States.

If the aim is to preserve peace for its own sake, however, rather than to use force to make the world the way we think it should be, strategists will seek ways to limit the utility of military instruments. This aim, rather than the implications of U.S. military primacy, is explored in this section, because it has been the subject of much debate among analysts as to whether and how it is possible to create stability in military relations through technical arms control.

One solution in principle can unite both realists satisfied with the status quo and liberals who deny the legitimacy of force as a means of change: military power should be distributed, configured, and usable only in ways that maximize confidence for defenders and risks for attackers. Force structures, strategies, and arms control agreements should be crafted to minimize the role of technologies that facilitate offensive operations and boost those that aid defensive tactics. The strategic implications of such "defense dominance" should be publicized in order to make governments realize that initiating the use of force is not necessary for defensive purposes or effective for aggressive ones. In "Cooperation Under the Security Dilemma," Robert Jervis outlines the theoretical logic behind these notions, and some examples to illustrate them.

Can such norms be institutionalized to keep peace in the future? Critics question how far the principle of defense dominance can be taken in practice. Scott Sagan points out several reasons that it did not solve all the strategic problems of states in 1914, especially the challenge of supporting exposed allies (this showed up starkly in 1939 when the French and British let defense dominate on the western front while the Germans gobbled up Poland).[1] Jack Levy raises questions

---

[1] The contrasting views that provoked Sagan's essay, and which drew on Jervis's arguments, can be found in Stephen Van Evera, "The Cult of the Offensive and the Origins of the First World War," *International Security* 9, no. 1 (Summer 1984) and Jack L. Snyder, *The Ideology of the Offensive: Military Decision Making and the Disasters of 1914* (Ithaca: Cornell University

about how clearly or consistently the concept of defense dominance can even be defined in principle or identified in practice.

Constraint of arms through treaty limitations became a staple of superpower negotiation during the Cold War. Many today assume that arms control is even more sensible, and easier to achieve, in a world of less tension and strategic competition. Charles Fairbanks and Abram Shulsky offer cautionary arguments, drawn from historical cases, about ways in which formal arms limitation can have unexpectedly destabilizing effects. Moreover, if there is now no important military enmity and strategic competition, why should formalized arms control be important? The selection by Betts in the Conclusion to this volume will discuss problems in designing safe standards for arms allotments in a world that lacks the clear political divisions of the Cold War.

Nuclear weapons remain a particularly sticky issue. The fewer of them in the world the better, according to conventional wisdom. In the Introduction to this volume, on the other hand, John Mearsheimer claimed that "managed" nuclear proliferation could be the least dangerous way to save Europe from the instability that will otherwise follow the end of the Cold War. The reasoning behind this argument was first elaborated by Kenneth Waltz in the essay included below. Many skeptics will remain unconvinced, but they should ask themselves whether it is consistent to reject the idea that nuclear deterrence may be stabilizing for Third World countries, and still believe, as so many do, that mutual nuclear deterrence between the United States and Soviet Union during the Cold War was quite stable.

Press, 1984). See the correspondence between Sagan and Snyder in *International Security* 11, no. 3 (Winter 1986–87). For an argument against interpreting the origins of World War I in terms of technical stability in force relationships, see Patrick Glynn, "The Sarajevo Fallacy," *National Interest* no. 9 (Fall 1987).

Cooperation Under the Security Dilemma

ROBERT JERVIS

The security dilemma: many of the means by which a state tries to increase its security decrease the security of others. In domestic society, there are several ways to increase the safety of one's person and property without endangering others. One can move to a safer neighborhood, put bars on the windows, avoid dark streets, and keep a distance from suspicious-looking characters. Of course these measures are not convenient, cheap, or certain of success. But no one save criminals need be alarmed if a person takes them. In international politics, however, one state's gain in security often inadvertently threatens others. In explaining British policy on naval disarmament in the inter-war period to the Japanese, Ramsey MacDonald said that "Nobody wanted Japan to be insecure."[1] But the problem was not with British desires, but with the consequences of her policy. In earlier periods, too, Britain had needed a navy large enough to keep the shipping lanes open. But such a navy could not avoid being a menace to any other state with a coast that could be raided, trade that could be interdicted, or colonies that could be isolated. When Germany started building a powerful navy before World War I, Britain objected that it could only be an offensive weapon aimed at her. As Sir Edward Grey, the Foreign Secretary, put it to King Edward VII: "If the German Fleet ever becomes superior to ours, the German Army can conquer this country. There is no corresponding risk of this kind to Germany; for however superior our Fleet was, no naval victory could bring

Robert Jervis, "Cooperation Under the Security Dilemma," *World Politics* Vol. 30, no. 2 (January 1978). Reprinted by permission of the author and the Johns Hopkins University Press.

[1]Quoted in Gerald Wheeler, *Prelude to Pearl Harbor* (Columbia: University of Missouri Press 1963), 167.

us any nearer to Berlin." The English position was half correct: Germany's navy was an anti-British instrument. But the British often overlooked what the Germans knew full well: "in every quarrel with England, German colonies and trade were ... hostages for England to take." Thus, whether she intended it or not, the British Navy constituted an important instrument of coercion....[2]

How a statesman interprets the other's past behavior and how he projects it into the future is influenced by his understanding of the security dilemma and his ability to place himself in the other's shoes. The dilemma will operate much more strongly if statesmen do not understand it, and do not see that their arms—sought only to secure the status quo—may alarm others and that others may arm, not because they are contemplating aggression, but because they fear attack from the first state. These two failures of empathy are linked. A state which thinks that the other knows that it wants only to preserve the status quo and that its arms are meant only for self-preservation will conclude that the other side will react to its arms by increasing its own capability only if it is aggressive itself. Since the other side is not menaced, there is no legitimate reason for it to object to the first state's arms; therefore, objection proves that the other is aggressive. Thus, the following exchange between Senator Tom Connally and Secretary of State Acheson concerning the ratification of the NATO treaty:

> *Secretary Acheson:* [The treaty] is aimed solely at armed aggression.
>
> *Senator Connally:* In other words, unless a nation ... contemplates, meditates, or makes plans looking toward aggression or armed attack on another nation, it has no cause to fear this treaty.
>
> *Secretary Acheson:* That is correct, Senator Connally, and it seems to me that any nation which claims that this treaty is directed against it should be reminded of the Biblical admonition that 'The guilty flee when no man pursueth.'
>
> *Senator Connally:* That is a very apt illustration. What I had in mind was, when a State or Nation passes a criminal act, for instance, against burglary, nobody but those who are burglars or getting ready to be burglars need have any fear of the Burglary Act. Is that not true?
>
> *Secretary Acheson:* The only effect [the law] would have [on an innocent person] would be for his protection, perhaps, by deterring someone else. He wouldn't worry about the imposition of the penalties on himself.[3]

---

[2]Quoted in Leonard Wainstein, "The Dreadnought Gap," in Robert Art and Kenneth Waltz, eds., *The Use of Force* (Boston: Little, Brown 1971), 155; Raymond Sontag, *European Diplomatic History, 1871–1932* (New York: Appleton-Century-Crofts 1933), 147. The French had made a similar argument 50 years earlier; see James Phinney Baxter III, *The Introduction of the Ironclad Warship* (Cambridge: Harvard University Press 1933), 149. For a more detailed discussion of the security dilemma, see Jervis, *Perception and Misperception in International Politics* (Princeton: Princeton University Press 1976), 62–76.

[3]U.S. Congress, Senate, Committee on Foreign Relations, *Hearings, North Atlantic Treaty*, 81st Cong., 1st sess. (1949), 17.

The other side of this coin is that part of the explanation for détente is that most American decision makers now realize that it is at least possible that Russia may fear American aggression; many think that this fear accounts for a range of Soviet actions previously seen as indicating Russian aggressiveness. Indeed, even 36 percent of military officers consider the Soviet Union's motivations to be primarily defensive. Less than twenty years earlier, officers had been divided over whether Russia sought world conquest or only expansion.[4]

Statesmen who do not understand the security dilemma will think that the money spent is the only cost of building up their arms. This belief removes one important restraint on arms spending. Furthermore, it is also likely to lead states to set their security requirements too high. Since they do not understand that trying to increase one's security can actually decrease it, they will overestimate the amount of security that is attainable; they will think that when in doubt they can "play it safe" by increasing their arms. Thus it is very likely that two states which support the status quo but do not understand the security dilemma will end up, if not in a war, then at least in a relationship of higher conflict than is required by the objective situation.

The belief that an increase in military strength always leads to an increase in security is often linked to the belief that the only route to security is through military strength. As a consequence, a whole range of meliorative policies will be downgraded. Decision makers who do not believe that adopting a more conciliatory posture, meeting the other's legitimate grievances, or developing mutual gains from cooperation can increase their state's security, will not devote much attention or effort to these possibilities.

On the other hand, a heightened sensitivity to the security dilemma makes it more likely that the state will treat an aggressor as though it were an insecure defender of the status quo. Partly because of their views about the causes of World War I, the British were predisposed to believe that Hitler sought only the rectification of legitimate and limited grievances and that security could best be gained by constructing an equitable international system. As a result they pursued a policy which, although well designed to avoid the danger of creating unnecessary conflict with a status-quo Germany, helped destroy Europe.

Geography, Commitments, Beliefs, and Security Through Expansion

... Situations vary in the ease or difficulty with which all states can simultaneously achieve a high degree of security. The influence of military technol-

[4]Bruce Russett and Elizabeth Hanson, *Interest and Ideology* (San Francisco: Freeman 1975), 260; Morris Janowitz, *The Professional Soldier* (New York: Free Press 1960), chap. 13.

ogy on this variable is the subject of the next section. Here we want to treat the impact of beliefs, geography, and commitments (many of which can be considered to be modifications of geography, since they bind states to defend areas outside their homelands). In the crowded continent of Europe, security requirements were hard to mesh. Being surrounded by powerful states, Germany's problem—or the problem created by Germany—was always great and was even worse when her relations with both France and Russia were bad, such as before World War I. In that case, even a status-quo Germany, if she could not change the political situation, would almost have been forced to adopt something like the Schlieffen Plan. Because she could not hold off both of her enemies, she had to be prepared to defeat one quickly and then deal with the other in a more leisurely fashion. If France or Russia stayed out of a war between the other state and Germany, they would allow Germany to dominate the Continent (even if that was not Germany's aim). They therefore had to deny Germany this ability, thus making Germany less secure. Although Germany's arrogant and erratic behavior, coupled with the desire for an unreasonably high level of security (which amounted to the desire to escape from her geographic plight), compounded the problem, even wise German statesmen would have been hard put to gain a high degree of security without alarming their neighbors. . . .

Offense, Defense, and the Security Dilemma

Another approach starts with the central point of the security dilemma— that an increase in one state's security decreases the security of others—and examines the conditions under which this proposition holds. Two crucial variables are involved: whether defensive weapons and policies can be distinguished from offensive ones, and whether the defense or the offense has the advantage. The definitions are not always clear, and many cases are difficult to judge, but these two variables shed a great deal of light on the question of whether status-quo powers will adopt compatible security policies. All the variables discussed so far leave the heart of the problem untouched. But when defensive weapons differ from offensive ones, it is possible for a state to make itself more secure without making others less secure. And when the defense has the advantage over the offense, a large increase in one state's security only slightly decreases the security of the others, and status-quo powers can all enjoy a high level of security and largely escape from the state of nature.

Offense-Defense Balance

When we say that the offense has the advantage, we simply mean that it is easier to destroy the other's army and take its territory than it is to defend one's own. When the defense has the advantage, it is easier to protect and to hold than it is to move forward, destroy, and take. If effective defenses can be erected quickly, an attacker may be able to keep territory he has taken in an initial victory. Thus, the dominance of the defense made it very hard for Britain and France to push Germany out of France in World War I. But when superior defenses are difficult for an aggressor to improvise on the battlefield and must be constructed during peacetime, they provide no direct assistance to him.

The security dilemma is at its most vicious when commitments, strategy, or technology dictate that the only route to security lies through expansion. Status-quo powers must then act like aggressors; the fact that they would gladly agree to forego the opportunity for expansion in return for guarantees for their security has no implications for their behavior. Even if expansion is not sought as a goal in itself, there will be quick and drastic changes in the distribution of territory and influence. Conversely, when the defense has the advantage, status-quo states can make themselves more secure without gravely endangering others. Indeed, if the defense has enough of an advantage and if the states are of roughly equal size, not only will the security dilemma cease to inhibit status-quo states from cooperating, but aggression will be next to impossible, thus rendering international anarchy relatively unimportant. If states cannot conquer each other, then the lack of sovereignty, although it presents problems of collective goods in a number of areas, no longer forces states to devote their primary attention to self-preservation. Although, if force were not usable, there would be fewer restraints on the use of nonmilitary instruments, these are rarely powerful enough to threaten the vital interests of a major state.

Two questions of the offense-defense balance can be separated. First, does the state have to spend more or less than one dollar on defensive forces to offset each dollar spent by the other side on forces that could be used to attack? If the state has one dollar to spend on increasing its security, should it put it into offensive or defensive forces? Second, with a given inventory of forces, is it better to attack or to defend? Is there an incentive to strike first or to absorb the other's blow? These two aspects are often linked: if each dollar spent on offense can overcome each dollar spent on defense, and if both sides have the same defense budgets, then both are likely to build offensive forces and find it attractive to attack rather than to wait for the adversary to strike.

These aspects affect the security dilemma in different ways. The first has its greatest impact on arms races. If the defense has the advantage, and if the status-quo powers have reasonable subjective security requirements, they can probably avoid an arms race. Although an increase in one side's arms and security will still decrease the other's security, the former's increase will be larger than the latter's decrease. So if one side increases its arms, the other can bring its security back up to its previous level by adding a smaller amount to its forces. And if the first side reacts to this change, its increase will also be smaller than the stimulus that produced it. Thus a stable equilibrium will be reached. Shifting from dynamics to statics, each side can be quite secure with forces roughly equal to those of the other. Indeed, if the defense is much more potent than the offense, each side can be willing to have forces much smaller than the other's, and can be indifferent to a wide range of the other's defense policies.

The second aspect—whether it is better to attack or to defend—influences short-run stability. When the offense has the advantage, a state's reaction to international tension will increase the chances of war. The incentives for pre-emption and the "reciprocal fear of surprise attack" in this situation have been made clear by analyses of the dangers that exist when two countries have first-strike capabilities.[5] There is no way for the state to increase its security without menacing, or even attacking, the other. Even Bismarck, who once called preventive war "committing suicide from fear of death," said that "no government, if it regards war as inevitable even if it does not want it, would be so foolish as to leave to the enemy the choice of time and occasion and to wait for the moment which is most convenient for the enemy."[6] In another arena, the same dilemma applies to the policeman in a dark alley confronting a suspected criminal who appears to be holding a weapon. Though racism may indeed be present, the security dilemma can account for many of the tragic shootings of innocent people in the ghettos.

Beliefs about the course of a war in which the offense has the advantage further deepen the security dilemma. When there are incentives to strike first, a successful attack will usually so weaken the other side that victory will be relatively quick, bloodless, and decisive. It is in these periods when conquest is possible and attractive that states consolidate power internally—for instance, by destroying the feudal barons—and expand externally. There are several consequences that decrease the chance of cooperation among status-quo states. First, war will be profitable for the winner. The costs will be low and the benefits high. Of course, losers will suffer; the fear of losing could induce states to try to form stable cooperative arrangements, but the temptation of victory will make this particularly difficult. Second, because wars are expected to be both frequent and short, there will be incentives for high levels of arms, and quick and strong reaction to the other's increases in arms. The state cannot afford to wait until there is unambiguous evidence that the other is building new weapons. Even large states that have faith in their economic strength cannot wait, because the war will be over before their products can reach the army. Third, when wars are quick, states will have to recruit allies in advance.[7] Without the opportunity for bargaining and re-alignments during the opening stages of hostilities, peacetime diplo-

---

[5] Thomas Schelling, *The Strategy of Conflict* (New York: Oxford University Press 1963), chap. 9.
[6] Quoted in Fritz Fischer, *War of Illusions* (New York: Norton 1975), 377, 461.
[7] George Quester, *Offense and Defense in the International System* (New York: John Wiley 1977), 105–06; Sontag (fn. 5), 4–5.

macy loses a degree of the fluidity that facilitates balance-of-power policies. Because alliances must be secured during peacetime, the international system is more likely to become bipolar. It is hard to say whether war therefore becomes more or less likely, but this bipolarity increases tension between the two camps and makes it harder for status-quo states to gain the benefits of cooperation. Fourth, if wars are frequent, statesmen's perceptual thresholds will be adjusted accordingly and they will be quick to perceive ambiguous evidence as indicating that others are aggressive. Thus, there will be more cases of status-quo powers arming against each other in the incorrect belief that the other is hostile.

When the defense has the advantage, all the foregoing is reversed. The state that fears attack does not pre-empt—since that would be a wasteful use of its military resources—but rather prepares to receive an attack. Doing so does not decrease the security of others, and several states can do it simultaneously; the situation will therefore be stable, and status-quo powers will be able to cooperate. When Herman Kahn argues that ultimatums "are vastly too dangerous to give because ... they are quite likely to touch off a preemptive strike,"[8] he incorrectly assumes that it is always advantageous to strike first.

More is involved than short-run dynamics. When the defense is dominant, wars are likely to become stalemates and can be won only at enormous cost. Relatively small and weak states can hold off larger and stronger ones, or can deter attack by raising the costs of conquest to an unacceptable level. States then approach equality in what they can do to each other. Like the .45-caliber pistol in the American West, fortifications were the "great equalizer" in some periods. Changes in the status quo are less frequent and cooperation is more common wherever the security dilemma is thereby reduced.

Many of these arguments can be illustrated by the major powers' policies in the periods preceding the two world wars. Bismarck's wars surprised statesmen by showing that the offense had the advantage, and by being quick, relatively cheap, and quite decisive. Falling into a common error, observers projected this pattern into the future.[9] The resulting expectations had several effects. First, states sought semi-permanent allies. In the early stages of the Franco-Prussian War, Napoleon III had thought that there would be plenty of time to recruit Austria to his side. Now, others were not going to repeat this mistake. Second, defense budgets were high and reacted

---

[8] Herman Kahn, *On Thermonuclear War* (Princeton: Princeton University Press 1960), 211.

[9] For a general discussion of such mistaken learning from the past, see Jervis (fn. 5), chap. 6. The important and still not completely understood question of why this belief formed and was maintained throughout the war is examined in Bernard Brodie, *War and Politics* (New York: Macmillan 1973), 262–70; Brodie, "Technological Change, Strategic Doctrine, and Political Outcomes," in Klaus Knorr, ed., *Historical Dimensions of National Security Problems* (Lawrence: University Press of Kansas 1976), 290–92; and Douglas Porch, "The French Army and the Spirit of the Offensive, 1900–14," in Brian Bond and Ian Roy, eds., *War and Society* (New York: Holmes & Meier 1975), 117–43.

quite sharply to increases on the other side. It is not surprising that Richard-son's theory of arms races fits this period well. Third, most decision makers thought that the next European war would not cost much blood and trea-sure.[10] That is one reason why war was generally seen as inevitable and why mass opinion was so bellicose. Fourth, once war seemed likely, there were strong pressures to pre-empt. Both sides believed that whoever moved first could penetrate the other deep enough to disrupt mobilization and thus gain an insurmountable advantage. (There was no such belief about the use of naval forces. Although Churchill made an ill-advised speech saying that if German ships "do not come out and fight in time of war they will be dug out like rats in a hole,"[11] everyone knew that submarines, mines, and coastal for-tifications made this impossible. So at the start of the war each navy pre-pared to defend itself rather than attack, and the short-run destabilizing forces that launched the armies toward each other did not operate.)[12] Fur-thermore, each side knew that the other saw the situation the same way, thus increasing the perceived danger that the other would attack, and giving each added reasons to precipitate a war if conditions seemed favorable. In the long and the short run, there were thus both offensive and defensive in-centives to strike. This situation casts light on the common question about German motives in 1914: "Did Germany unleash the war deliberately to be-come a world power or did she support Austria merely to defend a weaken-ing ally," thereby protecting her own position?[13] To some extent, this question is misleading. Because of the perceived advantage of the offense, war was seen as the best route both to gaining expansion and to avoiding drastic loss of influence. There seemed to be no way for Germany merely to retain and safeguard her existing position.

Of course the war showed these beliefs to have been wrong on all points. Trenches and machine guns gave the defense an overwhelming advantage. The fighting became deadlocked and produced horrendous casualties. It made no sense for the combatants to bleed themselves to death. If they had known the power of the defense beforehand, they would have rushed for their own trenches rather than for the enemy's territory. Each side could have done this without increasing the other's incentives to strike. . . .

---

[10]Some were not so optimistic. Gray's remark is well-known: "The lamps are going out all over Europe; we shall not see them lit again in our life-time." The German Prime Minister, Beth-mann Hollweg, also feared the consequences of the war. But the controlling view was that it would certainly pay for the winner.

[11]Quoted in Martin Gilbert, *Winston S. Churchill*, III, *The Challenge of War, 1914–1916* (Boston: Houghton Mifflin 1971), 84.

[12]Quester (fn. 7), 98–99. Robert Art, *The Influence of Foreign Policy on Seapower*, II (Beverly Hills: Sage Professional Papers in International Studies Series, 1973), 14–18, 26–28.

[13]Konrad Jarausch, "The Illusion of Limited War: Chancellor Bethmann Hollweg's Calculated Risk, July 1914," *Central European History*, II (March 1969), 50.

TECHNOLOGY AND GEOGRAPHY   Technology and geography are the two main factors that determine whether the offense or the defense has the advantage. As Brodie notes, "On the tactical level, as a rule, few physical factors favor the attacker but many favor the defender. The defender usually has the advantage of cover. He characteristically fires from behind some form of shelter while his opponent crosses open ground."[14] Anything that increases the amount of ground the attacker has to cross, or impedes his progress across it, or makes him more vulnerable while crossing, increases the advantage accruing to the defense. When states are separated by barriers that produce these effects, the security dilemma is eased, since both can have forces adequate for defense without being able to attack. Impenetrable barriers would actually prevent war; in reality, decision makers have to settle for a good deal less. Buffer zones slow the attacker's progress; they thereby give the defender time to prepare, increase problems of logistics, and reduce the number of soldiers available for the final assault. At the end of the 19th century, Arthur Balfour noted Afghanistan's "non-conducting" qualities. "So long as it possesses few roads, and no railroads, it will be impossible for Russia to make effective use of her great numerical superiority at any point immediately vital to the Empire." The Russians valued buffers for the same reasons; it is not surprising that when Persia was being divided into Russian and British spheres of influence some years later, the Russians sought assurances that the British would refrain from building potentially menacing railroads in their sphere. Indeed, since railroad construction radically altered the abilities of countries to defend themselves and to attack others, many diplomatic notes and much intelligence activity in the late 19th century centered on this subject.[15]

Oceans, large rivers, and mountain ranges serve the same function as buffer zones. Being hard to cross, they allow defense against superior numbers. The defender has merely to stay on his side of the barrier and so can utilize all the men he can bring up to it. The attacker's men, however, can cross only a few at a time, and they are very vulnerable when doing so. If all states were self-sufficient islands, anarchy would be much less of a problem. A small investment in short defenses and a small army would be sufficient to repel invasion. Only very weak states would be vulnerable, and only very large ones could menace others. As noted above, the United States, and to a lesser extent Great Britain, have partly been able to escape from the state of nature because their geographical positions approximated this ideal.

---

[14]Bernard Brodie, *Strategy in the Missile Age* (Princeton: Princeton University Press 1959), 179.

[15]Arthur Balfour, "Memorandum," Committee on Imperial Defence, April 30, 1903, pp. 2–3; see the telegrams by Sir Arthur Nicolson, in G. P. Gooch and Harold Temperley, eds., *British Documents on the Origins of the War*, Vol. 4 (London: H.M.S.O. 1929), 429, 524. These barriers do not prevent the passage of long-range aircraft; but even in the air, distance usually aids the defender.

Although geography cannot be changed to conform to borders, borders can and do change to conform to geography. Borders across which an attack is easy tend to be unstable. States living within them are likely to expand or be absorbed. Frequent wars are almost inevitable since attacking will often seem the best way to protect what one has. This process will stop, or at least slow down, when the state's borders reach—by expansion or contraction—a line of natural obstacles. Security without attack will then be possible. Furthermore, these lines constitute salient solutions to bargaining problems and, to the extent that they are barriers to migration, are likely to divide ethnic groups, thereby raising the costs and lowering the incentives for conquest.

Attachment to one's state and its land reinforce one quasi-geographical aid to the defense. Conquest usually becomes more difficult the deeper the attacker pushes into the other's territory. Nationalism spurs the defenders to fight harder; advancing not only lengthens the attacker's supply lines, but takes him through unfamiliar and often devastated lands that require troops for garrison duty. These stabilizing dynamics will not operate, however, if the defender's war matcriel is situated near its borders, or if the people do not care about their state, but only about being on the winning side. In such cases, positive feedback will be at work and initial defeats will be insurmountable.[16]

Imitating geography, men have tried to create barriers. Treaties may provide for demilitarized zones on both sides of the border, although such zones will rarely be deep enough to provide more than warning. Even this was not possible in Europe, but the Russians adopted a gauge for their railroads that was broader than that of the neighboring states, thereby complicating the logistics problems of any attacker—including Russia.

Perhaps the most ambitious and at least temporarily successful attempts to construct a system that would aid the defenses of both sides were the interwar naval treaties, as they affected Japanese-American relations. As mentioned earlier, the problem was that the United States could not defend the Philippines without denying Japan the ability to protect her home islands.[17] (In 1941 this dilemma became insoluble when Japan sought to extend her control to Malaya and the Dutch East Indies. If the Philippines had been invulnerable, they could have provided a secure base from which the U.S. could interdict Japanese shipping between the homeland and the areas she was trying to conquer.) In the 1920's and early 1930's each side would have been willing to grant the other security for its possessions in return for a reciprocal grant, and the Washington Naval Conference agreements were de-

---

[16]See, for example, the discussion of warfare among Chinese warlords in Hsi-Sheng Chi, "The Chinese Warlord System as an International System," in Morton Kaplan, ed., *New Approaches to International Relations* (New York: St. Martin's 1968), 405–25.

[17]Some American decision makers, including military officers, thought that the best way out of the dilemma was to abandon the Philippines.

signed to approach this goal. As a Japanese diplomat later put it, their country's "fundamental principle" was to have "a strength insufficient for attack and adequate for defense."[18] Thus, Japan agreed in 1922 to accept a navy only three-fifths as large as that of the United States, and the U.S. agreed not to fortify its Pacific islands.[19] (Japan had earlier been forced to agree not to fortify the islands she had taken from Germany in World War I.) Japan's navy would not be large enough to defeat America's anywhere other than close to the home islands. Although the Japanese could still take the Philippines, not only would they be unable to move farther, but they might be weakened enough by their efforts to be vulnerable to counterattack. Japan, however, gained security. An American attack was rendered more difficult because the American bases were unprotected and because, until 1930, Japan was allowed unlimited numbers of cruisers, destroyers, and submarines that could weaken the American fleet as it made its way across the ocean.[20]

The other major determinant of the offense-defense balance is technology. When weapons are highly vulnerable, they must be employed before they are attacked. Others can remain quite invulnerable in their bases. The former characteristics are embodied in unprotected missiles and many kinds of bombers. (It should be noted that it is not vulnerability *per se* that is crucial, but the location of the vulnerability. Bombers and missiles that are easy to destroy only after having been launched toward their targets do not create destabilizing dynamics.) Incentives to strike first are usually absent for naval forces that are threatened by a naval attack. Like missiles in hardened silos, they are usually well protected when in their bases. Both sides can then simultaneously be prepared to defend themselves successfully.

In ground warfare under some conditions, forts, trenches, and small groups of men in prepared positions can hold off large numbers of attackers. Less frequently, a few attackers can storm the defenses. By and large, it is a contest between fortifications and supporting light weapons on the one hand, and mobility and heavier weapons that clear the way for the attack on the other. As the erroneous views held before the two world wars show, there is no simple way to determine which is dominant. "[T]hese oscillations are not smooth and predictable like those of a swinging pendulum. They are uneven in both extent and time. Some occur in the course of a single battle or

---

[18]Quoted in Elting Morrison, *Turmoil and Tradition: A Study of the Life and Times of Henry L. Stimson* (Boston: Houghton Mifflin 1960), 326.

[19]The U.S. "refused to consider limitations on Hawaiian defenses, since these works posed no threat to Japan." William Braisted, *The United States Navy in the Pacific, 1909–1922* (Austin: University of Texas Press 1971), 612.

[20]That is part of the reason why the Japanese admirals strongly objected when the civilian leaders decided to accept a seven-to-ten ratio in lighter craft in 1930. Stephen Pelz, *Race to Pearl Harbor* (Cambridge: Harvard University Press 1974), 3.

campaign, others in the course of a war, still others during a series of wars."
Longer-term oscillations can also be detected:

> The early Gothic age, from the twelfth to the late thirteenth century, with its
> wonderful cathedrals and fortified places, was a period during which the at-
> tackers in Europe generally met serious and increasing difficulties, because
> the improvement in the strength of fortresses outran the advance in the
> power of destruction. Later, with the spread of firearms at the end of the fif-
> teenth century, old fortresses lost their power to resist. An age ensued during
> which the offense possessed, apart from short-term setbacks, new advantages.
> Then, during the seventeenth century, especially after about 1660, and until
> at least the outbreak of the War of the Austrian Succession in 1740, the de-
> fense regained much of the ground it had lost since the great medieval
> fortresses had proved unable to meet the bombardment of the new and more
> numerous artillery.[21]

Another scholar has continued the argument: "The offensive gained an advantage with new forms of heavy mobile artillery in the nineteenth century,
but the stalemate of World War I created the impression that the defense
again had an advantage; the German invasion in World War II, however, indicated the offensive superiority of highly mechanized armies in the field."[22]

The situation today with respect to conventional weapons is unclear. Until
recently it was believed that tanks and tactical air power gave the attacker an
advantage. The initial analyses of the 1973 Arab-Israeli war indicated that
new anti-tank and anti-aircraft weapons have restored the primacy of the defense. These weapons are cheap, easy to use, and can destroy a high proportion of the attacking vehicles and planes that are sighted. It then would
make sense for a status-quo power to buy lots of $20,000 missiles rather than
buy a few half-million dollar tanks and multi-million dollar fighter-bombers.
Defense would be possible even against a large and well-equipped force;
states that care primarily about self-protection would not need to engage in
arms races. But further examinations of the new technologies and the history of the October War cast doubt on these optimistic conclusions and
leave us unable to render any firm judgment. . . .[23]

[21]John Nef, *War and Human Progress* (New York: Norton 1963), 185. Also see *ibid.*, 237, 242–43,
and 323; C. W. Oman, *The Art of War in the Middle Ages* (Ithaca, N.Y.: Cornell University Press
1953), 70–72; John Beeler, *Warfare in Feudal Europe, 730–1200* (Ithaca, N.Y.: Cornell University Press 1971), 212–14; Michael Howard, *War in European History* (London: Oxford University Press 1976), 33–37.

[22]Quincy Wright, *A Study of War* (abridged ed.; Chicago: University of Chicago Press 1964), 142.
Also see 63–70, 74–75. There are important exceptions to these generalizations—the American Civil War, for instance, falls in the middle of the period Wright says is dominated by the
offense.

[23]Geoffrey Kemp, Robert Pfaltzgraff, and Uri Ra'anan, eds., *The Other Arms Race* (Lexington,
Mass.: D. C. Heath 1975); James Foster, "The Future of Conventional Arms Control," *Policy
Sciences*, No. 8 (Spring 1977), 1–19.

Offense-Defense Differentiation

The other major variable that affects how strongly the security dilemma operates is whether weapons and policies that protect the state also provide the capability for attack. If they do not, the basic postulate of the security dilemma no longer applies. A state can increase its own security without decreasing that of others. The advantage of the defense can only ameliorate the security dilemma. A differentiation between offensive and defensive stances comes close to abolishing it. Such differentiation does not mean, however, that all security problems will be abolished. If the offense has the advantage, conquest and aggression will still be possible. And if the offense's advantage is great enough, status-quo powers may find it too expensive to protect themselves by defensive forces and decide to procure offensive weapons even though this will menace others. Furthermore, states will still have to worry that even if the other's military posture shows that it is peaceful now, it may develop aggressive intentions in the future.

Assuming that the defense is at least as potent as the offense, the differentiation between them allows status-quo states to behave in ways that are clearly different from those of aggressors. Three beneficial consequences follow. First, status-quo powers can identify each other, thus laying the foundations for cooperation. Conflicts growing out of the mistaken belief that the other side is expansionist will be less frequent. Second, status-quo states will obtain advance warning when others plan aggression. Before a state can attack, it has to develop and deploy offensive weapons. If procurement of these weapons cannot be disguised and takes a fair amount of time, as it almost always does, a status-quo state will have the time to take countermeasures. It need not maintain a high level of defensive arms as long as its potential adversaries are adopting a peaceful posture. . . .

The third beneficial consequence of a difference between offensive and defensive weapons is that if all states support the status quo, an obvious arms control agreement is a ban on weapons that are useful for attacking. As President Roosevelt put it in his message to the Geneva Disarmament Conference in 1933: "If all nations will agree wholly to eliminate from possession and use the weapons which make possible a successful attack, defenses automatically will become impregnable, and the frontiers and independence of every national will become secure."[24] The fact that such treaties have been rare—the Washington naval agreements discussed above and the anti-ABM treaty can be cited as examples—shows either that states are not always willing to guarantee the security of others, or that it is hard to distinguish offensive from defensive weapons.

Is such a distinction possible? Salvador de Madariaga, the Spanish statesman active in the disarmament negotiations of the interwar years, thought not: "A weapon is either offensive or defensive according to which end of it

---

[24]Quoted in Merze Tate, *The United States and Armaments* (Cambridge: Harvard University Press 1948), 108.

you are looking at." The French Foreign Minister agreed (although French policy did not always follow this view): "Every arm can be employed offensively or defensively in turn.... The only way to discover whether arms are intended for purely defensive purposes or are held in a spirit of aggression is in all cases to enquire into the intentions of the country concerned." Some evidence for the validity of this argument is provided by the fact that much time in these unsuccessful negotiations was devoted to separating offensive from defensive weapons. Indeed, no simple and unambiguous definition is possible and in many cases no judgment can be reached. Before the American entry into World War I, Woodrow Wilson wanted to arm merchantmen only with guns in the back of the ship so they could not initiate a fight, but this expedient cannot be applied to more common forms of armaments.[25]

There are several problems. Even when a differentiation is possible, a status-quo power will want offensive arms under any of three conditions. (1) If the offense has a great advantage over the defense, protection through defensive forces will be too expensive. (2) Status-quo states may need offensive weapons to regain territory lost in the opening stages of a war. It might be possible, however, for a state to wait to procure these weapons until war seems likely, and they might be needed only in relatively small numbers, unless the aggressor was able to construct strong defenses quickly in the occupied areas. (3) The state may feel that it must be prepared to take the offensive either because the other side will make peace only if it loses territory or because the state has commitments to attack if the other makes war on a third party. As noted above, status-quo states with extensive commitments are often forced to behave like aggressors. Even when they lack such commitments, status-quo states must worry about the possibility that if they are able to hold off an attack, they will still not be able to end the war unless they move into the other's territory to damage its military forces and inflict pain. Many American naval officers after the Civil War, for example, believed that "only by destroying the commerce of the opponent could the United States bring him to terms."[26]

A further complication is introduced by the fact that aggressors as well as status-quo powers require defensive forces as a prelude to acquiring offensive ones, to protect one frontier while attacking another, or for insurance in case the war goes badly. Criminals as well as policemen can use bullet-proof vests. Hitler as well as Maginot built a line of forts. Indeed, Churchill reports that in 1936 the German Foreign Minister said: "As soon as our fortifications are constructed [on our western borders] and the countries in Central Europe realize that France cannot enter German territory, all these countries will begin to feel very differently about their foreign policies, and a

[25]Marion Boggs, *Attempts to Define and Limit "Aggressive" Armament in Diplomacy and Strategy* (Columbia: University of Missouri Studies, XVI, No. 1, 1941), 15, 40.
[26]Kenneth Hagan, *American Gunboat Diplomacy and the Old Navy, 1877–1889* (Westport, Conn.: Greenwood Press 1973), 20.

new constellation will develop."[27] So a state may not necessarily be reassured if its neighbor constructs strong defenses.

More central difficulties are created by the fact that whether a weapon is offensive or defensive often depends on the particular situation—for instance, the geographical setting and the way in which the weapon is used. "Tanks . . . spearheaded the fateful German thrust through the Ardennes in 1940, but if the French had disposed of a properly concentrated armored reserve, it would have provided the best means for their cutting off the penetration and turning into a disaster for the Germans what became instead an overwhelming victory."[28] Anti-aircraft weapons seem obviously defensive—to be used, they must wait for the other side to come to them. But the Egyptian attack on Israel in 1973 would have been impossible without effective air defenses that covered the battlefield. Nevertheless, some distinctions are possible. Sir John Simon, then the British Foreign Secretary, in response to the views cited earlier, stated that just because a fine line could not be drawn, "that was no reason for saying that there were not stretches of territory on either side which all practical men and women knew to be well on this or that side of the line." Although there are almost no weapons and strategies that are useful only for attacking, there are some that are almost exclusively defensive. Aggressors could want them for protection, but a state that relied mostly on them could not menace others. More frequently, we cannot "determine the absolute character of a weapon, but [we can] make a comparison . . . [and] discover whether or not the offensive potentialities predominate, whether a weapon is more useful in attack or in defense."[29]

The essence of defense is keeping the other side out of your territory. A purely defensive weapon is one that can do this without being able to penetrate the enemy's land. Thus a committee of military experts in an interwar disarmament conference declared that armaments "incapable of mobility by means of self-contained power," or movable only after long delay, were "only capable of being used for the defense of a State's territory."[30] The most obvious examples are fortifications. They can shelter attacking forces, especially when they are built right along the frontier,[31] but they cannot occupy enemy territory. A state with only a strong line of forts, fixed guns, and a small army to man them would not be much of a menace. Anything else that can serve only as a barrier against attacking troops is similarly defensive. In this category are systems that provide warning of an attack, the Russian's adoption of

---

[27]Winston Churchill, *The Gathering Storm* (Boston: Houghton 1948), 206.

[28]Bernard Brodie, *War and Politics* (New York: Macmillan 1973), 325.

[29]Boggs (fn. 25), 42, 83. For a good argument about the possible differentiation between offensive and defensive weapons in the 1930's, see Basil Liddell Hart, "Aggression and the Problem of Weapons," *English Review*, Vol. 55 (July 1932), 71–78.

[30]Quoted in Boggs (fn. 25), 39.

[31]On these grounds, the Germans claimed in 1932 that the French forts were offensive (*ibid.*, 49). Similarly, fortified forward naval bases can be necessary for launching an attack; see Braisted (fn. 19), 643.

a different railroad gauge, and nuclear land mines that can seal off invasion routes.

If total immobility clearly defines a system that is defensive only, limited mobility is unfortunately ambiguous. As noted above, short-range fighter aircraft and anti-aircraft missiles can be used to cover an attack. And, unlike forts, they can advance with the troops. Still, their inability to reach deep into enemy territory does make them more useful for the defense than for the offense. Thus, the United States and Israel would have been more alarmed in the early 1970's had the Russians provided the Egyptians with long-range instead of short-range aircraft. Naval forces are particularly difficult to classify in these terms, but those that are very short-legged can be used only for coastal defense. . . .

Four Worlds

The two variables we have been discussing—whether the offense or the defense has the advantage, and whether offensive postures can be distinguished from defensive ones—can be combined to yield four possible worlds.

The first world is the worst for status-quo states. There is no way to get security without menacing others, and security through defense is terribly difficult to obtain. Because offensive and defensive postures are the same, status quo states acquire the same kind of arms that are sought by aggressors. And because the offense has the advantage over the defense, attacking

	OFFENSE HAS THE ADVANTAGE	*DEFENSE HAS THE ADVANTAGE*
	1	*2*
OFFENSIVE POSTURE NOT DISTINGUISHABLE FROM DEFENSIVE ONE	Doubly dangerous	Security dilemma, but security requirements may be compatible.
	3	*4*
OFFENSIVE POSTURE DISTINGUISHABLE FROM DEFENSIVE ONE	No security dilemma, but aggression possible. Status-quo states can follow different policy than aggressors. Warning given.	Doubly stable

is the best route to protecting what you have; status-quo states will therefore behave like aggressors. The situation will be unstable. Arms races are likely. Incentives to strike first will turn crises into wars. Decisive victories and conquests will be common. States will grow and shrink rapidly, and it will be hard for any state to maintain its size and influence without trying to increase them. Cooperation among status-quo powers will be extremely hard to achieve.

There are no cases that totally fit this picture, but it bears more than a passing resemblance to Europe before World War I. Britain and Germany, although in many respects natural allies, ended up as enemies. Of course much of the explanation lies in Germany's ill-chosen policy. And from the perspective of our theory, the powers' ability to avoid war in a series of earlier crises cannot be easily explained. Nevertheless, much of the behavior in this period was the product of technology and beliefs that magnified the security dilemma. Decision makers thought that the offense had a big advantage and saw little difference between offensive and defensive military postures. The era was characterized by arms races. And once war seemed likely, mobilization races created powerful incentives to strike first. . . .

In the second world, the security dilemma operates because offensive and defensive postures cannot be distinguished; but it does not operate as strongly as in the first world because the defense has the advantage, and so an increment in one side's strength increases its security more than it decreases the other's. So, if both sides have reasonable subjective security requirements, are of roughly equal power, and the variables discussed earlier are favorable, it is quite likely that status-quo states can adopt compatible security policies. Although a state will not be able to judge the other's intentions from the kinds of weapons it procures, the level of arms spending will give important evidence. Of course a state that seeks a high level of arms might be not an aggressor but merely an insecure state, which if conciliated will reduce its arms, and if confronted will reply in kind. To assume that the apparently excessive level of arms indicates aggressiveness could therefore lead to a response that would deepen the dilemma and create needless conflict. But empathy and skillful statesmanship can reduce this danger. Furthermore, the advantageous position of the defense means that a status-quo state can often maintain a high degree of security with a level of arms lower than that of its expected adversary. Such a state demonstrates that it lacks the ability or desire to alter the status quo, at least at the present time. The strength of the defense also allows states to react slowly and with restraint when they fear that others are menacing them. So, although status-quo powers will to some extent be threatening to others, that extent will be limited.

This world is the one that comes closest to matching most periods in history. Attacking is usually harder than defending because of the strength of fortifications and obstacles. But purely defensive postures are rarely possible because fortifications are usually supplemented by armies and mobile guns which can support an attack.

... In the third world there may be no security dilemma, but there are security problems. Because states can procure defensive systems that do not threaten others, the dilemma need not operate. But because the offense has the advantage, aggression is possible, and perhaps easy. If the offense has enough of an advantage, even a status-quo state may take the initiative rather than risk being attacked and defeated. If the offense has less of an advantage, stability and cooperation are likely because the status-quo states will procure defensive forces. They need not react to others who are similarly armed, but can wait for the warning they would receive if others started to deploy offensive weapons. But each state will have to watch the others carefully, and there is room for false suspicions. The costliness of the defense and the allure of the offense can lead to unnecessary mistrust, hostility, and war, unless some of the variables discussed earlier are operating to restrain defection. ...

The fourth world is doubly safe. The differentiation between offensive and defensive systems permits a way out of the security dilemma; the advantage of the defense disposes of the problems discussed in the previous paragraphs. There is no reason for a status-quo power to be tempted to procure offensive forces, and aggressors give notice of their intention by the posture they adopt. Indeed, if the advantage of the defense is great enough, there are no security problems. The loss of the ultimate form of the power to alter the status quo would allow greater scope for the exercise of nonmilitary means and probably would tend to freeze the distribution of values.

This world would have existed in the first decade of the 20th century if the decision makers had understood the available technology. In that case, the European powers would have followed different policies both in the long run and in the summer of 1914. Even Germany, facing powerful enemies on both sides, could have made herself secure by developing strong defenses. France could also have made her frontier almost impregnable. Furthermore, when crises arose, no one would have had incentives to strike first. There would have been no competitive mobilization races reducing the time available for negotiations.

1914 Revisited

SCOTT D. SAGAN

The origins of the First World War continue to be of great interest today because there are a number of striking similarities between the events of 1914 and contemporary fears about paths by which a nuclear war could begin. July 1914 was a brinksmanship crisis, resulting in a war that everyone was willing to risk but that no one truly wanted. During the crisis, the political leaderships' understanding of military operations and control over critical war preparations were often tenuous at best. In 1914, the perceived incentives to strike first, once war was considered likely, were great, and the rapidity and inflexibility of offensive war plans limited the time available to diplomats searching for an acceptable political solution to the crisis. In a world in which the possibility of massive nuclear retaliation has made the deliberate, premeditated initiation of nuclear war unlikely, there is widespread concern that a repetition of the Sarajevo Scenario may occur: an apparently insignificant incident sparking—through a dangerous mixture of miscalculations, inadvertent escalation, and loss of control over events—a tragic and unintended war.[1] Indeed, for a student of the July crisis, even specific phrases in the current nuclear debate can be haunting: what former Secretary of Defense Harold Brown meant to be a comforting metaphor, that the Soviet Union would never risk its society on "a cosmic throw of the dice," is less reassuring to those who recall German Chancellor Theobald von Beth-

Scott D. Sagan, "1914 Revisited: Allies, Offense, and Instability," *International Security* Vol. 11, no. 2 (Fall 1986). Reprinted by permission of the MIT Press, Cambridge, Massachusetts. Copyright © 1986 by the President and Fellows of Harvard College and of the Massachusetts Institute of Technology.

[1]Recent discussions of nuclear strategy that utilize the 1914 analogy include Graham T. Allison, Albert Carnesale, and Joseph S. Nye, Jr., eds., *Hawks, Doves, and Owls* (New York: Norton, 1985), especially pp. 210–217; Paul J. Bracken, *The Command and Control of Nuclear Forces* (New Haven: Yale University Press, 1983), pp. 222–223, 239–240; and Miles Kahler, "Rumors of War: The 1914 Analogy," *Foreign Affairs*, Vol. 58, No. 2 (Winter 1979–80).

mann-Hollweg's statement, "If the iron dice are now to be rolled, may God help us," made just hours before Germany declared war against Russia on August 1, 1914.[2]

Prior to 1914, the general staffs of each of the European great powers had designed elaborate and inflexible offensive war plans, which were implemented in a series of mobilizations and counter mobilizations at the end of the July crisis. In August, all the continental powers took the offensive: the Germans attacked across Belgium and Luxembourg into France; the French army launched a massive assault against German positions in Alsace-Lorraine; and the Russian army, although not yet fully mobilized, immediately began simultaneous offenses against Germany and Austria-Hungary. In retrospect, the war plans of the great powers had disastrous political and military consequences. The negative political consequences were seen at the cabinet meetings during the July crisis, for the pressures to begin mobilization and launch offensives promptly, according to the military timetables, contributed greatly to the dynamic of escalation and the political leaderships' loss of freedom of action. In Berlin, for example, as Bethmann-Hollweg frankly admitted to the Prussian Ministry of State, once the Russians began to mobilize, "control had been lost and the stone had started rolling."[3] The military consequences were seen on the battlefield. Each of the major offensive campaigns was checked or repulsed with enormous costs: some 900,000 men were missing, taken prisoner, wounded, or dead by the end of 1914.[4]

Historians and political scientists have long sought to understand why the great powers all had offensive military doctrines when the military technology of 1914—barbed wire, machine guns, and railroads—appears to have favored the defense. The popular explanation is that European soldiers and statesmen blithely ignored the demonstrations of defensive firepower in the American Civil War and the Russo-Japanese War and simply believed that the next European war would be like the last (an offensive victory as in the Franco-Prussian war), but that has never been satisfactory. For, in fact, numerous European military observers were in the United States from 1861–65 and in Manchuria during the 1904–5 conflict. Observer reports were widely distributed, the German, French, and British armies sponsored multivolume official histories of the Russo-Japanese War, and throughout the period prior to 1914 prolonged and heated debates raged in European military

---

[2]Harold Brown, *Department of Defense Annual Report for Fiscal Year 1979* (Washington, D.C.: U.S. Government Printing Office, 1978), p. 63; and Karl Kautsky, ed., *Outbreak of the World War: German Documents* (New York: Oxford University Press, 1924), No. 553, p. 441. (Hereinafter, *German Documents*.)

[3]*German Documents*, No. 456, p. 382.

[4]The estimate is from Michael Howard, "Men Against Fire: The Doctrine of the Offensive in 1914," in Peter Paret, ed., *The Makers of Modern Strategy from Machiavelli to the Nuclear Age* (Princeton: Princeton University Press, 1986), p. 510.

journals about the relative effectiveness of offensive and defensive tactics and strategies.[5]

Recent scholarship has suggested a new explanation which, using organization theory, emphasizes the degree to which the organizational interests of the professional military are advanced by offensive military doctrines, regardless of whether offensives are recommended by perceived national interests or prevailing technology.[6] Jack Snyder and Stephen Van Evera have found, in the 1914 case, an extreme example of this phenomenon: the "cult of the offensive."[7] This new explanation for the origins of the First World War is becoming widely accepted, and no one has challenged its validity.[8]

This essay reviews the organizational theory arguments and their "cult of the offensive" application to the events of 1914. It concludes that this approach seriously misrepresents the *causes* of the offensive doctrines of 1914 and, therefore, the underlying causes of the war. By focusing on the organizational interests of the professional military, the "cult of the offensive" theory has overlooked the more fundamental causes of the World War I offensive doctrines: the political objective and alliance commitments of the great powers.

This essay also argues that the "cult of the offensive" theory misrepresents the *consequences* of the 1914 offensive military doctrines. Although offensive military doctrines were necessary, they were not sufficient to cause the strategic instability witnessed in the July crisis; the critical preemptive incentives

---

[5]These writings are reviewed in ibid.; and Michael Howard, "Men Against Fire: Expectations of War in 1914," in Steven E. Miller, ed., *Military Strategy and the Origins of the First World War: An International Security Reader* (Princeton: Princeton University Press, 1985), pp. 41–57. Also see T.H.E. Travers, "The Offensive and the Problem of Innovation in British Military Thought 1870–1915," *Journal of Contemporary History*, Vol. 13 (1978), pp. 531–553; Travers, "Technology, Tactics, and Morale: Jean de Bloch, The Boer War, and British Military Theory, 1900–1914," *Journal of Modern History*, Vol. 51, No. 2 (June 1979), pp. 264–286; and Jay Luvaas, *The Military Legacy of the Civil War: The European Inheritance* (Chicago: University of Chicago Press, 1959).

[6]See Barry R. Posen, *The Sources of Military Doctrine: France, Britain and Germany Between the World Wars* (Ithaca: Cornell University Press, 1984); and Stephen Van Evera, "Causes of War" (Ph.D. dissertation, University of California, Berkeley, 1984), especially chapter 7.

[7]Jack Snyder, "Civil-Military Relations and the Cult of the Offensive, 1914 and 1984" and Stephen Van Evera, "The Cult of the Offensive and the Origins of the First World War," both in Miller, *Military Strategy and the Origins of the First World War*. Also see Snyder, *The Ideology of the Offensive: Military Decision Making and the Disasters of 1914* (Ithaca: Cornell University Press, 1984); and Van Evera, "Why Cooperation Failed in 1914," *World Politics*, Vol. 38, No. 1 (October 1985), pp. 97–98.

[8]See Allison et al., *Hawks, Doves, and Owls*, p. 212; Robert Axelrod and Robert O. Keohane, "Achieving Cooperation under Anarchy: Strategies and Institutions," *World Politics*, Vol. 38, No. 1 (October 1985), pp. 230–231; Richard Ned Lebow, "The Soviet Offensive in Europe: The Schlieffen Plan Revisited?," *International Security*, Vol. 9, No. 4 (Spring 1985), pp. 52–53, 68–69; Jack S. Levy, "Organizational Routines and the Causes of War," *International Studies Quarterly*, Vol. 30, No. 2 (June 1986); and Steven E. Miller, "Introduction: The Great War and the Nuclear Age," in Miller, *Military Strategy and the Origins of the First World War*, p. 3.

and pressures to move quickly felt by the German General Staff would not have been so strong without specific military vulnerabilities of the Entente powers and Belgium. In addition, even given the German offensive doctrine and war plans, it appears likely that Berlin would have been deterred in 1914 if the British government had issued a clear and credible threat to intervene in a continental war early in the July crisis. Furthermore, while the "cult of the offensive" theory correctly identifies the problem of offensive instability during the July crisis, it ignores the critical strategic dangers that would have resulted if European statesmen had adopted purely defensive strategies in 1914. These conclusions are, finally, of more than historical interest, for they suggest that the explicit lessons that the "cult of the offensive" theorists offer for contemporary American deterrent strategy are quite misleading.

Offenses, Military Biases, and the Security Dilemma

International relations theory posits the existence of a common security dilemma between sovereign states and has stressed the pernicious impact of offensive military forces and doctrines in exacerbating the problem.[9] The security dilemma exists when actions taken by one state solely for the purposes of increasing its own security simultaneously threaten another state, decreasing its security. This dilemma can be vicious "even in the extreme case in which all states would like to freeze the status quo," when two conditions exist: first, when defensive weapons and strategies cannot be distinguished from offensive ones and, second, when offensive military operations are considered easier than defensive operations.[10] Such conditions are said to produce a number of dangers. When offense is easier, or when one cannot differentiate between offenses and defenses, "unnecessary" arms races are made more likely. Under such conditions, the incentives to launch preventive wars are increased whenever the balance of power is shifting in favor of an adversary. Likewise, when war is considered likely, preemptive incentives are increased to the degree that striking the first offensive blow is considered advantageous compared to waiting to be attacked.

Earlier work on the subject focused largely on the effect of military technology on the offensive/defensive balance, and many arms control negotiations have sought to promote "stability" by identifying and limiting offensive

[9]Robert Jervis, "Cooperation Under the Security Dilemma," *World Politics*, Vol. 30, No. 2 (January 1978), pp. 167–214. Also see George H. Quester, *Offense and Defense in the International System* (New York: John Wiley and Sons, 1977); Van Evera, "Causes of War," chapter 3; and Jack S. Levy, "The Offensive/Defensive Balance of Military Technology: A Theoretical and Historical Analysis," *International Studies Quarterly*, Vol. 28 (1984), pp. 219–238.
[10]Jervis, "Cooperation Under the Security Dilemma," pp. 167, 186–187.

weapons and promoting defensive ones.[11] This approach's assumption, that status quo powers will pursue defensive, "stabilizing" military capabilities if possible, is challenged by the new "cult of the offensive" literature which emphasizes that military organizations display a strong preference for offensive forces and doctrines, even if the predominant military technology favors defense.

Five related and reinforcing explanations are offered for the military's bias in favor of the offense. First, offensive doctrines enhance the power and size of military organizations.[12] Offenses are usually technologically more complex and quantitatively more demanding than defenses. They often require larger forces, longer range weapons, and more extensive logistic capabilities. Since military organizations, like other organizations, seek to enhance their own size and wealth, as a rule, they will prefer offenses. Second, offensive doctrines tend to promote military autonomy. As Jack Snyder explains, "The operational autonomy of the military is most likely to be allowed when the operational goal is to disarm the adversary quickly and decisively by offensive means."[13] Not only are defensive operations, because they tend to be less complex, easier for civilian leaders to understand, but defenses also can lead to prolonged conflict on one's own soil, increasing the likelihood of civilian interference. In addition, offensive doctrines may require professional armies, rather than more "civilianized" conscripted armies. Third, offenses enhance the prestige and self-image of military officers. Defensive operations are often seen as passive, less challenging, and less glorious. As Barry Posen puts it, offenses can make soldiers "specialists in victory," while defenses merely turn them into "specialists in attrition."[14]

The fourth explanation offered for the military's offensive bias is that offenses structure military campaigns in favorable ways. Taking the initiative helps ensure that your standard scenario and operations plans, instead of the enemy's, dominate at least in the initial battles of a war.[15] This advantage of offensive operations has been repeated in statements of the "principle of the initiative" in military manuals at least since Jomini's maxim of 1807: The general who takes the initiative knows what he is going to do; he conceals his

[11]Ibid., pp. 186–214. For related works see Quester, *Offense and Defense in the International System;* Marion W. Boggs, *Attempts to Define and Limit "Aggressive" Armament in Diplomacy and Strategy* (Columbia, Mo.: University of Missouri, 1941); and B.H. Liddell Hart, "Aggression and the Problem of Weapons," *The English Review,* July 1932, pp. 71–78.

[12]Posen, *Sources of Military Doctrine,* p. 49.

[13]Snyder, "Civil-Military Relations and the Cult of the Offensive," p. 121; see also Posen, *Sources of Military Doctrine,* pp. 49–50.

[14]Posen, *Sources of Military Doctrine,* p. 49. A recent examination of the causes of the persistence of offensive tactics on the part of the Confederacy emphasizes the influence of Southern culture's romantic notions of soldierly honor. See Grady McWhiney and Perry D. Jamieson, *Attack and Die: Civil War Military Tactics and Southern Heritage* (Tuscaloosa, Ala.: University of Alabama Press, 1982).

[15]Posen, *Sources of Military Doctrine,* pp. 47–48. It should be noted, however, that this advantage need not be a military bias, as the civilian leadership as well as the military would favor it.

movements, surprises and crushes an extremity or weak point. The general who waits is beaten at one point before he learns of the attack.[16]

The fifth explanation emphasizes the effect that military officers' training and duties have on their beliefs about the need for decisive military operations that tend to be offensive in nature. Officers, it is argued, are necessarily preoccupied with the possibility of war; they tend to see the adversary as extremely hostile and war as a natural, indeed often an inevitable, part of international politics. Such beliefs lead them to favor preventive wars or preemptive strikes when necessary and decisive operations when possible. "Seeing war more likely than it really is," Snyder concludes, "[military professionals] increase its likelihood by adopting offensive plans and buying offensive forces."[17]

The 1914 Cult of the Offensive

Jack Snyder and Stephen Van Evera have found, in the origins of the First World War, the most extreme example of what can go wrong if the endemic military bias in favor of offensive doctrines is allowed to determine a state's strategy. Why did all the continental powers immediately launch offensives at the outburst of war? Snyder argues, "The offensive strategies of 1914 were largely domestic in origin, rooted in bureaucratic, sociopolitical, and psychological causes."[18] In France, the offensive nature of Plan XVII is seen as the result of the professional military's use of offensive doctrine as a defense of its institutional interests. After the Dreyfus affair, political leaders sought to "republicanize" the French military, hoping to create an army based largely on reservists and capable of conducting only defensive operations. The French military countered this threat to its institutional "essence," Snyder explains, by adopting the *offensive à outrance* doctrine which required the discipline and élan that only a professional standing army's long training and service together could provide.[19] The offensive strategy of the Schlieffen Plan, according to Snyder, was adopted in Germany because of the Prussian General Staff's bias in favor of decisive operations and because an offensive strategy promoted their power, prestige, and autonomy. In Russia, the ambitious war plans calling for offensive operations against both Germany and

---

[16]Antoine-Henri Jomini, "L'art de la guerre," *Pallas: Eine Zeitschrift für Staats und Kreigs Kunst*, Vol. 1 (1808), pp. 32–40, as quoted in John I. Alger, *The Quest for Victory: The History of the Principles of War* (Westport, Conn.: Greenwood Press, 1982), p. 22.

[17]Snyder, "Civil-Miliary Relations and the Cult of the Offensive," p. 119.

[18]Ibid., p. 137.

[19]Ibid., pp. 129–133; and Snyder, *Ideology of the Offensive*, chapters 2 and 3. For a different argument, stressing that offensive doctrine was adopted so that the morale of patriotic French recruits could compensate for superior German material strength, see Douglas Porch, *The March to the Marne: The French Army, 1871–1914* (Cambridge: Cambridge University Press, 1981), chapter 11.

Austria-Hungary were adopted because the absence of a strong central political authority enabled each of the conflicting military factions, one favoring
an offense against Germany and the other supporting an offense against
Austria-Hungary, to pursue its own preferred campaign. Because a realistic
assessment of the chances of success would have threatened their fundamental beliefs, Russian military leaders resorted to what Snyder calls "need-
ful thinking," believing that both "necessary" offensives could succeed when
objective assessment would have shown that they would fail.[20] The conclusion is clear:

> Strategic instability in 1914 was caused not by military technology, which fa-
> vored the defender and provided no first-strike advantage, but by offensive war
> plans that defied technological constraints. The lesson here is that doctrines
> can be destabilizing even when weapons are not, since doctrine may be more
> responsive to the organizational needs of the military than to the implications
> of the prevailing weapon technology.[21]

While Snyder has focused on the causes of the "cult of the offensive," Van
Evera's work concentrates on its consequences; his detailed analysis of the
July crisis goes considerably further than earlier work on this subject in identifying precisely how the military plans of the European powers contributed
to strategic instability in 1914.[22] He finds the "cult of the offensive" to be the
"mainspring" driving the numerous mechanisms that led the great powers to
war and illustrates his argument by imagining what 1914 would have looked
like had military and civilian leaders not had such strong beliefs about the
efficacy of offenses. The expansionist aims of Germany, the perceived incentives for preventive war and preemptive strikes, and the dynamics of rapid escalation in the crisis could have all been avoided, Van Evera argues, had
European leaders "recognized the actual power of the defense":

> German expansionists then would have met stronger arguments that empire
> was needless and impossible, and Germany could have more easily let the Rus-
> sian military buildup run its course, knowing that German defenses could still
> withstand Russian attack. All European states would have been less tempted to
> mobilize first, and each could have tolerated more preparations by adversaries
> before mobilizing themselves, so the spiral of mobilization and counter-mobi-
> lization would have operated more slowly, if at all.[23]

---

[20]Snyder, "Civil-Military Relations and the Cult of the Offensive," pp. 125–129, 133–137; and
    Snyder, *Ideology of the Offensive*, chapters 4–7.

[21]Snyder, *Ideology of the Offensive*, pp. 10–11.

[22]Van Evera, "The Cult of the Offensive and the Origins of the First World War." Also see Levy,
    "Organizational Routines and the Causes of War." For earlier interpretations, see Herman
    Kahn, *On Thermonuclear War* (Princeton: Princeton University Press, 1960), pp. 357–375; and
    Thomas Schelling's discussion of "the dynamics of mutual alarm" in Schelling, *Arms and In-
    fluence* (New Haven: Yale University Press, 1966), pp. 221–244.

[23]Van Evera, "The Cult of the Offensive and the Origins of the First World War," p. 105.

Van Evera even concludes that the First World War might not have broken out at all if leaders had understood the strength of defenses: "If armies [had] mobilized, they might have rushed to defend their own trenches and fortifications, instead of crossing frontiers...." Indeed, "In all likelihood, the Austro-Serbian conflict would have been a minor and soon-forgotten disturbance on the periphery of European politics."[24]

An Alternative Explanation: Strategic Interests and Alliance Commitments

Snyder's work has identified a number of ways in which the organizational interests of the military can affect strategic doctrine, and Van Evera's writings have persuasively demonstrated the alarming consequences that specific aspects of the offensive war plans of 1914 had on the political leadership's ability to control events during the July crisis. But their "cult of the offensive" analysis greatly exaggerates the degree to which the offensive doctrines in 1914 were caused by military-motivated biases or misperceptions of the offense/defense balance. Moreover, by focusing exclusively on the problems of the 1914 offensive military doctrines, they have overlooked the negative consequences that would have resulted if the great powers had adopted purely defensive military doctrines.

Three related problems exist with the "cult of the offensive" theory explanation. First, the theory exaggerates the probability that critical offensive military operations would fail. This theory is perhaps the strongest in explaining the French military's *offensive à outrance* doctrine, which even Field Marshall Joffre admitted was influenced by "le culte de l'offensive."[25] But it was *not* this *French* offensive doctrine that produced the dynamic of rapid escalation during the July crisis. For the French, a decision to mobilize was *not* a decision to attack Germany, and the Paris government specifically ordered its army not to move within 10 kilometers of the German border upon general mobilization.[26] Instead, the most critical offensive war plan in 1914 was that of Germany, for it was the German military's perceived need to mobilize quickly to implement the Schlieffen Plan's preemptive attack on Liège and attack in the West before Russian mobilization was complete that caused the crisis to move beyond control.

---

[24]Ibid. For a similar argument, that the European armies should have been "rushing to their own trenches rather than the enemy's territory" in 1914, see Jervis,"Cooperation Under the Security Dilemma," p. 191.

[25]As quoted by Van Evera, "The Cult of the Offensive and the Origins of the First World War," p. 61, fn. 14.

[26]See Luigi Albertini, *The Origins of the War of 1914* (London: Oxford University Press, 1957), Vol. 3, pp. 66–111.

With 20–20 hindsight, however, it is too easy to argue that the German offensive plan for conquest was doomed to fail. Thus, when Snyder writes of the "*vain attempt* to knock France out of the war" and complains that the German General Staff "could not accept that a future war *would inevitably take the form of an inglorious, unproductive stalemate,*" he assumes that the historical outcome, the defeat of the Schlieffen Plan, was the only one possible.[27] Similarly, when Van Evera writes, "Had statesmen understood that in reality the defense had the advantage, they also would have known that *the possession of the initiative could not be decisive*" or that "German expansionists then would have met stronger arguments that empire was *needless and impossible,*" he assumes that the outcome of the war was a forgone conclusion.[28]

In fact, the Schlieffen Plan came very close to succeeding and the Germans almost did win the short war they had expected to fight. The French, who call the decisive battle outside Paris "the Miracle of the Marne," have a better sense of the probability of German victory than do those who assume that the German attack was bound to fail. It would be beyond the scope of this article to reexamine the long-standing debate among military analysts and historians on whether Moltke's timidity and poor judgment ruined what could have been a major German victory in September 1914. A number of major participants and historians have maintained that the German offense would have succeeded if Moltke had moved more vigorously and had not weakened the strength of the attacking right wing by moving forces to defend Alsace-Lorraine; others have countered that, even if the Germans had won an overwhelming victory at the Marne, the French would not have capitulated and a stalemate would still have developed. Defense-advocates have maintained that the Germans came close to an offensive victory only because the French launched their offensive Plan XVII.[29] Others have stressed, however, that knowledge that the French would attack in Alsace-Lorraine was the underlying premise of the Schlieffen Plan. The subtlety of the German offense was that, as Liddell Hart put it, "it would operate like a revolving door—the harder the French pushed on one side, the more sharply would the other swing around and strike their back."[30]

The key point for this critique of "cult of the offensive" theory is not how this counterfactual debate is resolved, but rather that it exists at all. For it demonstrates that the theory's assumption, that only gross misperceptions

---

[27]Snyder, "Civil-Military Relations and the Cult of the Offensive," p. 128; and Snyder, *Ideology of the Offensive,* p. 17. Emphasis added.

[28]Van Evera, "The Cult of the Offensive and the Origins of the First World War," pp. 75, 105. Emphasis added.

[29]Snyder, *Ideology of the Offensive,* p. 9.

[30]B.H. Liddell Hart, "Foreword" to Gerhard Ritter, *The Schlieffen Plan: Critique of a Myth* (London: Oswald Wolff, 1958), p. 6; see also Turner, "The Significance of the Schlieffen Plan," p. 204.

of the offensive/defensive balance can explain why offensive strategies were chosen in 1914, is questionable. In addition, it should be remembered that Schlieffen was acutely aware of the danger of frontal attacks against fortified positions, which was precisely why the German plan emphasized an enveloping attack on the French flanks.[31] Thus, although the professional military's excessive faith in "the offensive spirit" is likely to have played a role in the fruitless British and French frontal assaults along the Western Front during the war,[32] the "cult" explanation is far less persuasive in the case of the offensive Schlieffen Plan, which is what caused the dynamic of escalation in the July crisis.

The second major problem with the "cult of the offensive" explanation is that it ignores the fundamental issue of the military balances. After all, what do the terms used in this literature, "offense-dominance" and "defense-dominance," really mean? Robert Jervis's definition, that offense has the advantage when "it is easier to destroy the other's army and take its territory than it is to defend one's own" is problematic, because it has been generally recognized since Clausewitz that defense is almost always "easier" in land warfare because of advantages of cover and the capability to choose and prepare terrain and fortify positions.[33] This is why military analysts usually think in terms of the force ratios—the required superiority of the offensive forces (2:1, 3:1, etc.) in order to achieve victory—rather than in all-or-nothing terms such as "offense-dominance" or "defense-dominance."

By focusing on the effects of military technology on the "offense/defense balance," the "cult of the offensive" theory fails to consider adequately the quantity or quality of military forces opposed to one another in a particular territorial campaign. How "defense-dominant" was the world of 1914? Certainly the range and rate of fire of small-caliber magazine rifles, machine guns, and field artillery strongly favored the defensive. And yet, even if one assumes that the historical outcome of 1914–1918 was the likely one, it is doubtful that defenses were so dominant or advantageous as to make all states simultaneously secure if they had maintained defensive military doctrines.

---

[31]Ritter, *The Schlieffen Plan,* pp. 50–51.

[32]Michael Howard argues, however, that "the worst losses were those due not to faulty doctrine but to inefficiency, inexperience, and the sheer organizational problems of combining fire and movement on the requisite scale." Howard, "Men Against Fire: The Doctrine of the Offensive in 1914," p. 526.

[33]Jervis, "Cooperation Under the Security Dilemma," p. 187. For an excellent review of literature on the offense-defense balance, see Levy, "The Offensive/Defensive Balance of Military Technology." Also see Jack Snyder, "Perceptions of the Security Dilemma in 1914," in Robert Jervis, Richard Ned Lebow, and Janice Gross Stein (with contributions from Patrick M. Morgan and Jack L. Snyder), *Psychology and Deterrence* (Baltimore: Johns Hopkins University Press, 1985), pp. 157–160.

The point is best made by imagining what would have happened if individual armies had rejected offensive doctrines and had, as Stephen Van Evera and Robert Jervis recommend, "rushed to their trenches" instead of others' territory. Serbia did, after all, adopt what was essentially a defensive strategy and was eventually conquered by the overwhelming forces of the Central Powers.[34] What if the French had no offensive plans but had "rushed to their trenches," staying completely on the defensive in 1914? The outcome of the war in the East suggests that the Central Powers could have defeated the Russians even more soundly if there had been no Western Front. If the Germans, after defeating the Russians, had turned and quickly attacked the French, would the technology of 1914 have proven the "dominance" of the defense? One can, of course, only speculate on such a question, but the near victory of the German offensive in 1918 against the French, a fully mobilized and deployed British army, and the arriving Americans suggests that a massive German offensive against the French alone (or the French and the small British Expeditionary Force) would have stood a strong chance of success.

This leads to the third problem. The "cult of the offensive" argument, by focusing primarily upon narrow issues of military planning, ignores the critical role of the states' political objectives in determining their military doctrines. Here I am not referring to the expansionist war aims of Germany and the other great powers, for, as Jack Snyder correctly notes, the desire to annex territory had its most important influence on decision-making *after* the war began, and the doctrinal decisions of the military officers who prepared the prewar offensive war plans in France, Germany, and Russia were not strongly influenced by such territorial ambitions.[35] Yet, the "cult of the offensive" argument overlooks a key point: offensive military doctrines are needed not only by states with expansionist war aims, but also by states that have a strong interest in protecting an exposed ally. Unless sufficient capability to protect an ally at the point of attack exists, "protector" powers require offensive strategies even if their goals are defensive in nature. This consideration is often recognized with respect to extended deterrence today; it also, however, lay at the heart of the offensive doctrines of 1914.

Thus, the Russians needed an offensive capability against Austria-Hungary, in order to be able to prevent the Austrians from attacking Serbia with overwhelming offensive superiority. The French required offensive capabilities against Germany in order to support Russia. Germany needed an of-

---

[34]For a brief review of the campaigns in Serbia, see Trevor N. Dupuy and Molly R. Mayo, *Campaigns in Southern Europe* (New York: Franklin Watts, 1967), pp. 9–20, 38–46.

[35]Snyder, *Ideology of the Offensive*, pp. 19–20. Snyder does make an exception for Russia: the Russian offensive plans against Austria-Hungary were influenced by ambitions in the Balkans as well as military operational considerations. It should also be noted that Austria-Hungary, because of its punitive policy toward Serbia, required an offensive doctrine.

fense to protect Austria-Hungary if Russia launched an attack against Germany's ally. Particular conditions of the military balance in 1914—the slowness of the Russian mobilization and what General von Falkenhayn called "the almost unlimited power of the Russians to evade a final decision by arms"[36] due to its vast territory—resulted in the German plan to attempt to knock France out of the war first. This further complicated the issue, for the German offensive plans against France resulted in both a Russian need for an offensive against Germany and even Austrian plans to attack Russia as a "relief offensive" to give Moltke more time to defeat the French.

This need for offensive capabilities to provide support for allies can be seen as the root cause of the offensive war plans of the great powers. This argument does not mean that motivated biases, due to organizational or psychological factors, had no influence whatsoever on military doctrine prior to 1914. It does suggest that the states' strategic interests were dominant. For example, minor powers, such as Belgium and Serbia, may have had military cults of the offensive, but they did *not* have offensive military doctrines or war plans when war broke out in 1914.[37] In contrast, the great powers required offensive military doctrines because of their alliance commitments. This connection between alliance commitments and offensive doctrine was well understood in the years preceding the First World War. The Franco-Russian military convention, written in 1892, specified:

> If France is attacked by Germany or by Italy with Germany's support, Russia will bring all her available forces to bear against Germany. If Russia is attacked by Germany or by Austria with Germany's support, France will bring all her available forces to bear against Germany. . . . These troops will proceed to launch a vigorous and determined offensive, so that Germany will be forced to give battle in the East and West simultaneously.[38]

The spectre of Germany being able to defeat the French or the Russians in a piecemeal fashion haunted the allies before 1914: Joffre states that he replaced the more defensive-oriented Plan XVI with the offensive Plan XVII when he took office in part because the former failed to take into account "an eventuality which was altogether likely, namely, that the Germans might return to the old Von Moltke plan of an immediate offensive directed

[36]General Erich von Falkenhayn, *The German General Staff and Its Decisions, 1914–1916* (Freeport, N.Y.: Books for Libraries Press, 1971 reprint), p. 16.

[37]As Van Evera notes, some Belgian officers proposed that Belgium attack Germany at the outbreak of war. Van Evera, "The Cult of the Offensive and the Origins of the First world War," p. 61; and Van Evera, "Why Cooperation Failed in 1914," p. 84. It is important to note, however, that the "temerity of such an operation" was immediately pointed out by the Belgian Chief of Staff, and Belgium pursued a defensive strategy despite such "cult of the offensive" influences. The best discussion is Albertini, *The Origins of the War of 1914*, vol. 3, pp. 455–463, quoting Antonin Selliers de Moranville, *Contribution à l'histoire de la guerre mondiale 1914–19* (Paris, 1933), pp. 163–164.

[38]George Michon, *The Franco-Russian Alliance* (New York: Macmillan, 1929), p. 54.

against the Russians." Foreign Minister Poincaré promised the Russians in 1912 that France would launch an immediate offensive against Germany if war broke out and demanded that the Russians give similar assurances in writing. Furthermore, the French and Russian General Staffs specifically rejected the possibility of war being "conducted defensively" and confirmed the need for immediate offenses in their joint meetings in 1911, 1912, and 1913.[39]

Similarly, the Russian initial offensive against the Germans in 1914 demonstrates "wishful thinking" due to faith in the offensive less than the critical need to stop Germany from amassing its forces against France alone. According to Joffre, in 1912 Grand Duke Nicholas "fully understood the necessity of the Russian Army taking the offensive rapidly, whatever the risks such an attitude might seem to involve; for it was essential to bring some relief to our front at any price. . . ."[40] Thus, in the summer of 1914 Russian Foreign Minister Sazonov and the military commanders of the East Prussian front believed that a hasty offensive against Germany might indeed fail, but that, as Sazonov reportedly argued, "we have no right to leave our Ally in danger, and it is our duty to attack at once, notwithstanding the indubitable risk of the operation as planned."[41] The Chief of Staff of the Russian field army also stressed this point, telling his troops to attack Germany "by virtue of the same inter-allied obligations" that were demonstrated by the French offensive.[42]

The logic of the strategic situation was similarly understood in Germany. Offenses were required to support Austria-Hungary, albeit an offensive against France first, to be followed by the combined attack on Russia. When confronted with Austrian complaints that German offense in the West would leave them unprotected, Schlieffen responded that "the fate of Austria will be decided not on the Bug but on the Seine," a line that Moltke repeated to Conrad in February 1913.[43] The need for offensive action to protect Germany's ally was also the central argument of Moltke's urgent memorandum to Bethmann-Hollweg on July 29, 1914, written after Moltke learned that Russia had instituted only *partial* mobilization against Austria-Hungary:

[39] *The Personal Memoirs of Joffre* (New York: Harper and Brothers, 1932), Vol. 1, p. 20; Jan Karl Tannenbaum, "French Estimates of Germany's Operational War Plans," in Ernest R. May, ed., *Knowing One's Enemies: Intelligence Assessment Before the Two World Wars* (Princeton: Princeton University Press, 1984), pp. 167–168; Michon, *The Franco-Russian Alliance,* p. 54; and L.C.F. Turner, "The Russian Mobilization in 1914," in Paul M. Kennedy, ed., *The War Plans of the Great Powers, 1880–1914* (Boston: Allen & Unwin, 1979), pp. 256–258.

[40] *The Personal Memoirs of Joffre,* Vol. 1, p. 59.

[41] As quoted in Nicolas N. Golovine, *The Russian Army in the World War* (New Haven: Yale University Press, 1931), p. 213.

[42] Norman Stone, *The Eastern Front, 1914–1917* (New York: Scribner, 1975), p. 48.

[43] See Stone, "Moltke and Conrad: Relations between the Austro-Hungarian and German General Staffs, 1909–1914," pp. 224, 232.

If Germany is not to be false to her word and permit her ally to suffer annihilation at the hands of Russian superiority, she, too, must mobilize. And that would bring about the mobilization of the rest of Russia's military districts as a result.[44]

The German threat to Russia—that it would soon be forced to mobilize, which meant war, which meant the Schlieffen Plan's offensive, if Russia did not stop the *partial* mobilization against Austria-Hungary—underscores the importance of the alliance commitment in Berlin's calculations.[45] Moreover, it was the long-standing belief of the Russian military, which these threats reinforced in 1914, that the Germans would not passively tolerate Russian preparations for war against Austria-Hungary, which had led them to plan for and then in 1914 to insist upon, not a partial mobilization on the Austrian front, but rather a full mobilization against both Central Powers.[46] This decision was critical, for once the full mobilization of the Russian army began, Bethmann-Hollweg called off the attempt to avert war by having Austro-Hungarian forces "Halt in Belgrade." Thus, the alliance system—or more properly, the strategic interests the great powers had in maintaining their alliance partners—led not only to the offensive doctrines of 1914 but even to one of the specific conditions that contributed to the dynamic of rapid mobilization and counter-mobilization that constrained last minute efforts to prevent the outbreak of war.

The failure of the "cult of the offensive" theory to examine the influence of alliances on military doctrines is significant. While the theory has done a service by highlighting a number of the risks and instabilities that can result from offensive doctrines, it has ignored the risks and instabilities that result from purely defensive military strategies. For states with a security interest in preserving an exposed ally, offensive forces and strategies are necessary. Defensive military doctrines may not produce the same degree of preventive war or preemptive war incentives, but they can undercut extended deterrence by denying a government sufficient capability to protect its allies. As France discovered in 1938 and 1939, when the lack of offensive capabilities against Germany enabled Hitler to conquer France's East European allies in a piecemeal manner, a purely defensive military doctrine can also prove strategically disastrous.

---

[44]The Grand General Staff to the Imperial Chancellor, July 29, 1914, *German Documents*, No. 349, p. 307.

[45]See ibid., Nos. 342, 343, 401, and 490. It should be added, however, that both Bethmann-Hollweg and Jagow originally misled the Russians on this issue. See ibid., No. 219; and Albertini, *The Origins of the War of 1914*, Vol. 2, p. 481–485 and vol. 3, pp. 220–221.

[46]As General Kokovtzov put it, arguing against *partial* mobilization in 1912: "no matter what we chose to call the projected measures, a mobilization remained a mobilization, to be countered by our adversaries with actual war." Quoted in Turner, "The Russian Mobilization in 1914," p. 255. For detailed examinations of the interaction of mobilization plans, see Van Evera, "The Cult of the Offensive and the Origins of the First World War," pp. 85–94; and Ulrich Trumpener, "War Premeditated? German Intelligence Operations in July 1914," *Central European History*, Vol. 9, No. 1 (March 1976).

The Offensive/Defensive Balance of Military Technology

JACK S. LEVY

While many of the hypotheses regarding the consequences of the offensive/defensive balance are inherently plausible, there are critical analytical problems which must be resolved before they can be accepted as meaningful or valid. These problems have to do with the theoretical logic of the hypotheses, the definition of the offensive/defensive balance, and the empirical validity of the hypotheses.

The hypothesis that the likelihood of war is increased when the military technology favors the offense is theoretically plausible only on the basis of the rather strong assumption that decision makers correctly perceive the offensive/defensive balance. However, it is perceptions of one's psychological environment that determine decisions, not the 'objective' operational environment (Sprout and Sprout, 1965). The assumption of accurate perceptions is therefore open to question. The inherent difficulty of determining the offensive/defensive balance and the alleged tendency of the military to prepare for the last war rather than the next one may result in some profound misperceptions. It is widely agreed, for example, that in 1914 military technology favored the defense (Hart, 1932:75; Fuller, 1961: ch. 8–9; Montgomery, 1983:472) but that most decision makers perceived that it favored the offense. It was not the offensive/defensive balance that intensified worst-case analysis and increased the incentives for preemption, but decision mak-

Jack S. Levy, "The Offensive/Defensive Balance of Military Technology: A Theoretical and Historical Analysis," *International Studies Quarterly* Vol. 28, no. 2 (June 1984). Reprinted with permission of Blackwell Publishers.

ers' perceptions of that balance. If the offensive/defensive balance is not defined in terms of the perceptions of decision makers (and in most conceptualizations it is not so defined), then the hypothesis is technically misspecified. Hypotheses regarding the consequences of war, on the other hand, are properly defined in terms of the 'objective' balance.

The second problem relates to the definition of the offensive/defensive balance. What does it mean to say that the offense is superior to the defense, or *vice versa*? This will be treated at length in the following section, but one point should be made here. An hypothesis regarding the offensive/defensive balance has no explanatory power unless that concept can be nominally and operationally defined independently of its hypothesized effects. For example, Wright (1965:796–97) states that

> . . . it is difficult to judge the relative power of the offensive and defensive except by a historical audit to determine whether on the whole, in a given state of military technology, military violence had or had not proved a useful instrument of political change. . . . During periods when dissatisfied powers have, on the whole, gained their aims by a resort to arms, it may be assumed, on the level of grand strategy, that the power of the offensive has been greater. During the periods when they have not been able to do so, it may be assumed that the power of the grand strategic defensive has been greater.

It would be tautological to use this conception of the offensive/defensive balance to predict to the military success of the aggressor, though it would be legitimate to predict to the frequency of war. Similarly, it is meaningless to hypothesize that offensive superiority increases the incentive to strike first if the offensive/defensive balance is defined by the incentive to strike first. The separation of hypothesis construction from concept definition and the absence of rigorous definition has increased the dangers of tautological propositions.

The failure to subject these hypotheses to systematic empirical testing is another major problem. Most attempts to identify the offensive/defensive advantage in various historical eras are not guided by an explicit definition of the concept, and rarely is there a demonstration that a given balance had an effect on the frequency of wars occurring or on the decisions for a particular war. The apparent *a priori* plausibility of a particular hypothesis may derive more from its tautological construction than from its correspondence with reality. In the absence of a more thorough analytic treatment and a more systematic empirical analysis the validity of any of these hypotheses cannot be accepted.

Definitions of the Offensive/Defensive Balance

Use of the concept of offensive/defensive balance to refer to a variety of different things has led to a great deal of confusion. Theoretical propositions which are meaningful or interesting for one use of the term may not be very meaningful for another, and for this reason the various usages of the concept must be identified and examined.

Concern here is with the offensive/defensive distinction with respect to military technology and perhaps tactics but not with respect to policy. The question of whether national policy is offensive (aggressive) or defensive is not unimportant, but is analytically distinct and not directly relevant to the hypotheses surveyed earlier. These propositions all suggest that there is something about military technology itself that affects the likelihood or nature of war, and that what is important is whether technology gives an advantage to the offense or defense. This relative advantage may be one of several variables affecting the likelihood of war by affecting policy, but itself is analytically distinct from policy.

The offensive/defensive balance of military technology has been defined primarily in terms of the ease of territorial conquest, the characteristics of armaments, the resources needed by the offense in order to overcome the defense, and the incentive to strike first.

Territorial Conquest

The most common use of the concept of the offensive/defensive balance is based on territorial conquest and the defeat of enemy forces. Quester (1977:15) states that 'the territorial fixation then logically establishes our distinction between offense and defense.' Jervis (1978:187) argues that an offensive advantage means that 'it is easier to destroy the other's army and take its territory than it is to defend one's own.' 'The essence of defense,' on the other hand, 'is keeping the other side out of your territory. A purely defensive weapon is one that can do this without being able to penetrate the enemy's land' (1978:203). A defensive advantage means that 'it is easier to protect and hold than it is to move forward, destroy, and take' (Jervis, 1978:187). Wright (1965:793) includes these notions of defeat of enemy forces and territorial seizure in his rather complex definition:

> On a tactical level the offensive or defensive quality of a unit may be estimated by considering its utility in an attack upon an enemy unit like itself or in an attack upon some other concrete enemy objective, such as territory, commerce, or morale.

A primary purpose of protecting territory, of course, is the protection of people and property. What is perhaps implicit in the above definitions is made explicit by Tarr (1983): 'Defense refers to techniques and action, both active and passive, to repel attack, to protect people and property, to hold territory, and to minimize damage by the attacker.' This linkage of territorial conquest to population defense creates a problem, however. While territorial defense was sufficient for the protection of people and property in the pre-nuclear era (or at least in the era before strategic bombardment), that is no longer true. As Schelling (1966:ch. 1) and others have noted, the uniqueness of the nuclear age lies in the fact that the defeat of the adversary's military forces and territorial penetration are no longer necessary for the destruction of his population centers. The destruction of population and the coercive power that it makes possible are no longer contingent upon military victory. For this reason the protection of territory (from invasion) is analytically distinct from the protection of population. The inclusion of both in a definition of the offensive/defensive distinction only creates confusion (unless the use of that concept is explicitly restricted to the pre-nuclear era), for the hypothesized effects of an 'offensive' advantage are precisely the opposite for the two concepts. The likelihood of war presumably increases as territorial conquest becomes easier, because the probability of victory increases while its expected costs decrease. But the ability to destroy enemy population and industrial centers contributes to deterrence in the nuclear age, and therefore it decreases the likelihood of war (or at least nuclear war).

It is because of the distinction between deterrence and defense (Snyder, 1961:14–16) that the meaning of the offensive/defensive balance may differ in the nuclear and pre-nuclear eras. Whereas in the pre-nuclear era both deterrence and defense were based on the capacity to defeat the armed forces of the enemy, that is only true for defense in the nuclear age, for deterrence is ultimately based on countervalue punishment. The use of military force for the purpose of defeating enemy armed forces is analytically distinct from the use of force for coercion (Schelling, 1966:ch. 2). Consequently, traditional hypotheses (Wright and others) regarding the effects of the offensive/defensive balance of military technology are not necessarily applicable for nuclear powers at the strategic level. Neither the concepts nor the hypotheses are interchangeable.

Now let us return to the territorial conception of the offensive/defensive balance. Our earlier discussion leads to the question of what, besides the numbers of troops or weapons, contributes to the defeat of enemy forces and conquest of territory. One answer is provided at the tactical level, based on movement towards the armed forces, possessions, or territory of the enemy. A condition of relative passivity and immobility in waiting for the enemy to attack defines the strategic and tactical defensive (Wright, 1965:807). Clausewitz (as quoted in Boggs, 1941:68) states:

> What is defense in conception? The warding off a blow. What is then its characteristic sign? The state of expectancy (or of waiting for this blow) . . . by this sign alone can the defensive be distinguished from the offensive in war. . . .

Clausewitz also writes: 'In tactics every combat, great or small, is defensive if we leave the initiative to the enemy, and wait for his appearance on our front' (as quoted in Boggs, 1941:68).

Both offensive and defensive modes of war on the tactical level are necessary, of course, for the achievement of either offensive or defensive objectives. The pursuit of any offensive goal requires a supporting defense, and the defense alone can never bring victory but only stalemate. Mahan refers to 'the fundamental principle of naval war, that defense is insured only by offence' (Boggs, 1941:70). Clausewitz writes that an absolute defense is an 'absurdity' which 'completely contradicts the idea of war' (Boggs, 1941:71). At some point it is necessary to seize the tactical offensive in order to avoid defeat. Thus the familiar maxim: the best defense is a good offense. It is necessary, however, to distinguish between the strategic and tactical levels. A general fighting offensively in strategic terms needs only to invade and then hold territory to enable him to adopt the tactical defensive (Strachan, 1983). It may be strategically advantageous to maneuver the enemy into a position in which he is forced to take the tactical offensive under unfavorable conditions. As the elder Moltke stated in 1865, 'our strategy must be offensive, our tactics defensive' (Dupuy, 1980:200). In addition, military tactics may be offensive in one theater and defensive in another. The Schlieffen Plan, for example, required a holding action against Russia in the east in order to move against France in the west. Nevertheless, with certain types of weapons systems more movement and tactical mobility is possible than with others. It is difficult to measure movement historically while controlling for non-technological factors, however. This leads us to the question of whether the offensive/defensive balance can be defined by the characteristics of weapons systems themselves.

The Characteristics of Armaments

While nearly all weapons can be used for either the strategic or tactical offensive or the strategic or tactical defensive, the question is whether there are some weapons systems which contribute disproportionately more to one than to the other. As stated by the Naval Commission of the League of Nations Conference for the Reduction and Limitation of Armaments (1932–1936) (Boggs, 1941:82):

> Supposing one state either a) adopts a policy of armed aggression or b) undertakes offensive operations against another state, what are the weapons which, by reason of their specific character, and without prejudice to their defensive purposes, are most likely to enable that policy or those operations to be brought rapidly to a successful conclusion?

Hart (1932:73) argues that certain weapons 'alone make it possible under modern conditions to make a decisive offensive against a neighboring country.' What are the characteristics of such weapons?

Both Fuller and Hart identify mobility, striking power, and protection as the essential characteristics of an offensive weapon (Wright, 1965:808). Striking power (the impact of the blow) is not alone sufficient. A mobile gun contributes more to the tactical offensive than an immobile one, and its penetrating power is further enhanced if it is protected. But protection is even more important for the defense. Mobility and protection are inversely related, for it is easier to protect immobile weapons and wait passively for the enemy to attack. The offensive value of the medieval knight ultimately was negated by the heavy armor which protected him but restricted his mobility. Thus Dupuy and Eliot (1937:103) give particular emphasis to the offensive advantages of mobility and striking power, noting that they too may be in conflict. Boggs (1941:84–85) argues that 'the defense disposes especially of striking power and protection, to a lesser degree of mobility, while the offense possesses mobility and striking power, and protection to a lesser degree.' He concludes that mobility is the central characteristic of an offensive weapon and argues that 'armament which greatly facilitates the forward movement of the attacker might be said tentatively to possess relatively greater offensive power than weapons which contribute primarily to the stability of the defender' (Boggs, 1941:85). Our later survey of attempts by military historians to identify the offensive/defensive balance in various historical eras will show that tactical mobility is the primary criterion used to identify an advantage to the offense.

In terms of the characteristics of armaments, then, tactical mobility and movement toward enemy forces and territory are the primary determinants of the offense, at least in land warfare; protection and holding power contribute more to the defense. Other weapon characteristics such as striking power, rapidity of fire, and the range of a weapons system do not contribute disproportionately to either the offense or the defense. Much more work needs to be done here, however, because of the lack of precision of some of these concepts.

The classification of weapons systems by their contribution to mobility and tactical movement toward enemy forces and territory is much less useful for naval warfare. This was evident from the proceedings of the League of Nations Conference for the Reduction and Limitation of Armaments, where the problems and disagreements confronting the Naval Commission were even more serious than those confronting the Land Commission and where technical arguments were even more likely to follow the flag (Boggs, 1941:50–60). The United States, among others, declared that the qualitative distinction could not be applied to navies. Hart, a proponent of the qualitative principle in general, restricted it to the materials of land warfare (Boggs, 1941:50, 81). The main problem with attempts to apply these principles of mobility and tactical movement to naval warfare is the absence of anything comparable to the territorial standard occurring in land warfare. The command of the seas, the ultimate objective of naval warfare (Mahan, 1957), can be served by passive as well as aggressive action, for the neutralization of the enemy fleet by a blockade may serve the same function as its defeat. Moreover, aggressive action toward the enemy fleet does not always result in battle, for an inferior navy can often avoid battle without sacrificing major territorial objectives, unlike land warfare.

Application of the territorially-based criterion of tactical mobility to aerial weapons systems raises the question of whether the offensive or defensive character of these weapons is determined independently of land warfare or by their contribution to the defeat of enemy ground forces and territorial conquest. Many aerial weapons systems do contribute to the tactical offensive on the ground because of their striking power, mobility, and surprise (for example, in the Nazi *blitzkrieg*). Yet air power also has an independent capability to destroy the enemy's war making industrial capabilities, and hence contributes to deterrence in the nuclear age. This deterrent effect of air power takes place independently of its effect on the tactical offensive on the ground but cannot easily be incorporated into a conception of the offensive/defensive balance based on tactical mobility.

Some armaments that traditionally have been considered as defensive and therefore assumed to be 'stabilizing' (in the sense that they discourage aggression and reduce the likelihood of war) are often considered to be destabilizing in the nuclear age. Air defenses, anti-ballistic missile defenses, and even civil defenses are considered under the prevailing strategic doctrine to be destabilizing because by protecting populations they threaten to undermine deterrence. This reinforces our earlier point that the hypothesized consequences of a military technology favoring the offense (or the defense) may not be interchangeable between the nuclear and pre-nuclear eras.

The definition of the offensive/defensive balance, in terms of the characteristics of armaments, raises other questions as well. One is whether it is possible to define the offensive/defensive character of a weapon by its intrinsic performance characteristics alone, apart from the prevailing doctrine that determines it use. For example, essentially the same tank that was used in much of World War I as protected fire support was used in World War II as the organizing element of mobile offensive warfare (Fuller, 1945:ch. VI). The offensive character of Napoleonic warfare was due far more to the innovative tactics of Napoleon than to weapons systems themselves (Howard, 1976:75–76; Preston and Wise, 1979:189–191). It must be concluded that the offensive or defensive character of a weapons system must be defined by both its intrinsic characteristics and the tactical doctrine which determines its use.

What is important, of course, is not the characteristics of an individual weapon, but rather the aggregate impact of all weapons systems in a given arsenal. How is a given mixture of armaments, designed for different purposes and deployed for use in different theaters on land, sea, and air, to be aggregated so that their net effect on the offense and defense can be classified? This overall impact cannot be determined apart from the composition of an enemy's weapons systems and the terrain where the combat takes place. The offensive value of the tank, for example, was reduced by the development of new anti-tank technologies in the early 1970s. To complicate matters further, most hypotheses relating to the offensive/defensive balance treat that concept as a systemic-level attribute (the hypotheses that offensive superiority contributes to an increased frequency of war and to empire-building, for example). They suggest that at a given time the offensive/defensive balance can be characterized by a single value throughout the system. The balance must be aggregated not only over all weapons, functional roles, and theaters for a given state, but also over all states in the system. This is difficult given differential levels of industrialization and military power, uneven rates of technological diffusion, and doctrinal differences among various states in the system. Some of these problems are minimized, however, if the focus is restricted to the leading powers in the system, because they are often comparable in terms of power and technology.

Relative Resources Expended

Gilpin distinguishes between the offense and the defense in terms of an economic cost-benefit framework. 'To speak of a shift in favor of the offense means that fewer resources than before must be expended on the offense in order to overcome the defense' (Gilpin, 1981:62–63). Gilpin goes on to say that 'the defense is said to be superior if the resources required to capture territory are greater than the value of the territory itself; the offense is superior if the cost of conquest is less than the value of the territory' (p. 63).

Clearly the second definition does not follow from the first. Whereas the first uses the relative costs of overcoming the defense at two different times and independently of the resulting benefits, the second definition introduces an entirely new concept—the actual value of the territorial conquest itself. The value of territorial conquest is undoubtedly an important variable leading to war but it is analytically distinct from military technology and ought to be treated separately. Under Gilpin's second definition the hypothesis becomes equivalent to the statement that a positive (expected) utility of territorial conquest increases the likelihood of war. This may be true (Bueno de Mesquita, 1981), but it is not the hypothesis under consideration here. Moreover, the definition of the offensive/defensive balance by the utility of territorial conquest reduces to a tautology the hypothesis that offensive superiority increases the utility of territorial conquest.

One of the two conceptualizations of the offensive/defensive balance suggested by Jervis is more consistent with Gilpin's first formulation. Jervis (1978:188) poses the question as follows: 'Does the state have to spend more or less than one dollar on defensive forces to offset each dollar spent by the other side on forces that could be used to attack?' That is, what is the relative marginal utility of devoting military spending to the offense rather than to the defense? This approach is potentially valuable, but it is incomplete. It defines what it means to say that the offense (or the defense) has an advantage, but fails to provide any criteria for specifying what constitutes the offense or the defense in the first place. The marginal utilities cannot be compared until the offense and defense are first defined, and until this is done the concept is not particularly useful.

The definition of the offensive/defensive balance by the relative re-sources that must be expended on the offense in order to overcome the de-fense can be conceptualized in another way and related to the conception based on territorial conquest. This refers to attack/defense ratios rather than military spending. What ratio of troops does an attacker need in order to overcome an enemy defending fixed positions? This notion is mentioned but not developed by Quester (1977:212): 'The significant impact of defen-sive or offensive technology shows up in the minimum ratios of numerical superiority required for such an offensive.' It follows the same logic as Foch's comment regarding the power of the offensive prior to World War I: 'Formerly many guns were necessary to produce an effect. Today a few suf-fice' (Montross, 1960:686). The conventional wisdom is that the offense needs at least a three-to-one advantage, but the point here is that this ratio varies as a function of existing military technology and the tactical doctrine guiding its use. The offensive/defensive balance is then defined as being in-versely proportional to the minimum ratio of forces needed by the attacker in order to overcome an adversary defending fixed positions. The greater the minimum ratio, the greater the advantage of the defense.

It is important to note here that the minimum *ratio* of forces needed by the attacker in a particular era is analytically distinct from the relative *num-bers* of forces actually possessed by two adversaries in a particular situation. The probability of victory is a function of both. To say that the balance of military technology (as a function of attack/defense ratios) favors the of-fense does *not* mean the attacker is likely to win. That would be true only if the attacker actually possessed the requisite number of troops in a particular situation.

The problem arises as to what ratio should be used as a baseline, the zero-point indicating the transition from a defensive advantage to an offensive advantage. The most obvious ratio is one to one, but that is widely regarded as favoring the defense. While it would not be technically incorrect to say that the balance always favors the defense because the attacker always re-quires numerical superiority, this is neither interesting nor useful. If the of-fensive/defensive balance is defined as attack/defense ratios, it is preferable to conceive of this in relative rather than absolute terms. It is useful to speak of shifts in the balance and to compare the balance at different times, but not to speak about the absolute state of the balance. Thus the hypothesis should technically state that 'the higher the minimum ratio of forces needed by the attacker in order to overcome an adversary defending fixed positions, the lower the likelihood of war.'

This conception of the offensive/defensive balance is more useful than the others surveyed above, at least for land warfare. The attack/defense ratio could be measured in one of two ways. It could be determined empirically from an analysis of a variety of battles in a given era, with the force ratios and results determined for each and some kind of average computed. The prob-lem, of course, would be the need to control for asymmetries in geography, troop quality, and doctrine. Alternatively, the ratio could be conceived in perceptual terms and measured by the perceptions of military and political elites of what ratio of forces is necessary for either attack or defense. While this information is not readily available it might be inferred from an examination of the war plans of the leading states. The methodological problems involved in either of these approaches are quite serious, however.

The Incentive to Strike First

One of the questions asked by Jervis (1978:188) of the offensive/defensive balance is the following: 'With a given inventory of forces, is it better to attack or to defend? Is there an incentive to strike first or to absorb the other's blow?' This conceptualization is more flexible than earlier criteria based on tactical mobility and characteristics of armaments because it can incorporate considerations of deterrence and be applied to the nuclear age. It creates some problems, however, which Jervis may recognize but does not fully develop. For one thing, the hypothesis that a military technology favoring the offense increases the incentive to strike first is reduced to a tautology and hence carries no explanatory power. In focusing attention on the linkage between the incentive to strike first and war, it ignores the more basic question of what conditions create an incentive to strike first. These antecedent conditions possess the greatest explanatory power and operate through the intervening variable of the incentive to strike first. This leads to a related problem: there are numerous factors besides technology and doctrine affecting the incentive to strike first, including geographic constraints and diplomatic and domestic political considerations, factors which also have an independent effect on war. If the offensive/defensive balance is *defined* as the incentive to strike first, then it becomes confounded with these other variables and it becomes impossible to distinguish their independent effects. The incentive to strike first is best conceptualized as an intervening variable leading to war and as the product of several distinct variables, one of which is military technology and doctrine. One key issue is to elaborate the aspects of military technology or doctrine which affect the incentives to strike first, but this cannot be fully analyzed here.

It is important to distinguish the incentive to strike first from other concepts that have also been used to define the offensive/defensive balance. The incentive to strike first should not be confused with aggressive policy, which is influenced by a wide range of variables. A state may have revisionist ambitions but be constrained by a military technology favoring the tactical defense, as well as by other variables. Or, a state with purely defensive ambitions may rationally initiate war if it perceives that through a preemptive strike it can minimize its losses against an assumed aggressor. The distinction between the incentive to strike first and seizing territory is particularly likely to be confused. These are clearly distinct for naval and air warfare (particularly in the nuclear age) but the difference is more profound. One may simultaneously have a policy of not striking first *and* a strategy of active defense and territorial penetration in the event that war does break out. This was Bismarck's policy in the 1870s and 1880s (Langer, 1964) and perhaps Israel's in 1973. Germany's Schlieffen Plan called for passive defense (holding ground) in the East and rapid territorial penetration in northern France regardless of who initiated the war.

The failure to recognize these distinctions only creates confusion and may result in the incorrect use of hypotheses designed for other purposes. Hypotheses appropriate for a territorially-based definition of the offensive/defensive balance of military technology may not be valid for a definition based on the incentive to strike first. While the ease of territorial seizure may shorten wars and lower their costs (Wright, 1965:673), this may not necessarily be true for the incentive to strike first. Nor is an incentive to strike first in the nuclear age likely to have the same consequences as an attack/defense ratio which favors the offense. Further, it is not clear that the incentive to strike first itself has the same causes or consequences in the pre-nuclear period as it does in the nuclear age, though this might be an interesting area for future research.

The same types of problems arise with respect to the various other conceptualizations of the offensive/defensive balance examined above. The concept has been defined in terms of the defeat of enemy armed forces, territorial conquest, protection of population, tactical mobility, the characteristics of armaments, attack/defense ratios, the relative resources expended on the offense and the defense, and the incentive to strike first. These separate definitions are often not interchangeable, and hypotheses based on one definition are often either implausible or tautological for another definition. This is particularly true for applications of the offensive/defensive balance to the nuclear age. Because the most advanced weapons of this era are used primarily for coercive purposes and the weapons of earlier eras were used primarily to engage enemy armed forces, the concept of the offensive/defensive balance of military technology may mean entirely different things in the two different situations. Certainly one reason for the confusion and ambiguity among these hypotheses is the fact that they are based on common concepts such as 'offense', 'aggressor', and 'initiator' which have ordinary language meanings apart from more precise technical meanings. This is all the more reason why any attempt to use such a concept must first define it explicitly and be very clear regarding precisely which hypotheses are relevant.

Classification of the Offensive/Defensive Balance in History

The third section of this article surveys a variety of efforts to classify the offensive/defensive balance of military technology in the Western international system over the last eight centuries. This survey will be useful because of the absence of any previous review of this body of literature and because of the general failure of earlier studies to acknowledge or build upon each other. More importantly, it may reveal whether or not the concept has acquired an informal definition in its empirical application, in spite of the conceptual ambiguity demonstrated above. While the concept of the offensive/defensive balance of military technology has taken on a variety of meanings, the question arises as to how the concept has been used in attempts to classify the offensive/defensive balance in past historical eras. If different authorities have generally used the offensive/defensive balance to mean the same thing (even in the absence of any formal nominal or operational definition), and if they have generally agreed on the state of the balance in various historical eras, then it can be concluded that the ambiguity of the concept has not precluded its effective use in empirical analysis. Consistent usage and agreement by various authorities on the state of the balance in different historical eras would permit 'intercoder agreement' to be used as the basis for accurate historical measurement (provided these measurements are independent). Lack of agreement on classification, however, would suggest that the collective judgment of authorities cannot be used as the basis for measurement. It would also support the earlier conclusion that the offensive/defensive concept needs to be defined much more explicitly and rigorously before it can be used in historical analysis. . . .

[*At this point in the original article Levy includes a survey of several pages on varying interpretations of the offense/defense balance in several historical epochs.* (Ed.)]

There is unanimous agreement among the references cited that the period from 1200 to 1450 was characterized by defensive superiority and that the period from 1450 to 1525 was characterized by offensive superiority. The authorities are split on the 1525 to 1650 period. There is complete agreement that the defense was superior from 1650 to 1740. Some argue that this defensive superiority continues until 1789, though Frederick's emphasis on the tactical offensive leads some to assert the opposite and others to make no specific evaluation. The 1789 to 1815 period is generally regarded to favor the offense but because of innovations in tactics rather than armaments. Little attention is given to the 1815–1850 period. The next hundred years pose a problem because of the gap between the objective and perceived balance and the uncertain conceptual status of the latter. These authorities generally agree that from 1850 to 1925 or so the balance favored the defense but that nearly all statesmen perceived that it favored the offense from 1870 to 1914. Similarly, from 1930 to 1945 the balance favored the offense but that the actors themselves perceived that it favored the defense.

A rough calculation shows the following degree of consensus among our authorities. Of the 450 years from 1495–1945, only two periods totaling 55 years claim a definite consensus of offensive superiority. Two periods totaling at most 130 years claim a consensus of defensive superiority. Four periods constituting a minimum of 265 years are uncertain, either because of diverging views, or because of the diametric opposition of the evaluations of actors and analysts and the ambiguous conceptual status of perceptions in definitions of the balance. The inescapable conclusion is that there exists considerable divergence of opinion among leading authorities regarding the offensive/defensive balance during the last five centuries of the modern era, and that a method of 'intercoder agreement' cannot be used to provide a basis for classification during this period. . . .

To conclude, the concept of the offensive/defensive balance is too vague and encompassing to be useful in theoretical analysis. Many of the individual variables that have been incorporated into the more general idea may themselves be useful, however. Few would doubt the utility for deterrence theory of the concept of the incentive to strike first, for example, and the concept of attack/defense ratios suggested here deserves further exploration. Much more conceptualization is necessary before these individual variables can be effectively used in empirical analysis, however. There is already a body of theory regarding the consequences of an incentive to strike first. What is needed are comparable theories regarding the consequences of military technologies which contribute to tactical mobility or to the ease of territorial conquest, or which reduce the ratio of forces needed by the attacker to overcome an adversary defending fixed positions. Interaction effects between these separate variables also need to be explored. Further theoretical development of this kind is necessary, because in its absence there is little reason to believe that these individual concepts have an important impact on war, and therefore little reason to use these concepts in empirical analysis.

References

Boggs, M. W. (1941) 'Attempts to Define and Limit "Aggressive" Armament in Diplomacy and Strategy.' *University of Missouri Studies*, XVI, No. 1. Columbia, Missouri.

Bueno de Mesquita, B. (1981) *The War Trap*. New Haven: Yale University Press.

Dupuy, R. E. and G. F. Eliot (1937) *If War Comes*. New York: Macmillan.

Dupuy, T. N. (1980) *The Evolution of Weapons and Warfare*. Bloomington: Indiana University Press.

Fuller, J. F. C. (1945) *Armament and History*. New York: Charles Schribner's Sons.

———. (1961) *The Conduct of War, 1789–1961*. New Brunswick: Rutgers University Press.

Gilpin, R. (1981) *War and Change in World Politics*. Cambridge: Cambridge University Press.

Hart, B. H. L. (1964) *Strategy*. New York: Praeger.

Howard, M. (1976) *War in European History*. New York: Oxford University Press.

———. (1983) *Clausewitz*. Oxford: Oxford University Press.

Jervis, R. (1978) 'Cooperation Under the Security Dilemma.' *World Politics* 30: 167–214.

Langer, W. L. (1964) *European Alliances and Alignments, 1871–1890,* 2nd ed. New York: Vintage Books.

Mahan, A. T. (1957) *The Influences of Sea Power Upon History, 1660–1783.* New York: Hill and Wang.

Montgomery of Alamein, V. (1983) *A History of Warfare.* New York: William Morrow.

Montross, L. (1960) *War Through the Ages,* 3rd ed., rev. New York: Harper & Row.

Preston, R. A. and S. F. Wise (1979) *Men in Arms.* New York: Holt, Rinehart and Winston.

Quester, G. H. (1977) *Offense and Defense in the International System.* New York: Wiley.

Schelling, T. C. (1966) *Arms and Influence.* New Haven: Yale University Press.

Snyder, G. H. (1961) *Deterrence and Defense.* Princeton: Princeton University Press.

Sprout, H. and M. Sprout (1965) *The Ecological Perspective on Human Affairs.* Princeton: Princeton University Press.

Strachan, H. (1983) *European Armies and the Conduct of War.* London: George Allen & Unwin.

Tarr, D. (1984) 'Defense as Strategy: A Conceptual Analysis,' in S. J. Cimbala (ed.) *National Security Strategy.* New York: Praeger.

Wright, Q. (1949) 'Modern Technology and the World Order,' in W. F. Ogburn (ed.) *Technology and International Relations.* Chicago: University of Chicago Press.

———. (1965) *A Study of War,* rev. ed. Chicago: Chicago University Press.

Arms Control:
The Historical Experience

CHARLES H. FAIRBANKS, JR.
AND ABRAM N. SHULSKY

A new transformation of the arms control debate has overtaken us, though we are only half aware of it. This transformation is the gradual return of radical arms control, of proposals for real reductions in various categories of weapons or their complete elimination: the "zero option" for intermediate-range nuclear force (INF) systems, "deep cuts" for strategic offensive arms, the Reykjavik proposals to abolish all ballistic missiles, all strategic offensive arms, or eventually all nuclear weapons. (The Strategic Defense Initiative, while not an arms control measure as such, nevertheless proposes to make nuclear weapons "impotent and obsolete.") Perhaps this return to more radical arms control proposals has been obscured by its paradoxical relation to the conventional view that the Reagan administration is more skeptical of arms control than its predecessors.

This trend represents not so much a totally new direction in the history of arms control as a return on a different plane to the older notions of disarmament which, during the past 18 years, since the beginning of the near-continuous Strategic Arms Limitation Talks (SALT) with the Soviet Union, had been eclipsed by a more sophisticated notion of arms control as, in effect, a jointly-managed process by which both sides' arms development programs were to some extent stabilized or, at least, directed into more desirable channels.

Charles H. Fairbanks, Jr., and Abram N. Shulsky, "From 'Arms Control' to Arms Reductions: The Historical Experience," *Washington Quarterly* Vol. 10, no. 3 (Summer 1987). Reprinted by permission of the MIT Press, Cambridge, Massachusetts.

Faced with proposals for radical reductions in arms levels, it is surprising how little public discussion there has been of their wisdom and desirability. A major reason appears to be the prevalence of the notion that the danger of international tension or war comes not so much, or at all, from any given level (quantitative or qualitative) of arms, but from their uncontrolled growth—that is, from the "arms race." Thus, for example, the apparent views of the nuclear freeze movement, which seemed oblivious to the significance or consequences of any given level of armaments, but was concerned solely with stopping any increase in that level.

Our focus on arms races, and on arms control as a means of "stopping" them, has resulted in a lack of attention to the question of what role given levels of armaments play in maintaining a given international system, and what the consequences of radically reducing those levels are likely to be. Proposals for deep reductions, or for the elimination of classes of armaments, force us to look more carefully at these questions.

As a way of beginning to think about this problem—not so much a new issue as a new way of looking at a perennial one—we will look at several instances of deep reductions in, or steady and low levels of, armaments to see what kinds of issues they raise and what kinds of (mainly unintended) consequences they may have.

If we are entering an age of deep cuts, or even an age in which the arms control agenda centers on deep cuts, we must become more aware of the historical experience of deep reductions in all its diversity: not only of deep reductions that come through bilateral arms control agreements, but also deep reductions imposed on one side (as in the Versailles Treaty), of demobilizations (bilateral but not by agreement), and cases where countries have simply decided to make deep reductions in their own forces.

Demobilization: The USSR, 1945–1948

We can begin with demobilizations—probably the deepest cuts in our experience that are based on a nation's own choice. In the case of the Soviet Union after World War II, the ability to choose force levels freely was particularly great because the other great military powers, with the exception of the United States and Britain, had been shattered by the war. A far-reaching Soviet demobilization did take place, with army divisions of all types being cut down from 455 to 175, many of which would have needed to be brought back up to strength by remobilization before they could fight. Military aircraft decreased from 20,000 to 13,000.[1] The navy, reduced during the war to a marginal supplement to the ground forces, may have actually grown in mobilizable strength. Scrappings were offset by the transfer of many German and Japanese ships.

[1]Alexander Boyd, *The Soviet Air Force Since 1918* (New York: Stein and Day, 1977), pp. 180, 216.

There was thus a transformation of Soviet force posture, due to the fact that the air force and navy were not demobilized to the same extent as the ground forces. (One can compare this to the United States, where the Army Air Corps was reduced by three quarters, from 79,000 to 20,000.) Another way of expressing the same fact would be to say that, as a result of demobilization, Soviet forces suddenly became much more technology-intensive; elements of the armed forces reliant on high-technology weapons became much more important relative to the other elements. This shift took place on a much broader and deeper scale within many of the services. In the ground forces, for example, the ratio in 1945 of infantry division to tank and mechanized divisions had been ten to one. By 1947 it became two to one, a vast change in the character of the force.[2] The changes within the division were also great, as a recent book by Marshal Pavlovskii makes clear:

> In the table of organization of the [rifle] division was included a tank/self-propelled regiment, and in the rifle regiment a battery of SU76's. As a result of the change in establishments and the exchange of old weapons for new models the weight of the volley of a division's artillery and mortars grew *already by the end of 1946*, in comparison with 1944, from 1589 to 3500 kilograms, and the [small arms] shots per minute from 491,000 to 652,000. . . . The division as organized in 1948 already had 1,488 trucks, tank transporters and tractors, while in 1944 there were only 419 trucks and tractors.[3]

Such was the consequence of a deep reduction, Soviet demobilization. Of course, it is likely that a force in which the balance of elements was so different would require a different organization (that the air force and navy would obtain greater autonomy, for example). More tanks and trucks would tend to create more mobile tactics, and so forth; many ripples spread outward from the basic cut.

Why did Soviet demobilization bring such wide transformations in Soviet forces? One possibility is, of course, that Stalin decided to create a stronger rather than weaker military establishment. But there are reasons inherent in the situation, and seen in other countries, why demobilization tends to create such transformations to a greater or lesser degree. First, the demands of economic recovery drew more on the manpower in the army than any other part of the military structure. Second, the very nature of the forces is likely to create disproportionate shrinkage in the infantry. Tanks and planes do not want to go home at the end of the war, but men do. Finally, organizational interests (as well as desire for military strength) tend to go in the direction of retaining the best equipment within the shrunken structure of the active forces, thus raising their relative technological level.

---

[2]Cristann Gibson, "Patterns of Demobilization: the US and USSR after World War II," unpublished Ph.D. dissertation, University of Denver, 1983, p. 210.

[3]I.G. Pavlovskii, *Sukhoputniye voiska USSR* (Moscow: Voenizdat, 1985), p. 210.

In demobilizations, a cut is not just a cut. It is a massive disruption of an interconnected system made up of soldiers, organizations, weapons, reserves, supplies, and the tactics and strategy by which all these elements are employed. Thus demobilizations inevitably force deep cuts in some units, lesser cuts in other units, and increases in still others, leading to a general transformation of the military forces. If, for example, there are tanks in wartime armored formations that were not needed there in peacetime, but are reassigned to infantry divisions, the infantry divisions will need new logistics and maintenance units. This transformation is strongly shaped by the outside environment, by the needs of the economy, the desires of men who want to go home, or (certainly in Stalin's case) the opportunities and exigencies of the international situation.

Perhaps it is also true that the deeper the cut—and the cuts in demobilization are very deep—the greater the disruption of the system, and the greater the transformation finally produced.

The Effects of Low Armament Levels: The 1920s and 1930s

The last great period of history in which most nations' armaments levels were low was the 1920s: in Germany because of the arms limitations imposed on it in the Versailles Treaty, and in British (and to a lesser extent, French and Soviet) ground forces and air forces, because, given German weakness, there did not seem to be a threat. The case of the British, U.S., and Japanese navies, limited by the Washington Naval Arms Agreements, is discussed below. This period is thus important for understanding what reductions to low (or, in the case of Germany with respect to certain weapon systems, zero) levels of arms might mean.

Following World War I, Britain disarmed "explosively," with the exception of the brief naval arms race with the United States and Japan, which was ended by the Washington Naval Conference. At the end of demobilization, in October 1921, Britain had three air squadrons at home (other than those equipped solely for support of ground forces). The army, intended strictly for colonial wars, was far weaker in strength that could be mobilized for European service than it was before 1914.

It is easy to see why Britain acted as it did. There was great hope that the post–World War I peace settlement, including the creation of the League of Nations, would in fact achieve the war aim—an end to war—proclaimed by the victors during the fighting. This hope was encapsulated in the well-known "Ten Years' Rule," adopted by the cabinet in 1919 and confirmed, in this more definitive form, in 1928: "It should be assumed, in framing the Estimates of the Fighting Services, that at any given date there will be no major war for ten years."[4] Britain thus assumed that the favorable conditions it enjoyed (ultimately due to Germany's willingness to respect, more or less, the arms limitation provisions of the Versailles Treaty) would change only gradually. Britain further seemed to assume that its own disarmament would not tend to weaken this German willingness.

Britain was confronted in 1933 with German "breakout." The German aircraft production plan, adopted in June 1933, four months after Hitler came to power, envisaged moving from no air force to parity with Britain (51 squadrons) in a little over two years (by fall 1935). By November 1934 British intelligence had estimated the goal of this plan correctly, and unofficial British estimates were far higher. But by this time there was a new German plan, adopted in March 1934, which was aiming at a strength of 243 squadrons in four years, on the basis of a production of 17,015 aircraft (including 2,887 bombers and 2,225 fighters).[5]

German rearmament differed from any of the arms races before World War I or after World War II in that it violated an arms control treaty that had been imposed on Germany. One might have thought that its illicit character would have made France and Britain more reactive. This does not seem to have been the case. The buildup of the German armed forces was not officially proclaimed until 1935, though known to everyone. Although it was in violation of Germany's treaty obligations, Britain and France were at a loss as to what to do about it.

This is an important case for understanding the full problem involved in the violation of arms control agreements. U.S. writing on this question has tended to identify the problem posed by violation of arms control agreements with the problem of verification or detection of infringements. The case of German rearmament points out that there is at least as great a problem in what to do about arms control violations once detected.[6] As A.J.P. Taylor has pointed out, the disarmament of Germany "could only work with the cooperation of the German government":

> German disarmament worked if the Germans chose to make it work. And if not? Once more the Allies were faced with the problem of enforcement. The Germans had this measureless advantage that they could undermine the sys-

---

[4]N.H. Gibbs, *Rearmament Policy*, vol. I of *Grand Strategy, History of the Second World War*, United Kingdom Military History Series, Her Majesty's Stationery Office, London, 1977, p. 58.

[5]Edward L. Homze, *Arming the Luftwaffe: The Reich Air Ministry and the German Aircraft Industry, 1919–1939* (Lincoln, Nebraska: University of Nebraska Press, 1976), p. 75; Gibbs, *Rearmament Policy*, p. 136; R.J. Overy, "The German Pre-War Aircraft Production Plans: November 1936–April 1939," *The English Historical Review*, Vol. XC, no. 357 (October 1975), pp. 778–780.

[6]For a full discussion of this issue, see Fred C. Iklé, "After Detection—What?" in *Foreign Affairs*, vol. 39, no. 2 (January 1961), pp. 208–220.

tem of security against them merely by doing nothing; by not paying reparations and by not disarming. They could behave as an independent country normally behaves.[7]

Any British or French effort at enforcing German disarmament demanded an effort vaguely comparable to that of a war, and ran up against the problem that it offended contemporary customs of international good behavior. In this situation, the common British reaction was to try to trade legitimization of the German rearmament already accomplished for a halt to future rearmament.[8] As British Foreign Secretary Sir John Simon remarked in 1934 in a cabinet paper:

> If the alternative to legalizing German rearmament was to prevent it, there would be everything to be said for not legalizing it. But the alternative to legalizing it is for German rearmament to continue just the same. . . . The party that is bound [by disarmament agreements] has already burst his chains and nobody is going to put the shackles on him again.[9]

Although unwilling to enforce the Versailles Treaty provisions limiting German armaments, the Western allies did react by looking to their own rearmament. Successive British air armament programs called for rapid increases in air strength in response to what seemed to be the most worrying and most "strategic" threat from Germany, the establishment and rapid growth of the Luftwaffe.

The responsiveness of British air programs to estimates of German programs is sufficient to show that German aerial rearmament created enormous fear. The 1930s is obviously a case in which an arms race helped create tension. Upon examination, however, it appears that the instability created was not unrelated to the prior situation of low levels of armaments.

The intense fear of German air power was conditioned by the antagonistic political aims expressed by the German government and by the fact that German rearmament was emphasizing the quintessentially high-technology area of air power. In part, this fear was conditioned by the particular exaggeration of the effectiveness of bombing current in the 1930s. It also probably stemmed from the tendency to view air power as the single variable which best embodied the measure of a nation's overall military might.

But a very important precondition of the fear produced by German aerial rearmament was that this was not only illegal but unusually rapid rearmament. The building up of the Luftwaffe, completely forbidden (unlike the army) to Germany under the Versailles Treaty, produced what Tom Brown

---

[7]A.J.P. Taylor, *Origins of the Second World War*, pp. 28, 31.
[8]Gibbs, *Rearmament Policy*, pp. 141–142, 160.
[9]Ibid.

has called an "arms panic," as opposed to an arms race—an explosive mutual increase of weapons.[10] The rapidity of the German rearmament in the air was connected with its technological character. Viewed from outside, equipment rather than personnel determines the strength of an air force or a navy. Therefore mere production—the normal activity of industrial society—can, when shifted to aircraft, create a very quick impression of increased strength. The tremendous fear and tension generated by the revival of the Luftwaffe was grounded in this characteristic of industrial society. In the 1930s there was very little discussion, except to some degree in military circles, of the necessarily inadequate training and readiness of the new German air force; people were dazzled by the sudden appearance of equipment where there was none before.

Thus the rapidity of German aerial rearmament created the greatest fear. In other highly technological areas where the change of balance could not be rapid—as in the naval rearmament of the various powers—much less fear was created. These facts suggest an important point about arms control. The arms race in the air frightened people precisely because it moved so rapidly, and it moved so rapidly because it began from a very low level. In the case of Britain and France, a minute proportion of industrial effort was devoted to the air force. World War II showed that the major industrial states had the potential to produce military aircraft in the range of 25,000–100,000 a year, but their production in the early 1930s was a few dozen a year. Germany had similar production capacity, but was restricted to having no military aircraft under the Versailles Treaty. Thus on both sides there were perfect conditions for a sudden—and in the eyes of observers, enormous—increase when political conditions changed.

Germany's abandonment of the Versailles restrictions is the most important historical case of breakout from an arms control agreement. The effects of breakout, or of an arms panic more generally, in creating international tension are exacerbated by having low levels of armament to start with. In this sense, our world is safer than that of the 1920s and early 1930s, since most major states now maintain relatively larger forces and expend a larger proportion of their economic resources on defense than they did then. These forces provide a cushion against sudden disturbances of the military balance. One has to ask whether in this sense a continuous world arms competition, as opposed to an arms panic, may not actually be "stabilizing." This line of reasoning suggests that reduction of armaments to low levels can, in certain circumstances, risk endangering international harmony rather than aiding it.

[10]Thomas Brown, *What Is an Arms Race,* California Arms Control and Foreign Policy Seminar paper (unpublished, October 1975), pp. 16–17.

Reductions through Arms Control: The Washington Naval Agreements

The arms limitation provisions of the Versailles Treaty are an unrepresentative example of arms control in that they were not the result of agreement between potential adversaries, but rather were imposed by the allies on a Germany that had been rendered defenseless by defeat in the war. Thus they sought to embody a temporary relationship that did not reflect the real power of the countries involved.

The Washington Naval Treaty of 1922, on the other hand, represented a voluntary agreement which, unlike the SALT I and II agreements on strategic offensive arms, involved serious arms reduction: indeed, it is the only historical example of reductions of this magnitude. Each of the three main naval powers scrapped roughly half of their existing battleships and almost all of the enormous tonnage under construction. It was agreed that for a decade no new battleships would be built. The core of the treaty was a ratio freezing the parties' existing approximate relative strength in battleships and extending it to aircraft carriers. The ratio among the United States, Britain and Japan was 5:5:3.

Qualitative limits were imposed as well, limiting battleships to 35,000 tons and cruisers to 10,000 tons (with 8-inch guns). In the London Treaty of 1930, numerical limits were placed on other types of ships as well.

The Washington Treaty had real accomplishments. It saved all the countries involved a vast amount of money and stopped for nearly 20 years the increase in battleship size, just then swelling monstrously. The treaty also showed that in circumstances like these, where there was no deep opposition of political interests, stopping an arms race could indeed decrease international tension. Finally, the treaty provided a universal and principled covering which psychologically eased acceptance of shifts in power relationships—Britain's loss of naval superiority for the first time in 200 years and the abandonment of the Anglo-Japanese alliance—that could have been far more disturbing if boldly presented.

However, the treaty turned out not to be, as Lord Balfour, the head of the British delegation, proclaimed, an "absolute unmixed benefit to mankind, which carried no seeds of future misfortune." To begin with, it soon became apparent that the treaty had actually spurred the arms race in important ways. Stephen Roskill, the naval historian, writes that "all in all, the first effect of the limitation treaty on Britain . . . was to produce greater activity in naval building than at any time since the armistice [of 1918]."[11] No one fore-

---

[11]*Naval Policy Between the Wars* (London: Collins, 1968), p. 332.

saw this outcome, but it is hardly surprising. To negotiate, a nation needs to carefully compare its forces with those of other countries, highlighting areas of relative weakness. In the new situation created by the agreement, it may be felt to be necessary, or actually may be necessary, to remedy these weaknesses. Thus, the prospect of removing INF missiles from Europe has focused attention on the imbalance, favoring the Soviets, in shorter-range nuclear missiles. It is thus all too easy for the arms limitation process to wind up in incessant arms accumulation to remedy security weaknesses created or brought to light by the original negotiations—the equivalent of pouring water into a perforated bucket.

As soon as the battleship race was halted in the early 1920s, another race began in cruisers, which had been relatively neglected. The United States had only three modern cruisers, the British Empire 60. The cruisers constructed after the treaty displaced 10,000 tons and were armed with 8-inch guns (the treaty limits), while almost all existing cruisers were half this size and armed with 6- or 4-inch guns. The arms limitation treaty had quickly brought into existence a new and much more powerful weapon, the "treaty cruiser," the naval historians' ironic name for the new 10,000 ton, 8-inch gun warships.

It is easy to see why this was likely to take place. The pace of technological innovation in weapons is normally limited by the fact that military staffs, like all bureaucracies, are embedded in a mass of routine administrative duties. From these ordinary duties there are most likely to emerge conservative, incremental decisions on weapons: adding a few, or improving the type slightly, with each budget cycle.

A treaty negotiation, on the other hand, forces far-reaching reassessment of weapons policy. To develop their negotiating positions, the U.S., British, and Japanese governments needed to know from their naval staffs what was the most useful type of cruiser. It is scarcely surprising that the answer turned out to be that the optimum cruiser was one twice as big as existing cruisers.

By a somewhat similar process the Washington Treaty encouraged the emergence of the aircraft carrier. One of the mysterious events of modern military history is the rapid emergence of air power, and particularly carrier air power, so soon after the weapon was invented. The first ship originally designed as an aircraft carrier was completed in 1922, the year the Washington Naval Treaty was signed. Nevertheless, the treaty defined the aircraft carrier as a "capital ship," thus putting it in the same category as the battleship, a weapon some 300 years older. Only 19 years later, carrier air power was the weapon Japan chose—rather than battleships—to attempt a decisive victory. It is remarkable that a weapon so new, so far from the dominant strategy and tactics of the period, and so untested in combat was taken as seriously as it was.

The more one studies this transformation, the more it appears that it had something to do with arms control. In ordinary circumstances the battleship admirals then dominating every major navy would never have chosen to invest in aircraft carriers rather than battleships. Once their cherished battleship force had been cut to the bone in negotiations, however, they developed a sudden but natural awareness of the need for aircraft carriers, and discovered that the unfinished hulls of four battleships just stricken under the treaty terms could be converted quite nicely into giant aircraft carriers for the United States and Japan.

In this way, the treaty regime facilitated the emergence of air power at its very beginning. Subsequently, the environment created by the treaty continued to affect the role of air power in ways that were less visible and dramatic but perhaps even more important.

The treaty largely froze technological change in the battleship (and, shortly, in the cruiser as well), changing the particular relationship between technology, tactics, and strategy that had existed from the advent of the new *Dreadnought*-class battleship in 1904 up to World War I, and again from 1918 to 1922. The war itself had shown that although Britain and Germany had developed powerful battleships, they had only vague ideas about how to fight with them. An important reason seems to be the very pace of technological advance, which concentrated the energy of the naval bureaucracies on the development of more powerful battleships and the solution of immediate problems posed by them (e.g., fire control at long ranges).

The Washington Naval Treaty created an environment that was in many ways the opposite: technological development was frozen, and the naval officers were left free to concentrate on how to fight a real war with the existing technology. This was expressed in the Untied States and Japan in annual, detailed war games and in increasingly voluminous and concrete war plans. At first, the ideas were relatively crude, similar to those of 1914: a naval Armageddon fought between main battleship fleets in the Central Pacific. Increasingly, however, the planners were compelled to confront the many unanswered questions underlying this scenario, one of which was whether the battleships would suffer substantial attrition on their way to the battle area. Attention was thus gradually turned to the auxiliary weapons that could inflict or counter this attrition, and among them, to air power.

This logic particularly affected the inferior power, Japan, and attracted the Japanese to carrier air power as one means of righting the unfavorable balance (itself highlighted by the 5:5:3 ratio) with the United States. Thus the treaty created not only new weapons in a narrow sense, but new tactics and strategy for the employment of all naval weapons and a new seriousness about how to fight a war.

From the standpoint of defense policy and arms control, these results were of mixed value. The treaty probably encouraged serious planning for war within the U.S. Navy, while discouraging it within the wider public. Public opinion in the United States and Britain tended to be lulled by the treaty into ignoring defense. In 10 of the 18 years between the treaty and World War II, the U.S. Congress did not authorize the building of a single warship, while Japan laid down several ships every year. The result was that by the late

1930s Japan, entitled by the 1922 and 1930 treaties to 60 percent of U.S. strength, had actually been allowed to build to 80 percent of parity. It proved impossible to restore the treaty ratio by December 7, 1941.

In any case, the treaty undoubtedly hurried an evolution away from a weapon whose era was waning, the battleship, and toward the air power weapon of the future. But from the standpoint of arms control, this was a step backwards.

As Pearl Harbor made clear, the aircraft carrier was a weapon that, as compared with the battleship, encouraged striking first in a crisis, and therefore somewhat increased the chances of war. The aircraft carrier was far better adapted to carry out swift attack from a distance than the lumbering battleship, yet at the same time its thin, gasoline-laden hull could not withstand attack like the battleship's thick carapace.

At Midway and other carrier battles there was a strong tendency for the side that struck first to win. If one wanted to do everything that would make war less likely—the primary object of all arms limitation agreements—one did not want to encourage shifting the weapons mix toward weapons, like the aircraft carrier, that might have encouraged striking first. But the Washington treaty had precisely this effect.

Fortifications—a "weapon" that impedes successful offensive war—were actually prohibited by the treaty in the Western Pacific. This destabilizing concession had to be made to get Japan to accept the politically disagreeable 5:5:3 ratio. The general spirit that dominated arms limitation efforts in the 1920s as in SALT—the opposition to greater quantities of weapons in the abstract—tended to blind negotiators and planners to the particular effects of specific weapons on the preservation of peace.

When freed of the treaty limits by Japanese abrogation (as of 1936), the United States and Britain continued to build 35,000-ton battleships with 14-inch or 16-inch guns, while Japan went immediately to 64,000 tons and 18-inch guns.

As this suggests, the signatories had different conceptions of what the treaty meant. The United States and Britain tended to see their commitment to the treaty as a commitment to the spirit of the treaty, which might call for more than its formal provisions. Japan quite honorably interpreted the treaty to mean the letter of the treaty. To get around treaty limits, Japan laid down submarine tenders that could be quickly converted into aircraft carriers and cruisers whose 6-inch guns could be quickly exchanged for the 8-inch guns of heavy cruisers.

The United States also exploited the treaty provisions in less startling ways. By a somewhat sophistic interpretation of an apparently unrelated clause in the Washington treaty, U.S. officials squeezed out another 3,000-ton displacement for their new aircraft carriers, but then nervously did not list it in official tables.

These cases bring us to a further unintended consequence which the Washington and London Treaties share with other arms limitation agreements: they encourage attempts to extract from the treaty unforeseen advantage for one side, and, at the extreme, cheating. Deception is always an attractive possibility in arms races, but the need to work within the definite limits imposed by a formal agreement vastly increases the incentives for deception or for testing the limits of the treaty. This sort of behavior creates in turn new uncertainty, which is precisely one of the greatest aims of arms limitation agreements to avoid.

The end of the Washington–London Treaty system was clear in 1934 when Japan gave the required two years' warning to abrogate the treaty. It is little reproach to an arms limitation treaty that it could not dam up the volcanic forces that had begun to stir and crackle in Japan in the 1930s.

But this case does point out a final problem that all arms limitation agreements must face. Arms limitation agreements, which by their very nature involve precise ratios and numbers of arms permitted to each side, are far more specific and detailed than most treaties. They thus lack the flexibility that enables most international agreements to bend with change and be infused with a new political content—as the meaning of NATO, for example, has shifted substantially over the years. When the rigid structure of an arms limitation agreement can no longer contain changed political forces, it will snap apart. The cost may be heavy: after an arms limitation treaty not renewed, as after a divorce, one cannot return to the starting point. . . .

Conclusion

. . . Experience suggests that the power of arms control itself to stabilize political relationships is limited. The Washington Naval Treaty did stabilize the Anglo-American relationship, but the underlying tensions in that relationship were superficial. It could stabilize the Japanese-American relationship only temporarily.

Finally, the examples discussed suggest that the question of the appropriate level of armaments—for example, the levels at which arms control agreements ought to be aiming—is much more complicated than is suggested by the view which sees the primary purpose of arms control as that of breaking the "mad momentum" of the arms race. Such a view implies that once increases in arms levels have been stopped, there is no theoretical obstacle to reductions as deep as possible. The reason for this conclusion is that the role of arms in the international system is seen as totally negative: not only do they not resolve the political tensions in the system but, by causing mutual fear, they can easily exacerbate them.

The above examples suggest, on the other hand, that, given political tensions, armaments can, depending on the circumstances, be stabilizing for the international system as well. Large military forces may add to the sense of tension in some circumstances, such as those before World War I, but they can also provide a cushion that absorbs sudden fluctuations in the international political environment. Arms control treaties, because of their unusually specific and rigid character, are more likely to be broken by major political fluctuations than to absorb them.

Critics of a specific weapon system often complain that its proponents fail to take into consideration how the adversary will react to it, negating many of the benefits it is supposed to provide. Proponents of an arms control agreement must meet the same test of trying to foresee the inevitable adjustments both sides will make to this agreement and how they will alter a complicated web of political and military realities.

The Spread of Nuclear Weapons: More May Be Better

KENNETH N. WALTZ

Most people believe that the world will become a more dangerous one as nuclear weapons spread. The chances that nuclear weapons will be fired in anger or accidentally exploded in a way that prompts a nuclear exchange are finite, though unknown. Those chances increase as the number of nuclear states increases. More is therefore worse. Most people also believe that the chances that nuclear weapons will be used vary with the character of the new nuclear states—their sense of responsibility, inclination toward peace, devotion to the *status quo*, political stability, and administrative competence. If the supply of states of good character is limited, as is widely thought, then the larger the number of nuclear states, the greater the chances of nuclear war become. If nuclear weapons are acquired by countries whose governments totter and frequently fall, should we not worry more about the world's destruction than we do now? And if nuclear weapons are acquired by two states that are traditional and bitter rivals, should that not also foster our concern? . . .

The Effects of Nuclear Weapons

Nuclear weapons have been the second force [in addition to bipolarity] working for peace in the post-war world. They make the cost of war seem frighteningly high and thus discourage states from starting any wars that

Kenneth N. Waltz, *The Spread of Nuclear Weapons: More May Be Better*, Adelphi Paper No. 171 (London: International Institute for Strategic Studies, Autumn 1981). Reprinted with permission of the International Institute for Strategic Studies.

might lead to the use of such weapons. Nuclear weapons have helped maintain peace between the great powers and have not led their few other possessors into military adventures.[1] Their further spread, however, causes widespread fear. Much of the writing about the spread of nuclear weapons has this unusual trait: It tells us that what did *not* happen in the past is likely to happen in the future, that tomorrow's nuclear states are likely to do to one another what today's nuclear states have not done. A happy nuclear past leads many to expect an unhappy nuclear future. This is odd, and the oddity leads me to believe that we should reconsider how weapons affect the situation of their possessors. . . .

How can one state dissuade another state from attacking? In either or in some combination of two ways. One way to counter an intended attack is to build fortifications and to muster forces that look forbiddingly strong. To build defences so patently strong that no one will try to destroy or overcome them would make international life perfectly tranquil. I call this the defensive ideal. The other way to inhibit a country's intended aggressive moves is to scare that country out of making them by threatening to visit unacceptable punishment upon it. 'To deter' literally means to stop someone from doing something by frightening him. In contrast to dissuasion by defence, dissuasion by deterrence operates by frightening a state out of attacking, not because of the difficulty of launching an attack and carrying it home, but because the expected reaction of the attacked will result in one's own severe punishment. Defence and deterrence are often confused. One frequently hears statements like this: 'A strong defence in Europe will deter a Russian attack'. What is meant is that a strong defence will dissuade Russia from attacking. Deterrence is achieved not through the ability to defend but through the ability to punish. Purely deterrent forces provide no defence. The message of a deterrent strategy is this: 'Although we are defenceless, if you attack we will punish you to an extent that more than cancels your gains'. Second-strike nuclear forces serve that kind of strategy. Purely defensive forces provide no deterrence. They offer no means of punishment. The message of a defensive strategy is this: 'Although we cannot strike back, you will find our defences so difficult to overcome that you will dash yourself to pieces against them'. The Maginot line was to serve that kind of strategy.[2]

States may also use force for coercion. One state may threaten to harm another state not to deter it from taking a certain action but to compel one. Napoleon III threatened to bombard Tripoli if the Turks did not comply with his demands for Roman Catholic control of the Palestinian Holy Places.

---

[1]Cf. John J. Weltman, 'Nuclear Devolution and World Order', *World Politics,* vol. 32, January 1980, pp. 172–4.

[2]Cf. Robert J. Art and Kenneth N. Waltz, "Technology, Strategy, and the Uses of Force," *The Use of Force* (Boston: Little, Brown, 1971). For the different implications of defence and deterrence, see Glenn H. Snyder, *Deterrence and Defense* (Princeton: Princeton University Press, 1961).

This is blackmail, which can now be backed by conventional and by nuclear threats.

Do nuclear weapons increase or decrease the chances of war? The answer depends on whether nuclear weapons permit and encourage states to deploy forces in ways that make the active use of force more or less likely and in ways that promise to be more or less destructive. If nuclear weapons make the offence more effective and the blackmailer's threat more compelling, then nuclear weapons increase the chances of war—the more so the more widely they spread. If defence and deterrence are made easier and more reliable by the spread of nuclear weapons, we may expect the opposite result. . . .

Wars can be fought in the face of deterrent threats, but the higher the stakes and the closer a country moves toward winning them, the more surely that country invites retaliation and risks its own destruction. States are not likely to run major risks for minor gains. Wars between nuclear states may escalate as the loser uses larger and larger warheads. Fearing that, states will want to draw back. Not escalation but de-escalation becomes likely. War remains possible, but victory in war is too dangerous to fight for. If states can score only small gains, because large ones risk retaliation, they have little incentive to fight.

Second, states act with less care if the expected costs of war are low and with more care if they are high. In 1853 and 1854, Britain and France expected to win an easy victory if they went to war against Russia. Prestige abroad and political popularity at home would be gained, if not much else. The vagueness of their plans was matched by the carelessness of their acts. In blundering into the Crimean War they acted hastily on scant information, pandered to their people's frenzy for war, showed more concern for an ally's whim than for the adversary's situation, failed to specify the changes in behaviour that threats were supposed to bring, and inclined towards testing strength first and bargaining second.[3] In sharp contrast, the presence of nuclear weapons makes states exceedingly cautious. Think of Kennedy and Kruschev in the Cuban missile crisis. Why fight if you can't win much and might lose everything? . . .

Certainty about the relative strength of adversaries also improves the prospects for peace. From the late nineteenth century onwards the speed of technological innovation increased the difficulty of estimating relative strengths and predicting the course of campaigns. Since World War II, technology has advanced even faster, but short of an anti-ballistic missile (ABM) breakthrough, this does not matter very much. It does not disturb the American-Russian equilibrium because one side's missiles are not made obsolete by improvements in the other side's missiles. In 1906 the British *Dreadnought,* with the greater range and fire power of its guns, made older battle-

[3]See Richard Smoke, *War: Controlling Escalation* (Cambridge, Mass.: Harvard University Press, 1977), pp. 175–88.

ships obsolete. This does not happen to missiles. As Bernard Brodie put it: 'Weapons that do not have to fight their like do not become useless because of the advent of newer and superior types. . . .'[4]

Countries more readily run the risks of war when defeat, if it comes, is distant and is expected to bring only limited damage. Given such expectations, leaders do not have to be insane to sound the trumpet and urge their people to be bold and courageous in the pursuit of victory. The outcome of battles and the course of campaigns are hard to foresee because so many things affect them, including the shifting allegiance and determination of alliance members. Predicting the result of conventional wars has proved difficult.

Uncertainty about outcomes does not work decisively against the fighting of wars in conventional worlds. Countries armed with conventional weapons go to war knowing that even in defeat their suffering will be limited. Calculations about nuclear war are differently made. Nuclear worlds call for and encourage a different kind of reasoning. If countries armed with nuclear weapons go to war, they do so knowing that their suffering may be unlimited. Of course, it also may not be. But that is not the kind of uncertainty that encourages anyone to use force. In a conventional world, one is uncertain about winning or losing. In a nuclear world, one is uncertain about surviving or being annihilated. If force is used and not kept within limits, catastrophe will result. That prediction is easy to make because it does not require close estimates of opposing forces. The number of one's cities that can be severely damaged is at least equal to the number of strategic warheads an adversary can deliver. Variations of number mean little within wide ranges. The expected effect of the deterrent achieves an easy clarity because wide margins of error in estimates of probable damage do not matter. Do we expect to lose one city or two, two cities or ten? When these are the pertinent questions, we stop thinking about running risks and start worrying about how to avoid them. In a conventional world, deterrent threats are ineffective because the damage threatened is distant, limited, and problematic. Nuclear weapons make military miscalculations difficult and politically pertinent prediction easy. . . .

Nuclear Weapons and Regional Stability

. . . Many Westerners who write fearfully about a future in which third-world countries have nuclear weapons seem to view their people in the once familiar imperial manner as 'lesser breeds without the law'. As is usual with ethnocentric views, speculation takes the place of evidence. How do we know, someone has asked, that a nuclear-armed and newly hostile Egypt or a nuclear-armed and still hostile Syria would not strike to destroy Israel at the risk of Israeli bombs falling on some of their cities? More than a quarter of

[4]Bernard Brodie, *War and Politics* (New York: Macmillan, 1973), p. 321.

Egypt's people live in four cities: Cairo, Alexandria, Giza, and Aswan. More than a quarter of Syria's live in three: Damascus, Aleppo, and Homs.[5] What government would risk sudden losses of such proportion or indeed of much lesser proportion? Rulers want to have a country that they can continue to rule. Some Arab country might wish that some other Arab country would risk its own destruction for the sake of destroying Israel, but there is no reason to think that any Arab country would do so. One may be impressed that, despite ample bitterness, Israelis and Arabs have limited their wars and accepted constraints placed on them by others. Arabs did not marshal their resources and make an all-out effort to destroy Israel in the years before Israel could strike back with nuclear warheads. We cannot expect countries to risk more in the presence of nuclear weapons than they have in their absence.

Third, many fear that states that are radical at home will recklessly use their nuclear weapons in pursuit of revolutionary ends abroad. States that are radical at home, however, may not be radical abroad. Few states have been radical in the conduct of their foreign policy, and fewer have remained so for long. Think of the Soviet Union and the People's Republic of China. States coexist in a competitive arena. The pressures of competition cause them to behave in ways that make the threats they face manageable, in ways that enable them to get along. States can remain radical in foreign policy only if they are overwhelmingly strong—as none of the new nuclear states will be—or if their radical acts fall short of damaging vital interests of nuclear powers. States that acquire nuclear weapons will not be regarded with indifference. States that want to be freewheelers have to stay out of the nuclear business. A nuclear Libya, for example, would have to show caution, even in rhetoric, lest she suffer retaliation in response to someone else's anonymous attack on a third state. That state, ignorant of who attacked, might claim that its intelligence agents had identified Libya as the culprit and take the opportunity to silence her by striking a conventional or nuclear blow. Nuclear weapons induce caution, especially in weak states.

Fourth, while some worry about nuclear states coming in hostile pairs, others worry that the bipolar pattern will not be reproduced regionally in a world populated by larger numbers of nuclear states. The simplicity of relations that obtains when one party has to concentrate its worry on only one other, and the ease of calculating forces and estimating the dangers they pose, may be lost. The structure of international politics, however, will remain bipolar so long as no third state is able to compete militarily with the great powers. Whatever the structure, the relations of states run in various directions. This applied to relations of deterrence as soon as Britain gained nuclear capabilities. It has not weakened deterrence at the centre and need not do so regionally. The Soviet Union now has to worry lest a move made in Europe cause France and Britain to retaliate, thus possibly setting off Ameri-

[5]Shai Feldman, *Israeli Nuclear Deterrence: A Strategy for the 1980s?* (Berkeley, CA: Ph.D. Dissertation, 1980), Table 1.

can forces. She also has to worry about China's forces. Such worries at once complicate calculations and strengthen deterrence.

Fifth, in some of the new nuclear states civil control of the military may be shaky. Nuclear weapons may fall into the hands of military officers more inclined than civilians to put them to offensive use. This again is an old worry. I can see no reason to think that civil control of the military is secure in the Soviet Union, given the occasional presence of serving officers in the Politburo and some known and some surmised instances of military intervention in civil affairs at critical times.[6] And in the People's Republic of China military and civil branches of government have been not separated but fused. Although one may prefer civil control, preventing a highly destructive war does not require it. What is required is that decisions be made that keep destruction within bounds, whether decisions are made by civilians or soldiers. Soldiers may be more cautious than civilians.[7] Generals and admirals do not like uncertainty, and they do not lack patriotism. They do not like to fight conventional wars under unfamiliar conditions. The offensive use of nuclear weapons multiplies uncertainties. Nobody knows what a nuclear battlefield would look like, and nobody knows what happens after the first city is hit. *Uncertainty* about the course that a nuclear war might follow, along with the *certainty* that destruction can be immense, strongly inhibits the first use of nuclear weapons. . . .

Deterrence with Small Nuclear Forces

A number of problems are thought to attend the efforts of minor powers to use nuclear weapons for deterrence. In this section, I ask how hard these problems are for new nuclear states to solve.

The Forces Required for Deterrence

In considering the physical requirements of deterrent forces, we should recall the difference between prevention and pre-emption. A preventive war is launched by a stronger state against a weaker one that is thought to be gaining strength. A pre-emptive strike is launched by one state to blunt an attack that another state is presumably preparing to launch.

The first danger posed by the spread of nuclear weapons would seem to be that each new nuclear state may tempt an old one to strike preventively in order to destroy an embryonic nuclear capability before it can become mili-

---

[6]For brief accounts, see S. E. Finer, *The Man on Horseback* (London: Pall Mall Press, 1962), pp. 106–8; and Roy Medvedev, 'Soviet Policy Reported Reversed by SALT II', *Washington Star*, 7 July 1979, p. 1.

[7]Kenneth N. Waltz, 'America's European Policy Viewed in Global Perspectives', in Wolfram F. Hanrieder (ed.), *The United States and Western Europe* (Cambridge, Mass.: Winthrop, 1974), p. 31; Richard K. Betts, *Soldiers, Statesmen, and Cold War Crises* (Cambridge, Mass.: Harvard University Press, 1977), App. A.

tarily effective. Because of America's nuclear arsenal, the Soviet Union could hardly have destroyed the budding forces of Britain and France; but the United States could have struck the Soviet Union's early nuclear facilities, and the United States and the Soviet Union could have struck China's. Such preventive strikes have been treated as more than abstract possibilities. When Francis P. Matthews was President Truman's Secretary of the Navy, he made a speech that seemed to favour our waging a preventive war. The United States, he urged, should be willing to pay 'even the price of instituting a war to compel cooperation for peace'.[8]

The United States and the Soviet Union considered making preventive strikes against China early in her nuclear career. Preventive strikes against nuclear installations can also be made by non-nuclear states and have sometimes been threatened. Thus President Nasser warned Israel in 1960 that Egypt would attack if she were sure that Israel was building a bomb. 'It is inevitable', he said, 'that we should attack the base of aggression, even if we have to mobilize four million to destroy it'.[9]

The uneven development of the forces of potential and of new nuclear states creates occasions that seem to permit preventive strikes and may seem to invite them. Two stages of nuclear development should be distinguished. First, a country may be in an early stage of nuclear development and be obviously unable to make nuclear weapons. Second, a country may be in an advanced stage of nuclear development, and whether or not it has some nuclear weapons may not be surely known. All of the present nuclear countries went through both stages, yet until Israel struck Iraq's nuclear facility in June of 1981 no one had launched a preventive strike. A number of reasons combined may account for the reluctance of states to strike in order to prevent adversaries from developing nuclear forces. A preventive strike would seem to be most promising during the first stage of nuclear development. A state could strike without fearing that the country it attacked would return a nuclear blow. But would one strike so hard as to destroy the very potential for future nuclear development? If not, the country struck could simply resume its nuclear career. If the blow struck is less than devastating, one must be prepared to repeat it or to occupy and control the country. To do either would be difficult and costly.

In striking Iraq, Israel showed that a preventive strike can be made, something that was not in doubt. Israel's act and its consequences, however, make clear that the likelihood of useful accomplishment is low. Israel's strike increased the determination of Arabs to produce nuclear weapons. Arab states that may attempt to do so will now be all the more secretive and circum-

[8]Quoted in Walter H. Waggoner, 'U.S. Disowns Matthews Talk of Waging War to Get Peace', *New York Times,* 27 August 1950, p. 1.
[9]Quoted in William B. Bader, *The United States and the Spread of Nuclear Weapons* (New York: Pegasus, 1968), p. 96.

spect. Israel's strike, far from foreclosing Iraq's nuclear future, gained her the support of some other Arab states in pursuing it. And despite Prime Minister Begin's vow to strike as often as need be, the risks in doing so would rise with each occasion.

A preventive strike during the second stage of nuclear development is even less promising than a preventive strike during the first stage. As more countries acquire nuclear weapons, and as more countries gain nuclear competence through power projects, the difficulties and dangers of making preventive strikes increase. To know for sure that the country attacked has not already produced or otherwise acquired some deliverable warheads becomes increasingly difficult. If the country attacked has even a rudimentary nuclear capability, one's own severe punishment becomes possible. Fission bombs may work even though they have not been tested, as was the case with the bomb dropped on Hiroshima. Israel has apparently not tested weapons, yet Egypt cannot know whether Israel has zero, ten, or twenty warheads. And if the number is zero and Egypt can be sure of that, she would still not know how many days are required for assembling components that may be on hand.

Preventive strikes against states that have, or may have, nuclear weapons are hard to imagine, but what about pre-emptive ones? The new worry in a world in which nuclear weapons have spread is that states of limited and roughly similar capabilities will use them against one another. They do not want to risk nuclear devastation anymore than we do. Pre-emptive strikes nevertheless seem likely because we assume that their forces will be 'delicate'. With delicate forces, states are tempted to launch disarming strikes before their own forces can be struck and destroyed.

To be effective a deterrent force must meet three requirements. First, a part of the force must appear to be able to survive an attack and launch one of its own. Second, survival of the force must not require early firing in response to what may be false alarms. Third, weapons must not be susceptible to accidental and unauthorized use. Nobody wants vulnerable, hair-trigger, accident-prone forces. Will new nuclear states find ways to hide their weapons, to deliver them, and to control them? Will they be able to deploy and manage nuclear weapons in ways that meet the physical requirements of deterrent forces? . . .

Deterrent forces are seldom delicate because no state wants delicate forces and nuclear forces can easily be made sturdy. Nuclear weapons are fairly small and light. They are easy to hide and to move. Early in the nuclear age, people worried about atomic bombs being concealed in packing boxes and placed in the holds of ships to be exploded when a signal was given. Now more than ever people worry about terrorists stealing nuclear warheads because various states have so many of them. Everybody seems to believe that terrorists are capable of hiding bombs.[10] Why should states be unable to do what terrorist gangs are thought to be capable of?

[10]For example, David M. Rosenbaum, 'Nuclear Terror', *International Security*, vol. 1, Winter 1977.

It is sometimes claimed that the few bombs of a new nuclear state create a greater danger of nuclear war than additional thousands for the United States and the Soviet Union. Such statements assume that pre-emption of a small force is easy. It is so only if the would-be attacker knows that the intended victim's warheads are few in number, knows their exact number and locations, and knows that they will not be moved or fired before they are struck. To know all of these things, and to know that you know them for sure, is exceedingly difficult. How can military advisers promise the full success of a disarming first strike when the penalty for slight error may be so heavy? In 1962, Tactical Air Command promised that an American strike against Soviet missiles in Cuba would certainly destroy 90% of them but would not guarantee 100%.[11] In the best case a first strike destroys all of a country's deliverable weapons. In the worst case, some survive and can still be delivered.

If the survival of nuclear weapons requires their dispersal and concealment, do not problems of command and control become harder to solve? Americans think so because we think in terms of large nuclear arsenals. Small nuclear powers will neither have them nor need them. Lesser nuclear states might deploy, say, ten real weapons and ten dummies, while permitting other countries to infer that the numbers are larger. The adversary need only believe that some warheads may survive his attack and be visited on him. That belief should not be hard to create without making command and control unreliable. All nuclear countries must live through a time when their forces are crudely designed. All countries have so far been able to control them. Relations between the United States and the Soviet Union, and later among the United States, the Soviet Union, and China, were at their bitterest just when their nuclear forces were in early stages of development, were unbalanced, were crude and presumably hard to control. Why should we expect new nuclear states to experience greater difficulties than the old ones were able to cope with? Moreover, although some of the new nuclear states may be economically and technically backward, they will either have an expert and highly trained group of scientists and engineers or they will not produce nuclear weapons. Even if they buy the weapons, they will have to hire technicians to maintain and control them. We do not have to wonder whether they will take good care of their weapons. They have every incentive to do so. They will not want to risk retaliation because one or more of their warheads accidentally strikes another country.

Hiding nuclear weapons and keeping them under control are tasks for which the ingenuity of numerous states is adequate. Nor are means of delivery difficult to devise or procure. Bombs can be driven in by trucks from neighbouring countries. Ports can be torpedoed by small boats lying off shore. Moreover, a thriving arms trade in ever more sophisticated military

[11]Graham T. Allison, *Essence of Decision* (Boston: Little, Brown, 1971), p. 126.

equipment provides ready access to what may be wanted, including planes and missiles suited [to] nuclear warhead delivery.

Lesser nuclear states can pursue deterrent strategies effectively. Deterrence requires the ability to inflict unacceptable damage on another country. 'Unacceptable damage' to the Soviet Union was variously defined by Robert McNamara as requiring the ability to destroy a fifth to a fourth of her population and a half to two-thirds of her industrial capacity. American estimates of what is required for deterrence have been absurdly high. To deter, a country need not appear to be able to destroy a fourth or a half of another country, although in some cases that might be easily done. Would Libya try to destroy Israel's nuclear weapons at the risk of two bombs surviving to fall on Tripoli and Bengazi? And what would be left of Israel if Tel Aviv and Haifa were destroyed? . . .

Prevention and pre-emption are difficult games because the costs are so high if the games are not perfectly played. Inhibitions against using nuclear forces for such attacks are strong, although one cannot say they are absolute. Some of the inhibitions are simply human. Can country *A* find justification for a preventive or pre-emptive strike against *B* if *B*, in acquiring nuclear weapons, is imitating *A?* The leader of a country that launches a preventive or pre-emptive strike courts condemnation by his own people, by the world's people, and by history. Awesome acts are hard to perform. Some of the inhibitions are political. As Bernard Brodie tirelessly and wisely said, war has to find a political objective that is commensurate with its cost. Clausewitz's central tenet remains valid in the nuclear age.[12] Ultimately, the inhibitions lie in the impossibility of knowing for sure that a disarming strike will totally destroy an opposing force and in the immense destruction even a few warheads can wreak. . . .

In a nuclear world, conservative would-be attackers will be prudent, but will all would-be attackers be conservative? A new Hitler is not unimaginable. Would the presence of nuclear weapons have moderated Hitler's behaviour? Hitler did not start World War II in order to destroy the Third Reich. Indeed, he was surprised and dismayed by the British and French declaration of war on Poland's behalf. After all, the western democracies had not come to the aid of a geographically defensible and militarily strong Czechoslovakia. Why then should they have declared war on behalf of a less defensible Poland and against a Germany made stronger by the incorporation of Czechoslovakia's armour? From the occupation of the Rhineland in 1936 to the invasion of Poland in 1939, Hitler's calculations were realistically made. In those years, Hitler would almost surely have been deterred from acting in ways that immediately threatened massive death and widespread destruction

---

[12]See, for example, Bernard Brodie, 'The Development of Nuclear Strategy', *International Security,* vol. 2, Spring 1978, p. 12.

in Germany. And, if Hitler had not been deterred, would his generals have obeyed his commands? In a nuclear world, to act in blatantly offensive ways is madness. Under the circumstances, how many generals would obey the commands of a madman? One man alone does not make war.

To believe that nuclear deterrence would have worked against Germany in 1939 is easy. It is also easy to believe that in 1945, given the ability to do so, Hitler and some few around him would have fired nuclear warheads at the United States, Great Britain, and the Soviet Union as their armies advanced, whatever the consequences for Germany. Two considerations, however, work against this possibility. When defeat is seen to be inevitable, a ruler's authority may vanish. Early in 1945 Hitler apparently ordered the initiation of gas warfare, but no one responded.[13] The first consideration applies in a conventional world; the second in a nuclear world. In the latter, no country will press another to the point of decisive defeat. In the desperation of defeat desperate measures may be taken, but the last thing anyone wants to do is to make a nuclear nation feel desperate. The unconditional surrender of a nuclear nation cannot be demanded....

Arms Races among New Nuclear States

... Deterrent balances are inherently stable. If one can say how much is enough, then within wide limits a country can be insensitive to changes in its adversaries' forces. This is the way French leaders have thought. France, as former President Giscard d'Estaing said, 'fixes its security at the level required to maintain, regardless of the way the strategic situation develops in the world, the credibility—in other words, the effectiveness—of its deterrent force'.[14] With deterrent forces securely established, no military need presses one side to try to surpass the other. Human error and folly may lead some parties involved in deterrent balance to spend more on armaments than is needed, but other parties need not increase their armaments in response, because such excess spending does not threaten them. The logic of deterrence eliminates incentives for strategic arms racing. This should be easier for lesser nuclear states to understand than it has been for the US and the USSR. Because most of them are economically hard pressed, they will not want to have more than enough.

Allowing for their particular circumstances, lesser nuclear states confirm these statements in their policies. Britain and France are relatively rich countries, and they tend to over-spend. Their strategic forces are neverthe-

---

[13]Frederic J. Brown, *Chemical Warfare: A Study in Restraints*, excerpted in Art and Waltz, *op. cit.* in n. 2, p. 183.

[14]Valéry Giscard d'Estaing, 'Part II of the press conference by Valéry Giscard d'Estaing, President of the French Republic' (New York: French Embassy, Press and Information Division, 15 February 1979), p. 6.

less modest enough when one considers that their purpose is to deter the Soviet Union rather than states with capabilities comparable to their own. China of course faces the same task. These three countries show no inclination to engage in nuclear arms races with anyone. India appears content to have a nuclear military capability that may or may not have produced deliverable warheads, and Israel maintains her ambiguous status. New nuclear states are likely to conform to these patterns and aim for a modest sufficiency rather than vie with each [other] for a meaningless superiority.

Second, because strategic nuclear arms races among lesser powers are unlikely, the interesting question is not whether they will be run but whether countries having strategic nuclear weapons can avoid running conventional races. No more than the United States and the Soviet Union will lesser nuclear states want to rely on the deterrent threat that risks all. And will not their vulnerability to conventional attack induce them to continue their conventional efforts? . . .

The expense of mounting conventional defences, and the difficulties and dangers of fighting conventional wars, will keep most new nuclear states from trying to combine large war-fighting forces with deterrent forces. Disjunction within their forces will enhance the value of deterrence.

Israeli policy seems to contradict these propositions. From 1971 through 1978, both Israel and Egypt spent from 20% to 40% of their GNPs on arms. Israel's spending on conventional arms remains high, although it has decreased since 1978. The decrease followed from the making of peace with Egypt and not from increased reliance on nuclear weapons. The seeming contradiction in fact bears out deterrent logic. So long as Israel holds the West Bank and the Gaza Strip she has to be prepared to fight for them. Since they are by no means unambiguously hers, deterrent threats, whether implicit or explicit, will not cover them. Moreover, while America's large subsidies continue, economic constraints will not drive Israel to the territorial settlement that would shrink her borders sufficiently to make a deterrent policy credible.

From previous points it follows that nuclear weapons are likely to decrease arms racing and reduce military costs for lesser nuclear states in two ways. Conventional arms races will wither if countries shift emphasis from conventional defence to nuclear deterrence. For Pakistan, for example, acquiring nuclear weapons is an alternative to running a ruinous conventional race with India.[15] And deterrent strategies make nuclear arms races pointless.

Finally, arms races in their ultimate form—the fighting of offensive wars designed to increase national security—also become pointless. The success of a deterrent strategy does not depend on the extent of territory a state holds. . . .

---

[15]Richard K. Betts, 'Paranoids, Pygmies, Pariahs, and Nonproliferation', *Foreign Policy* no. 26, Spring 1977, pp. 161–2.

PART 7

Transnational Tensions: Religion, Migration, Environment

Some potential sources of conflict transcend borders and may not be caused or controlled by specific governments. Such problems were not well recognized during the Cold War era, or seemed less important then because the East-West struggle absorbed concern. Without that overwhelming problem confronting us, these other challenges to international stability may acquire a higher priority. How far such matters will become real issues of national security, however, is an open question. It would be a traditionalist conceit to ignore the emergence of novel grounds of conflict, yet not all new international problems turn into security problems.

Islam, for example, is a political force in countries as disparate as Egypt, Nigeria, Pakistan, and Indonesia. There is no evidence yet, however, of globally or even regionally coordinated action on the basis of religious motivation. In the past decade, much attention has focused on the notion of radical Islam's threat to the West, because of the Iranian revolution and the popular association of Islamic "fundamentalism" with fanaticism and terrorism. Since the crackup of Marxism-Leninism as a secular religion, moreover, Islam is the only major transnational ideological force currently posing an alternative to Western liberalism as a model for social organization. Some limitations on these views of Islam are noted in Graham Fuller's piece in this section.[1]

[1]This selection summarizes longer studies by Fuller: *Islamic Fundamentalism in Pakistan*, R-3964-USDP (Santa Monica: RAND Corporation, 1991) and *Islamic Fundamentalism in*

Myron Weiner points out the many ways in which the modern world's unprecedented transfers of population put new pressure on governments and prompt international friction. Large populations of political refugees contribute to violent conflict in many regions. Illegal immigration by economic refugees reflects one of the most enduring obstacles to the notion that market economics and free trade will be the font of peace. A world economy based on fully free markets and production according to comparative advantage would be one that allowed mobility of *both* major factors of production—not just capital, but labor as well—yet scarcely anyone dreams that rich countries will open their doors without restriction.

The third set of global problems that has become more salient involves international collective goods, access to resources and preservation of the natural environment that all countries need, but that none can control individually. The idea that security should be redefined to cover environmental and other non-military dangers is a recent vogue. Sometimes that definition of security is used as cover for the diversion of attention or resources earmarked for security studies, from military matters considered narrow and *passé* by the definers, to problems of real importance. Depletion of the ozone layer may indeed be a greater threat to our survival than the Russians ever were. If it is counted a matter of security, however, that term becomes so inclusive as to be meaningless. If "security" is synonymous with national interests in general, or with human safety, we might as well include educational policy and medicine in security studies.

Some environmental disasters, nevertheless, may affect security in the sense in which the term is traditionally used. The point at which the line should be drawn is where issues not traditionally addressed in security studies may cause social conflict and political violence. If one country were to contemplate using force against another to prevent it from releasing ozone-destroying chemicals into the atmosphere, for example, the ozone issue would qualify as a matter of security policy. Similarly, as John Cooley's discussion of control of water in the Middle East suggests, disputes over natural resources might easily become a source of armed conflict between states. Thomas Homer-Dixon shows how a wide range of developments that degrade the environment, thereby putting pressure on economies and societies (especially in Third World countries that live closer to the margin of subsistence) could also lead to significant political violence.[2]

The ultimate consequences of damage to the balance of nature are unknown, and are potentially significant beyond political and economic disputes. In the

---

Afghanistan, R-3970-USDP (Santa Monica: RAND Corporation, 1991). See also Abdulaziz A. Sachedina, "The Development of *Jihad* in Islamic Revelation and History," in James Turner Johnson and John Kelsay, eds., *Cross, Crescent, and Sword* (Greenwood Press, 1990).

[2]See also Norman Myers, "Environment and Security," *Foreign Policy* no. 74 (Spring 1989); Roy L. Thompson, "Water as a Source of Conflict," *Strategic Review* 6, no. 2 (Spring 1978); Richard Ullman, "Redefining Security," *International Security* 8, no. 1 (Summer 1983); Jessica Tuchman Matthews, "Redefining Security," *Foreign Affairs* 68, no. 2 (Spring 1989); and Robert L. Paarlberg, "Ecodiplomacy," in Kenneth Oye, Robert Lieber, and Donald Rothchild, eds., *Eagle in a New World* (New York: HarperCollins, 1992).

near term, however, environmental decline is likely to cause conflict mainly through its economic effects. The combination of these issues is also aggravating the old North-South clash over the international distribution of wealth. The developed countries progressed in earlier eras by exploiting nature's collective goods without a thought. Now they want poorer countries to exercise restraint and leave some of their natural resources intact, to preserve the collective goods.

Who should pay for that preservation? What compensation should go to those who do not despoil their forests, plunder the oceans, or run their industries on polluting fuels, and how should the prices for such transactions be determined? Who will make the rules? Could environmental regulation come to justify forcible intervention against those who refuse it? These are the questions that could lead to good old international conflict.

Islamic Fundamentalism

GRAHAM E. FULLER

Radical Islamic fundamentalism has taken power in only one country in the Muslim world to date: Iran. Not only is Iran's ideological vision Islamic, it is also uniquely Shi'ite, and it goes so far as to involve the clergy in the day-to-day running of the state. It is unfortunate that the main American experience with fundamentalist Islam has come via Iran and its Shi'ite supporters in the Persian Gulf and Lebanon, for this particular Iranian form carries with it a great deal more specifically Iranian political baggage than merely Islam. Iran is a country historically possessed of a unique sense of grievance and paranoia toward the West, stemming in part from its experience of heavy-handed domination at the hands of Western—especially British and Russian—imperialism. These grievances have been heightened by Shi'ite theology and a sense of historical martyrdom.

But the character of Islamic fundamentalism does not need to parallel the Iranian form in all respects. The United States has already had much experience with Saudi Arabia—a fundamentalist Islamic regime in many ways— and with Pakistan, where former President Zia ul-Haqq's Islamization campaign introduced a strong measure of Islamic ideology and religious austerity into the economic, political, and social aspects of life. Both of these countries have maintained good relations with the United States through the process.

... Radical Islamic fundamentalism is unlikely to come to power in the three remaining states of the Norther Tier: Turkey, Afghanistan, and Pakistan. Although the political, economic, and social conditions of these countries are all very different, a number of common factors suggest that Islamic fundamentalism, or "Islamism" as it is more accurately termed, faces considerable obstacles in coming to power.

Graham E. Fuller, *Islamic Fundamentalism in the Northern Tier Countries: An Integrative View*, R-3966-USDP (Santa Monica, CA: RAND Corporation, 1991), Summary. Reprinted with permission of the RAND Corporation.

But even though Islamism may not actually come to power, . . . it could exert considerable influence over the character of politics and policies in these countries, most of all in Pakistan and somewhat less so in Turkey.

Obstacles to an Islamic Takeover

Among the key obstacles to a takeover of power by radical Islamist forces in all three countries are the following:

- The lack of any single charismatic leadership in any country.
- The modest electoral showing of Islamic parties in free elections (Turkey and Pakistan).
- Opposition of the military to Islamism in power (Turkey and Pakistan).
- Serious divisions among the ranks of Islamists, including over the issue of how Islamic law should be implemented.
- Objection of Shi'ite minorities to the imposition of Islamic law—because it will invariably be Sunni law and signify Sunni religious domination over them.
- Competition to radical Islam from other political movements and trends, especially the left.
- Limited Iranian (Shi'ite) capability to sharply affect the evolution of Islamic politics and Sunni countries.

Factors Contributing to the Growth of Islamism

Despite Islamism's poor prospects for actually coming to power in these countries, Islam is likely to play an increasing role in the political, social, and economic arenas, rendering it a force that will have to be reckoned with by any government that comes to power in those states. Among the factors contributing to the growth and influence of Islam, we can note the following more generalized characteristics:

- The role of Islam as a native cultural vehicle for dissent, for the expression of nationalist grievances against the West, and as a legitimizing instrument for opposition to oppressive domestic rule.
- A general trend for Islam to be strong among the lower middle class (petty bourgeoisie), a class growing in salience in the Muslim world as it assumes a greater role in the economy and society at large.
- The tendency of Islamic organizations and parties to focus on social welfare work, including education and health, in societies where the stress of urbanization increases needs in this area.

- The role of Islam as an anchor for values and as a source of solace for those caught up in the trauma of the urbanization process.
- The increasing tendency of Islamist groups to turn to modern political instruments shunned by the traditional clergy, such as political parties and the use of the media, for influence.
- The impact of the growth of democracy, which has given the Islamists greater opportunity both for the expression of their political views and for election to national parliaments and city governments.
- The increasing influence of Islamists in the education system and the growth of Islamic schools, producing more students exposed to Islamic views.
- The modernist character of Islamist leadership, which, in sharp distinction to the traditional clergy, has received Western-style secular education, usually in such technical areas as engineering or medicine; this leadership perceives modernization and the use of technology as essential to the power of the modern Islamist state.

In these terms, it is probable that the role of Islam in the state will become more important in Afghanistan and Turkey, will diminish somewhat in Iran, and will remain a major force in Pakistan. In utilitarian terms, Islam is too politically powerful and emotive as a force for any political system to ignore.

Islamist Influence in Northern Tier States

Despite the many common features in the Islamist experience noted above, each of the Northern Tier countries under discussion differs sharply from the others in the character of its contemporary political situation.

Turkey

Turkey is a strongly secular state. Indeed, Turkey's modern secularism has almost anathematized it to the Islamists: once it had been the center of world Islam under the glorious Ottoman Empire, only to turn secular in the 1920s and abolish the very position of Caliphate, or leader of the Islamic faith—a post which to this day has never been resuscitated in the Muslim world. Turkey is thus at one extreme of the religious spectrum in the Muslim world. Turkey has also had a fairly functioning democracy over the past 40 years.

Afghanistan

Afghanistan is in a state of complete fluidity following the defeat and withdrawal of the Soviet Army. . . .

Because of the uncertainty of the military situation in Afghanistan and the lack of any political unity among the Islamic mujahidin parties, any prognosis on the future of Islam in Afghanistan is extremely difficult to make now. One thing is certain, however: the mujahidin consider that their victory over the Soviets, regardless of international aid, was a victory of Islam over the Soviet Union. "Islam is a superpower," as the mujahidin say. . . .

But the mujahidin almost surely will not be able to remain united, and the Islamists will be unable to control the country any more firmly than past Afghan regimes, including the communists, have been able to do. Any Islamic republic that might ever come into existence in Afghanistan will not replay the virulence and xenophobia of Iran, nor will it devote itself single-mindedly to opposition to the United States as Tehran has done.

Pakistan

Pakistan is unique in the modern world, a state whose very raison d'être in 1947 was to be a homeland for Muslims in the Indian subcontinent. Its Islamic character is central to its very existence and functioning, even today. Islam has also served as an instrument of political legitimation for a number of its leaders, especially former President Zia ul-Haqq. But despite his very active "Islamization" campaign, even Zia refrained from comprehensive implementation of Islamic law as the basis for the state and, as a military officer, opposed permitting the clerics or Islamists to come to absolute power in any case. Pakistan has additionally been considerably influenced by events in Afghanistan and the victory of the Islamist mujahidin over the Soviet Union—a victory achieved with key Pakistani support. Pakistani and Afghan Islamist groups have close links to each other, and each could considerably influence the strength of the other if one of them were to come to power. The political situation in Pakistan is also undergoing a period of transition since the unanticipated death of Zia in 1988, the holding of almost unprecedented free elections in late 1988, the unprecedented accession of a woman prime minister, Benazir Bhutto, into power (and opposed by the Islamists), and her subsequent loss of power in the elections of 1990. The future political role of Islam in Pakistan is thus also in a period of uncertainty.

The Islamists in Power

Should the Islamists attain power in Turkey, Afghanistan, or Pakistan, the regimes would be unlikely to take the extreme xenophobic positions of Iran, but they would share certain broad characteristics:

• All would be antipathetic to Western cultural influences, which Islamists view as lacking moral foundation and marked excessively by individualism, consumerism, sexual license, moral relativism, and secular values.

- All would oppose a major American presence in the country, although normal, correct relations would not be excluded; they would also oppose any U.S. military presence in the region, including the Persian Gulf and the Indian Ocean.
- All would oppose military ties with the United States, although each might, faced with a severe security problem (Pakistan in particular), turn to it for the purchase of weaponry. Turkey's NATO ties would be abolished.
- Economic ties with the world would remain much the same, but Turkey would almost certainly forgo membership in the European Community.
- All would be concerned with opposing "imperialist influence" from both East and West and would be extremely prickly about issues of national sovereignty.
- All would devote greater policy attention to the welfare of Muslims around the world, with particular emphasis on Muslims in India, the USSR, Palestine, Malaysia, and the Philippines.
- All would be active in "North-South politics" and the non-aligned movement—to the extent that that movement retains significance in a post–Cold War world.
- Unless the USSR were to regress to the ideological and expansionist policies that typified it under pre-Gorbachev rule, the Northern Tier states will probably be more relaxed about the USSR and will improve their ties with it. Islamists will view the USSR in general as less of a cultural threat to the Islamic world than the United States.
- Iran would lose a great deal of its prominence as a leader of the Muslim world and would probably encounter significant regional rivalry with its neighbors for the role of Islamic leadership.

Terrorism

Terrorism against the United States from Islamist policies in the Northern Tier countries is less likely than was the case with Iran; it could crop up, however, under specific situations in specific countries:

- Terror could certainly not be ruled out in Turkey if U.S. relations with Turkey were to undergo a rocky period. Key issues of friction could spring from serious disagreements within NATO, especially relating to the Greek-Turkish balance, human rights (especially relating to the Kurds in Turkey), or rejection of Turkish membership in the EC, or from U.S. efforts to engage Turkey in policies against Muslim states of the region. Terror against the U.S. presence in Turkey was active at one point during the period of "anarchy" in the 1970s, although it came almost exclusively from the left. It revived again during the Gulf War. An Islamist campaign against the United States under periods of severe national stress and friction with the West cannot be ruled out, especially if the U.S. presence in Turkey became a volatile issue in itself.

· The Afghans did not turn to international terror during the whole decade of struggle against the USSR, and there are likely to be few issues of genuine conflict with the United States in the future—short of a major U.S.-backed Pakistani confrontation with an Islamist Afghanistan, an unlikely contingency.

· Pakistan could move in an extremist direction, with mob action or terrorism against the United States, in the event of serious deterioration of relations over a strong U.S. tilt to India, nuclear proliferation, or human rights. While Pakistan does not have today a clandestine terrorist-oriented Islamist organization, violence has often been a feature of Islamist-supported anti-American agitation in the past.

U.S. Policies

There is not a great deal the United States can do specifically to influence the course of Islamic politics in the Northern Tier other than to observe national and Islamic sensitivities. Islamist tendencies tend to be stimulated by adversity, but they are not exclusively dependent upon that factor. Islam need not be a negative factor in general in the politics of these countries, it is only in its more extremist forms of political expression that it has strongly threatened American interests and lives.

U.S. confrontation with Islamic states anywhere can obviously have a bearing on Muslim world attitudes toward the United States. The continued festering of the Palestinian situation is one such issue, and solving it would serve to reduce at least one of the more salient conflicts in the Muslim world. The Gulf War also generated Islamist opposition to the U.S. military campaign against Iraq, most notably in Pakistan, but the reaction never got out of hand.

U.S. policymakers will need to remain sensitive to Islamic sentiment within these countries. But while such a statement is easy to make it is harder to implement. Latent reservoirs of anti-U.S. feeling exist in many parts of the Third World, and especially the Muslim world, based on a complex syndrome of grievances, many or most of which are not of American doing but for which the United States attracts censure simply because of its size, its wealth, its broad international presence, its pervasive official, private, cultural, and commercial influence, and its role as "center of the capitalist world." Some of this latent hostility cannot be overcome. U.S. policymakers and diplomats should remain sensitive to the Islamic element within Muslim societies, gauge its growth, and avoid assuming that the often pro-U.S. attitudes of the Westernized elites in power are representative of a country as a whole. Indeed, when power shifts abruptly out of the hands of one group into another, there can be unpleasant surprises if we have systematically ignored the views of an important segment of society not in power at the time. The United States will always have to live with the presence of many of these Islamist groups within these countries; we must recognize and accept that their views will inevitably constrain both U.S. policies and the acceptability of U.S. policies to the non-Islamist elite. To ignore these views and ride roughshod over them, or even to support local leadership that does the same, may bring highly negative and unforeseen returns in the future.

U.S. assistance to Muslim countries will clearly help improve attitudes. But we also know from experience that such aid, however well-intentioned and valuable, can be seen as heavy-handed cultural intervention when it assumes too high a profile in the life of a country. Under such circumstances, aid can become the spark for Islamist opposition.

In the end, democracy is probably the most effective instrument to prevent the growth of virulent Islamist forces. In countries such as Turkey, Egypt, and Tunisia, where Islamist parties have had to compete in open elections, espouse positions, and articulate a clear set of potential policies, such parties have received only a limited, but nonetheless significant, portion of the vote. Suppression generally serves to strengthen the radicalism of Islamist parties and groups and to increase their appeal to oppressed citizenry. Islamists are forced toward greater moderation and acceptance of democratic processes when they are required to compete in open elections.

Islamism is not inherently democratic in outlook, but its leadership recognizes that the movement has suffered deeply at the hands of totalitarian or authoritarian regimes around the world, making democracy a much safer and preferable system of government, even if it is not explicitly Islamist in character. U.S. support for democracy—a long-term policy goal that has sometimes suffered under the choices imposed by the Cold War—is the most effective instrument for helping deradicalize Islamic extremism.

The United States must above all avoid becoming paranoid about Islam. The Islamists occupy only a part of the whole spectrum of Islam. Other moderate Muslims in these countries find much to admire about the West, as well as much to criticize. They wish to maintain ties with the West. But to the extent that there are "objective" anti-American feelings for various reasons in different segments of Muslim societies, there will invariably be some Islamic expression of that hostility, which would in any case be expressed through some vehicle or other. This reality will not disappear, and the United States must learn to live with it while working over the longer term for the alleviation of the most serious problems of long-range economic, social, and political development of the Third World. We are well equipped to do so; our greatest weakness is perhaps our occasional heavy-handedness or cultural insensitivity in doing so owing to the sheer weight and exuberance of our culture and society.

In the end, we are talking about the problem of limiting extremism rather than limiting the idea or political expression of Islam per se which does not at all have to assume extremist or anti-U.S. form.

Security, Stability, and Migration

MYRON WEINER

Conceptual Approaches

. . . Consider the following:

- As a result of an international embargo following its invasion of Kuwait the government of Iraq seized western immigrants, placed them at strategic locations in order to prevent air strikes, and offered to exchange Asian immigrants for shiploads of food.
- Palestinian immigrants in Kuwait collaborated with the Iraqi invaders, thereby strengthening Iraq's hold on Kuwait but at the same time threatening the position of Palestinian immigrants in other countries in the Gulf.
- Iraq recruited 1.5 million Egyptian farm laborers as replacements for the nearly one million men conscripted into the military to serve in the war with Iran. Many remained in the country even as relations between Iraq and Egypt deteriorated.
- As a result of an exodus of East Germans to Austria through Czechoslovakia and Hungary in July and August 1989, the East German Government opened its western borders. The result was a massive flight to West Germany, clashes between refugees and the police, the fall of the East German government, and the absorption of East Germany by the Federal Republic of Germany.

Myron Weiner, "Security, Stability, and Migration," Defense and Arms Control Studies Program Working Paper (Cambridge: MIT Center for International Studies, December 1990). Reprinted with permission of Myron Weiner.

- Following an announcement by Palestinian radicals that they would launch terrorist attacks against airlines that carried Soviet Jews to Israel, several governments instructed their state-owned airlines not to carry the immigrants.
- A band of armed refugees in Uganda from the Tutsi tribe launched an invasion of Rwanda in an effort to overthrow the Hutu dominated government and restore Tutsi domination.
- Fearful that a large scale influx of Vietnamese refugees might jeopardize the security of Hong Kong, the British government ordered the return of the Vietnamese in spite of considerable international protest.

These developments suggest the need for a security/stability framework for the study of international migration which focuses on state policies toward emigration and immigration as shaped by concerns over internal stability and international security. Such a framework would consider political changes within states as a major determinant of international population flows, and migration—including refugee flows—both as a cause and a consequences of international conflict.

A security/stability framework can be contrasted with an international political economy framework which explains international migration primarily by focusing on global inequalities, the economic linkages between sending and receiving states, including the movement of capital, technology, and the role played by transnational institutions, and structural changes in labor markets linked to changes in the international division of labor. . . .

While at times complementary, the frameworks often yield different outcomes. A political economy perspective, for example, may lead the analyst to regard the movement of people from a poor to a rich country as mutually advantageous (the one benefitting from remittances, the other from needed additions to its labor force) whereas a security/stability perspective of the same migration flow may lead one to point to the political risks associated with changes in the ethnic composition of the receiving country and of the attending international strains that result if there are clashes between natives and migrants. A reverse assessment may also be rendered: a political economy perspective may lead the analyst to conclude that migration results in a brain drain from the sending country while worsening unemployment and creating housing shortages in the receiving country, while a security/stability framework may lead the analyst looking at the same migration flow to argue that internal security and international peace can be enhanced because the migrants are an ethnic minority unwelcomed in their home country but welcomed or at least readily accepted by another country. The movement of people may be acceptable to both countries even though each incurs an economic loss. Thus, a cost/benefit analysis may yield different assessments and policies depending upon which framework is chosen.

Much of the contemporary literature on international migration focuses on global economic conditions as the key determinants of population movements. Differentials in wages and employment opportunities—a high demand for labor in one country and a surplus in another—stimulate the movement of labor. According to economic theories of migration, individuals will emigrate if the expected benefits exceed the costs, with the results that the propensity to migrate from one region or country to another is viewed as being determined by average wages, the cost of travel, and labor market conditions. Accordingly, it is argued, changes in the global economy, such as a rise in the world price of oil or shifts in terms of trade and international flows of capital, will increase the demand for labor in some countries and decrease it in others. Moreover, the development strategies pursued by individual countries may lead to high growth rates in some and low growth rates and stagnation in others. Uneven economic development among states and a severe maldistribution of income within states may induce individuals and families to move across international boundaries to take advantage of greater opportunities.

These economic explanations go a long way toward explaining a great deal of international population movements but they neglect two critical political elements. The first is that international population movements are often impelled, encouraged, or prevented by governments or political forces for reasons that may have little to do with economic conditions. Indeed, much of the international population flows, especially within Africa and South Asia, are only marginally determined, if at all, by changes in the global or regional political economy. And secondly, even when economic conditions create inducements for people to leave one country for another it is governments that decide whether their citizens should be allowed to leave and governments that decide whether immigrants should be allowed to enter and their decisions are frequently based on non-economic considerations. Any effort, therefore, to develop a framework for the analysis of transnational flows of people must also take into account the political determinants and constraints upon these flows. . . .

Forced and Induced Emigrations: A Global Perspective

. . . First, governments may force emigration as a means of achieving cultural homogeneity or for asserting the dominance of one ethnic community over another. Such flows have a long and sordid world-wide history. The rise of nationalism in Europe was accompanied by state actions to eject religious communities that did not subscribe to the established religion, and ethnic minorities that did not belong to the dominant ethnic community. In the fifteenth century, the Spanish crown expelled the Jews. In the sixteenth century the French expelled the Huguenots. In the seventeenth and eighteenth centuries the British crown induced Protestant dissenters to settle in the American colonies. And in the nineteenth century minorities throughout Eastern Europe—Bulgarians, Greeks, Jews, Turks, Hungarians, Serbs, Macedonians—were put to flight.

Many of the population movements in post-independence Africa, the Middle East, South and Southeast Asia are similarly linked to the rise of nationalism and the emergence of new states. The boundaries of many of new post-colonial regimes divided linguistic, religious and tribal communities, with the result that minorities, fearful of their future and often faced with discrimination and violence, migrated to join their ethnic brethren in a neighboring country. Many third world countries also expelled their ethnic minorities, especially when the minorities constituted an industrious class of migrant origin in competition with a middle class ethnic majority. Governments faced with unemployment within the majority community and conflicts among ethnic groups over language and educational opportunities often regarded the expulsion of a prosperous, well placed minority as a politically popular policy. Minorities were often threatened by the state's antagonistic policies toward their religion, their language and their culture, as the state sought to impose a hegemonic ethnic or religious identity upon its citizens. Economically successful minorities were often told that others would be given preferences in employment, a policy of reverse discrimination which effectively made it difficult for minorities to compete on the basis of merit. Many governments expelled their minorities or created conditions which induced them to leave, and thereby forced other countries, on humanitarian grounds, out of cultural affinity, to accept them as refugees. The list is long: Chinese in Vietnam, Indians and Pakistanis in East Africa, Tamils in Sri Lanka, Bahais in Iran, Kurds in Turkey, Iran and Iraq, Ahmediyas in Pakistan, Chakmas in Bangladesh, and in Africa communities in Rwanda, Ethiopia and Sudan, to name a few.

Secondly, governments have forced emigration as a means of dealing with political dissidents and class enemies. The ancient Greeks were among the earliest to strip dissidents of citizenship and cast them to exile. Socrates himself was offered the option of going into exile rather than being executed. Contemporary authoritarian governments have expelled dissidents or allowed them to go into exile as an alternative to imprisonment. In the United States exiles from the third world—from Ethiopia, Iran, Cuba, South Korea, Nicaragua, Vietnam, Chile—have largely replaced exiles from Europe.

Governments may expel not only a handful of dissidents, but a substantial portion of the population hostile to the regime. Revolutionary regimes often see large scale emigration of a social class as a way of transforming the country's social structure. The exodus of more than a half million members of the Cuban middle class was regarded by the Castro regime as a way of disposing of a social class hostile to socialism. In 1971 the Pakistan government sought to weaken the insurgency in East Pakistan by forcing large numbers of Bengali Hindus out of the country. The Vietnamese government justified expulsions as a way of eliminating a bourgeois social class opposed to the regime. The Kampuchean government killed or forced into exile citizens tainted with French and other western cultural influences in an effort to reduce its cultural and economic ties with the west. And in Afghanistan, the Soviet and Afghan military forced populations hostile to the regime to flee to Pakistan and Iran.

A third type of forced emigration can be described as part of a strategy to achieve a foreign policy objective. Governments, for example, may force emigration as a way of putting pressure on neighboring states, though they may deny any such intent. The refugee receiving country, however, often understands that a halt to unwanted migration is not likely to take place unless it yields on a demand made by the country from which the refugees come. In the late 1970s, for example, the United States government believed that the government of Haiti was encouraging its citizens to flee by boat to Florida to press the United States to substantially increase its economic aid. (It did.) In the 1980s Pakistan officials believed that Soviet pressure on Afghans to flee was in part intended to force Pakistan to seek a settlement with the Afghan regime and to withdraw military aid to the insurgents. The Malaysian government feared that the government of Vietnam sought to destabilize them by forcing them to accept Chinese refugees. The Federal Republic of Germany believed that the German Democratic Republic was permitting Tamil refugees to enter through the Berlin border to force the FRG to establish new rules of entry that would tacitly recognize the East German state, or alternatively, as a bargaining ploy for additional financial credits (which it subsequently granted in return for halting the flow). . . .

When Is Migration a Threat to Security and Stability?

. . . Before turning to an analysis of how, why and when states regard immigrants and refugees as potential threats, it is first necessary to note that some obvious explanations are of limited utility. Plausibly a country with little unemployment, a high demand for labor, and the financial resources to provide the housing and social services required by immigrants would regard migration as beneficial while a country low on each of these dimensions would regard migration as economically and socially destabilizing. Using these criteria, therefore, one might expect Japan to welcome migrants and Israel to reject them!

A second plausible explanation is the volume of immigration. It is self-evident that a country faced with a large-scale influx would feel threatened, compared with a country experiencing a small influx of migrants. From this perspective one might have expected the Federal Republic of Germany to regard the influx of a trickle of Sri Lankans with equanimity, but to move swiftly to halt an influx of 2,000 East Germans daily, or for the countries of Africa to feel more threatened by the onrush of refugees and hence less receptive than the countries of Western Europe confronted with a trickle from the third world.

Economics does, of course, matter. A country willing to accept immigrants when its economy is booming is likely to close its doors in a recession. But economics does not explain many of the differences between countries nor does it explain the criteria countries employ to decide whether a particular group of migrants or refugees is acceptable or is regarded as threatening. Similarly, volume can matter, but again it depends upon who is at the door.

Ethnic affinity would appear to be the most likely explanation for accepting or rejecting migrants. Presumably a country is receptive to those who share the same language, religion or race, but may regard as threatening those with whom such an identity is not shared. While generally true, there are striking exceptions. For more than half a century Americans rejected "Oriental" immigrants while today most Americans regard Asians as a model minority whose educational and economic successes and patriotism make them more desirable immigrants than others who are in language, religion and race closer to most Americans but are less successful. Moreover, what constitutes cultural affinity for one group in a multi-ethnic society may represent a cultural, social and economic threat to another: note, for example, the response of Afro-Americans in Florida to Cuban migrants, Indian Assamese response to Bangladeshis, and Pakistan Sindhi response to Biharis. . . .

Refugees and Immigrants as a Source of International Conflict

Since refugees are legally defined by most countries as individuals with a well founded fear of persecution the decision to grant asylum or refugee status implies a severe criticism of another state. Thus, the bitter debate in Congress in January 1990 over whether Chinese students should be permitted to remain because of the persecutions in China was regarded by the People's Republic of China as "interference" in its internal affairs, a judgment which many members of Congress (but not the President) were prepared to make. Moreover, to classify individuals as refugees with a well founded fear of persecution is also to grant them the moral (as distinct from political) right to oppose a regime engaged in persecution so judged by the country that has granted them asylum. The view of the United Nations High Commissioner for

Refugees is that the granting of refugee status does not imply criticism of the sending by the receiving country, but such a view clearly contradicts the conception of the refugee as one with a fear of *persecution*. Moreover, democratic regimes generally allow their refugees to speak out against the regime of their country of origin, grant them access to the media, and permit them (to the extent the law permits) to send information and money back home in support of the opposition. The decision to grant refugee status thus often creates an adversary relationship with the country that produces refugees.

The receiving country may have no such intent, but even where its motives are humanitarian the mere granting of asylum can be sufficient to create an antagonistic relationship. In the most famous asylee related episode in this century, Iranian revolutionaries took violent exception to the U.S. decision to permit the Shah of Iran to enter the U.S. for medical reasons (which many Iranians regarded as a form of asylum) and used it as an occasion for taking American hostages.

A refugee-receiving country may actively support the refugees in their quest to change the regime of their country of origin. Refugees are potentially a tool in inter-state conflict. Numerous examples abound: the United States armed Cubans in an effort to overthrow the Castro regime at the Bay of Pigs; the United States armed Contra exiles from Nicaragua; the Indian government armed Bengali "freedom fighters" against the Pakistan military; the Indian government provided military support for Tamil refugees from Sri Lanka to give the Indian government leverage in the Tamil-Sinhalese dispute; Pakistan, Saudi Arabia, China and the U.S. armed Afghan refugees in order to force Soviet troops to withdraw from Afghanistan; the Chinese provided arms to Khmer Rouge refugees to help overthrow the Vietnamese-backed regime in Cambodia; the Palestinian refugees received Arab support against Israelis. Refugee-producing countries may thus have good reason for fearing an alliance between the refugees and their national adversaries. . . .

There are numerous examples of diasporas seeking to undermine the regime of their home country: South Koreans and Taiwanese in the United States (who supported democratic movements at home), Iranians in France (Khomeini himself during the reign of the Shah, and opponents of Khomeini's Islamic regime thereafter), Asian Indians in North America and the U.K. (after Mrs. Gandhi declared an emergency), Indian Sikhs (supporting secession), and dissident Sri Lankan Tamils and Northern Ireland Catholics among others.

The home country may take a dim view of the activities of its citizens abroad, and hold the host country responsible for their activities. Host countries, especially if they are democratic, are loath to restrict migrants engaged in lawful activities, especially since some of the migrants have already become citizens. The home country may even plant intelligence operators abroad to monitor the activities of its migrants and take steps to prevent further emigration. The embassy of the home country may also provide encouragement to its supporters within the diaspora. The diaspora itself may become a focal point of controversy: between the home and host countries, among contending groups within the diaspora, as well as between sections of the diaspora and the home government. Thus, struggles that might overwise only take place within a country become internationalized if the country has a significant overseas population.

Refugees and Immigrants as a Political Risk to the Host Country

Governments are often concerned that refugees to whom they give protection may turn against them if they are unwilling to assist them in their opposition to the government of their country of origin. Paradoxically, the risk may be particularly high if the host country arms the refugees against their country of origin. Guns can be pointed in both directions and the receiving country takes the risk that refugees will dictate the host country's policies toward the sending country. Two examples come to mind. The decision by Arab countries to provide political support and arms to Palestinian refugees from Israel created within the Arab states a population capable of influencing their own foreign policies and internal politics. Palestinians, for example, became a political force within Lebanon in ways that subsequently made them political and security problems for Lebanon, Syria, Jordan, Israel, France and the United States. The support of Iraqi invaders by Palestinians in Kuwait was an asset to Iraq since Palestinians (who number 400,000 in Kuwait) hold important positions in the Kuwaiti administration. Throughout the Middle East governments must consider the capacity of the Palestinians to undermine their regimes should they adopt policies that are unacceptable. Similarly, the arming of Afghan refugees in Pakistan limited the options available to the government of Pakistan in its dealings with the governments of Afghanistan and the Soviet Union. The Pakistan government armed the Afghans in order to pressure the Soviets to withdraw their forces and to agree to a political settlement, but the Pakistan government is also constrained by the knowledge that it cannot sign an agreement with the Soviet or Afghan governments that is unacceptable to the armed Afghan.

Refugees have launched terrorist attacks within their host country, illegally smuggled arms, allied with the opposition against host government policies, participated in drug traffic, and in other ways eroded a government's willingness to admit refugees. Palestinians, Sikhs, Croatians, Kurds, Armenians, Sri Lankan Tamils, and northern Irish, among others, are regarded with suspicion by intelligence and police authorities and their request for asylum is scrutinized not only for whether they have a well-founded fear of persecution; but for whether their presence constitutes a threat to the host country. . . .

Migrants Perceived as a Threat to Cultural Identity

Cultures differ with respect to how they define who belongs to or can be admitted into their community. These norms govern whom one admits, what rights and privileges are given to those who are permitted to enter, and whether the host culture regards a migrant community as potential citizens. A violation of these norms (by unwanted immigrants, for example) is often regarded as a threat to basic values and in that sense is perceived as a threat to national security.

These norms are often embedded in the law of citizenship, that is who by virtue of birth is entitled as a matter of right to be a citizen and who is permitted to become a naturalized citizen. The familiar distinction is between the concept of *jus sanguinis,* whereby a person wherever born is a citizen of the state of his parents, and *jus soli,* the rule that a child receives its nationality from the soil or place of birth. The ties of blood descent are broader than merely parentage for they suggest a broader "volk" or people to whom one belongs in a kind of fictive relationship. The Federal Republic of Germany has such a legal norm. Under a law passed in 1913—and still valid—German citizenship at birth is based exclusively on descent; thus the children of migrants born in Germany are not thereby entitled to citizenship. The Basic Law, as it is called, also accords citizenship to those Germans who no longer live in Germany and may no longer speak German but came (or their ancestors came) from the territories from which Germans were expelled after the war. Thus, thousands of immigrants who entered the Federal Republic from East Germany or from Poland were regarded as German citizens returning "home." Other countries share a similar conception. Israel, for example, has a Law of Return, under which all Jews, irrespective of where they presently live, are entitled to "return" home to reclaim, as it were, their citizenship. Nepal also has a law which entitles those who are of Nepali "origin," though they have lived in India, Singapore, Hong Kong or elsewhere for several generations, to reclaim their citizenship by returning home....

A norm of indigenousness may also be widely shared by a section of a country's population and even incorporated into its legal system. This norm prescribes differential rights between those who are classified as indigenous and those who, irrespective of the length of time they or their ancestors resided in the country, are not so classified. An indigenous people assert a superior claim to land, employment, education, political power, and to the central national symbols not accorded to others who live within the country. The indigenous—called *bhoomiputras* in Malaysia, sons of the soil in India, and native peoples in some societies—may assert an exclusiveness denied to others, often resting on the notion that they as a people exist only within one country, while others have other homes to which they can return. Thus, the Sinhalese in Sri Lanka, the Malays in Malaysia, the Assamese in Assam, and the Melanesians in Fiji, among others, subscribe to an ideology of indigenousness which has, in various guises, been enshrined in the legal system and which shapes the response of these societies to immigrants. The *bhoomiputras* in Malaysia regarded the influx of Chinese and others from Vietnam as a fundamental threat, indeed so threatening as to lead the government to sink Vietnamese boats carrying refugees. Similarly, the Assamese rejected the influx of Bengalis, Nepalis and Marwaris from the other parts of India (as well as immigrants from Bangladesh), fearing that any demographic change would threaten their capacity to maintain the existing legal arrangement under which native Assamese are provided opportunities in education and employment not accorded other residents of the state who are also citizens of India.

Nativism, a variant of the norm of indigenousness, played an important role in shaping the U.S. Immigration Act of 1924 with its national origins clause providing for national quotas. This legislation, and the political sentiment that underlay it, resulted in a restrictive policy toward refugees throughout the 1930s and early 1940s. After the war, however, the older American tradition of civic pluralism was politically triumphant. It shaped the 1965 Immigration Act which eliminated national quotas and gave preferences to individuals with skills and to family unification. The numbers and composition of migrants then significantly changed. From the mid 1960s to the later 1980s between five hundred thousand and one million migrants and refugees entered each year, with nearly half the immigrants coming from Asia.

Citizenship in the United States is acquired by birth or by naturalization. Originally, American law permitted naturalization only to "free white persons," but subsequent acts permitted naturalization to all irrespective of race. Apart from the usual residence requirements, U.S. naturalization law requires applicants to demonstrate their knowledge of the American Constitution and form of government and to swear allegiance to the principles of the U.S. Constitution. Political knowledge and loyalty are thus the norms for membership, not consanguinity. It is in part because the United States has political rather than ethnic criteria for naturalization that the United States has been more supportive of immigration and in the main has felt less threatened by immigration than most other countries.

For much of its history a low level of threat perception has also characterized the French response to immigration. While a concern for cultural unity is a central element in the French conception of nationhood, the French have also had a political conception of citizenship derived from the revolutionary origins of the notion of citizenship. The French, as Rogers Brubaker has written,[1] are universalist and assimilationist in contrast with the Volk-centered Germans. The result is that the French have been more willing to

---

[1]Brubaker, William Rogers, editor, *Immigration and the Politics of Citizenship in Europe and North America,* Lanham, MD: University Press of America, 1989.

naturalize immigrants than have the Germans and more open to political refugees than most other West European countries. . . .

Legal definitions of citizenship aside, most societies react with alarm when there is an unregulated large-scale illegal migration of people who do not share the same culture and national identity. Examples abound. The people of India's northeastern state of Assam are fearful that the influx of Bangladeshis will reduce them to a minority, a realistic fear given the precarious hold of the Assamese on the state. Illegal migration into Sabah from the Philippines and Indonesia—an estimated 700,000 or half of Sabah's 1.4 million indigenous population—has created anxieties in that state of Malaysia. The government of Malaysia is particularly uneasy since the Philippines lays claim to Sabah and some of its leaders insist that so long as the dispute continues Malaysia has no right to consider Filipinos as illegal aliens. Should the Filipinos acquire citizenship, it has been noted, they might win a third or more of Sabah's parliamentary seats and pursue a merger with the Philippines. The Philippines might thereby acquire through colonization what it is unable to win through diplomatic or military means.

Concern over colonization, it should be noted, can also be an internal affair in multi-ethnic societies. A central government may regard internal migration as a right of all citizens, but territorially based ethnic groups may regard an influx of people from other parts of the country as a cultural and political threat. Hence, the Moros in Mindanao revolted at the in-migration of people from other parts of the Philippines, Sri Lanka's Tamils oppose settlement by Sinhalese in "their" region, and a variety of India's linguistic communities regard in-migration as a form of colonization.

Colonization as a means of international conquest and annexation can in fact be the deliberate intent of a state. The government of Morocco, for example, moved 350,000 civilians into Western Sahara in an effort to claim and occupy disputed territory. The Israeli government provides housing subsidies to its citizens to settle on the West Bank. Since the annexation of the Turkic regions of central Asia in the 19th century the Czarist and Soviet regimes have encouraged Russian settlement while a similar policy of settling Han people has been pursued by the Chinese government in Sinkiang province.

Migrants Perceived as a Social or Economic Burden

Ethnicity aside, societies may react to immigrants because of their social behavior—criminality, welfare dependency, delinquency, etc.—or simply because their numbers are so large (or so poor) that they place a substantial economic burden on society even if the migrants are of the same ethnic community as that of the host society. This sense of threat can be particularly acute if the government of the sending country appears to be engaged in a policy of population "dumping" by exporting its criminals, unwanted ethnic minorities, and "surplus" population at the cost of the receiving country. The United States, for example, distinguished between those Cubans who fled the Communist regime and Cuban convicts removed from prisons and placed on boats for the United States. India accepted Hindus from Pakistan in the late 1940s and early 1950s who preferred to live in India, but regarded as destabilizing and threatening the forced exodus of East Pakistanis in the early 1970s, which India saw as a Pakistan effort to change the demographic balance between East and West Pakistan at India's expense. Governments also distinguished between situations in which ethnic minorities are permitted to leave (e.g., Jews from the Soviet Union) and situations in which minorities are forced to flee (e.g., Bulgarian Turks and Sri Lankan Tamils).

In the eighteenth and nineteenth centuries several European governments promoted emigration as a way of easing the social and political burdens that might result from poverty and crime. In the latter part of the eighteenth century the British exported prisoners to Australia. It has been estimated[2] that between 1788 and 1868 England exiled 160,000 of its criminals to Australia as a convenient way to get rid of prisoners and reduce the costs of maintaining prisons. In the middle of the nineteenth century the British regarded emigration as a form of famine relief for Ireland. In seven famine years, from 1849 to 1856, one and a half million Irish emigrated, mostly across the Atlantic.[3] In Germany, where 1,500,000 emigrated between 1871 and 1881, local officials believed that "a large body of indigent subjects constitute a social danger and a serious burden on meager public funds; better let them go."[4] Reacting to these policies one American scholar wrote in 1890 that "there is something almost revolting in the anxiety of certain countries to get rid of their surplus population and to escape the burden of supporting the poor, the helpless and the depraved."[5]

The fears of western countries notwithstanding, population dumping has not been a significant element in the flow of migrants from the third world to advanced industrial countries. To the extent that population dumping has occurred, it has largely been of ethnic minorities and the flight has been primarily to neighboring developing countries rather than to advanced industrial countries.

Forced population movements of ethnic minorities took place in eastern Europe during the interwar period, placing enormous economic and social strains upon the receiving countries, taking a heavy toll upon the migrants themselves, and worsening relations among states. But because there was an

[2]Hughes, Robert, *The Fatal Shore*, 1987.

[3]Jonston, H.J.M., *British Emigration Policy 1815–1830, Shovelling out Paupers*. Oxford: Clarendon Press, 1972.

[4]Walker, Mack, *Germany and the Emigration 1860–1885*. Cambridge: Harvard University Press, 1964.

[5]Mayo-Smith, Richard, *Emigration and Immigration: A Study in Social Science*. New York: Charles Scribner and Sons, 1890. Reprinted 1968, pp. 197–198.

element of exchange, and minorities moved to states in which their ethnic community was a majority, settlement was possible and violent international conflict was avoided. In 1922–23 Greeks fled Turkey and Turks fled Greece. An estimated 1.5 million people from both nations were involved. In a different though related population exchange, the Greek government in 1923, in an effort to Hellenize its Macedonian region, forced the exodus of its Bulgarian population. As the Bulgarian refugees moved into Greek-speaking areas of Bulgaria, the local Greek population fled southward to Greece.[6] The world's largest population exchange was in South Asia where fourteen million people moved between India and Pakistan between 1947 and 1950. But since both countries respected the wishes of ethnic minorities in each country to settle in the country in which they constituted a majority, the exchange took place without a conflict between the two countries. Similarly, the forced exit of Jews from North Africa to Israel in the 1950s was not a source of international conflict since the refugees were welcomed by Israel. In contrast, however, the flight of Arabs from Israel in 1948 led to an interminable conflict between Israel and its Arab neighbors since the Arab states did not recognize the legitimacy of the new state.

Where one state promotes or compels emigration to a state that limits or prohibits entry, the situation is fraught with a high potential for armed conflict.[7] The flow of refugees from East Pakistan to northeastern India, from Vietnam, Cambodia, and Laos to Thailand, from Burma to Bangladesh, and from Bangladesh to India has been the basis for regional conflicts that have often become violent. The magnitude of the flows, the element of forced emigration, the social and economic burden on the receiving country, a history of enmity between sending and receiving countries, the absence of a population exchange that might ease the land problem are all elements making these movements major inter-state crises. . . .

Migrants as Hostages: Risks for the Sending Country

Following the invasion of Kuwait on August 2, 1990, the government of Iraq announced a series of measures in which migrants were used as instruments for the achievement of political objectives. The first measure was to declare that westerners living in Iraq and Kuwait would be forcibly held as a shield against armed attack in an effort to deter the United States and its allies from launching airstrikes against military facilities where hostages might be

---

[6]Marrus, Michael R., *The Unwanted: European Refugees in the Twentieth Century.* New York: Oxford University Press, 1985.

[7]For an analysis of how conflicting rules of exit and entry affect interstate relations, see Weiner, Myron, "International Migration and International Relations," *Population and Development Review,* II (3), 1985, 441–456.

located. The Iraqi government then made distinctions among Asian migrants, indicating its willingness to treat more favorably those countries (such as India) which did not send troops to Saudia Arabia than those countries (Pakistan and Bangladesh) that did. The Iraqi government subsequently declared that food would not be provided for Asian migrants (including Indians) unless their countries sent food supplies and medicines, thereby weakening the United Nations embargo.

While the Iraqi strategy of using their control over migrants for international bargaining is unique, it should be noted that the mere presence of migrants in a country from which they could be expelled has been for some time an element in the behavior of the migrants' home country. The countries of South Asia have long been aware of their dependence upon migration to the Gulf and have recognized that any sudden influx of returning migrants would create a major problem for domestic security as remittances came to an end, balance of payments problems were created, families dependent upon migrant income were threatened with destitution, and large numbers of people were thrown into labor markets where there already existed substantial unemployment. All these fears have now materialized. In the past, sending governments aware of these potential consequences have hesitated to criticize host governments for the treatment of migrant workers. When workers have been expelled for strikes and other agitational activities, the home governments have sought to pacify their migrants—and the host government—in an effort to avoid further expulsions. Governments have often remained silent even when workers' contracts have been violated. Thus, the instinctive and understandable reaction of some governments with migrants in Kuwait and Iraq was to see first whether it was possible for their migrants to remain, and to assure the security of their citizens rather than to support international efforts against Iraqi aggression. . . .

Implications for Immigration and Refugee Policies

For the foreseeable future the numbers of people who wish to leave or are forced to leave their countries will continue to substantially exceed the numbers other countries are willing to accept. Indeed, for many reasons, the gap is likely to increase.

Democratization, or at least political liberalization of authoritarian regimes, is enabling some people to leave who previously were denied the right of exit. The removal of the Berlin wall resulted in an East German exodus although the government of the German Democratic Republic had hoped that by removing the wall they might thereby induce their citizens to remain at home. Under glasnost the Soviet Union has permitted a substantial number of Jews to obtain exit permits. And given the economic and political difficulties the new regimes in Eastern Europe are likely to encounter, we should anticipate a steady and perhaps rising demand for exit.

The political liberalization of multi-ethnic communist regimes has been accompanied by a reappearance of older conflicts among ethnic groups. There have been conflicts between Turks and Bulgarians in Turkey, Romanians and Hungarians in Transylvania, Armenians and Azerbaijanis in the Caucasus, Albanians and Serbians in Kosovo, and a variety of ethnic conflicts in Central Asia. There is thus a high potential for emigration from the multiethnic regions of Eastern Europe and from the Soviet Union, especially from the Baltic states, the Caucasus, and Central Asia.

Africa's authoritarian regimes have had little success in preventing conflicts among tribal and ethnic groups, although they have often justified one party states and military rule as necessary for avoiding violent conflict. But even if democratization begins to take root in Africa as it has in Eastern Europe, it is uncertain that ethnic conflicts, and the refugee movements that often result, will thereby decline. Indeed, the political transformations now under way in South Africa could result in increased conflicts as each of the various groups contends for control of the political system. Thus, struggles are already under way between Zulu supporters of Inkatha and Zulu supporters of the United Democratic Front in Natal, and among a variety of ethnic groups throughout the country.

A long-term decline in the birth rate in advanced industrial countries combined with continued economic growth is likely to lead employers to seek low-wage laborers from abroad. Transnational investment in manufacturing industries may reduce some of the manpower needs, but the demand for more workers in the service sector seems likely to grow, barring technological breakthroughs that will replace waiters, bus conductors, nurses, and household help. Employers in Japan, Singapore, and portions of the United States and Western Europe are prepared to hire illegal migrants, notwithstanding the objections of their governments and much of the citizenry. So long as employer demand remains high, borders are porous, and government enforcement of employer sanctions is limited, illegal migration seems likely to continue and in some countries increase. . . .

However many immigrants are admitted the numbers who want to enter will far exceed how many migrants countries are prepared to admit. Sealing borders is one response, but rarely wholly effective even in the case of islands. Control is difficult for any country with large coastlines or land borders. State regulation of employers (including penalties for employing illegals) and the use of identity cards has made a difference in the countries of Western Europe but is not an option readily usable for a country with large numbers of small firms, a poorly developed administrative structure, and officials who are easily corrupted. Moreover, however opposed the government and a majority of the population are to illegal migration, there are often elements within the society who welcome refugees and migrant workers: employers, ethnic kinfolk, political sympathizers, and officials willing to accept bribes.

Faced with unwanted flows whose entrance they cannot control, governments have increasingly turned to strategies for halting *emigration*. We can identify three such strategies.

The first is to pay for what one does not want. It has been suggested that an infusion of aid and investment, an improvement in trade, the resolution of the debt crisis and other measures that would improve income and unemployment in low income countries would reduce the rate of emigration. Meritorious as these proposals are there is no evidence that they can reduce emigration, at least not in the short run. Indeed, high rates of emigration have often been associated with high economic growth rates. It was so for Great Britain in the 19th century, and in recent years for South Korea, Taiwan, Turkey, Algeria and Greece. Moreover, economic aid is unlikely to affect the political factors which induce people to leave. Nonetheless, under some circumstances, economic assistance can reduce unwanted migrations, but primarily when the sending country has the means to prevent people from leaving. As noted earlier, U.S. economic assistance to Haiti halted a growing refugee flow; similarly, the flow of Sri Lankan refugees to West Germany from East Germany was reduced when the Federal Republic of Germany agreed to provide credits to the German Democratic Republic. In the Haitian case, government-to-government aid was intended by the donor country to persuade the recipient country to halt the exodus; in the German case, the aid was intended to persuade the recipient country to cease providing transit to unwanted refugees.

Assistance can also be used by governments to persuade other governments to retain their refugees. Thus, the United States and France have been willing to provide economic assistance to Thailand if the Thais would hold Vietnamese refugees rather than permit these refugees to seek entrance into the U.S. and France. The UNHCR [United Nations High Commission on Refugees] and other largely western-financed international agencies provide resources to refugee-receiving countries—especially in Africa—not only as an expression of Western humanitarian concerns, but also as a means of enabling refugees to remain in the country of first asylum rather than attempting to move elsewhere, especially to advanced industrial countries.

Secondly, where generosity does not work or is not financially feasible, receiving countries may employ a variety of threats to halt emigration. Diplomatic pressures may be exerted. The Indian government, for example, put the pressure on the government of Bangladesh to halt Bangladeshi land settlement in the Chittagong Hill tracts after land settlement led the local Chakma tribals to flee into India. The Indian government is in a position to damage Bangladesh trade and to affect the flow of river waters if the government is not accommodating. Where diplomatic means are not sufficient, the threat of force can be employed. When Muslim refugees moved from Burma into Bangladesh as a result of a similar policy of colonization, this time by the Burmese, the Bangladesh government threatened to arm the Burmese Muslim refugees if the colonization did not end. In both cases the threats worked to reduce or halt the flow. In another example, Palestinian supporters threatened international carriers who agreed to carry Jews emigrating from the Soviet Union to Israel, an instance of intervention by a third party which did not want an unimpeded flow between a sending and receiving country. The Arab League representative to the United Nations said that the influx of Soviet Jews into Israel could constitute a threat to international peace and security under the UN charter.[8]

Thirdly, there is the ultimate sanction of armed intervention to change the political conditions within the sending country. In 1971 an estimated ten million refugees fled from East Pakistan to India following the outbreak of a civil war between the eastern and western provinces of Pakistan. This refugee flow was regarded by India as the result of a deliberate policy by the Pakistan military to resolve Pakistan's own internal political problems by forcing upon India East Pakistan's Hindu population. Many Indian officials also believed that the Pakistan government was seeking to change the demographic balance between East and West Pakistan by shifting millions of East Pakistanis to India. The Indian government responded by sending its armed forces into Pakistan, occupied East Pakistan and thereby forced the partition of the country. Within months India moved the refugees home.

There were two other instances in South Asia where armed support for refugees was an instrument of policy by the receiving country. The Pakistan government armed a portion of the 3.7 million Afghan refugees who entered Pakistan following a communist coup in April 1978 and the subsequent Soviet invasion in December 1979. The aim of the Pakistan government was to arm the Afghans to force a Soviet withdrawal, to bring down the Soviet-supported Communist regime, and to repatriate the refugees. . . . The other instance of intervention was the initial Indian support for the Tamil Tigers, a militant group fighting against the Sri Lankan government. The Indian government supported Tamil Tiger refugees in India and enabled arms to flow into Sri Lanka in an effort to force a political settlement between the Tamils and the Sri Lankan government, but the result was that the ethnic conflict worsened and the refugee exodus continued, a factor which led to subsequent direct intervention by the Indian military. . . .

While the notion of sovereignty is still rhetorically recognized, a variety of internal actions by states are increasingly regarded as threats to others. Thus, the spewing of nuclear waste and other hazardous materials into the atmosphere and the contamination of waterways which then flow into other countries is no longer regarded as an internal matter. In the same spirit a

[8]*New York Times,* February 8, 1990.

country which forces its citizens to leave or creates conditions which induce them to leave has internationalized its internal actions.

A conundrum for liberal democratic regimes, however, is that they are reluctant to insist that governments restrain the exit of citizens simply because they or others are unwilling to accept them. Liberal democracies believe in the right of emigration by individuals but they simultaneously believe that governments retain the right to determine who and how many shall be permitted to enter. Liberal regimes may encourage or even threaten countries that produce refugees and unwanted immigrants to change the conditions which induce or force people to leave, but they are reluctant to press governments to prevent people from leaving or to force people to return home against their will. They do not want regimes to prevent political dissidents or persecuted minorities from leaving their country; rather, they want governments to stop their repression. Mass flight across international boundaries justifies actions by states or international organizations to provide incentives, inducements, withdrawal of assistance, or a variety of individual or collective sanctions (e.g., trade or investment restrictions) to change the conditions which create flight. . . .

For advanced industrial countries that admit immigrants there is a preference for a migration policy which creates the fewest domestic or international political problems. One policy option is to admit those who best satisfy the requirements of the receiving country: who have skills needed in the labor market, or capital to create new businesses, or relatives who would facilitate their integration into the society. The criteria for admission then become more meritocratic based upon an agreed upon point system.[9] It is more difficult, and morally contentious, to give preferences to those most acceptable by the home population, though "acceptable" can often mean education and skills rather than culture and race. Moreover, for a labor-short Western Europe, the incorporation of countries of Central and Eastern Europe into the European Community will be politically more palatable than opening borders to north Africans without raising awkward issues of culture and religion. But a limited, largely skill based immigration policy will leave large numbers of people banging on the doors, seeking to enter as refugees or, failing that, as illegals.

An alternative policy based upon the needs of immigrants and refugees is more difficult to formulate, more difficult to implement, and legally and politically more contentious, but morally more attractive. But no policy, short of the obliteration of international boundaries and sovereign states, can deal with the vast numbers of people who want to leave their country for another where opportunities are greater. A moral case can be made for giving preference to those in flight, even at the cost of limiting

[9]Wattenberg, Ben J. and Karl Zinsmeister, "The Case for More Immigration," *Commentary*, 89(4), 1990, 19–25, and Simon, Julian L., *The Economic Consequences of Immigration*, New York: Basil Blackwell, 1989.

the number of immigrants admitted to meet labor force needs or to enable families to reunite. If countries have a ceiling as to how many people they are willing to admit, there is a strong moral argument for providing admissions first to those who are persecuted or whose lives are in danger, and have few places to go. But for reasons indicated earlier only a narrow definition of what constitutes a refugee with a case-by-case review will enable states to put a cap on what they regard as potentially unlimited flows. We thus conclude with a paradoxical formulation, the large-scale unwanted mass population flows that threaten states require that states, individually or collectively through international organizations, seek ways to influence the domestic factors that force and induce people to leave their homeland, even though such interventions may themselves create international conflicts.

The War Over Water

JOHN K. COOLEY

"Water is not necessary to life but rather life itself," the French poet and aviator Antoine de Saint Exupéry wrote on the basis of his vast experience in arid countries. His observation highlights a fundamental of Middle East politics that has lately been forgotten by nearly everyone except Israel and its Arab neighbors. Indeed, long after oil runs out, water is likely to cause wars, cement peace, and make and break empires and alliances in the region, as it has for thousands of years.

The constant struggle for the waters of the Jordan, Litani, Orontes, Yarmuk, and other life-giving Middle East rivers, little understood outside the region, was a principal cause of the 1967 Arab-Israeli war and could help spark a new all-out conflict. It is also a major aspect of the Palestinian question and of the struggle over the future of the West Bank. Since 1947 many an attempt has been made to write peace documents or draw new cease-fire agreements between Israel and its neighbors. Each time, the water question has helped to block agreement. While the need for a rational, overall water-sharing scheme steadily grows more apparent, it seems less attainable, as water issues are aggravated by political tensions and by the fact that, while its neighbors' consumptions are rapidly rising, Israel still consumes roughly five times as much water per capita as each of its less industrialized and less intensively farmed neighbors.

In 1967 Israel went to war against Syria and Syria's ally, Egypt, partly because the Arabs had unsuccessfully tried to divert into Arab rivers Jordan River headwaters that feed Israel. During that war Israel captured Syria's Baniyas River, the last of the important Jordan headwaters not under Israel's control. Israel also succeeded in destroying the foundations and thus halting construction of a giant new dam at Mukheiba on the Yarmuk River,

John K. Cooley, "The War Over Water," *Foreign Policy* No. 54 (Spring 1984). Copyright © 1984 by the Carnegie Endowment for International Peace. Reprinted with permission.

which runs toward Israel between Jordan and Syria. This dam, still desired by Amman and enjoying American and World Bank (International Bank for Reconstruction and Development) backing, would have greatly augmented the water available to pre-1967 Jordan, including the West Bank, but might have deprived Israel of water supplies its planners coveted.

Today the threat of a war stems primarily from Israel's occupation of southern Lebanon. Launched ostensibly to drive out the Palestinian fighters, Israel's June 1982 invasion of Lebanon gave the Jewish state control of the lower reaches of a new river—Lebanon's Litani. The Litani has never flowed into Israel, and the invasion strengthened long-held Arab convictions that capturing its waters and diverting them into Israel has been an important long-term Israeli goal. Official Israeli government silence on the issue and continued expressions of interest in the Litani by Israeli hawks, such as former Defense Minister Ariel Sharon and Technology Minister Yuval Neeman, only serve to fuel Arab fears.

Meanwhile, as early as May 1983, Syrian officials informed the Lebanese government of President Amin Gemayel that Syrian troops would not leave Lebanon until Damascus had obtained, as part of an overall accord protecting Syrian interests in Lebanon, an ironbound water agreement. Syria wanted absolute guarantees that headwaters of the Orontes River, which rises in Lebanon's fertile Bekaa Valley, would never be seized by hostile forces. The Orontes irrigates much of Syria's best farm land and provides both drinking water and electric power for western Syria, the country's most populous region.

Meanwhile, the major project Israel has proposed to solve some of its own water and hydroelectric power problems poses some potentially serious difficulties for another neighbor, Jordan. This project, known as the Med-Dead Canal, would be a saltwater conduit linking the Mediterranean Sea near Gaza with the saline Dead Sea. The canal would use the drop of about 1,300 feet as the water flows east into the Dead Sea basin to drive electric turbines. Practical designs for the canal were drawn up by James Hayes and Joseph Cotton, American water consultants to the Water Planning Authority of Israel. At that time, Israeli Finance Minister Pinhas Sapir said the canal would "compensate the Dead Sea for the diversion of the Jordan River into the [Israeli] diversion system."

Yet the project has alarmed the Arab states, especially Jordan. They have studied delaying or halting the scheme. Specifically, Jordan fears that the rise in the level of the Dead Sea caused by the influx of Mediterranean water will destroy the phosphate extraction and other chemical industries Amman has built on its own side of the Dead Sea, opposite Israel's chemical and nuclear complexes at Arad and Dimona. This fear was heightened by the confirming findings of a 1981 Israeli parliamentary commission report. Jordanians have also feared for the last two generations that the Med-Dead Canal would ruin Jordan's already well-advanced plans for reclaiming for

Jordanian agriculture much of the salt-saturated Wadi Araba region south-
east of the Dead Sea and pollute much of the still-fresh waters of the Jordan
Valley's streams and aquifers. Israel's economic planning already takes these
effects into account; Jordan's economy would need to make costly adjustments.

Rainfall and Politics

The Middle East's problems of water and agriculture stem fundamentally
from its climate, not from politics. Seasonal temperature variations are wide
and rainfall is highly irregular. On the whole the region simply does not receive enough rainfall to support even subsistence agriculture without extensive irrigation. The scarcity of water has weighed upon the region's life since
prehistoric times.

Permanent farms require at least eight inches of water a year—enough to
sustain the grass needed to raise sheep, goats, donkeys, and camels. Somewhat more rainfall is needed to grow most vegetables and fruits. Wherever
rainfall reaches these levels, villages and towns can be built. And where water supplies are supplemented by rivers and wells, cities such as Alexandria,
Baghdad, Damascus, and Tehran have been able to grow. Inadequate or excessively erratic rainfall forces people to stay on the move and live as herds-
men or migrant farmers—like those of the American dust bowl of the 1930s.
They seek the oases: islands in the desert where spring water or cisterns can
be found. And if a season passes without restorative rain, desertification sets
in. Indeed, Arab literature is filled with delighted, sensitive accounts of the
coming of rain, a momentous event, and the Arabic language has a special
verb—*shama*—that means "to watch for lightning flashes to see where rain
will fall."

Despite all the talk of "making the desert bloom," cultivated land still represents no more than 5–7.5 per cent of the Middle East. The rest is mainly
desert, mountain, or swamp. Yet a large percentage of the region's population—including a majority in Syria—depends directly on agriculture for its
livelihood. Many others work as cotton and tobacco packers, fruit driers, or
canners of vegetables, fruit, or olive oil. Paradoxically, however, agriculture
represents less than half the gross national product of Egypt, Israel, Jordan,
Lebanon, and Syria. Thus for most Middle Eastern countries food production for domestic consumption or export remains the least successful aspect
of national economic development.

The Middle East's water problems are regional, deriving from common
sources, and cannot be regarded solely as an Arab-Israeli problem. In fact,
the Arab states have quarreled among themselves about water. But the water
problem's Arab-Israeli dimension is vitally important and is rooted in Israel's original diversion of Jordan River waters after 1948. Since the Palestin-

ian Arabs displaced during the Israeli war of independence and their Arab supporters considered the Israeli state to be illegitimate, they persistently decried the unilateral diversion of the Jordan as completely illegal and utterly nefarious. The Israelis responded that the surrounding Arabs were never willing to let Israel live in peace, that most remained in a state of war with Israel, and that Israel never intended to deprive Arab neighbors of water they needed.

The Jordan River rises in the hills and mountains that make up the Anti-Lebanon range in eastern Lebanon. As the Jordan flows south through the beginning of the Great Rift Valley, it is fed from underground sources and an intricate network of smaller rivers, rivulets, and streams at various points in Jordan, Israel, Syria, and Lebanon. The Jordan continues southward into the middle of the Jordan Valley, forming the border between East Jordan and Israeli-occupied West Jordan (Judaea and Samaria, in official Israeli parlance). The Jordan's main sources are the Hasbani River, which flows from Lebanon into Israel; the Yarmuk River, which rises near the Golan Heights and flows downward between Jordan and the Golan Heights; the Baniyas River, which also originates in Syria; and the Dan River, which rises and flows inside Israel.

The Litani flows entirely inside Lebanon. From its source in the north-central region of the country, it runs south through Lake Qir'awn to a point below steep cliffs where the 11th-century Crusader castle of Beaufort guards the Lebanese-Israeli frontier. The river then makes a sharp right turn in the gorges beneath Beaufort and empties into the Mediterranean. Along the way, it irrigates Lebanon's lush Bekaa Valley and many of the orchards, California-style truck farms, and tobacco fields of Lebanon's southwest.

As World War II still raged, the problem of accommodating the needs of the native Palestinian Jews and Arabs and the hundreds of thousands of new European Jewish immigrants crowding into Palestine became acute. Zionist leaders argued that exploiting the Jordan Valley's untapped water, electric power, and agricultural resources held the key to a peaceful future. One such scheme was proposed in 1944 by Walter Clay Lowdermilk, an American water engineer, in his book *Palestine: Land of Promise.* After extensive studies conducted in Palestine for the U.S. Department of Agriculture, Lowdermilk proposed using the waters of the Jordan, Yarmuk, Baniyas, Hasbani, Dan, and Zarqa (a river in East Jordan) in a comprehensive plan to irrigate the Jordan Valley, much of northern Galilee, and northern Palestine. Lowdermilk and other succeeding American consultants also suggested diverting the Litani in southern Lebanon to form an artificial lake in northern Palestine whose waters would be pumped southward to irrigate the Negev Desert. And Lowdermilk proposed an early version of the Med-Dead Canal as well.

The Arab-Israeli wars of 1947–1948, which surrounded Israel's creation, vastly complicated the task of those who sought a regional water solution. In particular, none of them could have foreseen that 420,000 Palestinian Arabs would flee eastward, to settle on either the Jordan River's West Bank, which Amman would soon annex, or on the East Bank, in Jordan proper.

The new state of Israel came to rely for most of its water on the diversion of between 50 and 75 percent of the Jordan River's flow, depending on whether one accepts Israeli or Arab figures. Israel's main diversion project is the National Water Carrier, a large conduit capable of channeling 11 billion cubic feet annually from the Sea of Galilee (Lake Tiberias) to Rosh Haayin, near Tel Aviv. To carry water from the Jordan and its headwaters as far as the Negev Desert, pipeline and canal systems such as the Yarkon-Negev project were built. These new waterways permitted cultivation of some additional desert land. But more important, they enabled Israelis to recultivate, by more intensive farming methods such as drip irrigation, the areas from which the Palestinian Arabs had fled.

According to early Israeli statistics, cultivated land increased from 400,000 acres in Israel's first full crop year, 1948–1949, to more than 1.1 million acres in 1977–1978, about 500,000 acres of which are irrigated. Since Operation Litani in 1978, Israel's first major invasion of southern Lebanon, which was intended to drive the forces of the Palestine Liberation Organization (PLO) back across the Litani, the Israeli government has not published full water and cultivation figures. The country's total 1980 water consumption, however, was authoritatively estimated at 64 billion cubic feet, of which about 42 billion cubic feet are used in agriculture.

It is impossible to say how much of this water Israel's less developed neighbors might have used in the past or could use in the future. What is certain is that all of the water development plans of the region's countries depend on tapping the region's rivers. Not surprisingly, to the Arabs in the 1950s the National Water Carrier became a symbol of Israel's aggressive expansionism. As early as 1953, Syrian artillery units opened fire on the construction and engineering sites behind the town and lake of Tiberias, forcing the Israelis to move the main pumping station.

The incident helped convince the United States that the water dispute both reflected and aggravated the political conflict sparked by the exodus of the Palestinian Arabs. President Dwight Eisenhower appointed motion picture magnate Eric Johnston to perform the herculean labor of negotiating regional watersharing arrangements. Johnston presented a series of proposals based largely on the work of Charles T. Main, Inc., a Boston, Massachusetts, consulting firm. A fundamental tenet of international law underlay these proposals: Water within one catchment area should not be diverted outside that area—regardless of political boundaries—until all needs of those within the catchment area are satisfied. Since it was already clear that nothing would deter Israel from sending Jordan River water as far as the Negev Desert, U.S. negotiators focused on other ways of meeting the needs of both Arabs and Israelis in the catchment areas of Galilee, southern Lebanon, and western Syria.

The Johnston proposals began with a series of dams on the Hasbani, Baniyas, and Dan rivers in Lebanon, Syria, and Israel, which would feed a canal to water Galilee farm land. The Huleh swamps were to be drained, a project soon carried out by Israel. A high dam was to be built on the Yarmuk River, a project still in abeyance. Finally, smaller works were called for to irrigate both sides of the Jordan Valley. One of these projects was Jordan's East Ghor Canal, eventually built mainly with U.S. foreign assistance.

The American planners thought that the Johnston proposals would preserve the catchment area principle. Indeed, the Israeli National Water Carrier was not yet complete. The proposals allotted Syria 1.6 billion cubic feet of water a year; Jordan, 27.3 billion; and Israel, 13.9 billion. But all three states objected to the scheme. The Arab states wanted larger shares, especially for Syria. They also insisted on an international board to supervise the allocation of regional water resources. Israel, too, wanted much more water and rejected giving a board containing Arab members any control over Israeli water supplies. A major Israeli counterproposal was prepared by Cotton in 1954. It differed from the Johnston proposals primarily by reviving the idea of diverting Lebanon's Litani River into Israel.

Notwithstanding these changes favored by Israel, the original Johnston proposals seemed, at times, to be drawing Israel and the Arab states toward a technical accord on sharing water resources that might have paved the way to wider political agreements. President Gamal Abdel Nasser of Egypt became actively involved in the process because Johnston submitted another set of proposals designed to deal with the Arab-Israeli conflict and the Palestinian problem simultaneously. Along with U.N. officials, Johnston envisaged using a canal from the Nile River to irrigate the western Sinai Desert and resettling some of the 2 million Palestinian Arab refugees in the one-time wasteland.

When the late Egyptian President Anwar el-Sadat revived this idea after his historic 1977 trip to Jerusalem, his seemingly cavalier treatment of the country's most precious natural resource outraged many Egyptians. Western interest in this concept revealed a total lack of understanding of the Palestinian problem. The refugees' concern was recovering their homes, farm lands, and jobs, not helping to make the Sinai Desert bloom. However, Egypt's involvement in the regional water controversy undoubtedly helped to spur its own grandiose projects for developing the Nile Valley—plans that centered around the highly political question of whether the Soviets or the Americans would build the high dam at Aswan.

The Egyptians also participated directly in the discussions on the Johnston proposals for the Israel-Jordan area: Johnston himself disclosed that Egypt was urging Jordan, Lebanon, and Syria to accept them. Indeed, then Egyptian Foreign Minister Mahmoud Riyad headed an Arab League committee set up to prepare a far-reaching, pan-Arab, regional water plan, which Nasser hoped that Israel would have no choice but to accept. According to his diaries, throughout the early 1950s dovish Israeli Prime Minister Moshe Sharett favored working with the American proposals and discussed a number of water plans with his cabinet, including the Litani diversion. Sharett also sought ways to open both public and secret conversations with Nasser.

Riyad, however, insisted that Israel's inclusion of the Litani River ruined any hopes of a regional agreement, since the project would doom Lebanon's hopes for developing its underdeveloped south and sully Arab honor. By the time Israeli leaders told Washington in early 1955 that they would drop the Litani idea, political tensions were rising for other reasons. Israel had responded to the beginning of guerrilla attacks from Gaza with a massive raid on the area: Nasser had decided to buy Soviet arms through Czechoslovakia; and the West had organized friendly regimes in Iraq, Jordan, and Turkey into the Baghdad Pact. There was talk of an Arab water diversion project that would pump the Hasbani River in Lebanon into the Litani, to prevent any of the Hasbani from watering Israel.

At this point, Sharett left the Israeli government. Doves began to vanish from the Mideast scene. Hawks moved into the ascendant, and Nasser's mood became more defiant. In July 1956 the United States refused to finance the Aswan High Dam, which the Soviets then took over as their showcase project in the Arab world. Nasser dropped the Johnston proposals and all of their offshoots, consigning the mission to history.

Water and the PLO

Arab-Israeli wars twice totally disrupted the economy and demography of Jordan, first in 1948, then again in 1967. The kingdom's annexation after the 1948 war of the 2,165 square miles of the West Bank, a rocky salient only partially suitable for irrigated cultivation, more than tripled its population, to 1.2 million. When Israel conquered the territory in 1967, about 300,000 of its inhabitants fled to unoccupied East Jordan. Today, about 1.9 million Arabs in the region are classified as refugees because their former homes or those of their parents were in Israel, Israeli-occupied territory, or pre-1948 Palestine.

Losing the West Bank in 1967 cost Jordan much of its foreign-exchange earning from tourism, which centered on East Jerusalem and the well-watered oasis region of Jericho; its grain production, which had helped to feed many of the Palestinians who had stayed on in their temporary or permanent homes in the West Bank; and worst of all, 80 per cent of its total fruit-growing and 45 per cent of its vegetable-growing land, both of which had become valuable sources of export revenues during the 1950s and 1960s.

Yet by 1948 it was already clear that the Arab refugees on both the East and the West Banks could subsist by their own efforts only if the Jordan's waters were augmented by waters from the Yarmuk River. The intensifying Arab-Israeli political conflict also made it clear that Jordan and Syria could not count on using water from the Sea of Galilee.

Enter Mills Bunger, a water expert on the U.S. Point Four aid team in Amman. In winter 1951, while flying over the Yarmuk River valley, Bunger spotted an intriguing basin he realized could be turned with the help of a dam into a natural reservoir to hold excess winter flood waters from converging rivers and streams. Soon, the U.S. and Jordanian governments and the U.N. Relief and Works Agency for Palestinian Refugees jointly planned a 480-foot high dam for the Yarmuk River at the site, named Maqarin, and allocated nearly $160 million for the venture. The dam was intended to store 18 billion cubic feet of water and feed canals that would water both the east and the west banks of the Jordan. A diversion dam would complete a system capable of irrigating both Jordanian and Syrian farm land without depending on Israel's Sea of Galilee.

To implement the Bunger plan, Syria and Jordan agreed in June 1953 on joint use of Yarmuk River water. But Israel, pushing to be included, laid claim to a share of the Yarmuk water. The Bunger plan quickly died, and the Syrians and Jordanians partially diverted the Yarmuk's flow for a brief time to irrigate farm lands in the eastern part of the Jordan Valley. The water controversy settled into a discouraging pattern for most of the decade. Local water projects went ahead, amid growing Arab anger over Israel's unilateral diversion of Jordan River waters and occasional military incidents that were sometimes raised in the U.N. Security Council.

But the Arabs also responded with their own diversion plans. As though to prove its Arab credentials, the Lebanese government showed an uncharacteristic zeal during the 1950s in attempting to thwart Israeli water plans. In 1959 the Arab League's technical committee called for boring a short tunnel to divert Lebanon's Hasbani River where it passed closest to the Litani, a place called Kaoukaba. Israel still takes this threat seriously. In 1982 Israeli invaders built a new road, a new bridge over the Litani, and a heavily fortified military camp, showing special vigilance over this area.

At this point, the water issue helped contribute to formation of the PLO. As long as the Israeli national water project was still under construction and Jordan River water was not actually flowing to the Negev Desert, Arab governments could oppose Israeli plans with safe rhetoric rather than potentially dangerous deeds. But Jordan's King Hussein and Nasser both realized the inherent threat they faced from the water problem. Action against the new Israeli water system might deprive Hussein, in the certain event of an Israeli counter-attack, of the West Bank (as it eventually did in 1967). Inaction could cost Nasser the claim to Arab leadership he had been so carefully carving out, following the embarrassing collapse in 1961 of his Egyptian-Syrian United Arab Republic after only three years. The Arab states needed a formula that would permit them to resist Israel's designs without provoking disastrous reprisals.

In January 1964 Arab representatives gathered in Cairo at Nasser's request for the first of a series of summit conferences to work out a joint strategy on water. Yet instead of fashioning a new water strategy, the conferees dumped the water issue and all the other Arab-Israeli political problems into the lap of the Palestinians. The Cairo conferees decided to create a "Palestinian entity" to mobilize the Palestinians themselves for the eventual "liberation of Palestine." The PLO became this entity's financial, political, and military expression. It was to be supported by all of the Arab participants in the summit meeting. But in 1964, when the ineffectiveness of the PLO's leadership and of its nascent "conventional" military arm, the Palestine Liberation Army, became apparent, Yasir Arafat decided to act. Arafat had already founded al-Fatah (the Palestine National Liberation Movement) in secret in 1959. In the groups' writings and indoctrination programs, Arafat and the other Fatah leaders laid great stress on Israel's usurpation of Arab land and water resources.

One of Arafat's closest associates, Dr. Nabil al-Shath, an American-trained engineer and business management specialist, told this writer in 1970, "The water issue was the crucial one. We considered our own impact on this to be the crucial test of our own war with Israel." Therefore, it was no accident that the first action of al-Assifa, Fatah's armed branch, was an unsuccessful attempt to sabotage the Israeli National Water Carrier on December 31, 1964.

Meanwhile, the Arab governments continued their own efforts to create an Arab counterdiversion project. Work aimed at diverting the Baniyas was begun on Syrian territory. But three times, in March and May 1965 and July 1966, the Israeli army and air force attacked the site. Nasser called another Arab summit meeting in Cairo, where he acknowledged that Arab states were unprepared to go to war with Israel and urged them to admit it and accept the consequences. Nasser evidently forgot his own advice in the months preceding the disastrous 1967 war.

The Syrian project and the Israeli attacks created what Harvard University political scientist Nadav Safran calls "a prolonged chain reaction of border violence that linked directly to the events that led to war" in June 1967. In that war Israel captured and bulldozed about 50 Syrian villages in the Golan Heights. The Israeli advance forced about 100,000 Syrians to flee eastward and become refugees in their own country. Victory enabled Israel not only to build a system of strategic Jewish settlements in the Golan but also to prevent the Baniyas diversion by capturing the site of its Golan Heights headwaters, a site that the Romans had garrisoned to protect their water supplies.

The Six-Day War led Mideast states to abandon finally regional water projects and focus on the resources within their own frontiers. For Israel, the central problem was husbanding its dwindling domestic supplies and efficiently using sources captured from Jordan and Syria. Water in the Arab farmers' wells in the West Bank became a key element in Israeli strategy to hold the West Bank, Golan Heights, and Gaza, as it has subsequently been in moves to annex and absorb them. Israeli journalists, military men, and water engineers have spoken and written often of the need to "protect Jewish water supplies from encroaching Arab water wells." Military government regulations now forbid West Bank Arabs from drilling new wells without special authorization, which is almost impossible to obtain. Many existing wells have been blocked or sealed by the occupation authorities, in some cases to prevent their use from draining nearby Jewish wells. Further, Arabs' access to water is determined by a rather restrictive consumption quota.

Israeli water experts explain that the ground water for northern and central Israel is supplied by two main aquifers. Both originate on the West Bank. They have apparently been augmented by another, originating from an underground lake, which extends beneath both banks of the Jordan.

Both of these aquifers drain westward toward the Mediterranean and are tapped by an elaborate system of wells along the coast between Haifa and Tel Aviv. Between these aquifers and the National Water Carrier, Israel draws its entire water consumption, although exact figures are closely guarded Israeli state secrets. Since 1967 the balanced functioning of the entire system has come to depend on a smooth, underground flow of water into Israel from the West Bank. The hydrological balance could be easily upset by interfering with the Hasbani, the Baniyas, the Dan, or the Yarmuk.

Keeping Tel Aviv, Haifa, and the other cities of the Israeli coastal plain from running dry depends on blocking Arab water development in the West Bank that could stop the aquifers' flow westward: hence the ban on Arab wells. Westward-flowing underground water also helps to stabilize pressure and prevent Mediterranean water from intruding into Israel's own coastal water wells. Some such saline pollution had befouled the Israeli coastal aquifers before the 1967 war and before the upper Jordan headwaters had been completely diverted.

The Golan Heights is as critical to Israeli water supplies as the West Bank's wells. About one-quarter of Israel's water is taken from the Sea of Galilee and channeled through the water carrier. Most of this water is used for consumption and industry in central and southern Israel. Syrian control of the Golan placed the upper Jordan basin's freshwater supplies beyond Israel's pre-emptive reach. Israel reversed this situation first by capturing the Golan Heights in 1967 and then by effectively annexing the region in 1981. Israeli leaders view maintaining access to this water largely as a military problem: Holding on to the territory is necessary to protect an intake system and pumping works embedded in rock cliffs just south of Kafer Nahum. The system can easily be hit by artillery on the Golan ridges overlooking the Sea of Galilee....

Since the Israeli invasion, the old and well-known Israeli-American plans for diverting the Litani have placed several developments in a worrisome light in Lebanese eyes. For example, when they captured the dam and lake at Qir'awn in June 1982 after a short battle with the Syrians, the Israelis immediately seized all the hydrographic charts and technical documents relating to the Litani and its installation. The Israelis were openly augmenting the flow of the Hasbani across the frontier into Israel by laying surface pipes to catch the run-off and other water from the mountains and nearby springs.

Moreover, a watchful American military observer claims to have seen Israelis burying pipes deep in a hillside near Marj'Uyn after the Israeli incursion of 1978, indicating that the Israelis might be secretly siphoning water underground from the Marj Plain in southern Lebanon into Israel, without affecting the measured flow of the Litani. Such a diversion would tap the extensive underground aquifer, which is fed by seepage from both the Litani and the Hasbani rivers and by underground streams from the Mount Hermon region. The site where the pipes and pumping equipment seem to have been secretly buried is near a World War II airfield built by the British and repaved and extended in fall 1983 by the Israeli Defense Forces.

In interviews, Technology Minister Neeman, a brilliant physicist from the far-right Techiya Party who has vowed to work for the "sharing" of Litani water with Lebanon, freely acknowledged Israel's long interest in Litani water. And he confirmed that seismic sounding and surveys had been conducted at a spot on the Litani gorges called Deir Mimas—sounding that Lebanese Litani River Authority officials were certain had been undertaken to find the optimum place for the inlet of a diversion tunnel to be dug about three miles into Israel.

Norwegian officers and soldiers of the U.N.'s Lebanon force have described how, in January 1983, an Israeli military bulldozer cut a steep road into the face of the rocky gorge below Deir Mimas. An engineering party then inserted rods into the rock outcroppings to take the sounding. In investigating these reports ABC News teams and other reporters in southern Lebanon encountered Israeli land survey parties taking measurements on the hills and hairpin turns of the roads near the Litani. The Israelis may simply be planning new military roads or improving topographical maps. A number of Israeli families in the Metullah area, however, hold deeds or other claims to land in southern Lebanon—just as Lebanese still hold similar claims to land south of the border in Israel. Should Israel decide to go ahead with the Litani plan, this Israeli-claimed land could be used for the artificial lake or reservoir or other irrigation works.

Neeman contended that such diversion tunnels might have been interesting when the Cotton plan and other earlier schemes were proposed in the past, but no longer. Neeman relates that when Sharon, his political ally, returned from the Lebanon campaign, Neeman asked, "What do you think about the Litani?" "The Litani?" Sharon allegedly responded, "Have you seen the Litani? It's only a trickle, not worth the taking." This meager flow, acknowledged Neeman, results from the intensive Lebanese power and irrigation projects upstream. Neeman added, however, if the Lebanese ever cared to sell some of the Litani water, "We would be glad to buy this little water and make good use of it in northern Galilee."

Lebanese water engineers estimate that an Israeli downstream diversion effort could cost the Litani at least 3.5 billion cubic feet annually. This loss would rule out effective irrigation of the southern Lebanon panhandle and would ultimately turn much of the region into a desert. Moreover, diversion, at least under schemes advanced in 1943 and 1954, would also require Israel to stay on in Lebanon and hold at least the entire Bekaa Valley south of the Damascus road in order to control the river's flow, to pre-empt Lebanon's use of the water to irrigate the panhandle if it regains the region, and to protect the diversion system from any Syrian counterattack. Any long-term harnessing by Israel of Lebanon's water resources would also require control of both slopes of the Lebanon mountain range. Otherwise, enemy spotters in the Shuf Mountains to the west, where the Israelis have upgraded and now operate a long-range radar station at Dar Barouk, could direct artillery fire or air strikes on diversion projects.

Israelis avoid public discussion of the sensitive subject of water resources. Never once did the Litani question come up during all of the Israeli-U.S.-Lebanese talks leading to the May 1, 1983, troop withdrawal agreement, even though the Lebanese were prepared to discuss the matter had it been raised by the Israelis. The Saudis have privately assured Lebanon that they would fully finance irrigation of the area south of the Litani, if the United States could provide a guaranteed date for Israeli withdrawal.

Israel's own water needs have been rising rapidly. Recent Israeli Water Administration statistics show that from 1948 to 1978 Israel's cultivated area increased at a slower rate than population. Yet 900,000 additional acres remain potentially available for irrigated agriculture, while 400,000 more acres are potentially suitable for dry farming. Upon considering that Israel's efficient farming methods require 100,000 cubic feet of water each year for the average acre of irrigated land, Israel's great need for water becomes clear.

Moreover, Israeli planners privately admit that unless the country concentrates purely on expensive desalination plants, or finds a way to increase substantially the present recycling of used irrigation and waste water, present aquifers can scarcely meet the country's current needs or greater levels of consumption much beyond 1990. Another major water source will be needed. The hydraulic imperative, from the Israeli point of view, is capturing either the Litani or a much greater share of the Yarmuk. Whether Israel moves unilaterally or whether the region returns to the Eisenhower-Johnston concepts of finding ways to share the Earth's most precious resource for the common good will help determine the future political geography of the Middle East. . . .

Environmental Changes as Causes of Acute Conflict

THOMAS F. HOMER-DIXON

How might environmental change lead to acute conflict? Some experts propose that environmental change may shift the balance of power between states either regionally or globally, producing instabilities that could lead to war.[1] Or, as global environmental damage increases the disparity between the North and South, poor nations may militarily confront the rich for a greater share of the world's wealth.[2] Warmer temperatures could lead to contention over new ice-free sea-lanes in the Arctic or more accessible resources in the Antarctic.[3] Bulging populations and land stress may produce waves of environmental refugees[4] that spill across borders with destabilizing effects on the recipient's domestic order and on international stability. Countries may fight over dwindling supplies of water and the effects of upstream pollution.[5] In developing countries, a sharp drop in food crop pro-

Thomas F. Homer-Dixon, "On the Threshold: Environmental Changes as Causes of Acute Conflict," *International Security* 16, no. 2 (Fall 1991). Reprinted by permission of the MIT Press, Cambridge, Massachusetts. Copyright © 1991 by the President and Fellows of Harvard College and of the Massachusetts Institute of Technology.

[1]For example, see David Wirth, "Climate Chaos," *Foreign Policy*, No. 74 (Spring 1989), p. 10.

[2]Robert Heilbroner, *An Inquiry into the Human Prospect* (New York: Norton, 1980), pp. 39 and 95; William Ophuls, *Ecology and the Politics of Scarcity: A Prologue to a Political Theory of the Steady State* (San Francisco: Freeman, 1977), pp. 214–217.

[3]Fen Hampson, "The Climate for War," *Peace and Security*, Vol. 3, No. 3 (Autumn 1988), p. 9.

[4]Jodi Jacobson, *Environmental Refugees: A Yardstick of Habitability*, Worldwatch Paper No. 86 (Washington, D.C.: Worldwatch Institute, 1988).

[5]Peter Gleick, "Climate Change," p. 336; Malin Falkenmark, "Fresh Waters as a Factor in Strategic Policy and Action," in Westing, *Global Resources*, pp. 85–113.

duction could lead to internal strife across urban-rural and nomadic-sedentary cleavages.[6] If environmental degradation makes food supplies increasingly tight, exporters may be tempted to use food as a weapon.[7] Environmental change could ultimately cause the gradual impoverishment of societies in both the North and South, which could aggravate class and ethnic cleavages, undermine liberal regimes, and spawn insurgencies.[8] Finally, many scholars indicate that environmental degradation will "ratchet up" the level of stress within national and international society, thus increasing the likelihood of many different kinds of conflict and impeding the development of cooperative solutions. . . .[9]

Poor countries will in general be more vulnerable to environmental change than rich ones; therefore, environmentally induced conflicts are likely to arise first in the developing world. In these countries, a range of atmospheric, terrestrial, and aquatic environmental pressures will in time probably produce, either singly or in combination, four main, causally interrelated social effects: reduced agricultural production, economic decline, population displacement, and disruption of regular and legitimized social relations. These social effects, in turn, may cause several specific types of acute conflict, including scarcity disputes between countries, clashes between ethnic groups, and civil strife and insurgency, each with potentially serious repercussions for the security interests of the developed world. . . .

The Salience of Environmental Issues

. . . The environmental system, in particular the earth's climate, used to be regarded as relatively resilient and stable in the face of human insults. But now it is widely believed to have multiple local equilibria that are not highly stable.[10]

[6]Peter Wallensteen, "Food Crops as a Factor in Strategic Policy and Action," Westing, *Global Resources,* pp. 151–155.

[7]Ibid., pp. 146–151.

[8]Ted Gurr, "On the Political Consequences of Scarcity and Economic Decline," *International Studies Quarterly,* Vol. 29, No. 1 (March 1985), pp. 51–75.

[9]"The disappearance of ecological abundance seems bound to make international politics even more tension ridden and potentially violent than it already is. Indeed, the pressures of ecological scarcity may embroil the world in hopeless strife, so that long before ecological collapse occurs by virtue of the physical limitations of the earth, the current world order will have been destroyed by turmoil and war." Ophuls, *Ecology,* p. 214.

[10]The development of chaos theory has contributed to this understanding. A chaotic system has nonlinear and feedback relationships between its variables that amplify small perturbations, thereby rendering accurate prediction of the system's state increasingly difficult the further one tries to project into the future. In chaos (not to be confused with randomness), deterministic causal processes still operate at the micro-level and, although the system's state may not be precisely predictable for a given point in the future, the boundaries within which its variables must operate are often identifiable. See James Crutchfield, J. Doyne Farmer, and Norman Packard, "Chaos," *Scientific American,* Vol. 255, No. 6 (December 1986), pp. 46–57; James Gleick, *Chaos: Making of a New Science* (New York: Viking, 1987).

In 1987, for example, geochemist Wallace Broecker reflected on recent polar ice-core and ocean sediment data: "What these records indicate is that Earth's climate does not respond to forcing in a smooth and gradual way. Rather, it responds in sharp jumps which involve large-scale reorganization of Earth's system. . . . We must consider the possibility that the main responses of the system to our provocation of the atmosphere will come in jumps whose timing and magnitude are unpredictable."[11]

A paradigm-shattering example of such nonlinear or "threshold" effects in complex environmental systems was the discovery of the Antarctic ozone hole in the mid-1980s. The hole was startling evidence of the instability of the environmental system in response to human inputs, of the capacity of humankind to significantly affect the ecosystem on a global scale, and of our inability to predict exactly how the system will change.

This altered perception of the nature of the environmental system has percolated out of the scientific community into the policymaking community. It may also be influencing the broader public's view of environmental problems. Scientists, policymakers, and laypeople are beginning to interpret data about environmental change in a new light: progressive, incremental degradation of environmental systems is not as tolerable as it once was, because we now realize that we do not know where and when we might cross a threshold and move to a radically different and perhaps highly undesirable system. . . .

Angus MacKay examines the relationship between climate change and civil violence in the kingdom of Castile (much of modern-day Spain).[12] During the fifteenth century, there were numerous well-documented episodes of popular unrest in Castile, and some seem to have been produced directly by climate-induced food shortages. In March 1462, for instance, rioters rampaged through Seville after floods forced the price of bread beyond the means of the poor. Usually, however, the causal connections were more complex. An important intervening factor was the fabric of religious and social beliefs held by the people and promoted by preachers, especially those beliefs attributing weather fluctuations to the sin of someone in the community.[13] MacKay thus argues against a simplistic "stimulus-response" model of

---

[11]Wallace Broecker, "Unpleasant Surprises in the Greenhouse?" *Nature,* Vol. 328, No. 6126 (July 9, 1987), pp. 123–126.

[12]Angus MacKay, "Climate and Popular Unrest in Late Medieval Castile," in T.M. Wigley, M.J. Ingram, and G. Farmer, *Climate and History: Studies in Past Climates and Their Impact on Man* (Cambridge: Cambridge University Press, 1981), pp. 356–376. For other historical case studies of climate–society interaction, see Hubert Lamb, *Weather, Climate and Human Affairs* (London: Routledge, 1988).

[13]Anger over food scarcity was sometimes turned against Jews and *conversos* (Jews who had converted to Christianity after Iberian pogroms in the late fourteenth century), and sometimes against small shopkeepers who were accused of the "sins" of creating shortages and overpricing food.

environment-conflict linkages and instead for one that allows for "culturally mediated" behavior.

Addressing a modern conflict, William Durham has analyzed the demographic and environmental pressures behind the 1969 "Soccer War" between El Salvador and Honduras.[14] Because of the prominence in this conflict of previous migration from El Salvador to Honduras, and because of the striking evidence of population growth and land stress in the two countries (most notably El Salvador), a number of analysts have asserted that the Soccer War is a first-class example of an ecologically driven conflict.[15] A simple Malthusian interpretation does not seem to have credibility when one looks at the aggregate data.[16] But Durham shows that changes in agricultural practice and land distribution—to the detriment of poor farmers—were more powerful inducements to migration than sheer population growth. Land scarcity developed not because there was too little to go around, but because of "a process of competitive exclusion by which the small farmers [were] increasingly squeezed off the land" by large land owners.[17] Durham thus contends that ecologists cannot directly apply to human societies the simple, density-dependent models of resource competition they commonly use to study asocial animals: a distributional component must be added, because human behavior is powerfully constrained by social structure and the resource access it entails.[18]

Others have analyzed environment-conflict linkages in the Philippines. Although the country has suffered from serious internal strife for many decades, its underlying causes may be changing: population displacement, deforestation, and land degradation appear to be increasingly powerful forces driving the current communist-led insurgency. Here, too, the linkages between environmental change and conflict are complex, involving numerous intervening variables, both physical and social. The Filipino population growth rate of 2.5 percent is among the highest in Southeast Asia. To help pay the massive foreign debt, the government has encouraged the expansion of large-scale lowland agriculture. Both factors have swelled

[14]William Durham, *Scarcity and Survival in Central America: The Ecological Origins of the Soccer War* (Stanford, Calif.: Stanford University Press, 1979).

[15]For instance, see Paul Ehrlich, Anne Ehrlich, and John Holdren, *Ecoscience: Population, Resources, Environment* (San Francisco: Freeman, 1977), p. 908.

[16]El Salvador was the most densely populated country in the Western Hemisphere (190 people per square kilometer in 1976; compare India at 186), with a population growth rate of 3.5 percent per year (representing a doubling time of about twenty years). Most of the country had lost its virgin forest, land erosion and nutrient depletion were severe, and total food production fell behind consumption in the mid-50s. Per capita farmland used for basic food crops fell from 0.15 hectares in 1953 to 0.11 hectares in 1971.

[17]Durham, *Scarcity and Survival*, p. 54.

[18]The importance of variables intervening between population density and conflict is emphasized in Nazli Choucri, ed., *Multidisciplinary Perspectives on Population and Conflict* (Syracuse, N.Y.: Syracuse University Press, 1984); see also Jack Goldstone, *Revolution and Rebellion in the Early Modern World* (Berkeley, Calif.: University of California Press, 1991).

the number of landless agricultural laborers. Many have migrated to the Philippines' steep and ecologically vulnerable uplands where they have cleared land or established plots on previously logged land. This has set in motion a cycle of erosion, falling food production, and further clearing of land. Even marginally fertile land is becoming hard to find in many places, and economic conditions are often dire for the peasants.[19] Civil dissent is rampant in these peripheral areas, which are largely beyond the effective control of the central government.

While these studies are commendable, a review of all of the recent work on environmental change and conflict reveals a number of difficulties, some methodological and some conceptual. First, researchers often emphasize human-induced climate change and ozone depletion to the neglect of severe terrestrial and aquatic environmental problems such as deforestation, soil degradation, and fisheries depletion. Second, much of the recent writing on the links between environmental change and conflict is anecdotal. These pieces do not clearly separate the "how" question (how will environmental change lead to conflict?) from the "where" question (where will such conflict occur?). . . .

Third, environmental-social systems are hard to analyze. They are characterized by multiple causes and effects and by a host of intervening variables, often linked by interactive, synergistic, and nonlinear causal relations. Empirical data about these variables and relations are rarely abundant. Although the underlying influence of environmental factors on conflict may be great, the complex and indirect causation in these systems means that the scanty evidence available is always open to many interpretations. Furthermore, understanding environmental-social systems involves specifying links across levels of analysis usually regarded as quite independent.

Fourth, the prevailing "naturalistic" epistemology and ontology of social science may hinder accurate understanding of the links between physical and social variables within environmental-social systems. In particular, it may be a mistake to conjoin, in causal generalizations, types of physical events with types of intentional social action. Fifth, researchers must acquire detailed knowledge of a daunting range of disciplines, from atmospheric science and agriculture hydrology to energy economics and international relations theory.

Sixth and finally, the modern realist perspective that is often used to understand security problems is largely inadequate for identifying and explaining the links between environmental change and conflict. Realism focuses on states as rational maximizers of power in an anarchic system; state behavior is mainly a function of the structure of power relations in the system. But

---

[19]Leonard notes that, around the planet, population growth, inequitable land distribution, and agricultural modernization have cause huge numbers of desperately poor people to move to "remote and ecologically fragile rural areas" or to already overcrowded cities. See Jeffrey Leonard, "Overview," *Environment and the Poor: Development Strategies for a Common Agenda* (New Brunswick, N.J.: Transaction, 1989), p. 5.

this emphasis on states means that theorists tend to see the world as divided into territorially distinct, mutually exclusive countries, not broader environmental regions or systems. Realism thus encourages scholars to deemphasize transboundary environmental problems, because such problems often cannot be linked to a particular country, and do not have any easily conceptualized impact on the structure of economic and military power relations between states. Realism thus encourages scholars to deemphasize transboundary environmental problems, because such problems often cannot be linked to a particular country, and do not have any easily conceptualized impact on the structure of economic and military power relations between states. Realism induces scholars to squeeze environmental issues into a structure of concepts including "state," "sovereignty," "territory," "national interest," and "balance of power." The fit is bad, which may lead theorists to ignore, distort, and misunderstand important aspects of global environmental problems.

Mapping Causes and Effects

... The total effect of human activity on the environment in a particular ecological region is mainly a function of two variables: first, the product of total population in the region and physical activity per capita, and second, the vulnerability of the ecosystem in that region to those particular activities. Activity per capita, in turn, is a function of available physical resources (which include nonrenewable resources such as minerals, and renewable resources such as water, forests, and agricultural land) and ideational factors, including institutions, social relations, preferences, and beliefs.... Environmental effects may cause social effects that in turn could lead to conflict. For example, the degradation of agricultural land might produce large-scale migration, which could create ethnic conflicts as migratory groups clash with indigenous populations. There are important feedback loops from social effects and conflict to the ideational factors and thence back to activity per capita and population. Thus, ethnic clashes arising from migration could alter the operation of a society's markets and thereby its economic activity....

The Range of Environmental Problems

Developing countries are likely to be affected sooner and more severely by environmental change than rich countries. By definition, they do not have the financial, material, or intellectual resources of the developed world; furthermore, their social and political institutions tend to be fragile and riven with discord. It is probable, therefore, that developing societies will be less able to apprehend or respond to environmental disruption.[20]

Seven major environmental problems might plausibly contribute to conflict within and among developing countries: greenhouse warming, stratospheric ozone depletion, acid deposition, deforestation, degradation of agricultural land, overuse and pollution of water supplies, and depletion of fish stocks. These problems can all be crudely characterized as large-scale human-induced problems, with long-term and often irreversible consequences, which is why they are often grouped together under the rubric "global change." However, they vary greatly in spatial scale: the first two involve genuinely global physical processes, while the last five involve regional physical processes, although they may appear in locales all over the planet. These seven problems also vary in time scale: for example, while a region can be deforested in only a few years, and severe ecological and social effects may be noticeable almost immediately, human-induced greenhouse warming will probably develop over many decades and may not have truly serious implications for humankind for a half century or more after the signal is first detected. In addition, some of these problems (for instance, deforestation and degradation of water supplies) are much more advanced than others (such as greenhouse warming and ozone depletion) and are already producing serious social disruption. This variance in tangible evidence for these problems contributes to great differences in our certainty about their ultimate severity. The uncertainties surrounding greenhouse warming, for example, are thus far greater than those concerning deforestation.

Many of these problems are causally interrelated. For instance, acid deposition damages agricultural land, fisheries, and forests. Greenhouse warming may contribute to deforestation by moving northward the optimal temperature and precipitation zones for many tree species, by increasing the severity of windstorms and wildfires, and by expanding the range of pests and diseases.[21] The release of carbon from these dying forests would reinforce the greenhouse effect. The increased incidence of ultraviolet radiation due to the depletion of the ozone layer will probably damage trees and crops, and it may also damage the phytoplankton at the bottom of the ocean food chain. . . .[22]

Four Principal Social Effects

Environmental degradation may cause countless often subtle changes in developing societies. These range from increased communal cooking as fuel-

[20]Gurr, "Political Consequences of Scarcity," pp. 70–71.

[21]WRI, et al., *World Resources 1990–91*, p. 111.

[22]Robert Worrest, Hermann Gucinski, and John Hardy, "Potential Impact of Stratospheric Ozone Depletion on Marine Ecosystems," in John Topping, Jr., ed., *Coping with Climate Change: Proceedings of the Second North American Conference on Preparing for Climate Change* (Washington, D.C.: The Climate Institute, 1989), pp. 256–262

wood becomes scarce around African villages, to worsened poverty of Filipino coastal fishermen whose once-abundant grounds have been destroyed by trawlers and industrial pollution. Which of the many types of social effect might be crucial links between environmental change and acute conflict? This is the first part of the "how" question. To address it, we must use both the best knowledge about the social effects of environmental change and the best knowledge about the nature and causes of social conflict.

In thus working from both ends toward the middle of the causal chain, I hypothesize that four principal social effects may, either singly or in combination, substantially increase the probability of acute conflict in developing countries: decreased agricultural production, economic decline, population displacement, and disruption of legitimized and authoritative institutions and social relations. These effects will often be causally interlinked, sometimes with reinforcing relationships. For example, the population displacement resulting from a decrease in agricultural production may further disrupt agricultural production. Or economic decline may lead to the flight of people with wealth and education, which in turn could eviscerate universities, courts, and institutions of economic management, all of which are crucial to a healthy economy.

AGRICULTURAL PRODUCTION   ... Decreased agricultural production is often mentioned as potentially the most worrisome consequence of environmental change.... The Philippines provides a good illustration of deforestation's impact.... Since the Second World War, logging and the encroachment of farms have reduced the virgin and second-growth forest from about sixteen million hectares to 6.8–7.6 million hectares. Across the archipelago, logging and land-clearing have accelerated erosion, changed regional hydrological cycles and precipitation patterns, and decreased the land's ability to retain water during rainy periods. The resulting flash floods have damaged irrigation works while plugging reservoirs and irrigation channels with silt. These factors may seriously affect crop production. For example, when the government of the Philippines and the European Economic Community commissioned an Integrated Environmental Plan for the still relatively unspoiled island of Palawan, the authors of the study found that only about half of the 36,000 hectares of irrigated farmland projected within the Plan for 2007 will actually be irrigable because of the hydrological effects of decreases in forest cover.[23]

... Degradation and decreasing availability of good agricultural land [are] problems that deserve much closer attention than they usually receive. Currently, total global cropland amounts to about 1.5 billion hectares. Opti-

[23]Christopher Finney and Stanley Western, "An Economic Analysis of Environmental Protection and Management: An Example from the Philippines," *The Environmentalist*, Vol. 6, No. 1 (1986), p. 56.

mistic estimates of total arable land on the planet, which includes both current and potential cropland, range from 3.2 to 3.4 billion hectares, but nearly all the best land has already been exploited. What is left is either less fertile, not sufficiently rainfed or easily irrigable, infested with pests, or harder to clear and work.

For developing countries during the 1980s, cropland grew at just 0.26 percent a year, less than half the rate of the 1970s. More importantly, in these countries arable land per capita dropped by 1.9 percent a year. In the absence of a major increase in arable land in developing countries, experts expect that the world average of 0.28 hectares of cropland per capita will decline to 0.27 hectares by the year 2025, given the current rate of world population growth. Large tracts are being lost each year to urban encroachment, erosion, nutrient depletion, salinization, waterlogging, acidification, and compacting. The geographer Vaclav Smil, who is generally very conservative in his assessments of environmental damage, estimates that two to three million hectares of cropland are lost annually to erosion; perhaps twice as much land goes to urbanization, and at least one million hectares are abandoned because of excessive salinity. In addition, about one-fifth of the world's cropland is suffering from some degree of desertification. Taken together, he concludes, the planet will lose about 100 million hectares of arable land between 1985 and 2000. . . .[24]

ECONOMIC DECLINE   . . . A great diversity of factors might affect wealth production. For example, increased ultraviolet radiation caused by ozone depletion is likely to raise the rate of disease in humans and livestock,[25] which could have serious economic results. Logging for export markets may produce short-term economic gain for the country's elite, but increased runoff can damage roads, bridges, and other valuable infrastructure, while the extra siltation reduces the transport and hydroelectric capacity of rivers. As forests are destroyed, wood becomes scarcer and more expensive, and it absorbs an increasing share of the household budget for the poor families that use it for fuel.

Agriculture is the source of much of the wealth generated in developing societies. Food production soared in many regions over the last decades because the green revolution more than compensated for inadequate or de-

---

[24]Smil gives a startling account of the situation in China. From 1957 to 1977 the country lost 33.33 million hectares of farmland (30 percent of its 1957 total), while it added 21.2 million hectares of largely marginal land. He notes that "the net loss of 12 million hectares during a single generation when the country's population grew by about 300 million people means that per capita availability of arable land dropped by 40 per cent and that China's farmland is now no more abundant than Bangladesh's—a mere one-tenth of a hectare per capita!" See Vaclav Smil, *Energy, Food, Environment* (Oxford, U.K.: Oxford University Press, 1987), pp. 223, 230.

[25]Janice Longstreth, "Overview of the Potential Health Effects Associated with Ozone Depletion," in Topping, *Coping with Climate Change*, pp. 163–167.

clining soil productivity; but some experts believe this economic relief will be short-lived. Jeffrey Leonard writes: "Millions of previously very poor families that have experienced less than one generation of increasing wealth due to rising agricultural productivity could see that trend reversed if environmental degradation is not checked."[26] Damage to the soil is already producing a harsh economic impact in some areas.

Gauging the actual economic cost of land degradation is not easy. Current national income accounts do not incorporate measures of resource depletion: "A nation could exhaust its mineral reserves, cut down its forests, erode its soils, pollute its aquifers, and hunt its wildlife to extinction—all without affecting measured income."[27] The inadequacy of measures of economic productivity reinforces the perception that there is a policy trade-off between economic growth and environmental protection; this perception, in turn, encourages societies to generate present income at the expense of their potential for future income.

POPULATION DISPLACEMENT   Some commentators have suggested that environmental degradation may produce vast numbers of "environmental refugees." Sea-level rise may drive people back from coastal and delta areas in Egypt; spreading desert may empty Sahelian countries as their populations move south; Filipino fishermen may leave their depleted fishing grounds for the cities. The term "environmental refugee" is somewhat misleading, however, because it implies that environmental disruption could be a clear, proximate cause of refugee flows. Usually, though, environmental disruption will be only one of many interacting physical and social variables, including agricultural and economic decline, that ultimately force people from their homelands. For example, over the last three decades, millions of people have migrated from Bangladesh to neighboring West Bengal and Assam in India. While detailed data are scarce (in part because the Bangladeshi government is reluctant to admit there is significant out-migration), many specialists believe this movement is a result, at least in part, of shortages of adequately fertile land due to a rapidly growing population. Flooding, caused by deforestation in watersheds upstream on the Ganges and Brahmaputra rivers, might also be driving people from the area. In the future, this migration could be aggravated by rising sea-levels coupled with extreme weather events (both perhaps resulting from climate change).

DISRUPTED INSTITUTIONS AND SOCIAL RELATIONS   The fourth social effect especially relevant to the connection between environment change and acute conflict is the disruption of institutions and of legitimized, accepted, and authoritative social relations. In many developing societies, the three social ef-

---

[26]Leonard, *Environment and the Poor,* p. 27.
[27]Robert Repetto, "Wasting Assets: The Need for National Resource Accounting," *Technology Review,* January 1990, p. 40.

fects described above are likely to tear this fabric of custom and habitual behavior. A drop in agricultural output may weaken rural communities by causing malnutrition and disease, and by encouraging people to leave; economic decline may corrode confidence in the national purpose, weaken the tax base, and undermine financial, legal, and political institutions; and mass migrations of people into a region may disrupt labor markets, shift class relations, and upset the traditional balance of economic and political authority between ethnic groups. . . .

Cornucopians and Neo-Malthusians

Experts in environmental studies now commonly use the labels "cornucopian" for optimists like Simon and "neo-Malthusian" for pessimists like Paul and Anne Ehrlich. Cornucopians do not worry much about protecting the stock of any single resource, because of their faith that market-driven human ingenuity can always be tapped to allow the substitution of more abundant resources to produce the same end-use service. Simon, for example, writes: "There is no physical or economic reason why human resourcefulness and enterprise cannot forever continue to respond to impending shortages and existing problems with new expedients that, after an adjustment period, leave us better off than before the problem arose."[28] Neo-Malthusians are much more cautious. For renewable resources, they often distinguish between resource "capital" and its "income"; the capital is the resource stock that generates a flow (the income) that can be tapped for human consumption and well-being. A "sustainable" economy, using this terminology, is one that leaves the capital intact and undamaged so that future generations can enjoy an undiminished income stream.

Historically, cornucopians have been right to criticize the idea that resource scarcity places fixed limits on human activity. Time and time again, human beings have circumvented scarcities, and neo-Malthusians have often been justly accused of "crying wolf." But in assuming that this experience pertains to the future, cornucopians overlook seven factors.

First, whereas serious scarcities of critical resources in the past usually appeared singly, now we face multiple scarcities that exhibit powerful interactive, feedback, and threshold effects. An agricultural region may, for example, be simultaneously affected by degraded water and soil, greenhouse-induced precipitation changes, and increased ultraviolet radiation. This makes the future highly uncertain for policymakers and economic actors; tomorrow will be full of extreme events and surprises. Furthermore, as numerous resources become scarce simultaneously, it will be harder to identify substitution possibilities that produce the same end-use services at costs that prevailed when scarcity was less severe. Second, in the past the scarcity of a given resource usually increased slowly, allowing time for social, eco-

[28]Julian Simon, *The Ultimate Resource* (Princeton: Princeton University Press, 1981), p. 345.

nomic, and technological adjustment. But human populations are much larger and activities of individuals are, on a global average, much more resource-intensive than before. This means that debilitating scarcities often develop much more quickly: whole countries may be deforested in a few decades; most of a region's topsoil can disappear in a generation; and critical ozone depletion may occur in as little as twenty years. Third, today's consumption has far greater momentum than in the past, because of the size of the consuming population, the sheer quantity of material consumed by this population, and the density of its interwoven fabric of consumption activities. The countless individual and corporate economic actors making up human society are heavily committed to certain patterns of resource use; and the ability of our markets to adapt may be sharply constrained by these entrenched interests.

These first three factors may soon combine to produce a daunting syndrome of environmentally induced scarcity: humankind will face multiple resource shortages that are interacting and unpredictable, that grow to crisis proportions rapidly, and that will be hard to address because of powerful commitments to certain consumption patterns.

The fourth reason that cornucopian arguments may not apply in the future is that the free-market price mechanism is a bad gauge of scarcity, especially for resources held in common, such as a benign climate and productive seas. In the past, many such resources seemed endlessly abundant; now they are being degraded and depleted and we are learning that their increased scarcity often has tremendous bearing on a society's well-being. Yet this scarcity is at best reflected only indirectly in market prices. In addition, people often cannot participate in market transactions in which they have an interest, either because they lack the resources or because they are distant from the transaction process in time or space; in these cases the true scarcity of the resource is not reflected by its price.

The fifth reason is an extension of a point made earlier: market-driven adaptation to resource scarcity is most likely to succeed in wealthy societies, where abundant reserves of capital, knowledge, and talent help economic actors invent new technologies, identify conservation possibilities, and make the transition to new production and consumption patterns. Yet many of the societies facing the most serious environmental problems in the coming decades will be poor; even if they have efficient markets, lack of capital and know-how will hinder their response to these problems.

Sixth, cornucopians have an anachronistic faith in humankind's ability to unravel and manage the myriad processes of nature. There is no *a priori* reason to expect that human scientific and technical ingenuity can always surmount all types of scarcity. Human beings may not have the mental capacity to understand adequately the complexities of environmental-social systems. Or it may simply be impossible, given the physical, biological, and social laws governing these systems, to reduce all scarcity or repair all environmental damage. Moreover, the chaotic nature of these systems may keep us from fully anticipating the consequences of various adaptation and intervention strategies. Perhaps most important, scientific and technical knowledge must be built incrementally—layer upon layer—and its diffusion to the broader society often takes decades. Any technical solutions to environmental scarcity may arrive too late to prevent catastrophe.

Seventh and finally, future environmental problems, rather than inspiring the wave of ingenuity predicted by cornucopians, may instead reduce the supply of ingenuity available in a society. The success of market mechanisms depends on an intricate and stable system of institutions, social relations, and shared understandings. . . . Cornucopians often overlook the role of *social* ingenuity in producing the complex legal and economic climate in which *technical* ingenuity can flourish. Policymakers must be clever "social engineers" to design and implement effective market mechanisms. Unfortunately, however, the syndrome of multiple, interacting, unpredictable, and rapidly changing environmental problems will increase the complexity and pressure of the policymaking setting. It will also generate increased "social friction" as elites and interest groups struggle to protect their prerogatives. The ability of policy makers to be good social engineers is likely to go *down,* not up, as these stresses increase. . . .

Types of Conflict

. . . I hypothesize that severe environmental degradation will produce three principal types of conflict. These should be considered ideal types; they will rarely, if ever, be found in pure form in the real world.

SIMPLE SCARCITY CONFLICTS   [We would expect] simple scarcity conflicts . . . when state actors rationally calculate their interests in a zero-sum or negative-sum situation such as might arise from resource scarcity. We have seen such conflicts often in the past; they are easily understood within the realist paradigm of international relations theory, and they therefore are likely to receive undue attention from current security scholars. . . . I propose that simple scarcity conflicts may arise over three types of resources in particular: river water, fish, and agriculturally productive land. These renewable resources seem particularly likely to spark conflict because their scarcity is increasing rapidly in some regions, they are often essential for human survival, and they can be physically seized or controlled. There may be a positive feedback relationship between conflict and reduced agricultural production: for example, lower food supplies caused by environmental change may lead countries to fight over irrigable land, and this fighting could further reduce food supplies.

The current controversy over the Great Anatolia Project on the Euphrates River illustrates how simple scarcity conflicts can arise. By early in the next century, Turkey plans to build a huge complex of twenty dams and irrigation systems along the upper reaches of the Euphrates.[29] This $21 billion project, if fully funded and built, would reduce the average annual flow of the Euphrates within Syria from 32 billion cubic meters to 20 billion.[30] The water that passes through Turkey's irrigation system and on to Syria will be laden with fertilizers, pesticides, and salts. Syria is already desperately short of water, with an annual water availability of only about 600 cubic meters per capita. Much of the water for its towns, industries, and farms comes from the Euphrates, and the country has been chronically vulnerable to drought. Furthermore, Syria's population growth rate, at 3.7 percent per year, is one of the highest in the world, and this adds further to the country's demand for water.

Turkey and Syria have exchanged angry threats over this situation. Syria gives sanctuary to guerrillas of the Kurdish Workers Party (the PKK), which has long been waging an insurgency against the Turkish government in eastern Anatolia. Turkey suspects that Syria might be using these separatists to gain leverage in bargaining over Euphrates River water. Thus in October, 1989, then Prime Minister Turgut Ozal suggested that Turkey might impound the river's water if Syria did not restrain the PKK. Although he later retracted the threat, the tensions have not been resolved, and there are currently no high-level talks on water sharing.

GROUP-IDENTITY CONFLICTS   Group-identity conflicts are . . . likely to arise from the large-scale movements of populations brought about by environmental change. As different ethnic and cultural groups are propelled together under circumstances of deprivation and stress, we should expect intergroup hostility, in which a group would emphasize its own identity while denigrating, discriminating against, and attacking outsiders. The situation in the Bangladesh-Assam region may be a good example of this process; Assam's ethnic strife over the last decade has apparently been provoked by migration from Bangladesh.[31]

As population and environmental stresses grow in developing countries, migration to the developed world is likely to surge. "The image of islands of affluence amidst a sea of poverty is not inaccurate."[32] People will seek to move from Latin America to the United States and Canada, from North Africa and the Middle East to Europe, and from South and Southeast Asia to Australia.

---

[29]Alan Cowell, "Water Rights: Plenty of Mud to Sling," *New York Times,* February 7, 1990, p. A4; "Send for the Dowsers," *The Economist,* December 16, 1989, p. 42.

[30]On January 13, 1990, Turkey began filling the giant reservoir behind the Ataturk Dam, the first in this complex. For one month Turkey held back the main flow of the Euphrates River, which cut the downstream flow in Syria to about a quarter of its normal rate.

[31]Myron Weiner, "The Political Demography of Assam's Anti-Immigrant Movement," *Population and Development Review,* Vol. 9, No. 2 (June 1983), pp. 279–292.

[32]Richard Ullman, "Redefining Security," *International Security,* Vol. 8, No. 1 (Summer, 1983), p. 143.

This migration has already shifted the ethnic balance in many cities and regions of developed countries, and governments are struggling to contain a xenophobic backlash. Such racial strife will undoubtedly become much worse.

RELATIVE-DEPRIVATION CONFLICTS Relative-deprivation [conflicts may arise] as developing societies produce less wealth because of environmental problems; their citizens will probably become increasingly discontented by the widening gap between their actual level of economic achievement and the level they feel they deserve. The rate of change is key: the faster the economic deterioration, it is hypothesized, the greater the discontent. Lower-status groups will be more frustrated than others because elites will use their power to maintain, as best they can, access to a constant standard of living despite a shrinking economic pie. At some point, the discontent and frustration of some groups may cross a critical threshold, and they will act violently against other groups perceived to be the agents of their economic misery or thought to be benefiting from a grossly unfair distribution of economic goods in the society. . . .

Conflict Objectives and Scope

Table 1 compares some attributes of the principal types of acute conflict that I hypothesize may result from environmental change. The table lists the objectives sought by actors involved in these conflicts (which are, once again, ideal types). There is strong normative content to the motives of challenger groups involved in relative-deprivation conflicts: these groups believe the distribution of rewards is unfair. But such an "ought" does not necessarily drive simple-scarcity conflicts: one state may decide that it needs something another state has, and then try to seize it, without being motivated by a strong sense of unfairness or injustice.

Table 1 also shows that the scope of conflict can be expected to differ. Although relative-deprivation conflicts will tend to be domestic, we should not underestimate their potentially severe international repercussions. The correlation between civil strife and external conflict behavior is a function of the nature of the regime and of the kind of internal conflict it faces. For example, highly centralized dictatorships threatened by revolutionary actions, purges, and strikes are especially prone to engage in external war and belligerence. In comparison, less centralized dictatorships are prone to such behavior when threatened by guerrilla action and assassinations.[33] External aggressions may also result after a new regime comes to power through civil strife: regimes born of revolution, for example, are particularly good at mobilizing their citizens and resources for military preparation and war.[34]

[33]Jonathan Wilkenfeld, "Domestic and Foreign Conflict Behavior of Nations," *Journal of Peace Research,* Vol. 5 (1968), pp. 56–69.

[34]See Theda Skocpol, "Social Revolutions and Mass Military Mobilization," *World Politics,* Vol. 40, No. 2 (January 1988), pp. 147–168.

Table 1. Comparison of Conflict Types.

Conflict Type	Objective Sought	Conflict Scope
Simple scarcity	Relief from scarcity	International
Group identity	Protection and reinforcement of group identity	International or domestic
Relative deprivation	Distributive justice	Domestic (with international repercussions)

While environmental stresses and the conflicts they induce may encourage the rise of revolutionary regimes, other results are also plausible: these pressures might overwhelm the management capacity of institutions in developing countries, inducing praetorianism[35] or widespread social disintegration. They may also weaken the control of governments over their territories, especially over the hinterland (as in the Philippines). The regimes that do gain power in the face of such disruption are likely to be extremist, authoritarian, and abusive of human rights.[36] Moreover, the already short time horizons of policy makers in developing countries will be further shortened. These political factors could seriously undermine efforts to mitigate and adapt to environmental change. Soon to be the biggest contributors to global environmental problems, developing countries could become more belligerent, less willing to compromise with other states, and less capable of controlling their territories in order to implement measures to reduce environmental damage.

If many developing countries evolve in the direction of extremism, the interests of the North may be directly threatened. Of special concern here is the growing disparity between rich and poor nations that may be induced by environmental change. Robert Heilbroner notes that revolutionary regimes "are not likely to view the vast difference between first class and cattle class with the forgiving eyes of their predecessors." Furthermore, these nations may be heavily armed, as the proliferation of nuclear and chemical weapons and ballistic missiles continues. Such regimes, he asserts, could be tempted to use nuclear blackmail as a "means of inducing the developed world to transfer its wealth on an unprecedented scale to the underdeveloped

[35]"Praetorian" is a label used by Samuel Huntington for societies in which the level of political participation exceeds the capacity of political institutions to channel, moderate, and reconcile competing claims to economic and political resources. "In a praetorian system, social forces confront each other nakedly; no political institutions, no corps of professional political leaders are recognized or accepted as the legitimate intermediaries to moderate group conflict." Samuel Huntington, *Political Order in Changing Societies* (New Haven: Yale University Press, 1968), p. 196.

[36]Ophuls notes that ecological scarcity "seems to engender overwhelming pressures toward political systems that are frankly authoritarian by current standards." Ophuls, *Ecology*, p. 163.

world."[37] Richard Ullman, however, argues that this concern is overstated. Third world nations are unlikely to confront the North violently in the face of the "superior destructive capabilities of the rich."[38] In light of the discussion in this article, we might conclude that environmental stress and its attendant social disruption will so debilitate the economies of developing countries that they will be unable to amass sizeable armed forces, conventional or otherwise. But the North would surely be unwise to rely on impoverishment and disorder in the South for its security.

---

[37]Heilbroner, *Inquiry,* pp. 39 and 95. These North-South disputes would be the international analogues of domestic relative-deprivation conflicts.

[38]Ullman, "Redefining Security," p. 143.

PART 8

Conclusion: Futures Between Euphoria and Despair

Which fork in the road will become the main thoroughfare as we approach the millennium? Will the stable northern hemisphere drag the rest of the world along to "perpetual peace" as the logic of political and economic liberalism becomes universally accepted? Or, with the removal of the imperative for cooperation formerly provided by the Communist threat, will the pacified north slide back into historic patterns of insecurity, competitive maneuvering, and resort to force? Was the Cold War the last act in history or an intermission?

We are unlikely to know for sure. For two hundred years or more, there have been too many surprises in world politics, too many events that confounded what one would expect from either the realist or liberal models, to give any reason for confidence in a final verdict. As analysts we can make any bet we want, since the consequences of being wrong are slight. As citizens, we owe ourselves more caution. How should governments proceed in trying to batten down a new world, codifying conditions favorable to peace while keeping a guard up for the return of those nasty patterns of behavior that optimists believe are gone for good?

The selections below reflect approaches between the extremes represented by Mueller or Mearsheimer in the introductory section, and do not conform rigidly to either realist or liberal paradigms. The selection by E. H. Carr is a remarkable statement of the deficiencies of realism by one of its main expositors. The Betts essay debunks reliance on collective security and arms control in the post-communist environment, but accepts the value of an eclectic approach which includes collective institutions. Jack Snyder outlines a course between the pitfalls of realist fatalism and overambitious liberalism in dealing with the economic and political conversion of the former Soviet empire. Hanns Maull suggests why two major states now represent a new and more pacific model of national power that could become increasingly relevant. Samuel Huntington places the issue of American power and strategy in a wider context and focuses on how Japan's significance may change radically with the end of the Cold War.

The Limitations
of Realism

EDWARD HALLETT CARR

The exposure by realist criticism of the hollowness of the utopian edifice is the first task of the political thinker. It is only when the sham has been demolished that there can be any hope of raising a more solid structure in its place. But we cannot ultimately find a resting place in pure realism; for realism, though logically overwhelming, does not provide us with the springs of action which are necessary even to the pursuit of thought. Indeed, realism itself, if we attack it with its own weapons, often turns out in practice to be just as much conditioned as any other mode of thought. In politics, the belief that certain facts are unalterable or certain trends irresistible commonly reflects a lack of desire or lack of interest to change or resist them. The impossibility of being a consistent and thorough-going realist is one of the most certain and most curious lessons of political science. Consistent realism excludes four things which appear to be essential ingredients of all effective political thinking: a finite goal, an emotional appeal, a right of moral judgment and a ground for action. . . .

Consistent realism, as has already been noted, involves acceptance of the whole historical process and precludes moral judgments on it. As we have seen, men are generally prepared to accept the judgment of history on the past, praising success and condemning failure. This test is also widely applied to contemporary politics. Such institutions as the League of Nations, or the Soviet or Fascist regimes, are to a considerable extent judged by their capacity to achieve what they profess to achieve; and the legitimacy of this test is implicitly admitted by their own propaganda, which constantly seeks

Edward Hallett Carr, *The Twenty Years Crisis, 1919–1939*, 2nd edition (London: Macmillan, 1946), Chapter 6. Copyright © 1969 by St. Martin's Press. Reprinted with permission of St. Martin's Press.

to exaggerate their successes and minimise their failures. Yet it is clear that mankind as a whole is not prepared to accept this rational test as a universally valid basis of political judgment. The belief that whatever succeeds is right, and has only to be understood to be approved, must, if consistently held, empty thought of purpose, and thereby sterilise and ultimately destroy it. Nor do those whose philosophy appears to exclude the possibility of moral judgments in fact refrain from pronouncing them. Frederick the Great, having explained that treaties should be observed for the reason that "one can trick only once", goes on to call the breaking of treaties "a bad and knavish policy", though there is nothing in his thesis to justify the moral epithet.[1] Marx, whose philosophy appeared to demonstrate that capitalists could only act in a certain way, spends many pages—some of the most effective in *Capital*—in denouncing the wickedness of capitalists for behaving in precisely that way. The necessity, recognised by all politicians, both in domestic and in international affairs, for cloaking interests in a guise of moral principles is in itself a symptom of the inadequacy of realism. Every age claims the right to create its own values, and to pass judgments in the light of them; and even if it uses realist weapons to dissolve other values, it still believes in the absolute character of its own. It refuses to accept the implication of realism that the word "ought" is meaningless.

Most of all, consistent realism breaks down because it fails to provide any ground for purposive or meaningful action. If the sequence of cause and effect is sufficiently rigid to permit of the "scientific prediction" of events, if our thought is irrevocably conditioned by our status and our interests, then both action and thought become devoid of purpose. If, as Schopenhauer maintains, "the true philosophy of history consists of the insight that, throughout the jumble of all these ceaseless changes, we have ever before our eyes the same unchanging being, pursuing the same course to-day, yesterday and for ever",[2] then passive contemplation is all that remains to the individual. Such a conclusion is plainly repugnant to the most deep-seated belief of man about himself. That human affairs can be directed and modified by human action and human thought is a postulate so fundamental that its rejection seems scarcely compatible with existence as a human being. Nor is it in fact rejected by those realists who have left their mark on history. Machiavelli, when he exhorted his compatriots to be good Italians, clearly assumed that they were free to follow or ignore his advice. Marx, by birth and training a *bourgeois,* believed himself free to think and act like a proletarian, and regarded it as his mission to persuade others, whom he assumed to be equally free, to think and act likewise. Lenin, who wrote of the imminence of world revolution as a "scientific prediction", admitted elsewhere that "no situation exist from which there is absolutely no way out".[3] In mo-

---

[1] *Anti-Machiavel,* p. 248.
[2] Schopenhauer, *Welt als Wille und Vorstellung,* ii. ch. 38.
[3] Lenin, *Works* (2nd Russian ed.), xxv. p. 340.

ments of crisis, Lenin appealed to his followers in terms which might equally well have been used by so thorough-going a believer in the power of the human will as Mussolini or by any other leader of any period: "At the decisive moment and in the decisive place, you *must prove* the stronger, you must *be victorious*".[4] Every realist, whatever his professions, is ultimately compelled to believe not only that there is something which man ought to think and do, but that there is something which he can think and do, and that his thought and action are neither mechanical nor meaningless.

We return therefore to the conclusion that any sound political thought must be based on elements of both utopia and reality. Where utopianism has become a hollow and intolerable sham, which serves merely as a disguise for the interests of the privileged, the realist performs an indispensable service in unmasking it. But pure realism can offer nothing but a naked struggle for power which makes any kind of international society impossible. Having demolished the current utopia with the weapons of realism, we still need to build a new utopia of our own, which will one day fall to the same weapons. The human will continue to seek and escape from the logical consequences of realism in the vision of an international order which, as soon as it crystallizes itself into concrete political form, becomes tainted with self-interest and hypocrisy, and must once more be attacked with the instruments of realism.

Here, then, is the complexity, the fascination and the tragedy of all political life. Politics are made up of two elements—utopia and reality—belonging to two different planes which can never meet. There is no greater barrier to clear political thinking than failure to distinguish between ideals, which are utopia, and institutions, which are reality. The communist who set communism against democracy was usually thinking of communism as a pure ideal of equality and brotherhood, and of democracy as an institution which existed in Great Britain, France or the United States and which exhibited the vested interests, the inequalities and the oppression inherent in all political institutions. The democrat who made the same comparison was in fact comparing an ideal pattern of democracy laid up in heaven with communism as an institution existing in Soviet Russia with its class-divisions, its heresy-hunts and its concentration camps. The comparison, made in each case between an ideal and an institution, is irrelevant and makes no sense. The ideal, once it is embodied in an institution, ceases to be an ideal and becomes the expression of a selfish interest, which must be destroyed in the name of a new ideal. This constant interaction of irreconcilable forces is the stuff of politics. Every political situation contains mutually incompatible elements of utopia and reality, of morality and power.

[4]Lenin, *Collected Works* (Engl. transl.), xxi. pt. i. p. 68.

Collective Security and Arms Control in the New Europe

RICHARD K. BETTS

Collective security is an old idea whose time keeps coming.[1] The term has been resurrected and revised in three generations of this century, once after each World War—the First, the Second, and the Cold War—and has been used to refer to: (1) the Wilsonian or ideal concept associated with the Fourteen Points and League of Nations; (2) the Rio Pact, the United Nations, and anti-communist alliances including the UN Command in Korea, NATO, the U.S.-Japan Mutual Security Treaty, SEATO, the Baghdad Pact, and CENTO;[2] and (3) current proposals for organizations to codify peace in Europe.[3]

Richard K. Betts, "Systems for Peace or Causes of War? Collective Security, Arms Control, and the New Europe," *International Security* Vol. 17, no. 1 (Summer 1992). A similar version appears as "Systems of Peace as Causes of War? Collective Security, Arms Control, and the New Europe," in Jack Snyder and Robert Jervis, eds., *Coping with Complexity in the International System* (Boulder: Westview Press, 1993). Reprinted by permission of Westview Press, Boulder, Colorado, and the MIT Press, Cambridge, Massachusetts. Copyright © 1993 by Westview Press.

[1]The concept can be traced back at least as far as the last millennium, when French bishops in a council at Poitiers and a synod at Limoges declared war on war, decided to excommunicate princes who broke the peace, and planned to deploy troops under a religious banner to use force against violators. Stefan T. Possony, "Peace Enforcement," *Yale Law Journal*, Vol. 55, No. 5 (1946).

[2]This was prevalent in official thinking in the first half of the Cold War. For example, see John Foster Dulles, *War or Peace* (New York: Macmillan, 1950), pp. 89–95, 204–207; and Dean Rusk, as told to Richard Rusk, and Daniel Papp, ed., *As I Saw It* (New York: Norton, 1990), pp. 503–505.

[3]For example, Richard Ullman, *Securing Europe* (Princeton: Princeton University Press, 1991); Gregory Flynn and David J. Scheffer, "Limited Collective Security," *Foreign Policy*, No. 80 (Fall

The protean character of collective security reflects the fact that many who endorse it squirm when the terms are specified or applied to awkward cases. This has occurred with all incarnations of the idea. The main problem is the gap between the instinctive appeal of the idea in liberal cultures as they settle epochal conflicts, and its inherent defects in relations among independent states as they move from peace toward war. When particular cases make the defects obtrusive the idea is revised rather than jettisoned. When revisions vitiate what essentially distinguishes the idea from traditional concepts it is supposed to replace, the urge to salvage the idea confuses strategic judgment. That is harmless only as long as strategy is not needed.

Among those who like the idea of collective security, negotiation of arms limitations among states is also popular. Many proponents of the League of Nations linked it closely to plans for general disarmament. That contributed to the association of Wilsonian collective security with utopian visions. In the second half of the Cold War, the shift from pursuit of complete disarmament to limitations aimed at fixing the distribution of military power in stable configurations made the enterprise more serious; indeed it became institutionalized over the past twenty years.

Arms control treaties designed to stabilize military relationships, however, are vestiges of the Cold War. They make sense between adversaries, not friends, and the Russians are on our side now. This may not last, but the size and identity of coalitions that would be arrayed in a new strategic competition—information essential for prescribing the regulation of military balances—cannot yet be known. Bureaucracies and peace strategists nevertheless continue to lobby for arms control as a means to reinforce the current amity. Although constituencies for collective security and arms control overlap, there is at best little connection between the logic of the two goals, and at worst a contradiction.

1990), pp. 77–101, Charles A. Kupchan and Clifford A. Kupchan, "Concerts, Collective Security, and the Future of Europe," *International Security*, Vol. 16, No. 1 (Summer 1991), pp. 114–161; Malcolm Chalmers, "Beyond the Alliance System," *World Policy Journal*, Vol. 7, No. 2 (Spring 1990), pp. 215–230; John Mueller, "A New Concert of Europe," *Foreign Policy*, No. 77 (Winter 1989–90), pp. 3–16; James E. Goodby, "A New European Concert" and Harald Mueller, "A United Nations of Europe and North America," *Arms Control Today*, Vol. 21, No. 1 (January/February 1991); John D. Steinbruner, "Revolution in Foreign Policy," in Henry J. Aaron, ed., *Setting National Priorities: Policy for the Nineties* (Washington, D.C.: Brookings, 1990). Steinbruner terms his overall vision "cooperative" rather than "collective" security, but the description is similar to the Wilsonian conception: "a global alliance . . . [where] all countries are on the same side and their forces are not directed against each other . . . [and] there are no neutrals." Ibid., pp. 68, 74, 109. For a mixed view of prospects, see Stephen F. Szabo, "The New Europeans: Beyond the Balance of Power," in Nils H. Wessell, ed., *The New Europe: Revolution in East-West Relations*, Proceedings of the Academy of Political Science, Vol. 38, No. 1 (New York: Academy of Political Science, 1991).

The main argument in this article is that reborn enthusiasm for collective security is fueled by confusion about which is the cause and which is the effect in the relation between collective security and peace, and by conflation of *present* security *conditions* (absence of a threat) with *future* security *functions* (coping with a threat). This conceptual confusion raises doubts about the congruence of form and function in a collective security system. Is the system designed in a form that will work in conditions where it is needed, or does the form reflect conditions where it is not needed? If changes in conditions prevent the system from functioning according to its design, it will not make war less likely, and will thus make coping with threats harder than if alternate security mechanisms had been developed.

The second possible danger is that instead of failing to perform according to design, collective security or arms control, in succeeding, would *worsen* military instability. Implementing collective commitments could turn minor wars into major ones, and equalizing military power of individual states through arms control without reference to their prospective alignment in war might yield unequal forces when alignments congeal. The usual criticism of collective security and arms control is that they will not work; the other criticism is that if they do work, we may wish they hadn't. . . .

Security Systems

The function of a security system is to produce security, and the system should be judged by how it does so rather than by other things associated with it. This also means that a system designed in good times to cope with bad times should be judged in terms of the bad times rather than the good times. By my reading, many current proposals for collective security do not fully share these assumptions. To judge the efficacy of the idea and the potential for perverse effects, we need to clarify what the system is supposed to do, how it is supposed to do it, and when.

For reasons argued below, the definition of collective security that we should use as a reference point is the classic Wilsonian ideal. Some charge that criticizing the ideal type prevents appreciation of more limited and realistic variants. We find on closer consideration, however, that most of the qualifications applied in current proposals make collective security more realistic by making it less collective and less automatic—and thus hard to differentiate from the traditional balance of power standards it is supposed to replace. Unless collective security *does* mean something significantly different from traditional forms of combination by states against common enemies, in alliances based on specific interests, the term confuses the actual choices.

The essential element in the Wilsonian concept is the *rejection of alliances,* expressed in the commitment of all members of the system to oppose any attack against another: "all for one, and one for all." Peace is indivisible. Alliances for defense are mandated only if collective security fails (on the same principle that a threatened citizen may rely on her own gun if the police fail to answer her call). Instead of planning against an identified adversary, security policy consists of the guarantee of united reaction against whoever might transgress. No grievance warrants resort to force to overturn the status quo; military force is legitimate only to resist attack, not to initiate it. States are to be legally accountable for starting wars. In contrast to traditional international relations, protection comes not from balance of power, but from preponderance of power against any renegade, guaranteed by universal treaty obligation to enforce peace whether doing so happens to be in a state's immediate interest or not. Community of power replaces balance of power.[4] The penalty for aggression is to be automatic economic or military sanctions. (Some collective security schemes rely primarily on economic punishment.[5] To keep discussion manageable within space constraints, my argument addresses the stronger form of the idea, which assumes military obligations.) . . .

What Kind of System?

A collective security system is a mechanism to guard the sovereignty of its members, one designed to function according to certain norms. Since it is not oriented to deterring a specific adversary, it does not function continuously in peacetime. It is an emergency safety mechanism, sitting on the shelf unless activated by emergence of a challenger to the status quo, in a sense

---

[4] G. F. Hudson, "Collective Security and Military Alliances," in Herbert Butterfield and Martin Wight, eds., *Diplomatic Investigations* (Cambridge, Mass.: Harvard University Press, 1966), pp. 175–176; Kenneth W. Thompson, "Collective Security," *International Encyclopedia of the Social Sciences* (New York: Free Press, 1968), pp. 565–566; Kenneth W. Thompson, "Collective Security Reexamined," *American Political Science Review*, Vol. 47, No. 3 (September 1953), pp. 753–756; Arnold Wolfers, *Discord and Collaboration* (Baltimore: Johns Hopkins University Press, 1962), chaps. 11–12; Inis L. Claude, Jr., *Power and International Relations* (New York: Random House, 1962), chap. 4; Claude, *Swords into Plowshares*, 4th ed. (New York: Random House, 1971), chap. 12; Roland M. Stromberg, "The Idea of Collective Security," *Journal of the History of Ideas*, Vol. 17, No. 2 (April 1956); Robert E. Osgood, "Woodrow Wilson, Collective Security, and the Lesson of History," *Confluence*, Vol. 5, No. 4 (Winter 1957), p. 344; M. V. Naidu, *Collective Security and the United Nations* (Delhi: Macmillan, 1974), chap. 2; Frederick H. Hartmann, *The Conservation of Enemies* (Westport, Conn.: Greenwood, 1982), chap. 13; Erich Hula, "Fundamentals of Collective Security," *Social Research*, Vol. 24, No. 1 (Spring 1957). Some have argued that collective security is really just an extension of the balance of power system (e.g., Edward Vose Gulick, *Europe's Classical Balance of Power* [New York: Norton, 1967], pp. 307–308), but this makes little sense unless one is defining it empirically rather than normatively.

[5] This helps to sell the idea to those skeptical of military entanglement. See, for example, James T. Shotwell, *War as an Instrument of National Policy and Its Renunciation in the Pact of Paris* (New York: Harcourt, Brace, 1929), p. 221.

comparable to the emergency back-up system in a nuclear power plant, which functions only in the highly unlikely event that normal operation goes awry.

To judge the effectiveness of an emergency system, it is useful to distinguish whether its most essential elements are automatic or volitional. That is, are the safety switches tripped by the alarm, or does the machine depend on *ad hoc* human choices to start it up and keep it going? If a set of conscious choices is required to run the machine, how many are real choices? Are there good reasons that those responsible might decide deliberately not to flip the switches necessary to keep the machine performing according to design? Are the "rules" for how the system works primarily empirical or normative? That is, do they describe how the linked components *do* work, in terms of laws of physics or evidence from experience; or prescribe how they should work or how they would work *if* the operators make the choices stipulated by the designers?

As Charles Perrow makes clear, the interactions in a complex system based on automatic switches may not be fully predictable.[6] They should be far more predictable, however, than the outputs of a system that depends on a combination of deliberate choices. In the latter, the probability of unanticipated interactions of components is potentially doubled, as mechanical uncertainties are compounded by decisional ones. The problem of predictability is further complicated by the strategic quality of decisions in a security system—statesmen trying not just to second-guess machines, but to outwit each other. These differences are of course what makes action in any system of politics harder to predict than in one of physics.

Realist theories of balance of power systems are both empirical and normative, but primarily the former. Just as automobiles in most countries should drive on the right side of the road because they must do so to avoid a crash, states *should* seek power because they *must*. The starkest versions of realism imply that precious little real choice is even available. The deterministic aspect of realism emphasizes automatic qualities of power-balancing in the international system more than do idealists who focus on cooperation or moral choices. Extreme realists see the rules of balance of power as almost a cybernetic process of constant adjustment to maintain equilibrium. If one state or coalition begins to dominate the system, the others, like thermostats, move to coalesce and right the balance.

A collective security system depends more on volition and normative rules. The design of collective security rests on the norm that states must subordinate their own immediate interests to general or remote ones. While there is disagreement about how thoroughly the theory and practice of balance of power systems have coincided in history, few claim that the case for collective security has yet been confirmed by experience. (As I argue below, the Concert of Europe is not a good example.) Indeed, the main theoretical

---

[6]Charles Perrow, *Normal Accidents* (New York: Basic Books, 1984), chap. 3.

argument against collective security is that its normative rules have been discredited by the empirically validated rules of balance of power.

All of this highlights the question of congruence between form and function. Will the system's performance correspond to the rules in its design? If not, will the design be just superfluous, or counterproductive? Or will it ever have to perform at all? The test of a security system is how it functions when a challenge to security arises. If it is never tested, its function is only symbolic, not substantive.

Testing, however, poses two problems. One is that the first test may kill the system if the design is flawed—if empirical rules contradict normative ones, and form does not govern function. There are no simulations or dry runs in international conflict comparable to what can be done with real machines. Another is that we may not know when a test occurs. As with deterrence in general, if the design is so good that a would-be challenger does not even dare to try, the system has worked, but no one can prove that it has because there is no certainty that the challenge would have been made otherwise. . . .

Collective Security as a Norm

. . . Those who identified the concept with the regional anti-communist alliance organizations spawned in the first decade of the Cold War were stretching the idea to cover arrangements really more consistent with traditional strategy. Dignifying regional coalitions like NATO by calling them collective security organs helped to brand communist states as outlaws and confirm the moralism in American policy, but the fact remained that they were alliances playing the power-balancing game. Many current proponents of collective security, in contrast, trim the concept to cover less than either the Wilsonian or Cold War variants, by allowing big exemptions from the obligation to discipline countries who resort to force. These variants evade what distinguished collective security from either traditional alliances or military isolation. If a collective institution is really to function as a security system rather than a slogan, the elements that are conceptually unique rather than those that are shared with other constructs should set the standard for assessing the idea. The principles of automaticity and universality are what most differentiate collective security from balance of power.

Many who now claim to endorse collective security demur on the ironclad obligation to join in countering any and all aggression. This vitiates the concept. Unless collective security requires states to act on the basis of the legal principle rather than their specific interests in the case at issue, and unless it forbids neutrality in the face of aggression, the concept adds nothing to traditional conventions of collective defense based on alliances and balance of power. Collective security, wrote Arnold Wolfers, "presumably would add nothing to the protection that victims of aggression would have enjoyed under the old system unless such victims could now expect more military assistance than they would have received otherwise." To add to the strength of defense and deterrence, nations must be willing to fight in situations where,

> if they had not been devoted to the principle of collective security, they would have remained neutral or fought on the side of the aggressor. Instead of being allowed to reserve their military strength for the exclusive task of balancing the power of countries considered a threat to themselves or their allies, nations committed to a policy of collective security must divert their strength to struggle in remote places or, worse still, take action against friends and allies.[7]

Nevertheless, in the generations after Wilson many felt the need to endorse collective security while defining it in ways that overlapped significantly with traditional arrangements. They did so because they recognized that the weakness of the League of Nations and the UN had embarrassed the pure concept as naive, yet they still resisted the argument that balance of power politics cannot be transcended.

What's Wrong with Collective Security?

Before confronting attempts to salvage the principle by softening it, we should note the reasons that so many have rejected it altogether. The main criticism has been that collective security does not work because states fail to honor commitments to automatic action. In the background of the many reasons that they renege is the problem that the animating motive for *constructing* a collective security system ("No More War") is in tension with the imperative required to make the system function when challenged ("No More Aggression"). The former reflects abhorrence of war, but the latter requires going to war where immediate self-interest might not. This reduces the odds that parties to the system will feel the same way about the principle when it comes to cases.

A second objection is that the collective security principle's legalism is too rigidly conservative, since it requires honoring the *status quo ante* irrespective of its merits.[8] Elihu Root complained about Article 10 of the League Covenant:

> If perpetual, it would be an attempt to preserve for all time unchanged the distribution of power and territory made in accordance with the views and exi-

---

[7]In the 1935 crisis over Ethiopia, "when faced with the choice of losing the support of Italy or else defaulting on collective security, France chose the latter course." Wolfers, *Discord and Collaboration,* pp. 167–169, 187.

[8]John H. Herz, *International Politics in the Atomic Age* (New York: Columbia University Press, 1959), pp. 85, 90–91.

gencies of the Allies in this present juncture of affairs. . . . It would not only be futile; it would be mischievous. Change and growth are the law of life, and no generation can impose its will in regard to the growth of nations and the distribution of power, upon succeeding generations.[9]

This is especially problematic because third parties often do not agree about which side in a war is the aggressor. The closest thing to a criterion that is both general and neutral would be "whoever strikes first across a national border," but this would never be universally accepted. For example, it would have required members of a collective security system to act against the British and Russians in World War II for occupying Iran, against Israel for preempting in June 1967, and against the United States in the 1980s for invading Grenada and Panama. Once we admit that justifications may exist for initial resorts to force, any standard for "aggression" becomes too slippery to serve consistently. "The problem is not, as the Wilsonians imagined, one of suppressing an infrequent case of diabolism. . . . To determine the aggressor is really to decide which is a bad nation. And a general law can never do this."[10]

Insensitivity to this ambiguity arose in part because, from the establishment of the League of Nations through the war in Korea, "aggressors" were ideologically repugnant states; for democracies "it was natural . . . to assume that committing themselves to deter or punish 'any aggressor anywhere' meant in fact committing themselves to oppose nondemocratic aggressors who were their national enemies anyway." Not until the Suez expedition of 1956 did assigning guilt become awkward.[11]

A third standard objection is that, in practice, organizing according to the principle of collective responsibility undermines preparations to balance the power of troublesome states. Potent alliances cannot be developed with a snap of the finger when innocent states suddenly lose faith in the collective guarantee. "No arrangement would be more likely to create conditions in which one nation can dominate," wrote Kissinger of the Wilsonian dream. "For if everybody is allied with everybody, nobody has a special relationship with anybody. It is the ideal situation for the most ruthless seeking to isolate potential victims."[12]

Fourth, the responsibility to counter every aggressor can endanger a threatened coalition, as when members of the League considered the obli-

---

[9]Quoted in Arthur S. Link, *Wilson the Diplomatist* (Baltimore: Johns Hopkins University Press, 1957), p. 136. "The dilemma of collective security has been that its major proponents have been driven to oppose social change in the name of the sanctity of treaties." Thompson, "Collective Security Reexamined," p. 770.

[10]Stromberg, "The Idea of Collective Security," pp. 255, 258.

[11]Wolfers, *Discord and Collaboration*, pp. 185–186.

[12]Henry A. Kissinger, "Germany, Neutrality and the 'Security System' Trap," *Washington Post,* April 15, 1990, p. D7.

gation of resisting the Soviet attack on Finland after Britain and France were already at war with Germany.[13] The counterproductive effect of collective security came closer to actuality earlier, in the case of efforts to punish Italy for its aggression against Ethiopia. Where proponents of the norm see those efforts as feeble, conservative realists charge that they helped push Italy into the Axis alliance. This argument also cuts against current proponents of "limited" collective security as an alternative to the unrealistic demands of the ideal type. The problem in the 1930s was precisely the limitation of the concept, a compromise response; either of the extremes would have been preferable. Had *pure* collective security been applied, the fascist powers could have been crushed early; or had pure balance-of-power strategy been applied, Italy might have been kept in the allied camp by ignoring its depredations in Africa. Falling between the stools, however, truncated collective security and left France and Britain with the worst of both worlds. . . .

The main reason that liberals lost interest in collective security in earlier generations was that it did not work, and the challenge to it had to be met with traditional means. The League Covenant and Kellogg-Briand Pact neither deterred nor defeated fascist aggressions in the 1930s, because the volitional elements of the system faltered; when principle came to practice, statesmen chose not to honor the commitment of the covenant to united action; they chose not to flip the switches on the collective security machine.

Conservative realists, however, do not just fear that the principle would not work; to them it can be awful if it *does* work. Their criticism is that if abstract commitments are honored, the system inevitably turns small conflicts into big ones, by requiring states to get involved when it is not in their interest to do so. This was the main reason that realists like Hans Morgenthau and George Kennan fell out with liberal hawks over the Vietnam War. The Cold War redefinition of collective security as the global coalition against communist aggression, in rhetoric from Dean Acheson to Dean Rusk, fed the domino theory: South Vietnam was important not in itself, but as a matter of principle. Fighting in Vietnam meant avoiding the mistakes of the 1930s in not fighting in Manchuria or Ethiopia. Morgenthau posed the counterproductive effect of the principle:

> It is the supreme paradox of collective security that any attempt to make it work with less than ideal perfection will have the opposite effect from what it is supposed to achieve. . . . If an appreciable number of nations are opposed to the status quo . . . the distribution of power will take on the aspects of a balance

---

[13]"We still read that the path to Nazi aggression was made possible by the failure of the League to coerce Japan in 1931 and Italy in 1935. We have the absurdity, to which collective security is always being reduced, of saying that war in 1931 would have prevented war in 1941. It is implied that had the western states been fighting Japan in Asia they could have fought Germany better in Europe. The verdict of careful history might be that the ill-conceived effort to apply 'sanctions' against Italy in 1935 weakened, not strengthened, the front against Germany." Stromberg, "The Idea of Collective Security," p. 254.

of power. . . . The attempt to put collective security into effect under such conditions . . . will not preserve peace, but will make war inevitable. . . . It will also make localized wars impossible and thus make war universal. For under the regime of collective security as it actually works under contemporary conditions, if A attacks B, then C, D, E, and F might honor their collective obligations and come to the aid of B, while G and H might try to stand aside and I, J, and K might support A's aggression. . . . By the very logic of its assumptions, the diplomacy of collective security must aim at transforming all local conflicts into world conflicts . . . since peace is supposed to be indivisible. . . . Thus a device intent on making war impossible ends by making war universal.[14]

Realist arguments against a collective security system for Europe rest on both fears—that it would not work when needed, or that it would work when it should not. If commitments falter in a crunch, defense against a rogue power will be weaker than if the regular NATO alliance had remained the guarantor of security. If it does work, however, it precludes denying protection to Eastern European countries against each other or a great power. This makes a crisis in that cauldron of instabilities more likely to erupt than to stew in its own juices. Concern with this implication of the classic scheme of collective security for involvement in the Balkans, embodied in Article 10 of the League Covenant (to "preserve as against external aggression the territorial integrity of all members"), was a specific reason for U.S. domestic opposition to joining that organization over seventy years ago.[15]

Why Does Collective Security Keep Coming Back?

The Wilsonian ideal of collective security was buffeted by history from all sides in the 1930s, and again after the anti-fascist alliance split. Redefinitions in the first half of the Cold War were also driven from favor—for hawks, by disappointment with the development of the UN after Korea, and for doves, by disillusionment with the crusade in Vietnam. The term's renewed popularity does not come from a change of mind about the earlier disillusionments, but from the apparent inadequacy of alternative constructs for adjusting to the outbreak of peace, and because some now define the concept in narrow ways that avoid troublesome implications. At the same time, there is no agreement on whether the most troublesome commitment would be to counter aggression by a great power or to pacify wars between Eastern European states over borders and ethnic minorities.

Many proponents of a collective security system for post–Cold War Europe are ambivalent or opposed outright to requiring intervention in a new generation of Balkan wars. Richard Ullman proclaims that "Europe's peace has

---

[14]Hans J. Morgenthau, *Politics Among Nations,* fifth ed. (New York: Knopf, 1973), pp. 411–412. See also Stromberg, "The Idea of Collective Security," pp. 258–259.
[15]Henry L. Stimson and McGeorge Bundy, *On Active Service in Peace and War* (New York: Harper, 1948), pp. 102–103.

become a divisible peace," yet endorses a European Security Organization (ESO) that would include "a generalized commitment to collective security. Each member state should commit itself . . . to come to the aid of any other if it is the victim of an armed attack." The obligation, however, would not extend to little victims. Eastern Europe's fate is to be excluded as "a vast buffer zone between the Soviet Union and Germany." If cross-border violence erupts over national minorities in Kosovo or Transylvania, "the major powers would be unlikely to get involved to an extent greater than through diplomacy and perhaps economic pressure." Besides "walling off" local conflicts, the benefit of the buffer zone that Ullman anticipates is to facilitate great power confidence in a shift toward defensively-oriented military doctrines.[16] Similarly, Charles Kupchan and Clifford Kupchan prescribe collective security, yet at the same time make a gargantuan concession to traditional balance of power by endorsing tacit recognition of "areas of special interest" such as a Russian *droit du regard* in Eastern Europe.[17] These notions recognize the defects in the Wilsonian ideal type, and they may reassure the great powers about their security, but they de-collectivize collective security.

Uncertainty about whether the system would cover Eastern Europe is crucial. There are two essential trends in Europe today: in the West, economic and political integration, consensus on borders, and congruence between nations and states; in the East, the reverse—disintegration and lack of consensus or congruence. Will the stability of the West be protected by holding the mess in the East at arm's length? Ullman believes the new collective system would handle misbehavior by one of the great powers, but not small ones,[18] presumably because the stakes are higher. By the same token, however, the costs and risks (such as involvement of nuclear weapons) would be higher too, so the balance of costs and benefits does not obviously make pacification of small wars in Eastern Europe a less attractive objective.

It should hardly be as daunting for the system to settle a fight between Hungary and Rumania or between Ukraine and Poland as to confront one between Russian or Germany and the rest of the continent. At the same time, apparent sideshows in Eastern Europe may offer occasions for abrasions and misperceptions among the great powers if they disagree about intervention. One nightmare would be a Russian attack on Ukraine (far less fanciful than a Soviet attack on NATO ever was; Russian vice president Rutskoi has already broached the issue of recovering the Crimea for Russia). Under true collective security, members of the system would have to aid Ukraine—doing what NATO would not do for Hungary in 1956—thus invoking the danger of escalation and nuclear war. Under realist norms, the West should leave Ukraine to its fate—tragic for the Ukrainians, but safer for

[16]Ullman, *Securing Europe*, pp. 28, 29, 68, 73–74, 78, 147.

[17]Kupchan and Kupchan, "Concerts, Collective Security, and the Future of Europe," pp. 156–157.

[18]Ullman, *Securing Europe*, p. 68.

everyone else. If we prefer the latter course, why try to dress it up by associating it with collective security? . . .

Confusion of Causes and Consequences

Since the collapse of communism it has not always been clear whether the invocation of collective security is meant to enforce peace or to celebrate it. Less emphasis is usually placed on how the system would restore peace in the face of war than on why war (or at least war worthy of concern) will not arise. Ullman writes:

> If one were to rely on the historical record of generalized commitments to collective security, one could not be hopeful. . . . But it is arguable that the conditions now emerging in Europe make the past a poor predictor. . . . No major state has revisionist ambitions that its leaders think they could satisfy by sending troops across borders. . . . A genuine congruence of interest and goals sharply distinguishes the present from previous eras . . . *it is unlikely that the great powers will soon find their commitments to collective security put to the test of a large, searing, and escalating crisis.*[19]

Ullman does recognize that things could go bad, and urges taking advantage of the current window of opportunity to get an ESO going, so that the regime could buttress stability in fouler weather. Why collective security should work any better in the face of the many logical and historical criticisms noted earlier, however, remains unclear, apart from the idea that it can work because it will not have to (since there will be no rampaging rogue state), or because not all aggressions will have to be countered (so statesmen and strategists can pick and choose, just as they have traditionally). Such hopes may also deflect reservations about automatic commitment to combat unidentified future aggressors, but they imply that *peace is the premise of the system rather than the product, that peace will cause peace rather than that collective security will cause peace.* If we fasten on the import of the current calm, we muddle the difference between the current need for a security organization (which we can see is low) and the future efficacy of such an organization (which we should want to be high).[20]

One can argue that even if peace may be the cause rather than the consequence at the beginning, it can become the consequence as a regime, once

---

[19]Ullman, *Securing Europe*, p. 66 (emphasis added).

[20]An analogous issue for nuclear power safety is suggested by the Nuclear Regulatory Commission's inability in the early 1980s to think of a way to deal with the potential problem of genetic damage from a plant accident. "If the risks of an accident are kept low enough, they said, there will be no problem with ignoring inter-generational effects. This conclusion answers the question about consequences of accidents by saying they will be trivial because there will be so few accidents." Perrow, *Normal Accidents*, p. 69, citing U.S. Nuclear Regulatory Commission (NRC), "Safety Goals for Nuclear Power Plants: A Discussion Paper," *NUREG* 0880 (Washington, D.C.: NRC, February 1982), p. 15.

established, promotes cooperation and takes on a life of its own. Speaking of the Concert of Europe, Robert Jervis notes that the expectation that it "could continue to function helped maintain it through the operation of familiar self-fulfilling dynamics. . . . There were no 'runs on the bank'." Rules, reciprocity, and institutionalization reinforced opposition to attempts to change the status quo. Recently, the Kupchans argue, the norm of reciprocity is growing again, as reflected in mutual concessions such as Soviet and Western troop withdrawals from Central Europe.[21] These examples are weak reeds.

First, while the nineteenth-century Concert "influenced the behavior of states in ways that made its continuation possible even after the initial conditions had become attenuated," when the conditions eroded, the regime's efficacy did too. By 1823, a mere eight years after the Napoleonic Wars, the Concert was fraying.[22] The Concert "worked" well only as long as the great powers' disagreements were minor; when the consensus cracked over the Crimea in 1854, and again later in the century, so did the Concert.

As to the second argument, the idea that growing reciprocity characterized East-West relations in recent years misreads the end of the Cold War. The peace settlement was no compromise; it was a series of outright victories for the West. The Soviet Union surrendered in arms control negotiations, accepting NATO's terms which required grossly asymmetrical reductions in both the treaties on Intermediate Range Nuclear Forces (INF) and Conventional Forces in Europe (CFE). Moscow gave up political control of Eastern Europe without a fight in 1989, getting nothing in return. Within a year the Warsaw Pact was defunct while NATO lived on. The West did not reciprocate Soviet concessions, it just pocketed them. There was more reciprocity during the Cold War when both sides were bargaining with each other (as in SALT I and II or the Helsinki accords) than there was in the ending, as the Russians rolled over belly-up. . . .

When exceptions to the applicability of collective security are pointed out, few reasons are offered for continuing to believe in the idea that do not come back to citations of peace, satisfaction with the status quo, and consensus on legitimate behavior as preconditions for their own enforcement. If Europe remains at peace, it is likely to be not because a collective security system causes it, but because the nations and states of Europe are satisfied.

Few dare propose a pure collective security system, but some argue that realistically limited versions are at least more effective than traditional "balancing under anarchy."[23] This misunderstands the choice. Collective security commitments do not obviate international anarchy any more than an alliance does; only political federation would. And if the salvage job for the concept is completed by dispensing with the unrealistic requirements of

---

[21]Robert Jervis, "Security Regimes," in Stephen D. Krasner, ed., *International Regimes* (Ithaca: Cornell University Press, 1983), pp. 181–182; Richard N. Rosecrance, *Action and Reaction in World Politics* (Boston: Little, Brown, 1963), p. 56; Kupchan and Kupchan, "Concerts, Collective Security, and the Future of Europe," p. 130.

[22]Jervis, "Security Regimes," p. 184.

[23]Kupchan and Kupchan, "Concerts, Collective Security, and the Future of Europe," p. 116.

universality and automaticity, what then is really left that is not consistent with traditional "balancing under anarchy" to which collective security is ostensibly opposed?

Stripping away the rhetoric of collective security, the actual results that seem to be envisioned by the more realistic proposals that invoke the term are: (1) marginal peacekeeping functions comparable to what the UN has attempted in the Congo, Cyprus, Sinai and Gaza (until Nasser evicted the UN force just before the 1967 war), and Lebanon; (2) a collective security cachet on what really amounts to policing by a single dominant power, comparable to the UN actions in Korea and Kuwait where many nations sent token forces but the preponderance of power was imposed by the United States; (3) a condominial system of great power tutelage modeled on the nineteenth-century Concert; or (4) a *de jure* overlay of collective security norms on a *de facto*, unorganized security system, comparable to the Rio Pact "system" in South America.

The limitations of the first of these are well recognized. Cases of UN peacekeeping have generally been modest monitoring and interposition operations,[24] not forthright defeat of aggression as supposed in the basic model of collective security (in large part because there was no international consensus on which sides were the aggressors). The UN missions intervened impartially to separate contending forces under truces which the contenders accepted. Peacekeeping is not peacemaking. Even the peacekeeping was dubious: when the contenders fell out violently again (as in the June 1967 war, the Greek Cypriot coup and Turkish invasion in 1974, or the Israeli invasion of Lebanon in 1982), the UN troops were brushed aside by the combatants. After Korea, UN forces "kept" peace only where and when local contenders did not try to break it.

U.N.-mandated action in the Korean War and against Iraq in 1991 come the closest to real collective security, and the symbolic value of the large number of nations sending combat units was indeed quite significant. In neither case, however, was the military participation of countries other than the United States vital to the outcome. In the recent war, for example, it is implausible that the anti-Iraq coalition forces could have liberated Kuwait without the Americans, or that the Americans could have failed to do so without the assistance of the other forces (although it would have needed the bases in Saudi Arabia). The principle of collective security, however, was indeed vital in motivating the American decision to attack Iraq.[25]

[24]See *The Blue Helmets: A Review of United Nations Peace-keeping* (New York: United Nations Department of Public Information, October 1985).

[25]Once Saudi oil was guarded by the Desert Shield deployment, there was no crucial material interest requiring the United States to spend blood and treasure for tiny Kuwait. Nor was enthusiasm for democracy an explanation. After booting Iraq out, Bush handed Kuwait back to the Sabah family oligarchy that had suspended the country's reasonably democratic constitution (and he then stood aside as Saddam Hussein slaughtered the Shi'ites and Kurds, who rose against Baghdad). Opposition to aggression as a matter of principle is the primary explanation of the U.S. decision for war.

The third and fourth variants suggested above deserve more scrutiny. The relevance of the Concert model has been overestimated, and that of the unorganized system has been underestimated.

The Old Concert and the New Europe

If we had to find a reasonable hybrid version of collective security, the nineteenth-century Concert of Europe would be it. As a modification, the Concert does not go so far as to become identical with eighteenth- or late nineteenth-century balance of power models. The Concert departs from important aspects of the ideal definition, however, and it also rests on archaic ideological premises. These problems may not disable it as a model for twenty-first century collective security, but they do weaken it.

One discrepancy between ideal collective security and the concert is that the former sanctifies the security of all nations while the latter subordinates the sovereignty of the weak to the interests of the strong. Under the Concert the great powers colluded to keep peace by keeping each other satisfied; the rights of a Poland were not in the same class as those of an Austria, Prussia, or Russia. The security nurtured by the Concert was selectively collective.[26] To be accurate rather than confusing, we should call it *condominial* rather than collective. Also, maintaining a balance of power (by cooperation rather than competition) remained an important object of the nineteenth-century Concert regime.

The moral glue of much of the Concert (at least of the Holy Alliance in the East) was monarchical conservatism and opposition to liberalism and nationalism. Yet liberalism and nationalism are precisely what most characterize the recent revolution in Europe. This weakens the proposition that the time for another Concert is ripe because the underlying conditions "are once again present," and because burgeoning democracy is conducive to it.[27] Only if the fact of ideological consensus *per se* were all that mattered, irrespective of its content, would this be convincing.

The liberal consensus in today's world, however, has different implications for the rights of great powers. Outside of academic hothouses, liberals are unlikely to rejoice in the pacifying effects of transcontinental democracy in one breath and endorse a two-class system of policy making and security rights in the next. They cannot easily promote collective security for the big

---

[26]See Richard B. Elrod, "The Concert of Europe," *World Politics*, Vol. 28, No. 2 (January 1976), pp. 163–165. Consider that the United Nations in 1945 resembled a Concert. The role of the Security Council apart from the General Assembly accorded special rights to the great powers, and Poland's pre-war borders were changed to suit the Soviet Union.

[27]Kupchan and Kupchan, "Concerts, Collective Security, and the Future of Europe," pp. 116, 149. On achievements of the regime, see Paul W. Schroeder, "The 19th-Century International System," *World Politics*, Vol. 39, No. 1 (October 1986). It is true that in the West the Concert did accommodate the new forces, as in the creation of Belgium. British and French ideological disagreements with the eastern powers, however, reduced the Concert's unity. See F. H. Hinsley, *Power and the Pursuit of Peace* (New York: Cambridge University Press, 1963), chaps. 9–10.

boys on the block, and every-man-for-himself for benighted weak states in Eastern Europe. The point was clear in the statement by Czechoslovakia's Foreign Minister Jiri Dienstbier that "the core of any collective system of European security must be a treaty committing every party to provide assistance, including military assistance, in the event of an attack against any participant."[28]

Can we imagine the western powers giving the back of their hand to the new heroes of the liberated zones? Maybe in whispered back alley conclaves, but not in the formal conferences such as defined the Concert system at its height. Even then, as Gregory Flynn and David Scheffer note in dismissing the Concert as a form of collective security, "No one is prepared to redraw the map of Europe for balance-of-power purposes. . . . International law has evolved substantially to protect the integrity of all states."[29] A Concert today would have more trouble juggling two contradictory sets of values: national self-determination, and the sanctity of existing state borders.

Nor can a collective security regime be shorn of ideology, because the essence of the concept is an assumption of legal order and moral obligation independent of immediate national interest. To ignore this is hardly feasible when the flush of enthusiasm for collective security comes mainly from teleological liberalism.[30] The mechanics of the system and the prediction of how it would function cannot easily be separated from the values that are integral to its design.

Is an Organized System Necessary?

Collective security is popular, despite all the logical problems, because it is hard to think of what else should replace the Cold War alliance system. It seems to go without saying that there must be a grand design and formal regulatory structure. If the structure is not to be designed in terms of bipolar alliances like the Cold War, or multipolar alliances like the classical balance of power, or a fully United Europe, or American dominance, then collective security becomes appealing by process of elimination. Coupled with the celebration of peace, collective security becomes a talisman, a security blanket legitimizing relaxation, rather than a serious action plan for collective war against yet unknown "aggressors." Analysts, however, should bite the bullet and ask what this means about the substance of the security order.

If what we are facing is really a durable condition of natural security in Europe, a post-Hobbesian pacific anarchy, why assume the need for an organized functioning security system of any sort? Why is strategic *laissez faire*, with *ad hoc* adaptation as we go along, unthinkable? What would be wrong if the organization of security on the European continent became like that in

[28]Quoted in Flynn and Scheffer, "Limited Collective Security," p. 88.
[29]Flynn and Scheffer, "Limited Collective Security," p. 81.
[30]For example: "There is an inherent logic to the emerging era. . . . The basis of security is being altered by a natural historical progression." Steinbruner, "Revolution in Foreign Policy," p. 66.

South America for the past half-century, where symbolic organs like the Rio Pact continue to exist without substantive import, and states dispense with significant alliance arrangements because there is little concern with the prospect of major international war. Instead of an ESO, why not a UPE (Unorganized Pacified Europe)? If something goes wrong, states could look for allies or other tried and true solutions when the time comes. If this is what ambivalent fans of collective security are implicitly getting at, the two could coexist: an ESO overlay of symbolic commitment in principle to collective security, left sufficiently ambiguous to allow the evolution of traditional initiatives for self-protection in the underlying UPE. In Perrow's terms this would be a "loosely coupled" collective security system, with more potential for adapting to unforeseen circumstances,[31] but its substantive significance would be low; sensible states would not count on it in a pinch. . . .

Arms Control Without Alignment

Most enthusiasts for collective security also favor negotiated limitations on armament. Collective security organizations and arms control treaties alike aim to establish legal orders that deter challenges to peace. The rationales behind them, however, are not consistent.

The two forms of regulation deal in different currencies. Collective security is based on commitments of *intent* (that states will act against aggressors). Arms control is based on constraint of *capabilities*. These could be complementary, but there is still a difference between the political logic of one and the military logic of the other. Arms control relies on balance of power, aiming to construct a military balance that in itself dissuades states from thinking that they can use force effectively for attack; moral status in disputes between the parties to arms control is irrelevant to a treaty's impact on the stability of deterrence. Collective security, in contrast, relies on imbalance of power, a preponderance of the law-abiding many against the lawbreaking few; moral claims of the states involved are everything.

The impact of arms limitations on military stability depends in principle on beliefs about what would happen if the forces allowed under the agreement were to crash into each other in battle: stability implies that neither side could win by striking first. Thus a stable agreement would be evaluated according to force ratios calculated in terms of dyads. If there is any strategic logic to an arms treaty, it must assume knowledge of who would be on whose side in event of war. It would be nonsensical for A, B, and C to agree to binding constraints of equal armament, forswearing options of unilateral military buildup, if they think that in a pinch two of them are likely to combine against the third. There is nothing stable about a peacetime ratio of 1:1:1 if it translates into a wartime ratio of 2:1. A country expecting that it may have

---

[31]Perrow, *Normal Accidents*, pp. 88–97.

to fight alone will want the option to increase its power unilaterally, and will not logically settle for limits that prohibit that option. . . .

Military Criteria for Limitations

Few proposals address in detail what standards or formulas would mesh limits for armament with the logic of a collective security system. Those who embrace the treaty on Conventional Forces in Europe (CFE), or who endorse further reductions along its lines, would base arms control on the old Cold War framework of bipolar alliances that is already gone. The CFE Treaty itself makes no strategic sense (at least for Russia) since the dissolution of the old order. It says nothing about what forces should be allowed to the successor states of the Soviet Union, and aside from that problem the formula for military balance in the treaty is logical only as long as the former members of the Warsaw Pact are assumed to have more strategic affinity with Moscow than with the countries of western Europe.

Another proposal does attempt to supersede the old framework, but with dubious implications. It would establish a supranational "organization, to which all states belong, that regulates the conditions of military deployment for everyone."[32] What would be the benchmarks for regulation? At one point John Steinbruner suggests that "standardized criteria for setting force ceilings *would ensure that no state faced a decisive advantage against any other single state,* and the residual alliances would offer protection against the formation of aggressive coalitions." In the next breath, however, it is proposed that each state be allowed force levels proportional to the length of its borders. By the author's own estimates this showed the old Soviet Union with *more than double* the "offensive potential" of Germany and a far higher margin against any other European state; Turkey with nearly four times as much as its enemy Greece; and Germany with more than twice as much as either Poland or France. All of this contradicts the prior criterion of no decisive advantage between any two states,[33] and shows that the identification of coali-

---

[32]Steinbruner, "Revolution in Foreign Policy," pp. 108–109.

[33]Steinbruner, "Revolution in Foreign Policy," pp. 74–76 (emphasis added). The estimates also include figures for "defensive potential," but the bar on the graph for the Soviet Union's offensive potential is still longer than the bars for any of the other countries' defensive potentials, and Germany's offensive bar is longer than the defensive ones for any other countries in the compilation except the Soviet Union. (The United States and the United Kingdom do not appear on the chart. Also, the figures for the Soviet Union appear to include only the portions of its border west of the Urals.) A better rationale for the figures is available, ironically, if we substitute assumed coalitions for the notion of "global alliance." This can be read into Steinbruner's mention of "residual alliances," although there is only one alliance of any sort on the continent anyway, since the Warsaw Pact has dissolved and many of its former members would like to join NATO. Allotting to Russia forces that are grossly superior to any other state in the region might bring the actual situation closer to balance if we assume that solitary Russia were to face a coalition of many of the others. Moreover, as Malcolm Chalmers suggests ("Beyond the Alliance System," p. 245), an ESO would limit obligations to Europe, and thus would not guarantee Russia against security problems in Asia or challenges to its southern borders, so Moscow would have another justification for a surplus of capability.

tions would remain absolutely essential to assessing the stability of military relationships on the continent.

If the prior criterion were to take precedence, the arms control order should be denominated in terms of force-to-force rather than force-to-space ratios, and should accord absolutely equal forces, battalion for battalion, to all states, irrespective of their size, population, or other asymmetries; Belgium's forces should equal Germany's. The proposal does not do so, because it seeks to endow the new military allotments with a technical character more favorable to defensive operations than to attack, and assumes that this is related to capacity to cover borders with satisfactory force-to-space ratios. To take that criterion seriously, however, contradicts the aim of significant reductions of forces, or for many of the countries in Europe, of any reductions at all.

Ensuring a linear defense means maximizing the density of forces covering the line, to prevent probing attacks from finding a gap or weak point that can be penetrated. Yet the Steinbruner proposal, although denominated in terms of force-to-space ratios, seeks to reduce density rather than maximize it. It aims at an allowance of one brigade per seventy-five kilometers of front, which is a mere one-fifth of the ratio considered adequate (and only a tenth of the optimum) in tactical doctrines of modern armies.[34] This could conceivably be rationalized by compensating for thinner ground forces along the line with unusually large amounts of mobile firepower from air forces, yet the proposal seeks to reduce that dimension of capability as well, and to do so disproportionately (on grounds that airpower is an offensive capability).[35] Low density on the ground, uncompensated by other sources of firepower, opens up much larger possibilities for offensive movement. If total force levels were low enough on both sides, this would prevent penetrations from occupying much of the defender's territory, operations could degenerate into the raiding/counterraiding style of medieval warfare, and strategy would move from denial or conquest toward punishment, but it would all be hardly conducive to linear defense.[36]

---

[34]John J. Mearsheimer, *Conventional Deterrence* (Ithaca: Cornell University Press, 1983), pp. 181, 265 n.

[35]Steinbruner, "Revolution in Foreign Policy," p. 77. He argues that because "it is generally believed that a standard brigade would have to be concentrated in less than a five-kilometer segment of front ... in order to overcome well-prepared, competently positioned defenses," overall reduction of force levels would require an attacker to concentrate a larger proportion of its ground units, thus exposing its own defense in other sectors to greater risk of counterattack (p. 75). This, however, appears to lose sight of the relativity of requirements. If the defender's line is much thinner than the standard norm, the concentration an attacker needs to penetrate will be lower as well.

[36]See Archer Jones, *The Art of War in the Western World* (Urbana: University of Illinois Press, 1987), pp. 558–560, 652–653, 666–667. At one end of the continuum of force-to-space ratios would be the western front in World War I, where density was so high that sustained penetration proved impossible for most of the war. At the other end would be guerrilla wars, where

Defense-dominance is easier with high force levels and low tech than with low force levels and low tech.[37] If one really wants to base operational doctrine on linear defense and force-to-space ratios, and simultaneously to reduce the mobile firepower available to defenders for quick movement to threatened sectors, the answer would be to *increase* ground forces (while limiting their mobility), not reduce them. The most effective capability for defense that posed the least capability for attack would be, in effect, heavily armed infantry, lined up shoulder-to-shoulder all along the border, with their legs cut off. To increase forces, however, is hardly a plausible response to the end of the Cold War, no matter what the military logic.

Tactical complexities aside, endorsement of technological and doctrinal "defense dominance" by proponents of collective security is reasonable, but not unambiguously so. Compared with traditional strategic arrangements, which usually develop war plans, deployments, and doctrine in regard to an identified enemy, collective security is likely to *delay* reaction to attack, because the members of the system must react, mobilize, and coordinate their response *ad hoc*. Since preponderant power is not arrayed against an attacker before transgression occurs (if it were, the system would be a regular alliance, not collective security), and strategic initiative can often negate tactical advantage,[38] defeat of aggression will usually have to rely on counterattack to take back lost territory, rather than on direct defense. In that case the tactical advantage of defense passes to the original aggressor, and the

the ratios are so low that governments cannot cover all points they need to defend, while rebels can concentrate at will to raid those left vulnerable. Force-to-space ratios are certainly not all-determining, especially given big differences in equipment and tactical doctrines between forces. For the most extensive survey of the question, see Stephen D. Biddle, et al., *Defense at Low Force Levels: The Effect of Force to Space Ratios on Conventional Combat Dynamics,* IDA Paper P-2380 (Alexandria, Va.: Institute for Defense Analyses, August 1991).

[37]This point must be emphasized because the Steinbruner proposal uses the counter-argument that high-tech defenses and surveillance, coupled with limits on advanced offensive weapons, allow forward defense with low force levels. This is dubious for two reasons. First, it implicitly assumes that defensive forces can move and reconcentrate instantly, in response to instant intelligence detection of concentration by the attacker. No reasons are suggested as to why the strategic initiative, and the prerogative of choosing circumstance of weather and terrain, give the attacker no significant advantage in timing. Second, the proposal is unrealistic about the strategic flexibility of combined arms operations, which blurs simple distinctions between dominantly defensive or offensive characteristics of weapons. For example, in October 1973 the Egyptians used surface-to-air missiles and precision-guided anti-tank munitions (both normally tagged as inherently defensive weapons) to screen the advance of armored forces into the Sinai: similarly, the Israelis used "offensive" attack aircraft to defend against the advancing Egyptian tanks. Had both sides been limited to the "defensive" elements of force structure only, the Israelis might have held if they had manned the Suez Canal Bar-Lev Line with high force-to-space ratios, but the line was lightly manned.

[38]See Carl von Clausewitz, *On War,* Michael Howard and Peter Paret, eds. and trans. (Princeton: Princeton University Press, 1976), pp. 363–364, 367; Richard K. Betts, *Surprise Attack* (Washington, D.C.: Brookings, 1982), p. 15; and Betts, "Conventional Deterrence," *World Politics,* Vol. 37, No. 2 (January 1985), pp. 163–172.

counterattack has to rely on its disproportionate strength or offensive ingenuity at the strategic level to succeed. This was indeed the case in the two international actions of the past half-century that came closest to the collective security model: the responses to the North Korean attack in 1950 and to the Iraqi invasion of Kuwait in 1990.

Political Criteria for Limitations

The legalism of collective security, which establishes obligations in terms of hypothetical rather than actual enemies, is an apolitical guide to arms control. If no danger of war ever arose, the various potential dyadic power balances affected by treaty limits would not matter strategically, and the arms control agreements' value would depend on how much they facilitated cuts in military expenditure. Nor would limits matter much if a challenge to collective security did arise and all the members of the system honored the obligation to roll back the aggressor. If war were to break out more raggedly, however, with a great power or a set of states challenging the status quo while a number of the others stood aloof from combat, the balances established by apolitical criteria could be disastrous; having been decided without reference to the wartime lineups, it would be only fortuitous if the distribution of capabilities happened to favor the side with defensive objectives.

Worse, formal limitations, especially if they do not produce a balance of power in the relevant dyad, could have more directly dangerous effects. Accords can provide advance warning of aggression, arms controllers claim, facilitating timely countermobilization. As the Kupchans write, "a significant military buildup would *automatically* be interpreted as a sign of aggressive intent, *triggering* a response."[39] If the agreement is violated in order to prepare to commit aggression, automatic reaction would be a good thing; if the violation is motivated by anxiety about military vulnerability, on the other hand, such reaction would be destabilizing, producing the stereotypical escalation of tension that "spiral" theorists worry about. It is quite plausible that anxious states facing an unfavorable balance of forces with emerging enemies could feel compelled to abrogate limitations on their own options imposed by prior apolitically designed arms control formulas. Had legal constraints not existed, their military buildups could seem more innocent or ambiguous, and response could be determined according to the merits of the balance of power rather than the legal order of allowed armament.

This is a particular problem if we have any reason to worry about a future change in Russian attitudes toward traditional security. The Soviet Union let the Warsaw Pact crumble not simply because it had no choice; there is no reason to assume that laying down the law with a little violence before November 1989 (as in East Germany in 1953, Hungary in 1956, Czechoslovakia

---

[39]Kupchan and Kupchan, "Concerts, Collective Security, and the Future of Europe," p. 127 (emphasis added).

in 1968, and as would have happened in Poland in 1981 had Jaruzelski not imposed martial law) would not have kept Communist governments in power. Instead, Gorbachev adopted a liberal foreign policy, mouthing all the axioms about cooperation, trust, insanity of the arms race, and obsolescence of traditional concepts of security that we have always heard from doves in the West. If we can unwind the coiled spring of mutual suspicion and tension, Gorbachev believed, we would jointly conquer not just the symptom but the cause of conflict. "New thinking" embraced collective security because the new thinkers, like many liberals in the West, believed security was an artificial problem more than a real one, that there was nothing to fear but fear itself. These were the same new thinkers, however, who believed that the Soviet Union would survive as a state if it reduced its reliance on coercion.

The concessions that happily ended the Cold War were a precipitous loss of security for Russia in the hoary terms of balance of power. The Reds may never come back, but what if the Realists do? What if economic disaster, apparent failure of western liberal models, nasty maneuvers by newly free republics, oppression of Russian minorities in those areas, and upsurge of populist and nationalist bitterness bring the principle of "Looking Out for Number One" back into favor? Will noticing that the old subservient buffer of Eastern Europe is not only gone, but aligned with the West, spur no Russian interest in rearmament? The limits in the CFE agreement, conceived in the context of the two old alliances, preclude parity between Russia and a new western coalition that could include former members of the Warsaw Pact (and even some former Soviet republics). In a meaner world, such military inferiority might seem less tolerable to Moscow than it does now, when it seems irrelevant. . . .

Other Perverse Effects

In the present atmosphere most governments will rush to cut military budgets unilaterally, and with less attention to the effects on arcane calculations of military stability than in the past. Negotiating on prospective legal regulations, however, necessarily fixes more attention on technical calculations and nuances of disparity. This will especially be a problem if countries seeking arms control *do* worry about how it will affect stability. The goal of arms control might produce ongoing negotiations that reach no conclusion but retard unilateral cuts. The parties "will strain to be sure that all dangers and contingencies are covered," John Mueller writes. "Participants volunteer for such regulation only with extreme caution because once under regulation they are often unable to adjust subtly to unanticipated changes. . . . Arms *reduction* will proceed most expeditiously if each side feels free to reverse any reduction it later comes to regret."[40]

[40]Mueller, " A New Concert of Europe," pp. 6, 9.

Cold War critics claimed that arms control stimulated military spending (or at least failed to constrain it), as when Kennedy's Limited Test Ban Treaty, Ford's Vladivostok Accord, or Carter's SALT II Treaty coincided with defense budget increases. More indicative of the post–Cold War world should be the 1922 Washington Naval Treaty that fixed capital ship ratios among the great powers, since it was concluded in a period of minimal international tension and was multilateral rather than bipolar in construction. Britain responded to that agreement "with greater activity in naval building than at any time since the armistice."[41] That treaty is also sometimes charged with having stimulated competition in unregulated dimensions of weaponry (for example, the "treaty race" in bigger and better cruisers, replacing the battleship race), and having channelled innovation away from defensive developments (fortifications were prohibited in the western Pacific to secure Japanese agreement to the battleship ratio) and into weaponry of more offensive, destabilizing, "first-strike" capability (aircraft carriers).[42]

Finally, contrary to conventional wisdom, arms control designed in the context of peacetime could endanger crisis management. Collective security proponents usually claim that arms control will reinforce crisis stability because treaty provisions for monitoring and verification will create "transparency" and rules of the road that will reduce chances of accidental escalation in a crisis confrontation.[43] This argument means the most to those who worry that uncontrolled interactions of military forces operating in alert conditions are a more probable cause of war than premeditated resort to force.

Positive reasons for such controls certainly exist. Their relative importance after the Cold War, however, is oversold, while their potential negative consequences are overlooked. Primary concern with crisis interactions as an autonomous cause of war—the notion of "inadvertent" or "accidental" war—is inconsistent with faith in the durability of the current causes of peace. You cannot get hair-trigger alert operations like those in the crisis of October 1962, or mobilization spirals like those in the crisis of July 1914, without a crisis. Yet crisis presupposes conflict. A crisis does not arise through a *deus ex machina,* with no prior clash of interests. A conflict serious enough to produce a military confrontation will mean that the premise of continental contentment has been shattered, in which case *that* problem looms much larger than the technical one of crisis instability due to communication breakdowns.

---

[41]Stephen Roskill, *Naval Policy Between the Wars* (London: Collins, 1968), p. 332, quoted in Charles H. Fairbanks, Jr. and Abram N. Shulsky, "From 'Arms Control' to Arms Reductions: The Historical Experience," *Washington Quarterly,* Vol. 10, No. 3 (Summer 1987), p. 65.

[42]Fairbanks and Shulsky, "From 'Arms Control' to Arms Reductions," pp. 66–67. See also Robert Gordon Kaufman, *Arms Control During the Pre-Nuclear Era* (New York: Columbia University Press, 1990).

[43]Ullman, *Securing Europe,* pp. 141–142; Kupchan and Kupchan, "Concerts, Collective Security, and the Future of Europe," p. 131; Steinbruner, "Revolution in Foreign Policy," p. 75.

As others have often noted, it is hard to think of any case of a genuinely accidental war (that is, one due to causes beyond political authorities' control, as distinct from one due to their miscalculation).[44] World War I, the favorite case for those who worry about the problem, does not qualify. Marc Tracht-enberg has shown how strategic mythology over the last several decades grossly exaggerated the political "loss of control" in the July 1914 crisis, even if one rejects the Fritz Fischer thesis that German aggression caused the war.[45] To promote arms control measures in order to limit accidental escalation elevates the secondary to the essential. This was reasonable in the Cold War context, when the essential problem endangering security—the ideological and power competition between East and West—was well recognized and addressed steadily through alliances and defense plans, but not now, when the principal problem is to anticipate what basic conflict of interest could arise.

It is also short-sighted to assume that treaty arrangements for verification in peacetime will help defuse crises. Inspection regimes are unlikely to be operating and "transparency" will probably have gone by the boards by the time a crisis erupts. Treaty obligations are usually abrogated before that point is reached. There are no bolts from the blue; wars do not explode at the instant a conflict of interest develops. Germany junked the arms control provisions of the Versailles Treaty long before 1939, and Japan renounced the 1922 Naval Treaty five years before Pearl Harbor. While abrogation may provide political warning of crisis, it is misguided to count on the monitoring provisions of arms control agreements to provide strategic warning of war or tactical warning of attack.

If inspection regimes or other agreements oriented to crisis management did remain in place during the run-up to crisis, they could just as easily have a counterproductive effect as a dampening one, since the effect of abrogating *during* the crisis could seem much more threatening. It is more likely

---

[44]Alexander George defines *inadvertent* war as one "neither side wanted or expected at the outset of the crisis." "Findings and Recommendations," in George, ed., *Avoiding War: Problems of Crisis Management* (Boulder, Colo.: Westview Press, 1991), p. 545. This is expansive enough to include deliberate decisions by political authorities to initiate combat, which are not the same as hypothetical cases where decentralization of authority could produce military operational activities that elude policymakers' control and provoke escalation autonomously. See Paul Bracken, *The Command and Control of Nuclear Forces* (New Haven: Yale University Press, 1983), pp. 48, 53, 231–232; or John D. Steinbruner, "An Assessment of Nuclear Crises," in Franklyn Griffiths and John C. Polanyi, eds., *The Dangers of Nuclear War* (Toronto: University of Toronto Press, 1980), pp. 39–40. For a study that admits the importance of the danger in principle but shows persuasively the overwhelmingly powerful restraints against it in practice, see Joseph F. Bouchard, *Command in Crisis* (New York: Columbia University Press, 1991). Geoffrey Blainey persuasively debunks the notion that accidental wars have occurred, but argues that if miscalculation is included in the definition, virtually all wars could be considered accidental. Blainey, *The Causes of War*, 3rd ed. (New York: Free Press, 1988), chap. 9, especially pp. 144–145.

[45]Marc Trachtenberg, *History and Strategy* (Princeton: Princeton University Press, 1991), chap. 2, especially pp. 54–60, 77–80, 84–87, 90–92, 97–98.

then than in normal peacetime that an anxious state would rush to revoke restraints on its options for self-defense, or intrusive inspections helpful to its adversary, and that such actions could be read by the adversary as preparations to strike first. "Transparency" can only apply to capabilities, not intentions. If the value of such greater openness depends on the assumption that actions inconsistent with arms control agreements will be presumed evidence of aggressive intent, the regime could harm crisis management as much as help it.

Conclusion

If there is any time when establishing a collective security institution should be feasible, this is it, but collective security will hardly matter unless the present peace goes bad. If there is any time when negotiated arms control should *not* matter, this is it, but agreements achieved now would leave equations of power whose significance could be utterly different, and dangerous, if peace goes bad. Conservative realism, on the other hand, is too fatalistic a guide, since it underestimates the potential grounds for pacific anarchy in Europe. Anarchy, and the competition for power that it encourages, are necessary but not sufficient causes of war. They need a *casus belli* to push conflict over the edge.[46] The "Unorganized Pacified Europe" described above is not markedly less probable than John Mearsheimer's hyper-realist nightmare. Either one, however, is more plausible than a *functioning* collective security system or a politically disembodied arms control regime.

Instituting a collective security organization might be acceptable, nevertheless, for its symbolic value. Despite the negative emphasis in the rest of this article, I am not set against the idea, provided that it is not taken seriously enough in practice to bar parallel security arrangements that should be considered incompatible with it in principle. Similarly, serious and comprehensive arms regulation may never be achieved if leaders lose their sense of urgency and get wrapped up in more important problems, while their bureaucracies get bogged down in technical questions. In any event, arms control constraints that could prove destabilizing in a Europe riven by new alignments would probably be abandoned long before a crisis at the brink of war, so strategists should not fall on their swords to prevent such agreements. But beware of too much insouciance.

---

[46]World War I is sometimes cited as caused by pure power rivalry, but without nationalist-imperialist ideologies, territorial disputes, and militarist romanticism it would have been much harder to get the war started. Blainey argues against viewing motives, grievances, or substantive aims as causes on grounds that they are only "varieties of power." Blainey, *The Causes of War*, chap. 10. That all-inclusive definition, however, makes the argument practically tautologous.

In another context Jack Snyder has argued that "neo-liberal institution-building will do great damage if it is attempted, but doesn't work."[47] The same is true of pressures for transforming old security institutions in Europe into a collective security organization, or concluding new arms control agreements, unless we are disingenuous or subtle enough to couple them with other initiatives that work in different directions. If collective security and arms control were important only as symbols, we could accept them as harmless or reject them as diversionary. But symbols can have substantive effects. The effects may be consistent with the symbol if it motivates statesmen to conform with the value that it enshrines; this is what regime theorists hope collective security might do. Or the effects may be antagonistic to the symbol if it obscures reality and prevents properly adaptive action; this is what Realists fear it might do.

All this implies accepting three different but partially overlapping rings of security organization. One ring would be a new European Security Organization, including all the countries in the Conference on Security and Cooperation in Europe (CSCE), but without replacing the second ring, the old NATO. This combination is accepted by many current fans of collective security, although some would turn NATO into the sole ESO by admitting Russia, which would be a mistake. The latter aim should be accomplished in the third ring, a discreet concert of the United States, Britain, France, Germany, and Russia, without highly publicized formal meetings like the economic summits (if that model were followed, membership of the concert would have to expand in response to pleas from other big states in the system). We might also want to accept arms control agreements as long as they are modest enough not to confine freedom of adaptation (e.g., alliances according to emergent threats, decisions to refrain from intervention in wars between small states).

The risk in this recommendation is that it will sound either stupid—a mindless endorsement of anything in response to uncertainty about everything—or cynical—a deliberate commitment to institutions whose rationales contradict each other. In either case the idea would prove infeasible. If governments devote themselves symbolically to collective security in a way substantial enough to have any beneficial effects, we cannot count on them to be cynical enough to pursue divergent policies in an equally substantial way. If the happily pacific order of the new post–Cold War Europe goes bad, then the process of traditional adaptation will probably be more hesitant and delayed than otherwise. That might leave us the worst of both worlds: a collective security organization that falters when the chips are down, and a hysterical scramble to establish a better balance of power that goes in such a hurry that it aggravates political tensions.

---

[47]Jack Snyder, "Averting Anarchy in the New Europe," *International Security*, Vol. 14, No. 4 (Spring 1990), p. 40.

But what else should we do if not tread water by dabbling in several somewhat inconsistent solutions? While a UPE may be possible, at least for some period of time, it would be reckless to bank on it; while NATO may last, it may wither if nothing new and big and scary replaces the Marxist menace; and while a collective security commitment may capture imaginations, it could leave us in the lurch if we count on it. The problem is, we cannot prescribe a system (if we expect actual statesmen to make it work) based on a principle without reference to cases; we cannot compose a definite new solution until we confront a definite new problem. The current peace is not what makes some novel solution to security suddenly plausible, it is what makes it *harder* to settle on any formula, and what encourages the logically inconsistent policy of overlaying various schemes, regimes, or organizations on each other.

Inconsistency is reasonable if we do not yet know when and against whom we will once again need a functioning security system for Europe. Relying on any single scheme is too risky in the new world where the current threat is uncertainty. Yes, the idea that post–Cold War strategy must define itself against "uncertainty" is becoming a tiresome and suspiciously facile cliché. That is unfortunate, but cannot be helped, because it happens to be true.

Averting Anarchy
in the New Europe

JACK L. SNYDER

This article presents three views of the demise of the bipolar division of Europe. First, some Western observers have seen these developments as all to the good: Liberal "end of history" optimism envisions that, as illegitimate Communist rule is rolled back and replaced by liberal, market-oriented regimes, the sources of conflict in Europe will be eliminated and peace will break out. But the difficulties facing *perestroika* in the Soviet Union and the potential for nationalist conflicts throughout the erstwhile Soviet bloc raise the possibility of a much grimmer outcome.

Hobbesian pessimism anticipates a reversion to pre-1945 patterns of multipolar instability and nationalism. While agreeing with some of the diagnosis of Hobbesian pessimism, I question its policy prescriptions of shoring up the Cold War status quo ante and, if that fails, keeping at arm's length from the impending East European maelstrom.

As an alternative to these solutions, I explore a third view that is conditionally optimistic: neo-liberal institutionalism prescribes the implantation of cooperative international institutions as an antidote to the consequences of Hobbesian anarchy.

The Soviet Union and Eastern Europe are facing the classic problem that Samuel Huntington described in *Political Order in Changing Societies:* a gap between booming political participation and ineffectual political institutions. In Huntington's analysis, this gap is typically filled by the pernicious pattern of "praetorian" politics. "In a praetorian system," says Huntington:

Jack L. Snyder, "Averting Anarchy in the New Europe," *International Security* Vol. 14, no. 4 (Spring 1990). Reprinted by permission of the MIT Press, Cambridge Massachusetts. Copyright © 1990 by the President and Fellows of Harvard College and of the Massachusetts Institute of Technology.

> social forces confront each other nakedly; no political institutions, no corps of professional political leaders are recognized or accepted as the legitimate intermediaries to moderate group conflict. Equally important, no agreement exists among the groups as to the legitimate and authoritative methods for resolving conflicts. . . . Each group employs means which reflect its peculiar nature and capabilities. The wealthy bribe; students riot; workers strike; mobs demonstrate; and the military coup.[1]

Other studies of praetorian societies add that nationalist demagogy becomes a common political instrument to advance group interests and to help unstable governments rule.[2]

Praetorian societies such as Germany and Japan have accounted for most of this century's international security problems among the great powers.[3] In both cases, weak democratic institutions were unable to channel the exploding energies of increasing mass political participation in constructive directions. Instead, elite groups interested in militarism, protectionism, and imperialism used nationalist appeals to recruit mass backing for their parochial ends. Consequently, the Western democracies have a powerful incentive to head off the emergence of more states of this type, especially in the Soviet Union but also in Eastern Europe.

One possible solution to the contemporary dangers signaled by Huntington's model would be to recruit reformist Eastern regimes into the West's already well-developed supra-national political order, especially the European Community. As in the cases of Spain and Greece, this would create incentives for the emergence of liberal rather than praetorian political patterns, as well as a ready-made institutional framework for acting on those incentives. . . .

---

[1]Samuel P. Huntington, *Political Order in Changing Societies* (New Haven: Yale University Press, 1968), p. 196. Philip Roeder, "Modernization and Participation in the Leninist Developmental Strategy," *American Political Science Review,* Vol. 83, No. 3 (September 1989), pp. 859–884, also invokes Huntington in analyzing current Soviet developments.

[2]Myron Weiner, "The Macedonian Syndrome: An Historical Model of International Relations and Political Development," *World Politics,* Vol. 23, No. 4 (July 1971), pp. 665–683, examines praetorian-type states from this aspect. Huntington, *Political Order,* pp. 304–305, writes about nationalism as a response to foreign domination.

[3]The Nazi period was not praetorian in my use of the term, because central state authority dominated parochial interests, but the foreign policy ideology that spurred Hitler's expansionism was an outgrowth of earlier praetorian periods. It developed from ideas that flourished in the political competition among imperialists, militarists, and protectionist groups in the Wilhelmine era. See Woodruff Smith, *The Ideological Origins of Nazi Imperialism* (New York:- Oxford University Press, 1986). More generally, arguments about the international aggressiveness of praetorian regimes dominated by imperialist elite coalitions are developed in Jack Snyder, *Myths of Empire: Domestic Politics and International Ambition* (Ithaca: Cornell University Press, 1991).

Liberal End-of-History Optimism

Liberal optimism anticipates that the erosion of the bipolar division of Europe will make the European political order more peaceful. The Cold War division of the continent has been, in this view, an inherently tense, war-prone situation. The imposition of illegitimate regimes in Europe's Eastern half has been a cause of political frustration and potential violent conflict. If these illegitimate Communist regimes in Eastern Europe and the Soviet Union are replaced by liberal, market-oriented, democratic regimes, neither internal nor international bloodshed is likely. As the historical record shows, liberal democratic regimes do not fight wars against each other. . . .

Hobbesian Pessimism

The currently prevailing Realist theory of international politics holds that the bipolar stalemate between the two superpowers is the most stable possible power configuration, given the realities of an anarchic international system.[4] This brand of Realism anticipates that the waning of Soviet power and the erosion of the bipolar division of Europe are likely to lead to the breakup of NATO, the reunification of Germany, and the consequent emergence of an unstable, multipolar balance-of-power system. As a result, major war may come again for the same reasons it came in 1914 and 1939, through the uncertain workings of the multipolar balancing process.[5] Likewise, the balance-of-power policies of small East European states, released from the grip of Soviet hegemony, may help catalyze war among the great powers, as they did before the First World War. . . .

A more innovative Hobbesian strategy might be to give up the bipolar stalemate as lost, and switch to a Bismarckian strategy of defensive multipolar alliances.[6] For example, France, Britain, and the United States might

[4]Kenneth Waltz, *Theory of International Politics* (Reading, Mass.: Addison-Wesley, 1979). In the following discussion, I use the word "anarchy" when I mean the lack of a central authority to adjudicate disputes between competitors; I use "disorder" or "chaos" to describe the results of anarchic political conflict. On conceptual confusion in the use of the term "anarchy," see Helen Milner, "Anarchy and Interdependence," *International Organization,* Vol. 44, No. 2 (Spring 1990).

[5]Thomas Christensen and Jack Snyder, "Chain Gangs and Passed Bucks: Predicting Alliance Patterns in Multipolarity," *International Organization,* Vol. 44, No. 2 (Spring 1990), present a discussion of the pathologies of multipolar balancing in these cases that builds on, but revises, Waltz's basic insights.

[6]Stephen Van Evera mentions this approach in "The Future of Europe," unpublished ms., November 1989. On the distinction between Bismarck's defensive alliances and the offensive ones that supplanted them, see Stephen Van Evera, "The Cult of the Offensive and the Origins of the First World War," *International Security,* Vol. 9, No. 1 (Summer 1984), pp. 96–103.

guarantee the security of a reunited Germany against attack by Russia, while also insuring Russia against aggression by Germany. Likewise, small East European states would be guaranteed security assistance only if they were the party attacked, not if they were the attacker. The Locarno Treaty's two-way guarantee of Germany's Western border might also provide a model for such a strategy.

Such a scheme might be stabilizing, but history and theory point to many pitfalls along that path. Neither Bismarck's defensive alliances nor Locarno lasted very long. In the multipolarity of the interwar period, some states were tempted to ride free, relying on the balancing efforts of others, so defensive alliances lost credibility. Conversely, alliance commitments that were originally defensive had by 1914 come to be unconditional, because the power of each major ally was considered essential to maintaining the balance. In such circumstances, as with the German blank check to Austria in 1914, allies had to be supported even if they were the aggressors.[7] Moreover, in checkerboard multipolar alliance patterns, it may be difficult to honor alliance commitments, even defensive ones, without the development of offensive military capabilities and strategies to attack an aggressor in the rear.[8] But such capabilities would exacerbate security fears and undermine the pacific aims of a system of defensive alliances. There is little reason to believe that a strategy of defensive alliances would by itself produce stability. Still, this does not exclude the possibility that in a system moderated by other factors, such as benign patterns of domestic politics, defensive alliances might make a beneficial contribution.

Finally, reliance on a multipolar nuclear stand-off to insure stability also seems problematic. First, the Soviet Union's nuclear arsenal will not protect it from the real challenges to its integrity as a state: economic colonization of its periphery by more advanced powers, and ethnic separatism. Second, most of the newly emerging power centers, including Germany, will not have nuclear weapons. In light of the nuclear allergy which currently dominates European thinking, decisions to acquire nuclear weapons might well take place only *after* a severe worsening of international tension had made them seem necessary. In that context, the uneven proliferation of nascent, vulnerable nuclear forces could be a provocation to war, not a deterrent against it.

The enormity of Hobbesian predictions and the weakness of Hobbesian prescriptions virtually demand asking whether other kinds of measures can be devised to head off such dire developments. If the pressure of international and domestic anarchy is indeed likely to foster a miscarriage of the

---

[7]Waltz, *Theory of International Politics,* pp. 166–169; Christensen and Snyder, "Chain Gangs and Passed Bucks."

[8]Stephen Van Evera, "Offense, Defense, and Strategy: When Is Offense Best?" Paper presented to the annual meeting of the American Political Science Association, Chicago, 1987; and Scott Sagan, "1914 Revisited: Allies, Offense, and Instability," *International Security,* Vol. 11, No. 2 (Fall 1986), pp. 151–176.

balance of power and the spread of militaristic nationalism, then it is natural to ask whether steps can be taken to mitigate this anarchic pressure. Neo-liberal institution-building takes up this issue.

Neo-Liberal Institutionalism

Neo-liberal institution-building offers a more constructive perspective on the creation of a stable political order in Europe. This approach assumes that the Hobbesian condition can be mitigated by an institutional structure that provides legitimate and effective channels for reconciling conflicting interests. Whereas liberal optimism sees political order as arising spontaneously from a harmony of interests, and Hobbesian pessimism sees it as imposed by hegemonic power, neo-liberal institutionalism sees it as arising from organized procedures for articulating interests and settling conflicts among them.[9]

When institutions are strong, there is order; the effects of anarchy are mitigated. When institutions are weak, there is disorder; politics are marked by the perverse effects of anarchy.[10] Thus, from this perspective, the problem of creating a new European security order to supplant that of the bipolar stalemate is above all a problem of building institutions. Institutionalist theories borrowed from the fields of comparative politics and international political economy can illuminate the task ahead.

The classic statement of the institutionalist understanding of political order is Samuel Huntington's *Political Order in Changing Societies*. Huntington is concerned with the consequences for political order when intense political demands are advanced by a mobilized society, but governing institutions are too weak to reconcile those competing claims effectively. In particular, he examines the disorder that emerges in a modernizing society when industrialization, urbanization, and expanding literacy lead to an expansion of political demands, which the traditional political institutions of the *ancien regime* cannot process efficiently and authoritatively.[11]

In such circumstances, politics becomes disordered. Groups and individuals cannot defend their interests by appealing to legitimate governing institutions and orderly procedures for resolving conflicts, because such channels are unavailable. As a result, narrow groups form to defend their parochial interests through self-help, including direct violent action, as in any anarchical environment. Social groups like students and organized la-

---

[9]Differentiating between neo-liberal institutionalism and classical liberalism is Robert Keohane, *International Institutions and State Power* (Boulder, Colo.: Westview, 1989), pp. 10–11.

[10]Two influential studies embodying this type of analysis are Stephen Krasner, ed., *International Regimes* (Ithaca: Cornell University Press, 1983), first appearing as a special issue of *International Organization*, Vol. 36, No. 2 (Spring 1982); and Robert Keohane, *After Hegemony* (Princeton: Princeton University Press, 1984).

[11]Huntington, *Political Order,* chapter 1.

bor may take to the streets or use other means of direct, coercive action, like political strikes, to advance their self-interested goals. Government institutions, unable to create order and pursue the state's interests on the basis of legitimate authority, also act as narrowly self-interested, coercive groups. The military, because the dominant means of violent coercion lie in its hands, tends to play a central role in this pattern of "praetorian" politics. As Huntington quotes Hobbes, "when nothing else is turned up, clubs are trumps."[12]

In praetorian societies the problem is not in a lack of organization, but in the character of the institutions that are well organized. Various parochial interests—e.g., the military and the trade unions—may be well organized. But institutions for aggregating competing interests—e.g., elected representative institutions and mass political parties—are weak and ineffective. . . .[13]

International Consequences of Praetorian Politics

The emergence of praetorian societies in Eastern Europe would have grave implications for international politics. Two such societies, Japan and Germany, have been the most egregious disturbers of the peace in this century. In Eastern Europe in the first half of this century, even small powers with praetorian political systems provoked international conflicts, which embroiled the great powers.

Wilhelmine Germany, again, illustrates why this occurred.[14] Wilhelmine aggressiveness stemmed from two sources. The first source was the terms of the intra-elite logroll. Many of the elite groups had vested interests in policies that embroiled Germany with other powers—e.g., the interests of heavy industry and the navy in fleet construction, the Army's offensive Schlieffen Plan, the Junkers' need for farm tariffs that hurt Russian interests. In the praetorian Wilhelmine society, there was neither a strong central authority nor strong accountability to the median voter to constrain these parochial interests and establish strategic priorities. As a result, Germany made too many enemies, and once encircled, tried to break out of that encirclement through aggression.

The second element feeding Wilhelmine aggressiveness was the relationship between the elites and the mass groups suddenly mobilized into German political life in the 1880s and 1890s. This sudden burst of political participation was due in part to the processes of industrialization and urban-

---

[12]Quoted in Huntington, *Political Order*, p. 196; chapter 4 discusses praetorian systems.

[13]Huntington, *Political Order*, chapter 4, can be read this way.

[14]The following discussion of German politics is based on Hans-Ulrich Wehler, *The German Empire, 1871–1918* (Leamington Spa/Dover, N.H.: Berg, 1985); Geoff Eley, *Reshaping the German Right* (New Haven: Yale University Press, 1980); and ideas developed in the chapter on Germany in Snyder, *Myths of Empire*.

ization, and in part also to the strategies of elite groups who sought to recruit mass allies against competing elites. Thus, Junker landowners recruited small-holding agrarian populists, while industrial and naval circles
used the middle class Navy League to create popular pressure for their pet
project. Many of these agricultural and middle class groups had been whip-
sawed by market forces which had disrupted their traditional economic activities in the late 19th century. Because liberal *laissez faire* had been
discredited by its disruption of traditional, regulated markets, these mass
groups were not hard to recruit for the elites' illiberal protectionist and imperialist schemes. Added to this volatile mixture was nationalistic propaganda, which the elites used as part of their "social imperialist" strategy for
managing the explosion of popular participation in politics.

A similar pattern can also be observed in the history of Eastern Europe's
small powers during the first half of the twentieth century. Myron Weiner
has noted what he calls the "Macedonian syndrome," in which the weak,
modernizing states of Central and Eastern Europe were often captured by
ethnic groups, the military, and intellectuals touting nationalist themes as
tools for their parochial purposes.[15] Their irredentist nationalism embroiled
these states in conflicts with their neighbors, contributing further to the hy-
per-patriotic cultural atmosphere and the praetorian character of domestic
politics. Squabbles among the praetorian East European states gave rise to
the familiar multipolar "checkerboard" balance-of-power pattern and triggered interventions by outside great powers. In short, nationalistic, praetorian domestic politics both fed and was fed by sharp competition in the
anarchical international setting.[16]

Despite Weiner's findings, the broader historical record does not show
that praetorian societies necessarily become nationalistic and expansionist.
Huntington's instances of praetorianism include many societies that turned
their violence strictly inward. Perhaps the East Europeans internationalized their praetorian violence because of the prevalence of ethnic irredenta
in their region, an historical pattern which largely persists today.[17] Another
difference between Weiner's cases and Huntington's might be the distinctive historical role played by praetorian Germany as a model of belligerence
for its smaller East European praetorian neighbors. If so, a well-behaved
Federal Republic of Germany might exert a more benign influence on Eastern Europe in the present era.

How likely is it that the Soviet Union will recapitulate the Wilhelmine pattern of domestic and foreign policy, or that Eastern Europe will relive the

---

[15]Myron Weiner, "The Macedonian Syndrome: An Historical Model of International Relations
  and Political Development," *World Politics*, Vol. 23, No. 4 (July 1971), pp. 665–683. Weiner's
  cases include almost every East European and Balkan state, before either World War I or II.
[16]The best extended treatment of these problems is Joseph Rothschild, *East Central Europe be-*
  tween the Two World Wars (Seattle: University of Washington Press, 1974).
[17]Zbigniew Brzezinski, "Post-Communist Nationalism," *Foreign Affairs*, Vol. 68, No. 5 (Winter
  1989–90), p. 3.

Macedonian syndrome? Some obvious parallels can be mentioned. The Soviet Union is a state undergoing a huge leap in mass political participation in the context of an authoritarian tradition and a demonstrable de-legitimation of its previous governing institutions. "Traditional" elite groups, in this case the conservative sectors of the Party and the military, have corporate interests that in the past have inclined them toward a conflictual approach to international politics.[18] Labor, ethnic groups, the military, and intellectuals are forming organized groups. Existing institutions, including the Communist government and truncated democratic bodies, are hard pressed to reconcile competing demands of these groups in ways that serve collective rather than parochial interests. The mass populace, moreover, is being mobilized into political life at the same time as it is being threatened with unparalleled economic disruptions due to the introduction of market reforms. Potential or actual ethnic conflicts in the Soviet periphery and between some East European states may contribute to an international environment where intense nationalism seems the norm and where peace and security cannot be taken for granted. . . .[19]

International Causes of Praetorian Politics

Whether a society takes the praetorian path is determined largely by its domestic pattern of development. The prime candidates are late, rapid developers with elites who have a strong interest in resisting the diffusion of political power.[20] But the international environment may also play a role either for good or ill.

Among small states, one would expect the international environment to play a major role in shaping domestic institutions and their expression in foreign policy. Small, vulnerable states must adapt to their international position, since they cannot buffer themselves from its influence. As I suggested above, the especially malign international setting may explain why Weiner's aggressive "Macedonian syndrome" prevailed in Eastern Europe in the first half of this century, whereas it was less prevalent in praetorian states else-

---

[18]Jack Snyder, "The Gorbachev Revolution: A Waning of Soviet Expansionism?" *International Security*, Vol. 12, No. 3 (Winter 1987/88), pp. 93–131. Celeste Wallander, "Third-World Conflict in Soviet Military Thought: Does the 'New Thinking' Grow Prematurely Grey?" *World Politics*, Vol. 42, No. 1 (October 1989), pp. 31–63, presents evidence that the Soviet military has manifested such tendencies even after the emergence of "new thinking" among Soviet civilians.

[19]For a theoretically informed analysis of Soviet nationality problems, see Alexander Motyl, *Will the Non-Russians Rebel? State, Ethnicity, and Stability in the USSR* (Ithaca: Cornell University Press, 1987).

[20]Barrington Moore, *Social Origins of Dictatorship and Democracy* (Boston: Beacon, 1966); and Alexander Gerschenkron, *Bread and Democracy in Germany* (Ithaca: Cornell University Press, 1989; orig. ed. 1943).

where.[21] Likewise, Peter Katzenstein finds that an "authoritarian version" of corporatism was prevalent in small European states in the 1930s, whereas later a "democratic form of corporatism" was "nourished by the strong effect of a liberal United States on the postwar global economy."[22]

The effect of the international setting on large, would-be praetorian states is just as dramatic. In the 1920s, for example, Weimar Germany and Taisho Japan were societies on the cusp of emerging from praetorian patterns. Liberal, democratic, free-trading, non-militarist institutions were potentially emerging in these two states in the 1920s facilitated in part by a fairly benign international environment. The Washington Naval Treaty of 1922 and the Locarno Pact of 1925 institutionalized a security environment that made aggressive behavior seem unnecessary for achieving security. Financial flows from America, in the form of Dawes Plan loans to Germany and Japanese profits from the textile trade, bankrolled liberal, free-trading coalitions, which counted on an expanded electoral franchise to maintain their position against military, protectionist, and conservative elites. When this relatively liberal international order collapsed with the Depression at the end of the 1920s, however, the liberal regimes in Germany and Japan collapsed along with it.[23]

The lessons of this case may cut both ways. One lesson is cautionary: unless links between a tentatively liberalizing state and a liberal international order are strong and permanent, they may be counterproductive. Forging such ties and then having them broken is probably more disruptive to domestic political order than never forging them at all.

A more optimistic lesson, however, is that even a relatively weak liberal international order can exert positive effects, even on hard-case praetorian societies like Germany and Japan, by creating incentives for the formation of liberal coalitions. By implication, a much stronger liberal regime, like the one that the advanced capitalist countries have forged today, should be able to exert an even stronger positive effect on easier cases, like most of today's East bloc states.

The next section uses the neo-liberal institutionalist theory of international regimes to examine the current policy implications of this proposition.

---

[21]For a related argument and evidence about the 1930s, see Deborah Welch Larson, "Bandwagon Images in American Foreign Policy: Myth or Reality?" in Robert Jervis and Jack Snyder, eds., *Dominoes and Bandwagons: Strategic Beliefs and Superpower Competition in the Eurasian Rimland* (New York: Oxford University Press, 1991).

[22]Peter Katzenstein, *Small States in World Markets* (Ithaca: Cornell University Press, 1985), p. 38. The corporatism of the 1930s included both democratic and authoritarian variants, but the latter were more prevalent in the 1930s than in the liberal international order after 1945.

[23]Jack Snyder, "International Leverage on Soviet Domestic Change," *World Politics*, Vol. 42, No. 1 (October 1989), pp. 6–8; Peter Gourevitch, *Politics in Hard Times* (Ithaca: Cornell University Press, 1986). Of course, Weimar's comparatively restrained foreign policy was also due in part to its military weakness.

How International Institutions May Create Political Order

How might international institution-building contribute to the creation of a stable, democratic order in the former Soviet bloc? In addressing this question, it will be worthwhile to consider theories of international regimes and to look back to the origins of the postwar order.

Neo-liberal regime theory, as articulated by such students of international political economy as Stephen Krasner and Robert Keohane, accepts the proposition that cooperation rarely emerges spontaneously in anarchic conditions.[24] To overcome problems of organizing collective action, successful cooperation requires a push from some powerful provider of incentives to cooperate, and then creation of institutions that coordinate the participants' expectations and actions. But once in place, a cooperative regime and its institutions tend to create habits and constituencies that make them self-perpetuating.

One version of the institutionalist view places particular stress on the role of the structures of institutions in channeling interests toward certain outcomes. This is the part of the institutionalist argument that I draw on most heavily. Kenneth Arrow's famous "impossibility theorem" showed that it is impossible to predict a unique outcome of pluralistic policy-making from the preferences of the participants. A variety of different coalitions and policy outcomes are all possible; there is no stable equilibrium. Subsequent theorists have shown, however, that the prevailing institutional setting increases the probability of certain outcomes and favors the emergence of some potential coalitions over others.[25]

The canonical example of a successful attempt to use international institution-building to load the dice in favor of liberal outcomes is the post-1945 international economic regime. Initially underwritten by American power and leadership, this regime is now firmly rooted in its participants' domestic and international institutions in ways that go beyond simple power relations among states. In light of the frequent calls for a "new Marshall Plan" for Eastern Europe, it is especially appropriate to remember precisely how the original Marshall Plan worked to forge the liberal postwar order.

The Marshall Plan's effectiveness lay in its political and institutional strategy, not just in its dollar amount. American money was only a small fraction of the total investment in Western Europe in the late 1940s. America did not

---

[24]Krasner, *International Regimes;* and Keohane, *After Hegemony.* See also Joseph Grieco, "Anarchy and Cooperation: A Realist Critique of the Newest Liberal Institutionalism," *International Organization,* Vol. 42, No. 3 (Summer 1988), pp. 485–508.

[25]A good review of this literature is Kenneth Shepsle, "Studying Institutions: Some Lessons from the Rational Choice Approach," *Journal of Theoretical Politics,* Vol. 1, No. 2 (April 1989), pp. 131–147. The seminal work is Kenneth Arrow, *Social Choice and Individual Values,* 2d ed. (New Haven: Yale University Press, 1963).

just buy a liberal international order. Rather, the Marshall Plan worked primarily because it linked its financial aid to the beneficiary countries' acceptance of institutions of transnational economic cooperation. These included multilateral institutions like the General Agreement on Tariffs and Trade (GATT), and also regional European cooperative efforts like the European Coal and Steel Community (ECSC) and the European Payments Union (EPU). This had a multiplier effect on economic efficiency, while politically it strengthened internationally-oriented sectors and coalitions against their insular, protectionist competitors. In short, the Marshall Plan worked because it created international institutions to channel domestic interests in a direction favorable to international cooperation and stability.[26]

Proponents of a new Marshall Plan for Eastern Europe should think in similar terms. More than just economic investment, the former Soviet bloc needs to develop a workable set of economic and political institutions that will allow that investment to be put to stable, productive use. Western loans and investment in Eastern Europe in the 1970s failed to spark meaningful economic growth and political change because they were not tied to institutional reform. Moreover, just as Marshall aid backed regional European organizations like ECSC and EPU, so too today's efforts might work best through regional European institutions like the European Community.

Specific Proposals for Building Pan-European Institutions

Like the original Marshall Plan, the "new Marshall Plan" needs a strategy for using international institutions to fill the gap between booming political participation and a weak domestic order threatened by the competing demands of illiberal organized interests. Below I evaluate some ideas of this type that have already been advanced by prominent figures in the West, and add some specific ideas of my own to this framework.

The most effective scheme would gradually integrate reforming Soviet bloc states into the European Community. The EC is a strong, well-developed supranational institution with a proven record of successfully assimilating less-developed European states into its economic system, with favorable effects on their political development. West Germany, the nation that Soviet bloc states are most eager to trade with, is a member of the EC. With backing from Washington and a benign attitude from Moscow, the EC would surely have sufficient resources to play the leadership role that is helpful in setting up a strong international regime. There are economic incentives for the EC to play a more active role in the East, as well as ideological and security incentives.

---

[26]Robert Pollard, *Economic Security and the Origins of the Cold War, 1945–1950* (New York: Columbia, 1985), pp. 158–167, 248–249.

This is *not* a scheme that relies simply on the erroneous notion that economic interdependence breeds peace. The favorable political effect comes not just from interdependence, but from the institutional structures and changes in domestic interests that may or may not accompany high levels of interdependence. In previous eras of extensive foreign trade and loans, multilateral economic institutions were weaker, as were the effects of interdependence on domestic economic structure. Though trade may have been at high levels, the production process of individual firms was rarely internationalized, as it is now. Consequently, the political effects of a liberal order were not deeply rooted in international institutions and domestic interests.[27] Thus, merely pointing out that high levels of trade preceded World War I is not an argument against a strategy of neo-liberal institution-building in the former Soviet bloc.

How would such a strategy work? According to the most commonly discussed ideas, different East European states would be granted different levels of association with the EC and integrated into its institutions at varying paces. Progress toward market reforms and full-fledged electoral democracy would be the price of admission to greater participation. Access to capital and markets would be the carrot. The institutionalized, legal character of the relationship would make for predictability, irreversibility, and deeply penetrating effects on the domestic order of the state.

The regime should also have a security component. Alliances that the Soviet Union would find threatening (e.g., between NATO and Poland) should be forsworn. Arms control should be designed to stabilize not only the East-West balance but also East-East balances.[28]

Two principles should be considered in designing military postures. First, states that have potential irredentist ethnic claims should not be militarily stronger than their neighbors. Thus, Hungary is—and should be—militarily weaker than Rumania, which deters irredentism over Transylvania. Rumania, in turn, is weaker than the Soviet Union, which deters irredentism over the status of Rumanian-speaking Soviet Moldavia. Poland is stronger than East Germany, which could have hypothetical historical claims against Polish territory. However, Poland would of course be much weaker than a militarily united Germany, which for that reason (among others) should be avoided.

Second, individual states and the two alliances should have force postures that are optimized for defense. Tank-heavy mobile strike forces and deep-strike ground-attack aircraft should be sharply limited, whereas fixed defenses should be encouraged.[29] Whenever possible, states should prepare to

---

[27]On the internationalization of firms' operations and interests, see Helen Milner, *Resisting Protectionism* (Princeton: Princeton University Press, 1988). On the institutional aspect, see Robert Keohane and Joseph S. Nye, Jr., *Power and Interdependence* (Boston: Little, Brown, 1977).

[28]Henry Kissinger, "Untangling Alliances," *Los Angeles Times,* April 16, 1989, part V, pp. 1, 6, discusses conventional arms control in the context of the broader European political order.

[29]For details, see Jack Snyder, "Limiting Offensive Conventional Forces: Soviet Proposals and Western Options," *International Security,* Vol. 12, No. 4 (Spring 1988), pp. 48–77.

defend their allies by moving forces into defensive positions on the allies' own territory, not by preparing to attack the aggressor on the aggressor's home territory. For non-contiguous allies, this might involve plans to airlift troops into prepared defensive positions.

A cooperative, pan-European security regime should also lay out the rights and responsibilities of ethnic and religious minorities. The purpose would be to head off nationalistic conflicts before they got started. Adherence to such a regime would be a precondition for the extension of a state's participation in East-West economic ties. Social science has developed a number of ideas about how to prevent ethnic tension from creating political instability. Applied social scientists should think about how to use these ideas in the construction of a European minorities regime.[30]

One new institution that could advance a stabilizing minorities regime would be an International Academy for Nationalities Studies. Its aim would be to get local intellectuals out of their self-created hothouses of nationalistic mythology and into the broader Euro-Atlantic intellectual community. Throughout the history of nationalism, intellectuals and publicists have played a major role by creating a wave of nationalist myth and then riding it to positions of prestige and influence. The international community should try to create alternative incentives for restless intellectuals and on-the-make journalists. Conferences, fellowships, and mid-career retraining at the Academy should expose them to objective accounts of the history of their region and its relations with others, and to modern theories of conflict management in multi-ethnic societies. To participate, intellectuals and their local institutes would have to be accredited by some international body (much as the international psychiatric organization now imposes professional preconditions that have affected Soviet participation). Conditions might include international standards of archival openness, availability of books by international authors, accurate labeling of fact and opinion in journalistic writings, and academic promotions based on international scholarly standards. . . .

How International Institutions Could Prevent Praetorianism

A system of international institutions would work to prevent the emergence of praetorian regimes in the former Soviet bloc, first, because increased openness to trading on the world market would help break the power of the self-interested cartels that are characteristic of praetorian politics. As con-

---

[30]See Arend Lijphart, *The Politics of Accommodation: Pluralism and Democracy in the Netherlands* (Berkeley: University of California Press, 1968); and other works discussed and cited in Katzenstein, *Small States*, pp. 35, 88, 185, 213–215. Note also the proposals for voluntary ethnic confederations in Brzezinski, "Post-Communist Nationalism."

ventional wisdom has phrased it, "the tariff is the mother of trusts."[31] The Bismarckian marriage of iron and rye, for example, was consummated expressly to establish tariff protection for both sectors, which would have been severely weakened without it. In contrast, free trading would make it impossible to return to the domestic political alliances, comprising obsolete industry, the military, and the orthodox Communist Party, that characterized Brezhnev's Russia and Gierek's Poland.

Second, a negotiated security environment would undercut the plausibility of nationalist appeals and threat exaggeration by the military. Since civilian control over the military would be thereby easier, one of the ingredients of praetorian politics—military intervention in domestic politics—would be missing. At the same time, by co-opting intellectuals into pan-European networks, another potential source of virulent nationalism would be channeled toward more benign pursuits.

Third, a democratic institutional requirement for EC membership would directly strengthen the moderating voice of the average citizen in Eastern Europe. Recent developments in Hungary already show this process at work. The Hungarians admit that one motive for their democratic constitutional reforms is to make Hungary an acceptable economic partner for EC countries. Democratic voting, in turn, has helped to stymie a would-be Communist-nationalist ruling cartel in that country.

Finally, successful economic integration into the EC would expand the economic pie in Eastern countries, and thus lubricate the process of political transformation, just as the mid-Victorian economic boom, fueled by expanding international trade, facilitated Britain's transition to a full-fledged, two-party, universal-suffrage democracy.

In short, given the importance of heading off the emergence of praetorian states in the former Soviet bloc, the West has an incentive to extend its successful international regimes eastward in order to help fill the gap between rising political participation and weak governing institutions. One promising scheme would center on an expanded EC as its core, with the United States and the Soviet Union as more loosely associated members of a Euro-Atlantic Common Home.

Evaluating the Competing Perspectives

The burden of this paper is to clarify the reasoning behind three competing perspectives on security in the changing European order, and in particular to explore the logic behind the neo-liberal institutionalist view. A definitive

---

[31]Ronald Rogowski, *Commerce and Coalitions: How Trade Affects Political Alignments* (Princeton: Princeton University Press, 1989); Mancur Olson, *The Rise and Decline of Nations,* (New Haven: Yale University Press, 1982), chapter 5.

evaluation of the three views remains a task for the cumulative work of many scholars and public commentators.

Nonetheless, a few judgments are in order. First, liberal optimism seems more like ideological self-indulgence or politicians' rhetoric than a serious analytical position. Any worthwhile analysis must recognize that the dismantling of a stable political order entails grave dangers.

Hobbesian pessimism, in contrast, enjoys a firmer theoretical foundation and offers some insightful diagnoses, but suffers from a few significant flaws. It exaggerates the inevitability that international conflict and nationalistic excesses will flow from the erosion of the bipolar division of Europe. Its assumption, that profound changes in the domestic character of states since the interwar period will be readily reversed as a consequence of changes in the structure of the international system, is untenable. The past pathologies of German politics, for example, were caused not primarily by Germany's vulnerable position in the multipolar system, but by the social tensions associated with Germany's pattern of late development. Since this particular phase of development was outgrown long ago, the coming period of multipolarity will take place in a more benign domestic context. If this favorable pattern is reinforced by liberal international institutions, there is no reason to expect a revival of the Hobbesian war of all against all in Europe.

Nor does the Hobbesian viewpoint generate any plausible solutions to the problem of European order. The solution that *is* consistent with its theoretical assumptions—maintaining the bipolar Cold War division of Europe—is no longer available. Russia is too weak and irresolute and East European publics too restive for the *status quo ante* to be restored. More plausible would be a unilateral decision by the NATO alliance to insulate itself from the coming crisis in the East, but this fits poorly with the theoretical assumptions of Hobbesian theory, which posits as unlikely that a state would impose on itself a geopolitical sphere of abstention, and that an alliance would be maintained after the opposing alliance breaks up. In particular, it is hard to imagine West Germany remaining completely indifferent to the fate of reforms in East Germany, under Hobbesian or any other plausible assumptions.

The third Hobbesian solution, Bismarckian defensive alliances, had a weak track record when it was tried before. If it is to do better this time, it will have to be embedded in a political order of more favorable domestic and international institutions. Insuring that all states in the multipolar checkerboard are simultaneously secure will require elaborate arms control arrangements negotiated on the principles of non-offensive defense in a well-institutionalized setting. Otherwise, the logic of the strategic situation will increase pressures to develop offensive military capabilities to come to the aid of non-contiguous allies.

Neo-liberal institutionalism also entails several serious problems. It envisages a cooperative security regime involving all of the world's great powers, which would be a historical event almost unprecedented, apart from the short-lived post-Napoleonic Concert of Europe. Moreover, it fails to reckon with the problem of compensating the many powerful social groups who would be losers in any scheme integrating Eastern societies into the Western political order—e.g., internationally uncompetitive economic sectors, those who control locally scarce resources,[32] and the institutional remnants of the Soviet period. Integrating these societies into Western market economies is bound to be disruptive, if not outright explosive.

Inclusion of the Soviet Union in the Western order is the *sine qua non* of the whole scheme, yet it is by far the most difficult to accomplish. Its economy is too big for the EC to digest as it could a Spain, a Greece, or a Hungary. Moreover, the Soviet economy and polity seem more inherently resistant to successful reform than does, for example, Hungary's. The nuclear-armed Soviet Union must be included because a praetorian outcome there would do the most damage, but it is the country for which that outcome may be hardest to prevent.[33]

Finally, neo-liberal institution-building will do great damage if it is attempted, but doesn't work. It will damage the West by engaging it deeply in the possibly insoluble problems of the East. A new Marshall Plan may convince Americans that to spread liberalism in Eastern Europe is their "manifest destiny," and they may get so absorbed in the task that they refuse to give it up if it turns sour. As the example of the 1920s suggested, international institution-building might also damage the East by engaging it in disruptive, but unsustainable economic ties with the West. Shaking up the social order in order to forge such links, and then breaking them if they fail to work, could generate more profound social disorder than would failing to forge them in the first place.

On balance, a middle road between the Hobbesian instinct for insulation and the neo-liberal instinct for institutionalized activism is probably best. East Germany, Hungary, and Czechoslovakia should probably eventually be admitted into the Western institutional framework. It is especially important

---

[32]Rogowski, *Commerce and Coalition*, pp. 106–107, 121–122, 175–177, discusses Eastern Europe and the USSR in light of the hypothesis that increasing exposure to trade harms holders of locally scarce factors of production (land, labor, or capital), but benefits holders of the locally abundant factors.

[33]According to some critics, EC expansion into Central Europe might strengthen a German-dominated European Community, creating what amounts to a tripolar configuration of power: the United States, the Soviet Union, and the EC. If, as Waltz argues in *Theory of International Politics*, p. 163, tripolar configurations are unstable, this outcome could be dangerous. But the United States and the Soviet Union should be included as major participants in the European regime, which thus would not exist as a separate pole. Moreover, if the institutional scheme worked, the consequences of tripolar anarchy would be muted. In any event, Waltz's deductions about the instability of tripolar configurations are speculative and not logically compelling. (By the broader logic of Waltz's own theory, an attack by one pole should lead to an alliance of the other two, to prevent the achievement of system-wide hegemony by the attacker. The attacker, anticipating this, should be dissuaded from aggression.) Finally, adding Japan and/or China would make the global configuration multipolar, not tripolar.

that the EC solution be adopted for the German Democratic Republic. Poland's role in western institutions should be tailored to fit Soviet sensitivities, which would probably tolerate a high degree of Polish economic integration with the West, but not close military ties.

The Soviet Union should be offered generous security guarantees, a full seat in Europe's diplomatic councils, and beneficial economic relationships with the West. Given the apparent unripeness of the Soviet economy for reform, however, it is highly risky to encourage a leap into the dark in the form of total integration of the Soviet economy into Western markets. Judging from current evidence, this would disrupt Soviet society more than it would spur increased productivity, and consequently might provoke praetorian tendencies rather than dampen them

Analyzing European security can no longer be reduced to positing the vectors of billiard-ball states and counting their tanks. The European order is being remade by social and economic change, no less than by shifts in the international configuration of power. Strategies to maintain international security must, in this new world, comprehend all of these varied facets of social life.

Germany and Japan:
The New Civilian Powers

HANNS W. MAULL

As the postwar international order dissolves, some of the initial concerns that informed and shaped it are resurfacing. One key objective of this old order was the containment of Japanese and German military expansionism and its threat to the international status quo in the Far East and Europe. This was achieved brilliantly by embracing both countries in an American-led alliance system directed against a new adversary, the Soviet Union. This rationale is rapidly fading now, and old specters once more raise their ugly heads; the power of Japan and Germany has again become a cause of concern for their partners in the alliance.

Some observers fear a return of either state (or both) to traditional temptations of military power politics and suspect that Japan or Germany may revert to challenging the status quo, or perhaps even try to replace it with a "Pax Nipponica" or "Pax Teutonica." Others worry about the implications of a changing distribution of economic power as a result of Germany's and Japan's single-minded pursuit of economic gain abroad and tendencies toward parochial and closed societies and economics at home.

Most fears about Japanese and/or German revanchism turn less on perceived political strategies by today's leaderships in Tokyo or Bonn than on the dynamics of ungovernable change. German unification and its impact on the alliance are seen in terms of a "runaway freight train" headed for collision as a result of sheer momentum and the inability or unwillingness of the drivers to apply the brakes. And as for Japan, we are told by a "revision-

Hanns W. Maull, "Germany and Japan: The New Civilian Powers," *Foreign Affairs* Vol. 69, no. 5 (Winter 1990/1991). Reprinted with permission of *Foreign Affairs*. Copyright © 1990 by the Council on Foreign Relations.

ist" that nobody really is in charge there.[1] The forces of change in the post-war era, which have worked so powerfully in favor of the West and against the East, are now seen as threatening American control over events.

Those concerns no doubt reflect certain realities. The redistribution and growing diffusion of economic weight is a fact (although it is often not appreciated that the U.S. share of gross world product actually grew in the 1980s). It also seems correct to suggest that the dynamics of international relations have shifted from the military-political sphere to economic and social developments—a shift that favors Japan and Germany, as economically dynamic and socially cohesive countries.

Yet on balance the alarmists are probably wrong—not because they do not identify trends correctly, but because they fail to put them in the proper perspective. International relations are not just undergoing a reshuffling of power hierarchies, but a sea-change affecting both the structure and substance of international politics. It is hardly surprising that the demise of the East-West conflict should direct our eyes (invited and guided along by Paul Kennedy's *The Rise and Fall of the Great Powers*) toward the traditional play of geopolitics—balance-of-power calculations, the struggle of nation-states for power and a relentless security dilemma. The question is whether this perspective really captures the essence of today's international relations. I would submit it does not, because elements of fundamental change have become more important than those of continuity. This implies, *inter alia,* that the term "power" no longer means what it used to: "hard" power, the ability to command others, is increasingly being replaced by "soft" (persuasive) power. Neither Japan nor Germany, then, is about to become a new superpower, for this role no longer exists in the old sense.

Nor is the United States about to be dethroned as the leader of the Western alliance, thought this role, too, will continue to change. Rather, the United States will have to evolve into a new type of international power, of which Germany and Japan are already in a sense prototypes: it must become a civilian power. This implies: a) the acceptance of the necessity of cooperation with others in the pursuit of international objectives; b) the concentration on non-military, primarily economic, means to secure national goals, with military power left as a residual instrument serving essentially to safeguard other means of international interaction; and c) a willingness to develop supranational structures to address critical issues of international management.[2]

---

[1] This is the central thesis of Karel van Wolferen's *The Enigma of Japanese Power,* New York: Knopf, 1989.

[2] Richard Rosecrance has coined the term "trading state" to define this new paradigm (see his *The Rise of the Trading State,* New York: Basic Books, 1986). It basically conveys the same notions as the term "civilian power" but suggests a primarily economic orientation.

The central argument of this essay is that international relations are undergoing a profound transformation that offers an opportunity to take history beyond the world of the nation-state, with its inherent security dilemmas and its tendency to adjust to change through war. As a result of their own hubris, the farsightedness of the American victors in World War II and a series of historical accidents, Germany and Japan now in some ways find themselves representing this new world of international relations. Circumstances, in a supreme example of irony, have turned them from "late modernizers" into prototypes of a promising future.

II

Although historical parallels between Japan and Germany extend from the mid-nineteenth century, the starting point of this exploration of the similarities in Germany's and Japan's roles in the modern world is their position at the end of World War II.

Both nations had lost ruthless gambles for regional supremacy and world power. The victors' most immediate and pressing concern was to ensure that German and Japanese militaristic expansionism would never again pose a threat to the international status quo. Sharp divisions developed among the former allies, however, and these came to supersede their concern about Germany and Japan. The result was the American strategy of "double containment," in which Germany and Japan were embraced as junior partners in the effort to contain the Soviet Union; at the same time they were firmly anchored in the U.S.-centered alliance system by a web of security, political and economic ties.[3] The logic of this strategy was put bluntly, but quite appropriately, by Lord Ismay, in his famous dictum about NATO's purpose in Europe (which could also have described, with a minor adjustment, U.S. policies toward the Japanese): "Keep the Americans in, the Russians out, and the Germans down."

Western policies toward Japan and Germany in the decade from 1945 to 1955, as well as the defeated nations' respective policy responses, thus bore considerable resemblances. Both Germany and Japan were subjected to selective screening and weeding out of the old elites, the dismemberment of industrial concentrations, and democratic reforms by the occupying powers. While the scope and intensity of those programs differed importantly between Japan and Germany (with the latter, for understandable reasons, being treated much more thoroughly), they helped indigenous democratic tendencies in both countries sufficiently to clear the path toward establish-

---

[3]The term "double containment" is Wolfram Hanrieder's (see his *Germany, America, Europe,* New Haven: Yale University Press, 1989).

ing sound democracies. Democracy in Japan and Germany today may not be perfect, but it looks strong enough to prevent any return toward militarism, fascism or nationalistic authoritarianism.[4]

The military defeat resulted for both countries in very substantial territorial amputations and—in the case of Germany—division between East and West. Japan saw its whole overseas empire dismantled. Less justifiably from the Japanese viewpoint, Japan also lost Okinawa and the Northern islands—territories that had clearly and firmly belonged to Japan proper for a long time. Germany lost the areas east of the Oder-Neisse line and (temporarily) the Saarland. It also was divided into separate entities (although it must be added that this was not the result of a deliberate dismemberment—something that was considered during the war by the Allies, but eventually discarded—but of the escalation of the Cold War). Overall, this confronted both states with the loss of more than forty percent of their prewar territorial expanse, and a massive (and proportionately comparable) influx of people from those areas.

In territorial terms, the settlement of World War II was harsh—harsher in fact than that of World War I against Germany. This reflected the desire of the victors to weaken the two states decisively, but also was a result of the onset of the Cold War, which prevented territorial revision and deepened the partition of Germany. The results of the settlement have been challenged by both Germany and Japan, which have been unwilling to accept fully the postwar territorial status quo—let alone, in the case of Germany, the division of the nation. Revanchism nonetheless never became a serious problem in the postwar world. One reason was the democratic transformation of both countries.

More important, however, may have been another element: German and Japanese territorial demands were rapidly drawn into the East-West conflict. In this context, Germany and Japan were able to secure the return of territories taken over by the West (Saarland, Okinawa), while their demands directed against the Soviet Union were tied into the patterns of the broader international antagonism between East and West. As long as the Soviet Union was unwilling to consider concessions to German or Japanese territorial demands, both countries had to pursue their goals by enlisting U.S. support. Alternatively, a Soviet willingness even to consider territorial concession offered Moscow opportunities to pry those countries away from their alliance with the West. Not surprisingly, therefore, Washington played an important role in scuttling exploration of Soviet signals to allow German re-

---

[4]To substantiate this point would go beyond the scope of this article. For West Germany, perhaps the simplest way to support the arguments is to point to the fact that West German democracy has already passed the ultimate test, a peaceful change in government, twice—in 1969 and in 1982. For Japan, this test still remains to be passed, and the democratic character of the Japanese political system has recently been subjected to much critical scrutiny.

unification (1952, 1954–1955) and to return two of the four Northern islands to Japan (1956). The allies also withheld support for West Germany's territorial demands east of the Oder-Neisse, but gave qualified backing to German reunification.

After the late 1950s, West German and Japanese demands for the territorial revision of the results of World War II acquired an unrealistic quality. The superpowers' interest in reducing tensions between the blocs collided with the position of Germany and Japan. Any serious revision of the territorial results of the postwar settlement would inevitably have undermined the whole postwar order. It was, therefore, hardly surprising that such demands found less and less serious support not only among the allies, but also among the foreign policy establishments in West Germany and Japan; the status quo was more stable, more predictable and, in the last analysis more advantageous.

Insistence on the return of the lost territories and the reunification of Germany did provide internal political fodder and some external leverage, but this had no real effect on the disputed borders. Japan's political parties used the issue of the Northern Territories to bolster electoral support and to underpin their anti-Soviet orientation; West German conservatives saw reunification as a way to mobilize nationalist voters and those who had fled the East, and to strengthen sentiments of anticommunism and orientation toward the West. Unlike Japan, however, which could pursue this course at little real cost, Germany confronted a serious dilemma: insistence on reunification and territorial revision contributed to tensions in Europe and blocked possibilities for alleviating the human burden of German and European partition. This eventually led to the *Ostpolitik* of the Social Democratic/Liberal coalition from 1969 onward, which explicitly recognized the Oder-Neisse boundary and the existence of a second German state, albeit as part of the German nation. The rationale of this policy was twofold: it was to be a means to reduce East-West tensions and a way, ironically, to undermine the partition of Germany and Europe by first recognizing it.

Both Japan and Germany accepted a renunciation of autonomous security policies. This monumental step profoundly transformed international politics in the direction that had been suggested by the European visionary, Jean Monnet—toward an international order created through mutually accepted reciprocal dependence. By ensuring that neither Germany nor Japan would be able to resume its past quest for military supremacy, it also removed or at least weakened regional security dilemmas arising out of fears of a revival of military expansionism, and thus enabled both Germany and Japan to integrate themselves better in their respective regions. In that sense, the postwar security arrangements by and for Germany and Japan were probably the key ingredient in the transformation of this postwar order: they made possible the effective stabilization of two critical regions, Europe and Northeast Asia, and thus established the military and political stability required to shift the emphasis of international relations to enhancing prosperity. The postwar settlement also enabled Japan and Germany to turn their national energies toward economic resurgence. Both became prototypes of the modern trading state.

A number of factors inclined Germany and Japan toward becoming economic superpowers. The security alliance with America provided both countries with a comparatively cheap solution for their defense problems, and gave them new international respectability. Blocked national aspirations could be rechanneled toward economic achievements through international exchanges—an ideal path for states that had seen their ambitions as traditional nation-states profoundly discredited and had renounced defense sovereignty. The American strategy of double containment also provided for economic integration into an open world economy, offering both countries initial financial support and a stable international economic environment.

To underline the parallels between Japan and Germany is not to ignore very substantial differences between the experiences of the two nations. The transformation has undoubtedly been more profound in the case of Germany; even after unification, it will be anything but a reborn Bismarckian empire. It will be a democratic and federal state, economically integrated, solidly anchored in the European Community and preoccupied with internal and regional problems of reconstruction and development, to which traditional military power has no relevance whatsoever. The webs of interdependence tying Germany to its partners in Europe and across the Atlantic are much more varied and broad than those between Japan and the West—the importance of European integration in this context can hardly be overestimated.

Japan, by comparison, has benefitted less from the reappraisal that, on the whole, accepts the entrance of Germany into the mainstream of Western democracies. Thus, the burden of Japan's past (which arguably is much less extraordinary than Germany's) seems more of a political impediment than is the case with Germany; Japan's domestic political transformation from militarism to democracy seems less complete.

But Japan, too, has been profoundly changed in the past 45 years. There are few signs of a serious radical or militaristic threat to the present political system, and there remains a powerful undercurrent of pacifism with which the experience of the Second World War imbued Japanese society. Japan, like Germany, has traded significant parts of its sovereignty in favor of interdependence—by accepting American bases, by developing its defense capabilities in close coordination with the United States and by the sheer weight of its economic presence in America and other parts of the world.

Both Germany and Japan must now define their interests and objectives in the context of integration and interdependence, and pursue them through cooperation and negotiations with their partners. This makes a return to old policies nearly impossible.

III

Nevertheless, Japan and Germany have once more become sources of concern to many Americans. Those concerns may be grouped around the following themes: old-fashioned national expansionism, either military or economic; a shift of international leadership from America to Japan and/or Germany; and maintaining international stability and prosperity, as it were, "under new management."

To expect a revival of traditional militarism in Germany or Japan at present requires a considerable leap of imagination; it is hard to construct plausible scenarios for such a return of history. Even if domestic developments were to evolve in this direction, however, it would be enormously difficult for either country to extricate itself from the complex webs of integration in which they have allowed themselves to be bound and to develop their own, independent military capabilities. Such moves would also immediately trigger powerful reactions and no doubt involve very serious economic and foreign policy costs. In short, those fears simply seem unrealistic.

But what about new, economic forms of nationalist expansionism? Opinion polls show a high percentage of Americans perceiving Japan as a greater threat to their future than the Soviet Union. But because those polls invite comparisons between vastly different types of problems, such answers are deceptive. The real issues behind American fears are the economic successes of German and Japanese industries in comparison to those of the United States.

Economic imbalances reflecting differences in national savings rates and the relative competitiveness of certain sectors of industry do not in themselves constitute "threats." Basically, the concerns about Japan and Germany are that their economic systems are not compatible with a liberal world economy, that their economic values and priorities differ profoundly from those of America, and that their inability to change course, combined with the inability of others to achieve levels of international competitiveness similar to those of Germany or Japan, risks producing a proliferation of protectionist and interventionist measures. Such developments, it is feared, could gradually destroy the open world economy and transform it into a system of relatively closed regions: a European economic space dominated by Germany, an East Asian "Greater Co-Prosperity Sphere" dominated by Japan.

Those fears are based on the assumption that Germany and Japan direct their economic activities toward a noneconomic goal—the pursuit of national power. The economies of Germany and Japan are seen as qualitatively different from other Western economies. At its most pointed, this argument sees the Japanese economy orchestrated by faceless bureaucrats, politicians and managers aiming at world domination through a relentless pursuit of market share abroad and the effective closure of the market at home. West Germany has been singled out less frequently but it, too, has been accused of running a "corporatist" economy with excessive emphasis on exports and a strictly regulated domestic market.

Considerable evidence supports an alternative conclusion: that the forces of global interdependence will produce changes and mutual adjustments of the economic imbalances between Japan and the outside world. Some of those pressures will be economic, others will be political; some will be international, others domestic. Their effects can already be detected in changing corporate strategies of Japanese firms, which are restructuring themselves toward becoming global entities. One result has been a shift from trade to foreign direct investment, and hence a shift from one form of interdependence to another (which ironically has not only failed to diffuse trade conflicts, but has instead opened a new arena of economic conflict concerning Japanese investments abroad).

But it is not only international economic and political counterpressures that will force domestic adjustments in the Japanese and German economies. Economies following mercantilist strategies act against the interests of their own societies, and against the notion of "vertical interdependence" between state and society: export surpluses represent under consumption and hence a suppression of domestic well-being; excessive regulation results in inflated prices, hence again a restraint on welfare. In Japan economic success has been achieved on the back of the urban consumers. American pressure for change can thus, in principle, count on powerful domestic social forces to support its objectives. In Germany the bias toward deflation, underconsumption and regulation may be wrenched open by the challenges of unification and reconstruction in Eastern Europe.

The fear about German or Japanese economic domination also fails to take adequately into account the nature of technological and economic power. Such power today differs profoundly from traditional state power. First, the resources of these forms of power are in the hands of economic actors such as firms or banks, which pursue their own objectives and strategies. Economic "power" thus cannot be easily manipulated and targeted by governments. Moreover, this power grows out of firms' interaction in markets that are rapidly becoming transnational, even global—and this again militates against a straightforward political manipulation of economic capabilities. Finally, economic power thus embedded in webs of interdependence implies substantial vulnerabilities even where interdependence is highly asymmetrical; the implications of interfering with interdependence may be unpredictable and very costly for all concerned.

None of this is to say that economic mercantilism can be discarded as a real danger. Dynamic interdependence implies rapid change and thus requires substantial adjustment to changing circumstances. This is painful, and will produce resistance. Mercantilism could develop as the cumulative result of defensive interventions to protect domestic constituencies against the burden of adjustment, as well as offensive industrial policy efforts to secure national economic advantages. But why should such a development be triggered by Japan or Germany, which have been the principal beneficiaries of the present system? It seems much more plausible that they would try their utmost to defend this system, even if doing so means allowing changes that somewhat reduce their relative benefits.

It is also profoundly wrong to see Germany or Japan as immune to change; their international economic successes reflect, if anything, a superior capacity to adjust to changing circumstances. The same must also be said about the evolution of domestic politics. The direction and implications of those changes may not be precisely what critics would like to see—yet it should be clear from the preceding discussion that many of the pressures to which Germany and Japan have responded are global in nature, and have forced them to become even more international. Still, there can be no doubt that the management of the German and Japanese economies reflects values and forms of social organization that differ from (and may be more effective than) those of other industrialized countries. An emphasis on stability, social consensus, cohesion and continuity amid change can be found in both societies. It is possible that such orientations and forms of social organization could become important features at the level of the global economy as well.

American worries about being pushed aside and replaced as the leading Western power also largely miss the real point. For one thing, U.S. leadership is not really threatened, although it is undergoing qualitative changes. Moreover, as Herbert Stein has rightly pointed out, the American concern about losing preeminence confuses leadership with dominance and economic strength with economic monopoly.[5] Put differently, these worries look at today's world of international relations—shaped by the dynamics of interdependence—through yesterday's lenses of balance-of-power politics among nation states obsessed with territorial insecurity and expansion. The political debate in the United States simply seems to be catching up with the realities of interdependence, which Germany and Japan have been used to for a long time. The United States will not be replaced in its leading role within the alliance by Japan or Germany; ours is no longer an international system of superpower hegemony, but one of cooperation and conflict among highly interdependent partners.

It is true, of course, that interdependence implies a loss of autonomy. In that sense, American worries are real. This autonomy, however, cannot be retrieved without a concomitant loss of benefits from interdependence. Japan and Germany have long accepted this logic, and have opted against autonomy, with good results. Opting against interdependence and for autonomy has often produced disastrous results—witness the socialist experience in Eastern Europe and the Soviet Union. To suggest seriously that Japanese companies could withhold their chips from the United States and sell them to the Soviet Union, and thus change the military balance of

[5]Herbert Stein, "Who's Number One? Who Cares?" in *The Wall Street Journal*, March 5, 1990.

power, as Shintaro Ishihara and Akio Morita have done in *The Japan That Can Say No,* seems breathtakingly unrealistic. Such a move would endanger Japan's access to the American market, unravel its ties with the West and even risk confrontation with it, and destabilize the whole Northeast Asian region, with potentially huge costs for Japan.

Interdependence, however, does not by itself supply a vision of world order, other than to offer material welfare and comforts. It is thus hardly surprising that the trading states Germany and Japan have been criticized for the lack of such vision, and for the arcane and parochial quality of their domestic politics. Moreover, the outcomes of interdependence, the distribution of its costs and benefits, will as a rule not be symmetrical. They will also not necessarily reflect values such as social equity or environmental stability; the burdens of adjustment will tend to be pushed onto marginal actors and global institutions, while each nation will strive to maximize its own benefits.

Thus, interdependence will imply intense conflicts over the distribution of its costs and benefits—and continue heavily to involve national governments. If the outcomes of those political bargaining processes do not reflect values other than maximization of overall benefits and the relative bargaining strength of participants, the results of interdependence may threaten political legitimacy in those countries that do not benefit proportionately. Systemic legitimacy will also suffer if issues such as the protection of the global environment or the gap between rich and poor are not addressed.

IV

The core of the American problem with Germany and Japan is not the redistribution of power within the alliance but the overall change in the international system. This change affects both the substance and the power structure of world politics, and requires major foreign policy adjustments from all powers. It also demands a willingness to think about, and act upon, a new model of international politics—complex interdependence[6]—which is based on three fundamental preconditions: a security framework that guarantees systemic political stability and permits a sustained focus on interdependence; the ability of interdependence to satisfy people's aspirations; and the effective and socially just management of interdependence to avoid breakdowns and crises in the processes of modernization and transformation.

The critical challenges and risks for the future will largely come from economic, social and cultural dislocations and their potential for producing political crises and turmoil. Social changes in this broad sense have been at the roots of the crisis of the Soviet empire and the revolution in Iran; they foster

---

[6]The seminal work for this paradigm is Robert O. Keohane and Joseph S. Nye, Jr., *Power and Interdependence,* Boston: Little, Brown, 1977; revised edition 1989.

new security problems such as migration, drugs and international terrorism. Military power seems to have become a residual, rather than a central, element in international politics. This is not to deny the continued relevance of the security dimension for international relations; nuclear deterrence and conventional force still play a role in guaranteeing the state-centered character of the international system, and war and civil war have, if anything, become more, rather than less, frequent and destructive in the Third World. The proliferation of weapons of mass destruction and of missile technology in the Third World add to such concerns. Nevertheless, military force is likely to be largely irrelevant in confronting such new challenges as political instability and crises in Eastern Europe or the Third World, terrorism, drugs or environmental dangers.

The interpenetration of state and society ("vertical interdependence"), which has resulted from the shift toward the modern welfare state in the postwar era, implies a much more intense interplay of domestic and foreign relations and a much higher importance for economic success as a means to secure political legitimacy. Failure to exploit the potential of interdependence resulted in the fall of the Soviet empire and the transformation of the East-West conflict. The future of East-West relations will depend on the management of political and security interdependence (arms control, development of new security structures in Europe) and the development of economic and social interdependence—or, if such efforts fail, on the containment of turmoil and violence spawned by the bitter Soviet legacy of economic, social and political distortions.

The ability to shape international processes of conflict and cooperation will depend strongly on technological and economic capabilities. As events in Eastern Europe have demonstrated, individual aspirations have become highly relevant for international politics. These aspirations, insofar as they are focused on basic needs, material well-being and quality of life, can only be met through economic growth. But technological and economic strengths differ qualitatively from military capabilities: they are increasingly produced in transnational networks linking firms across the globe.

To think and act in terms of complex interdependence will not be easy. Reservations about giving up national sovereignty with all its symbolic and political paraphernalia are bound to interfere; the necessary domestic adjustments will be hard to organize; and patience will be required to carry through extensive bargaining to find compromises between diverging national interests and conditions.

Whether complex interdependence will be viable will depend importantly on the future behavior of Germany, Japan and the United States. There can be no doubt that both Germany and Japan have very strong reasons to remain tied to the West. Economically, a loosening of integration could only be achieved at tremendous cost; politically, Germany's and Japan's integration in a broader security context ensures regional stability, defuses the legacy of the past and offers the best chance to maintain the reorientation of international politics away from military competition and war and toward the exploitation of benefits from interdependence. This fundamental interest in continued close alignment with the United States and Western Europe is well recognized by public opinion, and the strong institutional ties that bind Japan and Germany to the West also work in the same direction.

Although the integration of Japan and Germany into the Western "club" has undoubtedly changed both countries and laid solid foundations for the future, it is unlikely to provide in itself the answers to new questions of identity and national purpose. These questions arise out of asymmetries between economic weight and political roles, and they are given additional urgency by the transformation of the East-West conflict both in Europe and the Far East, which will involve a redefinition of alliance relations.

In the case of Germany, there is, of course, the need to define a united Germany's place in Europe and the world. For Germany, Europe provides an important dimension of supranational identity. While the emotional appeal of Europe may have receded recently, it is interesting to note that opinion polls now show a certain revival of interest in and attachment to Europe as a counterweight to the emotional uncertainties stirred up by the prospect of German unification. Although this European orientation has developed considerable strength, West Germany's sense of international identity in the postwar era has been largely economic, rather than political, and pragmatic, rather than emotional. It has also never been entirely persuasive, as recurrent debates about West Germany's identity and role in the world have demonstrated. The unification of Germany, as well as the new environment of international relations, will make it imperative for Germany to reexamine and develop its European identity.

At present, however, everything indicates that this process will strengthen, rather than weaken, Germany's European identity. There is also a strong factual basis for such an identity: for many practical purposes, the West German economy has become submerged in a wider European economy, and the European Community is developing a substantial supranational identity of its own. Europe, in fact, has become a functioning laboratory of the new international order; in many ways, it no longer makes sense to talk about Germany as a distinct national unit.

Germany's new identity will thus have to be supranational and European. At its outset, it will have to reaffirm the basic choices made in the early 1950s—the choices for security integration with America and political and economic integration with Europe. The core identification with the European Community will become more difficult to sustain, however, as processes of deepening West European integration are synchronized with efforts to bring Eastern Europe and eventually the Soviet Union into the webs of economic and political interdependence. Both processes, moreover, will have to be kept open for participation by the United States and Japan. This development of European relations with the other principal industrial centers will no doubt be complicated by the dissolution of the unifying threat to all from the Soviet Union, and by the macroeconomic imbalances caused by the erosion of U.S. economic competitiveness. This makes for a fairly complicated set of requirements; Germany's future identity ought to be West European at the core, marked by a strong sense of solidarity with Eastern Europe, and open for intensified ties with America, Japan and Russia.

In the case of Japan, the transformation of East-West relations has prompted a vigorous debate about the future of the U.S.-Japan Security Treaty. For Japan, the development of a purely regional identity seems inconceivable. Through its very close trans-Pacific ties with the United States, and its worldwide economic presence, Japan has become the first global civilian power. Its political identity will have to follow those ties. This means that Japan's sense of responsibility must be shaped around its alliance with the United States, and around global challenges such as Third World development and environmental reconstruction. There are some signs that such a sense of identity may be developing: the United Nations has long enjoyed very strong support in Japan, the "internationalization" of Japan has been a popular obsession for several years now, and public opinion reactions to the recent crisis in American-Japanese relations show some considerable understanding of the need to make concessions to Washington. Official assistance to developing countries has rapidly increased in recent years. There is also the strong aversion of Japanese society to militarism. Yet in spite of all these positive signs, Japan clearly still has a long way to go toward developing a sense of global political responsibility.

Both Germany and Japan thus face the need to develop international identities that explicitly recognize and accept the facts of interdependence. Even if they do, however, this will in no way make U.S. world leadership redundant. Its substance and policies, of course, will have to change to accommodate pressures for supranational cooperation and a partial transfer of sovereignty. Only effective political cooperation between North America, Europe and Japan will be able to provide sufficient resources to meet the challenges the world will face in coming years.

Sovereignty has already, in reality, been transferred. National foreign policies will now have to recognize this, accept the conclusions, and build on them. Transfer of sovereignty allows the development of the rule of law in international relations and thus helps to push forward the process of "civilizing" international politics. It also offers an important set of values. Solidarity with other societies, and a sense of responsibility for the future of the world—and particularly the global environment—are values that will have to be inculcated. Those values must be developed domestically to make effective international interdependence policies possible. Paradoxically, the new challenges of international relations will thus require a much more active emphasis on the domestic political side of international relations—and particularly so in Germany and Japan.

America's Changing Strategic Interests

SAMUEL P. HUNTINGTON

Introduction

The world changed in 1990, and so did strategic discourse. In the late 1980s, after four decades of Cold War, discussions among American strategists had come to focus on relatively narrow and highly technical issues: the merits of particular weapons systems, the minutiae of arms-control proposals and methodologies for estimating the European military balance. The end of the Cold War in 1990 and the dramatic changes in the international environment deprived many of these once hotly contested issues of their significance or made them totally irrelevant. Suddenly a new array of truly big strategic questions assumed center stage. What is the nature of the post–Cold War world? What are America's interests and from whence will those interests be threatened? What policies should the United States follow in order to protect its interests? What military forces and other capabilities will be required to carry out those policies?

This article does not answer these questions, which undoubtedly will be debated for years before a consensus, if any, emerges in the American foreign-policy community. It does, however, attempt to provide a possible prologue to dealing with these issues by: (i) calling attention to how the US has reacted to comparable changes in the international environment in the past; (ii) identifying three major strategic interests of the US that appear to flow from the geopolitical realities of the post–Cold War world; and (iii) briefly suggesting some of the implications of these interests for American military and other policies.

Samuel P. Huntington, "America's Changing Strategic Interests," *Survival* Vol. 33, no. 1 (January/February 1991). Reprinted with permission of the International Institute for Strategic Studies.

Evolution of the International System and American Strategy

In the first two hundred years of the American republic from the 1780s to the 1980s, the international system and the American role in it evolved through four phases. In the first phase, dominated by the French Revolution and Napoleon, Europe was almost continually at war and the United States was effectively a European power, deeply involved in European politics, European diplomacy and European wars. American statesmen did not like this situation but, leading a minor power, they could not do much about it. 'Were I to indulge my own theory,' Jefferson declared in 1787, 'I should wish them [the United States] . . . to stand with respect to Europe precisely on the footing of China.' In a similar vein, Richard Henry Lee supported 'our just wishes to be detached from European politics and European vices. But unfortunately Great Britain is upon our Northern quarter and Spain upon the Southern. We are therefore compelled to mix with their Councils in order to be guarded against their ill designs.[1] The United States had to pursue a policy not of isolation, which was impossible, but of neutrality. American leaders quite explicitly held up Switzerland as their model. The principal American goals during this period were to defend American independence, territorial integrity, and commerce in the North Atlantic and Mediterranean. To achieve these goals efforts were made to develop a strong militia system to guard against European incursions and a small but capable Navy to protect American shipping against the depredations of the British Navy, French privateers and the Barbary pirates. These military forces fought an undeclared war against France, the war of 1812 against Britain, and engaged in various military actions against the *beys* of North Africa.

In 1815 the Napoleonic threat to Europe disappeared and a few years later European colonialism in the Americas came to an effective end. International relations entered a new phase, the *Pax Britannica*, in which the United States was sheltered behind the British fleet and British diplomacy. Isolation became the American condition; continental expansion and economic development the American priorities. The structure of American forces changed accordingly. The militia gave way to a small, long-service, active-duty, Indian-fighting Army. The Navy declined in importance and was oriented away from European contingencies to combating the slave trade, protecting American merchantmen in Asia, and providing navigational support to commerce. The United States fought two major wars during this pe-

---

[1]The quotations are from J. Fred Rippy and Angie Debo, *The Historical Background of the American Policy of Isolation*, Smith College Studies in History, IX (Northampton, MA: 1924), pp. 125, 131. For a somewhat more extensive analysis of the evolution of American military policy from the 1780s to the Cold War, see Samuel P. Huntington, 'Equilibrium and Disequilibrium in American Military Policy', *Political Science Quarterly*, vol. 76, December 1961, pp. 481–502.

riod, both in North America, the first to expand the Union and the second to preserve it.

The *Pax Britannica* ended with the century and the rise of Germany, Japan, Russia and the United States as competing centers of power. As a result of its victory over Spain in 1898, the United States emerged as a minor colonial power and a major actor on the world scene. For a half century the international system was dominated by the efforts of Germany and Japan to secure pre-eminence in their regions of the world. American strategy shifted from continental expansion to intermittent involvement to restore disrupted balances of power in Europe and Asia. In connection with these changes, the United States replaced its small, dispersed Navy with a massive battle fleet second to none, designed to win command of the seas in any conflict and thus make possible the projection of American power into Eurasia. The Indian-fighting Army gave way, first to a larger but much more cerebral force with a General Staff and War College dedicated to developing plans for a major war overseas and, second, to a totally new system of military reserves which could be mobilized for combat in such wars. And three times the United States did go to war to restore the balances of power in Europe and Asia.

The elimination of the German and Japanese challenges in 1945, of course, marked the beginning of a fourth phase in the international system dominated by the Cold War. The American goal was to prevent the Soviet Union from achieving total hegemony in Eurasia. The grand strategy to achieve this purpose was containment; the military strategy was deterrence. The six key components of the American military structure developed to implement these strategies were: (*i*) a very large active-duty military establishment; (*ii*) a massive invulnerable strategic nuclear force; (*iii*) forward deployment of ground, air and naval forces in Europe and Asia; (*iv*) an extraordinarily complex system of alliances and mutual security relationships; (*v*) force-projection capabilities for Third World contingencies; and (*vi*) technological or qualitative superiority in weapons. All six of these elements of American military policy represented major changes from previous practice.

In 1989 and 1990 American policies of containment and deterrence achieved their objectives. The Cold War ended and 1990 joined 1815, 1898 and 1945 as a symbolic year of change in the international system and the American role in it. Like them, 1990 signalled the beginning of debates about the nature of the new system, American interests in this new environment, and the policies which the United States should pursue to advance its interests.

The Post–Cold War Security Environment

The changes that appear to be taking place in the international system are bewildering in their number and diversity. They can, however, be generally grouped under three main headings.

First, there are *systemic changes,* that is changes in the structures of domestic and international politics. These include: the emergence of a truly global economy and of powerful transnational economic organizations; the electronic revolution in communications; the global movement towards democratic political systems and market economies; the declining importance and power of the nation-state for some purposes and the intensification of national and ethnic identities for others; and the rise of international organizations and procedures—what political economists call regimes—to deal with almost every conceivable international issue. Perhaps the most important consequence of these systemic changes is the seeming shift in the relevance and usefulness of different power resources, with military power declining and economic power increasing in importance.[2]

Second, there are *changes in the distribution of power* in the international system. These include: the relative decline in American economic power after World War II; the rise of Japanese economic power; the unification of Germany and the consolidation of its position as the preeminent West European power; the rise of locally dominant powers in many regions; the general diffusion of economic and military capabilities in the Third World; and the social mobilization of publics in the Third World. Most significant and dramatic of the power changes, however, is the decline and perhaps collapse of Soviet power, now manifest in its economic weakness and its withdrawal from Eastern Europe. The break-up of the Soviet empire appears to be under way. After 1992, the coming apart of the Soviet Union may be counterbalanced by the coming together of Western Europe and the emergence of the European Community as a powerful actor on the political as well as the economic scene.

Some people label the new world multipolar. Others point out that the end of the Cold War world left only one superpower. Both observations are true. The emerging world is perhaps best described as a 'uni-multipolar' world. The United States is clearly the only country that could be called a superpower. At least six other countries—the Soviet Union, Japan, China, Germany, the UK and France—are major powers, with particularized strengths, weaknesses and interests. Behind them are the emerging powers of the Third World, among which India is currently the most prominent in asserting its regional dominance.

Third, there are *changes in the relations among countries.* During the Cold War, the relations among key countries were relatively stable and clear. There were allies, antagonists and neutrals. With only a few exceptions, China being the most notable, countries did not change their role. Diplomatic surprises were rare. Stability and predictability prevailed. In the post–Cold War world, relationships among countries are likely to be very different. American-Soviet relations have changed dramatically. So also have

---

[2]See, in this connection, Joseph S. Nye, Jr., 'The Changing Nature of Power', *Political Science Quarterly*, vol. 105, Summer 1990, pp. 177–92.

German-Soviet relations. Other countries have similarly moved to establish new relationships cutting across the old Cold War battle lines and more directly reflecting their own immediate interests. Overall, it seems likely that the new world will be without an overriding cleavage such as characterized the Cold War, but will have a welter of ethnic, national, religious, economic and cultural antagonisms. International relations in this world are likely to have two characteristics.

First, the relations between countries may be more volatile and possibly more duplicitous than they were in the Cold War years. Today's friend may be tomorrow's enemy, and vice versa. Nations will have fewer commonly perceived serious threats and hence more frequently will pursue unilateral interests. Permanent multilateral alliances like NATO will become less important while *ad hoc* coalitions on particular issues, such as that assembled for the Gulf Crisis, will be more important.

Second, relations among countries are likely to be more ambivalent; the world of 'good guys and bad guys' will give way to a world of 'grey guys'. Relations among the major powers may converge towards a mean mixing of elements of co-operation and of competition. The Cold War, in upper case letters, may be replaced by a variety of lesser cold wars, lower case, among the major powers. The United States and Japan may remain military allies but are also likely to be intense economic competitors. While some truly special relationships, such as that between the United States and the United Kingdom, may endure, American relations with the Soviet Union are unlikely to be much more competitive than its relations with the countries with whom it has been allied.

The international politics of the Persian Gulf could be an extreme foretaste—almost a caricature—of what global politics could be like in the future. Iraq invades Iran. Iran mobilizes its strength and threatens to defeat Iraq. Kuwait, the United States and other countries provide assistance to Iraq. An end to the fighting is negotiated. Iraq invades its former backer, Kuwait. The United States comes to Kuwait's help and puts together a coalition of diverse countries, including both NATO allies and the Soviet Union, both Egypt and Syria. The US continues to classify Syria as a state supporting terrorism. Shifting and ambivalent relationships like these did not typify the Cold War but they may be typical of the post Cold War world. All in all, the emerging world is likely to lack the clarity and stability of the Cold War and to be a more jungle-like world of multiple dangers, hidden traps, unpleasant surprises and moral ambiguities.

US Strategic Alternatives in the New World

The changes in the international environment are prompting a re-examination of US priorities and strategy comparable to those after 1815, 1898 and

1945. Back in the early years of the Cold War, public discussion and confidential planning papers, such as NSC-68 in 1950 and NSC-162 in 1953, argued the merits of alternative grand strategies: isolationism, liberation, preventive war, containment, multilateralism, unilateralism, globalism. A similar debate with comparable alternatives is now under way in the United States. Arguments are being made for what is often called containment-plus, disengagement or isolationism of the nineteenth- or twentieth-century variety, global reform, world order, economic nationalism, the promotion of democracy and social justice everywhere, hard-boiled power politics, and for variations on and combinations of these alternatives. Anti-military liberals and anti-communist conservatives urge substantial American disengagement from an active role in world affairs. Some Congressmen promote protectionism and economic nationalism; others see international law and the United Nations as the desirable lodestars of American policy. Secretary of State James Baker, supported by some moderate Democrats, argues that the principal goal of US foreign policy should be the promotion and consolidation of democracy throughout the world.[3]

At some level and in some respects, each of these alternatives makes some sense and intelligent arguments could be made on behalf of each of them. This article, however, is an effort to analyze strategic interests, not to articulate policy preferences. Consequently, it will not make a case for the promotion of democracy, *realpolitik*, economic nationalism, or any of the other broad alternatives. Let us instead assume, with the 'realist' approach to international politics, that the root concerns of a nation-state are with power and security, accept the general trends and the probable nature of the post–Cold War world outlined above, and attempt to identify the principal American strategic interests in that world. Three such interests are:

(i)   to maintain the United States as the premier global power, which in the coming decade means countering the Japanese economic challenge;
(ii) to prevent the emergence of a political-military hegemonic power in Eurasia; and
(iii) to protect concrete American interests in the Third World, which are primarily in the Persian Gulf and Middle America.

Meeting the Japanese Economic Challenge

Throughout the Cold War, the United States was the number one power in the world: economically, technologically, militarily, diplomatically, politically and culturally. At times, its pre-eminence in these various arenas of power was challenged, and it responded to those challenges, sometimes more successfully than others. In the post–Cold War world the United States

[3]James Baker, 'Democracy and American Diplomacy', Address, World Affairs Council, Dallas, Texas, 30 March 1990.

will continue to have an interest in maintaining itself as the number one power in the world. The claims of domestic needs may moderate this priority but they will not eliminate it, and in some important respects they may strengthen it.

The Soviet Union long ago lost the ideological competition with the United States. Now it is abandoning the military competition. No country is presently in a position to challenge the primacy of the US in terms of global ideological, military, diplomatic or cultural influence. The one area of US weakness is economics and the challenge in that arena comes from Japan. In a world where economic power and economic issues are increasingly important, that challenge is a real one.

Non-Americans often ask: 'What is it with you Americans and the Japanese? Why is your country so obsessed with Japan?' The answer is that the United States is obsessed with Japan for the same reasons that it was once obsessed with the Soviet Union. It sees that country as a major threat to its primacy in a crucial arena of power. In 1980 in the United States, the Soviet military threat was on the public mind: discussions focused on the comparative statistics of Soviet and American missiles, warheads, throw-weight, bombers, tanks and submarines. Today, the Japanese economic threat is on people's mind. The concern is not missile vulnerability but semiconductor vulnerability. Public discussions focus on comparative Japanese and American figures for economic growth, productivity, high-technology exports, savings, investment, patents, research and development. These are where the threat to American primacy lies and where it is perceived to lie.

In recent decades, Japanese performance in almost every one of these areas has exceeded, often substantially, the performance of the United States. In the 1950s and 1960s the American public was concerned with 'bomber gaps' and 'missile gaps' with the Soviet Union. It is now, with much greater justification, concerned with economic performance gaps with Japan. Between 1980 and 1987, Japanese saved 20.3% of their net national income; Americans saved 4.2%. During the 1980s the investment gap between the two countries widened significantly. In 1989 Japan had a gross national product that was 60% of that of the United States and invested 24% of that product, or about $750 billion. The United States invested about 10% of its gross national product, or about $500 billion. In the late 1980s the productivity of American workers still exceeded that of Japanese workers, but the gap was narrowing. Between 1980 and 1987, the gross domestic product per worker grew at a rate of 0.8% in the United States, but at a rate of 2.8% in Japan. Over the course of 15 years, the Japanese share of US patents rose from 4% to 19%, while the American share declined from 73% to 54%.[4] These are only some of the comparisons that worry Americans.

[4]These figures come from Barry P. Bosworth and Robert Z. Lawrence, 'America in the World Economy', *The Brookings Review*, vol. 7, Winter 1988–9, p. 44; *New York Times*, 8 January 1989, p. A16; *The Economist*, 3 February 1990, p. 67; *International Herald Tribune*, 12 April 1990, p. 11.

Superior economic performance generates greater economic power: increased control over capital, facilities, markets and technology. Japanese investment in the United States increased dramatically in the 1980s. The bulk of this was in US government securities, but there was also substantial investment in real estate and physical facilities, as well as the purchase of US companies. Four of the ten largest banks in California, for instance, are under Japanese control. The market share of Japanese companies increased in a variety of industries, particularly in electronics. In 1983, for example, the Japanese share of the market for semiconductor manufacturing equipment was roughly 40% of that of the United States; by 1989 it was roughly equal to the American share. In 1983 the US had 65% of the market for wafer steppers, which are essential to the manufacturing of semiconductors, and Japan 35%. In 1989 the US share had dropped drastically to 20%, while the Japanese share had risen dramatically to 70%.[5]

The increases in Japanese economic power have produced reactions in the United States similar to those produced during the Cold War by increases in Soviet military power. Public opinion polls depict a striking ambivalence towards Japan on the part of the Americans. They still see Japan as a friendly country, but increasing numbers also see it as a threat. Between 1987 and 1990, the proportion of Americans having a favorable view of the Soviet Union increased from 25% to 51%; the proportion having a favorable view of Japan decreased from 70% to 56%. In 1989, some 72% of the American public said that they thought the US and Japan could be close friends. Yet 73% also believed that 'the greatest threat to American security is the economic challenge posed by Japan', and supported the shifting of resources from military purposes 'to domestic investment to make America more economically competitive'.[6] In the view of the American public, in short, the political-military threat from the Soviet Union is waning, while the economic challenge from Japan is rising. These popular concerns are reflected in the large number and large sales of books dealing with the 'Japanese menace'. The hostile attitudes in the United States towards Japan are mirrored in increasing Japanese criticisms of the United States, manifested most dramatically in the best-selling book, *The Japan That Can Say 'No'*.[7]

'Economics', Daniel Bell has observed, 'is the continuation of war by other means.' In effect, an economic cold war is developing between the United States and Japan, and Americans have good reason to be concerned about the consequences of doing poorly in that competition. First, and most specifically, American national security, in the narrow sense, could be affected if the Japanese expand their lead in a variety of militarily important

---

[5] *New York Times*, 10 December 1989, pp. 1, 44.

[6] See World Policy Institute, Defining American Priorities: Results of Survey Conducted for World Policy Institute (New York, 1989), pp. 3–4; *New York Times*, 10 July 1990, p. A11; *Washington Post National Weekly Edition*, 24–30 September 1990, p. 37; 'How We See Japan', *The American Enterprise*, vol. 1, November-December 1990, p. 86ff.

[7] By Shintaro Ishihara (New York: Simon & Schuster, February 1991).

technologies. In 1988, for instance, the Defense Science Board identified 22 areas of critical technology and judged the Soviet Union to be 'significantly' ahead of the United States in 'some niches of technology' in two areas but Japan to be ahead in six. In 1990 a Commerce Department study found Japan to be ahead of the United States in five of 12 emerging technologies and rapidly gaining in another five.[8] American national security obviously is weakened to the extent to which the United States becomes dependent upon Japanese technology for its sophisticated weapons.

Second, the growth of Japanese economic power threatens American economic well-being. The loss of markets means the loss of jobs and profits. Japanese purchase of American companies increases Japanese access to American technology and the shift of high value-added manufacturing from the United States to Japan.

Third, the increase in Japanese economic power means an increase in Japanese influence and a relative decline in American influence. Japanese penetration of and influence in American media, academic institutions and policy-making processes have increased significantly.[9] In the 1940s the Soviet Union used its ideology to enlist influential Americans to serve its interests. The United States itself is, of course, the principal target of Japanese efforts to use its economic resources to advance its economic and political interests. Those resources also enhance its ability to influence developments in third countries in directions which conflict with American interests. Unless current trends are reversed, Tokyo's influence in other capitals will go up and Washington's will go down.

In the Cold War, the United States and the Soviet Union had common interests in not destroying themselves in a nuclear exchange and they carefully avoided any significant direct military conflict with each other. In their economic competition, the US and Japan will have much stronger common interests in limiting the methods they use and the damage they cause each other. Arms-control negotiations and agreements helped to define and restrain the Cold War military competition. Trade negotiations and broader efforts such as the Structural Impediments Initiative are their strategic equivalents in the US-Japanese competition and conceivably can direct that competition into more constructive channels.

American unilateral actions in the Cold War sometimes served its interests well and sometimes did not. Similarly, while Japan should be pressured to open its economy, 'Japan-bashing' and protectionism are non-productive or counter-productive in terms of US interests. A positive and constructive American strategy would aim to correct the economic weaknesses that have

[8]US Department of Defense, *Critical Technologies Plan* (Washington DC: March 1989, revised May 1989), p. 11; *The Economist,* 7 July 1990, p. 29.

[9]See Pat Choate, *Agents of Influence: How Japan's Lobbyists in the United States Manipulate America's Political and Economic System* (New York: Knopf, 1990), *passim;* Steven Kelman, 'The "Japanization" of America', *The Public Interest,* no. 98, Winter 1990, pp. 70–83; *New York Times,* 10 December 1989, pp. 1F, 6F.

made possible the relative growth of Japanese economic power. These weaknesses include: first, the on-going budget deficit, with which Congress has wrestled but has taken only a first step towards solving; second, the low savings rate of Americans, which shows some signs of improving but is still much too low to provide the resources needed for investment; third, inadequate spending on research and development, particularly for non-military purposes; and, fourth, and most important, the potentially catastrophic deficiencies in the education and training of American youth and the resulting decline in the quality of the workforce.

Maintaining the Eurasian Balance of Power

Coping with the Japanese economic challenge is a new strategic interest for the United States. For two hundred years, in contrast, the United States has had an interest in promoting balances of power first in Europe and then in Asia so as to prevent any country or combination of countries from achieving a predominance that would threaten American interests. American statesmen have rarely acknowledged, almost never articulated and often denounced this goal, but they have nonetheless consistently returned to it. In its first 40 years, the United States attempted diplomatically to play off one major European power against another, most centrally, of course, France against Britain. After 1815 the British took on the role of promoting a balance of power on the continent, and the United States turned its attention westward. When a new constellation of powers arose at the turn of the century, the United States continued to remain relatively isolated from European international politics and, somewhat less so, from East Asian international affairs. Apart from the Open Door policy in China and the naval arms agreements of the 1920s, the United States did not actively attempt to promote peacetime balances of power in Europe and Asia and, as a result, had to go to war to restore those balances. With the elimination of German and Japanese power, massive American power was deployed to balance Soviet and communist threats in both Europe and Asia. Containment and deterrence were the Cold War policies to achieve what had been a long-standing American goal.

The Soviet Union remains a formidable military power, second only to the United States. Yet the unification of Germany, the liberation of Eastern Europe, the continuing withdrawal of Soviet forces to Soviet territory, and the economic and political decay of the Soviet Union, all mark the virtual disappearance of the Soviet hegemonic threat. A multipolar situation, involving the UK, France, Germany and the Soviet Union as the major actors, appears to be emerging in Europe; a comparable situation involving China, Japan, and the Soviet Union exists in Asia. No single power now appears able to dominate Europe, Asia, or both. At the end of 1990, indeed, the principal threat to stability and the balance of power in Eurasia appeared to be the possibility of a major vacuum of power emerging in Mackinder's heartland.

Conceivably, however, a hegemonic threat could develop in the future. For centuries before 1917, Russian governments regularly intervened militarily in Eastern Europe, suppressed revolutions in Poland and Hungary, and participated in the partitions of Poland. The Soviet Union or its successor state could find compelling geopolitical reasons to intervene once again in Eastern European affairs, even as the United State regularly finds reasons to intervene in Central America and the Caribbean. United Germany could attempt to use its economic power not only to dominate the European Community, but also to extend its economic hegemony and political control through Central and Eastern Europe. That, too, is a course which German governments—imperial, democratic and Nazi—have followed in the past. The political integration of the European Community, if that should occur, would also bring into existence an extraordinarily powerful entity which could not help but be perceived as a major threat to American interests.

In East Asia, an economically dominant Japan conceivably could use its formidable economic resources to establish through investment and trade the co-prosperity sphere it failed to create by military means. China, however, is a more likely source of East Asian instability. The external expansion of the UK and France, Germany and Japan, the Soviet Union and the United States coincided with phases of intense industrialization and economic development. China will undoubtedly be moving into such a phase in the coming decades. Apart from a possible power vacuum in the heartland, none of these potential threats to the Eurasian balance is immediate or even likely in the near future. None, however, is impossible at some point, and one, Chinese expansion, while more distant is both more probable and more threatening than the others.

In this new environment, the overall strategic interest of the US does not lie in deterring an existing threat, but rather in preserving an equilibrium and in preventing the emergence of new threats. Pursuing equilibrium rather than containment requires less emphasis on military force and more on diplomatic, economic and institutional means. The problem for the United States is to reduce its military involvement in Eurasia, which was required to contain Soviet power in the second half of this century, without producing the American absence from Europe that led to two world wars in the first half of the century. The United States is, in some respects, in the position of Britain after 1815, when the end of the Napoleonic threat created the need to produce a Concert of Europe, incorporating France, and the need to promote a continuing balance of power in Europe so that no country could again threaten British interests. In 1990 UK Foreign Secretary Douglas Hurd pointed to the post-1815 parallel and said that as a result he was reading a biography of Castlereagh. The person who should be reading that book, however, is President George Bush.

If the overall US strategic interest is to promote a stable equilibrium of power in Eurasia, presumably flowing from that are specific interests:

(i)   to prevent the total disintegration of the Soviet Union and to promote the emergence of a stable, democratic, economically capable successor state composed of those republics which voluntarily choose to join it;

(ii)   to prevent the reimposition of Soviet or Russian military or political control in Eastern Europe, which presumably can best be achieved by NATO guaranteeing the national independence, territorial integrity, political democracy and diplomatic neutrality of the former Soviet-bloc states;

(iii) to limit German power in the new Europe, by encouraging German involvement in NATO and European international organizations, while at the same time working with the UK, France and other countries to constrain German control over those organizations;

(iv)   to encourage stability in Central and Eastern Europe by strengthening the new democracies;

(v)   to promote evolution of the European Community in the direction of a looser, purely economic entity with broader membership rather than a tighter political entity with an integrated foreign policy;

(vi)   to provide constraints on Japanese power in East Asia by continuing the US-Japanese military alliance, encouraging movement towards Korean unification, retaining a reduced military presence in East Asia, and providing an alternative source of economic and technical assistance to developing South-east Asian countries; and

(vii) to prevent or to limit possible Chinese expansion by encouraging trends towards political pluralism and a market economy in China.

Protecting Concrete Third World Interests

During the Cold War the United States had three types of interests in the Third World. First, it had general interests which included promoting human rights, democracy, market economies, economic development, and preventing aggression, political instability and weapons proliferation. Second, the United States had competitive interests in the Third World which derived from its Cold War with the Soviet Union. Much US involvement in the Third World was designed to minimize Soviet influence there and to counter developments that appeared to further Soviet interests in the Third World. Third, it had concrete interests in particular countries or areas which supplied it with crucial raw materials, which had substantial American investments or were markets for American goods, which were geopolitically significant, or which had close historical connections with the United States.

In the coming era, the United States will continue to have an interest in promoting democracy, development, peace and other general goals in the Third World. Its changing relations with the Soviet Union, however, will substantially remove the competitive impetus to involvement in the Third World. While the USSR is still active in some Third World areas, that activity has decreased, and it seems probable that Soviet-American competition will not be a significant factor in the Third World in this new era. If this happens, one major reason for American involvement in many Third World situations will disappear. Without the Cold War it is hard to see how much interest the United States will have in who governs Afghanistan or whether India or Pakistan controls Kashmir. South Asia is simply not an American strategic property. The same is true for many parts of South-east Asia and for most of Africa. The attitude that will become increasingly prevalent was well expressed in a 1990 *New York Times* editorial entitled 'Why Bankroll Mobutu?' The newspaper answered that question by saying: 'The end of the Cold War removes any possible justification for this taxpayer subsidy to a repellent dictator.'[10]

The end of the Cold War should also see a constriction of US strategic involvement in Latin America. Before the 1930s the United States had almost no strategic interests in South America south of its northern littoral. In the 1930s the United States became concerned about the possible spread of Nazi influence in Brazil and Argentina. During the Cold War the United States had a major interest in preventing the spread of communism and Soviet influence throughout South America. With the end of the Cold War and the dramatic decline in the appeal of leftist ideologies in Latin America, US strategic interest in Latin America south of Venuzuela, Colombia and, marginally, Peru are likely to revert downward towards their pre-1930s levels.

In the absence of the incentive to compete with the Soviet Union, American strategy will focus on those areas where the US has substantial concrete interests. These are, first, Mexico, Central America, the Caribbean and the northern tier of South America. Concerns arising from propinquity, security, demography, economics and drugs all serve to direct increasing American attention to that part of the world. Many countries around the world, including the Soviet Union, teeter on the brink of economic and political collapse. The country whose political and economic collapse would most adversely affect the United States is Mexico.

Second, so long as the United States remains heavily dependent upon imported oil, it will have a major interest in the Persian Gulf. Implementation of the Carter Doctrine designed to promote security in that area consumed a major share of the Reagan defence build-up. Those resources were justified by the threat from the Soviet Union. The justification, however, was not the reason. The reason was the potential threat from local wars, like the Iran-Iraq conflict and the Iraqi invasion of Kuwait, or from domestic instability, such as the possible overthrow of regimes in Saudi Arabia or the Gulf emirates. Those dangers, now dramatically visible, presumably will remain for a long time to come.

---

[10]*New York Times*, 21 April 1990, p. 22.

Third, the United States has concrete interests, for historical and political reasons, in some individual Third World countries, such as Israel, South Korea and the Philippines. In the past the US has also had competitive or Cold War interests in these countries, particularly Israel and South Korea. To the extent that the Cold War is over, that interest will decline; the interests stemming from domestic politics and historical association will remain.

A Few Implications

Nations do not necessarily pursue their strategic interests; their strategic interests are not necessarily their best interests; and they may subordinate their best interests to parochial and short-term concerns. If the United States were to pursue the strategic interests outlined above, significant changes would be required in US policies and resource allocations. The military policies, programmes and forces required to promote these interests would be significantly different from those required for the Cold War. The armed forces could be considerably reduced in size. The massive US deployments abroad required by deterrence could be replaced by much more modest 'presence' forces designed to underline US interests in preserving a stable equilibrium in Eurasia and defending its concrete interests in Southwest Asia and Middle America. These forces would be designed not so much for immediate combat as to receive and support major combat units deployed from the United State when they were needed to cope with a crisis. Reserve forces would be strengthened, and major improvements would be required in the mobility of US forces, particularly in sea-lift. An unstable and unpredictable world would require increased support for intelligence capabilities and for the research and development, although not necessarily the procurement, of sophisticated weapons.

In this new environment, however, military capabilities are likely to be less important than they have been in the past. Economic measures will be central to dealing with the Japanese challenge; diplomacy and economics will be crucial to promoting a political-military equilibrium in Eurasia. The promotion of US strategic interests will involve not only foreign and defence policy but also domestic policy on the budget, taxes, subsidies, industrial policy, science and technology, child care, education, and other topics.

If the United States is to promote its interests in the new world, a first requirement is to create the institutional means to develop a more comprehensive approach to national security policy, to pull together what is foreign and domestic, and what is military and economic. In the 1940s the United States created the National Security Council, the Department of Defense, the Central Intelligence Agency and other institutions that played central roles in producing victory in the Cold War. Meeting the threats to its interests in the post–Cold War era will probably require institutional innovations no less significant.

More important is the question: To what extent will the American public and American leaders want to pursue their strategic interests in the new era? After fighting and winning what were in effect three world wars in 75 years, Americans may well want a respite. In this century, the United States became deeply involved in Eurasian political-military affairs only in the face of obvious threats. In the absence of a hateful enemy—the Kaiser, Hitler, Japanese warlords, Stalin—the American people may be less willing to support a sustained US involvement in Eurasia and the expenditures that would entail. In the Cold War, moreover, the interests of power and the interests of morality generally coincided. The Soviet Union was powerful and hence a threat to be countered; it was also a godless totalitarian dictatorship and hence an evil to be eradicated. No such easy identity of the demands of power politics and those of morality is likely to exist in the future. After the Iraqi invasion of Kuwait, some Americans engaged in an orgy of recrimination about earlier US support for Iraq in its war against Iran, and some were equally unhappy about the US co-operating against Iraq with President Assad of Syria. Playing the balance-of-power game and engaging in the moral compromises and odious associations that often involves will not come easy to the American public and American politicians.

Meeting the Japanese economic challenge may also require significant changes in US attitudes and behavior. The Cold War was a competition between two very different political-economic systems in which one eventually proved to be superior to the other. The differences between the Japanese and US political-economic systems are nowhere near as great, but they are real. The one stresses collectivity, consensus, authority, hierarchy, discipline; the other individualism, competition, dissent, egalitarianism, unbridled self-interest. One finds on the long haul and saves and invests; the other focuses on the short term and spends and consumes. In the competition that is developing, success is likely to go to that country which is best able to absorb some of its adversary's virtues.

The issue for the United States is whether it can meet the economic challenge from Japan as successfully as it did the political and military challenges from the Soviet Union. If it cannot, at some future time the United States could find itself in a position relative to Japan that is comparable to the position the Soviet Union is now in relative to the United States. Having lost its economic supremacy, the United States would no longer be the world's only superpower and would be simply a major power like all the others.

Such a development might produce some benefits for the United States, but it would not serve American strategic interests. It is unclear whether it would serve the world's strategic interests. What is preferable in terms of global security and stability? A world with the United States as the presiding superpower, chairman of the board, leading and working with various combinations of major powers and lesser countries to deal with the world's problems? Or a truly multipolar world of seven or more roughly equal major powers, including the United States, each pursuing its own interests and competing with and co-operating with each other in a variety of permutations and combinations? Or a world in which some other country replaces the United States as the presiding superpower? The choices the United States made after 1898 and 1945 significantly shaped the international environment in each half of this century. The choices the United States makes in the coming decade will have at least a comparable impact on the international environment in the opening years of the twenty-first century.